T0202853

Lecture Notes in Computer Science   10864

Commenced Publication in 1973
Founding and Former Series Editors:
Gerhard Goos, Juris Hartmanis, and Jan van Leeuwen

Editorial Board

David Hutchison
  Lancaster University, Lancaster, UK
Takeo Kanade
  Carnegie Mellon University, Pittsburgh, PA, USA
Josef Kittler
  University of Surrey, Guildford, UK
Jon M. Kleinberg
  Cornell University, Ithaca, NY, USA
Friedemann Mattern
  ETH Zurich, Zurich, Switzerland
John C. Mitchell
  Stanford University, Stanford, CA, USA
Moni Naor
  Weizmann Institute of Science, Rehovot, Israel
C. Pandu Rangan
  Indian Institute of Technology Madras, Chennai, India
Bernhard Steffen
  TU Dortmund University, Dortmund, Germany
Demetri Terzopoulos
  University of California, Los Angeles, CA, USA
Doug Tygar
  University of California, Berkeley, CA, USA
Gerhard Weikum
  Max Planck Institute for Informatics, Saarbrücken, Germany

More information about this series at http://www.springer.com/series/7409

Ian F. C. Smith · Bernd Domer (Eds.)

Advanced Computing Strategies for Engineering

25th EG-ICE International Workshop 2018
Lausanne, Switzerland, June 10–13, 2018
Proceedings, Part II

 Springer

Editors
Ian F. C. Smith
Applied Computing and Mechanics
 Laboratory (IMAC)
School of Architecture, Civil and
 Environmental Engineering (ENAC)
Swiss Federal Institute of Technology,
 Lausanne (EPFL)
Lausanne
Switzerland

Bernd Domer
Institute for Landscape, Architecture,
 Construction and Territory (inPact)
Construction and Environment
 Department (CED)
University of Applied Sciences,
 Geneva (HEPIA)
Geneva
Switzerland

ISSN 0302-9743   ISSN 1611-3349   (electronic)
Lecture Notes in Computer Science
ISBN 978-3-319-91637-8   ISBN 978-3-319-91638-5   (eBook)
https://doi.org/10.1007/978-3-319-91638-5

Library of Congress Control Number: 2018943445

LNCS Sublibrary: SL3 – Information Systems and Applications, incl. Internet/Web, and HCI

© Springer International Publishing AG, part of Springer Nature 2018
This work is subject to copyright. All rights are reserved by the Publisher, whether the whole or part of the material is concerned, specifically the rights of translation, reprinting, reuse of illustrations, recitation, broadcasting, reproduction on microfilms or in any other physical way, and transmission or information storage and retrieval, electronic adaptation, computer software, or by similar or dissimilar methodology now known or hereafter developed.
The use of general descriptive names, registered names, trademarks, service marks, etc. in this publication does not imply, even in the absence of a specific statement, that such names are exempt from the relevant protective laws and regulations and therefore free for general use.
The publisher, the authors and the editors are safe to assume that the advice and information in this book are believed to be true and accurate at the date of publication. Neither the publisher nor the authors or the editors give a warranty, express or implied, with respect to the material contained herein or for any errors or omissions that may have been made. The publisher remains neutral with regard to jurisdictional claims in published maps and institutional affiliations.

Printed on acid-free paper

This Springer imprint is published by the registered company Springer International Publishing AG
part of Springer Nature
The registered company address is: Gewerbestrasse 11, 6330 Cham, Switzerland

Preface

The architecture–engineering–construction (AEC) industry worldwide spending is over ten trillion dollars annually[1]. The industry is the largest global consumer of raw materials, and constructed assets account for 25–49% of the world's total carbon emissions[2]. Also, the World Bank has estimated that each year, demand for civil infrastructure exceeds supply (new plus existing infrastructure) creating an annual shortfall of one trillion dollars[3]. This cannot continue. Engineers must find new ways to design, build, manage, renovate, and recycle buildings and civil infrastructure.

Advanced computing strategies for engineering will be the enablers for much of this transformation. Until recently, new computing strategies have not been able to penetrate into the AEC industry. Owners and other stakeholders have observed little return on investment along with excessive risk associated with a fragmented industry where computing competence is far from homogeneous. This is changing quickly as efficient information modeling, the foundation of many computing strategies in this field, becomes more accessible. Also, important advances in fields such as construction management, life-cycle design, monitoring, diagnostics, asset management, and structural control are being made thanks to fundamental computing advances in fields such as machine learning, model-based reasoning, and human–computer interaction. In parallel, studies of full-scale AEC cases are uncovering additional scientific challenges for computer scientists.

The European Group for Intelligent Computing in Engineering (EG-ICE) was established in Lausanne in 1993 to promote research that lies on the interface between computing and engineering challenges. The primary goals of the group are to promote engineering informatics research across Europe by improving communication and trust between researchers, fostering collaborative research, and enhancing awareness of recent research. The EG-ICE group maintains contact with similar groups outside Europe and encourages contact with experts wherever they reside.

This volume contains papers that were presented at the 25th Workshop of the European Group for Intelligent Computing in Engineering (EG-ICE), which was held in Lausanne, Switzerland, June 10–13, 2018. Of the 108 abstracts that were submitted, 57 papers made it through the multi-step review process of evaluating abstracts, commenting on full papers, and assessing subsequent revisions so that they could be presented at the workshop.

---

[1] https://www.statista.com/statistics/788128/construction-spending-worldwide/.

[2] Shaping the Future of Construction, World Economic Forum, Geneva, 2016.

[3] https://futureofconstruction.org/blog/infographic-six-megatrends-impacting-the-ec-industry/.

We are grateful to the many reviewers who worked hard to provide constructive comments to authors. The scientific results presented here are a sample of the diversity and creativity of those who are planting the seeds of the exciting transformation that is coming over the next decade. It is not too soon.

April 2018

Ian F. C. Smith
Bernd Domer

Organization

Organizing Committee

Ian Smith (Workshop Co-chair)	Swiss Federal Institute of Technology, EPFL, Switzerland
Bernd Domer (Workshop Co-chair)	University of Applied Sciences, HEPIA, Switzerland
Raphaël Wegmann (Workshop Secretary)	Swiss Federal Institute of Technology, EPFL, Switzerland
Pierino Lestuzzi (Member)	Swiss Federal Institute of Technology, EPFL, Switzerland
Sai Pai (Member)	Swiss Federal Institute of Technology, EPFL, Switzerland
Yves Reuland (Member)	Swiss Federal Institute of Technology, EPFL, Switzerland
Gennaro Senatore (Member)	Swiss Federal Institute of Technology, EPFL, Switzerland
Ann Sychertz (Member)	Swiss Federal Institute of Technology, EPFL, Switzerland

EG-ICE Committee

Pieter de Wilde (Chair)	University of Plymouth, UK
Timo Hartmann (Vice-chair)	Technical University of Berlin, Germany
Haijiang Li (Secretary)	Cardiff University, UK
Philipp Geyer (Treasurer and International Representative)	Catholic University of Leuven, Belgium
Georg Suter (Chair, Best Paper Award Committee)	Technical University of Vienna, Austria
Jakob Beetz (Committee Member)	RWTH Aachen University, Germany
Christian Koch (Committee Member)	Bauhaus University, Weimar, Germany
André Borrmann (Past Chair)	Technical University of Munich, Germany
Ian Smith (EG-ICE Fellow)	Swiss Federal Institute of Technology, EPFL, Switzerland

Scientific Committee

Jamal Abdalla	American University of Sharjah, UAE
Burcu Akinci	Carnegie Mellon University, USA

Robert Amor	University of Auckland, New Zealand
Chimay Anumba	University of Florida, USA
Burcin Becerik-Gerber	University of Southern California, USA
Jakob Beetz	RWTH Aachen University, Germany
Mario Berges	Carnegie Mellon University, USA
André Borrmann	Technical University of Munich, Germany
Frédéric Bosché	Heriot-Watt University, UK
Manfred Breit	University of Applied Sciences, FHNW, Switzerland
Ioannis Brilakis	University of Cambridge, UK
Hubo Cai	Purdue University, USA
Jack Cheng	Hong Kong University of Science and Technology, SAR China
Symeon Christodoulou	University of Cyprus, Cyprus
Lorenzo Diana	Swiss Federal Institute of Technology, EPFL, Switzerland
Semiha Ergan	New York University, USA
Esin Ergen	Istanbul Technical University, Turkey
Boi Faltings	Swiss Federal Institute of Technology, EPFL, Switzerland
Martin Fischer	Stanford University, USA
Ian Flood	University of Florida, USA
Adel Francis	École de Technologie Supérieure, ÉTS, Canada
Renate Fruchter	Stanford University, USA
James Garrett	Carnegie Mellon University, USA
David Gerber	University of Southern California, USA
Philipp Geyer	Catholic University of Leuven, Belgium
Mani Golparvar-Fard	University of Illinois at Urbana-Champaign, USA
Ewa Grabska	Jagiellonian University, Poland
Carl Haas	University of Waterloo, Canada
Amin Hammad	Concordia University, Canada
Timo Hartmann	Technical University of Berlin, Germany
Markku Heinisuo	Tampere University of Technology, Finland
Shang-Hsien (Patrick) Hsieh	National Taiwan University, Taiwan
Raja Raymond Issa	University of Florida, USA
Farrokh Jazizadeh	Virginia Polytechnic Institute and State University, USA
Vineet Kamat	University of Michigan, USA
Peter Katranuschkov	Technical University of Dresden, Germany
Arto Kiviniemi	University of Liverpool, UK
Christian Koch	Bauhaus University, Weimar, Germany
Bimal Kumar	UK
Markus König	Ruhr University of Bochum, Germany
Debra Laefer	New York University, USA
Kincho Law	Stanford University, USA
SangHyun Lee	University of Michigan, USA
Fernanda Leite	University of Texas at Austin, USA
Haijiang Li	Cardiff University, UK
Ken-Yu Lin	University of Washington, USA

Jerome Lynch	University of Michigan, USA
John Messner	Pennsylvania State University, USA
Edmond Miresco	École de Technologie Supérieure, ÉTS, Canada
Ivan Mutis	Illinois Institute of Technology, USA
Hae Young Noh	Carnegie Mellon University, USA
William O'Brien	University of Texas at Austin, USA
Esther Obonyo	Pennsylvania State University, USA
Feniosky Peña-Mora	Columbia University, USA
Yaqub Rafiq	University of Plymouth, UK
Yves Reuland	Swiss Federal Institute of Technology, EPFL, Switzerland
Uwe Rüppel	Technical University of Darmstadt, Germany
Rafael Sacks	Technion - Israel Institute of Technology, Israel
Eduardo Santos	University of Sao Paulo, Brazil
Sergio Scheer	Federal University of Parana, Brazil
Raimar Scherer	Technical University of Dresden, Germany
Gennaro Senatore	Swiss Federal Institute of Technology, EPFL, Switzerland
Kristina Shea	Swiss Federal Institute of Technology, ETH Zurich, Switzerland
Kay Smarsly	Bauhaus University, Weimar, Germany
Lucio Soibelman	University of Southern California, USA
Sheryl Staub-French	University of British Columbia, Canada
Georg Suter	Technical University of Vienna, Austria
Pingbo Tang	Arizona State University, USA
Jochen Teizer	Ruhr University of Bochum, Germany
Walid Tizani	University of Nottingham, UK
Žiga Turk	University of Ljubljana, Slovenia
Xiangyu Wang	Curtin University, Australia
Nobuyoshi Yabuki	University of Osaka, Japan
Yimin Zhu	Louisiana State University, USA
Pieter de Wilde	University of Plymouth, UK

Contents – Part II

BIM and Engineering Ontologies

Contents – Part I

Computer Supported Construction Management

Life-Cycle Design Support

Monitoring and Control Algorithms in Engineering

Disaster Economics and Networked Transportation Infrastructures: Status Quo and a Multi-disciplinary Framework to Estimate Economic Losses

Fang Wei[1] , Eyuphan Koc[2(✉)] , Lucio Soibelman[2] , and Nan Li[1]

[1] Department of Construction Management, Tsinghua University,
Beijing 100084, China
`wei-f17@mails.tsinghua.edu.cn, nanli@tsinghua.edu.cn`
[2] Department of Civil and Environmental Engineering, University of Southern California,
Los Angeles, CA 90089, USA
`{ekoc,soibelman}@usc.edu`

Abstract. In recent years, the frequency and severity of catastrophic events triggered by natural hazards have increased. Meanwhile, man-made hazards, such as terrorist attacks, and their impacts on infrastructure systems have gained increasing attention. These hazards (both natural and man-made) can cause catastrophic physical damage to transportation infrastructure systems that are essential to the wellbeing of the society. Moreover, the direct economic losses (e.g., physical damage to infrastructure) diffuse and expand continually through the disruption of economic activities between different regions and industries, resulting in enormous and complex indirect losses. A comprehensive investigation of total losses, including direct and indirect losses, requires the use of economic impact analysis models. However, most of the economic impact analysis methods and models introduced in the existing literature fail to incorporate the spatially distributed and networked nature of transportation infrastructures. To achieve a comprehensive and a realistic understanding of the economic impacts caused by the disturbances to the transportation infrastructure, the spatial distribution and the networked nature of transportation systems has to be accounted for, and realistic and locally relevant hazard scenarios must be incorporated into the economic analyses. This paper first provides a detailed account of the status-quo in economic modeling associated with impact analysis of transportation disturbances to identify the gaps in this domain. Next, focusing on the commuting related economic impacts of transportation disturbances as an example, the paper introduces a multidisciplinary framework designed to demonstrate an understanding on how to address the gaps. Preliminary results from a Los Angeles case study are presented.

Keywords: Disasters · Economic impact analysis · Transportation
Interindustry economics

© Springer International Publishing AG, part of Springer Nature 2018
I. F. C. Smith and B. Domer (Eds.): EG-ICE 2018, LNCS 10864, pp. 3–22, 2018.
https://doi.org/10.1007/978-3-319-91638-5_1

1   Introduction

Natural and man-made hazards disturb transportation systems that are essential to the wellbeing of the society at an increasing rate and severity to cause extensive physical damage. Direct economic losses resulting from physical damages diffuse and expand continually through economic activities between different regions and industries, resulting in enormous indirect losses. Research on transport-related economic losses caused by the Niigata-Chuetsu earthquake shows that 40% of total losses occurred in the Kanto region and other non-ignorable losses reached remote regions such as Okinawa [1]. In this context, understanding the economic impacts of hazards beyond the direct losses and studying the inter-industry and inter-regional diffusion of the impact is critical. A comprehensive investigation of total losses (including direct, indirect and induced costs) requires the use of tools from interindustry economics in the form of economic impact analysis models.

Many researchers have been trying to estimate economic losses due to natural and man-made hazards using models for economic impact analysis. Among varieties of models that have been used the Input-Output models (IO) and the Computable General Equilibrium (CGE) models are the most common approaches. In a pioneering study, Cochrane [2] applied IO models to estimate disaster losses. Hallegatte [3] introduced adaptive behaviors into IO models and proposed the Adaptive Regional Input-Output model. Park et al. [4] and Park et al. [5] constructed demand-driven and supply-driven regional Input-Output models based on IMPLAN and CFS data, and applied them to evaluate the U.S. economic losses of various types of infrastructure disruptions caused by hypothetical terrorist attacks. Rose [6] and Rose and Liao [7] estimated the regional economic impacts of water supplies disruptions using a CGE model, and considered resilience measures. Some researchers also integrated other non-economic methods, such as Inoperability Input-Output Model [8]. However, the literature in hazards and economic impact analysis mostly focuses on individual infrastructure components (e.g. a bridge instead of the road network) and almost always fails to incorporate the spatially distributed and networked nature of civil infrastructures into the impact assessment. This is a major shortcoming of the works in this domain, as individual infrastructure components depend on the well-being of the network to carry out the desired functions. Thus, e.g. if one studies the impact of a hazard on a port and does not consider the post event condition of the inland highway network supporting the port's functionality, the analysis cannot provide insight into the totality of impacts induced on the supply chains going through the port. Only a handful of studies attempted to estimate the economic impacts of disturbances to spatially distributed and networked transportation systems. In addition, a predominant number of these studies assumed - hypothetically or based on hazard information - the failure of a small subset of infrastructure components and did not study the full spectrum of the potential impacts, i.e. functionality losses that spread well beyond a small subset of infrastructures, due to a locally relevant natural or man-made hazard.

To achieve a comprehensive and a realistic understanding of the economic impacts caused by the disturbances to the transportation systems, (1) the spatial distribution and the networked nature of transportation systems has to be accounted for, and (2) realistic and locally relevant hazard scenarios must be incorporated into the economic analyses. Surveying the literature, we provide a detailed account of the status-quo in economic modeling associated with the impact analysis of transportation disturbances to identify the gaps in this domain. We also introduce an exemplary and a multidisciplinary framework developed to demonstrate an understanding on how to begin addressing these gaps. The framework consists of an integration of engineering and economic domains, and incorporates hazard-specific features to investigate the earthquake risk and the potential impacts on commuting in the Greater Los Angeles Area. Direct impact indicators (in terms of commuting times and distances) are selected in order to represent the performance of the urban transportation network and how commuting based mobility can be disrupted due to simulated functionality losses. These indicators are coupled with economic impact analysis.

2 Literature Review

To draw a picture of the status-quo of this domain at the interface of economics and engineering, a literature review was conducted. To find the articles studying economic impact analysis and specifically focusing on transportation disturbances, Web of Science was accessed. Initially, various combinations of the keywords or keyword groups such as 'economic losses', 'hazard', 'disaster', 'disruption', 'transportation', 'economic impact analysis', 'supply chain disruption' were used to list the previous works in the area.

During the search process, a cut-off date was not used as we did not identify an earlier review with a similar scope. From the results of the search, articles that are authored in languages other than English were excluded. Note that our review did not include the articles that exclusively used engineering approaches to study transportation disturbances as well, i.e. studies that do not intend to analyze economic impacts were excluded. These include works that focus on, among many other branches of engineering, transportation safety, traffic engineering and optimization, infrastructure management, and so on. Lastly, articles from the field of economics that study direct and indirect economic losses due to man-made or natural hazards were excluded from the review if they investigated the impacts on several industries without clearly specifying the extent of losses in transportation related sectors [9–11]. The attempts at the initial keyword-based search helped us reveal 23 papers that satisfy our criteria. Studying the citation network of these 23 papers, 17 additional papers were discovered and added to the review inventory. Among these studies, 34 are published in peer-reviewed journals, 5 of them are published in conference proceedings and one is a technical report.

We present a categorization and elaborate on the reviewed studies based on this categorization. Originating from the motivation of this paper, the reviewed studies were categorized according to the following three dimensions: *(1) Scope of Network Modeling and Analysis*, to distinguish studies that achieve explicit transportation network modeling and analysis from the ones that do not attempt the same; *(2) Scope of Hazard Impact Information*, to identify studies that base their hazard impact information on simple assumptions, reported or reviewed impacts, or on realistic simulations of locally relevant hazards, or studies that simply do not have hazard information; *(3) Scope of Economic Modeling*, to identify the spectrum of economic impact analysis methods and tools utilized in reviewed studies. The remainder of this section is structured with respect to the first two dimensions of this categorization scheme.

2.1 Category 1: Papers that Use Simple Assumptions for Hazard Impacts (Direct Losses) and Do not Use Explicit Network Modeling

Among the reviewed studies, most have not used explicit transportation network modeling and analysis, and only used simple assumptions for the treatment of hazard impacts. Oztanriseven and Nachtmann [12] applied a Monte Carlo simulation model to estimate the potential losses of waterway disruptions on the MKARNS (McClellan–Kerr Arkansas River Navigation System), and calculated related holding cost, penalty cost and transportation cost. Other studies tried to quantify the indirect economic impacts of disruptions with initial losses spreading over numerous sectors. Lian and Haimes [13] applied a DIIM (dynamic inoperability input-output model) to estimate the economic impacts of a potential terrorist attack in Virginia which results in the inoperability of truck transportation, broadcasting and telecommunications and utilities sectors, at a level of 20%, 50% and 60%, respectively. It is essential to note that, in the case of terrorist attacks, it is hard to simulate the hazard realistically due to the innate randomness of these events. This leaves the researchers with simplistic assumptions about the damages to the infrastructure. Li et al. [14] examined the economic impacts of a hypothetical flooding scenario in London through an input-output analysis with initial losses in labor, service and other sectors. Park et al. [15] proposed NIEMO (national interstate economic model) and the supply-side NIEMO with a succeeding study [16] and applied the models to evaluate port closure scenarios. However, the final demand losses were estimated based on the reduction of imports and exports without any realistic hazard simulation. Park [16] also conducted demand-side and supply-side models on hypothetical port shutdown scenarios and looked at potential substitution effects estimated by econometric simulation models.

Other researchers estimated the economic impacts of supply chain disruptions without leveraging explicit network models. Wei et al. [17] estimated the direct and indirect supply-chain-related losses of Chinese white alcohol industry caused by several earthquakes in Sichuan using IIM (Inoperability Input-Output model). Gueler et al. [18] built a coal delivery network including coal mines and power plants and calculated the total transportation cost of partial or full disruption of the Ohio River as a transportation mode. Tan et al. [19] and Zhang and Lam [20] investigated the direct and total import/export related losses of port disruptions based on a Petri Net model for the Shenzhen port, respectively, in which they illustrated the flow of the supply chain of printer business of HP through the Shenzhen port.

Rose and Wei [21] estimated the total economic impacts of a 90-day seaport shutdown scenario based on supply-driven and demand-driven IO models. Santos and Haimes [22] estimated the economic impacts of airline transportation sector disruption caused by terrorism using IIM. Pant et al. [23] applied an MRIIM (multi-regional inoperability input-output model) to assess the economic losses of a two-week shutdown of the Port of Catoosa without considering disturbances to commodity flows transported through other ports. Thekdi and Santos [24] introduced a modified DIIM to quantify the economic impacts of sudden-onset port disruptions with scenario-based methods. Irimoto et al. [25] quantified the economic losses caused by regional and international transport links interruptions based on inter-regional and trans-national IO models, respectively. Tatano and Tsuchiya [1] used a SCGE (spatial computable general equilibrium model) to estimate the economic impacts of transportation infrastructure disruptions caused by Niigata-Chuetsu earthquake of 2004. The economic losses were calculated based on a simple assumed two-period disruption scenario. Ueda et al. [26] proposed a SCGE model to estimate the economic damage caused by railway traffic interruption due to earthquake. In the model, the price of transport services was set at 1 to 10 times higher than usual. In his study presenting a conceptual framework only, Thissen [27] pointed out that additional costs on transportation and commuting could have larger economic impacts on the society due to permanent increase in transport cost caused by increased security measures. The author proposed a SAGE (spatial applied general equilibrium model) and analyzed how the surging transportation costs would affect the production and labor market. However, the author did not deploy his framework on a case study.

2.2 Category 2: Papers that Use Reported/Reviewed Hazard Impacts (Direct Losses) and Do not Use Explicit Network Modeling

Only a few studies managed to introduce the impacts of past disasters (based on reported or reviewed disaster information) on transportation networks into economic models. Jaiswal et al. [28] estimated the direct and landslide risk (in monetary value) in a transportation line in Southern India by simple math approach. Catastrophic events of the recent past drew a lot of research attention. Kajitani et al. [29] investigated the 2011 Tohoku earthquake and tsunami to summarize the disaster related losses and estimated the capacity losses. MacKenzie et al. [30] examined the production related losses of the same event based on a multi-regional input-output model. Tokui et al. [31] calculated the indirect economic losses caused by supply chain disruptions using modified forward linkage model (a revised input-output model) based on self-estimated direct damages to economic sectors; however, the process of finding the damage ratios was not discussed in elaborate detail. These studies investigating the losses from the 2011 Tohoku earthquake and tsunami do not particularly focus on transport systems; however, disturbance to transportation is treated as a major source of economic loss. Xie et al. [32] used a CGE model and estimated the indirect economic impacts of 15.6% decrease in road freight service inputs to other sectors, which was triggered by transportation disruption due to the Great 2008 Chinese Ice Storm. Yu et al. [33] estimated the economic losses based on an IIM model when the transportation sector of Luzon, Philippines experienced a 15% of inoperability according to World Bank estimates.

2.3 Category 3: Papers that Use Realistic Simulated Hazard Impacts (Direct Losses) but Do not Use Explicit Network Modeling

Only two studies in the review inventory calculated the economic losses based on realistic simulated hazard impacts but without explicit network modeling. Zhang and Lam [34] estimated the probability of port disruptions based on climate analysis and then calculated the transportation related losses by a simple math approach. Rose et al. [35] used CGE and IO models to quantify the total economic impacts of port cargo disruptions caused by the SAFRR tsunami scenario which is based on extensive prior research.

2.4 Category 4: Papers that Use Simple Assumptions for Hazard Impacts (Direct Losses) but Use Explicit Network Modeling

Only a handful of studies estimated the impacts of transportation disruptions with explicit network modeling. Xie and Levinson [36] estimated the traffic related losses caused by the increase in travel time triggered by the collapse of the I-35 Bridge on the Mississippi river. However, they did not take the ripple effect across the national highway system caused by the bridge collapse into account. Omer et al. [37] proposed the NIRA framework (networked infrastructure resiliency assessment) and applied it on estimating the resilience of a regional transportation network-transportation corridor between Boston and New York City. Economic losses for Hartford-New York City Link under different levels of disruptions were calculated based on simple indicators such as average cost per hour per person. Ashrafi et al. [38] measured the costs of highway closures based on commodity values and the increase in time cost, however, the authors only investigated a single link disruption and could not accommodate commodity types due to data shortage. It is worth mentioning that only transportation related costs were calculated in these papers, as a result, the accounting of the ripple effects across other industries caused by network disruptions was missing.

On the other hand, some studies leveraged advanced economic models and managed to capture the ripple effects in the economy. Tsuchiya et al. [39] formulated an SCGE-transportation integrated model and applied it to estimate the economic losses due to links disconnection in hypothetical earthquake scenarios. However, they assumed that there is no congestion and travel times were estimated based on shortest paths. Kim and Kwon [40] built an integrated model consisting of a sub-transport model and a SCGE model and applied it to assess the impacts of traffic accessibility disruptions and production losses due to nuclear and radiation accidents in Japan. A multi-disciplinary group of researchers combined transportation network analysis with the National Interstate Economic Model (NIEMO), and evaluated the economic impact of disruptions on major elements of the highway network (bridges and tunnels) based on commodity flow data [41, 42]. However, the selection of disrupted bridges was not based on hazard considerations and was largely hypothetical being based on auxiliary metrics such volume of truck traffic crossing the bridge, number of alternative routes available, etc. Moreover, TransNIEMO is computationally expensive due to data acquisition and reconciliation, which limits the extensive application of the model.

2.5   Category 5: Papers that Use Reported/Reviewed Hazard Impacts (Direct Losses) and Use Explicit Network Modeling

Some researchers were able to gather data on past hazards to investigate impacts on transport networks. Mesa-Arango et al. [43] estimated the economic impacts of highway segments closure due to severe floods based on FAF3 data and historical disruptions records. Torrey [44] quantified the volumes of trucks and the amount of travel delay based on public data in order to estimate the impacts of congestions on trucking industry by region, metropolitan, state and national levels. However, both studies considered transport related operational costs by simple math operations and did not investigate the problem from inter-industry economics perspective. On the other hand, Tirasirichai and Enke [45] applied a regional CGE model to evaluate the indirect economic losses induced by increasing travel costs due to increased travel costs caused by damages to highway bridges. The increased travel costs data was based on earlier studies [46, 47]. However, the indirect losses were calculated on a set of random elasticity values, which are essential values to calibrate and identify all other parameters.

2.6   Category 6: Papers that Use Realistic Simulated Hazard Impacts (Direct Losses) and Use Explicit Network Modeling

Lastly, very few studies estimated the economic impacts of transportation infrastructure disruptions in a comprehensive way that incorporates explicit network modeling, and realistically simulated and locally relevant hazard impacts. Cho et al. [48] integrated seismic, transportation network, spatial allocation and economic models, and applied their methodology on the Elysian Park earthquake scenario. Studying the same scenario, Gordon et al. [49] estimated the structural damage, business interruptions, network disruption and bridge repair costs of the earthquake based on an integrated, operational model. Sohn et al. [50] estimated the final demand losses and increased transport costs of 1812 New Madrid earthquake based on functionality losses in the transportation network, final demand loss function, and an integrated commodity flow model. Postance et al. [51] combined disaster simulation and network modeling by quantifying increased travel time based on susceptible road segments and disruption scenarios. The scenarios were identified through a susceptibility analysis. However, economic losses in this study are measured by an increase travel time multiplying national user generalized cost without considering ripple effects across other industries.

Based on all of the above, we draw the following conclusions from our literature review. The existing economic impact analysis methods are sophisticated to the extent that transportation disturbances due to natural and man-made hazards can be investigated in a comprehensive way. However, most of the literature in this area does not leverage explicit transportation network models. This shortcoming undermines the spatially distributed nature of and the interdependencies that exist within today's transport systems. Moreover, hazards that create the disturbances are not incorporated into the investigation in a systematic way, where researchers often use simplistic assumptions to fill the gap of missing hazard impact information that is locally relevant to the study area. Having identified these gaps in the literature, we propose a framework in the next section to demonstrate a multi-disciplinary understanding on how to begin addressing these gaps.

3   Economic Impact Analysis of Commuting Disturbances

Here we introduce a multidisciplinary framework that was developed to demonstrate possible approaches to address the gaps identified in the literature. It is essential to note that the primary focus of this paper is the economics facet of the larger framework, however, we broadly introduce the other facets as well. The framework was designed to investigate the economic impacts of a potential earthquake event in the Greater Los Angeles Area. It takes advantage of public domain hazard simulation software to estimate damage states and restoration timelines for the bridge inventory[1] of a metropolitan area. The results from earthquake hazard simulations are used to construct the degraded versions of the network given the restoration information, to mimic the recovery of a transportation network following an earthquake[2].

In addition, the version of the framework introduced in this paper only focuses on the impact on commuting (home-workplace-home trips taken on a daily basis) in the study area and its economic consequences. Commuting is a rarely studied facet in economics of transportation disturbances compared to some other services provided by these networks (e.g., movement of freight goods). Leveraging fine grain public domain data on commuters and an open source routing engine, the framework calculates commuting costs (in terms of driving times and distances) for all of the commuters that use the metropolitan transportation network to access their workplaces. First, routing is done for the undamaged network (business-as-usual) to establish a pre-event baseline for comparing the increasing commuting costs on the degraded, i.e. damaged network versions. These costs are converted to monetary values and become inputs to the economic impact analysis. Figure 1 illustrates the conceptual framework.

The economic impact analysis facet of the framework takes increasing commuting costs as its input. Note that, during network analysis, it is assumed that commuters will maintain trips to their workplaces as usual, i.e. the earthquake event does not cause loss of employment, migration of labor or businesses, etc. This constant trip demand assumption is widely used in literature [52]. However, the commuting trips become costlier due to the hazard-related disturbance to transportation. We assume that increasing costs of commuting will be fully passed on to the consumers. Therefore, increasing costs result in increasing prices for the outputs of every sector that uses transportation services as an input. This increasing price effect throughout the economy and leads to a shrinkage in consumer expenditures. Decreasing consumer expenditure has a direct inhibiting impact on final demand. Consequently, the reduction in final demand results in a loss of total economic output in the region. Quantifying the loss of economic output over the

---

[1]   We assume that most critical components of the transportation network are its bridges. This is well established by the literature in transportation safety.

[2]   Earthquakes present a different opportunity for economic impact analysis than some of the other hazards. This is due to the advanced ability of scientists to forecast the impact of these events which gives way to policy initiatives directed to mitigation [50].

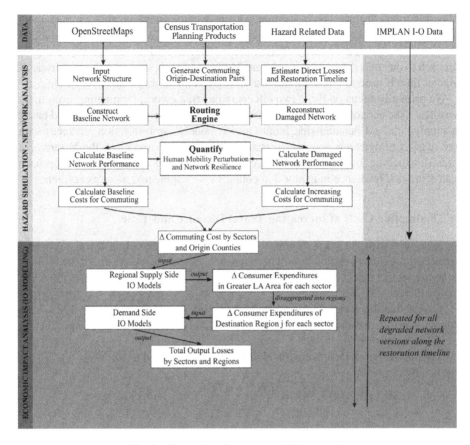

Fig. 1. Illustrating the conceptual framework.

restoration timeline of the network for its multiple degraded versions will allow us to estimate the total economic impact due to the earthquake related disturbance of commuting.

There are multiple ways for traffic network disruptions to induce increases in commuting costs. One of the ways is through the increase in operation costs. Commuters that have to travel on suboptimal routes due to the loss of functionality in the transportation network will travel over longer distances for longer durations. Increasing consumption in fuel, maintenance, repair, etc. follows from this adverse effect. In addition, for businesses that are paying mileage reimbursements to their employees, it will be costlier to provide the same benefit given a disrupted network. The mileage reimbursements are usually paid in terms of a constant dollar amount per unit distance traveled (e.g., $0.5/km). Last but not least, that people spending more time driving means they tend to spend less time on income generating or leisure activities. Here, there would be time-money tradeoff effects.

To estimate the economic cost of commuting disturbance, two factors need to be examined, namely the increase in travel distance and travel time. The economic cost of increasing travel distance can be estimated using average operation and reimbursement costs. However, the cost of travel time is difficult to quantify as it is a non-market intangible item and related to many factors [53]. There is still no universally accepted approach to quantify the cost of travel time. However, in this study, the average tradeoff value of time is used to represent the market price value of travel time.

We primarily focus on these two effects in our framework. Originating from these two effects, the economic impact of the commuting disturbance can be estimated based on supply-side and demand-side Input-Output models. As restoration advances with time, e.g. as bridges are opening to traffic, the economic impact of the hazard will diminish with time. In our future work, we will use the results of this step-wise approach as an economic resilience indicator that couples with engineered network resilience.

3.1   Estimating Costs of Increasing Travel Distance and Time

We quantify the direct impact indicators in the form of increasing travel times and distances through network analysis. The increasing traveling costs are distributed among economic sectors based on the Census data on commuters regarding the industries that employ them.

Assume that there are M regions and N industries, and assume i, j (i, j = 1, 2, ... M) denote the origin and destination regions, respectively. Finally, we denote production sectors with k (k = 1, 2, ... N).

Economic costs of increasing travel distance are quantified as follows:

$$\Delta TDC_{ij}^k = TRC_{ij}^k + \Delta TOC_{ij}^k \tag{1}$$

where

ΔTDC_{ij}^k is the cost of increasing travel distance (referenced to business-as-usual baseline network) from origin region[3] i to destination region j for sector k.

ΔTRC_{ij}^k is the increase in total reimbursement cost paid by employers to commuters traveling from origin region i to destination region j for sector k.

ΔTOC_{ij}^k is the increase in total operation cost from origin region i to destination region j, in which higher fuel consumption is the biggest part.

ΔTOC_{ij}^k is calculated simply by multiplying the total driving distance summed up for all commuting trips from i to j by the average cost of driving. The former comes from our network analysis and the latter is a statistic offered by the Bureau of Transportation Statistics[4].

---

[3] The economic region in the full deployment of the framework will be the regions in Los Angeles that we have the input-output table for.

[4] These values are published annually by Bureau of Transportation Statistics. Average cost of driving includes fuel, maintenance, and tires. Available online at: www.rita.dot.gov/bts.

For increasing travel time, the cost would be:

$$\Delta TTC_{ij}^k = \Delta TT_{ij}^k \times ATC_{ij}^k \qquad (2)$$

where

ΔTTC_{ij}^k is the total cost of increasing travel time from origin region i to destination region j for sector k.

ΔTT_{ij}^k is the increase in total travel time summed up for commuting trips from region i to j referenced to the baseline total.

ATC_{ij}^k is the average tradeoff value of time. This is to account for the time spent by commuters in driving instead of income generating or leisure activities.

In this way, the total cost of increasing travel distance and time:

$$\Delta TC_{ij}^k = \Delta TDC_{ij}^k + \Delta TTC_{ij}^k \qquad (3)$$

where

ΔTC_{ij}^k is the increase in total travel cost from origin region i to destination region j for sector k.

3.2 Estimating the Impact Through Interindustry Economics: Supply-Side IO Model

In 1958, Ghosh [54] proposed the supply-driven IO model. It has fixed allocation coefficients similar to the Leontief Input-Output model [55]. Following its inception, the model received criticism regarding its plausibility [56], however, Dietzenbacher [57] proposed a way to address this problem by interpreting the Ghosh model as a price model.

The designed framework uses a supply-side IO model to estimate the impact of increasing commuting costs in the regional economy. It should be noted that the impact of price inflation (caused by increasing transportation costs) on consumer expenditure cannot be treated independently for every region as consumers may spend their money on goods and services in any region in the Greater Los Angeles Area. Therefore, we take the Greater Los Angeles Area as a single region and use a supply side IO model to estimate the decreased consumer expenditures. To be specific, the inflation in sector k's goods and services caused by increasing travel costs in all regions results in decreasing consumer expenditures in the Greater Los Angeles Area. In the supply-side IO model, increasing travel costs are aggregated in order to estimate the whole impact on consumer expenditure in the Greater Los Angeles Area.

The total increasing travel cost for sector k by all regions is aggregated as following:

$$\Delta TC^K = \sum_{i=1}^{M} \sum_{j=1}^{M} \Delta TC_{ij}^k \qquad (4)$$

The decreasing consumer expenditure is calculated as following:

$$\Delta CE^K = \Delta TC^k \times (I - B)^{-1} \qquad (5)$$

where

ΔTC^k_{ij} is the total price inflation for sector k due to increasing commuting costs.
ΔCE^K is the decrease in total consumer expenditure for sector k after price inflation effect.

$(I - B)^{-1}$ is the output inverse matrix and B is the direct output coefficients matrix of the Greater Los Angeles Area.

In the short term, it is assumed that producers will not be closed or new ones will not be established but the existing producers will change their production quantity. Therefore, the impact of reduced consumer expenditure on total output losses for each region is not the same given different output levels for each region. Then the decreased expenditures will be reallocated to each region.

The reallocation process of decreasing consumer expenditures is as following:

$$\Delta CE^k_j = c^k_j \times \Delta CE^K \qquad (6)$$

where

ΔCE^k_j is the total decreased consumer expenditure in region j for sector k.

c^k_j is the consumer expenditure ratio of region j to the whole area.

Next, we use a demand side IO model to estimate the economic impacts based on reductions in final demand.

3.3 Estimating the Impact Through Interindustry Economics: Demand-Side IO Model

Demand-side IO models have been proposed and widely-used to assess the economic impact of reduction in final demand. Here, we make the assumption that there is no substitution effect and consumer expenditures have direct impacts on final demand. This assumption was proposed and used in TransNIEMO [42]. Then, the total output losses can be calculated based on NIEMO, a demand-driven Input-Output model. This demand-side version of NIEMO is useful to analyzing the backward linkage impacts. In our framework, we estimate total output losses with an approach similar to [15] as follows.

Using the decreasing consumer expenditures from the supply-side, we use a demand-side Input-Output model to estimate the total output loss for sector k due to the losses in final demand in destination region j.

$$\Delta X^k_j = (I - A)^{-1}_j \times \left(-\Delta CE^k_j\right) \qquad (7)$$

where

ΔX_j^k is the decrease in total output in destination region j for sector k.

$(I - A)_j^{-1}$ is input inverse matrix and A is direct input coefficients matrix in destination region j.

Based on that, the total impacts of commuting disturbances can be summed up by regions and by sectors.

The total impacts by regions are:

$$\sum_{k=1}^{N} \Delta X_j^k \qquad (8)$$

And the total impacts by sectors are:

$$\sum_{j=1}^{M} \Delta X_j^k \qquad (9)$$

In this way, the total output losses induced by increasing commuting costs due to transportation infrastructure disruptions can be calculated. Sectors and regions that are more easily affected by network disturbances can be identified. Prevention measures can be taken and limited resources can be distributed wisely to mitigate the general economic impacts. Note that, this economic impact estimation methodology will be carried out for all the degraded versions of the transportation network. This will enable us to observe the economic recovery along with the recovery in the road network.

4   Case Study: Quantifying Economic Impacts of Increasing Travel Time for Commuting in Los Angeles

To deploy the economic facet of the framework that the authors focus on in this study, results from a sister paper by Koc et al. [58] on coupled assessment of mobility-infra-structure network resilience were used. In their work, Koc et al. carried out the hazard analysis and the network analysis encapsulated in the framework for a case study investigating the commuting in Los Angeles and the potential impacts of the governing seismic hazard in Downtown Los Angeles Area. Using state-of-the-art earthquake hazard analysis, Koc et al. found the disturbances in the physical transportation network (bridges only) along with the downtimes of the damaged components. Consequently, using the Census Transportation Planning Products (CTPP) data [59], they quantified the increasing travel times and distances that commuters (the dominant driving mode only in Los Angeles) would have to bear at the Traffic Analysis Zone (TAZ) level of detail. During the restoration and recovery of the network, the improving travel times and distances were also quantified to achieve an understanding of resilience. Adopting these results at an aggregated level for the 5 counties in the Greater Los Angeles Area commuting zone, the authors carried out preliminary economic analysis to deploy the economic facet of the framework. Within the scope here, economic impacts are quantified only from an increased travel time standpoint where the authors use the average tradeoff value of time values published by California Department of Transportation [60]. Local input-output data are obtained from IMPLAN Group [61]. The industry break-down scheme is aggregated by the authors to transform the 536 industries in IMPLAN data into 7 industries to match the industry aggregation in the CTPP dataset. There are 5 counties in the Greater Los Angeles Area, including Los Angeles, Orange, Riverside, San Bernardino and Ventura counties. For each county, direct-input coefficients matrix (A matrix) and direct-output coefficients matrix (B matrix) are generated. Model year is set to be 2017.

4.1 Data Processing and Preliminary Results from Economic Analysis

With the gathered data, economic analysis was carried out as follows. First, treating 5 counties as origins and destinations, total travel times per economic sector between all origins and destinations were calculated by simply multiplying the number of commuters with average travel times before and after the earthquake. This is done at 5 discrete time intervals, between day 0 (before the hazard) and day 1, from day 1 to 7, from day 7 to 30, from day 30 to 90, and from day 90 to 1 year, respectively. This way, changes in total travel times during restoration are obtained at a reasonable resolution in terms of timeline. Take the interval from day 1 to day 7 as an example, the increase in total travel time for all commuters from region i to region j in sector k can be calculated as:

$$\Delta TT_{ij}^{k,\,day\,1\,to\,day\,7} = (7 - 1) * \left(TT_{ij}^{k,\,day\,7} - TT_{ij}^{k,\,day\,1} \right) \tag{10}$$

Then, the total cost of increasing travel time, ΔTTC_{ij}^k, can be calculated based on Eq. (2). The average tradeoff value of time for automobiles are taken from Vehicle Operation Cost Parameters[5] table to represent the average tradeoff value of time.

These costs are then aggregated by sectors. The decreasing consumer expenditure for each sector is calculated based on a supply-side IO model as shown in Eq. (5), and is allocated to each county using average household income levels obtained from IMPLAN.

Lastly, a supply-side IO model is used to estimate the total output losses based on Eq. (7). Accounting for the tradeoff value of time only, the annual total output loss in the Greater Los Angeles Area is estimated to be over 270 million USD. Table 1 shows the total output losses for five counties, and Table 2 shows the direct and indirect losses for seven industries in the study region. Direct losses refer to the total tradeoff value of increasing travel times. Total losses are estimated economic impacts across the whole economy, in which the impacts of economic transactions are taken into consideration. The indirect economic loss caused by increased commuting times is about 117 million dollars, accounting for 42.36% of total economic losses. According to Tables 1 and 2,

---

[5] The Vehicle Operation Cost Parameters are statewide representative average values recommended by California Department of Transportation [60] to be used in the economic analysis of highway and other projects.

sectors of information, finance, real estate, and technology services etc. suffer the most, and these losses are exacerbated during the process of economic activities.

Table 1. Estimated total output losses in five counties (million USD).

	Los Angeles	Orange	Riverside	San Bernardino	Ventura
1. Agriculture, forestry, fish & hunting, mining, construction	4.26	4.60	3.19	3.09	4.37
2. Manufacturing	7.81	7.78	4.82	5.01	7.08
3. Transportation & warehousing, utilities, wholesale trade, retail trade	12.52	12.84	8.39	8.34	12.02
4. Finance & insurance, real estate & rental, scientific & technology services, information, management of companies, administrative & waste services	22.85	24.72	13.88	13.14	22.36
5. Education services, health & social services	8.09	8.63	5.49	5.69	8.09
6. Arts, entertainment & recreation, accommodation & food services	4.11	4.32	2.77	2.81	4.05
7. Other services	4.64	4.82	3.24	3.31	4.64
Total	64.27	67.73	41.79	41.40	62.62

Table 2. Direct and indirect output losses in the Greater Los Angeles Area (million USD).

	Direct losses	Indirect losses	Total losses
1. Agriculture, forestry, fish & hunting, mining, construction	11.26	8.25	19.51
2. Manufacturing	19.65	12.85	32.50
3. Transportation & warehousing, utilities, wholesale trade, retail trade	32.89	21.22	54.11
4. Finance & insurance, real estate & rental, scientific & technology services, information, management of companies, administrative & waste services	35.4	61.56	96.96
5. Education services, health & social services	32.35	3.65	36.00
6. Arts, entertainment & recreation, accommodation & food services	13.8	4.26	18.06
7. Other services	14.78	5.88	20.66
Total	160.14	117.66	277.80

5   Limitations of the Framework

One major limitation of this study is that it only captures the economic impacts of increasing transportation costs. Other direct economic losses such as costs of physical damages to infrastructure and increasing freight shipping costs are not included. Therefore, there might be some underestimation of economic losses in the current version of the framework.

Second, some assumptions and simplifications have to be made in order to obtain the direct losses. The assumption that people will maintain their commuting trips as usual after earthquakes ignores the possibility that some commuters choose to work from home or change their transport mode considering changes in travel costs and travel time. In addition, the value of travel time is intangible. It is hard to capture the effects of spending more time on commuting trips holistically with the averaged tradeoff value of time. Also, the accuracy of the indicators to estimate the increasing transportation costs are crucial, such as mileage reimbursement rates. These indicators vary by regions as well as industries and may not be readily available.

Lastly, the inherent shortcomings of the IO models cannot be ignored, such as linearity and the assumption of no substitution effects. In this paper, supply-side and demand-side IO models are chosen because of modest data demand compared to alternatives such as CGE models. As a result, some realism may be sacrificed. More advanced modeling can achieve a more realistic analysis.

6   Conclusion and Future Work

The relationship of hazards and transportation systems will be a focus of increasing attention in the coming decades, mostly because hazardous events are becoming more frequent and more severe, threatening the civil infrastructure at increasing rates with unprecedented risks. With this paper, we pressed on the need of advancing the multi-disciplinary research in this domain without losing the individual contributions of participating disciplines for the sake of simplicity. The gaps in the area were identified through a literature review and results were presented based on a categorization designed according to the objective of the paper. We find that more than often, networked transportation systems are abstracted from economic analyses. Moreover, despite the advances in hazards science, realistic simulations of locally relevant hazards are not fully integrated into economic studies. These will limit our ability to comprehensively quantify the economic impacts of infrastructure disruptions caused by disasters. Building on this foundation, we presented an exemplary impact analysis framework that is designed to study the adverse economic impacts of earthquakes on commuting in metropolitan areas. This paper did not include a full case study, however, we are currently deploying the framework in Los Angeles, where commuting to work is a daily undertaking for most working Angelenos. This initial effort will help us refine the framework. Other items in our future work agenda include incorporation of comprehensive direct losses (e.g., dollar value of physical damage to infrastructure), and multimodal mobility analysis into the framework. The latter will enable us to study mode-choice behavior in disaster settings. Overall, we will improve upon the current version of the framework presented here towards more accurate economic impact analysis.

Acknowledgements. This material is based upon work supported by National Key R&D Program of China under grant No. 2017YFC0803308, National Natural Science Foundation of China (NSFC) under grant No. U1709212, 71741023, and Tsinghua University Initiative Scientific Research Program under grant No. 2014z21050 and 2015THZ0. The authors are thankful for the support of Ministry of Science and Technology of China, NSFC and Tsinghua University. Any opinions, findings, and conclusions or recommendations expressed in this paper are those of the authors and do not necessarily reflect the views of the funding agencies.

References

1. Tatano, H., Tsuchiya, S.: A framework for economic loss estimation due to seismic transportation network disruption: a spatial computable general equilibrium approach. Nat. Hazards **44**, 253–265 (2008)
2. Cochrane, H.C.: Predicting the Economic Impacts of Earthquakes (1974)
3. Hallegatte, S.: An adaptive regional input-output model and its application to the assessment of the economic cost of Katrina. Risk Anal. **28**, 779–799 (2008)
4. Park, J., Gordon, P., Kim, S., Kim, Y., Moore, J.E.I., Richardson, H.W.: Estimating the State-by-State Economic Impacts of Hurricane Katrina (2005)
5. Park, J.Y., Gordon, P., Moore, J.S.E., Richardson, H.W.: The state-by-state economic impacts of the 2002 shutdown of the Los Angeles-Long Beach ports. Growth Change **39**, 548–572 (2008)
6. Rose, A.: Defining and measuring economic resilience to disasters. Disaster Prev. Manag. Int. J. **13**, 307–314 (2004)
7. Rose, A., Liao, S.Y.: Modeling regional economic resilience to disasters: a computable general equilibrium analysis of water service disruptions. J. Reg. Sci. **45**, 75–112 (2005)
8. Crowther, K.G., Haimes, Y.Y., Taub, G.: Systemic valuation of strategic preparedness through application of the inoperability input-output model with lessons learned from Hurricane Katrina. Risk Anal. **27**, 1345–1364 (2007)
9. Aloughareh, I.R., Ashtiany, M.G., Nasserasadi, K.: An integrated methodology for regional macroeconomic loss estimation of earthquake: a case study of Tehran. Singap. Econ. Rev. **61**, 1550025 (2016)
10. Koks, E.E., Thissen, M.: A multiregional impact assessment model for disaster analysis. Econ. Syst. Res. **28**, 429–449 (2016)
11. Koks, E.E., Carrera, L., Jonkeren, O., Aerts, J.C.J.H., Husby, T.G., Thissen, M., Standardi, G., Mysiak, J.: Regional disaster impact analysis: comparing input-output and computable general equilibrium models. Nat. Hazards Earth Syst. Sci. **16**, 1911–1924 (2016)
12. Oztanriseven, F., Nachtmann, H.: Economic impact analysis of inland waterway disruption response. Eng. Econ. **62**, 73–89 (2017)
13. Lian, C., Halmes, Y.Y.: Managing the risk of terrorism to interdependent infrastructure systems through the dynamic inoperability input-output model. Syst. Eng. **9**, 241–258 (2006)
14. Li, J., Crawford-Brown, D., Syddall, M., Guan, D.: Modeling imbalanced economic recovery following a natural disaster using input-output analysis. Risk Anal. **33**, 1908–1923 (2013)

15. Park, J., Gordon, P., Ii, J.E.M., Richardson, H.W.: Simulating the State-by-State Effects of Terrorist Attacks on Three Major U.S. Ports: Applying NIEMO (National Interstate Economic Model) (2005)
16. Park, J.Y.: The economic impacts of dirty- bomb attacks on the los angeles and long beach ports: applying the supply-driven NIEMO (national interstate economic model). J. Homel. Secur. Emerg. Manag. **5**, Article 21 (2008)
17. Wei, H., Dong, M., Sun, S.: Inoperability input-output modeling (IIM) of disruptions to supply chain networks. Syst. Eng. **13**, 324–339 (2010)
18. Gueler, C.U., Johnson, A.W., Cooper, M.: Case study: energy industry economic impacts from ohio river transportation disruption. Eng. Econ. **57**, 77–100 (2012)
19. Tan, X.M., Zhang, Y., Lam, J.S.L.: Economic impact of port disruptions on industry clusters: a case study of Shenzhen. In: Yan, X.P., Hu, Z.Z., Zhong, M., Wu, C.Z., Yang, Z. (eds.) 3rd International Conference on Transportation Information and Safety (ICTIS 2015), pp. 617–622. IEEE, New York (2015)
20. Zhang, Y., Lam, J.S.L.: Estimating economic losses of industry clusters due to port disruptions. Transp. Res. Part A-Policy Pract. **91**, 17–33 (2016)
21. Rose, A., Wei, D.: Estimating the economic consequences of a port shutdown: the special role of resilience. Econ. Syst. Res. **25**, 212–232 (2013)
22. Santos, J.R., Haimes, Y.Y.: Modeling the demand reduction input-output (I-O) inoperability due to terrorism of interconnected infrastructures. Risk Anal. **24**, 1437–1451 (2004)
23. Pant, R., Barker, K., Grant, F.H., Landers, T.L.: Interdependent impacts of inoperability at multi-modal transportation container terminals. Transp. Res. Part E Logist. Transp. Rev. **47**, 722–737 (2011)
24. Thekdi, S.A., Santos, J.R.: Supply chain vulnerability analysis using scenario-based input-output modeling: application to port operations. Risk Anal. **36**, 1025–1039 (2016)
25. Irimoto, H., Shibusawa, H., Miyata, Y.: Evaluating the economic damages of transport disruptions using a transnational and interregional input-output model for Japan, China, and South Korea. In: AIP Conference Proceedings, p. 110002 (6 p.). AIP - American Institute of Physics, College Park (2017)
26. Ueda, T., Koike, A., Iwakami, K.: Economic damage assessment of catastrophes in high speed rail network. In: Proceedings of 1st Workshop for Comparative Study on Urban Earthquake Disaster Management, pp. 13–19 (2001)
27. Thissen, M.: The indirect economic effects of a terrorist attack on transport infrastructure: a proposal for a SAGE. Disaster Prev. Manag. **13**, 315–322 (2004)
28. Jaiswal, P., Van Westen, C.J., Jetten, V.: Quantitative assessment of direct and indirect landslide risk along transportation lines in southern India. Nat. Hazards Earth Syst. Sci. **10**, 1253–1267 (2010)
29. Kajitani, Y., Chang, S.E., Tatano, H.: Economic Impacts of the 2011 Tohoku-oki earthquake and tsunami. Earthq. Spectra. **29**, S457–S478 (2013)
30. MacKenzie, C., Santos, J., Barker, K.: Measuring changes in international production from a disruption: case study of the Japanese earthquake and tsunami. Int. J. Prod. Econ. **138**, 293–302 (2012)
31. Tokui, J., Kawasaki, K., Miyagawa, T.: The economic impact of supply chain disruptions from the Great East-Japan earthquake. Japan World Econ. **41**, 59–70 (2017)
32. Xie, W., Li, N., Li, C., Wu, J.D., Hu, A., Hao, X.: Quantifying cascading effects triggered by disrupted transportation due to the Great 2008 Chinese Ice Storm: implications for disaster risk management. Nat. Hazards **70**, 337–352 (2014)

33. Yu, K.D.S., Tan, R.R., Santos, J.R.: Impact estimation of flooding in manila: an inoperability input-output approach. In: 2013 IEEE Systems and Information Engineering Design Symposium (SIEDS), pp. 47–51. IEEE, New York (2013)
34. Zhang, Y., Lam, J.S.L.: Estimating the economic losses of port disruption due to extreme wind events. Ocean Coast. Manag. **116**, 300–310 (2015)
35. Rose, A., Sue Wing, I., Wei, D., Wein, A.: Economic impacts of a California Tsunami. Nat. Hazards Rev. **17**, 4016002 (2016)
36. Xie, F., Levinson, D.: Evaluating the effects of the I-35W bridge collapse on road-users in the twin cities metropolitan region. Transp. Plan. Technol. **34**, 691–703 (2011)
37. Omer, M., Mostashari, A., Nilchiani, R.: Assessing resilience in a regional road-based transportation network. Int. J. Ind. Syst. Eng. **13**, 389–408 (2013)
38. Ashrafi, Z., Shahrokhi Shahraki, H., Bachmann, C., Gingerich, K., Maoh, H.: Quantifying the criticality of highway infrastructure for freight transportation. Transp. Res. Rec. J. Transp. Res. Board **2610**, 10–18 (2017)
39. Tsuchiya, S., Tatano, H., Okada, N.: Economic loss assessment due to railroad and highway disruptions. Econ. Syst. Res. **19**, 147–162 (2007)
40. Kim, E., Kwon, Y.J.: Indirect impact of nuclear power plant accidents using an integrated spatial computable general equilibrium model with a microsimulation module on the Korean transportation network. In: Kim, E., Kim, B.H.S. (eds.) Quantitative Regional Economic and Environmental Analysis for Sustainability in Korea. NFRSAP, vol. 25, pp. 141–152. Springer, Singapore (2016). https://doi.org/10.1007/978-981-10-0300-4_8
41. Park, J., Cho, J., Gordon, P., Moore II, J.E., Richardson, H.W., Yoon, S.: Adding a freight network to a national interstate input-output model: a TransNIEMO application for California. J. Transp. Geogr. **19**, 1410–1422 (2011)
42. Cho, J.K., Gordon, P., Moore, J.E., Pan, Q., Park, J.Y., Richardson, H.W.: TransNIEMO: economic impact analysis using a model of consistent inter-regional economic and network equilibria. Transp. Plan. Technol. **38**, 483–502 (2015)
43. Mesa-Arango, R., Zhan, X., Ukkusuri, S.V., Mitra, A.: Direct transportation economic impacts of highway networks disruptions using public data from the United States. J. Transp. Saf. Secur. **8**, 36–55 (2016)
44. Torrey, W.F.: Estimating the cost of congestion to the trucking industry standardized methodology for congestion monitoring and monetization. Transp. Res. Rec. 57–67 (2017)
45. Tirasirichai, C., Enke, D.: Case study: applying a regional CGE model for estimation of indirect economic losses due to damaged highway bridges. Eng. Econ. **52**, 367–401 (2007)
46. Enke, D.L., Tirasirichai, C., Luna, R.: Estimation of earthquake loss due to bridge damage in the St. Louis metropolitan area. II: indirect losses. Nat. Hazards Rev. **9**, 12–19 (2008)
47. Chen, G., Anderson, N., Luna, R., Stephenson, R., El-Engebawy, M., Silva, P., Zoughi, R., Hoffman, D., Enke, D., Rogers, D.: Assessment and Mitigation of New Madrid Earthquake Hazards to Transportation Structure Systems (2005)
48. Cho, S., Gordon, P., Moore, J.E., Richardson, H.W., Shinozuka, M., Chang, S.: Integrating transportation network and regional economic models to estimate the costs of a large urban earthquake. J. Reg. Sci. **41**, 39–65 (2001)
49. Gordon, P., Moore II, J.E., Richardson, H.W., Shinozuka, M., An, D., Cho, S.: Earthquake disaster mitigation for urban transportation systems: an integrated methodology that builds on the Kobe and Northridge experiences. In: Okuyama, Y., Chang, S.E. (eds.) Modeling Spatial and Economic Impacts of Disasters, pp. 205–232. Springer, Heidelberg (2004). https://doi.org/10.1007/978-3-540-24787-6_11
50. Sohn, J., Kim, T.J., Hewings, G.J.D., Lee, J.S., Jang, S.G.: Retrofit priority of transport network links under an earthquake. J. Urban Plan. Dev. **129**, 195–210 (2003)

51. Postance, B., Hillier, J., Dijkstra, T., Dixon, N.: Extending natural hazard impacts: an assessment of landslide disruptions on a national road transportation network. Environ. Res. Lett. **12**, 014010 (2017)
52. Evangelos, S., Kiremidjian, A.S.: Treatment of Uncertainties in Seismic Risk Analysis of Transportation Systems (2006)
53. Tirasirichai, C.: An indirect loss estimation methodology to account for regional earthquake damage to highway bridges. ProQuest dissertations theses, p. 147 (2007)
54. Ghosh, A.: Input-output approach in an allocation system. Economica **XXV**, 58–64 (1958)
55. Leontief, W.: Quantitative input and output relations in the economic systems of the United States. Rev. Econ. Stat. **18**, 105–125 (1936)
56. Oosterhaven, J.: On the plausibility of the supply-driven input-output model. J. Reg. Sci. **28**, 203–217 (1988)
57. Dietzenbacher, E.: In vindication of the Ghosh model: a reinterpretation as a price model. J. Reg. Sci. **37**, 629–651 (1997)
58. Koc, E., Akhavan, A., Castro, E., Cetiner, B., Soibelman, L., Wang, Q., Taciroglu, E.: Framework for coupled assessment of human mobility and infrastructure resilience under extreme events (in review). J. Comput. Civ. Eng. Spec. Collect. Comput. Approaches Enable Smart Sustain. Urban Syst. (2018)
59. CTPP, Census Transportation Planning Products. http://ctpp.transportation.org/Pages/5-Year-Data.aspx. Accessed 19 Mar 2018
60. California Department of Transportation, Vehicle Operation Cost Parameters. http://www.dot.ca.gov/hq/tpp/offices/eab/benefit_cost/LCBCA-economic_parameters.html. Accessed 19 Mar 2018
61. Minnesota IMPLAN Group (MIG), Impact Analysis for Planning (IMPLAN) System. http://www.implan.com. Accessed 19 Mar 2018

Data-Driven Operation of Building Systems: Present Challenges and Future Prospects

Mario Bergés[1]([⊠]), Henning Lange[1], and Jingkun Gao[2]

[1] Civil and Environmental Engineering Department, Carnegie Mellon University,
5000 Forbes Avenue, Pittsburgh, PA, USA
marioberges@cmu.edu
[2] Alibaba Group, Hangzhou, China

Abstract. In this paper we review the current landscape of data-driven decision making in the context of operating residential and commercial building systems with energy management objectives. First, we present results from a literature review focused on identifying new sources of data that have become available (e.g., smart-phone sensors, utility smart meters) and their potential to impact the decision making processes involved in operating these facilities. Existing obstacles to realizing the full potential of these novel data sources are discussed and later explored more in depth through case studies. These include limited interoperability and standardization practices, high labor and/or maintenance costs for installing and maintaining the instrumentation and computationally expensive inference procedures for extracting useful information out of the measurements. Finally, two specific research projects that address some of these challenges are presented in detail: one on disaggregating the total electricity consumption of a building into its constituent loads for informing predictive maintenance practices; and another on standardizing meta-data about sensors and actuators in existing Building Automation Systems (BAS) so that software applications targeting building systems can be deployed in different buildings without the need for manual configuration. Our case studies reveal that the rapid proliferation of sensing/control devices, alone, will not improve the building systems being monitored or significantly alter the way these systems are managed or controlled. When data about the physical world is a commodity, it is the ability to extract actionable information from this resource what generates value and, more often than not, this process requires significant domain expertise.

1 Introduction

Buildings account for approximately 40% of the annual energy consumption in the U.S., and similar proportions of the energy used in other countries. Commercial buildings, in particular, represent 45% of that figure (i.e., 20% of the total) [1]. There are great opportunities to reduce these numbers through efficiency

© Springer International Publishing AG, part of Springer Nature 2018
I. F. C. Smith and B. Domer (Eds.): EG-ICE 2018, LNCS 10864, pp. 23–52, 2018.
https://doi.org/10.1007/978-3-319-91638-5_2

upgrades, optimized operation and user engagement, as evidenced by many different studies (e.g., [2,3]). For example, research shows that up to 40% of the energy used by HVAC systems is wasted due to faulty operation [4], so merely identifying and correcting these faults would result in a substantial reduction of the total energy used.

It can be argued that there has been no better time to seize these opportunities than now. Advances in sensing and communication technologies have made it possible for us to instrument more and more of our buildings, which has led to numerous new opportunities to better understand and optimize their energy consumption patterns. However, though there are significantly more sensing and actuation points in buildings today, leveraging them to make improved data-driven decision making poses engineering and scientific challenges spanning areas as diverse as computing (e.g., devising efficient algorithms for data processing), hardware (e.g., designing low-power, low-cost sensors) and even government (e.g., enacting and promoting standard information models).

In this paper we review the current landscape of data-driven decision making in the context of operating residential and commercial building systems. First, we present results from a literature review focused on identifying new sources of data that have become available (e.g., smart-phone sensors, utility smart meters) and their potential to impact the decision making processes involved in operating these facilities. Existing obstacles to realizing the full potential of these novel data sources are presented in general and later explored in more depth through two case studies: one on disaggregating the total electricity consumption of a building into its constituent loads for informing predictive maintenance practices; and another on standardizing meta-data about sensors and actuators in existing Building Automation Systems (BAS) so that software applications targeting building systems can be deployed in different buildings without the need for manual configuration.

1.1 Flying Blind: Building Energy Management Today

In general terms, managing a building's energy demand is a cost-minimization task (i.e., an optimization problem). Two broad types of objectives are being minimized: (a) monetary and comfort costs to the building owner/tenant or occupant and (b) operational costs to grid operators and utilities (i.e., via demand response programs). Needless to say, solutions to this problem need to also meet many constraints and, because of the large number of decision variables involved and their continuous nature (e.g., zone-level temperature set-points, equipment schedules) the solution space is large and complex. To further complicate matters, there are significant uncertainties associated with most of the variables in this type of optimization problem (e.g., human comfort, weather patterns, noisy sensor measurements), and due to the heterogeneity of the building stock and the dynamic environments/functions that buildings need to operate in and support, each of these optimization problems are very much building-specific and time-dependent.

In more concrete terms, we can define a model for a building's thermodynamic behavior to better understand the challenges that these optimization problems present. A discrete dynamic system is generally used in the literature to express relationships between the building's internal state, and all of the known influences (e.g., [5]). Paired with a model for the measurements (e.g., sensor data) we have of the building, these two relationships define the system and our observations of it:

$$\mathbf{s}_{t+1} = f(\mathbf{s}_t, \mathbf{u}_t, \mathbf{w}_t) \tag{1}$$
$$\mathbf{y}_t = h(\mathbf{s}_t, \mathbf{u}_t, \mathbf{w}_t) \tag{2}$$

Here $\mathbf{s}_t$ is the state vector (e.g., temperature of all zones); $\mathbf{u}_t$ is the input vector, which describes the controllable parameters (e.g., set-points, fan speeds, chiller status, etc.); $\mathbf{w}_t$ is a vector capturing the disturbances to the system or the uncontrollable input (e.g., outside temperature, user-requested setpoints, solar irradiance, etc.); and $\mathbf{y}_t$ are the measurements. These measurements could be a subset of the state variables, or any other quantity related to the current state of the building, such as the building's total electrical power consumption p_t.

Equations 1 (the plant model) and 2 (the observation model), if known, can then be used to design input sequences ($\mathbf{u}_t$) that optimize some objective function. For instance, imagine that we can find a function mapping from the set of measurements we have $\mathbf{y}_t$ to both the total power consumed by the building p_t as well as the average daily discomfort of occupants c_d. Given these, an operator can try to find a sequence of, say, temperature setpoints for every room $\mathbf{u}_t$ as follows:

$$\min_{\{\mathbf{u}_t\}_{t \in T_d}} J(p_{t+1}, \dots, p_{t+T}, c_d)$$

Here J is a cost function in terms discomfort and power, T is a time horizon for the optimization, and T_d is the set of all times within that period. We have purposefully omitted any mention of the constraints in this problem but even with this simplistic and general model, it is easy to see why building energy management is complicated. Among the many challenges (most of which exceed the scope of this paper), one can easily identify the following:

- Many parameters contain significant uncertainty (e.g., $\mathbf{w}_t$, $\mathbf{y}_t$), and this uncertainty propagates.
- Functions f and h are seldom known and there is reason to believe they may be unidentifiable [6]. Furthermore, these functions evolve over time with the building.
- The cost function J may not be simple and/or convex, thus making the optimization more challenging.
- To identify and properly evaluate these models we need to have well-curated historical records of the different measurements (e.g., $p_t, \dots, p_{t+T}$).

A more insidious problem not easily deduced from the above formulation is that we rarely have measurements $\mathbf{y}_t$ that directly map to concepts that a facility manger or occupant would care about. In other words, many of the useful objectives require auxiliary functions mapping observations to higher-level concepts such as occupant discomfort. For instance, facility operators care about minimizing the energy supplied to unoccupied spaces, or tracking the energy consumed by an individual appliance, yet these observations are rarely elements of the set of measurements $\mathbf{y}_t$.

1.2   Are More Sensors the Answer?

Currently, a lack of understanding of the determinants of building energy demand forces building managers to control the building's energy use in a conservative, heuristic manner. For example most of the control policies for Heating, Ventilation and Air Conditioning (HVAC) systems are rule-based and pre-determined, making little to no use of models like the ones described earlier.

At first glance, incorporating more sensors seems to be beneficial as this could directly decrease the uncertainty in some of the parameters and overall decrease the relevance of many of the challenges listed at the end of the previous section. Fittingly, a significant number of so-called Internet of Things (IoT) devices are expected to penetrate the buildings market in the coming years [7]. Already there are a large number of products making their way into homes and commercial buildings worldwide such as voice-activated controllers, wireless occupancy counters, power meters, etc. [8,9]. However, the explosion in the adoption of sensing and control technologies in buildings has also increased the complexity of our building systems. For example, facility managers and engineers now rely on hundreds of different sensing/control points for each building and, despite the advances made in technologies and standards for describing and analyzing sensor data, a large portion of the processes involving the use of these sensor streams is still manual [10,11], primarily due to problems related to data exchange [11]. Questions pertaining to static information about the sensors, such as where they are located and what physical phenomena they are measuring, oftentimes cannot be answered directly. Similarly, questions about dynamic information from sensor data, such as mapping measurements to process stages, or detecting and diagnosing process faults, also require manual analysis.

A recent report from the National Renewable Energy Laboratory (NREL) assessed the needs of the building owners in the Commercial Building Energy Alliances (CEBAs) of the Department of Energy (DOE), and summarized the situation as follows: "building owners can collect massive amounts of energy-related building data, but they have difficulty transforming the data into usable information and energy-saving actions" [11]. The same report identified the following problems, among others: (a) assigning metadata to raw measurements, and making it available to end-users, is a tedious and error prone process; (b) "there are too many data to manage with current technology". Similarly, in a recent review of the communication systems for building automation systems (BAS) [12], the authors conclude that there is a need for automated tools to support the integration of different systems and identify the location of the sensing nodes within a building.

The integration of different building automation systems is an unsolved challenge that researchers have attempted to solve via novel middleware systems to homogenize the hardware and communication layers (e.g., [13–16]), or attempting to solve the schema matching problem [17,18]. But despite these advances, many case studies conclude that the vast majority of the data being collected by these systems today is almost never used in a proactive fashion (e.g., [19]), perhaps because of this lack of metadata and/or integration across systems [20,21]. For example, hundreds of different automated fault detection and diagnosis (FDD) algorithms for heating, ventilation and air conditioning (HVAC) systems have been developed in the past few decades by researchers [22]. Yet, despite their proven ability to significantly reduce the energy consumed for HVAC, these algorithms are seldom used by facility managers.

1.3   Contextual Inference to the Rescue

In many applications, humans are still much better than computers at inferring content and context (metadata) from measurements, which is why generating metadata is still largely a manual process. Yet, the increasing volume of data being generated and the lack and/or limitation of standard information models to describe these measurements suggests that computerized analysis of these data will be required. Hence, there is increased interest by the research community in formulating approaches to automatically annotate and extract meaningful content out of raw sensor streams from buildings for the purpose of improving their self-managing and self-improving capabilities. Metadata about building measurements is scarce and, even when there are information models available (e.g., [23,24]) and/or self-describing sensors (e.g., [25]) there are still a number of reasons why further analyzing sensor streams is still warranted:

– **Indirect Measurements:** Sensors are usually deployed in order to infer some specific property of a physical phenomena or process in buildings, yet these properties are rarely measured directly and require that we perform inference on the data.
– **Security and Sensor Fault Detection:** Assumptions made about the sensor properties and the phenomena being monitored should be checked against the data to confirm that the sensor is providing accurate measurements.
– **Varying Processes:** Some sensors measure a variety of different processes over time (e.g., plug-level power meters measure any appliance connected to the plug), therefore requiring further interpretation of the sensor stream to identify what is being measured.
– **Aggregated Phenomena:** In some cases, sensors measure a combination of different phenomena of interest, thus requiring that the sensor stream be segmented and annotated in order to track each phenomenon separately.
– **Inexisting Static Metadata:** Basic information about the sensors, such as their location within the building, is not known and inferring this from data would be useful.

If recent technology development trends continue at the current pace, there will come a time in the not too distant future when the vast majority of the physical phenomena taking place in buildings will be measured and/or controlled through digital automation either directly (with purposefully installed devices) or indirectly (through mobile devices, surveillance systems, etc.). That time will likely coincide with when we are able to provide inexpensive, compact and low-power computing platforms capable of remarkable computing power. It is reasonable then to imagine that each building will be equipped with both of these and, thus, the question that remains is: how can we harness these resources (computing power and pervasive instrumentation) in order to allow the facility to self-manage its operation?

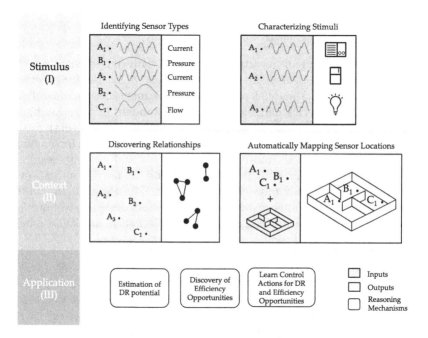

Fig. 1. Opportunities for automated inference from sensor streams in buildings.

Figure 1 shows a high-level depiction of this problem and generalized solutions. In it we show different levels of processing that can be performed on data obtained from building information models (shown as a floorplan) and instrumentation systems (shown as dots), organized from top to bottom. The first layer (i.e., layer I) involves an analysis of the raw sensor streams to (a) identify the sensor types, and (b) characterize the stimulus that generated the measurements. The challenge then is how to automatically recognize what type of system or space is causing the stimuli measured by the sensors. The case shown in the diagram, for example, corresponds to the automatic identification of electrical loads in a building from measurements of their current draw. The present state of affairs for sensor data from buildings is similar to that of other rich sensor media formats available in other domains (e.g., sound and video recordings): we typically know information about the sensor and the process by which measurements were acquired (e.g., 3 megapixel camera, 32 frames per second), but identifying and understanding the content of those sensor streams remains primarily a task reserved for humans (compared to the successful state of machine vision today).

Following this, the next steps in the processing stack revolve around an analysis of the relationships between the sensing and control points, as well as the functional and spatial relationships between these instruments and the building spaces/systems as obtained from digital information models. These two goals are depicted in layer II of Fig. 1. Lastly, the layer III is the inference layer, where using the identified relationships, algorithms are applied in order to enable applications such as the discovery of energy efficiency opportunities, estimating the potential for demand response (DR) participation, and learning control actions to achieve these DR and efficiency opportunities, among other desired goals.

It is important to reiterate that in many cases these contextual inference procedures can be used to derive the needed information from unintuitive sources. For instance, it may be possible to infer the existence and operational schedule of individual appliances in a building from high-frequency measurements obtained from a photo-resistor in a room where there is artificial light sharing the same power source as the appliance of interest. Figure 2 shows a short burst of 30 kHz measurements from such an experiment. The sudden change in intensity between 2 and 4 s (in the spectrogram) can be directly related back to the voltage fluctuations caused by a vacuum cleaner operating in the same electrical circuit. Other examples of this include the identification of multimedia content in televisions derived solely from power measurements [26].

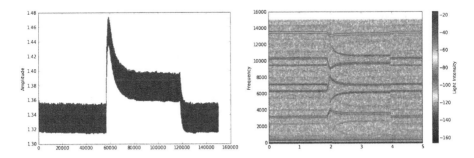

Fig. 2. Light intensity as measured by a photoresistor in a room lit by an incandescent light bulb (left), with sample number (30 kHz sampling rate) on the horizontal axis. The corresponding spectrogram is shown on the right, with number of seconds in the horizontal axis.

1.4   Organization of the Paper

In the remainder of the paper, we will present two case studies exploring computational tools which, when aided by domain knowledge, can efficiently perform contextual inference of the kind illustrated in Fig. 1. The first investigates one aspect of disaggregating the total electricity consumption of a building into its constituent loads for informing predictive maintenance practices. The second explores the feasibility of automatically identifying different sensor types in buildings (e.g., temperature, humidity, light intensity) so that software applications targeting building systems can be deployed in different buildings without the need for manual configuration.

2   Case Study: Residential Electricity Disaggregation

Often times facility managers only have access to aggregate electrical power measurements but need to answer questions pertaining to individual electrical appliances (e.g., how much power is a particular air handling unit consuming?). With the rapid growth of Advanced Metering Infrastructure (AMI) in the power sector worldwide [27], there is an increased interest by academia and industry to so solve this problem also known as Non-Intrusive Load Monitoring (NILM) or energy disaggregation.

In this case study we focus on a particular sub-challenge in this domain. In particular, we assume our measurements $\mathbf{y}_t$ contain only aggregate electrical current consumed by a building (let's call them x_t), and we are interested in obtaining an efficient and tractable model for the multivariate posterior distribution $p(z_{1:T}|x_{1:T})$ where z is a multivariate binary vector indicating whether or not any of the N constituent appliances in the building is operating at any moment t. Though the true distribution is intractable, we show how one can find an auxiliary distribution that closely approximates the true one by making use of domain knowledge and variational inference procedures.

2.1   Background

Energy disaggregation, the problem of inferring the power consumption of appliances given voltage and current measurements at a limited number of sensing points in a building, has received increasing attention in recent years [28,29]. However, despite decades of research into this problem, many technical and scientific challenges remain unsolved. Real-time inference of appliance power usage, for instance, has remained an elusive goal as the proposed solutions thus far are either computationally very expensive, or are very sensitive to changes in the hand-crafted features used to recognize appliances ultimately leading to poor performance over time or across buildings.

Early NILM approaches identified sudden changes in the power time series (also called events) and extracted features of these events, mostly active and reactive power, which were subsequently clustered in the hopes that the clusters would characterize the *on*-transitions or *off*-transitions of appliances. In order to infer power traces of individual appliances, *on*-transition clusters were matched with *off*-transition clusters. These approaches, however, sometimes do not perform well because temporal patterns of state transition sequences cannot be directly modeled. Variants of Factorial Hidden Markov Models (FHMMs) were soon employed to overcome some of the weaknesses [30–33].

FHMMs [34] are a natural choice for modeling the generative process of energy disaggregation [32, 35–37]. FHMM are a generalization of Hidden Markov Models were multiple hidden chains evolve independently in parallel. Usually, the state of a single appliance is modeled by a single HMM chain, whereas the aggregate power measured at the main distribution panel is modeled by the aggregate observation. Let $z \in \mathcal{Z} = \{0,1\}^{N \times T}$ be the latent variable and $x \in \mathbb{R}^{S \times T}$ be the aggregate observation with T number of time steps, N number of parallel HMM chains and S being the observation dimensionality. The joint distribution is defined as:

$$p(x_{1:T}, z_{1:T}) = \prod_{t}^{T} p(x_t|z_t) \prod_{i}^{N} p(z_{t,i}|z_{t-1,i})p(z_{0,i})$$

However, reasoning about the posterior of P is usually difficult because the latent variables become conditionally dependent given the observation, specifically for the forward and filtering distribution the following equations hold, respectively:

$$p(x_{1:t}, z_t) = p(x_t|z_t) \sum_{z' \in \mathcal{Z}} p(z_t|z')p(z_{t-1}, x_{1:t-1}) \tag{3}$$

$$p(z_t|x_{1:t}) = \frac{p(x_{1:t}, z_t)}{\sum_{z' \in \mathcal{Z}} p(x_{1:t}, z')} \tag{4}$$

Note that (3) and (4) both contain summations over $\mathcal{Z}$ and that the cardinality of $\mathcal{Z}$ grows exponentially with N.

Throughout this case study, for illustration purposes, we will consider a simpler distribution that nevertheless faces the same difficulty. Consider the graphical model that arises from removing the temporal dependencies between latent variables (Fig. 3a). Similar to FHMMs, latent variables become dependent conditioned on the observation x (Fig. 3b). For the joint density, the following holds:

$$p(x_{1:T}, z_{1:T}) = \prod_{t=1}^{T} p(x_t, z_t) \tag{5}$$

As for FHMMs, the posterior of (5) is intractable, i.e. the number of states grows exponentially with the latent dimensionality rendering the denominator of the posterior intractable. However, previously, statistical tools such as Variational Inference [38] have been applied to reason about intractable posterior distributions in the context of energy disaggregation [35, 36]. The main idea of Variational Inference is to introduce a tractable auxiliary distribution Q_ψ parameterized by the variational parameters ψ. Inference is then turned into an optimization problem, i.e. Q_ψ is optimized in such a way that it best approximates P as measured

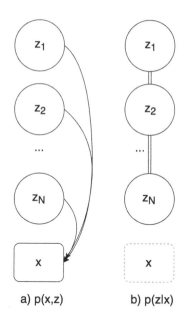

a) p(x,z)   b) p(z|x)

Fig. 3. (a) latent variables of the proposed distribution are marginally independent, however, become (b) conditionally dependent given the observation

by the KL-divergence. Then, instead of performing inference on the intractable posterior P, inference can be carried out on Q_ψ instead. Since Q is required to be tractable, usually additional independence assumption are made and specifically, in the context of energy disaggregation, in order to deal with the difficulty of dependent latent variables, independence between latent states in the posterior is usually assumed. Note that Q is generally required to be simpler than P, i.e. to have less capacity than P. However, because inference is carried out on a simpler distribution, Variational Inference maximizes a lower bound on the data likelihood $p(x)$, i.e. it performs inference up to a constant and it can be shown that this constant is the KL divergence between P and Q. Note too that because Q is required to be simpler than P, the KL divergence usually never becomes 0.

Furthermore, if independence between latent states is assumed in Q, then the posterior can be factored as follows:

$$q_\psi(z_t|x_t) = \prod_i f_\psi(x_t)_i^{z_i}(1 - f_\psi(x_t)_i)^{1-z_i} \qquad (6)$$

With f being bounded by $[0,1]$, Q_ψ is often overly simple. It is easy to show that depending on whether the forward or backward KL divergence is employed as a divergence measure, the Q in (6) either learns the mean or the mode of P. Specifically, for energy disaggregation, this means that such a unimodal Q is unable to learn *either* this appliance *or* the other.

Consider a scenario with 2 two-state appliances with comparable power draw and an aggregate observation that is similar to the power consumption of each one of the appliances. Thus we can assume that for the posterior the following holds:

$$p(z|x) = \begin{pmatrix} 0 & 0.5 & 0.5 & 0 \end{pmatrix}$$
$$\text{with } z = \begin{pmatrix} (0,0) & (0,1) & (1,0) & (1,1) \end{pmatrix}$$

Note that approaches that assume independence between latent states of the auxiliary distribution fail at capturing the *either-or* relationship between appliance states. Let ψ_f^* and ψ_b^* be optimal variational parameters that minimize the forward and backward KL-divergence between P and Q, respectively. It can be shown that:

$$q_\psi(z|x) = \begin{pmatrix} 0.25 & 0.25 & 0.25 & 0.25 \end{pmatrix}$$
$$q_{\psi_f^*}(z|x) = \begin{pmatrix} 0 & 1 & 0 & 0 \end{pmatrix} \text{ or } q_{\psi_b^*}(z|x) = \begin{pmatrix} 0 & 0 & 1 & 0 \end{pmatrix}$$

It is easy to see that independent of the choice of divergence measurement, Q cannot capture a significant proportion of the information present in P, specifically the fact that one of the appliances is active but not both or none.

That is why we argue that previous approaches based on Variational Inference can be improved by a better choice of the auxiliary distribution. Thus, we introduce a tractable auxiliary distribution g that despite being tractable can approximate any discrete distribution arbitrarily well. To sum up, we propose an auxiliary distribution that has the following characteristics:

1. No independence assumptions and therefore unlimited capacity, i.e. in general, any multivariate Bernoulli distribution can be approximated arbitrarily well
2. The posterior can be trained efficiently based on samples of the joint $p(x, z)$
3. Computing the mode and drawing independent samples can be achieved in $\mathcal{O}(N)$

In the next section we will provide a brief introduction to Variational Inference and introduce FactorNet, the proposed auxiliary distribution. We then conduct experiments in and show the power of this distribution (Fig. 4).

2.2   Variational Inference and FactorNet

Variational Inference (VI) has experienced a recent surge in attention from various academic communities [39, 40]. One of the key advantages of VI over its alternatives such as Markov Chain Monte Carlo [41] (MCMC) is speed. Since, as stated earlier, VI translates statistical inference into an optimization problem that produces a tractable distribution that best approximates the true posterior, inference can be amortized, i.e. time training the auxiliary distribution is spend once and after training, inference can be carried out extremely fast. This

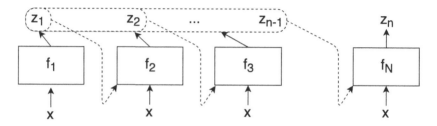

Fig. 4. A graphical depiction of the cascaded neural networks that factorize the joint probability distribution.

characteristic has direct implications in the context of energy disaggregation: VI-based approaches allow for inference on cheap hardware such as an electricity meter located in the premises whereas MCMC would require remotely collecting, storing and processing data. However, even in the asymptotic regime, VI is an approximate inference technique whereas (albeit slowly) MCMC is known to converge to the true posterior. The quality of the VI-based approximation crucially depends on the choice of the auxiliary distribution which can be seen when investigating the commonly used Expectational Lower Bound as the variational objective:

$$\log p(x) = \sum_z \log p(x|z)p(z) \tag{7}$$

$$= \sum_z \frac{q(z|x)}{q(z|x)} \log p(x|z)p(z) \tag{8}$$

$$\geq D_{KL}[q(z|x)||p(z)] + \mathbb{E}_{q(z|x)}[\log p(x|z)] \tag{9}$$

This inequality is tight if and only if $p(z|x) = q(z|x)$, however, this cannot be achieved when Q is simpler than P. Furthermore note that (9) is typically evaluated by Monte Carlo techniques, i.e. evaluating the expectation by sampling from Q. Thus, in order for a Variational approach to be successful, Q needs to be complex enough to be fit to P tightly but simple enough to be sampled from efficiently.

For continuous distributions the problem of choosing a suitable posterior distribution has recently been addressed by introducing normalizing flows [42], i.e. a succession of invertible non-linear transformations of the random variable z. However, for discrete random variables this approach does not seem to be possible since the flow-operators are required to be differentiable but to be mapping into the same domain (in this case $\{0,1\}^N$). Or in other words, the flow-operator cannot at the same time be mapping into the discrete domain whilst being smooth and differentiable.

Furthermore, another difficulty that arises for VI-based approaches is the fact that the true posterior is usually not obtainable, thus all updates need to be made based on samples of the joint $p(x,z)$. Typically, this is circumvented by maximizing the variational objective (9), however, in the experience of the authors (9) has suboptimal convergence properties.

Thus, in this case study, we follow a different strategy. We directly learn the conditional factorization of the joint and show that once the joint is factorized, obtaining the posterior can be done efficiently. First, we note that any joint probability distribution can be factored according to the chain rule of probabilities:

$$p(z_t, x_t) = p(z_{t,1}, x_t)p(z_{t,2}, x_t|z_{t,1})...p(z_{t,N}, x_t|z_{t,N-1}, ..., z_{t,1})$$

$$= \prod_{n=1}^{N} p(z_{t,n}, x_t|z_{t,1:n})$$

The goal now is to learn this factorization. This is achieved by approximating every factor of the probability distribution by a neural network that takes the respective condition as input and produces the conditional probability. Thus, let g be the FactorNet distribution and f_n and $\overline{f}_n$ with $1 \leq n \leq N$ be the N neural networks approximating the *on* and *off* factors of the posterior distribution, i.e.:

$$f_i(x_t, z_1, ..., z_{i-1}) \approx p(x_t, z_i = 1|z_1, ..., z_{i-1})$$
$$\overline{f}_i(x_t, z_1, ..., z_{i-1}) \approx p(x_t, z_i = 0|z_1, ..., z_{i-1})$$

therefore:

$$p(z_i = 1|x_t, z_1, ..., z_{i-1})$$
$$\approx \frac{f_i(x_t, z_1, ..., z_{i-1})}{f_i(x_t, z_1, ..., z_{i-1}) + \overline{f}_i(x_t, z_1, ..., z_{i-1})}$$
$$= f_i^*(x_t, z_1, ..., z_{i-1})$$

For the FactorNet joint distribution the following then holds:

$$g(z_t, x_t) = \prod_{i}^{N} f_i(x_t, z_1, ..., z_{i-1})^{z_i} \overline{f}_i(x_t, z_1, ..., z_{i-1})^{(1-z_i)}$$

and for its posterior:

$$g(z_t|x_t) = \prod_{i}^{N} f_i^*(x_t, z_1, ..., z_{i-1})^{z_i} (1 - f_i^*(x_t, z_1, ..., z_{i-1}))^{(1-z_i)}$$

Note that because the joint instead of the posterior probability is factorized, $f_i(x_t, z_1, ..., z_{i-1}) + \overline{f}_i(x_t, z_1, ..., z_{i-1}) \neq 1$ and that even though no independence assumption between latent variables has been made, evaluating the joint as well as the posterior probability is linear in the latent dimensionality as opposed to exponential for evaluating P. Furthermore, we can take independent samples from the posterior of G efficiently, i.e. linear time. That is, we do not have to resort to Markov Chain Monte Carlo techniques for drawing samples from g,

Result: Sample or Mode of $g(z|x_t)$
$z = \{\};$
for $n = 1, ..., N$ **do**

$\quad p_n = f_n(x_t, z)/(f_n(x_t, z) + \overline{f}_n(x_t, z));$
$\quad$ **if** $p_n >$ *threshold* **then**
$\quad\quad |$ Append 1 to z
$\quad$ **else**
$\quad\quad |$ Append 0 to z;
$\quad$ **end**
end

Algorithm 1. Outputs either an independent sample or the mode of $g(z|x_t)$. If the mode is desired, set *threshold* $= 0.5$ and to a sample from $g(z|x_t)$ set *threshold* $\sim U[0, 1]$, i.e. to a sample from a uniform distribution.

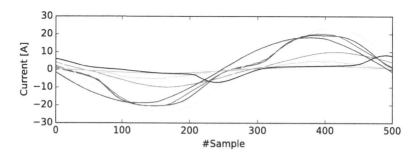

Fig. 5. The current waveforms used in the synthetic experiment taken from PLAID datasets. Current waveforms were extracted by alignment to zero-crossings in the voltage line.

which would, in principle, allow for an efficient Monte Carlo approximation of the expectation of (9) given the samples from Q. See Algorithm 1 for how to sample from $g(z|x)$.

However, as stated above, (9) has suboptimal convergence properties that can be circumvented by exploiting the fact that G allows to efficiently obtain the joint as well as the posterior. That is why we propose a learning objective that directly minimizes the KL-divergence between the joint distributions, i.e.:

$$\mathcal{L} = -g(z_t, x_t) \log \frac{p(z_t, x_t)}{g(z_t, x_t)}$$

Note that we do not allow the gradients to flow into the fraction, i.e. we treat $g(z_t, x_t)$ in the denominator as a constant.

2.3 Experiments

The efficacy of FactorNet is evaluated on a synthetic experiment in the context of supervised waveform disaggregation. Specifically, we choose 8 appliances from the PLAID dataset [43] and extract a single steady-state current waveform for

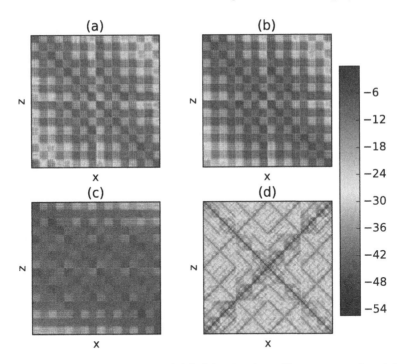

Fig. 6. (a) The true posterior $\log p(z|x)$ (b) The FactorNet posterior $\log g(z|x)$ (c) The posterior $\log q(z|x)$ minimizing the forward KL-divergence (d) The posterior $\log q(z|x)$ minimizing the backward KL-divergence. Note that all probabilities were clipped between 0.001 and 0.999 to avoid $\log(0)$

every appliance aligned by zero-crossing of the voltage line. PLAID is a publicly available dataset containing high-frequency current and voltage measurements of single appliances. Since PLAID is collected at 30 kHz, approximately 500 samples are collected per voltage cycle. Thus a matrix $W \in \mathbb{R}^{500 \times 8}$ was extracted from PLAID and Fig. 5 shows the waveforms used in the experiments. The 8 appliance waveforms were then mixed up, i.e. all 256 possible combinations of waveforms were created and corrupted by Gaussian noise: $X = \{Wz + \mathcal{N}(0, 0.1I)|z \in \{0, 1\}^8\}$. The probability of the aggregate observation was defined as:

$$p(x_t|z_t) = \mathcal{N}(x_t|Wz_t, 0.1I)$$

with W being a matrix containing the appliance waveforms and I being the identity matrix. Thus, for the posterior, the following holds:

$$p(z_t|x_t) = \frac{\mathcal{N}(x_t|Wz_t, 0.1I)}{\sum_z \mathcal{N}(x_t|Wz, 0.1I)}$$

For every combination of $z \in \{0, 1\}^8$ and $x \in X$, $\log p(z|x)$ was computed and stored. See Fig. 6(a) for a plot of the resulting 256×256 matrix.

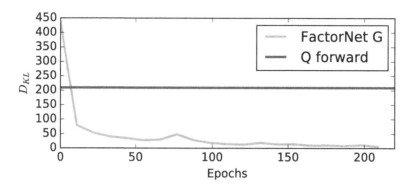

Fig. 7. The KL-divergence $D_{KL}(p(z|x)||f(z|x))$ summed over all x. In this case f is either the FactorNet distribution g or the q_ϕ minimizing the forward KL divergence. Note that q_ψ minimizing the backward KL divergence did not fit onto the plot with a divergence of approximately 3800.

Eight neural networks with a similar topology were created with an input dimensionality of $500 + (n-1)$, two intermediate *relu*-layers with 512 hidden units and two-unit *sigmoid* output-layer for f and $\overline{f}$ respectively. The network was trained by minimizing the loss $\mathcal{L}$ introduced earlier. The objective was minimized by drawing mini-batches of 144 samples uniformly from the joint distribution $p(z, x)$. The training procedure did not assume knowledge of the posterior $p(z|x)$ and was solely presented with sampled of the joint. The performance of the algorithm is compared to distributions $q_{\psi_f^*}$ and $q_{\psi_b^*}$ introduced earlier, i.e. distributions that assume independence between latent states in the posterior and minimize the forward and backward KL-divergence respectively. The parameters ψ_f^* and ψ_b^* were obtained with the knowledge of the true posterior that usually is not available, thus we compare to distributions in their globally optimal configuration.

Figure 6 shows a visual comparison of the different resulting posterior distributions. One can see that FactorNet G (Fig. 6b) captures much more information present in P compared to Q in both settings (Fig. 6c and d). Figure 7 emphasizes this fact as it shows the KL-divergence over time during training. One can see that FactorNet reaches a KL-divergence of practically 0 after approximately 100 epochs.

3 Case Study: Metadata Inference for Commercial Building Systems

Deployment of software applications for building systems remains a challenge due to the non-trivial efforts of organizing, managing and extracting metadata associated with sensors (e.g., information about their type, function, etc.), which is required by them. Going back to our plant and measurement models (Eqs. 1 and 2), one can cast this problem as having access to a $\mathbf{y}_t$ for which the identity of each of the entries in the vector is unknown (i.e., it is not clear what sensor they are referring to). One of the reasons leading to this problem is that varying conventions, acronyms, and standards are used to define this metadata. Though standards and government-mandated policies may lift these obstacles and enable these software-based improvements to our building stock, this effort could take years to come to fruition and there are alternative technical solutions, such as automated metadata inference techniques, that could help reign in on the non-standardized nature of today's BASs.

3.1   Background

From an academic perspective, there is little past work on the problem of identifying the location, or any other meta-data of sensors in a building directly from their measurements. Some researchers have focused on auto-generating room connectivity graphs from sensor data [44], discovering co-located sensors using non-parametric feature transformations and correlation analysis [45], as well as generating blueprints [46] through various heuristics. Similarly, discovering relationships between two or more information models by analyzing the similarities in topological relationships between components contained in them, has been a successful approach to map control points and building systems [47]. However, these approaches have been developed primarily for residential buildings, which generally have simpler floor-plans and less complex building systems, and it is not yet known how well they will generalize to more complex environments, especially given some of the assumptions that support them (e.g., single-story buildings).

In the specific domain of time series based sensor metadata inference for BAS, many approaches have been proposed using different features [48–51]. These approaches use hand-crafted engineered features (e.g., descriptive statistics, maximum, minimum and standard deviation) and very often overlook the sequential information that can be extracted. For the curious reader, we note that this phenomenon is further explained in [52]. In short, different datasets with varying appearance could have identical statistics[1], which makes such statistical features less sensitive to the change of the sequence (order) of values. Although researchers have tried to overcome such issues by dividing time series data into multiple windows, extracting features from each window, and then taking another summary statistics of features from multiple windows [53], the power of these features to incorporate the sequential information could still be limited.

Recent work on sensor metadata inference, including research by the authors, has shed light on the feasibility of this automated approach to the problem. Using data from more than 400 buildings in the US it was found that using simple statistical summaries of historical time-series data from the sensors, it is possible to classify its type with an average accuracy of 75% [54]. In this case

---

[1] An animation can be seen at https://www.autodeskresearch.com/publications/samestats.

study we extend this line of work and explore the possibility of avoiding the use of pre-defined summary statistics as features for identifying the sensor type. Instead, we learn an approximate mapping using a more expressive and flexible family of functions such as convolutional neural networks.

3.2 Time-Series Based Inference Using Deep Learning

We explore a new metadata inference approach to infer the type of BAS points from time series data based on convolutional neural networks. The purpose is to investigate the inference problem from a purely data-driven perspective where the efforts to design hand-crafted features are avoided. To incorporate sequential information in this type of problems, other efforts have been made to exploit deep neural networks, especially convolutional neural networks (CNN) for end-to-end time series classification [55]. With different processing units (e.g., convolution, pooling, rectifiers), CNNs have also shown success in computer vision, natural language processing, speech recognition, and time series analysis [56]. CNNs have been mostly used as a supervised classification model when initially being designed. However, one special architecture of CNN has been proposed as an unsupervised feature extraction method directly using an auto-encoder (AE) structure [57]. Convolutional neural network auto-encoders (CAE) learn how to map the original data into a latent representation (encoding process) which is then mapped back to the original data (decoding process) using a convolutional layer in the middle. This lower-dimensional latent representation can then be used to interrogate the time series. Due to the convolution operations performed by continuously sliding windows of different scales to the time series, the sequential information is preserved in the latent layer. Like any other neural network architecture, CAEs have several variations made possible by the choice of pooling and unpooling operations [58], convolution and deconvolution operations [59], tied weights for encoder and decoder layers [60], predicting noise as targets instead of the original inputs [61], etc. As CAEs reduce the efforts to build hand-crafted engineered features and can incorporate sequential information, we attempt to build a specific architecture of CAE for the purpose of inferring sensor metadata from time series in buildings. Additionally, as a comparison of supervised method versus unsupervised feature extraction methods, we will also build a CNN as a classier directly. The detailed description of the proposed method will be presented in the next section.

3.3 Data

We use the same dataset used in [54] extracting the top 20 most frequent BAS points (see [62]) as shown in Fig. 8. Specifically the dataset contains historical measurements for sensors and control points in Air Handling Units (AHUs) from 421 buildings across 35 different building sites in the United States. We limit our scope to a single month (January) from the whole dataset. This eventually gives us a raw data matrix X of size 4822×2976, representing 4822 BAS points with each having 2976 samples in January of the year 2015 (i.e., 1 sample every

15 min). It is worth noting that the sensor tags shown in Fig. 8 actually encode the metadata information including point types, physical quantities, medium, and functions. For example, "DischargeAirTemperatureSetpoint" represents a set point controlling the temperature of the air to be discharged out of an AHU.

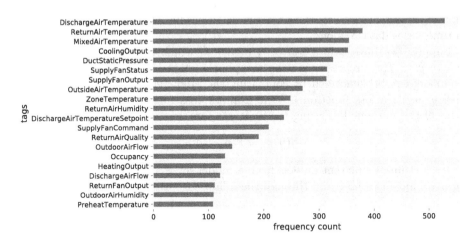

Fig. 8. Frequency counts for 20 most frequently appearing sensor/actuator tags in the dataset.

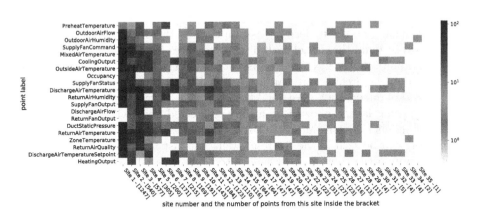

Fig. 9. Frequency counts of each point label across 35 different sites, the number in the horizontal axis represents the total number of points at this site

To better understand how these 20 different types of point labels spread over building sites, Fig. 9 shows the number of counts of each label across sites, sorted from the site with most numbers to the least. We can see the distribution is quite unbalanced with some sites having up to 1247 points and some only have 1 point.

3.4 Methodology

We start by defining the problem of time series classification using more specific notation. Given N one-dimensional time series of length T from N sensors in a building $X^{N \times T} = \{x_1, \cdots, x_i, \cdots, x_N\}$, where $x_i \in \mathbb{R}^T$ and the corresponding class labels are $Y^{N \times 1} = \{y_1, \cdots, y_i, \cdots, y_N\}$ and $y_i \in \{1, 2, \cdots, C\}$ (C is the number of unique classes), the objective is to predict the class labels Y based on time series data X alone.

Suppose we have a function or a model f, which is able to map x to y. Denote $\hat{y}_i = f(x_i)$ representing the mapping relationship. The performance of the model can be quantified by comparing the predicted label $\hat{y}_i$ with the true label y_i using a loss function h. One example loss function can be defined in terms of the zero-one loss using the indicator function:

$$h(y, \hat{y}) = \mathbb{1}(y = \hat{y}) \tag{10}$$

If we evaluate different models from a model set $\mathcal{F}$ using N time series, the optimal model can be found through the following optimization problem:

$$f^* = \arg \min_{f \in \mathcal{F}} \sum_{i=1}^{N} h(y_i, f(x_i)) \tag{11}$$

This model f is typically trained using a portion of labeled data (both x and y are given) and then evaluated on the remaining unlabeled data (only x is given). The model involves two parts, namely feature extraction and classification. Feature extraction aims to find the feature, which is another representation of the original data X, that allows the classifier to better discriminate data of different types. Depending on the underlying assumptions of the data, various strategies can be used to build the model with distinct features and diverse classifiers.

In this approach, the CNN is used as a supervised classifier on raw time series data directly. The architecture can be seen in Fig. 10 where we feed data with batch size B of dimension T. We build the network with two convolutional layers and two pooling layers followed by a fully connected layer with 30% drop-out ratio. The number of convolutional filters and the size for convolution as well as the pooling can be seen in the figure as well. The last layer is based a softmax function to map the continuous variables to C discrete labels. This model can be trained from the data with known labels and then used to infer the metadata for points with unknown labels.

In the implementation phase, we use a batch size of 200 with the dimension of the data being 2976 (one-month-long) to predict 20 different classes. The training and testing strategy will be discussed later. We refer to this approach as **cnn-clf**.

3.5 Convolution Neural Network Auto Encoder

A simple one hidden layer auto-encoder takes an input $x_i \in \mathbb{R}^T$ and maps it to a latent representation $h_i \in \mathbb{R}^d$ using an encoder function $h_i = f_E(x_i) =$

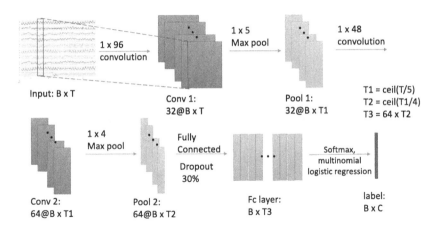

Fig. 10. Architecture of the convolutional neural network for time series data classification

$\sigma(Wx_i + b)$ where $W \in \mathbb{R}^{d \times T}$ and $b \in \mathbb{R}^d$ are the weight and bias parameters respectively, and $\sigma(\cdot)$ is an activation function[2]. The latent representation h_i is then mapped back to the reconstructed input $\hat{x}_i \in \mathbb{R}^T$ using an decoder function $\hat{x}_i = g_D(h_i) = \sigma(W' h_i + b')$ where weights (W) are normally tied with the parameters from the symmetric encoder layer forcing $W^T = W'$. This reduces the number of parameters to train and regularizes the model to be simple. By minimizing the following loss among all samples iteratively, we can find values for weight and bias parameters that minimize the reconstruction error:

$$Loss = \sum_{i=1}^{N} ||x_i - \hat{x}_i||_2 = \sum_{i=1}^{N} || \{x_i - g_D [f_E(x_i)]\} ||_2 \qquad (12)$$

Normally, the auto-encoder can have multiple encoder and decoder layers which allows one to learn a deeper representation. The loss function can be represented as follows with a chain structure if we have m encoder layers and decode layers:

$$Loss = \sum_{i=1}^{N} || [x_i - g_D^1(g_D^2(\cdots g_D^m(f_E^m(\cdots (f_E^1(x_i))))))] ||_2 := ||X - \mathcal{D}_\phi(\mathcal{E}_\theta(X))||_F \qquad (13)$$

where $\mathcal{D}$ and $\mathcal{E}$ are notations used to represent all decoder and encoder layers respectively, with weights and biases denoted as ϕ and θ.

CAE essentially has the same structure as a regular auto-encoder with the difference being that the encoder function is based on convolution and pooling operations and the decoder function is based on deconvolution and unpooling operations. A good explanation with 2D images can be found in [59]. An example of the CNN architecture for time series can be seen in Fig. 11.

---

[2] The activation function σ is normally in the form of sigmoid, tanh or ReLU.

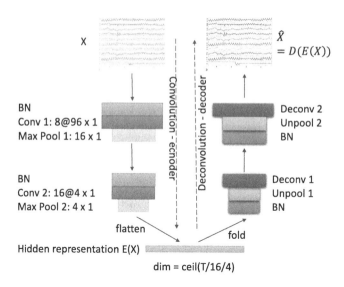

Fig. 11. Architecture of the convolutional neural network autoencoder for feature extraction

To explain the architecture, we use an auto-encoder with two encoder layers and two decoder layers. The structure of the layers has the transformation from $h_i^{E1} = f_{E1}(x_i), h_i = f_{E2}(h_i^{E1}), h_i^{D2} = g_{D2}(h_i), \hat{x}_i = g_{D1}(h_i^{D2})$. Suppose we are using k filters to apply the convolution on input X with a stride of 1 and padding 0 to make sure each filter slides T times, then we will have h^{E1} of dimension $N \times T \times k$, and $h_{i,k}^{E1} = \sigma(x_i \star W^k + b^k)$ where $\star$ is the convolution operation by sliding the window on the data and take the weighted summation. A good illustration of common operations including convolution, deconvolution, pooling and unpooling can be seen in [59].

In addition to these typical operations for CAE, we also adopt the batch normalization (BN) technique to avoid the problem of vanishing gradients as is suggested in [63]. Due to the fast speed of rectified linear units (ReLU), we will use it as the σ activation function after the convolution operation. The weights will also be tied to the encoder and decode layers. However, since there exist negative values in the time series data and ReLU will force them to be zero, we will not apply any activation for the last layer in order to reconstruct the original input. Hence, the weights on the last layer will not be tied with weights from the first layer while the weights on the rest layer are tied in a symmetric fashion.

Once the network is trained, we can use the latent representation $f_E^m(\cdot)$ in the hidden layer as the feature on which to perform classification. In the implementation phase, we use the same parameter for the convolutional layers and pooling layers specified in the figure. We mark this feature **caeF**. Such feature incorporating sequential information will be evaluated on a classifier to compare with the existing hand-crafted engineered features.

3.6   Baseline Approach

Instead of using the same list of features in [54], which are based on existing approaches, directly as the baseline, we group the features into several categories based on the literature:

– Statistical feature (**statF**): Descriptive statistics such as mean, median, standard deviation, etc. of the time series.
– Window feature (**winF**): We divide the data into multiple sliding windows and calculate features within each window. For each feature calculated over multiple windows, other statistics can be used to generate a higher level of abstraction.
– Time-frequency feature (**tfaF**): Features derived from time-frequency analysis information including fast Fourier transform (FFT) and wavelet analysis.
– Distance-based similarity feature (**dtwF**): We use dynamic time warping (DTW) as a distance measure to quantify the similarity between any pair of time series.

Additionally, we will also concatenate the above features to produce a combined feature (**combF**). For each of the features above, a Random Forest will be used as the classification model since it showed the best performance in [54].

It is worth noting that the above categories of features could have overlaps, for example, STFT in time-frequency analysis can also be considered as a window feature. Thus, by **winF** we mean applying statistics on windows, and by time-frequency feature, we mean applying Fourier transform and wavelet decomposition on the whole time series without using windows. Also, for the combined feature, we will simply combine all of the features. The study of mixing and combining different features is not the focus of this work.

To summarize, we will use five approaches based on existing literatures including **statF**, **winF**, **tfaF**, **dtwF** and **combF**, and two approaches based on convolutional neural networks namely **cnn-clf** and **caeF**. These approaches are all feature extractions methods which will be combined with random forest to make predictions except for **cnn-clf** which can classify point types directly.

3.7   Experiments

To explore the generalizability of the neural network based approaches versus the baseline approach, we use data from all but one sites to train and use the data from the remaining sites to test, and we iterate over sites.

The average accuracy over different testing sites of the 20-class classification problem can be seen in Table 1 for each approach. The two approaches yielding

Table 1. Average accuracy for each approach

	statF	winF	tfaF	dtwF	combF	cnn-clf	caeF
Accuracy	0.60	0.61	0.45	0.57	0.61	0.57	0.61

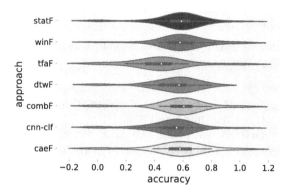

Fig. 12. Violin plots over 35 sites for different approaches

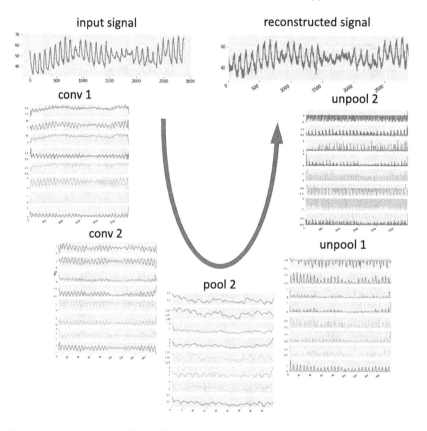

Fig. 13. An example of how CAE is used to reconstruct the time series signal

the best score are **winF** and **caeF**, suggesting CNN based approaches can reach comparable performance with respect to the existing approaches.

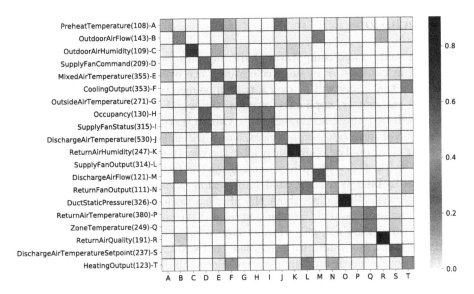

Fig. 14. Confusion matrix normalized by row using CAE and Random Forest. The number inside the bracket besides the label name on the vertical axis represents the number of testing instances for this class

To better understand how the accuracy vary when different test sites are being used, we present the accuracy distribution over 35 sites using violin plots in Fig. 12. As we can see they all have very similar performance near 60%, with **winF** and **caeF** having slightly better results. This confirms that CNN-based unsupervised approach can perform similarly compared with existing statistical-based approaches. Note that for this 20-class classification problem with unbalanced samples in each class (seen in Fig. 8), if we have a baseline model predicting every testing samples as belonging to the most frequent class, the resulting accuracy would be just 11%.

To visualize the reconstruction capability of CAE, we show an example of how one time series signal can be reconstructed going through convolution, pooling, unpooling, and deconvolution operations in Fig. 13. The plot under the title is the output of the signal after each operation. The operation after second pooling will produce the latent representation, which is also illustrated in Fig. 11. The reconstructed signal shown in Fig. 13 is very close to the input signal, which implicitly suggests the hidden latent representation could be a good approximation (feature) of the original time series.

To further understand how this approach performs for each class, we plot the normalized confusion matrix in Fig. 14 for **caeF**. As we can see, all temperature sensors, air flow sensors, fan outputs, along with heating and cooling outputs are easily confused. This motivates us to explore the idea of using a hierarchical classifier where we group 20 different types into larger groups and use two nested classifiers to recognize point types.

4   Conclusions

Sensing, actuation and computation hardware have been decreasing in cost and increasing in capabilities at an accelerating pace over the last few decades. It is projected that there will be over a trillion connected objects (e.g., electricity, water and gas meters, appliances, etc.) in the world in the next decade, most of which will be housed inside buildings. Our case studies reveal that the rapid proliferation of sensing/control devices, alone, will not improve the building systems being monitored or significantly alter the way these systems are managed or controlled as there is a steep requirement for carefully designed computational approaches to infer rich contextual information from the measurements made by these devices. When data about the physical world is a commodity, it is the ability to extract actionable information from this resource what generates value and, more often than not, this process requires significant domain expertise.

In our first case study, we presented FactorNet: an auxiliary distribution capable of approximating any multivariate Bernoulli distribution arbitrarily well whilst at the same time having a functional form that is simple enough to allow for drawing samples as well as computing the mode of the posterior efficiently. This distribution was then used to disentangle current waveforms of different appliances from measurements in which they were linearly combined together. Furthermore, using the auxiliary function, the joint and posterior distributions can be obtained in linear time by approximating the chain rule factorization by a succession of neural networks which allows for using a training objective that minimizes the divergence between the joint distributions directly circumventing the need for ELBO minimization.

However, experiments in which FactorNet incorporates temporal dependencies have not yet been conducted. Note that FactorNet was conceived out of the realization that auxiliary distributions that assume independence in the posterior are detrimental when modeling temporal dependencies, i.e. the posterior collapses onto a single state and most of the uncertainty falsely explained away. This prohibits temporal models from reversing previous decisions like e.g. the Viterbi [64] algorithm would. FactorNets performance with temporal dependencies needs yet to be determined.

For our second case study, we explored a purely data-driven approach to the problem of building automation system metadata inference based on convolutional neural networks. The approach can generate similar and sometimes better performance than existing approaches. However, when the model makes incorrect predictions, it is difficult to ascertain why it erred. Thus, there is a need to develop new methods to understand the behaviors of the metadata inference approaches and recognize when the model will fail and why it fails. Here the moral of the story is different than in the first study: fully data-driven approaches, though capable and flexible to complete certain inference procedures as well as other approaches, lack the explanatory power that simpler approaches may have.

Acknowledgments. We would like to acknowledge the Siebel Foundation for the funding that partially supported the research presented in this paper. This research was also partially funded by the Pennsylvania Infrastructure Technology Alliance (PITA), and the Department of Energy project grant DE-EE0007682. We would also like to sincerely thank Dr. Youngchong Park, Erik Paulson, and Andrew Boettcher from Johnson Controls International for providing the data used in the second case study; Dr. Michael Brambley and Dr. Andrew Stevens from the Pacific Northwest National Laboratory for their guidance and comments about the second case study; as well as Aarti Singh and Alex Davis for conversations that crystalized the general description provided in Sect. 1.1. The opinions expressed here are those of the authors and do not necessarily reflect the views of the sponsors.

References

1. U.S. Energy Information Administration: Annual Energy Review 2011. None, annual edition. Energy Information Administration, October 2012
2. Kiliccote, S., Piette, M.A., Hansen, D.: Advanced controls and communications for demand response and energy efficiency in commercial buildings. Technical report, Lawrence Berkeley National Laboratory (LBNL), January 2006
3. Froelich, J., Everitt, K., Fogarty, J., Patel, S., Landay, J.: Sensing opportunities for personalized feedback technology to reduce consumption. In: The CHI Workshop on Defining the Role of HCI in the Challenge of Sustainability (2009)
4. Roth, K.W., Westphalen, D., Feng, M.Y., Llana, P., Quartararo, L.: Energy impact of commercial building controls and performance diagnostics: market characterization, energy impact of building faults and energy savings potential. Technical report TIAX LLC D0180, TIAX LLC, Cambridge, August 2005
5. Ma, Y., Borrelli, F., Hencey, B., Coffey, B., Bengea, S., Haves, P.: Model predictive control for the operation of building cooling systems. IEEE Trans. Control Syst. Technol. **20**(3), 796–803 (2012)
6. Agbi, C., Song, Z., Krogh, B.H.: Parameter identifiability for multi-zone building models. In: CDC, pp. 6951–6956 (2012)
7. Gubbi, J., Buyya, R., Marusic, S., Palaniswami, M.: Internet of things (IOT): a vision, architectural elements, and future directions. Future Gener. Comput. Syst. **29**(7), 1645–1660 (2013)
8. Horch, A., Kubach, M., Roßnagel, H., Laufs, U.: Why should only your home be smart?-a vision for the office of tomorrow. In: 2017 IEEE International Conference on Smart Cloud (SmartCloud), pp. 52–59. IEEE (2017)
9. Chilipirea, C., Ursache, A., Popa, D.O., Pop, F.: Energy efficiency and robustness for IOT: building a smart home security system. In: 2016 IEEE 12th International Conference on Intelligent Computer Communication and Processing (ICCP), pp. 43–48. IEEE (2016)
10. Ploennigs, J., Dibowski, H., Ryssel, U., Kabitzsch, K.: Holistic design of wireless building automation systems. In: 2011 IEEE 16th Conference on Emerging Technologies Factory Automation (ETFA), pp. 1–9 (2011)
11. Livingood, W., Stein, J., Considine, T., Sloup, C.: Review of current data exchange practices: providing descriptive data to assist with building operations decisions. Technical report NREL/TP-5500-50073, National Renewable Energy Laboratory, Golden, May 2011
12. Kastner, W., Neugschwandtner, G., Soucek, S., Newmann, H.: Communication systems for building automation and control. Proc. IEEE **93**(6), 1178–1203 (2005)

13. Dawson-Haggerty, S., Jiang, X., Tolle, G., Ortiz, J., Culler, D.: sMAP: a simple measurement and actuation profile for physical information. In: Proceedings of the 8th ACM Conference on Embedded Networked Sensor Systems, SenSys 2010, pp. 197–210. ACM, New York (2010)
14. Krioukov, A., Fierro, G., Kitaev, N., Culler, D.: Building application stack (BAS). In: Proceedings of the Fourth ACM Workshop on Embedded Sensing Systems for Energy-Efficiency in Buildings, BuildSys 2012, pp. 72–79. ACM, New York (2012)
15. Rowe, A., Berges, M., Bhatia, G., Goldman, E., Rajkumar, R., Garrett, J.H., Moura, J.M.F., Soibelman, L.: Sensor Andrew: large-scale campus-wide sensing and actuation. IBM J. Res. Dev. 55(1.2), 6:1–6:14 (2011)
16. Agarwal, Y., Gupta, R., Komaki, D., Weng, T.: BuildingDepot: an extensible and distributed architecture for building data storage, access and sharing. In: Proceedings of the Fourth ACM Workshop on Embedded Sensing Systems for Energy-Efficiency in Buildings, BuildSys 2012, pp. 64–71. ACM, New York (2012)
17. Liu, X., Akinci, B., Berges, M., Garrett Jr., J.H.: An integrated performance analysis framework for HVAC systems using heterogeneous data models and building automation systems. In: Proceedings of the Fourth ACM Workshop on Embedded Sensing Systems for Energy-Efficiency in Buildings, BuildSys 2012, pp. 145–152. ACM, New York (2012)
18. Rahm, E., Bernstein, P.A.: A survey of approaches to automatic schema matching. VLDB J. 10(4), 334–350 (2001)
19. Granderson, J., Piette, M.A., Ghatikar, G.: Building energy information systems: user case studies. Energ. Effi. 4(1), 17–30 (2011)
20. Jagpal, R.: Computer aided evaluation of HVAC system performance: technical synthesis report. Technical report, International Energy Agency (2006)
21. Katipamula, S., Brambley, M.R.: Review article: methods for fault detection, diagnostics, and prognostics for building systems—a review, part I. HVAC&R Res. 11(1), 3–25 (2005)
22. Liu, X., Akinci, B., Berges, M., Garrett Jr., J.H.: Extending the information delivery manual approach to identify information requirements for performance analysis of HVAC systems. Adv. Eng. Inf. 27(4), 496–505 (2013)
23. Botts, M., Percivall, G., Reed, C., Davidson, J.: OGC® sensor web enablement: overview and high level architecture. In: Nittel, S., Labrinidis, A., Stefanidis, A. (eds.) GSN 2006. LNCS, vol. 4540, pp. 175–190. Springer, Heidelberg (2008). https://doi.org/10.1007/978-3-540-79996-2_10
24. Whitehouse, K., Zhao, F., Liu, J.: Semantic streams: a framework for composable semantic interpretation of sensor data. In: Römer, K., Karl, H., Mattern, F. (eds.) EWSN 2006. LNCS, vol. 3868, pp. 5–20. Springer, Heidelberg (2006). https://doi.org/10.1007/11669463_4
25. Potter, D.: Smart plug and play sensors. IEEE Instrum. Meas. Mag. 5(1), 28–30 (2002)
26. Greveler, U., Glösekötterz, P., Justusy, B., Loehr, D.: Multimedia content identification through smart meter power usage profiles. In: Proceedings of the International Conference on Information and Knowledge Engineering (IKE), The Steering Committee of The World Congress in Computer Science, Computer Engineering and Applied Computing (WorldComp), p. 1 (2012)
27. Mohassel, R.R., Fung, A., Mohammadi, F., Raahemifar, K.: A survey on advanced metering infrastructure. Int. J. Electr. Power Energy Syst. 63, 473–484 (2014)
28. Zeifman, M., Roth, K.: Nonintrusive appliance load monitoring: review and outlook. IEEE Trans. Consum. Electron. 57(1), 76–84 (2011)

29. Zoha, A., Gluhak, A., Imran, M.A., Rajasegarar, S.: Non-intrusive load monitoring approaches for disaggregated energy sensing: a survey. Sensors **12**(12), 16838–16866 (2012)
30. Jia, R., Gao, Y., Spanos, C.J.: A Fully Unsupervised Non-intrusive Load Monitoring Framework (2015)
31. Johnson, M.J., Willsky, A.S.: Bayesian nonparametric hidden semi-markov models. J. Mach. Learn. Res. **14**(1), 673–701 (2013)
32. Kolter, J.Z., Jaakkola, T.: Approximate inference in additive factorial HMMs with application to energy disaggregation. In: International Conference on Artificial Intelligence and Statistics, pp. 1472–1482 (2012)
33. Lange, H., et al.: Disaggregation by State Inference a Probabilistic Framework for Non-intrusive Load Monitoring (2016)
34. Ghahramani, Z., Jordan, M.I.: Factorial hidden Markov models. Mach. Learn. **29**(2–3), 245–273 (1997)
35. Lange, H., Berges, M.: Variational bolt: approximate learning in factorial hidden Markov models with application to energy disaggregation. In: AAAI (2018)
36. Ng, Y.C., Chilinski, P.M., Silva, R.: Scaling factorial hidden Markov models: stochastic variational inference without messages. In: Advances in Neural Information Processing Systems, pp. 4044–4052 (2016)
37. Hart, G.W.: Nonintrusive appliance load monitoring. Proc. IEEE **80**(12), 1870–1891 (1992)
38. Jordan, M.I., Ghahramani, Z., Jaakkola, T.S., Saul, L.K.: An introduction to variational methods for graphical models. Mach. Learn. **37**(2), 183–233 (1999)
39. Hoffman, M.D., Blei, D.M., Wang, C., Paisley, J.: Stochastic variational inference. J. Mach. Learn. Res. **14**(1), 1303–1347 (2013)
40. Kingma, D.P., Welling, M.: Auto-encoding variational bayes. arXiv preprint arXiv:1312.6114 (2013)
41. Geman, S., Geman, D.: Stochastic relaxation, Gibbs distributions, and the Bayesian restoration of images. IEEE Trans. Pattern Anal. Mach. Intell. **6**, 721–741 (1984)
42. Rezende, D.J., Mohamed, S.: Variational inference with normalizing flows. arXiv preprint arXiv:1505.05770 (2015)
43. Gao, J., Giri, S., Kara, E.C., Bergés, M.: PLAID: a public dataset of high-resolution electrical appliance measurements for load identification research: demo abstract. In: Proceedings of the 1st ACM Conference on Embedded Systems for Energy-Efficient Buildings, BuildSys 2014, pp. 198–199. ACM, New York (2014)
44. Ellis, C., Scott, J., Constandache, I., Hazas, M.: Creating a room connectivity graph of a building from per-room sensor units. In: Proceedings of the Fourth ACM Workshop on Embedded Sensing Systems for Energy-Efficiency in Buildings, BuildSys 2012, pp. 177–183. ACM, New York (2012)
45. Hong, D., Ortiz, J., Whitehouse, K., Culler, D.: Towards automatic spatial verification of sensor placement in buildings. In: Proceedings of the 5th ACM Workshop on Embedded Systems for Energy-Efficient Buildings, BuildSys 2013, pp. 13:1–13:8. ACM, New York (2013)
46. Lu, J., Whitehouse, K.: Smart blueprints: automatically generated maps of homes and the devices within them. In: Kay, J., Lukowicz, P., Tokuda, H., Olivier, P., Krüger, A. (eds.) Pervasive 2012. LNCS, vol. 7319, pp. 125–142. Springer, Heidelberg (2012). https://doi.org/10.1007/978-3-642-31205-2_9
47. Liu, X., Akinci, B., Garrett Jr, J.H., Berges, M.: Requirements and development of a computerized approach for analyzing functional relationships among HVAC components using building information models. In: CIB W078–W102, France (2011)

48. Koc, M., Akinci, B., Bergés, M.: Comparison of linear correlation and a statistical dependency measure for inferring spatial relation of temperature sensors in buildings. In: Proceedings of the 1st ACM Conference on Embedded Systems for Energy-Efficient Buildings, BuildSys 2014, pp. 152–155. ACM Press, New York, November 2014

49. Gao, J., Ploennigs, J., Bergés, M.: A data-driven meta-data inference framework for building automation systems. In: Proceedings of the 2nd ACM International Conference on Embedded Systems for Energy-Efficient Built Environments, BuildSys 2015 (2015)

50. Holmegaard, E., Kjærgaard, M.B.: Mining building metadata by data stream comparison. In: Proceeding of the 2016 IEEE Conference on Technologies for Sustainability, pp. 28–33 (2016)

51. Hong, D., Gu, Q., Whitehouse, K.: High-dimensional time series clustering via cross-predictability. In: Singh, A., Zhu, J. (eds.) Proceedings of the 20th International Conference on Artificial Intelligence and Statistics, Fort Lauderdale, FL, USA. Proceedings of Machine Learning Research, PMLR, vol. 54, pp. 642–651 (2017)

52. Matejka, J., Fitzmaurice, G.: Same stats, different graphs. In: Proceedings of the 2017 CHI Conference on Human Factors in Computing Systems, CHI 2017, pp. 1290–1294. ACM Press, New York (2017)

53. Hong, D., Wang, H., Ortiz, J., Whitehouse, K.: The building adapter. In: Proceedings of the 2nd ACM International Conference on Embedded Systems for Energy-Efficient Built Environments, BuildSys 2015, pp. 123–132. ACM Press, New York, November 2015

54. Gao, J., Berges, M.: A large-scale evaluation of automated metadata inference approaches on sensors from air handling units. In: Advanced Engineering Informatics (2018, to appear)

55. Wang, Z., Yan, W., Oates, T.: Time series classification from scratch with deep neural networks: a strong baseline. arXiv:1611.06455 [cs, stat] (2016)

56. LeCun, Y., Bengio, Y.: Convolutional Networks for Images, Speech, and Time Series, pp. 255–258. MIT Press, Cambridge (1998)

57. Masci, J., Meier, U., Cireşan, D., Schmidhuber, J.: Stacked convolutional auto-encoders for hierarchical feature extraction. In: Honkela, T., Duch, W., Girolami, M., Kaski, S. (eds.) ICANN 2011. LNCS, vol. 6791, pp. 52–59. Springer, Heidelberg (2011). https://doi.org/10.1007/978-3-642-21735-7_7

58. Turchenko, V., Chalmers, E., Luczak, A.: A Deep Convolutional Auto-Encoder with Pooling - Unpooling Layers in Caffe, January 2017

59. Noh, H., Hong, S., Han, B.: Learning Deconvolution Network for Semantic Segmentation, May 2015

60. Dong, J., Mao, X.J., Shen, C., Yang, Y.B.: Learning Deep Representations Using Convolutional Auto-encoders with Symmetric Skip Connections, November 2016

61. Bojanowski, P., Joulin, A.: Unsupervised learning by predicting noise. arXiv:1704.05310 [cs, stat] (2017)

62. Gao, J.: A metadata inference framework to provide operational information support for fault detection and diagnosis applications in secondary HVAC systems. Ph.D. thesis, CEE Department, Carnegie Mellon University, December 2017

63. Ioffe, S., Szegedy, C.: Batch Normalization: Accelerating Deep Network Training by Reducing Internal Covariate Shift, February 2015

64. Viterbi, A.J.: Error bounds for convolutional codes and an asymptotically optimum decoding algorithm. IEEE Trans. Inf. Theor. **13**(2), 260–269 (1967)

A Prototype Tool of Optimal Wireless Sensor Placement for Structural Health Monitoring

Weixiang Shi, Changzhi Wu$^{(\boxtimes)}$, and Xiangyu Wang

Australian Joint Research Centre for Building Information Modelling,
Curtin University, Bentley, WA 6102, Australia
C.Wu@exchange.curtin.edu.au

Abstract. With increasing collapses of civil infrastructures and popularized utilization of large-scale structures, worldwide deployment of structural health monitoring (SHM) systems is of importance in emerging and future SHM industry. A reliable and practical tool of optimal wireless sensor placement (OWSP) can promote implementation of wireless-based SHM systems by reducing construction cost, extending lifetime and improving detection accuracy. This paper presents a prototype of wireless sensor placement (WSP) for bridge SHM based on multi-objective optimisation (MOO) technique and bridge information modelling (BrIM) technology. MOO technique is used to determine sensor locations by simultaneously searching for multiple trade-offs among structural engineering, wireless engineering and construction management. The BrIM model will be used as a platform to validate and visualize the proposed MOO. A BrIM integrated design tool will be developed to improve the efficiency in design stage through visualisation capabilities and semantic enrichment of a bridge model. As future applications, 4D BrIM that combines time-related information in visual environments with the 3D geometric and semantic BrIM model will help engineers and contractors to visualise possible defects and project costs in the real world.

Keywords: Structural health monitoring (SHM)
Optimal wireless sensor placement (OWSP)
Multiple objective optimization (MOO)
Bridge information modelling (BrIM)

1 Introduction

The failure of a civil infrastructure is a serious issue around the world. Though total collapses of civil infrastructures are exceedingly rare, distress caused by hazard effects and frequent loads is increasingly occurring during the life of a civil structure. For example, from the public report between 2009 and 2012, 8 bridges collapsed in China and more than 20 people dead for these accidents. In the United States, 1254 bridge failures that occurred from 1980 to 2012 has been reported [1]. In Australia, over 60% of bridges of all local roads are used over 50 years and approximately 55% of all highway bridges are used more than 20 years [2]. The qualified civil infrastructure is originally good, but continued neglect of health state during the life could cause fatal

© Springer International Publishing AG, part of Springer Nature 2018
I. F. C. Smith and B. Domer (Eds.): EG-ICE 2018, LNCS 10864, pp. 53–73, 2018.
https://doi.org/10.1007/978-3-319-91638-5_3

disasters. Thus, the uncertain state of the civil infrastructure without health monitoring might threat the safety of people around the world.

SHM is to use advanced technology in order to evaluate structural performance and identify structural damage. Recently it is extensively implemented on infrastructures throughout the world [3]. However, the current engineering practices based on wire-based SHM systems require a tremendous labour cost and implementation time. For example, the cost of the wire-based SHM systems deployed on the Bill Emerson Memorial Bridge and TsingMa Bridge reach $1.3 and $8 million [4]. Moreover, especially in some complex civil infrastructures of high-rise buildings and long-span bridges, that could be more costly. In Australia, there are around 22,500 bridges with a replacement value of about AUD$ 3 billion, and an annual maintenance expenditure of about AUD$300 million [5]. The increasing demand of SHM systems promotes cost-effective and easily deployed wireless-based SHM system as substitutes for conventional wire-based SHM systems. As such, installation and maintenance costs can be reduced from several thousand dollars per sensing channel to $100 per channel in the wireless-based SHM [6].

Monitoring infrastructure performance requires a significant amount of knowledge in structural engineering that computer science researchers are usually unfamiliar with. As a result, most previous works on wireless-based SHM systems were done by researchers in civil engineering without considering performance of wireless sensor network (WSN) and number of sensors [7]. However, the performance of WSN with respect to connectivity, reliability, energy efficiency and fault tolerance must be considered in addition to the accurate modal information from perspective of civil domain. Thus, how to develop an approach of wireless sensor placement (OWSP) for wireless-based SHM systems considering construction cost and wireless transmission quality is important, especially on large-scale structures. Multi-objective optimization (MOO) technique is a potential technique to balance the most optimal result in accuracy of modal information, reliability of wireless link and number of sensors. Traditionally, researchers attempted to determine OWSP problems for SHM systems usually modelled as a constrained single objective function through aggregating multiple objectives into a single objective with weighted function. However, in practice, how to determine the weight for each objective function is still subjective and challenging.

In this work, we tackle above issues and draw attention to formulate the mathematical model of OWSP for wireless-based SHM system by considering modal information, wireless link, energy consumption and number of sensors as a multi-objective optimization problem. Then, we will develop a MOO technique for searching all the possible best configurations of SHM-specific wireless sensor network applications under the sense of Pareto-front. Then, a decomposition-based firefly algorithm is developed to solve this multi-objective optimization problem. To the best of our knowledge, there are rather limited methods available for OWSP under MOO framework. Our developed method is then integrated with BrIM technology for better visualization.

The rest of paper is organised as follow. In Sect. 2, we make a literature review of OWSP, MOO technique and importance of integration with BrIM. In Sect. 3, we provide a study framework of our research. In Sect. 4, a case study is presented. In Sect. 5, we conclude our research and highlights our future work.

2 State-of-the-Art

In this section, we first summary the traditional approaches of OWSP for SHM systems. There is still limited applicability and flexibility in those proposed OWSP determinations designed to address the configuration problem of wireless-based SHM systems. Then we review the recent development of MOO technique and its applications in generic OWSP problem. The reason of recent MOO techniques for generic OWSP problem which cannot be directly used in SHM systems will be clarified.

2.1 Approaches of OWSP

In past few years, researchers from civil engineering have proposed numerous approaches of OWSP for SHM systems. Examples include effective independence (EI) method which ranks sensor locations by determinant of FIM results [8], effective independence method with driving point residue which DPR was considered as an index to weight the relative contribution of each node [9], kinetic energy (KE) method which is supposed to ranks the KE instead of the determinant of FIM [10], modified variance (MV) method which can optimize sensor configuration and test all targets by reducing computation time [11]. Recent advances in computation engineering have paved the new way for approaches of OWSP because of these approaches are more efficient in blind searching and global optimization. The genetic algorithm (GA) can be used in OWSP as a substitute for conventional optimization methods [12] and lots of developed GAs have been published, such as generalized genetic algorithm (GGA) [13]. The monkey algorithm applied in OWSP for SHM also can obtain optimal sensor configuration [14]. The firefly algorithms (FA) which is a metaheuristic algorithm has been developed for OWSP [15]. The above methods for addressing OWSP are mainly based on single objective optimization method. In single objective optimization, the aim is to maximise or minimise a single objective under various constraints.

In fact, there are multiple objectives existing in real cases, such as energy consumption, number of sensor nodes, system lifetime. Although researchers try to convert multiple objectives into single objective using weighting method and then to solve the problem with single objective optimization method, this conversion could make the optimization results unreal or insufficient for commercial use when the multiple objectives conflict with each other while subjective weights are adopted. Unfortunately, multiple objectives in OWSP of wireless-based SHM systems are nature conflicting. Thus, we need to develop methods to optimize multiple objectives under various constraints without conversion. In this paper, we will develop a multi-objective optimization technique into OWSP for wireless-based SHM.

2.2 MOO Techniques

Many real problems involve multiple objectives are complex, since multiple conflicting objectives have to be faced with several kinds of constraints. Therefore, MOO techniques are more practical and efficient for the OWSP problems due to multiple objectives are simultaneously optimized in MOO techniques [16, 17]. Researchers have proposed various MOO techniques in generic applications of WSN, but these approaches for generic applications cannot be directly used in SHM due to specific difficulties in damage detection [18, 19]. For example, a multi-objective evolutionary algorithm based on decomposition (MOEA/D) with fuzzy dominance for searching of a trade-off among overage, lifetime, energy consumption and connectivity has been proposed for addressing OWSP problems in generic WSN applications. This proposed approach is only tested in mathematical model with prior information of coverage area for each sensor which can not detect damage in SHM cases [19]. A MOO technique based on wavelet particle swarm algorithm has been developed for OWSP in specific bridge dynamic monitoring. Due to the lack of considering number of sensors and knowledge of real structural responses, it is still far away from real cases [20, 21]. An optimization approach of wireless ad hoc network planning have been proposed for finding the optimal performance region of a wireless ad hoc network when multiple performance metrics are considered, but it still did not specifically study the specific metrics in SHM [22, 23]. The multi-object optimization method has also been presented in industry automation control and potentially to be practically solve two-objective conflict control problem. This approach could be to find a more efficient controller for greenhouse environment control but it is still hard to apply in SHM systems since each node in wireless-based SHM systems do not have specific coverage area [24, 25].

In general, existing MOO techniques have been proposed only for generic wireless sensor network applications, such as fire detection, environment monitoring [26–29]. In these generic applications, MOO do help them to get a better optimization results compared to single objective optimization method because all objectives, such as energy consumption and data transmission quality, can be optimised simultaneously where some important points in the optimization process may not be ignored. However, OWSP of wireless-based SHM systems is different from generic WSN applications. In SHM application, damage is detected via the vibration responses. These dynamic responses are based on the data of multiple sensor nodes. So each sensor node, no matter how close it is to damage location, is not able to detect the damage by itself. This indicates, it is hard for researchers to define a specific sensing area for each sensor node like the other generic WSN applications, which is the basic assumption in all the existing MOO techniques for generic WSN applications.

2.3   Integration with BrIM

Traditionally, an initial finite element model is created based on the existing documentary of design information to define both geometric and structural parameters of the model. Otherwise, the finite element model should be adjusted to include specific elements which are not usually included in a designed model. These components may influence the dynamic response of the infrastructure. For example, the additional elements like diaphragms, sidewalks and curbs may not be included in the design model. The BrIM refined model with semantic information can reflect the true behaviour of the real case. By tackling a key issue on integrating the BrIM model with finite element analysis software, such as ANSYS or MATLAB, a BrIM refined finite element model will be established as the baseline model for the further system identification.

Furthermore, a BrIM integrated system will be developed to help improve the decision-making process and performance evaluation through visualisation capabilities. For example, 4D that combines infrastructure in visual environments with the 3D geometric model will help engineers to visualise sensor locations and possible defects in the operation system. A framework of BIM-based multi-disciplinary collaboration platform has been proposed, but the procedure of sensor configuration has been sadly neglected [30–33].

3 Study Framework

The objective of this work is to create a framework by integrating our new approach of OWSP based on developed MOO techniques with BrIM technology so that optimal sensor placement locations can be visualised and discussed in integrated research groups in design stage. The research consists of 4 stages: (1) 3D model creating and modal parameters extraction; (2) developing wireless-based SHM system models consisting of communication model (CM), quality model (QM) of structure and energy consumption model (ECM); (3) problem solving through using MOO technique for determining optimal sensor placement locations; (4) integration with BrIM software In the first stage, 3D model will be created through 2D drawing. Then, modal parameters will be extracted from 3D model. In the second stages, modal, energy consumption, transmission distance parameters will be used for building system models and then OWSP problems will be formulated with mathematical models. In the third stage, the developed MOO technique for determining sensor placement locations will be applied in addressing OWSP problems in wireless-based SHM system. Finally, the developed approach of OWSP are then integrated with BrIM technology and visualised results will be discussed by all research teams before making final decision.

3.1 3D Model Creating and Modal Parameters Extraction

3D Model Creating. For the 3D bridge simulation modelling settings, real 2D geometric information data of bridge will be used and 3D bridge model can be developed in Revit (Autodesk 2017). Developed 3D bridge model (See Fig. 1) could be organised with families, types and instances with detailed geometric information and material information (See Fig. 2).

Modal Parameters (Mode Shape and Natural Frequency) Extractions. Mode shape and corresponding natural frequency widely serve as important data for detecting damage location and estimating structural conditions [34]. As a result, it is important to properly install sensors in the right locations in order to improve the quality of collected modal parameters information. Otherwise, it will degrade the accuracy of mode shape based methods for damage identification and increase the error of condition evaluation. The relationship between sensor location and identified mode shape will be explained in Sect. 3.2.

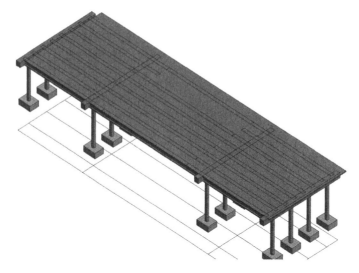

Fig. 1. View of a simulated bridge structure

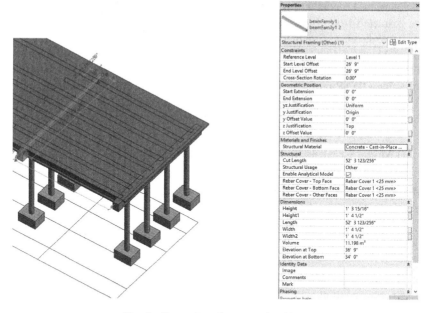

Fig. 2. Properties of parametric object

Mode Shape and Natural Frequency. Every mechanical structure has a vibration pattern with n-degree of freedoms (DOFs) called mode shape at a specific natural frequency f^k.

$$f = \left[f^1, f^2, ..f^n\right]',$$ (1)

$$\Phi = \left[\Psi^1, \Psi^2, ...\Psi^n\right] = \begin{pmatrix} \emptyset_1^1 & \cdots & \emptyset_1^n \\ \vdots & \ddots & \vdots \\ \emptyset_M^1 & \cdots & \emptyset_M^n \end{pmatrix},$$ (2)

where f^k ($k = 1, 2, ..n$) is the kth natural frequency, Ψ^k is the mode shape corresponding to f^k, $\emptyset_i^k$ ($i = 1, 2, ..M$) is the value of Ψ^k at the i th DOF. Table 1 shows an example of target mode shapes Φ (this example matrix contains 50 DOFs and 10 natural frequencies, but in the Table 1 we only select first 7 DOFs of first 3 natural frequency).

Table 1. Fragment of mode shapes Φ with 7 DOFs at first 3 natural frequency

	Frequency at 4.8 Hz, 1st natural frequency	Frequency at 19.4 Hz, 2nd natural frequency	Frequency at 43.6 Hz, 3rd natural frequency
1st DOF	0.0075	−0.0150	0.0224
2nd DOF	0.0150	−0.0298	0.0440
3rd DOF	0.0224	−0.0440	0.0641
4th DOF	0.0298	−0.0576	0.0819
5th DOF	0.0370	−0.0730	0.0968
6th DOF	0.0440	−0.0819	0.1083
7th DOF	0.0509	−0.0922	0.1159

Degree of Freedom. In Eq. (2), we could find $\emptyset_i^k$ contains spatial information corresponding to sensor locations because each DOF has been used to identify location of damage.

Unfortunately, we cannot place all the sensor nodes on locations which are selected by FEM at each DOF even though this is the best way to give highly accurate modal parameters. In a practical wireless-based SHM system, we have to choose a set of sensor locations by considering number of sensors, system lifetime and reliability of wireless link rather than only highly accurate modal parameters.

Through finite element analysis in MATLAB with BrIM refined bridge model, the bridge will be simplified into finite small elements which contains modal parameters of this bridge. All locations of the given elements are candidate locations for placing wireless sensor node which provide the target mode shape matrix Φ.

For example, Fig. 3 shows the first 3 mode shapes of a typical 10 m beam with 50 DOFs.

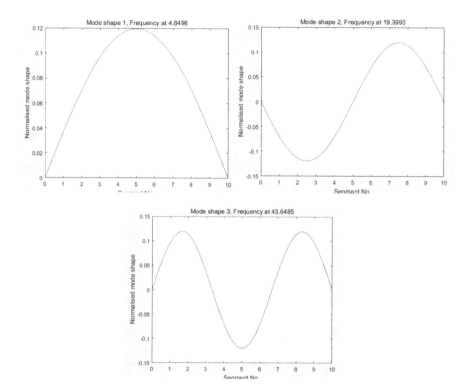

Fig. 3. The first 3 mode shapes of a typical 10 m beam with 50 DOFs.

3.2 System Models

In order to formulate a multi-objective OWSP in SHH, we will introduce several models which are accuracy of modal parameters, wireless link quality and energy consumption efficiency before addressing this OWSP problem based on a developed MOO technique.

Quality Model (QM). In practical engineering, it is vital to place sensors on proper locations where identified mode shapes can be as linearly independent as possible. Quality metric (QM) is considered to evaluate the linear independence among identified mode shapes which are estimated by a scheme of sensor placement. The ith element of independence distribution vector E_D corresponding to linear independence of each sensor location can be formulated as diagonal of the matrix E [35]:

$$E = \Phi_s [\Phi_s^T \Phi_s]^{-1} \Phi_s^T, \tag{3}$$

$$QM_i = E_D^i, \quad 0 \le E_D^i \le 1, i \in 1, \ldots, M \tag{4}$$

where Φ_s is the matrix of mode shapes structured by selected sensor configuration. M is the number of sensor nodes. E is the fisher information matrix (FIM), E_D is diagonal vector of matrix E which is to rank the linear independence of each sensor location in the selected configuration and thus E_D^i is the linear independence indicator of each sensor location which has a range $0 \leq E_D^i \leq 1$. A value of E_D^i that is close to 1 indicates this location is vital to the linear independence and identified mode shapes, otherwise 0 indicates this location is dispensable.

Communication Model (CM). We assume the WSN as a graph in a two dimensional plane, G = (V, E) where V represents the sensor nodes with number of N and E represents the wireless communication link in order to address problem of network connectivity. We assume that each node has a communication range (C_r) and its maximum communication range is R_{max}, $0 < C_r \leq R_{max}$ and $d_{i, j}$ is Euclidean distance between two neighbouring sensor nodes v_i and v_j. The wireless link $e_{i, j}$ can be directly connected if and only if $d_{i, j} \leqslant R_{max}$, which can be defined as

$$l_{i,j} = \begin{cases} 1, & if\ v_i, v_j \text{ connected and } i \neq j \\ 0, & \text{otherwise} \end{cases} \tag{5}$$

The adjacency matrix A of the graph and connectivity judgement matrix J are defined as

$$A = \begin{pmatrix} 0 & \cdots & l_{n1} \\ \vdots & \ddots & \vdots \\ l_{1n} & \cdots & l0 \end{pmatrix}, \tag{6}$$

$$J = \sum_{s=1}^{W-1} A^s, \tag{7}$$

where J denotes the judgement matrix and A^s is the sth power of adjacency matrix A.

The edge between i and j in the graph G = (V,E) is connected if and only if the element in the judgement matrix $J_{i,j} \neq 0$. If the graph is connected, the percentage of packet losses between two directly connected sensors could be calculated by $Pl_{i,j}$. From the view of practical application, percentage of packets loss could be the best way to predict WSN performance. We calculate $Pl_{i,j}$ mainly based on the experimental evaluations in different environment of a bridge structure [36].

$$Pl_{i,j} = \alpha d_{i,j} + \beta \ (unit : \%), \tag{8}$$

where α and β are coefficients of packet loss in different materials of bridge and obstructed environment.

Then, the link quality in the two directly connected wireless sensor nodes can be formulated as

$$Q_{i,j} = l_{i,j}(1 - Pl_{i,j}) = l_{i,j}(1 - (\alpha d_{i,j} + \beta)) \tag{9}$$

where i, j = 1,2, ...,k a and i $\neq$ j.

Energy Consumption Model (ECM). In most of existing results, the ECM often only considers energy consumption at the cost of wireless communication. To improve energy consumption model, we will create a model to include comprehensive energy consumption: data sensing, data processing, and wireless communication, which are denoted as $E_s(v_i)$, $E_p(v_i)$, and $E_C(v_i)$, respectively.

$$EC = E(v_i) = E_s(v_i) + E_C(v_i) + E_P(v_i), \tag{10}$$

For each sensor node v_i, the data sensing cost $E_s(v_i)$ is:

$$E_s(v_i) = N_s \cdot e_s \tag{11}$$

where N_s is the amount of sensing samples and e_s is the sensing energy consumption per sample.

For each sensor node v_i, the data processing cost $E_p(v_i)$ is:

$$E_p(v_i) = e_{FFT}(N_s) + e_{SVD}(|V|), \tag{12}$$

where e_{FFT} is the processing energy used in the sensor node when it transferred data into frequency domain. e_{SVD} is dependent on the number of sensor nodes communicated with v_i, denoted as $|V|$, and E_p is generally complex since the process consists of many kinds of computations such as Fast Fourier Transform (FFT) and Singular Value Decomposition (SVD) [37].

For each sensor node v_i, the data communication cost $E_C(v_i)$ is:

$$E_C(v_i) = e_t \cdot N_t + e_r \cdot N_r \tag{13}$$

where e_t is the transmitting energy cost used in the sensor node v_i, N_t is the number of transmitting data samples, e_r is the receiving energy cost in the sensor node v_i, N_r is the number of receiving data samples. Several parameters, such as e_s, e_r, e_t and e_{ERA}, are defined by real tests [38, 39].

3.3   Problem Formulation

Problem Definition. Consider a flat rectangular area A as bridge span and place M homogenous wireless sensor nodes with initial energy E_{node} on the span as instructed by finite element model, and a static sink v_{sink} with unlimited energy on the middle of bridge span. Wireless sensor nodes can directly communicate with other sensor nodes located within their communication range C_r. The sensors are responsible for monitoring the area A and transferring the collected data to the v_{sink}. Thus, each sensor node is able to transmit its data to the v_{sink} directly or via multi-hop communication. This SHM-specific OWSP problem can be described as to find an optimal sensor configuration $S = (v_1, \ldots, v_n)$ out of M candidate sensor locations $\Omega = (v_1, \ldots, v_M)$ obtained by FEM analysis with multiple objectives and defined constraints, where $(v_1, \ldots, v_n)$ are deployed sensors and Ω is decision variable space. These multiple objectives and constraints will be described in details as below.

Decision Variables. $\mathbf{x} = S = (v_1(x_1, y_1), \ldots v_n(x_n, y_n))$, $\mathbf{x} \in \Omega$ denotes a scheme of sensor configuration, $v_i(x_i, y_i)$ denotes coordinates of each sensor location and n is defined number of sensors.

Multiple Objectives. We have mentioned energy consumption by each node is calculated as Eq. (9). If we set initial energy of each sensor node is E_{node}, the system stops to work when the first sensor node is depleted of energy. Therefore the system lifetime T can be measured by minimum lifetime t_i in the first depleted sensor node:

$$T = min(t_i), \tag{14}$$

and the lifetime of ith sensor node is defined as defined as number of detection round t_i:

$$t_i = \frac{Enode}{E(vi)}, \tag{15}$$

Therefore the system lifetime T defined as the minimum lifetime of a sensor node in the system is our first objective function:

$$f_1(\mathbf{x}) = T = min\left(\frac{Enode}{E(vi)}\right), \tag{16}$$

As we mentioned in last section, wireless link quality at each link is considered as $Q_{i,\,j}$. It is obviously that we need to improve $Q_{i,\,j}$ in entire system if the WSN graph is connected. So we need to model this problem by maximising poorest wireless link quality in entire system and the second objective function link quality could be expressed as:

$$f_2(\mathbf{x}) = min(Q_{i,j}) \tag{17}$$

where $Q_{i,j}$ is a link quality indicator of each directly connected link in the WSN $G = (V, E)$ and $min(Q_{i,j})$ is the poorest wireless link in system. Note that those sensors which cannot directly communicate will be removed because of the value of $l_{i,j} = 0$.

The third objective is to maximise the accuracy metric of modal parameters and could be describes as:

$$f_3(\mathbf{x}) = min(E_D^i), \tag{18}$$

where $min(E_D^i)$ represents the minimum term in linear independence indicator which means worst sensor location for identifying mode shapes in the current sensor configuration.

Constraints

(1) Connectivity constraints. The edge between i and j in the graph $G = (V, E)$ is connected if and only if the element in the judgement matrix $J_{i,j} \neq 0$. In the connected WSN graph, there exists at least one disjoint path between any two nodes v_i and v_j, $v_{i,j} \in V, i \neq j$.

(2) Energy constraints. Due to energy limitation $\sum_{j=1} EC(v_i) * t_j \leq E_{node}$, $v_j \in \mathbf{x}$ and $t_j \in (1, 2 \ldots, k)$, where t_j is defined as number of detection round.

(3) Number of sensor nodes. By considering construction cost, we will set N as defined number of nodes to address this OWSP problem.

Thus, this multiple objective optimal wireless sensor placement problem can be formulated as,

$$Max\, F(\mathbf{x}) = (f_1(\mathbf{x}), f_2(\mathbf{x}), f_3(\mathbf{x})), \tag{19}$$

subject to the following constraints:

$\forall v_{i,j} \in V, \min(J_{i,j}) > 0$, such that it is a connected graph,
$\forall v_i \in V, \sum_{j=1} EC(v_i) * t_j \leq E_{node}$,
$\exists \mathbf{x} \in \Omega$, such that $|S| = N$, $|S|$ is defined as the number of sensor nodes in a scheme.

In the next section, we will develop a decomposed based firefly algorithm to present all the solutions in the Padreto-front.

3.4 Multi-Objective Firefly Algorithm Based on the Decomposition (MOFA/D)

The aim of MOO technique is to search for the best trade-off determination within a series of complex or even conflicting objective functions and multiple models or metrics are used to evaluate the functions. Firefly algorithm is a popular swarm intelligence tool which finds optimal solutions based on population search. In this research, a developed multi-objective fly algorithm based on the decomposition (MOFA/D) is used in this research since it is evident that MOFA/D is a better way to address the above problem. The developed MOFA/D in this research could be expressed as below:

Coding and Spreading Fireflies for OWSP Problem. The fireflies are coded with a dual-structure coding system, a firefly represents a scheme of sensor configuration and defined as $F_i = (v_i, g_i)^T = (x_{i1}, y_{i1}), \ldots, (x_{iM}, y_{iM}); g_{i1}, \ldots, g_{iM})^T, i = 1, 2, \ldots, n$. Here, n is the population size and M is the number of defined sensor locations. v_i is the location vector contains coordinates of each wireless sensor node in F_i. g_i is the state vector which indicates scheme of sensor selections. The element in state vector $g_{ip} = 1$ if the pth sensor in the ith scheme is used, otherwise $g_{ip} = 0$. Note that the number of ones in state vector is equal to the number of all candidate sensor locations. The g_{ip} is randomly defined as 0 or 1 and then F_i needs to be re-arranged with coordinates in an ascending order. If the location of a sensor node is near to one of the previous chosen sensor, then the state of sensor will be reset to be 0. As a result, the code includes state vector and coordinates vector is need to be updated.

Evaluating the Objective. Evaluating the objective function of chosen firefly F_i which represents a scheme of sensor configuration in order to approximate the Pareto front of this OWSP problem. After a feasible scheme of sensor configuration is produced, the value of $(f_1(F_i), f_2(F_i), f_3(F_i))$ then can be computed. Note that it is vital to deploy movement of fireflies.

Updating Individual Firefly. In FA, it is assumed that fireflies move toward other brighter fireflies which are more attractive. The attractiveness β can be defined as:

$$\beta(d) = \beta_0 e^{-\gamma d^2}, \tag{20}$$

where d denotes the Hamming distance between two individual firefly i and j, β_0 denotes the attractiveness of firefly at d = 0.

Individual firefly F_i is updated by state vector. To avoid frequent change of F_i, only one sensor is chosen in updating process. A sigmoid function is introduce to update variables:

$$\text{sigmoid}(x) = \frac{1}{1 + \exp(x)}, \tag{21}$$

$$g_{ip} = sig\left(\beta_o e^{-\gamma r_{ij}^2}\left(g_{ip} - g_{jp}\right) + \alpha\left(rand(0, 1) - \frac{1}{2}\right)\right), \tag{22}$$

where p is the chosen sensor to update, β_o is the attractiveness of a firefly source, γ is the light absorption coefficient, $r_{i,j}$ is the distance two individual fireflies, and α is a random parameter. Then the function g_{ip} is defined as

$$g_{ip} = \begin{cases} 1, & \text{if } rand(0, 1) < sigmoid(x_i) \\ 0, & \text{if } rand(0, 1) \geq sigmoid(x_i) \end{cases}, \tag{23}$$

After the sensor is selected, then the individual firefly F_i is updated by coordinated vector according to brightness of firefly F_j, the new v_i' is defined as

$$v_i' = v_i + \beta_0 e^{-\gamma d^2}\left(v_i - v_j\right) + \alpha\varepsilon, \tag{24}$$

where α is generated from the interval [0,1] and ε is generated from a Gaussian distribution. The new position will be updated iteratively until meets the stop criterion.

Framework of MOFA/D. Tchebycheff approach for multi-objective decomposition is widely used to search trade-off in multiple objectives. Let $\vec{W} = (\vec{w}^1, \ldots, \vec{w}^n)$ be weights vector for n sub-problems and $z^* = (z_1^*, \ldots z_m^*)$ be the reference points for n objective functions. $z_i^* = \max\{f_i\{\vec{X} | \vec{X} \in \Omega\}\}, i = 1, 2 \ldots, n.$ Then the problem can be decomposed into n single problems optimization.

The objective function of the jth decomposed single objective problem is:

$$g^{te}(\vec{X} | \overrightarrow{W}, \vec{z}^*) = \max_{1 \leq i \leq m}\{w_i^j | (f_i(x) - z_i^*)|\}, \tag{25}$$
$$\text{for each } i = 1, 2, \ldots m \text{ and } j = 1, 2, \ldots, n$$

where MOFA/D can maximize all m objective functions with conflicting natures simultaneously by using the Tchebycheff approach. In this approach, a neighbourhood of weight vector w^i is defined as a set $w^j = (w_1, \ldots, w_n)$. The neighbourhood of ith sub-problem also contains n weight vectors from w^j and the population consists of the best solution found so far for each sub-problem.

The developed MOFA/D algorithm is shown as Table 2. The input parameters consist of coordinates information, topology information, initial energy of sensor node, limited number of sensors, population size and maximum generation. Hence EP denotes the Pareto set output by this algorithm.

Table 2. Developed specific MOFA/D algorithm

Algorithm

Input: All feasible sensor locations Ω , WSN parameters, sensor node parameters, population size N, maximum number of generations K.

Output: After the maximum number of generations K is reached, the final External Population outputs as optimal solutions in the search space. (Project leader can choose one of them by satisfying all members in integrated research group) ;

Step1) Initialization:

Step 1.1) Set EP$\in \Omega$

Step 1.2) Compute the Hamming distances between any two weight vectors and then work out the p closest weight vectors to each weight vector, $w^{i1}, \ldots, w^{ik}$ are the k closet weight vectors to w^i

Step 1.3) Randomly produce an individual firefly F_i. Compute fitness value FV^i

Step 1.4) Initialize its reference points $\vec{z}^* = (z_1, z_2, z_3)^T$

Step 1.5) Initialize neighbour of each firefly by closet weight vectors.

Step 2) Update:

For i=1,...,n, do

Step 2.1) Individual updating: Evaluating firefly F_i. If F_j satisfy $g^{te}(f_j|\vec{W}, \vec{z}^*) < g^{te}(f_i|\vec{W}, \vec{z}^*)$, then move F_i to F_j, otherwise a random walk will be introduced.

Step 2.2) Neighbour Updating: For each index k $\in$ ($w^{i1}, \ldots, w^{ip}$), select individual firefly F_k from neighbours of F_i, k=0. If F_k satisfy $g^{te}(f_i|\vec{W}, \vec{z}^*) < g^{te}(f_k|\vec{W}, \vec{z}^*)$, then update F_k by new individual f_i, otherwise find another F_{k+1}. It is limited by k < $neighbour\ size$.

Step 2.3) Update of reference points: for each j =1, s... m, if $z_j < f_j(x^*)$, then set $z_j = f_j(x^*)$.

Step2.4) Update of EP:

Remove all the vector from EP dominated by F(x*),
Add F(x*) to EP if no vectors in EP dominate F(x*).

Step 3) Stopping Criteria: If maximum number of generations K is satisfied, then stop and output optimal results (sensor configuration and values of three objectives). Otherwise, go to **step 2**.

At each generation t, MOFA/D with the Tchebycheff approach maintains:

- A population of N fireflies $F_1, \ldots, F_N \in \Omega$, where F_i is the current solution to the ith sub-problem.

- $FV^1, \ldots, FV^n$, where FV^i is the fitness value of F_i, $FV^i = FV(F_i) = \max_{1 \leq j \leq 3} w_j^i |f_j(F_i) - z_j^*|\}$ for each i = 1,...,n, j = 1,2,3; $f_j(F_i)$ is the value of jth objective, z_i^* are the reference points, $w_j^i = (w_1^i, w_2^i, w_3^i)$ are weight vectors for firefly F_i.

- There are 3 objectives in this OWSP, $\mathbf{z} = (z_1, z_2, z_3)^T$, where z_1, z_2, z_3 are the best values found so far for each objective f_1, f_2, f_3.
- Fireflies movement is described as Eqs. (23) and (24) and updated simultaneously according to Eq. (25)
- Individual firefly will be updated only if the neighbouring firefly dominates it.

An external population (EP), which is used to store non-dominated solutions found by every generation.

The developed MOFA/D algorithm is shown as Table 2.

3.5   Integration with BrIM

Visualized optimal sensor locations on the case bridge will be performed with Revit. Though Revit provides a 3D modelling bridge and we could get optimal results from MATLAB, we still need to make a further development by integrating them together. In the future, integrated research group could use the 3D model bridge updated with detailed optimal locations results from toolbox directly for facilitating design of SHM systems.

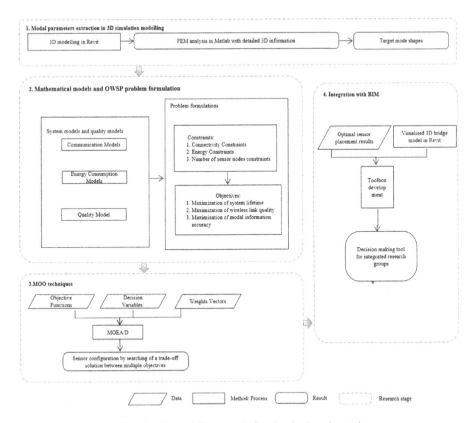

Fig. 4. General framework for developing the tool

To develop the tool used to locate and record optimal sensor locations in a 3D model bridge formed by Revit, we need to define the following capabilities: (1) Mark the sensor node at a location in built-up model along linking geometric parameters to informative 3D model's database; (2) The Revit model could be updated with a user interface for ease of design and documentation; (3) Wireless sensor nodes can be placed on any elements of 3D bridge model built by Revit except for some optimal locations on the bridge may be unavailable. Semantic information in nodes include the location, size, number and energy capacity.

In general, the framework of this optimal sensor placement tool for SHM systems on bridge structure are depicted in Fig. 4.

4   Case Study

As a primary example, we begin by implementing the 3D model of a beam defined as Table 3 and modified FEM model to generate target mode shapes. In Table 3, detailed beam properties and WSN parameters are given.

Table 3. Properties of study case

Weight	Width	Height	Flange Thickness	Web Thickness	Root Radius	Moment of Inertia-XX	Moment of Inertia-YY
14 kg/m	750mm	150mm	7mm	5mm	8mm	6.66 million mm**4	0.495 million mm**4

Communication range	Node initial energy	Sensing energy	Receiving energy	Transferring energy	Number of sensors
12m	1 Ah	$1.1e^{-4}$ mAh	$5e^{-4}$ mAh	$5e^{-4}$ mAh	10

On the MATLAB platform, we simulate the beam in a flat area 100 m * 0.75 m where the beam is divided into 50 number of elements. As discussed, we get target mode shape Φ_{ex} from FEM analysis and take it as input data to formulate objective function of accuracy metric corresponding to sensor locations. Parameters used in Table 2 also will be used to formulate objective function of system lifetime and link quality.

In this case, we present the Pareto front between 3 objectives: accuracy metric, link quality and system lifetime. Figure 5 shows the approximated Pareto front for considering of 10 nodes case. So the leader of integrated research group could choose an optimal configuration as required by conditions of project and meanwhile can achieve higher performance with 3 objectives simultaneously.

This is done to provide several optimal results with considering lifetime metric, wireless link quality and modal information accuracy. The multiple configurations of optimal results with a matter of primary interest can suggest project leader for choosing the best one in accordance with project conditions. Compared to traditional single objective optimization, optimal results of MOFA/D are carried out at the same time. For an instance, Table 4 shows the sample results of 5 different compromised configurations considering of 10 sensor nodes.

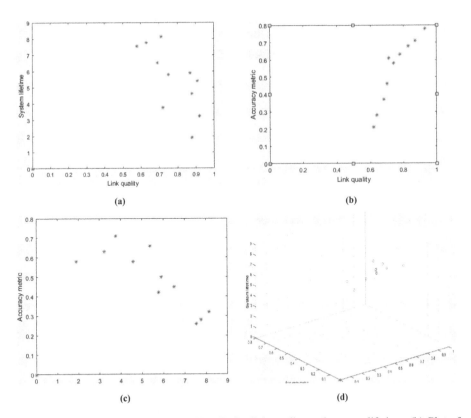

Fig. 5. (a) Plot of Pareto front by MOFA/D for link quality and system lifetime; (b) Plot of Pareto front by MOFA/D for link quality and accuracy metric; (c) Plot of Pareto front by MOFA/D for system lifetime and accuracy metric; (d) Plot of Pareto front by MOFA/D for link quality, accuracy metric and system lifetime.

Table 4. Results of different compromised configurations with 3 objectives when number of sensor nodes is 10

Node = 10	S_1	S_2	S_3	S_4	S_5
Objective 1: Accuracy metric	0.38	0.43	0.52	0.63	0.57
Objective 2: Link quality	0.69	0.75	0.87	0.91	0.88
Objective 3: System lifetime	6.51	5.78	5.89	5.38	4.59

A sample configuration for wireless-based SHM system is shown in in Fig. 6. This figure is a configuration of S_4 in 2D plan with accuracy metric is 0.63, link quality is 0.91 and system lifetime is 5.78. The corresponding decision variables are:

$$S = ((106, 47), (186, 13), (224, 33), (315, 39), (611, 41), (715, 19), (811, 21), (876, 26), (910, 31), (987, 25))$$

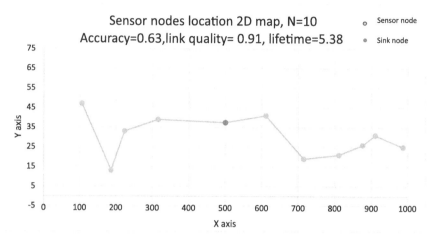

Fig. 6. A sample configuration of 10 nodes with MOEA/D

From multiple optimal results obtained by the MOFA/D approach, integrated research groups can choose one configuration corresponding to specific requirement of project. Next, we need to realise and visualise it in Revit environment to help specific

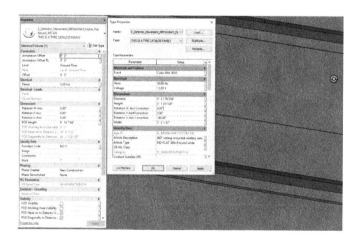

Fig. 7. Visualised placement design in 3D environment

domain engineers can make final decisions in an easy way. Meanwhile, sub-constructors from industry could potentially mark some unfeasible placement locations or location with potential function will be used by other mechanical, electrical and plumbing (MEP) teams. Figure 7 shows the visualised placement design and detailed sensor information.

5 Conclusion and Future Work

Large and complex civil structures are being placed in new and extreme conditions for extended periods. As a result, the need for design SHM System in an optimal way continues to grow. This problem that should be solved by the engineers from all the related groups in the construction project. The worldwide implementation of an effective and affordable SHM system should consider number of sensor nodes and optimal locations can be accepted by isolated MEP teams. This paper has presented a framework to trade off the installation cost, the quality of the collected data and the consummated energy for wireless sensor placement in bridge SHM. Different from existing work, our method will present all the potential solutions to the owner and a potential solution can be selected based on owner's preference. Our method is further embedded with BrIM for visualization and validation which could be more practically for civil engineers, wireless engineers and related sub-contractors. In the future, we will select a test bed from our collaborated industrial partner to validate our proposed method. The prototype will be further linked with commercial software required, such as BrIM and ANSYS, to realize automatic wireless sensor placement based on the given BrIM.

Acknowledgements. This research was partially supported under Australian Research Council Linkage Project scheme (project number: LP160100528).

References

1. Lee, G.C., Mohan, S., Huang, C., Fard, B.N.: A study of US bridge failures (1980–2012). MCEER Technical report 13-0008 (2013)
2. Austroads: Investigating the Development of a Bridge Assessment Tool for Determining Access for High Productivity Freight Vehicles, Research report (2012)
3. Park, S., Savvides, A., Srivastava, M.B.: Simulating networks of wireless sensors. In: Proceedings of the 33nd Conference on Winter Simulation, pp. 1330–1338. IEEE Computer Society (2001)
4. Wong, K.Y.: Instrumentation and health monitoring of cable-supported bridges. Struct. Control Health Monit. **11**, 91–124 (2004)
5. Austroads: Guidelines for Ensuring Specified Quality Performance in Bridge Construction (2003)
6. Lynch, J.P., Loh, K.J.: A summary review of wireless sensors and sensor networks for structural health monitoring. Shock Vibr. Digest **38**, 91–130 (2006)

7. Spencer, B.F., Jo, H.K., Mechitov, K.A., Li, J., Sim, S.H., Kim, R.E., Cho, S., Linderman, L. E., Moinzadeh, P., Giles, R.K., Agha, G.: Recent advances in wireless smart sensors for multi-scale monitroing and control of civil infrastructure. J. Civil Struct. Health Monit. **6**(1), 17–41 (2015)

8. Li, J., Hao, H., Chen, Z.: Damage identification and optimal sensor placement for structures under unknown traffic-induced vibrations. J. Aerosp. Eng. **30**, B4015001 (2015)

9. Yi, T.-H., Li, H.-N., Zhang, X.-D.: Sensor placement on Canton Tower for health monitoring using asynchronous-climb monkey algorithm. Smart Mater. Struct. **21**, 125023 (2012)

10. Chang, M., Pakzad, S.N.: Optimal sensor placement for modal identification of bridge systems considering number of sensing nodes. J. Bridge Eng. **19**, 04014019 (2014)

11. Bhuiyan, M.Z.A., Wang, G.: Sensor placement with multiple objectives for structural health monitoring. ACM Trans. Sens. Netw. **10**, 68 (2014)

12. Yi, T.-H., Li, H.-N., Zhang, X.-D.: A modified monkey algorithm for optimal sensor placement in structural health monitoring. Smart Mater. Struct. **21**, 105033 (2012)

13. Yi, T.-H., Li, H.-N., Gu, M.: Optimal sensor placement for health monitoring of high-rise structure based on genetic algorithm. Math. Probl. Eng. **2011**, Article ID 395101, 12 p. (2011)

14. Hou, L., Wu, C., Wang, X., Wang, J.: A framework design for optimizing scaffolding erection by applying mathematical models and virtual simulation. Comput. Civil Build. Eng. **2014**, 323–330 (2014)

15. Hou, L., Zhao, C., Wu, C., Moon, S., Wang, X.: Discrete firefly algorithm for scaffolding construction scheduling. J. Comput. Civil Eng. **31**, 04016064 (2016)

16. Liang, J., Liu, M., Kui, X.: A survey of coverage problems in wireless sensor networks. Sens. Transducers **163**, 240 (2014)

17. Zhu, J., Wright, G., Wang, J., Wang, X.: A critical review of the integration of geographic information system and building information modelling at the data level. ISPRS Int. J. Geo-Inf. **7**, 66 (2018)

18. Bhuiyan, M.Z.A., Wang, G., Cao, J., Wu, J.: Deploying wireless sensor networks with fault-tolerance for structural health monitoring. IEEE Trans. Comput. **64**, 382–395 (2015)

19. Sengupta, S., Das, S., Nasir, M.D., Panigrahi, B.K.: Multi-objective node deployment in WSNs: in search of an optimal trade-off among coverage, lifetime, energy consumption, and connectivity. Eng. Appl. Artif. Intell. **26**, 405–416 (2013)

20. Wang, T., Wang, J., Wu, P., Wang, J., He, Q., Wang, X.: Estimating the environmental costs and benefits of demolition waste using life cycle assessment and willingness-to-pay: a case study in Shenzhen. J. Clean. Prod. **172**, 14–26 (2018)

21. You, T., Jin, H., Li, P.: Optimal placement of wireless sensor nodes for bridge dynamic monitoring based on improved particle swarm algorithm. Int. J. Distrib. Sens. Netw. **9**(12), 390936 (2013)

22. Cheng, L., Niu, J., Cao, J., Das, S.K., Gu, Y.: QoS aware geographic opportunistic routing in wireless sensor networks. IEEE Trans. Parallel Distrib. Syst. **25**, 1864–1875 (2014)

23. Jaffres-Runser, K., Schurgot, M.R., Wang, Q., Comaniciu, C., Gorce, J.-M.: A cross-layer framework for multiobjective performance evaluation of wireless ad hoc networks. Ad Hoc Netw. **11**, 2147–2171 (2013)

24. Hu, H., Xu, L., Zhu, B., Wei, R.: A compatible control algorithm for greenhouse environment control based on MOCC strategy. Sensors **11**, 3281–3302 (2011)

25. Lee, C.-Y., Chong, H.-Y., Liao, P.-C., Wang, X.: Critical review of social network analysis applications in complex project management. J. Manag. Eng. **34**, 04017061 (2017)

26. Long, Q., Wu, C., Huang, T., Wang, X.: A genetic algorithm for unconstrained multi-objective optimization. Swarm Evol. Comput. **22**, 1–14 (2015)

27. Song, Y., Tan, Y., Song, Y., Wu, P., Cheng, J.C., Kim, M.J., Wang, X.: Spatial and temporal variations of spatial population accessibility to public hospitals: a case study of rural-urban comparison. GISci. Remote Sens. 1–27 (2018)
28. Tao, S., Wu, C., Sheng, Z., Wang, X.: Space-time repetitive project scheduling considering location and congestion. J. Comput. Civil Eng. **32**, 04018017 (2018)
29. Zhao, C., Wu, C., Chai, J., Wang, X., Yang, X., Lee, J.-M., Kim, M.J.: Decomposition-based multi-objective firefly algorithm for RFID network planning with uncertainty. Appl. Soft Comput. **55**, 549–564 (2017)
30. Chi, H.-L., Kang, S.-C., Wang, X.: Research trends and opportunities of augmented reality applications in architecture, engineering, and construction. Autom. Constr. **33**, 116–122 (2013)
31. Chong, H.Y., Lopez, R., Wang, J., Wang, X., Zhao, Z.: Comparative analysis on the adoption and use of BIM in road infrastructure projects. J. Manag. Eng. **32**, 05016021 (2016)
32. Li, J., Wang, Y., Wang, X., Luo, H., Kang, S.-C., Wang, J., Guo, J., Jiao, Y.: Benefits of building information modelling in the project lifecycle: construction projects in Asia. Int. J. Adv. Rob. Syst. **11**, 124 (2014)
33. Wang, Y., Wang, X., Wang, J., Yung, P., Jun, G.: Engagement of facilities management in design stage through BIM: framework and a case study. Adv. Civil Eng. **2013**, Article ID 189105, 8 p. (2013)
34. Fan, W., Qiao, P.: Vibration-based damage identification methods: a review and comparative study. Struct. Health Monit. **10**, 83–111 (2011)
35. Bhuiyan, M.Z.A., Wang, G., Cao, J., Wu, J.: Sensor placement with multiple objectives for structural health monitoring. ACM Trans. Sens. Netw. (TOSN) **10**, 68 (2014)
36. Bae, S.-C., Jang, W.-S., Woo, S.: Prediction of WSN placement for bridge health monitoring based on material characteristics. Autom. Constr. **35**, 18–27 (2013)
37. Liu, X., Cao, J., Tang, S.: Enabling fast and reliable network-wide event-triggered wakeup in WSNs. In: 2013 IEEE 34th Real-Time Systems Symposium (RTSS), pp. 278–287. IEEE (2013)
38. Cheng, P., Chuah, C.-N., Liu, X.: Energy-aware node placement in wireless sensor networks. In: Global Telecommunications Conference, GLOBECOM 2004, pp. 3210–3214. IEEE (2004)
39. Olariu, S., Stojmenovic, I.: Design guidelines for maximizing lifetime and avoiding energy holes in sensor networks with uniform distribution and uniform reporting. In: INFOCOM 2006, pp. 1–12 (2006)

A System Analytics Framework for Detecting Infrastructure-Related Topics in Disasters Using Social Sensing

Chao Fan, Ali Mostafavi[(✉)], Aayush Gupta, and Cheng Zhang

Texas A&M University, College Station, TX 77840, USA
{chfan,ayu2224,czhang}@tamu.edu, amostafavi@civil.tamu.edu

Abstract. The objective of this paper is to propose and test a system analytics framework based on social sensing and text mining to detect topic evolution associated with the performance of infrastructure systems in disasters. Social media, like Twitter, as active channels of communication and information dissemination, provide insights into real-time information and first-hand experience from affected areas in mass emergencies. While the existing studies show the importance of social sensing in improving situational awareness and emergency response in disasters, the use of social sensing for detection and analysis of infrastructure systems and their resilience performance has been rather limited. This limitation is due to the lack of frameworks to model the events and topics (e.g., grid interruption and road closure) evolution associated with infrastructure systems (e.g., power, highway, airport, and oil) in times of disasters. The proposed framework detects infrastructure-related topics of the tweets posted in disasters and their evolutions by integrating searching relevant keywords, text lemmatization, Part-of-Speech (POS) tagging, TF-IDF vectorization, topic modeling by using Latent Dirichlet Allocation (LDA), and K-Means clustering. The application of the proposed framework was demonstrated in a study of infrastructure systems in Houston during Hurricane Harvey. In this case study, more than sixty thousand tweets were retrieved from 150-mile radius in Houston over 39 days. The analysis of topic detection and evolution from user-generated data were conducted, and the clusters of tweets pertaining to certain topics were mapped in networks over time. The results show that the proposed framework enables to summarize topics and track the movement of situations in different disaster phases. The analytics elements of the proposed framework can improve the recognition of infrastructure performance through text-based representation and provide evidence for decision-makers to take actionable measurements.

Keywords: System analytics framework · Social sensing
Infrastructure-related topics · Disaster resilience · Text mining

1 Introduction

Infrastructure systems such as water networks, highways, and power grid are critical components to human lives and community functions [1]. The performance of

© Springer International Publishing AG, part of Springer Nature 2018
I. F. C. Smith and B. Domer (Eds.): EG-ICE 2018, LNCS 10864, pp. 74–91, 2018.
https://doi.org/10.1007/978-3-319-91638-5_4

infrastructure systems can affect other systems due to their interdependencies [2, 3]. Timely mapping of infrastructure disruptions and damages is essential for response and restoration of infrastructure services. However, the limited resources and accessibility inhibit situational awareness and effective detection of infrastructure disruptions. Social sensing and crowdsourced data collection (such as social media), processes in which social posts deliver the users' observations and emotions regarding their physical environment [4], have been shown to be potentially useful in improving the situational awareness of agencies involved in disaster response. The advantages of using social sensing data are twofold: (1) sheer volume of messages and users; and (2) high velocity of generating posts. In existing studies, for example, Olteanu et al. [5] showed that more than 2.7 million tweets relative to hurricane Sandy were generated in three days, while 3.3 million tweets relative to Boston Bombings were generated in five days. Lu and Brelsford [6] collected 14.2 million messages in the 2011 Japanese Earthquake and Tsunami, where over 2000 tweets per second were generated following this disaster [7]. As such, social media impart a great opportunity for obtaining important information in disasters.

In order to use social sensing in assessing infrastructure service disruptions and resilience, there are two technical issues that should be addressed: event detection and tracking. Infrastructure-related events exhibit the severity and duration of failures. Detecting those events is essential for disaster responders to recognize the situation and distribute the resources for relief. On the other hand, the situations associated with infrastructure systems were changing over time since the intervention from humans or other interdependent systems. Tracking the evolution of the events is necessary for evaluating the performance of infrastructure and making response decisions. Some research [8–10] involving text mining approaches in detecting and tracking domain-specific events has been conducted on social media. For example, Ashktorab et al. [11] classified tweets, extracted tokens, and phrases that reported damages and casualties based on predefined terms by using a Twitter-mining tool, Tweedr. Yin et al. [12] investigated natural language processing and data mining techniques to conduct some burst detection, tweet classification, and geotagging by employing empirical search terms. Bala et al. [13] applied regression analysis to text data for finding the course of the disaster by counting the frequencies of sample words. Tien et al. [1] detected damages and failures in transportation and energy systems by using given search terms. However, all outputs in the literature were binary: can or cannot be detected, since the events were predefined by keywords. Another stream of research concentrates on the tentative analysis of filtered relevant social data. For example, Olteanu et al. [5] employed crowdsourcing and supervised learning to create a lexicon of crisis-related terms. Prasetyo et al. [14] conducted content analysis, emotion analysis, activity analysis and network analysis on social posts that were retrieved by selected keywords in the case of Singapore Haze. However, the existing studies still cannot be applied to understanding the extent of detecting and tracking infrastructure-related events on social media.

To address this gap, this study proposes a framework integrating social sensing and text mining for building a detailed text-based representation of infrastructure-related events and tracking the evolution of those major events. It enables to precisely filter infrastructure-related social posts, classify tweets into different clusters, summarize relevant events, and analyze the changes of these events during the development of disasters. This paper is organized into two parts: system analytics framework and a case study. In section two, the architecture of our novel framework including innovative algorithms is presented and explained. In section three, a case study of hurricane Harvey in Houston area is conducted, relevant events are summarized in four disaster phases (e.g., before Harvey landed, hurricane period, flooding period, and after flooding receded), and the changes of the events over time are explored. Section four presents the limitation of current results and discusses the future work that is potentially capable of improving the outputs. Section five concludes the study in this paper and the contributions of this work towards situational awareness of infrastructure disruptions.

2 System Analytics Framework

The proposed system analytics framework supports a series of social sensing methods and text-mining approaches, such as text classification, vectorization, topic modeling, data clustering, and text-based representation. The overall framework of this study is shown in Fig. 1. This framework includes four components: (1) context recognition; (2) data collection and preprocessing; (3) text classification; (4) topic modeling and representation. First, context recognition is to learn basic information about disasters (e.g., spatial distribution, severity, measures, and prominent events) for figuring out the inputs (e.g., geolocations and keywords) to the algorithms. The novelties of this framework are two important iterations which contribute to: (1) stop words and keywords updates; (2) dynamic changes of the number of classes in text classification. The update of keywords in the first iteration is to obtain a comprehensive list of keywords for retrieving relevant social posts, while the update of stop words is to delete some common words that also appear in other irrelevant documents for reducing the size of datasets and improving the accuracy and efficiency of following procedures. The process of updates is manual but adopts POS (Part-of-Speech) tagging to filter out new relevant keywords and stop words. The iteration of text classification is to determine the number of major topics in each dataset without predefined numbers. Meanwhile, text classification integrates text-mining elements such as TF-IDF (term frequency-inverse document frequency) vectorization, K-means clustering, LDA (Latent Dirichlet Allocation) topic modeling for precisely extracting specific topics. These two iterations contributed to making the algorithm be more adaptive to the evolving streaming data than previous studies. The merits of these iterations will be validated by their applications. The last component, topic representation, is to make a detailed summary of each detected topic so that the results can be used directly by decision makers for developing strategies. In the following subsections, we present the functions and merits of each component.

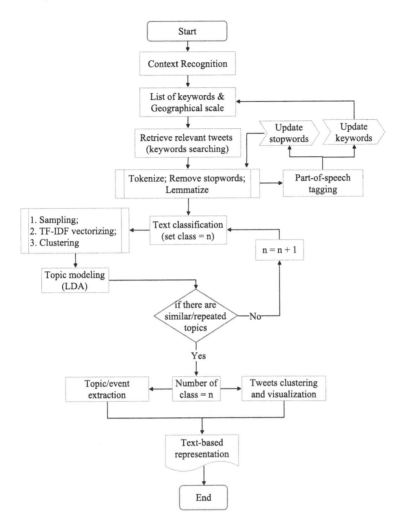

Fig. 1. The architecture of the system analytics framework.

2.1 Context Recognition

In the first component, context recognition and awareness of users are fundamental requirements of conducting social sensing and text mining, because the context of disasters provides the basis for data collection and processing. As the architecture of this framework shows, data retrieval includes keyword-based and geolocation-based retrieval on social media. The understanding of context is helpful to preliminarily identify relevant keywords and define the scale of affected areas for data collection. Further, defining phases based on the context is essential for dividing the life cycle of disasters into several time periods, in order to analyze the changes of detected events over time. In the proposed framework, disaster phases are defined by the dominant events and threats so that the derived damages and disruption of infrastructure systems by those dominant events can be summarized and assessed. In the end, the extracted topics in each disaster phase will be validated by the context. As such, context recognition and disaster phases definition are significant for users to conduct this framework. For details of context recognition, there are a vast number of sources (e.g., news articles, web portals, governmental reports, photos as well as interviews) relative to disasters can be accessed. Thus, deep understanding of the development of disasters is easy to be achieved.

2.2 Data Collection and Preprocessing

After getting to know the context of the disasters, we can determine a list of keywords describing the disaster and geolocation of affected areas for identifying and gathering relevant tweets from Twitter. Due to the rate limitation of Twitter's public API (i.e., the constraints of login and scraping data), both keyword-based and location-based collection are commonly used in the current social sensing literature [15]. Keywords (e.g., disruption, damage, sad, emergency, and survivor) are constructed by human reaction to the effects of disasters and are representative of the sentences in messages. In this framework, the list of keywords is the combination of two parts: infrastructure-related keywords and disaster event-related keywords, for collecting domain-specific data. These search terms contribute to obtaining precise topics relative to infrastructure performance in the following components of this framework. However, keyword-based collection always leads to a lot of noise in datasets since similar keywords or events may appear in other areas around the world. Thus, a combination of the location-based and keyword-based collection is particularly helpful for reducing noise in our datasets and improving the accuracy of collected data in our specific research domain. Then, the lexicon and geographical scale can be applied to retrieve microblogged communications and messages.

The next step in processing social data before text classification is data cleaning to get focused content which includes tokenization, removing stop words as well as lemmatization. Tokenization is a process of splitting the text into meaningful tokens [16]. As the microblogged communications are always no more than 140 words, so the complexity of tokenization is much lower than dealing with fictions and scripts. However, because the users are used to using a lot of symbols and punctuations (e.g., "(: - :)", "???", and "\^ - ^/") to express their emotions and feelings, it is necessary to remove these symbols and punctuations by employing regular expressions. After getting the clean datasets, lemmatization including multiple rules of converting all tokens to their root words is utilized. For example, "affect" and "affects" have the same meaning in out topics. Thus, "affects" should be converted to "affect" so that these tokens can be filtered into the same category. It is essential for updating keywords, stop words as well as text classification since almost every derived word can be identified. Furthermore, in order to get more representative content, removing the words that occur commonly across all the other documents, called stop words, are used as a preprocess in natural language processing (NLP). In our infrastructure-specific research domain, the stop words and relevant keywords are not very discriminative and cannot be determined previously and completely. Therefore, an iteration with POS tagging and identification is designed for updating stop words and relevant keywords from retrieved datasets. It categorizes tokens into different part-of-speech categories so that the users can filter keywords in certain categories. For example, the word with symbol (SYM) tag is straightforward to be identified and assigned to the stop words category, while the word with NN (noun, singular or mass) tag can be filtered to recognize whether it is relevant or not.

2.3 Text Classification

Text classification is a machine learning algorithm for reducing the dimensionality of social media messages and employing NLP applications (e.g., vectorization, counting the frequency of words, clustering and topic modeling). The content of texts from social media covers several different disaster topics, such as power outage, heavy rain, strong wind, and governmental relief. Therefore, clustering the tweets with the same topic into the same class is a preliminary step to understand the content of texts. First, the overall dataset should be divided into two parts: training set and test set. It can be split randomly for simplicity, or based on well-researched approaches (e.g., probability distribution, Bayesian networks, and empty network) to improve accuracy. Then, as all machine learning methods are developed for numeric features, the text corpus of social communications should be converted in a format with numeric features as well. In our framework, the texts are transformed to vectors because computers are good at handling vectors in an efficient way. As such, different words in the dataset can be the elements of a matrix, while the frequencies of the words in each tweet are the values. In this way, each tweet can be represented by a vector. In this framework, the transformation is conducted by employing a refinement of term frequency method to downscale weights for words that are commonly used in other documents. This approach is called term frequency-inverse document frequency (TF-IDF) [17]. In the context of infrastructure resilience domain, some words such as "nervous", "strong", "washer", and "repose" are not highly relevant but may appear with infrastructure-related keywords in the same tweet. The weights of those words should be very low even if their frequencies are a little bit high. Thus, TF-IDF plays a critical role to address these conditions. Subsequently, a term-document matrix is obtained after vectorization of the texts. The next step is to train a text classifiers such as Naïve Bayes classifier, decision trees, stochastic gradient descent, and support vector machines which are widely used for this purpose. However, these classification algorithms are supervised algorithms which require historic pre-labeled training data. Also, the disruptions and bursts of infrastructure services are changing over time since disruptions and bursts are sensitive to the intervention of human activities and interdependent system. For example, a large-scale power outage can be solved by utility companies rather than continuing after flooding receded. Thus, for simplicity and flexibility for dynamic data streams, the proposed framework adopts an unsupervised learning, called K-means clustering, which does not need any labeled data but can identify important hidden patterns in unlabeled data. However, K-means clustering method requires the number of clusters to be predefined. To obtaining the exact number of major clusters and topics from social media datasets, an iteration involving topic modeling and repeatability detecting is implemented for determining a precise number of clusters (see Fig. 1). As discussed earlier, when the topics are repeated, the number of clusters should be reduced to maintain their uniqueness. For example, if two clusters of tweets are both talking about the road closure, it should be combined and get a complete a dataset for this topic. Thereby, the extracted topics from clusters are representative of the majority of texts and precise enough to be used for topic evolvement analysis.

2.4 Topic Modeling and Representation

In the infrastructure-specific domain, the detailed representation and development of events on social media communications can provide evidence for performance under-standing and assessment (e.g., how severe is the interruption, how many people are affected by this disruption, and what further effects by this disruption should be taken into account). For example, the highway, Interstate-10 from Texas to Louisiana, closed when it was covered by floodwaters during Harvey, but it reopened after six days because the water receded. Thus, people who need to use this road should be presented with information in accordance to the situation of this road including which section of this road was closed, when it was closed, when it would reopen, and what damage of this road was caused by floodwaters. Therefore, not only the detailed representation, but also the evolvement of events should be carefully analyzed on the social data. In this frame-work, the events are detected based on the summarization of topics. By definition, topics are the summary and representation of certain clusters of tweets and are practical for tracking the development of disasters and resilience performance of infrastructure. For example, the airport was closed, and all flights were canceled when hurricane Harvey landed, while it reopened and played an important role in disaster relief when Harvey passed. Based on the extracted topics about the airport, disaster responders can further detect potential issues (e.g., deficient in the capacity of transporting and distributing resources) in this cluster of tweets. To get the initial insights regarding the unlabeled social posts, topic modeling is an effective approach to deal with large volumes of texts through Latent Dirichlet Allocation (LDA) and reduce the dimensionality of the dataset for further studies (e.g., specific entities detection, geo-tagging, and relation extraction). Intuitively, the topic modeling technique is based on the probability of the words in each document and the latent semantic structures of the text. For example, if a document is 80% talking about "flooding" and 20% talking about "birthday party", the topic about "flooding" will definitely be extracted in priority. As such, the clusters of text can be represented by semantic coherent keywords, while the trend of topics can be tracked over different disaster phases.

3   A Case Study of Hurricane Harvey

The presented system analytics framework provides chances to identify developments of events related to the performance of infrastructure systems in disaster situations based on social media. In this paper, the process on a set of tweets relative to hurricane Harvey shows the possibilities of the application. Using this system analytics framework, we filtered out relevant tweets, cleaned data sets, classified texts, and modeled topics with the context of Harvey in Texas. The findings in this specific case study show the potential of the proposed framework for detecting and tracking the disasters using tweets.

3.1   Context Recognition

The proposed framework is examined in a case study of hurricane Harvey, which made a landfall in Texas on 25th August 2017 [3]. The rainfall level during hurricane Harvey in Texas is shown in Fig. 2 [18]. Harvey caused severe disruptions in infrastructure systems. Based on a Texas Department of Transportation report [19], more than 200 highway locations were closed or flooded, and all flights were suspended in the Houston Airport System. Customers served by 166 water systems received boil-water orders and another 50 water systems were shut down completely due to storm impact [20].

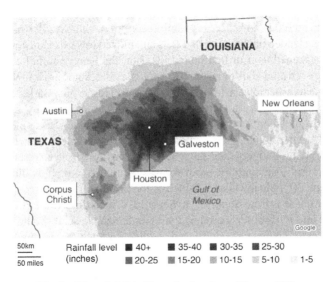

Fig. 2. The rainfall in Texas by hurricane Harvey [18].

In the case study, we identified relevant keywords including infrastructure-related, and disaster event-related keywords (see Table 1) from multiple online sources such as news articles, government reports, and social media. We applied the proposed framework to retrieve relevant tweets through the process of keyword-based collection and geography-based collection, process texts, update stop words and keywords, and iterate retrieving tweets. This process was repeated until a complete dataset is collected, at which point no stop words and keyword needed to be updated and no more tweets would be retrieved. In this paper, 63263 tweets were gathered from Aug. 23rd to Sept. 30th in the 150-mile radius around Houston.

Table 1. Keywords used for collecting relevant tweets.

Infrastructure-related keywords	Disaster event-related keywords
Shelter, power outage, electricity, road, closure, floodwater, water, watersheds, drainage, infrastructure, damage, restoration, transport, shortage, devastation, flight, airport, bridge, car, neighborhood, river, gas, build, rebuild, debris, sewage, electric, energy, utilities, roadway, Addicks, Barker, bayou, sh6, I10, reservoir	Harvey, flood, flooding, Hurricane, flooding, recovery, storm, surge, warning, evacuation, emergency, remnants, survivor, disaster, FEMA, medicine, rescue, rainfall, relief, victims, food, safety, health, donate, insurance, wind, response, rainy, refuge, resources, aid, demand, volunteer, landfall, needs, restore

The authors defined specific time periods of disaster phases to map the temporal distribution of infrastructure-related events. In this study, the disaster phases were defined based on time of duration (see Table 2): before the hurricane landed (preparedness phase), after the hurricane landed (response phase). From Aug. 23rd to Aug. 24th, people began to be aware of the threats of hurricane Harvey and prepare for the response (e.g., stocked up on food and water, and reinforced roofs). August 25th was the date that hurricane Harvey landed on the coast of Texas and moved towards Houston. After Aug. 29th, Harvey weakened as it drifted inland [3]. But, the heavy rainfall continued and caused flooding even after Harvey passed Houston. Besides, some areas in West Houston were flooded due to water release from two flood control reservoirs, Barker and Addicks. Thus, neighborhoods in West Houston continued to be affected by flooding until surcharge release ended on Sept. 14th. Hence, the flooding phase was defined from Aug. 30th to Sept. 14th. After flooding, residents, responders, government agencies, and infrastructure agencies took emergency response measures for disaster rescue and infrastructure restoration. Although the recovery was continued, our study did not retrieve tweets after Sept. 30th. Meanwhile, considering the limitation of the size of the dataset, the last disaster phase is from Sept. 15th to Sept. 30th. Accordingly, the collected tweets were separated into four subsets based on their predefined phase. It should be noted that the tweets processed in this case study were original tweets without retweeting. These tweets can reflect the actual condition at the time when they were posted.

Table 2. Time periods of disaster phases.

Disaster phases	Time of duration
Before Harvey landed	Aug. 23rd–Aug. 24th
Hurricane period	Aug. 25th–Aug. 29th
Flooding period	Aug. 30th–Sept. 14th
After the flooding receded	Sept. 15th–Sept. 30th

3.2 Text Classification and Topic Modeling

In the next component, text sampling, vectorization, clustering and topic modeling were conducted. The output of this component is listed in Table 3 and mapped in Fig. 3. Because the duration of time in different phases was various and the physical environment was dynamic in disasters, the number of clusters in each disaster phase was different. This process was controlled by the iteration that increased the number of classes until repeated topics appear.

As shown in Table 3, before the Harvey landed, three major topics were dominant: (1) George Bush Intercontinental airport was affected and needed to take rapid response to the hurricane; (2) Pearland is humid so that residents and infrastructure agencies should prepare; (3) City of Houston encourage citizens to get prepared. The relevant tweets were clustered into three categories (see Fig. 3). Topic 1 which is associated with the airport and topic 3 which is associated with the early warning in Houston area are more frequent than topic 2 which is associated with the early warning in Pearland since the size of tweets cluster of topic 1 and topic 3 are distinctively larger than the size of the cluster of topic 2. In addition, topic 2 showed its significance in early warning before the disaster since the water sewage treatment system in Pearland was sensitive to storms and flooding [21].

When Harvey landed, topics were more about the devastation and severity of the disaster. As displayed in Table 2, five topics were detected in the hurricane phase: (1) Because Houston was attacked by Harvey at that time, the public was conducting relief and donating for damaged properties; (2) the intensity of rainfall in Pasadena was heavy so that residents and responders were encouraged to be careful; (3) freeway and tollway were both closed because of flooding and extreme weather; (4) the floodwaters level and status of freeway were reported for the public and responders; (5) downtown and East-side were highly affected by the hurricane. Most of the topics were talking about the damage in infrastructure systems. For example, the freeway was the most sensitive infrastructure for hurricane due to rainfall, and it was essential for evacuation, search and rescue, and refuge. As shown in Table 3, a technical challenge remained in which some noisy words (e.g., "bitlyhsijn", "bublyusahrz") were scratched inevitably should be mentioned here. The reason for that is there are some technical issues (e.g., decode error) of parsing texts from the Twitter platform. The problem can be addressed when cleaning up the data, but it is possible to delete some critical and relevant information at the same time. Therefore, in this case study, some noisy words were left to keep the semantic integrity of the texts.

After the hurricane passed through Houston, flooding continued, not only because of the rainstorm but also due to water release from reservoirs that was recognized in context recognition. In addition, the public, agencies, and organizations were joining in the relief efforts. Thus, the topics in this phase were: (1) Bush intercontinental airport started operation for relief; (2) reducing mph when driving in Houston was important since some roads were still humid; (3) freeway and tollway were still closed in the Westside; (4) The residents in Pasadena should still be in response to heavy wind; (5) fund was raised for aid and shops were open. The severe flooding after hurricane appeared on the Westside of Houston. Thus, the freeway and tollway in the west of Houston were still closed for security. In topic 3, a damage on the highway, Sam, in west Houston was detected and the Sam tollway reopened when the 14 feet of water drained from it [22]. Meanwhile, other parts of Houston gradually restored from the disasters. A dominate event was that the airport resumed its operation. It helped stranded passengers leave Houston and transport resources from other states. Thus, a large

Table 3. Extracted topic in four disaster phases.

Phases	Topic 1	Topic 2	Topic 3	Topic 4	Topic 5
Before the Harvey landed	mph	mph	hurricane		
	Houston	pressure	Houston		
	Harvey	current	Texas		
	airport	weather	Harvey		
	wind	humidity	mph		
	hurricane	wind	ready		
	bush	Pearland	wind		
	intercontinental	sky	tropical		
	George	clear	Hurricane Harvey		
Hurricane period	Houston	humidity	fwy	Houston	main
	Harvey	pressure	closed	Harvey	affecting
	hurricane	weather	Sam	repost	high
	Texas	intensity	flooding	bitlyhsijn	downtown
	water	heavy	lane	help	eastside
	storm	Pasadena	traffic	Texas	bublyusahrz
	relief	rain	tollway	fwy	lane
	donate	wind	frontage	water	fwy
Flooding period	make	hurricane	temperature	weather	raise
	money	Houston	Sam	pressure	shop
	travel	humidity	traffic	cloud	aid
	airport	relief	flooding	wind	unique
	bush	wind	closed	Pasadena	sale
	lifestyle	mph	fwy	sky	help
	intercontinental	Harvey	tollway	current	Obama
	start	Texas	Westside	humidity	fund
After the flooding receded	car	need	energy	Harvey	buy
	need	food	need	benefit	coming
	Houston	warning	water	relief	hopefully
	water	power	service	concert	does
	recovery	info	health	Houston	flight
	fund	ppb	power	strong	airport
	relief	Houston	get	car	know

percentage of tweets were associated with this topic. However, some topics such as power outage were not among the topics based on the modeling on current dataset. This was because the power outage just appeared in some parts of Houston areas so that it was not the commonly concerned issues among the public. Except for the infrastructure-related topics, human behaviors about raising funds, opening shops, and relief were discussed as well.

When flooding receded, the damaged infrastructure systems were in need of recovery. Thereby, the topics in this phase were: (1) many cars in Houston were destroyed by flooding so the victims were seeking funds for recovery; (2) food and power were needed in some parts of Houston; (3) the public were concerned about the health impacts of contaminated flood water; (4) stakeholders were conducting relief during this period; (5) airport performed very well for transporting resources by flights. Because of severe flooding, 300,000 to 500,000 vehicles in Houston were destroyed by Harvey [23]. Thus, victims and companies were seeking funds for making up for a loss. After the disaster, resources including power, oil, and boiled water were the most urgent needs for all victims. Thus, topic 2 and 3 account for a large proportion of the collected tweets in Fig. 3 (e.g., green and yellow nodes). A serious issue detected in the results is the contaminated floodwaters with Nasty and dangerous bacteria that people with under-lying illness, the elderly and children were susceptible to [24]. Thus, this cluster of tweets was warning for the public to be careful of the floodwaters and for the agencies to develop strategies for reducing the health effects.

The summarized topics were used to analyze the infrastructure conditions in disasters from relevant tweets. Figure 3 mapped the tweets based on spring layout, a force-directed layout in graph theory. The lengths of the edges and the locations of nodes were based on Hooke's law which was used to attract pairs of endpoints of the edges towards each other [25]. It should be mentioned that the clusters in each figure were mapped randomly

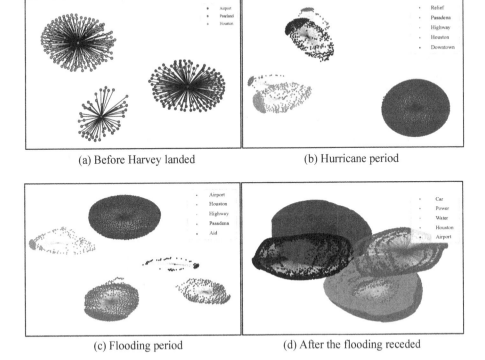

(a) Before Harvey landed   (b) Hurricane period

(c) Flooding period   (d) After the flooding receded

Fig. 3. Clusters of tweets in four disaster phases. (Color figure online)

and automatically by computers. Thus, as the limitation of the size of the figures, some clusters were partially overlapping. In addition, different colors represent different clusters. For example, in the first phase, three topics were represented by three colors: red, yellow, and blue. As Fig. 3 shows, the tweets were connected to their centroid topics. Although the number of major topics in last three phases was equal, the topics are quite different, and the trend of these topics will be discussed in the following section.

3.3   Topic Evolution and Resilience Analysis

Analyzing the evolution of topics over the development of disasters is essential for understanding the effects of disasters on infrastructure systems. For example, Harris County Tolls started up all toll roads on September 7th except Sam Houston Tollway because a section of Sam was still closed [22]. This situation can be an indicator of the performance of Sam Houston Tollway during flooding. Also, the performance of the tollway can be the evidence for decision makers to develop mitigation plans including repairing or replacing road drainage systems for improving the flood resistance. Because of the importance of infrastructure performance in disasters, we summarized the detected topics, and computed the percentage of relevant tweets in each topic among the dataset in certain disaster phase in Fig. 4. Figure 4 shows the trend of the major topics as well as the importance of the topic in each disaster phase. For example, the topic about airport appeared before the Harvey landed, in flooding period, and after the flooding receded. When the Harvey began to affect the airport, all flights were canceled for the purpose of security, and passengers were trapped in the airport, waiting for rescue. Thus, the public was worried about their journey and tweeted their situations for help. Hence, the tweets about airport topic account for 40% of the total number of tweets in first disaster phase. During Harvey, the airport was closed and only allowed a few flights for relief such as transporting rescue staffs and resources. Therefore, the topic about the situation of the airport did not become a core topic in this disaster phase. In flooding period, the airport restored and operated for transporting relief supplies and passengers, playing a critical role in disaster relief. Thereby, the tweets about airport conditions account for 58% of the dataset in this phase. After flooding receded, affected communities started recovery measures, such as cleaning up the ruins, restoring transportation systems, and repairing power grid. The topic about highway appeared and increased significantly during hurricane and flooding period since sections of important roads such as Interstate-10 were closed by water. But, after the hurricane, the percentage of tweets about highway dropped from 11% to 6% since flooding receded in most parts of Houston but still affected the Westside. For example, in flooding period, outbound interstate 45 North to and from Dallas was accessible, and US-290 was open, even though the State Highway 225 at Richey in and out of Pasadena remains covered in water and still closed [26]. Meanwhile, in the last disaster phase, three new topics about car and power were detected by the framework. It is because floodwaters destroyed more than 300,000 cars and power grid in some communities.

To support the results from topic modeling in this framework, the daily frequencies of infrastructure-related keywords were computed and displayed in Fig. 5. Before the Harvey landed, social communications were hardly related to infrastructure service and their damages. Thus, the frequencies of the keywords were lower than the frequencies of these keywords in other disaster phases. During Harvey, however, the keywords including "roadway", "lanes", "freeway (fwy)", and "blocked" were obviously increased and accounted for a large proportion. It should be mentioned that "power" and "outage" were not frequent in the collected datasets even though the power outage appeared in some areas during hurricane Harvey. After the Harvey passed, the size of tweets about infrastructure damages was decreased since the stakeholders were conducting recovery measures in full swing at that time. It was evidenced by the high frequency of "relief" in the phase of flooding period. Due to the limitation of the dataset which will be discussed in next section, the size of the dataset in this disaster phase was larger than the sizes of datasets in other phases. Thus, the word frequencies were higher than the corresponding frequencies in other phases. Nevertheless, comparing the word frequencies in this dataset, "car", "electric", "power", "road", "energy", "tollway", and "gas" reached high frequencies in this disaster phase. The results proved the conclusions made from topic modeling. Thus, the summarized topics in each disaster phase were precise enough for representing the situations of some infrastructure systems.

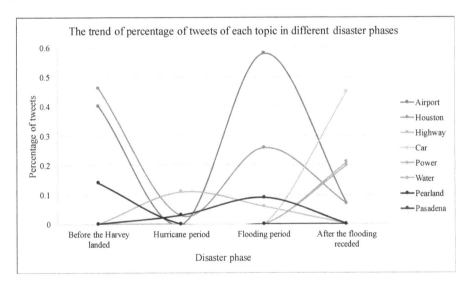

Fig. 4. The trend of percentage of tweets of each topic in different disaster phases

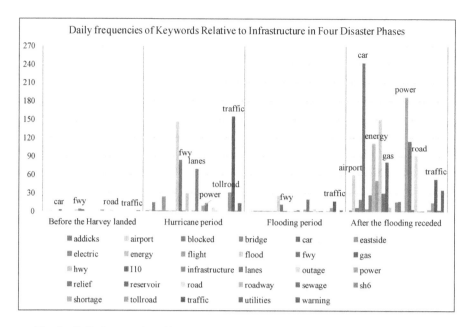

Fig. 5. Daily frequencies of keywords relative to infrastructure in four disaster phases

4   Limitations and Future Work

This paper answered the research question: to what extent can infrastructure-related events be detected and tracked in disasters on social media, through a system analytics framework and a case study of hurricane Harvey. However, limitations exist in our current work. First, the dataset of tweets used in this case study is incomplete. This dataset was not collected by Twitter Rest API or Streaming API during disasters, instead, it was collected by a web crawler through Twitter search platform. The limitation of using Twitter search platform was that part of relevant tweets in two weeks ago cannot be scrapped. Thus, the size of tweets in first three disaster phases was relatively smaller than the size of tweets in last disaster phase. In further studies, we will employ a complete dataset with 21 million tweets over Houston area in Harvey and flooding period.

The proposed framework can incorporate more text mining approaches (e.g., Named Entity Recognition, and event detection) [27, 28] for detecting detailed information in social communications. For example, among the blocked roads was Interstate 45 from Dallas to Houston [29]. This event did not appear in the major topics, but it is essential for the people who want to evacuate themselves or providing helps to victims through this road. Therefore, detecting detailed entities and related events are needed for situational awareness and relief operation. However, there is no well-trained model to conduct detection and summarization of infrastructure-specific entities and events. So, supervised learning algorithms can be employed to train a model which can identify the domain-specific entities and events automatically. The procedure for the supervised learning approach can be: (1) cleaning, vectoring, and clustering the data; (2) sampling the corpus into training set and test set, and labeling the data in training set with infra-structure-specific labels (may need crowdsourcing); (3) adopting an appropriate machine learning algorithm to train the model; (4) applying the model to the test set. The larger the training set is, the better the output will be. Furthermore, the well-trained model can be enveloped into a system which can provide evidence of damage and support for decision making automatically.

5   Conclusion

This paper presented and examined a system analytics framework involving social sensing and text mining for text-based representation of infrastructure resilience performance in disasters. The framework creatively developed an iteration for building a complete infrastructure-specific lexicon and a stop-words list to retrieve and clean relevant tweets. In addition, this framework integrated text classification (e.g., K-means clustering) and topic modeling (e.g., LDA) for summarizing the major topics in clusters of tweets. Therefore, the topics that the public and agencies were highly concerned were detected and analyzed for understanding the extent that the events were discussed on social media. The application of the proposed framework was shown in a preliminary study of infrastructure-related event detection and tracking in 2017 hurricane Harvey and derived flooding around Houston area. The case study investigated 63263 tweets in four disaster phases which were defined by the duration of disasters. The results showed that the computational algorithm exhibits capabilities of gathering complete and relevant datasets, classifying tweets into several clusters, modeling major topics in each cluster, and analyzing the changes of infrastructure-related topics along with the development of disasters. Thus, the results well addressed the gap of applying social sensing to assessing infrastructure service disruptions and highlighted the extent of the public and agencies discussing infrastructure on social media. Based on the output of the framework and the results of the analysis, the disaster responders and residents can develop their measures for enhancing the resilience of infrastructure systems, including improving the drainage capacity of the highways and early warning for airports. Their implemen-tation can eventually contribute to the improvement of infrastructure resilience perform-ance and property safety in times of disasters.

The framework proposed in case study can integrate the machine learning algorithms and disaster informatics on social media for data collection, cleaning, clustering and topic modeling relative to infrastructure systems. This system analytics framework can be further developed into several aspects: (1) apply it to other domain-specific research (e.g., sports event, finance & stock, and business marketing), and adjust some compo-nents to make it more adaptive to varieties of different domains; (2) incorporate other data processing and analyzing methods (e.g., dependency parsing, chunking, and word sense disambiguation) to explore new features of the collected data; (3) extend this framework to conduct some other analysis such as dynamic network analysis from systematic operation or civil engineering perspectives.

Acknowledgement. This material is based in part upon work supported by the National Science Foundation under Grant Number IIS-1759537. Any opinions, findings, and conclusions or recommendations expressed in this material are those of the authors and do not necessarily reflect the views of the National Science Foundation.

References

1. Tien, I., Musaev, A., Benas, D., Pu, C.: Detection of damage and failure events of critical public infrastructure using social sensor big data. In: Proceedings of International Conference on Internet of Things and Big Data, April 2016
2. Eusgeld, I., Nan, C., Dietz, S.: "System-of-systems" approach for interdependent critical infrastructures. Reliabil. Eng. Syst. Saf. **96**(6), 679–686 (2011)
3. Wikipedia Contributors: Hurricane Harvey. Wikipedia, The Free Encyclopedia. https://en.wikipedia.org/wiki/Hurricane_Harvey. Accessed 10 Dec 2017
4. Wang, D., Abdelzaher, T., Kaplan, L.: Social Sensing: Building Reliable Systems on Unreliable Data. Morgan Kaufmann, Burlington (2015)
5. Olteanu, A., Castillo, C., Diaz, F., Vieweg, S.: CrisisLex: a lexicon for collecting and filtering microblogged communications in crises. In: ICWSM, June 2014
6. Lu, X., Brelsford, C.: Network structure and community evolution on twitter: human behavior change in response to the 2011 Japanese earthquake and tsunami. Sci. Rep. **4**, 6773 (2014)
7. iRevolutions Contributors: What is Big (Crisis) Data? iResolutions. https://irevolutions.org/2013/06/27/what-is-big-crisis-data/. Accessed 10 Dec 2017
8. Imran, M., Castillo, C., Diaz, F., Vieweg, S.: Processing social media messages in mass emergency: a survey. ACM Comput. Surv. (CSUR) **47**(4), 67 (2015)
9. Imran, M., Elbassuoni, S., Castillo, C., Diaz, F., Meier, P.: Extracting information nuggets from disaster-related messages in social media. In: ISCRAM, May 2013
10. Acar, A., Muraki, Y.: Twitter for crisis communication: lessons learned from Japan's tsunami disaster. Int. J. Web Based Commun. **7**(3), 392–402 (2011)
11. Ashktorab, Z., Brown, C., Nandi, M., Culotta, A.: Tweedr: mining twitter to inform disaster response. In: ISCRAM, May 2014
12. Yin, J., Lampert, A., Cameron, M., Robinson, B., Power, R.: Using social media to enhance emergency situation awareness. IEEE Intell. Syst. **27**(6), 52–59 (2012)
13. Bala, M.M., Navya, K., Shruthilaya, P.: Text mining on real time Twitter data for disaster response. Int. J. Civ. Eng. Technol. **8**(8), 20–29 (2017)
14. Prasetyo, P.K., Gao, M., Lim, E.P., Scollon, C.N.: Social sensing for urban crisis management: the case of Singapore haze. In: SocInfo, pp. 478–491, November 2013
15. Bruns, A., Liang, Y.E.: Tools and methods for capturing Twitter data during natural disasters. First Monday **17**(4), 1–8 (2012)
16. Hardeniya, N.: NLTK Essentials. Packt Publishing Ltd., Birmingham (2015)
17. Sarkar, D.: Text Analytics with Python: A Practical Real-World Approach to Gaining Actionable Insights from Your Data. A Press, New York (2016)
18. BBC NEWS Contributor: In maps: Houston and Texas flooding. http://www.bbc.com/news/world-us-canada-41094872. Accessed 31 Dec
19. ENR Editors: How badly has hurricane Harvey damaged Texas infrastructure? In: Engineering News-Record, August 2017
20. Hernandez, A.R., Zezima, K., Achenbach, J.: Texas faces environmental concerns as wastewater, drinking water systems compromised. In: Washington Post, September 2017

21. Nix, K.: Hurricane Harvey brings record rains to Pearland, September 2017. http://www.chron.com/neighborhood/pearland/news/article/Hurricane-Harvey-brings-record-rains-to-Pearland-12169450.php. Accessed 14 Jan

22. KHOW Contributor: Sam Houston Tollway fully reopens after Harvey flooding, damage. http://www.khou.com/news/hctra-sam-houston-tollway-southbound-to-reopen-sunday-night/473114404. Accessed 19 Jan

23. Fortune Contributor: Hurricane Irma and Harvey damaged 1 million cars. What happens now? http://fortune.com/2017/09/20/hurricane-irma-harvey-damaged-cars/. Accessed 14 Jan

24. Scutti, S., CNN Contributor: Sewage, fecal bacteria in hurricane Harvey floodwaters, September 2017. http://www.cnn.com/2017/09/01/health/houston-flood-water-contamination/index.html. Accessed 19 Jan

25. Kobourov, S.G.: Spring embedders and force-directed graph drawing algorithms (2012). Freely accessible: arXiv:1201.3011

26. Whaley, K., Eyewitness NEWS Contributor: Check out Houston freeway conditions post-Harvey. http://abc13.com/traffic/check-out-houston-freeway-conditions-post-harvey/2358197/. Accessed 19 Jan

27. Gao, X., Yu, W., Rong, Y., Zhang, S.: Ontology-based social media analysis for urban planning. In: 2017 IEEE 41st Annual Computer Software and Applications Conference (COMPSAC), vol. 1, pp. 888–896. IEEE, July 2017

28. Kryvasheyeu, Y., Chen, H., Obradovich, N., Moro, E., Van Hentenryck, P., Fowler, J., Cebrian, M.: Rapid assessment of disaster damage using social media activity. Sci. Adv. **2**(3), e1500779 (2016)

29. QUARTZ Contributor: One map shows just why the Texas flooding is so disastrous: it's preventing people from escaping, August 2017. https://qz.com/1066033/hurricane-harvey-highways-closed-by-record-rainfall-are-trapping-texans-in-flooded-communities/. Accessed 31 Dec

Community Engagement Using Urban Sensing: Technology Development and Deployment Studies

Katherine A. Flanigan and Jerome P. Lynch[✉]

Department of Civil and Environmental Engineering, University of Michigan,
Ann Arbor, MI 48109, USA
kaflanig@umich.edu, jerlynch@umich.com

Abstract. There is considerable interest globally in "smart cities" due to the emergence of game changing technologies including IoT platforms, cloud computing, and powerful automation architectures. A host of smart city applications exist including connected and autonomous vehicles, controlled urban watersheds, pedestrian and vehicle tracking, among others. However, a general-purpose urban sensing architecture has not yet emerged that empowers all stakeholders in a city to partake in data collection and data-driven decision making. This paper describes the development of the *Urbano* sensing architecture designed for dense deployments in cities for a wide variety of smart city applications. The design of the architecture is based on the belief that urban sensing can play a major role in empowering communities to collect data on urban processes and transform how communities engage with city stakeholders to make decisions. *Urbano* does not require persistent power sources nor wired communication mediums, and is an ultra-low power wireless sensor node that is capable of collecting sensor measurements, supporting embedded computing, and communicating using cellular wireless communication.

The *Urbano* sensor node has been deployed in several smart city engagements in Michigan. The first uses GPS-enabled *Urbano* nodes to track food trucks in Grand Rapids as part of a larger effort in curbside management. The second monitors pedestrian traffic and air quality along the Detroit waterfront to better understand public utilization of spaces to guide future investments. The third packages *Urbano* nodes in a kit called "Sensors in a Shoebox" for youth and community deployment in southwest Detroit to measure air quality.

Keywords: Urban sensing · Embedded data processing · Wireless sensing
Curbside management · GPS · Mobility · Air quality

1 Introduction

1.1 Smart Cities and Current Limitations

There has been considerable interest globally in "smart cities" due to the emergence of game changing technologies including Internet of Things (IoT) platforms, cloud computing, and powerful automation architectures. The application of heterogeneous IoT technologies and network services to sensing in urban environments enables the

© Springer International Publishing AG, part of Springer Nature 2018
I. F. C. Smith and B. Domer (Eds.): EG-ICE 2018, LNCS 10864, pp. 92–110, 2018.
https://doi.org/10.1007/978-3-319-91638-5_5

development of smart cities, which are those cities in which the use of IoT sensor networks, massive sets of urban data, and ubiquitous access to cloud computing enhance the performance of urban systems and experiences of citizens. Already, a host of smart city applications have been advanced and deployed including connected and autonomous vehicles, controlled urban watersheds, environmental sensing, pedestrian and vehicle tracking using cameras, among many others [1, 10, 14]. In addition to the realization of these applications in cities, various conceptual criteria have also been proposed regarding the integration of IoT technologies into smart cities [6, 7, 11, 19].

However, a general-purpose urban sensing architecture has not yet emerged that is diverse enough to enable the management of diverse arrays of heterogeneous IoT technologies and empower all stakeholders in a city to partake in data collection and data-driven decision making [10]. This may be in large part due to the commercial sector and their marketing approach tailored to government stakeholders. Consequently, the proliferation of sensors and government-centric data aggregation in urban cities has disproportionately focused on improving city cores, with less attention paid to residential neighborhoods and areas. This is worsened by technological obstacles associated with current IoT platforms, such as the high power demand of existing hardware which requires access to power sources (e.g. light poles, electrical trash receptacles, and other powered street furniture), thus limiting the potential of mobile sensors and deployments in cities like Detroit where community access to power sources is severely limited in residential areas. This lack of connection between citizens and smart city initiatives is particularly pronounced in depopulated American cities (e.g., Detroit, Flint, St. Louis, Baltimore) where there has been no notable success in using smart city technologies to connect populations to their larger communities.

While most urban cities in the United States have undergone sustained periods of economic growth since the 1940s, a small number of cities have seen dramatic drops in population and economic activity [15]. For example, Detroit experienced population reductions from 1.8 million people in 1950 to less than 700,000 in 2015 [2]. However, major revitalization efforts in Detroit's business core are starting to rapidly transform the city. However, the residential areas and neighborhoods of Detroit remain underpopulated, with scarce access to important city services. Shrinking cities have resulted in extreme levels of poverty and inequality that result in stressors that disproportionately impact urban youth, who are at risk of losing connectivity to their cities and communities [8]. As a result, there is a need to expand the use of sensing, especially by the general public, through the development of a more democratized approach to urban data collection and post-collection data uses to fully and more broadly reap the promise of smart cities. This, in part, entails engaging urban youth and citizens with their communities by architecturally embedding them within a smart city's urban cyber-physical-*social* system (CPSS). As seen in Fig. 1, this expanded cyber-physical system (CPS) architecture directly integrates humans into the CPS framework by taking into account a citizen's ability to observe and take action in response to physical and CPS elements [18]. By empowering communities to collect their own data in their neighborhoods and cities, city governments, local organizations *and* citizens can work in a more meaningful partnership with each other, leading to more resilient modes of smart city governance.

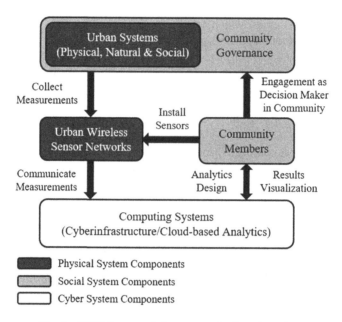

Fig. 1. CPSS framework for community-based sensing.

In addition to the lack of current urban sensing strategies that can empower *all* stakeholders in a city to partake in data collection and data-driven decision making, there are several technological obstacles that impede the emergence of a successful general-purpose urban sensing architecture for widespread use. These include the development of a sensing platform that supports interoperability among diverse arrays of heterogeneous IoT devices, preserves privacy and trust among citizens, supports cloud-based analytics, and supports low-power and low-cost sensing and communication, which is particularly difficult to achieve with platforms that require a continuous source of energy [10]. For example, the Array of Things (AoT) deployment in Chicago provides environmental and air quality sensors tied to a Linux-based sensing node [1]. The high power demand of the hardware requires access to power sources supplied by street furniture (e.g. light poles) which limits its deployment potential in less populated areas and residential neighborhoods where power sources are severely limited. In addition, Placemeter is a novel camera-based sensing solution designed to track vehicles and pedestrians in city spaces [14]. While Placemeter promises to anonymize data by processing video footage using automated data processing tools, many communities might be resistant to camera-based monitoring due to infringements on privacy and overarching notions of "Big Brother" within the community.

1.2 Introduction to the *Urbano* IoT Platform

In response to these needs, this paper describes the development of the *Urbano* sensing node which is designed for dense and rapid deployment in cities for a wide variety of smart city applications. In particular, the design of the architecture is based on the belief that urban sensing can play a major role in empowering communities to collect data on urban processes of interest, and can transform how communities engage with other city stakeholders to make decisions. Hence, the design of *Urbano* emphasizes ease of use and minimizes dependence on required infrastructure for which a stakeholder may have limited or no access. *Urbano* is designed as an ultra-low power, low-cost, wireless sensor node that is capable of collecting diverse and heterogeneous sensor measurements, supporting embedded computing, and communicating using cellular or wireless communication. A major differentiator of *Urbano* from other smart city IoT platforms is that it does not require a persistent power source (e.g., grid power available from street furniture) nor a wired communication medium (e.g., fiber network). Rather, it is designed to operate using solar energy and leverages a cellular radio to push data to the cloud. The case studies presented in this paper avoid the use of cameras in order to respect the anonymity of citizens. For example, passive infrared (PIR) sensors are used for pedestrian counting instead of using cameras or Bluetooth, and GPS modules are only integrated into *Urbano* nodes with the consent of the relevant parties (e.g. food truck vendors).

Due to *Urbano's* low-power design, low cost, and independence from continuous power sources, nodes can be densely and rapidly deployed as stationary or mobile sensing units anywhere in a city. *Urbano* has analog and digital sensing interfaces, and a wide variety of sensing transducers have already been integrated with *Urbano* and deployed in urban cities. These include digital sensors such as air quality sensors (NO_2, SO_2, O_3, and particulate matter (PM)) and GPS receivers, in addition to analog sensors such as geophones for vibration measurements, strain gages, accelerometers, PIR sensors for pedestrian tracking, and temperature sensors. Sensors are connected to *Urbano's* analog and digital sensing interfaces (Figs. 3 and 4) and are either housed inside of the node enclosure or connected to the *Urbano* externally through a water tight connection through the enclosure.

To emphasize its ability to support community uses, *Urbano* has been assembled in a user-friendly packaging with all components integrated, and consists of a variety of libraries of data processing blocks that support the different sensing applications (including those that require onboard data analytics); community members can simply deploy, turn on the device, and see the data stream to a data portal of their choice. *Urbano* nodes are designed to push their data to a database server hosted in a commercial cloud environment. A variety of data portals are exposed. The cellular modem integrated with *Urbano* can be used to issue data and alerts in the form of SMS messages and Twitter posts to allow nodes to essentially tweet alerts and updates to users subscribed to their feed. This specific approach to data dissemination is well suited to presenting urban data and information using a user-friendly interface. The second approach adopts a more robust cloud-based data management platform well suited for storage and management of time history series. Here, Exosite's One Platform [5] is adopted as a time series database that is ideally suited to collect and manage *Urbano* data streams. Graphical representations of the data are provided using Exosite's internal standard and customizable visualization portals. This paper details the hardware design, software architecture, and data processing approaches implemented in an analytics layer that queries data from the database.

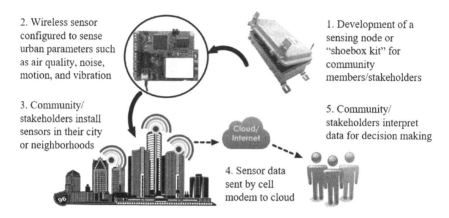

2. Wireless sensor configured to sense urban parameters such as air quality, noise, motion, and vibration

1. Development of a sensing node or "shoebox kit" for community members/stakeholders

3. Community/ stakeholders install sensors in their city or neighborhoods

5. Community/ stakeholders interpret data for decision making

4. Sensor data sent by cell modem to cloud

Fig. 2. Overview of the implementation of the *Urbano* platform.

The *Urbano* sensor node has been deployed in a number of smart city engagements in Michigan. These applications incorporate a wide variety of stakeholders including city governments, local organizations, urban youth, and communities. As outlined in Fig. 2, each of the three applications described in this paper is carried out using the single *Urbano* cloud-based sensing IoT platform. The first test case highlights the use of GPS-enabled *Urbano* nodes to track food trucks in Grand Rapids, MI to assess compliance with permit rules and curbside management by city planning officials. The second application deploys *Urbano* nodes to monitor pedestrian traffic and air quality along the Detroit waterfront; this data is desired by the Detroit Riverfront Conservancy (DRC) to under-stand utilization of public spaces to guide future investments. Finally, the third test case packages *Urbano* nodes in a kit called "Sensors in a Shoebox" for community deployment in southwest Detroit to measure air quality. Residents in southwest Detroit reside in one of the most polluted regions of the state due to the presence of heavy industries including oil refining, steel mills, and coal fired power plants. As a result of poor air quality there have been high rates of youth asthma and long-term cardiovascular disease in the community [4].

2   Hardware Architecture

The hardware of the *Urbano* wireless sensing node is separated into three primary subsystems: analog and digital sensing interfaces, computational core, and wireless communication. The flexible sensing interface is compatible with a diverse array of heterogeneous analog and digital sensing transducers, the computational core is programmed to operate the hardware and carry out on-chip data processing, and the wireless communication system incorporates a cellular modem to push and pull data from the cloud. In addition to an overview of wireless sensing, the following sub-sections provide a detailed overview of the hardware design, cellular communication design, and packaging of the *Urbano* wireless sensing node to demonstrate how the hardware satisfies the needs identified in Sect. 1. The general architecture of the hardware design is shown in Fig. 3.

2.1 Introduction to Wireless Sensing

Wireless sensing has emerged as a major platform for collecting and transmitting data, both within and outside of cities, over the past several decades. This is especially prominent within the context of structural health monitoring (SHM), where wireless sensing systems are installed on infrastructure around the world in order to detect damage and use data to help guide decisions to repair, rehabilitate, or replace a structure [16]. Wireless sensing technologies for monitoring infrastructure originally emerged as an alternative to existing wired systems, which require high upfront costs due to material procurement, and labor intensive installation, not to mention extensive installation times [17]. Using commercial off-the-shelf electrical components, researchers have successfully developed and deployed wireless systems for use in monitoring infrastructure [9]. However, there remain several limitations to current wireless sensing platforms. Specifically, limited ranges of wireless transceivers and the dependence of wireless sensing nodes on connections to wireless communication infrastructure, such as local base stations (that house single-board computers), hinder low-cost dense and rapid deployments over large areas, and the ability to have mobile sensors.

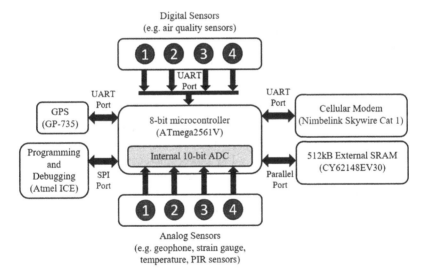

Fig. 3. Hardware design for sensing interface, computational core, and wireless communication.

The limitations associated with current wireless sensing platforms used for monitoring single asset infrastructure are particularly important to recognize as more attention turns toward monitoring multi-asset infrastructure, physical systems, and environmental parameters within urban environments where connectivity and automation are inherent features. Due to the need for a wireless sensing platform for which stakeholders with sensing needs in a city can deploy dense networks (possibly up to hundreds of sensors) of stationary *and* mobile sensors rapidly for data collection, wireless sensing nodes must be completely autonomous, with no dependence on additional communication infrastructure (such as base stations).

While smart city IoT applications continue to emerge that are reliant on short range technologies such as Bluetooth, Zigbee, and Wi-Fi [10], it quickly becomes less feasible for citizens to engage in and initiate smart city applications in neglected areas of cities, such as in neighborhoods outside of city centers, where the power and access to additional communication infrastructure necessary to enable these means of communication, are scarce. On the other hand, with typical coverage of 5–30 km [10], long range technologies such as cellular modems are a much more feasible and autonomous method of communication that gives city governments, local organizations, and citizens the flexibility to sense a diverse array of parameters throughout a city. A drawback to using cellular communication for data transmission is that cellular modems have high energy consumption during active communication. However, as outlined in the following subsections, the hardware and software architectures of the *Urbano* IoT cloud-based flexible sensing platform are designed to minimize power consumption such that each node is able to use solar energy harvesting with a small solar panel to realize full autonomy from access to power and communication infrastructure aside from a cellular network (applications in this paper use various solar panels between 3.4–10 W).

2.2 Hardware Design

Computational Core. The computational core is programmed to carry out three main functions: the operation of the hardware, data interrogation and on-chip processing, and network communication. At the center of the computational core of the *Urbano* node is an Atmel AVR ATmega 2561 V 8-bit microcontroller with 8 MHz system clock, which operates at a 3.3 V supply voltage. An 8-bit microcontroller was selected to avoid the significantly higher power consumption and costs associated with 16- and 32-bit microcontrollers. In addition, an 8-bit internal data bus is sufficient for the required on-chip processing. The ATmega 2561 V is a low power microcontroller that has a current consumption of 7.3 mA in active mode. Strategic software manipulation of the microcontroller's sleep modes allows for reduced power consumption when the node is not actively collecting data, as the microcontroller consumes 4.5 μA in power-save mode, and 0.18 μA in power down mode. As a result, the microcontroller is able to perform data processing computations and operate the sensing and communication subsystems using very little power.

The ATmega 2561 V has more than sufficient read-only memory, with 256 kB of flash and 4 kB of EEPROM, which reduces constraints on data interrogation and on-chip processing. The microcontroller has 8 kB of internal SRAM. Since 8 kB of internal SRAM is not sufficient when large amounts of data need to be stored, the microcontroller is configured to include an extended 512 kB of external SRAM to augment the internal memory using the Cypress CY62148EV30. Since *Urbano* nodes do not require a continuous power source and the cellular modem consumes the most power in the system, additional SRAM is valuable so that it is possible to execute embedded data-processing algorithms on large amounts of data and only transmit necessary, pre-processed information. Using the solar harvesting configuration, the *Urbano* node is capable of the periodic transmission of both raw continuous time-series data and pre-processed data. In the case where the node has access to a power source (i.e. solar harvesting is not necessary), there is no limit on the frequency of data transmission.

Analog and Digital Sensing Interface. Controlled by pre-programmed data collection schemes in the microcontroller, the sensing interface includes four analog and four digital sensing channels. The sensing channels support heterogeneous sensing transducers so that each node can sense a diverse array of parameters, such as environmental *and* physical parameters. An internal 10-bit 200 kHz analog-to-digital converter (ADC) in the microcontroller is used for digitizing analog signals to enable embedded processing and transmission of data to the cloud using the cellular modem. For sensing infrastructure systems such as bridges and buildings (i.e. structural health monitoring), a higher resolution 16-bit ADC would be more appropriate. However, for sensing urban parameters such as mobility (e.g. vehicle and pedestrian movement), and various environmental parameters, 10-bits is sufficient. While an external 16-bit ADC can be easily integrated into the *Urbano* node, it is desirable to avoid the additional power consumption and cost that accompany higher resolution external ADCs.

Cellular Wireless Communication. Wireless communication is achieved using the Nimbelink Skywire 4G/LTE Cat 1 Cellular Embedded Modem. A standard XBee hardware interface is used to connect the cellular modem to the printed circuit board (PCB) (Fig. 4). The cellular modem connects to Verizon or AT&T's 4G LTE network and is the lowest power fully developed LTE technology available in the market [12]. The Nimbelink Cat 1 modem consumes 616 mA of current during active cellular communication and 48 mA when idle, but the utilization of sleep modes can reduce current consumption to 8.6 mA in low power mode and 44 µA when it is off. To minimize the amount of power consumed by the cellular modem, the computational core is programmed with robust timing and interrupt schemes to ensure the cellular modem remains off whenever active read and write transmissions are not necessary. In addition, the modem is Federal Communications Commission (FCC) and end-device pre-certified, meaning that it does not require carrier certification, which significantly reduces the cost and eliminates the time associated with the certification process (which can take up to months in the United States). In addition, the cell modem supports multiple LTE bands (B4(1700) and B13(750)) with fallback capabilities, and has a small U.FL port for antenna flexibility. The Nimbelink Cat 1 is based on the Gemalto ELS31 chipset and achieves excellent speeds of 10 Mbps download and 5 Mbps upload. The Gemalto ELS31 is designed for power optimization and speed which make it an excellent candidate for machine-to-machine and IoT applications. In addition, the Nimbelink Cat 1 has a commercially available development kit that allows users to connect the cell modem to a PC via a USB-to-UART converter, and send AT commands to the modem through any serial terminal application. This direct and simple method of communication enables rapid development and debugging.

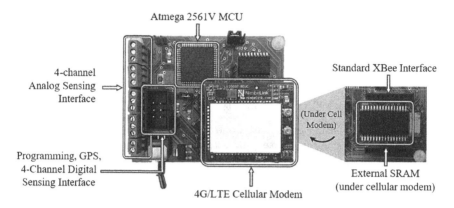

Fig. 4. *Urbano* node with key components highlighted.

2.3 Packaging

To emphasize its ability to support community uses, *Urbano* has been assembled in a user-friendly packaging (smaller than the size of a shoebox). All components are integrated into a single enclosure, and the *Urbano* node is programmed with a variety of libraries of data processing blocks that support the different sensing applications. Without making significant changes to the physical structure of the node, community members can simply deploy, turn on the device, and see the data stream to a data portal of their choice (visualization portals discussed in Sect. 3). For the three applications discussed in Sect. 4, two different methods of packaging are used. For deployments by the City of Grand Rapids planning officials and the Detroit Riverfront Conservancy, these two stakeholders desired a compact assembly. As seen in Fig. 5(a), the *Urbano* node, sensing components, rechargeable lithium ion battery, solar controller, and a small 3.4 W solar panel were assembled in a small 20.32 cm × 10.16 cm × 7.62 cm weatherproof box. Figure 5(b) shows the *Urbano* node installed on the roof of a food truck in Grand Rapids, MI, complete with solar panel. On the other hand, an alternative packaging scheme (Fig. 5(c)) is used for the "Sensors in a Shoebox" kit (Sect. 4.3), which allows for more room and clearly labeled and identifiable components. For educational purposes, a clear lid is included with the kit so that students and community members can observe the contents of the box even when it is deployed and collecting data.

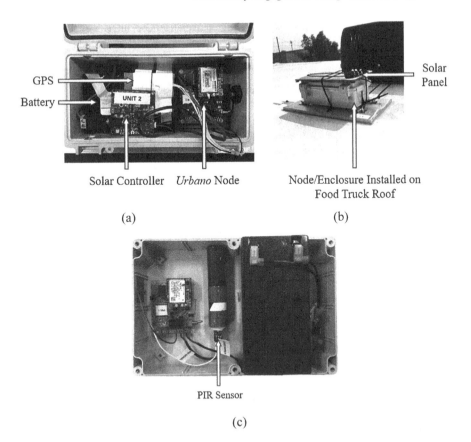

Solar Controller   *Urbano* Node   Node/Enclosure Installed on
                                              Food Truck Roof

(a)   (b)

PIR Sensor

(c)

Fig. 5. (a) *Urbano* node assembled for studying food truck curbside management, (b) *Urbano* node installed on the roof of a food truck with solar panel mounted to top of packaging, and (c) "Sensors in a Shoebox" kit for pedestrian sensing.

3   Software Architecture

The success of a diverse sensing solution for smart city applications relies on the implementation of a scalable cloud-based database system for the storage, processing, and analysis of sensor data transmitted from the *Urbano* nodes. In response to this need, *Urbano* nodes are designed to push collected data to a database server hosted in a commercial cloud environment. An additional requirement is that data be accessible and able to be interpreted by all stakeholders, including city governments, local organizations, and citizens, regardless of their education level or familiarity with IoT technologies and cloud computing. As a result, a variety of data portals are exposed. For example, pre-programmed code on *Urbano's* microcontroller (computational core) enables the Nimbelink Cat 1 cellular modem to send data and issue alerts in the form of SMS messages and Twitter posts to allow the nodes to tweet their notifications to users subscribed to their feed. This specific approach to data dissemination is well suited for presenting urban data and information using a user-friendly interface. The second approach adopts a more robust data management web server platform that is well suited for storage, cloud-based analytics, and management of time history data.

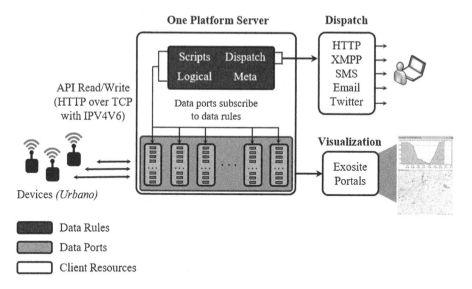

Fig. 6. One platform architecture.

Urbano's software architecture utilizes Exosite's commercially available One Platform as a time series database that is ideally suited to store and manage data collected and transmitted by each *Urbano* node. Exosite was selected due to its manageable system development, user friendly visualization tools, and primary focus as an IoT software platform. As seen in Fig. 6, each user maintains a client, which consists of several resources such as data ports, data rules, meta, dispatch functions, and visualization portals. Each client is identified by an assigned Client Identifier Key (CIK) that is used for accessing application programming interface (API) calls to the One Platform and mapping to a client's resource identifier (RID). Data that is written from a device (*Urbano* node) is tagged with an alias that is used to map the data to a corresponding data port in the One Platform database. The data is then stored in the appropriate data port's data-store. Each data port can subscribe to user-defined algorithms, known as data rules, which are scripts and logical statements that are written in the Lua language to process data. Data rules are also used to call dispatches, which are outputs from the One Platform in forms such as HTTP, XMPP, SMS, email, and Twitter. This means that data can even be seamlessly integrated to another robust server or cloud service, such as Amazon Web Services, or to a user-friendly interface such as Twitter.

The software that is embedded onto *Urbano's* microcontroller (C language) is programmed to issue and receive AT commands through the Nimbelink Cat 1 cell modem to connect and interact with the server. For data transmission, the *Urbano* network utilizes unconstrained protocol stacks where requests and responses between the devices and web server are managed by HTTP application layer protocols. Under the HTTP protocol, TCP is used as a transport layer protocol to handle the HTTP traffic. For the network layer protocol, the Nimbelink Cat 1 is an IP capable device and the microcontroller is programmed to utilize an IPV4V6 dual stack PDP context that simultaneously supports both IPv6 and IPv4 using the cellular modem.

Graphical representations of the data are provided using Exosite's internal standard and customizable visualization portals so that data can be easily interpreted by all stakeholders. The applications described in this paper (Sect. 4) leverage several of these portals. For example, Exosite's GIS tools are leveraged to track the movement of food trucks throughout the city of Grand Rapids, numerous data time series associated with environmental parameters are plotted, and Twitter dispatches are enabled to tweet data to subscribers. In addition, portals are leveraged to show the current air quality associated with several pollutants (e.g. NO_2, SO_2, O_3, and PM), which are automatically colored green, yellow, or red, to indicate the value's relationship to pre-defined "Safe Level," "Warning Level," and "Alert Level" thresholds as defined by the Environmental Protection Agency (EPA).

4   Applications

The *Urbano* sensing node has been deployed in a number of smart city engagements in Michigan. The three applications described in the following subsections incorporate a wide variety of stakeholders including city governments, local organizations, urban youth, and communities. These diverse applications demonstrate the flexibility of the *Urbano* platform, as a wide variety of analog and digital sensors are interfaced on both mobile and stationary sensing nodes using only the single *Urbano* platform.

4.1   Food Trucks as Mobile Sensors

Using the *Urbano* platform, an array of GPS-enabled mobile *Urbano* nodes were deployed on food trucks (Fig. 5(b)) in the city of Grand Rapids in order to observe the behavior and locations of these mobile assets for two months. This first test case was desired by the city's planning and transportation officials in order to assess compliance with permit rules and to explore novel curbside management models. Monitoring the food trucks was mutually beneficial for both the city's officials *and* the food truck vendors. Food truck vendors readily volunteered for this pilot program, as it allows them to provide information in real-time to their customer base regarding their current location.

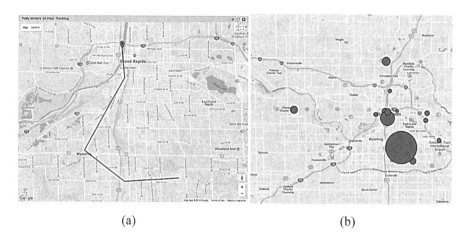

Fig. 7. Patty matters food truck (a) 24 h tracking period, and (b) duration spent parked at curbside locations for one month.

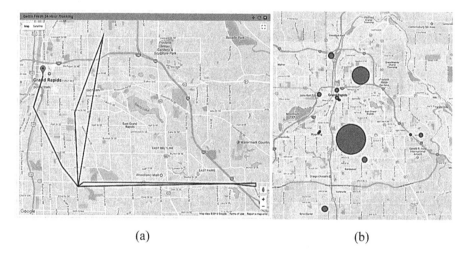

Fig. 8. Gettin' fresh food truck (a) 24 h tracking period, and (b) duration spent parked at curbside locations.

In addition to storing GPS output data in the One Platform's database, an Exosite trail map portal is used to visualize each truck's movement within the past 24 h (Figs. 7(a) and 8(a)). In addition, Matlab is leveraged to help visualize the duration of time each truck spends parked at various curbside locations. The time that a food truck spends stationary at a known curbside location is proportional to the area of each circle associated with that location (Figs. 7(b) and 8(b)). In addition to leveraging the One Platform's server, database, and user-friendly visualization tools, the *Urbano* platform is flexible enough to be directly integrated into the City of Grand Rapid's existing GIS platform. In upcoming engagements with the City, dispatch scripts will be configured to output data from the relevant data ports (corresponding to various food trucks) to an existing ArcGIS server that is currently used by the City. Collected data showed that the food trucks spend a considerable amount of time at a wide range of locations, including colleges, community parks, downtown business areas, and residential neighborhoods. As a result, a diverse array of air quality sensors, including NO_2, SO_2, O_3, and PM, will be added to each mobile *Urbano* node to monitor air pollution throughout the city. This allows for air quality to be monitored in areas outside of the city core that are often neglected because power and access to additional communication infrastructure necessary to enable existing smart city technologies, are scarce.

4.2   Pedestrian Counting and Air Quality Sensing Along the Detroit Riverfront

Depopulation of the residential sectors of Detroit has left many public spaces and parks neglected. Of the city's 307 parks, the city is quietly closing some of them [13]. As the city decides on its plan for public spaces, various stakeholders are interested in observing and assessing the use of their public and park spaces. For the second application, *Urbano* nodes are deployed along the Detroit Riverfront to monitor pedestrian traffic and air quality (NO_2, SO_2, O_3, and PM) in this popular park area along the Detroit River. This data is desired by the Detroit Riverfront Conservancy to monitor important environmental parameters that impact people using the space, and to understand utilization of public spaces to guide future investments.

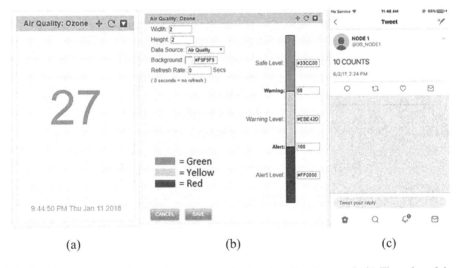

(a)   (b)   (c)

Fig. 9. (a) Live stream of current O_3 readings displayed on Exosite portal. (b) The color of the reading corresponds to pre-defined safety level thresholds as defined by the EPA. (c) Example of pedestrian counting readings being rerouted and displayed in real time as Twitter posts.

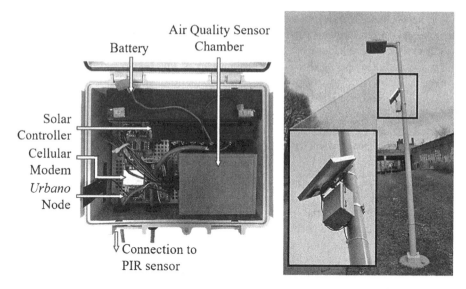

Fig. 10. Air quality and pedestrian counting (a) node configuration and assembly and (b) node installed on the Detroit Dequindre Cut for DRC deployment.

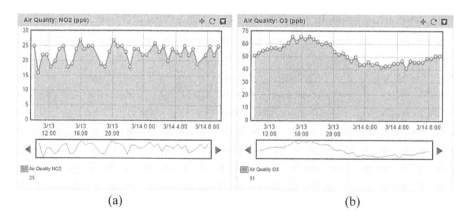

Fig. 11. (a) NO_2 and (b) O_3 data collected from nodes for the DRC air quality and pedestrian counting deployment.

The Detroit Riverfront Conservancy already uses commercially available pedestrian counting technology to monitor the use of public spaces in several parks throughout Detroit [3]. However, the costs associated with the existing commercial technology, in particular, the cost to continuously replace the device-specific battery, are too high. As a result, low-cost, self-sustaining solar powered *Urbano* nodes have been installed along the Detroit Riverfront and Dequindre Cut to measure pedestrian traffic and air quality. Low power PIR sensors are installed at the base of lamp posts along the park (Fig. 10(b)), and point out towards the river across the park's busy pedestrian pathway along the riverfront. Each PIR sensor is connected to an *Urbano* node that is attached higher up on the light post to prevent theft. The air quality sensors are housed inside of a 3D printed chamber (Fig. 10(a)) within the node that exposes the air quality sensors to the outside environment while keeping the node's internal circuitry weatherproof. Since many citizens and communities are resistant to the use of camera-based sensors due to infringements on privacy, PIR sensors were selected to ensure completely anonymized data. In addition to storing this information as time series data in the database, an additional Exosite portal is leveraged for real-time visualization that is easy for community members to interpret (Fig. 11). As depicted in Fig. 9(a), a live stream of current air quality pollutants (O_3 for this example) is displayed. The color of the reading corresponds to pre-defined safety level threshold as defined by the EPA (as set by end-users in Fig. 9(b)). For pedestrian counting, the One Platform's Twitter output dispatch is used to tweet live pedestrian count updates for the nodes distributed along the Riverfront (Fig. 9(c) shows an example of a tweet of pedestrian counts at the Detroit Riverfront).

While assessing the use of public park spaces is of particular importance to the DRC, the same platform can easily be implemented in other parts of the city to help quantify community mobility more generally. As Detroit communities begin to fortify and rebound, communities would benefit from understanding the mobility of their neighbors. In particular, quantitative data on the utilization of roads and pedestrian pathways could inform them in the quest to secure transportation infrastructure investments.

4.3 "Sensors in a Shoebox"

The third test case packages *Urbano* nodes in a "Sensors in a Shoebox" kit to offer youth and citizens the opportunity to deploy sensors in their communities to observe and analyze urban processes occurring in their communities. In order to move towards the realization of Detroit as a smart city, there is a need to support citizens and, importantly, urban youth, in developing the basic skills necessary to engage with the Shoebox kit so that they can be connected to their communities in a meaningful way. In addition to providing Detroit youth with the sensing kit, they were engaged in after school programming, where they learned how sensors collect and transmit data. As a preliminary application, the youths deployed an *Urbano* sensing node on the roof of Detroit's Voyageur Academy in order to track environmental conditions, such as temperature. The deployment lasted for one week and demonstrated the data acquisition capabilities of the *Urbano* sensing kit to students, and allowed students to learn how to process time series data (Fig. 12).

After the initial deployment the students then outlined their own research problems that could be studied by deploying sensing technologies within their communities. The youths identified several problems, including water quality, space usage, air quality, and noise levels within the city. Since many of the students participating in the program are afflicted by asthma, they elected to monitor air quality. Residents in southwest Detroit reside in one of the most polluted regions of Michigan due to the presence of heavy industries including steel mills, oil refining, and coal fired power plant. As a result of poor air quality there have been high rates of cardiovascular disease and youth asthma [4]. For the second deployment, students attached air quality sensors to the *Urbano* node (measuring NO_2, SO_2, O_3, and PM), initiated data collection at Voyageur Academy, rode a school bus out to the Delray Recreation Center and Park, and continued to collect data for one hour. This allowed students to compare air quality measurements at different locations throughout Detroit. Students selected to visit the Delray Recreation Center and Park because it is surrounded by the eight most polluted zip codes in the Detroit area so that air quality measurements. The park is surrounded by Zug "Industrial" Island, an oil refinery, wastewater treatment facility, steel mills, a coal burning power plant and busy freeways. Data was streamed to Twitter so that students could practice inputting and analyzing data in Excel.

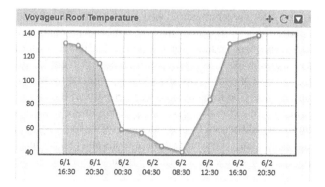

Fig. 12. Exosite portal showing time series data of temperature (deg. F) of the Voyageur Academy roof over 24 h of data collection during the one week of data collection.

Through this work in engaging citizens in smart city applications, youth are positioned to better understand their communities and how their cities work, thereby empowering them as connected citizens in their communities. However, the concept of packaging the *Urbano* sensing node as a "Sensors in a Shoebox" kit is not just beneficial for urban youth. This platform offers a scalable and sustainable solution for enabling communities to help strengthen their city neighborhoods. In addition to helping connect citizens to their communities, this platform provides a scientific and technological foundation for the extension of CPS to include humans. These CPSS human-in-the-loop systems have the potential to transform a variety of application areas including transportation, building energy management, among others.

5   Conclusions

The *Urbano* IoT cloud-based sensing node proposed in this paper serves as a flexible sensing platform that can be densely and rapidly deployed throughout cities. The hardware and software architecture of *Urbano* nodes are designed to ensure ultra-low power consumption so that they can rely solely on solar energy harvesting to be self-sustaining. Since *Urbano* nodes are not reliant on continuous power sources (e.g. light poles or powered street furniture) and operate autonomously aside from connection to a cellular network, they can be deployed as stationary or mobile sensing units not only in city centers, but also in residential neighborhoods and areas where access to power and communication infrastructure can be scarce. This design architecture is based on the belief that urban sensing can play a major role in empowering communities to collect data on urban processes of interest, and can transform how communities engage with other city stakeholders to make decisions. To demonstrate the utility of the *Urbano* platform to a wide range of city stakeholders, three preliminary deployment studies were successfully carried out that engaged city governments, local organizations, urban youth, and communities. All stakeholders were able to use a variety of analog and digital sensors to deploy both stationary and mobile sensing nodes, all using the same *Urbano* platform. While stakeholders have access to data in a time series database, a variety of user friendly visualization portals were leveraged to make data easy to interpret and accessible to community members. To maximize the utility of urban sensing, the engineering field is pioneering new methods of power management including the use of edge-computing in urban sensor networks that minimize demands on high-power wireless communications.

For future work, the focus of this research will continue to shift towards presenting additional contributions in computing software architecture to enable and optimize operations for a wide range of applications. The embedded microcontroller of the *Urbano* node will be used for extensive on-chip data processing as part of a more broad edge-computing structure associated with dense networks of *Urbano* nodes deployed in smart and connected cities. This will focus on automating the operation of the node to maximize the net utility of all collected data given a certain power budget.

Acknowledgements. The authors would like to gratefully acknowledge support from NSF EAGER Grant #1637232 and the Knights Foundation, in addition to assistance from Elizabeth Moje and Jacqueline Handley from the University of Michigan School of Education.

References

1. AOT: Array of Things (2015). https://arrayofthings.github.io/. Accessed 01 Feb 2016
2. The Detroit News: Detroit Population Rank is Lowest Since 1850 (2016). www.detroitnews.com/story/news/local/detroit-city/2016/05/19/detroit-population-rank-lowest-since/84574198. Accessed 08 Jan 2018
3. Eco Counter (2017). https://www.eco-compteur.com/en/applications/parks-recreation. Accessed 08 Jan 2018
4. EPA: Environmental Issues in Southwest Detroit (2015). https://archieve.epa.gov/region5/swdetroit/web/html/index.html. Accessed 21 Feb 2016
5. Exosite (2017). https://exosite.com. Accessed 01 Jan 2018
6. Ganchev, I., Ji, Z., O'Droma, M.: A generic IoT architecture for smart cities. In: 25th IET Irish Signals & Systems Conference and China-Ireland International Conference on Information and Communications Technologies, Limerick, Ireland, pp. 196–199 (2013)
7. Jin, J., Gubbi, J., Marusic, S., et al.: An information framework for creating a smart city through internet of things. IEEE Internet Things J. **1**(2), 112–121 (2014)
8. Luthar, S.S.: Vulnerability and resilience: a study of high-risk adolescents. Child Dev. **62**(12), 600–616 (1991)
9. Lynch, J.P., Loh, K.J.: A summary review of wireless sensors and sensor networks for structural health monitoring. Shock Vib. Dig. **38**(2), 91–128 (2006)

10. Mehmood, Y., Ahmad, F., Yaqoob, I., et al.: Internet-of-Things-based smart cities: recent advances and challenges. IEEE Commun. Mag. **55**(9), 16–24 (2017)
11. Mitton, N., Papavassiliou, S., Puliafito, A., et al.: Combining cloud and sensors in a smart city environment. EURASIP J. Wirel. Commun. Netw. **2012**(1), 1–10 (2012)
12. Nimbelink: Skywire LTE CAT 1 (2017). https://nimbelink.com/Documentation/Skywire/4G_LTE_Cat_1/30154_NL-SW-LTE-GELS3_ProductBrief.pdf. Accessed 13 Jan 2017
13. NPR: Shh! Detroit's little-known success story: its parks are getting better (2015). http://michiganradio.org/post/shh-detroit-s-little-known-success-story-its-parks-are-getting-better#stream/0. Accessed 22 Feb 2016
14. Placemeter: The Placemeter Sensor (2015). https://www.placemeter.com/. Accessed 29 Feb 2016
15. Ryan, B.D.: Design after Decline: How America Rebuilds Shrinking Cities, 1st edn. University of Pennsylvania Press, Philadelphia (2012)
16. Straser, E., Kiremidjian, A., S.: Modular, wireless damage monitoring system for structures. Report #128, John A. Blume Earthquake Engineering Center, Stanford, CA (1998)
17. Swartz, A.R., Zimmerman, A., Lynch, J.P.: Structural health monitoring system with the latest information technologies. In: Proceedings of 5th Infrastructure & Environmental Management Symposium, Ube, Yamaguchi, Japan (2007)
18. Wang, F.Y.: The emergence of intelligent enterprises: From CPS to CPSS. IEEE Intell. Syst. **25**(4), 85–88 (2010)
19. Zanella, A., Bui, N., Castellani, A., et al.: Internet of Things for smart cities. IEEE Internet Things J. **1**(1), 22–32 (2014)

Actuator Layout Optimization for Adaptive Structures Performing Large Shape Changes

Arka P. Reksowardojo$^{(\boxtimes)}$ ⓘ, Gennaro Senatore ⓘ, and Ian F. C. Smith ⓘ

Applied Computing and Mechanics Laboratory (IMAC), School of Architecture, Civil and Environmental Engineering (ENAC), Swiss Federal Institute of Technology (EPFL), 1015 Lausanne, Switzerland
arka.reksowardojo@epfl.ch

Abstract. Adaptive structures are sensed and actuated to modify internal forces and shape to maintain optimal performance in response to loads. The use of large shape changes as a structural adaptation strategy to counteract the effect of loads has been investigated previously. When large shape changes are employed, structures are designed to change shape as the load changes thus giving the opportunity to homogenize stresses. In this way, the design is not governed by peak loads that occur very rarely. Simulations have shown a significant amount of embodied energy can be reduced with respect to optimized active structures limited to small shape changes and with respect to passive structures. However, in these previous studies, the actuator layout was assigned a-priori.

This paper presents a new method to search for an actuator layout that is optimum to counteract the effect of loads via large shape changes. The objective is to design the actuation system allowing the structure to 'morph' into shapes optimized to maximize material utilization for each load case. A combination of simulated annealing and the nonlinear force method is proposed to meet both the actuator placement problem and to determine appropriate actuator commands. A heuristic for near-neighbor generation based on the actuator control efficacy is employed to explore effectively the large search space. Case studies show the proposed method converges to the global optimum for simple configurations and generally produces actuator layouts enabling shape control even with a low number of actuators.

Keywords: Adaptive structures · Shape control · Actuator layout optimization
Nonlinear force method · Stochastic search

1 Introduction

The construction industry contributes to more than a third of the global energy demand and consumes almost a half of all mined raw materials [1]. For this reason, it is becoming important to include energy and material efficiency into the design rationale of civil structures.

Civil structures are generally designed to meet strength and deformation requirements for all possible load cases, including rare extreme loads. Thus, most structures are overdesigned for most of their life time.

© Springer International Publishing AG, part of Springer Nature 2018
I. F. C. Smith and B. Domer (Eds.): EG-ICE 2018, LNCS 10864, pp. 111–129, 2018.
https://doi.org/10.1007/978-3-319-91638-5_6

Shape optimization methods have been employed to design structures having ideal geometry under permanent load resulting in significant mass reduction as shown by several previous studies including [2–4]. However, because the shape cannot change, to deal with loading conditions different to the permanent load, additional material is distributed locally which is only utilized during peak demands.

Adaptive structures are structures with embedded sensors and actuators that can modify internal forces and shape to maintain optimal performance in response to loads. Previous work has shown that through well-conceived adaptive-design strategies [5] substantial whole-life energy savings can be achieved compared with traditional passive designs [6]. The whole-life energy consists of an embodied part in the material and an operational part for structural adaptation. Embodied energy is the energy consumed by the combined processes associated with the production of a material, such as mining, manufacturing and transportation. Operation energy is the energy consumed by the actuation needed for structural adaptation. Through actuation, the internal load-path of a given structure can be redistributed (such that stress concentration is reduced) thus increasing material efficiency. Whole-life energy savings are achieved by finding an optimum design that minimizes the energy embodied in the material at a small cost of energy required for sensing and actuation [7]. However, the formulations given in [5–7] are based on the assumption of small deformations hence control is limited to small shape changes.

The use of large shape changes as a structural adaptation strategy to counteract the effect of loads has been investigated previously [8]. In this study adaptive truss structures are designed to change shape as the load changes, thus providing an opportunity to further homogenize stresses. This way, peak loads that occur very rarely do not govern the design. Simulations on a simply supported beam truss, have shown that when large shape changes are employed 41% and 45% of embodied energy reduction is achieved with respect to optimized active structures limited to small shape changes and to passive structures respectively. However, in [8], the actuator layout was assigned a-priori.

For adaptive structures, it is important to optimize simultaneously the structure and control system to reach an integrated design [9, 10]. Design methods minimizing a cost function based on the linear-quadratic regulator performance index were successfully used for active vibration control [11–14].

Within the scope of damage tolerance such as in [15], the actuator locations were determined to meet safety and serviceability (deflection-governed) requirements in an event of damage via control. A Pareto front [16] of possible actuator layouts compromising between stress and deflection control requirements was computed. The best solution was selected via a ranking method. It was assumed that stress and deflection control requirements are competing criteria and therefore the actuator placement was framed as a multi-objective problem. However, a structure can be designed to change shape as the load changes thus employing shape control as a strategy to redistribute the stress as shown in the formulations given in [7, 8] and in this paper.

The search for optimal actuator layouts in [15] is carried out without employing suitable heuristics which might result in slow convergence for structures having complex topology. The Dynamic Relaxation (DR) method was employed to simulate shape changes given a set of actuator commands. DR is an efficient method to handle geometric nonlinearity. It can be proven that for matrix based implicit methods the operation count is proportional to the number of elements $O(m^{7/3})$ while for DR is $O(m^{4/3})$ (m is the number of elements) thus making the latter better suited for systems with larger number of elements [17]. However, DR cannot be used directly for the inverse ('backward') problem which is to obtain actuator commands to control the structure into a given target shape and load-path.

Within the scope of whole-life energy minimization such as in [5], the actuator placement was carried out via ranking the actuator efficacy of the structural elements. This criterion evaluates the contribution of a structural element assumed to be active towards the required load-path and shape control. A computationally efficient routine based on the integrated force method [18] and *eigenstrain* assignment was formulated to solve the actuator placement problem [19]. This method produces optimal actuator layouts for reticular structures under quasi-static loading. However, the method works within the assumption of small deformations and therefore is less reliable when implemented in systems with geometric nonlinearity.

Given a truss structure and an actuator layout, a previous study [20] presented a formulation called nonlinear force method (NFM) to determine suitable actuation commands to control large shape changes. Based on work by [21–23], the computation of actuator commands is formulated as an iterative process based on the solution of a linear least-square problem. NFM generally requires low number of iterations, thus it is suitable to be implemented within a nested optimization scheme.

This paper presents a method to find an actuator layout that is optimum to counteract the effect of loads via large shape changes. The method is formulated for statically determinate reticular structures (i.e. truss systems). The objective is to find an optimum actuator layout allowing the structure to 'morph' into efficient shapes that counteract the effect of peak load. The actuators are thought of as linear motor which are strategically fitted within selected elements. Since large shape changes may induce geometric nonlinearity, small deformations cannot be assumed. The formulation proposed in this paper is based on a combination of simulated annealing (SA) and the nonlinear force method (NFM). NFM is chosen because it can be used to solve the 'backward' problem to obtain actuator commands to control the structure into a given target shape and load-path [20]. A nested optimization scheme is proposed to solve the actuator placement problem. Actuator positions and actuator commands (i.e. length changes) are the variables of the external and internal process respectively. In the internal process, shape control is simulated while in the external process, the actuator layout is evaluated in terms of control efficacy. Illustrative examples are presented to demonstrate the feasibility of the proposed method.

2   Structure Cross-section Area, Load-Path and Shape Optimization

Adaptive structures can be designed to be fully compliant in terms of ultimate limit state but ignoring deflection requirements. Instead of using more material to meet serviceability requirement, strategically placed active elements keep deflections within limits by changing the shape of the structure [5]. The method is formulated for statically deter-minate reticular structures (i.e. truss systems). The structural joints are referred as nodes.

However, rather than having a fixed shape, the structure can be designed to morph into optimum shapes as the external load changes. The formulation described in this paper extends a previous work [5] by including nodal coordinates in the optimization. In the proposed formulation, the design variables $\mathbf{x}$ comprises cross-section area vector $\boldsymbol{\alpha} \in \mathbb{R}^m$, load-path vector $\mathbf{t} \in \mathbb{R}^m$ and nodal coordinate change vector $\Delta \mathbf{d} \in \mathbb{R}^n$:

$$\mathbf{x} = \begin{bmatrix} \boldsymbol{\alpha} & \mathbf{t}_1 & \cdots & \mathbf{t}_o & \Delta\mathbf{d}_1 & \cdots & \Delta\mathbf{d}_o \end{bmatrix}^T, \tag{1}$$

where m, n and o are the number of elements, degrees of freedom and load cases respec-tively. Optimal load-paths and shapes are searched for each load case to minimize the embodied energy (i.e. material usage) of the structure. The process can be thought of as a mapping between external load and shape/load-path, which are optimized to maximize material utilization for each load case.

The optimization is subject to force equilibrium, stress and element buckling constraints (ULS). The problem is nonlinear because each iteration: (1) the cross-section areas change and thus the self-weight changes; (2) the shape of the structure changes and thus the equilibrium matrix changes. Because the search space is generally contin-uous and convex, optimization is carried out using sequential quadratic programming (SQP).

The absence of compatibility constraint between element deformation and node position in the optimization implies that the resulting optimal shapes are not compatible ones. In other words, it is impossible to achieve optimal shapes perfectly unless the length of all elements in the structure are adjustable (i.e. all elements are actuators). The adaptive system will be used to enforce compatibility by controlling the shape as close as possible to the optimal ones.

The optimal shape can be thought of as the shape of the structure would have if it was pre-stressed. Conventionally, pre-stressing is a one-time process that carried out during the construction phase. In the proposed adaptive structure, on the other hand, both load-path and shape change as the load changes.

3   Actuator Layout Optimization

The actuator layout design is an inverse problem (i.e. abductive inference) whose solu-tions are searched given a set of desired behaviors. In this case, the problem is to deter-mine the locations where the actuators are most effective to change the shape of the structure into the optimal shapes (Sect. 2) via controlled length changes (e.g. expansion or contraction). Due to compatibility, the optimal shapes could only be matched perfectly if all elements were active. Therefore, the problem is to determine the location of the minimum number of actuators to ensure feasible controlled shapes that are as close as possible to the optimal shapes.

The degrees of freedom allowed to move during shape optimization (Sect. 2) are set as controlled degrees of freedom. This is to match the optimal shapes within reasonable accuracy. However, other degrees of freedom might be chosen to be controlled to set additional constraints including deflection limits for serviceability.

The problem is of combinatorial nature. The task of selecting n^{act} actuators from m feasible locations has a search space size of:

$$\frac{m!}{n^{act}!(m - n^{act})!} \tag{2}$$

When the number of structural elements is large, a full enumeration of the problem (i.e. evaluation of all possible solutions) is computationally impossible.

A nested optimization (bilevel optimization) scheme is proposed here to solve the actuator placement problem. The scheme contains two levels of optimization tasks where one optimization task is nested within the other. Actuator positions and actuator commands (i.e. length changes) are the variables of the external and internal process respectively. The actuator commands are obtained using the nonlinear force method (NFM), which is akin to an iterative least-square minimization process, while the optimal actuator layout is determined via a global stochastic search using simulated annealing (SA).

3.1 Internal Process: Computation of Actuator Commands Given an Actuator Layout

In the internal optimization process the actuator layout is given, this being a variable of the external process. The objective here is to obtain suitable actuator-length changes to control the structure into the required optimal shapes and load paths (Sect. 2).

Solution of structural mechanics problems generally should satisfy the equilibrium, compatibility and material constitutive requirements. Good solutions can be obtained no matter in which order and in respect to which variable the requirements are being satisfied. Two well-known methods to solve structural mechanics problems are the displacement method and the force method having displacements and forces as solution variables respectively. While commonly used, the displacement method is not easily adapted to simulate self-stress or shape changes induced by expansion or contraction of structural elements. In addition, the displacement method lacks generality to be extended for cases with kinematic indeterminacies [24, 25] which often arise in cable-strut structures. Through the force method (FM), such cases can be solved within the assumption of small deformations [26]. To account for geometric nonlinearity (e.g. large shape changes) a nonlinear force method (NFM) [20, 23] is proposed.

The NFM solves equilibrium and compatibility using the Newton-Raphson iterative method [27]. For explanation on the formation of the equilibrium and compatibility matrix, readers are referred to [26]. The NFM is used as 'forward' method to compute nodal displacements and internal forces caused by a given set of actuator commands. Even if the structures considered in this paper are statically determinate, the actuator length changes affect the internal forces due to geometric nonlinearity caused by large shape changes. Conversely, the 'backward' NFM is used to compute actuator length changes to control the structure into the required shapes and load-paths. This method offers an efficient derivation of actuator commands given required shapes.

In the backward NFM there is no assumption of the deformation path to move from the deformed shape (i.e. shape without control) to the target shape. The method starts by computing the inverse of the compatibility matrix which is then reduced to the rows and columns corresponding to the controlled degrees of freedom and active elements respectively. This matrix relates changes of nodal coordinates (i.e. shape) to the actuator commands and it is defined here as the shape influence matrix. Because this scheme is iterative, this matrix can be thought of as the tangent of the shape influence matrix. Computing the pseudoinverse of the shape influence matrix multiplied by the target shape change (i.e. nodal shift) gives the actuator length-change vector each iteration:

$$\delta \mathbf{l} = \mathbf{A}_d^+ \delta \mathbf{d}^* \tag{3}$$

where $\delta \mathbf{l}$ is the actuator length change vector, $\mathbf{A}_d^+$ is the pseudoinverse of the shape influence matrix and $\delta \mathbf{d}^*$ is the target shape change.

The actuator commands obtained this way are input to a forward NFM to verify that the controlled shapes match the required ones within a set tolerance (i.e. each iteration of the backward NFM contains a forward NFM). The process continues until convergence. The method can be summarized in the following steps:

(1) The influence matrix based on the initial state of the structure is computed via the inverse of the compatibility matrix. At this stage, the structure is in its undeformed shape (i.e. there is no shape change caused by either external loads or actuator length changes).

(2) A reduced influence matrix is formed by extracting the rows and columns corresponding to controlled degrees of freedom and active elements respectively.

(3) Actuator length changes to move towards the target shape are obtained computing the pseudoinverse of the influence matrix multiplied by the target shape change (i.e. target nodal shifts). Note this is only an incremental actuator command vector, the total actuator command is obtained at convergence.

(4) The actuator length changes obtained from step (3) are applied using a forward NFM to compute resulting changes of shape and internal forces and thus updating the equilibrium matrix.

(5) A new influence matrix is obtained based on the new state of the structure.

(6) Loop step (2) to (5) until the difference between the controlled shape and the target shape is less than a threshold.

The process requires updating the equilibrium matrix at each iteration and within each iteration several updates are required by the forward NFM. For detailed mathematical formulation of NFM as well as explanation and examples on the forward NFM and backward NFM, readers are referred to [20, 23]. To improve computational efficiency, the equilibrium matrix is updated using the connectivity matrix (a matrix that describes element-to-node connectivity of the structure) [28] which is constant because the topology of the structure is invariant.

3.2   External Process: Search for Actuator Layout

The objective of the external process is to find an actuator layout that maximizes the actuation control efficacy. That is to determine the locations (i.e. element sites) where the actuators are most effective to control the structure into the required optimal shapes and load-paths.

The problem is formulated as a constrained maximization of the closeness between the nodal displacements caused by the actuator length changes and the optimal shapes. The objective function is defined in Eq. 4:

$$\max_{\mathbf{y}} \left\{ \frac{1}{2} \left(1 + \frac{1}{n} \sum_{j=1}^{n} \frac{\delta\mathbf{d}^T \delta\mathbf{d}^*}{\sqrt{(\delta\mathbf{d}^T \delta\mathbf{d})(\delta\mathbf{d}^{*T} \delta\mathbf{d}^*)}} \right) \right\}, \tag{4}$$

where $\delta\mathbf{d}$ and $\delta\mathbf{d}^*$ correspond to controlled shape change and target shape change, respectively. The search is subject to stress constraints and element buckling (ULS). The variable $\mathbf{y} \in \mathbb{Z}^{n^{act}}$ is the vector of element indices that are assigned as active elements. The number of actuators n^{act} is assigned a-priori. The shape closeness is evaluated for each load case j. An average value over n load cases is taken.

The objective function is inspired from the modal assurance criterion (MAC) [29] which is used for evaluating closeness between mode shapes in the field of dynamics. The MAC function returns value between 0 and 1. To evaluate similarity between two shapes, the closer the function value to one, the closer the shapes. However, this function returns one even when two shapes are identical in terms of nodal displacements but phased by 90° (i.e. mirrored), leading to a misinterpretation. For this reason, the MAC function was changed by omitting the absolute value at the numerator and taking the square root of the ratio. The objective function formulated here returns values between 0 and 1. The closer the objective function to one, the closer the actuated shapes are to optimal ones. The selection of such objective function is motivated by the need for a normalized measure of the closeness between two given shapes. A normalized measure is necessary when multiple load cases are considered because actuation efficacy may vary across load cases.

A global stochastic search algorithm based on the simulated annealing (SA) method is used. SA is a widely used algorithm to solve combinatorial processes [30]. SA mimics the cooling process of molten metals through annealing. Annealing is a physical process through which particles are randomly arranging themselves towards a low energy-state configuration as the temperature is slowly lowered. In SA, the physical particle configurations correspond to minimization solutions and the energy-state to the objective value. A control parameter called 'temperature', taking a direct analogy to the physical temperature, determines the probability of accepting a potential solution [31]. Within a group of feasible solutions, called neighborhood, a solution is randomly selected to be close to the current one. While the temperature is high, a neighbor is likely to be accepted, regardless of its fitness. As the temperature decreases, neighbor solutions having a worse fitness than the current one are increasingly more likely to be rejected; in other words, the search around good solutions is increasingly intensified [31]. SA has been successfully applied to a variety of engineering problems [4, 32–34].

The generation of solutions is carried out by using an efficacy measure of a given element to contribute towards the attainment of the optimal shapes via its length changes. The efficacy measure will be used as a heuristic to generate the initial solution (solution at the first iteration) and to define the neighborhood structure that is a set of feasible solutions close to the current solution. Having a problem-specific initial solution and neighborhood structure is not a requirement, but often it offers improvements in terms of convergence when compared with a complete randomization [35].

Actuator Efficacy Heuristics and Initialization
At this stage all elements are taken to be active. To compute the actuator efficacy, a two-step method is formulated. First, the actuator length changes to control the structure into the required optimal shapes are obtained from the backward NFM. Second, the shape changes (for each load case) resulting from the length changes of each element in turn is computed using the forward NFM by extracting the corresponding entry from the actuator command vector and setting all other entries to zero. Finally, the shape changes obtained in the second step are evaluated using Eq. 4. which is a measure of how close the controlled shapes are to the optimal ones.

This method is inspired by [5] which was formulated within the assumption of small displacements. For geometric nonlinear structures, the actuator influence matrix (Sect. 3.1) updates as the shape changes and thus nodal trajectories due to length change of multiple actuators cannot be obtained through superposition. In other words, the contribution of multiple actuators is not equivalent to the sum of the individual contributions. For this reason, the actuator efficacy is used here as a heuristic to obtain the initial actuator layout by selecting the topmost ranked n^{act} elements. This solution is optimal if geometric nonlinearity is neglected and therefore represents only an initial guess.

Neighborhood Generation
The actuator efficacy heuristic is also used for neighborhood generation. The actuator efficacy is normalized to be used as a discrete probability distribution $\mathbf{P}^{act}$. This distribution gives the probability of an element to be selected as an actuator based on its efficacy as defined previously. Conversely, the inverse of $\mathbf{P}^{act}$ gives the probability of an element to be removed from the current solution.

To generate neighbor solutions a random integer is drawn from a uniform distribution representing the number of actuator locations to be replaced n^{rep}. An actuator location is drawn from the inverse of $\mathbf{P}^{act}$ to be removed from the current solution. The removed actuator is then replaced through drawing from $\mathbf{P}^{act}$ which is updated after each draw to avoid selecting the same element more than once (i.e. drawing without replacement). This process is repeated as many times as the number of actuators to be replaced (n^{rep}) to form the new neighbor solution.

3.3   Method Summary

Figure 1 shows the schematic flowchart of the proposed method. The actuator layout optimization process is initialized by computing the first solution based on the actuator efficacy rank. Each iteration begins with the generation of a new neighbor solution (i.e.

candidate actuator layout) using the procedure described in Sect. 3.2. Based on the candidate actuator layout, actuator commands are derived applying the backward NFM and the controlled shapes are computed using the forward NFM (Sect. 3.1). If the controlled load-paths do not satisfy ultimate limit states constraints the candidate actuator layout is rejected. Otherwise, the objective value of the neighbor solution is evaluated and compared with that of the previous solution using Eq. 4. If the objective value of the neighbor solution is greater, it is accepted.

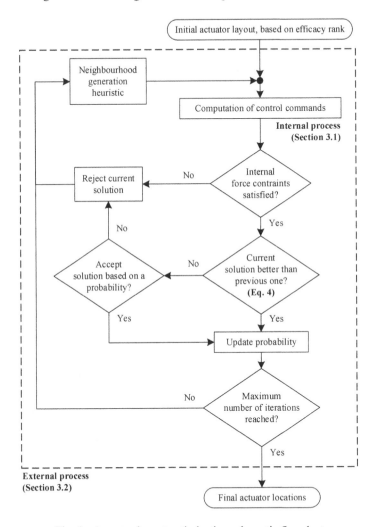

Fig. 1. Actuator layout optimization schematic flowchart

Inferior neighbor solutions are accepted subject to a certain probability which is a function of the temperature parameter. The probability of a candidate actuator layout to be accepted, even if it results in a lower objective value, decreases as the number of iterations increases.

4   Case Study

4.1   Initial Geometry and Loading

To illustrate the application of the method presented in Sects. 2 and 3, a simply supported 20:1 span-to-depth truss-beam is taken as a case study. The truss has a 2000 mm span and it is constrained as indicated in the diagram shown in Fig. 2. This structure, which can be thought of as a roof system reduced to two dimensions, is 1:5 scale of a test prototype currently under development at EPFL Applied Computing and Mechanics Laboratory (IMAC). The purpose of this test prototype is to assess the feasibility of the proposed design method. All elements are made of aluminum assuming an average Young's modulus of 70 GPa and have a circular section.

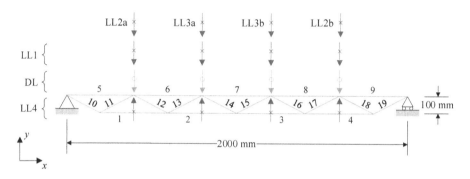

Fig. 2. Base layout and loads, DL indicated by [○], LL indicated by [×]

The dead load (DL) is applied to the top chord as distributed load of magnitude 0.25 kN/m. Self-weight (SW) is computed iteratively during the first process of the optimization (Sect. 2). Four live loads (LL) are considered, namely LL1, LL2, LL3 and LL4. LL1 is a uniformly distributed load of magnitude 0.5 kN/m representing a snow load applied on top chord. LL2 and LL3 are point loads offset from mid span, representing general payloads (e.g. static object, maintenance personnel, etc.), of magnitude 0.8 kN. For symmetry, LL2 and LL3 are applied twice i.e. as LL2a and LL3a mirror LL2b and LL3b respectively. LL4 is a uniformly distributed uplift of magnitude 0.5 kN/m applied to the top chord which could be thought of as resulting from wind pressure. These loads have been drawn from standard loading [36] to be practically applied to a 2 m span truss beam. Table 1 summarizes all load-case combinations.

Table 1. Load combinations

Load case	Combinations
Permanent load case	DL + SL
Load case #1	DL + SL + LL1
Load case #2	DL + SL + LL2
Load case #3	DL + SL + LL3
Load case #4	DL + SL + LL4

4.2 Size, Load-Path and Shape Optimization

During size, load-path and shape optimization (Sect. 2) each node except the supports is allowed to change position vertically within a range of ±30 as indicated in Fig. 3.

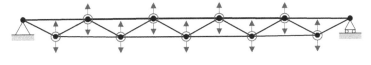

Fig. 3. Selected degrees of freedom

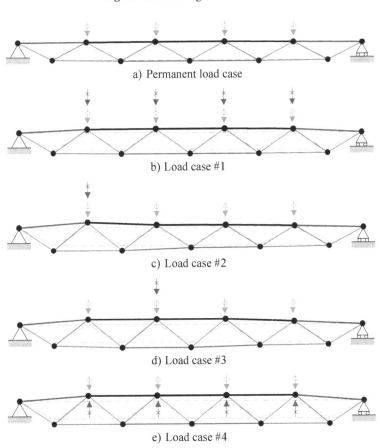

a) Permanent load case

b) Load case #1

c) Load case #2

d) Load case #3

e) Load case #4

Fig. 4. Optimal shapes, DL indicated by [○], LL indicated by [×]

Figure 4 shows the optimized layouts. Element diameters are indicated by line thickness variation and color shading. Referring to Fig. 4, it can be noted that the structure increases its depth when load case #1 is applied (Fig. 4b) with respect to the shape under permanent load (Fig. 4a). The optimal shape for load case #2 and #3 are shown in

Fig. 4c and d respectively. These shapes are asymmetrical because the load is applied with an offset from the mid span.

The structure obtained with the method proposed here is benchmarked against one obtained using the method given in [5] which does not employ shape optimization (i.e. the adaptive structure is limited to small shape changes). Figure 5 shows a comparison of the cross-section sizes obtained with the two methods. Employing large shape changes to optimize the load-path generally yields a lower cross-section distribution compared to the same optimization process without considering large shape changes – a 16.4% embodied energy reduction is achieved in this case. Note that the energy assessment is carried out without taking into account the weight of the actuators. The actuator weight is highly dependent on the type of actuation technology. The actuator embodied energy share will be investigated in future works.

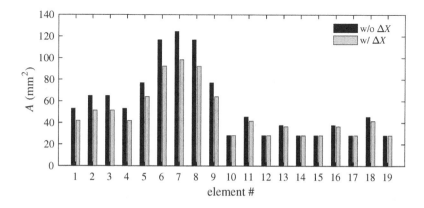

Fig. 5. Optimal section size distribution with shape change vs. without shape change

4.3 Actuator Layout Optimization

The structure is assumed to be built using the optimal shape under permanent load. This means that when the live load is applied, the active system will control the structure into the required optimal shapes and load-paths starting from the shapes and load-path under the permanent load. The controlled degrees of freedom are the same as those ones selected for shape optimization indicated by circles in Fig. 3.

The actuator layout optimization formulated in Sect. 3 requires setting the number of actuators n^{act} whose optimal locations will be determined. Generally, a low number of active elements is desired to reduce cost and control complexity. However, below a certain number of actuators, controllability cannot be achieved. The minimum number of actuators can be determined by testing convergence multiple times each time decreasing the number of active elements. The search is repeated starting from all elements set as active and then decreasing the number of actuators 14, 10, 7, 5 and 4.

Figure 6 shows the actuator layouts obtained for all cases. Table 2 gives metrics for all tested layouts including the Euclidean norm of the difference between optimal and controlled shapes $\|\delta \mathbf{d} - \delta \mathbf{d}^*\|_2$ and the maximum element demand over capacity ratio obtained after control for each layout. No feasible solution can be found for any number of actuators less than five. For instance, when the total number of actuators is set to 4, the maximum element demand over capacity ratio is approximately 2 thus ultimate limit state (ULS) constraints are not satisfied. As expected, the higher number of actuators the closer the controlled shapes achieved via actuation match the optimal shapes.

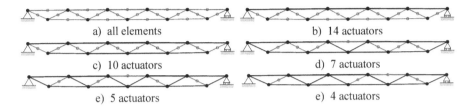

a) all elements   b) 14 actuators

c) 10 actuators   d) 7 actuators

e) 5 actuators   e) 4 actuators

Fig. 6. Optimal layouts for 19, 14, 10, 7, 5 and 4 actuators

Table 2. Comparison of optimal layouts for 19, 14, 10, 7, 5 and 4 actuators.

n^{act}	1 – objective value [1 – (Eq. 2)]	Norm of shape discrepancy (mm)	Max. shape discrepancy (mm)	Norm of load-path discrepancy (kN)	Max. demand/ capacity ratio
19	5.804×10^{-7}	8.4	5.25	0.146	0.832
14	1.553×10^{-6}	9.2	5.46	0.389	0.855
10	6.299×10^{-6}	19.9	7.55	0.375	0.861
7	1.347×10^{-5}	148	44.4	1.81	0.899
5	2.211×10^{-5}	182	52.5	1.69	0.992
4	2.981×10^{-5}	190	54.0	3.71	2.09*

Because 5 is the minimum number of actuators allowed to control the structure, a more detailed analysis of this case is presented in the following. For clarity, the optimal actuator layout obtained with 5 actuators is shown again in Fig. 7. Note that the solution is symmetrical, despite symmetry not being explicitly imposed as a constraint.

Fig. 7. Optimal layout for 5 actuators

Figure 8 shows the shapes achieved via actuation with element stress mapped onto the geometry. Optimal shapes (previously shown in Fig. 4) are shown in the background for comparison. As expected, the shapes achieved via actuation are not identical to optimal shapes since not all elements are capable of changing their lengths. The actuator maximum expansion is 53.2 mm for element 11 and 18 under load case #4, while maximum contraction is 51.6 mm for element 7 under load case #4. Under the permanent

124   A. P. Reksowardojo et al.

load case the actuator maximum expansion is of 0.6 mm for element 7 and maximum contraction is 0.2 mm for elements 13 and 17. These values are considered to determine the required stroke capacity of the actuators. For the permanent load case the actuator effort is lower because the structure is assumed to be built according to the corresponding optimal shape. Element numbers are shown in Fig. 2.

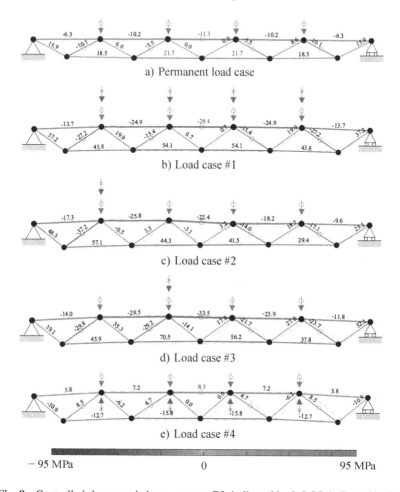

Fig. 8. Controlled shapes and element stress, DL indicated by [○], LL indicated by [×]

The bar charts shown in Fig. 9 illustrate the difference between the optimal and controlled load-path for all load cases. The element capacity (ULS) is shown by horizontal lines. Generally, the controlled forces have a higher magnitude with respect to the optimal ones. However, ULS criteria are satisfied for all load cases.

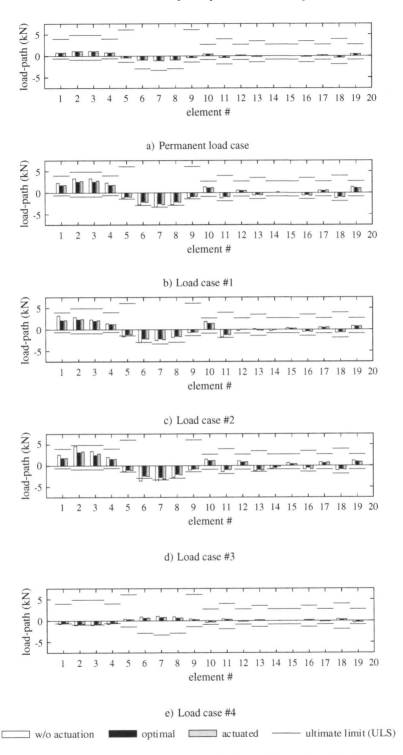

a) Permanent load case

b) Load case #1

c) Load case #2

d) Load case #3

e) Load case #4

☐ w/o actuation   ■ optimal   ▨ actuated   ── ultimate limit (ULS)

Fig. 9. Optimal, controlled and non-controlled internal forces for all load cases

Also shown in white are the internal forces caused by the load when the structure is not controlled (i.e. does not change its shape). In this case the internal forces are higher with respect to the controlled forces. In fact, without shape changes, the internal force of element 5 to 9 exceeds the ultimate limit for load case #1, # 2 and #3. The same can be seen for elements 1 to 4 in load case #4.

As expected, using the proposed method, optimum actuator layouts were obtained after a much lower number of evaluations with respect to a full enumeration. For example, for the case with 5 actuators convergence is achieved only after 234 evaluations on average (of 20 runs) while full enumeration requires 11628 evaluations.

Figure 10 shows the objective value (Eq. 4) as a function of the number of iterations for a single run of the process. A single run of the process represents the search from the initial solution until convergence is reached. In this paper, convergence is defined as the attainment of the global optimum solution. Because the case study discussed in this paper is a structure made of small number of elements, the global optimum can be obtained through full enumeration while using manageable computing resources thus providing the opportunity to validate the proposed method. Across multiple runs, the solution at convergence does not vary between different runs; the objective value remains at 2.211×10^{-5} and the final actuator layout is identical.

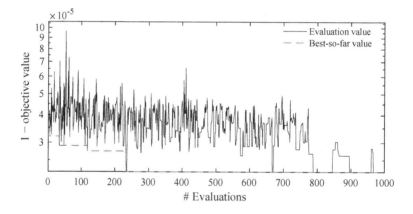

Fig. 10. Search process convergence (y-axis in logarithmic scale)

To assess the effectiveness of the proposed heuristics based on actuator efficacy (Sect. 3), the same problem (5 actuators layout optimization) is solved using the same method implemented using an SA without heuristics, a genetic algorithm (GA) and a full enumeration. Table 3 gives average, maximum and minimum number of evaluations to achieve convergence obtained from 20 runs of each method. The proposed heuristics, based on the actuator efficacy (Sect. 3.2), enabled the convergence within an average number of evaluation which is only 15%, 18% and 5% that required by the SA without heuristics, GA and full enumeration respectively.

Table 3. Performance of various search methods

Method	Average number of evaluations	Maximum number of evaluations	Minimum number of evaluations
Full enumeration	11628	11628	11628
GA	3281	6761	873
SA without heuristic	3755	6819	1189
SA with heuristic	579	1557	7

5 Conclusions

The study presented in this paper focuses on the implementation of an optimization scheme to search for optimum actuator layouts to control adaptive structures designed to counteract the effect of loads via large shape changes. This is a challenging task because of the combinatorial nature of the problem which includes geometric nonlinearity as discussed in Sects. 2 and 3. A search method is proposed combining simulated annealing and nonlinear force method to explore the solution space of the actuator placement problem and to determine appropriate actuator commands. A heuristic based on the actuator efficacy is employed to explore effectively the large search space. Results from the case studies presented in this paper lead to the following conclusions:

(1) The proposed method successfully converges to optimal solutions for the case under study, thus showing potential for generality.
(2) The heuristic for near-neighbor generation based on the actuator control efficacy improves convergence properties which is important for structures having complex layouts made of several elements.
(3) This method successfully produces actuator layouts whereby it is possible to control the shape and satisfy ULS even with a low number of actuators.

Future work will include considerations on the whole-life energy of the structure comprising the energy embodied in the material and the operational energy for structural adaptation to achieve a compromise between optimal states (i.e. shape and load-path) and actuation effort. The method will be further developed to include statically indeterminate structures. In addition, the structure taken as a case study in this paper will be built and experimentally tested to validate numerical predictions.

Acknowledgements. The research presented in this paper is supported by the Swiss Government Excellence Scholarship (ESKAS-Nr: 2016.0749).

References

1. Straube, J.: Green building and sustainability. Building Science Digests, 24 October 2006
2. Gil, L., Andreu, A.: Shape and cross-section optimisation of a truss structure. Comput. Struct. **79**, 681–689 (2001)
3. Wang, D., Zhang, W., Jiang, J.: Truss shape optimization with multiple displacement constraints. Comput. Methods Appl. Mech. Eng. **191**, 3597–3612 (2002)

4. Shea, K., Smith, I.F.C.: Improving full-scale transmission tower design through topology and shape optimization. Struct. Eng. **132**(5), 781–790 (2006)
5. Senatore, G., Duffour, P., Hanna, S., Labbe, F., Winslow, P.: Adaptive structures for whole life energy savings. Int. Assoc. Shell Spat. Struct. (IASS) **52**(170), 233–240 (2011)
6. Senatore, G., Duffour, P., Winslow, P.: Whole-life energy and cost assessment of adaptive structures - case studies. J. Struct. Eng. (ASCE) (in press)
7. Senatore, G., Duffour, P., Winslow, P., Wise, C.: Shape control and whole-life energy assessment of an "infinitely stiff" prototype adaptive structure. Smart Mater. Struct. **27**(1), 015022 (2017)
8. Reksowardojo, A., Senatore, G., Smith, I.: Large and reversible shape changes as a strategy for structural adaptation. In: Proceeding of International Association for Shell and Spacial Structures (IASS) (2017)
9. Skelton, R.E., Sultan, C.: Integrated design of controllable tensegrity structures. Adapt. Struct. Mater. Syst. **54**, 27–35 (1997)
10. Soong, T.T., Manolis, G.D.: Active structures. J. Struct. Eng. **113**(11), 2290–2302 (1987)
11. Manning, R.A.: Optimum design of intelligent truss structures. In: Structures, Structural Dynamics, and Materials Conference, Co-located (1991)
12. Furuya, H., Haftka, R.Z.: Placing actuators on space structures by genetic algorithms and effectiveness indexes. Struct. Optim. **9**, 69–75 (1995)
13. Begg, D.W., Liu, X.: On simultaneous optimization of smart structures – part II: algorithms and examples. Comput. Methods Appl. Mech. Eng. **184**(1), 25–37 (2000)
14. de Jager, B., Skelton, R.: Input/output selection for planar tensegrity models. In: Proceedings of 40th IEEE Conference on Decision and Control, Orlando (2001)
15. Korkmaz, S., Ben Hadj Ali, N., Smith, I.F.C.: Configuration of control system for damage tolerance of a tensegrity bridge. Adv. Eng. Inform. **26**, 145–155 (2012)
16. Grierson, D.: Pareto multi-criteria decision making. Adv. Eng. Inform. **22**, 371–384 (2008)
17. Sauve, R.: Advances in dynamic relaxation techniques for nonlinear finite element. J. Press. Vessel Technol. **117**, 170–176 (1995)
18. Patnaik, S.: An integrated force method for discrete analysis. Int. J. Numer. Meth. Eng. **6**, 237–251 (1973)
19. Senatore, G.: Adaptive building structures. Doctoral dissertation, University College London, London (2016)
20. Yuan, X., Liang, X., Li, A.: Shape and force control of prestressed cable-strut structures based on nonlinear force method. Adv. Struct. Eng. **19**(12), 1917–1926 (2016)
21. Pellegrino, S.: Structural computations with the singular value decomposition of the equilibrium matrix. Int. J. Solids Struct. **30**(21), 3025–3035 (1993)
22. You, Z.: Displacement control of prestressed structures. Comput. Methods Appl. Mech. Eng. **144**, 51–59 (1997)
23. Luo, Y., Lu, J.: Geometrically non-linear force method for assemblies with infinitesimal mechanisms. Comput. Struct. **84**, 2194–2199 (2006)
24. Kahla, N., Kebiche, K.: Nonlinear elastoplastic analysis of tensegrity systems. Comput. Struct. **22**, 1552–1566 (2000)
25. Xu, X., Luo, Y.: Non-liear displacement control of prestressed cable structures. J. Aerosp. Eng. **223**, 1001–1007 (2009)
26. Pellegrino, S., Calladine, C.: Matrix analysis of statically and kinematically indeterminate frameworks. Int. J. Solids Struct. **22**, 409–428 (1986)
27. Lax, P., Burstein, S., Lax, A.: Calculus with Applications and Computing. Courant Institute of Mathematical Sciences, New York University, New York (1972)

28. Achtziger, W.: On simultaneous optimization of truss geometry and topology. Struct. Multidiscipl. Optim. **33**, 285–304 (2007)
29. Pastor, M., Binda, M., Harčarik, T.: Modal assurance criterion. Procedia Eng. **48**, 543–548 (2012)
30. Kirkpatrick, S., Gelatt, J.C., Vecchi, M.: Optimization by simulated annealing. Science **220**, 671–679 (1983)
31. Metropolis, N., Rosenbluth, A., Teller, A., Teller, E.: Equation of state calculations by fast computing machines. J. Chem. Phys. **21**, 1087–1092 (1953)
32. Reddy, G., Cagan, J.: An improved shape annealing algorithm for truss topology generation. ASME J. Mech. Des. **117**, 315–321 (1995)
33. Onoda, J., Hanawa, Y.: Actuator placement optimization by genetic and improved simulated annealing algorithms. AIAA J. **31**, 1167–1169 (1992)
34. Arora, J., Elwakeil, O., Chahande, A.: Global optimization methods for engineering applications: a review. Struct. Optim. **9**, 137–159 (1995)
35. Cheh, K., Goldberg, J., Askin, R.: A note on the effect of neighborhood structure in simulated annealing. Comput. Oper. Res. **18**(6), 537–547 (1991)
36. Eurocode 1 Actions on structures—General actions—Part 1–4: Wind (1991)

Unsupervised Named Entity Normalization for Supporting Information Fusion for Big Bridge Data Analytics

Kaijian Liu[✉] [iD] and Nora El-Gohary

Department of Civil and Environmental Engineering,
University of Illinois at Urbana-Champaign, Urbana, IL 61801, USA
{kliu15,gohary}@illinois.edu

Abstract. The large amount of multi-type and multi-source bridge data open unprecedented opportunities to big data analytics for better bridge deterioration prediction. Information fusion is needed prior to the analytics to transform the heterogeneous data from different sources into a unified representation. Resolving the ambiguities in the named entities extracted from bridge inspection reports is one of the most important fusion tasks. The ambiguity stems from the use of different and ambiguous surface forms to the same target named entity. There is, thus, a need for named entity normalization (NEN) methods that can map these ambiguous surface forms into their canonical form – an identifier concept. However, existing NEN methods are limited in this regard. This is because they mostly require pre-established knowledge (e.g., dictionaries or Wikipedia) and/or training data, and mostly ignore the impact of the normalization on data analytics. To address this need, this paper proposes an unsupervised NEN method. It includes two main components: candidate identifier concept generation based on multi-grams of each named entity set, and candidate identifier concept ranking based on a proposed ranking function. The function uses the TF-IDF (term frequency–inverse document frequency) weight and is further improved by considering the impacts of gram lengths and positions on the ranking. It aims to balance the abstractness and detailedness of the identifier concepts, so as to ensure that the resulting data are neither too dense nor too sparse for the analytics. A set of experiments were conducted to evaluate the performance of the proposed method. It achieved an accuracy of 84.5%.

Keywords: Named entity normalization · Big data analytics
Bridge deterioration prediction

1 Introduction

Bridge deterioration is a long-lasting problem faced by many countries across the world [1]. Many agencies have been reporting the deterioration problems of their bridges, since the 1980s [2]. For example, the Commonwealth Bureau of Roads reported that 39% of the highway bridges in Australia were deficient as of 1986 [3]. The Organisation for Economic Cooperation and Development reported that, among the 800,000 bridges sampled from18 developed countries, 40% of them were found structurally deficient as of 1988 [4]. To date, the problem is still present. For example, as reported by the 2017

© Springer International Publishing AG, part of Springer Nature 2018
I. F. C. Smith and B. Domer (Eds.): EG-ICE 2018, LNCS 10864, pp. 130–149, 2018.
https://doi.org/10.1007/978-3-319-91638-5_7

American Society of Civil Engineers (ASCE) Infrastructure Report Card, 9.1% and 13.6% of the bridges in the U.S. are structurally deficient and functionally obsolete, respectively [5]. The poor conditions of the bridges threaten the safety of highway and bridge users. As reported in [1], a total of 71 major bridge failures have occurred around the world since 1970, with 24 and 13 failures in North America and Europe, respectively. The failures are catastrophic, resulting in many fatalities and injuries. For example, in the collapse of the I-35 W Mississippi River Bridge alone, 13 people were killed and 145 were injured [6]. Despite the imperativeness of improving the conditions of bridges for public safety and economic well-being, bridge agencies are still struggling to make cost-effective bridge maintenance decisions [7, 8]. This is because their maintenance decisions are largely constrained by the limited maintenance funding. For instance, in the U.S. alone, in order to eliminate the nation's deficient bridge backlog by 2028, a $20.5 billion investment in bridge construction and maintenance is needed annually; however, only $12.8 billion is being invested currently [5]. Bridge deterioration prediction plays an important role towards addressing the challenges in making cost-effective bridge maintenance decisions under the current funding constraints [7–10].

As such, in their previous work [11–13], the authors proposed a big bridge data analytics framework. The proposed framework capitalizes on the increasing availability of multi-type and multi-source data in the bridge domain. It aims to learn from the data to better predict future bridge deterioration for enhancing bridge maintenance decision making. Such data include structured National Bridge Inventory (NBI) and National Bridge Elements (NBE) data, unstructured textual data from bridge inspection reports, unstructured multisensory data from various sensors, and semi-structured traffic and weather data. The NBI and NBE data contain bridge condition rating information at the bridge level and the element level, respectively. The reports contain technically-detailed data about bridge conditions (e.g., the types, quantities, and severities of deficiencies) and maintenance history (e.g., maintenance actions and material). The sensory data are collected from structural health monitoring. The traffic data are about traffic volumes, vehicle classification counts, and vehicle weights; and, the weather data are about temperature, wind, precipitation, etc.

Information fusion is at the cornerstone of the proposed big bridge data analytics framework. It aims to transform these multi-type and multi-source bridge data into a unified representation. Resolving the ambiguities in the named entities extracted from bridge inspection reports is one of the most important fusion tasks. The ambiguity stems from the use of different and ambiguous surface forms to refer to the same target named entity. For example, these two named entities "east approach pavement" and "bituminous approach pavement" are used to refer to the same entity "approach pavement". Despite that several guidelines have defined vocabularies that should be used for recording structured bridge data (e.g., bridge element concepts used for collecting NBE data) across bridge agencies and inspectors, there are no such guidelines when it comes to the vocabulary used in writing textual bridge inspection reports. As a result of such practice, the text in the reports is "uncontrolled" (as seen in the example above). There is, thus, a need for named entity normalization (NEN) methods that can map the ambiguous surface forms of different named entities – referring to the same target named entity – into their canonical form, i.e., an identifier concept. However, as further analyzed in

Sect. 4.2, existing NEN methods are limited in this regard. This is because they mostly require pre-established knowledge (e.g., dictionaries and Wikipedia) and/or human annotated data, and mostly ignore the impact of the normalization on subsequent data analytics. To address this need, the authors propose a new unsupervised NEN method. This paper focuses on presenting the authors' research efforts in defining the research problem, developing the unsupervised NEN method, and evaluating its performance.

2   Research Objectives and Contributions

The objectives and contributions of this paper are threefold:

- Defining the research problem: This paper provides an overview of the proposed big bridge data analytics framework. The research problem that this paper aims to address manifests itself in the fusion step of the framework.
- Introducing the background of NEN: This paper provides an overview of the current state of the art in the area of NEN. It also identifies the main knowledge gaps in this area through an analysis of the state of the art.
- Presenting the proposed NEN method and its evaluation: To address these knowledge gaps, this paper proposes a new unsupervised NEN method. The details of the proposed NEN method are highlighted, and the evaluation of the NEN method and the experimental results are discussed. This paper, thus, contributes to the body of knowledge by providing a new NEN method for better normalizing named entities in natural language text.

3   Overview of the Proposed Big Bridge Data Analytics Framework

The proposed big bridge data analytics framework is depicted in Fig. 1. It includes three primary components: information and relation extraction, data linking and information fusion, and data analytics. An example case is provided in Fig. 2. This case details how

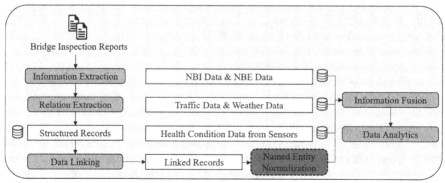

Big Bridge Data Analytics Framework

Fig. 1. Proposed big bridge data analytics framework.

the information about bridge conditions and maintenance actions buried in bridge inspection reports is extracted and represented in a semantically-rich structured way (i.e., into structured records), how the records referring to the same entity are linked, and how the named entities in the linked records are normalized and then fused. This case intends to provide the readers with a better understanding about the research problem (i.e., normalizing the named entities) at hand.

o **Sample sentences from 2009 South Park Bridge Inspection Report, Washington**

• East walls of north abutment have rotated outward, with map cracking (not new condition).
• Several old vertical cracks in abutment wall up to 1/8 " wide.
• Leaching at corner of north abutment and bottom of deck.
• South abutment settled downward and retaining walls of abutment rotated outward, allowing span between abutment and bent 2 to settle as well during earthquake.

o **Extracted information represented in a semantically-rich structured way**

• <ET>East walls of north abutment</ET>, <DY>rotated outward</DY>
• <ET>East wall of north abutment</ET>, <DY>map cracking</DY>
• <ET>abutment wall</ET>, <DY>vertical cracks</DY>, <QM>Several</QM>, <NM>1/8</NM>, <NU>"</NU>
• <ET>north abutment</ET>, <DC>Leaching</DC>
• <ET>bottom of deck</ET>, <DC> Leaching</DC>
• <ET>South abutment</ET>, <DY> settled downward</DY>
• <ET>retaining walls of abutment</ET>, <DY>rotated outward</DY>
• <ET>span</ET>, <DY>settle</DY>
ET = Bridge element, DY = Deficiency, DC = Deficiency cause, QM = Categorical quantity measure, NM = Numerical measure, NU = Numerical measure unit.

o **Linked records that refer to the same entity (partial)**

• <ET>East walls of north abutment</ET>, <DY>rotated outward</DY>
• <ET>retaining walls of abutment</ET>, <DY>rotated outward</DY>

o **Named entity normalization for the bridge element concepts**

• <ET>abutment wall</ET>, <DY>rotated outward</DY>

Fig. 2. An example case of the named entity normalization in the proposed big bridge data analytics framework.

3.1 Information and Relation Extraction

Information extraction aims to extract information about bridge conditions and maintenance actions from unstructured textual bridge inspection reports. In the proposed framework, the extraction is formulated as a named entity recognition (NER) task – identify the entity type of each term in the reports. The following entity types are defined and extracted: bridge element (ET), deficiency (DY), deficiency cause (DC), maintenance action (MA), maintenance material (MM), numerical measure (NM), numerical measure unit (NU), categorical quantity measure (QM), categorical severity measure (SM), date (DT), and other (OT). For the NER from the reports, an ontology-based semi-supervised conditional random fields (CRF) algorithm [14] was proposed and utilized in the framework.

Relation extraction aims to extract relations from the reports for linking the isolated terms into concepts (i.e., the named entities) and representing the semantically-low concepts in a semantically-rich structured way (i.e., representing the extracted information as structured records). In the proposed framework, relation extraction is formulated as a dependency parsing (DP) task. The DP aims to perform grammar analysis to extract dependency relations between "head" words and "modifier" words from a sentence. The extracted dependency relations are then used for the linking and representation. For the DP, a semantic neural network ensemble (NNE) algorithm [15] was proposed and utilized. For more details about the information and relation extraction, the readers are referred to [14, 15].

3.2   Data Linking and Information Fusion

Data linking aims to link the records that refer to the same entity. In this proposed framework, the linking of the records is formulated as a clustering task. It aims to cluster the records referring to the same entity into the same cluster. For the data linking, a hierarchical spectral clustering algorithm [16] was proposed and utilized.

Information fusion aims to resolve the ambiguities and the conflicts between the linked records as well as between the linked records and the other bridge data (as per Fig. 1). In this framework, resolving the conflicts in the bridge data from multiple sources is formulated as a fuzzy logic and reasoning task. The ambiguities mainly arise from the named entities in the linked records, because of the use of a number of different surface forms that a target named entity has. Thus, resolving the ambiguities is formulated as a named entity normalization (NEN) task. For more details about the data linking and fusion, the readers are referred to [16]. Figure 2 provides an example case that explains why NEN is needed in the framework. This paper focuses on presenting the background of NEN and the proposed NEN method.

3.3   Data Analytics

Data analytics aims to use machine learning methods to learn from the multi-type and multi-source bridge data for predicting future bridge deterioration and learning how to better maintain bridges. As seen in Fig. 1, these data get integrated – data from different sources are linked, and the ambiguities as well as the conflicts in the data are resolved by information fusion – before being used in the data analytics. Here, the bridge deterioration prediction is formulated as a multi-type and multi-attribute prediction task. "Multi-type" means that the prediction has the capability to predict the types of deficiencies at both the bridge and the element levels. For example, the following main deficiency types (defined based on [17]) will be predicted: corrosion, cracking, decay, delamination, efflorescence, scaling and spalling, scour, and settlement. "Multi-attribute" means that, in addition to the deficiency types, the other attributes of the deficiencies are also predicted. For example, the following main attributes (defined based on [17]) will be considered in the prediction: quantity, severity, onset timing, condition rating, and propagation in quantity and severity with time.

4   Background of Named Entity Normalization

4.1   State of the Art

Named entity normalization (NEN) aims to transform non-standard surface forms of the named entities that refer to the same target entity into their canonical form, i.e., an identifier concept [18, 19]. Many NEN methods, including dictionary-based and machine learning (ML)-based methods, have been proposed in recent years for the normalization [20]. Despite the existence of some ML-based methods, the majority of the methods in the domain of NEN are still dictionary-based [20].

Dictionary-based methods rely heavily on pre-established knowledge of how different named entities of the same identifier concept should be normalized. For example, [21] developed a hybrid approach that utilized both dictionary-based and rule-based methods for normalizing location names. The candidate identifier concepts of location names were generated from a location gazetteer list and the final identifiers were selected based on the rules that were developed based on the local contexts and the global graphs of the location names in text. [22] employed a domain-specific knowledge base, which includes synonyms, hypernyms, hyponyms, lexical variants and related concepts, for normalizing entities in an information retrieval setting. Similarly, [23] developed a dictionary-based NEN system for normalizing protein names, where the dictionary was built from five databases in the medical informatics domain. In addition to the aforementioned research efforts, extensive amounts of efforts have been undertaken towards developing domain-specific dictionaries for supporting NEN (e.g., [20, 24–26]). On the other hand, some studies also utilized the open-domain Wikipedia as a knowledge source. For example, for normalizing named entities in user-generated content, [27] developed an NEN system that employed within-document coreference resolution to link the entities referring to the same identifier concept and utilized the Wikipedia disambiguation page to generate an identifier for the linked entities. [19] normalized the entities extracted from Tweets by representing the linked entities using their corresponding Wikipedia entry. Also, [28] evaluated the impact of using a Wikipedia-based NEN method on information retrieval for question answering.

ML-based NEN methods use ML algorithms to learn how to normalize named entities from training examples. For example, [29] developed a support vector machines (SVM) classifier to learn from the lexical, orthographic, phonetic, and morphological features of named entities for NEN. [30] developed a CRF model to learn from edit operations of labeled data and from the features induced from unlabeled data by character-level neural text embeddings for named entity normalization. [31] utilized a CRF algorithm to perform character-level labeling to generate the variants of names for supporting the normalization. Other ML algorithms and models have also been used in this regard, such as random walks [32], unsupervised noisy-channel models [33], semi-Markov models [34], etc.

4.2   Knowledge Gaps

Despite the importance of the aforementioned efforts, two main knowledge gaps in the area of NEN are identified. First, existing NEN methods heavily rely on external knowledge sources and/or training data. In existing dictionary-based methods (e.g., [20–26]), domain-specific dictionaries or knowledge bases are generally required. However, it is very challenging to develop such domain-specific knowledge sources, especially given the dynamic nature of knowledge. For example, bridge inspection reports are continuously generated from different inspectors/writers, who have different writing styles and come from various bridge agencies. Hence, the named entities in the reports exhibit different levels of variations in their surface forms, and the variations keep evolving across time. It would be challenging, in terms of comprehensiveness and representativeness, to capture the knowledge of how to map these entities into identifier concepts. Although some methods (e.g., [19, 27, 28]) attempted to use Wikipedia as the knowledge source to reduce the effort of building dictionaries, they are insufficient in dealing with domain-specific text. For example, most of the names/concepts and their variations in bridge inspection reports are not listed on Wikipedia. On the other hand, in existing ML-based methods, training data are generally needed in order to develop NEN models (e.g., [29–31]). Similar to building dictionaries, developing a comprehensive yet representative training dataset is rather challenging. Despite that some unsupervised NEN methods have been proposed (e.g., [33]), they mostly still require prior knowledge about how to map named entities to identifier concepts from dictionaries or lexicons.

Second, and more importantly, existing NEN methods mostly ignore the impact of the normalization on data analytics. As presented in Sect. 3, the named entities in the linked records need to be normalized and then used in the subsequent data analytics for predicting bridge deterioration. Thus, the level of detail of the resulting normalized identifier concepts directly affects the performance of the data analytics. The following example scenario illustrates how different detail levels of the identifier concepts would affect the performance of the subsequent data analytics. If the normalized identifier concepts have a high detail level (i.e., for example, each set of the linked records has an identifier concept that is different from the others), the data analytics will suffer from the curse of dimensionality. This is because each identifier concept would act as a feature in the analytics, and the size of the feature space would become unnecessarily too large. Conversely, if the detail level is low (i.e., for example, most of the linked records have the same identifier concept), the analytics will not be able to sufficiently capture the distinctive patterns about different deterioration cases, which would lead to errors in the prediction. Therefore, balancing the abstractness and detailedness levels of the identifier concepts during the normalization is critical.

5   Proposed Unsupervised Named Entity Normalization Method

To address the aforementioned knowledge gaps, the authors propose a new unsupervised named entity normalization (NEN) method. The proposed NEN method consists of two main components: candidate identifier concept generation and candidate identifier concept ranking.

5.1 Candidate Identifier Concept Generation

Candidate identifier concept generation aims to enumerate all possible identifier concepts that the named entities in the linked records could have. In this paper, the authors formulate this task as an n-gram generation problem. For a set of linked named entities, the n-gram generation aims to generate all possible grams (e.g., unigrams, bigrams, trigrams, etc.) based on and for each of the named entities in the set. To better illustrate the n-gram generation, an example case is provided in Table 1.

Table 1. An example case of candidate identifier concept generation.

Linked named entity entities	Candidate identifier concepts (multi-grams)[a,b]
Deck	Deck (9)
Deck	Bridge (1)
Deck	Concrete (1)
Deck	Approach (2)
Deck	Span (2)
Bridge deck	Surfaces (2)
Concrete deck	Bridge deck (1)
Approach span deck surfaces	Concrete deck (1)
Approach span deck surfaces	Approach span (2)
–	Span deck (2)
–	Deck surfaces (2)
–	Approach span deck (2)
–	Span deck surfaces (2)
–	Approach span deck surfaces (2)

[a]The numbers in the parenthesis indicate the frequencies of the grams.
[b]The candidate identifier concepts were generated based on the original named entities. Unigrams, bigrams, trigrams, and four-grams of the named entities were used for generating the concepts.

This approach is adopted because of two main reasons. First, it allows for capturing different variations of the named entities at different abstraction (or detail) levels. For example, the following grams (partial) for the named entity "asphalt deck wearing surface" would be generated: "deck", "wearing surface", and "deck wearing surface". As seen, these grams have different levels of abstraction in describing this bridge element entity: at the highest level of abstraction, the entity would be normalized as "deck" (i.e., a wearing surface is a part of a deck system); and, at the lowest level of abstraction, the entity would be normalized as "asphalt deck wearing surface" (a much more descriptive gram than "deck", by also indicating the material and the sub-element of the deck). Second, the n-gram generation allows for preserving the sequence of the terms in a named entity, and thus generates meaningful grams. For example, when generating bigrams for the named entity "asphalt deck wearing surface", the concept "deck asphalt" that does not carry any real-word semantic meaning will not be generated. This helps assure that the resulting grams are technically and semantically meaningful and can be used as features in the data analytics.

5.2 Candidate Identifier Concept Ranking

Candidate identifier concept ranking aims to rank the generated grams of each named entity set. The top-ranking grams are then used as the final, normalized identifier concepts for representing their corresponding named entities in a set. To rank the grams, a new ranking function, as per Eq. (1), is proposed in this paper.

$$Ranking\ score = TF\text{-}IDF\ weight \times GL\ weight \times GP\ weight \times SW\ weight \qquad (1)$$

TF-IDF Weight. In Eq. (1), the TF-IDF weight is determined by term frequency (TF) and inverse document frequency (IDF). The TF, as defined in Eq. (2), captures the frequencies of the grams in each set of the linked entities, where $f_{g,d}$ denotes the frequency of a gram, g, in a "document", d. In this paper, each named entity set is considered as a "document". In ranking the candidate identifiers (grams), the TF favors those that have high frequency rates per each entity set. For example, only based on the TF, unigrams and bigrams would have a higher probability to be selected as the identifiers, because they are the constituent parts of the named entities and are thus more common and frequent in the dataset. The IDF, as defined in Eq. (3), captures the frequency rates of the grams across all the "documents" in the dataset (i.e., how many "documents" contain a specific gram), where N is the total number of "documents" in the dataset. In ranking the candidate identifiers, the IDF favors those that appear only in a few "documents". For example, only based on the IDF, the grams with longer lengths would have a higher probability to be selected as the identifiers. This is because such grams are less common in most of the "documents", and thus have a higher IDF score. As noted, the TF and IDF weights favor different types of grams – the former prefers shorter grams while the latter prefers longer ones. The TF-IDF weight, the multiplication of the TF and IDF weights, is thus applied to balance these two types of preferences. This helps balance the abstractness and the detailedness of the final identifier concepts (used as features in the data analytics), resulting in a feature space that is neither too dense nor too sparse for the analytics.

$$TF = 0.5 + 0.5 \times \frac{f_{g,d}}{max_{\{g' \in d\}} f_{g',d}} \qquad (2)$$

$$IDF = log \frac{N}{|\{d \in D : g \in d\}|} \qquad (3)$$

Gram Length Weight. In Eq. (1), the gram length (GL) weight is determined by the length of the current gram and the greatest gram length in a "document". The GL weight is defined in Eq. (4), where $|g|$ denotes the length of a gram. As seen, this weight gives a higher score to the grams with shorter lengths, which has a similar effect in the ranking as the TF weight. Here, the GL weight is further applied in the ranking because the effect of the IDF is much stronger than that of the TF, resulting in that the ranking prefers the identifier concepts with longer lengths (more detailed, less-frequent concepts). The stronger effect of the IDF is caused by two main reasons. First, the number of "documents" is much greater than the highest frequency of the grams. Second, as per Eq. (2), the TF scores are within the range of 0.5 to 1.0; while, the IDF scores are generally much greater than the TF scores. As a result, although TF is used, less-frequent grams are always selected because of their IDF weights. Therefore, the GL weight is proposed to further balance the two types of preferences.

$$GL = 1.0 - \frac{|g|}{max_{\{g' \in d\}} |g'|} \quad (4)$$

Gram Position Weight. In Eq. (1), the gram position (GP) weight is determined by the position of the current unigram in the longest gram in a "document". This weight is defined in Eq. (5), where $I(g)$ denotes the ordinal number of the gram in the longest gram. It is used to ensure that, in the case of selecting a unigram as an identifier, the selected unigram is meaningful. As seen in Eq. (5), this weight gives a higher score to the unigrams that are placed at the ending position(s) of the longest grams. This is because such unigrams carry more meanings than those at the beginning positions. For example, the following unigrams are generated from the named entity "asphalt overlay": "asphalt" and "overlay". Compared to the former one, the unigram "overlay" carries more meaning towards representing its original named entity.

$$GP = 1.0 + \frac{I(g)}{max_{\{g' \in d\}} |g'|} \quad (5)$$

Stop-Word Weight. In Eq. (1), the stop-word (SW) weight is determined by a pre-defined stop-word list. This weight is defined in Eq. (6), where a gram is associated with a stop-word weight of 0.0 if it is in the stop-word list; otherwise, it is associated with a weight of 1.0. The initial stop-word list was developed by enumerating the grams whose TF-IDF weights are smaller than 2.0. Here, the TF scores were calculated by using the frequencies of the grams in the entire collection of the "documents". Then, the meaningful grams in the original stop-word list that are important to consider when normalizing the named entities were removed based on engineering judgement. The developed stop-word list is shown in Table 2.

Table 2. Developed stop-word list.

Grams in the stop-word list[a]			
Lower	South	*(Bar)*	*(Paint System)*
(Bolt)	Top	*(Lacing bar)*	*(Overlay)*
North	Surface	South approach	Member
Concrete	*(Web)*	*(Connection)*	*(Lower chord)*
Paint	East	*(Joint)*	*(Bent)*
Timber	North abutment	System	–
Steel	*(Lacing)*	End	–

[a]The grams in parenthesis with italic font were removed from the original list based on engineering judgement. The resulting list contains words that are less informative (i.e., adjectives) and contribute less (if any) to generating gold standard identifier concepts (e.g., "deck" is preferred over "south deck" as an identifier concept).

$$SW = \begin{cases} 1.0, & \textit{gram not in the stopword list}; \\ 0.0, & \textit{otherwise}. \end{cases} \quad (6)$$

6 Experimental Setup

A set of experiments were conducted to evaluate the performances of the proposed NEN method and its variations. The experimental setup for these experiments included three main steps: dataset creation and human annotation, NEN method implementation, and NEN method evaluation.

6.1 Dataset Creation and Human Annotation

Dataset creation aimed to create a representative set of named entities for evaluating the performance of the proposed NEN method. In creating the dataset, five bridge inspection reports were selected and collected. The information about these reports is summarized in Table 3. These reports are considered representative, because they are from different reporting years and are form different state Departments of Transportation in the U.S. The information about bridge conditions and maintenance actions were extracted and represented in a semantically-rich structured way – representing the unstructured information as a set of structured data records. The records that refer to the same entity were linked together. The extraction, representation, and linking were implemented by following the methods presented in Sect. 3. Finally, all the named entities about bridge element were included in the dataset.

Table 3. Information about the bridge inspection reports in the created dataset.

Report no.	State	Reporting year
1	Virginia	2016
2	New Mexico	2007
3	New Mexico	2008
4	Montana	2011
5	Washington	2009

Human annotation aimed to manually assign each set of the linked named entities with an identifier concept by human annotators. The dataset was annotated by the first author and two other researchers [with expertise in civil engineering, natural language processing (NLP), and ML]. During the annotation, two main annotation rules were followed. First, the manually-assigned concepts should be neither too detailed nor too abstract. Second, the annotation should be an iterative process – the gold standard identifier concepts are iteratively refined by balancing their abstractness and detailedness levels across the entire dataset. This process terminated until no more refinement can be done by the annotator. As a result, three initial sets of annotations were generated. For example, for the first named entity set (as per Table 4), each of the annotators annotated the concept as "deck", "deck", "concrete surface", respectively. Such discrepancies across the annotation sets were discussed until mutual agreement was achieved, resulting in a final set of agreed-on annotations (e.g., "deck" for the aforementioned example) that formed the gold standard.

Table 4. Examples of the linked named entities in the dataset.

Named entity set 1	Named entity set 2
Deck	Walls
Deck	Abutment wall
Deck	East walls of north abutment
Deck	East walls of north abutment
Deck	Retaining walls of abutment
Bridge deck	West wall of north abutment
Concrete deck	–
Approach span deck surfaces	–
Approach span deck surfaces	–

6.2 NEN Method Implementation

The implementation of the proposed NEN method included three main steps. First, all the named entities in the dataset were stemmed. Stemming aimed to analyze how terms of the entities are formed based on morphological derivation and inflection, and to map them into their root forms. Stemming was conducted because it captures the variations in the term/entity surface forms, and thus supports better analysis of the TF and IDF of the candidate identifier concepts (grams) in the dataset. For example, the unigrams "cracks" and "cracking" were stemmed into the same root "crack", which helped better count their frequencies. The stemming was conducted using the natural language toolkit (NLTK) Porter stemmer [35]. Second, the candidate identifier concepts were generated based on and for each set of the linked named entities. The candidate identifier concept generation was implemented using the NLTK n-gram module [35]. Third, for each set of the multi-grams, the grams were ranked based on Eq. (1). The ranking was implemented by the authors in the Python programming language environment [36].

6.3 NEN Method Evaluation

The evaluation aimed to benchmark the performance of the proposed NEN method using an evaluation metric. Two main steps were conducted. First, the algorithm-generated identifier concepts were compared with the gold standard concepts. Second, the performance of the proposed NEN method was reported using an evaluation metric. In this study, accuracy was selected as the metric. As defined in Eq. (7), accuracy is the percentage of the number of correctly-generated concepts out of the total number of the generated concepts.

$$Accuracy = \frac{Number\ of\ correctly\ generated\ concepts}{Total\ number\ of\ generated\ concepts} \tag{7}$$

7 Preliminary Experimental Results and Analysis

Three main groups of experiments were conducted. The experiments were conducted using the TF, the IDF, and the TF-IDF as the base weights for each group, respectively. The methods that only used these base weights served as the baseline methods. Each group also contained the experiments using different combinations of the base weight and the other weights (as per Sect. 5.2). The performances of these experiments are presented in Fig. 3. To facilitate the analysis of the experimental results, example cases of using these weights for the normalization are provided in Tables 4 and 5.

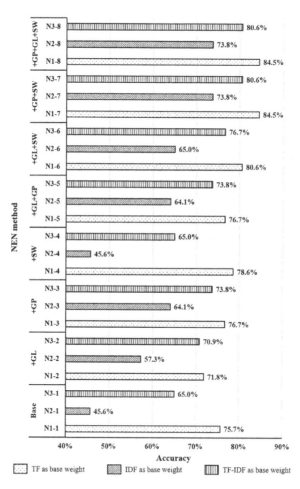

Fig. 3. The performances of the proposed unsupervised named entity normalization (NEN) method and its variations. The indices of these methods follow those defined in Table 5.

Table 5. Identifier concepts generated by the proposed NEN method and its variations.

No.	NEN methods	Identifier concepts	
		Named entity set 1	Named entity set 2
N1-1	TF	Deck	Wall
N1-2	TF + GL	Deck	Wall
N1-3	TF + GP	Deck	Abutment
N1-4	TF + SW	Deck	Wall
N1-5	TF + GL +GP	Deck	Abutment
N1-6	TF + GL + SW	Deck	Wall
N1-7	TF + GP + SW	Deck	Abutment
N1-8	TF + GL + GP + SW	Deck	Abutment
N2-1	IDF	Span deck	North abutment wall
N2-2	IDF + GL	Bridge	Retaining
N2-3	IDF + GP	Surface	Of
N2-4	IDF + SW	Span deck	North abutment wall
N2-5	IDF + GL +GP	Surface	Of
N2-6	IDF + GL + SW	Bridge	Retaining
N2-7	IDF + GP + SW	Span	Of
N2-8	IDF + GL + GP + SW	Span	Of
N3-1	TF-IDF	Span deck	Wall of
N3-2	TF-IDF + GL	Deck	Of
N3-3	TF-IDF + GP	Deck	Of
N3-4	TF-IDF + SW	Span deck	Wall of
N3-5	TF-IDF + GL +GP	Deck	Of
N3-6	TF-IDF + GL + SW	Deck	Of
N3-7	TF-IDF + GP + SW	Deck	Of
N3-8	TF-IDF + GL + GP + SW	Deck	Of
–	Annotation	Deck	Abutment wall

7.1 Effect of the TF-IDF Weight

The experimental results of the NEN methods that only used the TF, IDF, and TF-IDF weighs are shown in Fig. 3 (N1-1, N2-1, and N3-1 in Fig. 3). These methods achieved an accuracy of 75.7%, 45.6%, and 65.0%, respectively. Two main observations are drawn from the results and the examples. First, the TF weight prefers the identifier concepts that are more abstract, whereas the IDF weight prefers those that are more detailed. For example, using the TF weight, the following two concepts were generated for the named entities in sets 1 and 2 (as per Table 4), respectively: "Deck" and "Wall". Using the IDF weight, these concepts were generated as "Span deck" and "North abutment wall". This further supports the analysis in Sect. 5.2 that these two types of weights have opposite effects in normalizing the entities. Second, combining the TF and IDF weights seems – conceptually – to be a better solution to the NEN than using any of the weights alone (because the TF-IDF balances the opposite preferences of the TF and IDF in terms of the abstractness and the detailedness); but, the experimental results indicate that the TF-IDF did not further improve the NEN performance. As noted, compared to the TF weight, when the TF-IDF weight was used, the accuracy dropped by around 10.7%. This might be attributed to the fact that the IDF weight is dominating in the TF-IDF weight, and the performance of the TF-IDF weight was thus much affected by that of the IDF. The examples in Table 5 provide further evidence to this observation. As seen, the identifier concepts generated by the IDF and TF-IDF weights are quite similar.

7.2   Effect of the Gram Length and Position Weights

The experimental results of the NEN methods that used the gram length and position weights are shown in Fig. 3 (N1-5, N2-5, and N3-5 in Fig. 3). These methods achieved an accuracy of 76.7%, 64.1%, and 73.8%, respectively. Three main observation are drawn from the experimental results and the examples. First, the gram length and position weights were able to improve the accuracy performance. Compared to the methods that did not use these weights (N1-1, N2-1, and N3-1), the accuracy was improved by around 1.0%, 18.5%, and 8.8%, respectively, when the gram length and position weights were used.

Second, the gram length and position weights show larger positive impacts on the IDF and TF-IDF weights than on the TF weight. This is because, as presented in Sect. 5.2, the gram length and position weights are used in order to select more abstract identifier concepts that are at the ending positions of the longest named entities, over those that are more detailed and at the beginning positions. As seen in the examples in Table 5, the TF weights already considered such preference to some extent, whereas the other weights did not. For example, without the gram length and position weights, the identifier concepts generated by the TF, IDF, and TF-IDF are "Deck", "Span deck", and "Span deck", respectively. When these weights were included, these concepts changed to "Deck", "Surface", and "Deck", respectively. As seen, including these weights did not change the identifier concepts generated by the TF weight. However, it changed those generated by the IDF and TF-IDF weights.

Third, at the presence of the gram position weight, the gram length weight showed a minimum (if any) impact on the normalization. For example, when the TF-IDF weight was used as the base weight (N3-1), by incorporating the length, the position, and the combination of the length and position weights (N3-2, N3-3, and N3-5), the accuracy was improved by 5.9%, 8.8%, and 8.8%, respectively. The gram position weight achieved the same accuracy improvement rate as the combination. This observation also holds in the case where the TF and IDF weights were used as the bases. This might be attributed to that the position weight already gives higher weights to the abstract concepts.

7.3   Effect of the Stop-Word Weight

The experimental results of the NEN methods that used the stop-word weight (list) are shown in Fig. 3. These results indicate that the use of stop-word weight is effective in normalizing the named entities. For example, compared to the methods that included the gram length weight into the base methods (N1-2, N2-2, and N3-2 in Fig. 3), further including the stop-word weight (N1-6, N2-6, and N3-6) improved the accuracy by 8.8%, 7.7%, and 5.8%. Similarly, compared to the methods that included the gram position weight into the base methods (N1-3, N2-3, and N3-3), using the stop-word weight (N1-7, N2-7, and N3-7) improved the accuracy by 7.8%, 9.7%, and 6.8%, respectively. This indicates the effectiveness of using a stop-word list for improving the NEN performance.

7.4 Error Analysis and Overall Performance

An error analysis was conducted. Accordingly, two main sources of error were identified. First, although the TF-IDF (and it constituent parts) was effective in supporting the normalization, some normalization errors were generated because of its use. For example, for the named entities in set 2 (as per Tables 4 and 5), the gold standard identifier concept is "abutment wall". However, the proposed NEN method and its variations all failed to generate a correct concept for this set. For instance, even when the NEN method that achieved the highest accuracy (i.e., TF + GP + SW) was used, an incorrect identifier concept "abutment" was still generated. This is mainly due to the fact that TF-IDF and its constituent parts are not always able to adequately capture the distribution characteristics of the grams in the dataset, and thus sometimes fail to balance the abstractness and detailedness of the identifier concepts – resulting in some errors in the normalization. Second, the way of generating multi-grams sometimes limited the method in achieving further improved performance. In this paper, the grams were generated by strictly following the term orders in their original named entities. In some cases, the gold standard identifier concepts are not even in the generated grams, hence resulted in errors. For example, the gold standard concepts for these two named entities "east nose of pier" and "east nose of pier" is "pier nose". Based on the conditions on how the grams were generated, the "pier nose" was not even in the gram list, which makes the method fail to conduct correct normalization.

Overall, when the TF, gram position, and stop-word weights were used, the proposed NEN method achieved the highest accuracy of 84.5%. This shows the promise of the proposed NEN method in supporting the normalization.

8 Conclusions and Future Work

In this paper, the authors proposed an unsupervised named entity normalization (NEN) method for normalizing the named entities extracted from bridge inspection reports. The NEN is an important component in the authors' big bridge data analytics framework towards using and learning form big bridge data for better predicting bridge deterioration for enhancing cost-effective bridge maintenance decision making. In this framework, the information about bridge conditions and maintenance actions is extracted from unstructured bridge inspection reports and is represented in a semantically-rich structured way, and then the structured records that refer to the same entity are linked and the conflicts in the linked records are fused.

Normalizing the named entities in the linked records, who have different and ambiguous surface forms, into the same identifier concept is one of the most important tasks of the fusion. To this end, an unsupervised NEN method was proposed. This paper focused on presenting the proposed NEN method and its evaluation. The NEN method includes two primary components: candidate identifier concept generation and candidate identifier concept ranking. At the backbone of the NEN method is a proposed ranking function. The function relies on TF-IDF, gram length, gram position, and stop-word weights for the ranking of candidate identifier concepts. A set of experiments were conducted to evaluate the performance of the proposed NEN method. Overall, it achieved an accuracy of 84.5%. Three main conclusions were also drawn from the experimental results. First, the TF weight alone (without using the IDF weight) served as a better base weight in the ranking. Second, the gram length and position weights were effective in improving the NEN performance. However, at the presence of the position weight, the gram length weight did not further improve the performance. Third, the use of the stop-word list was effective in the normalization. Also, one main limitation of this paper is acknowledged. The performance of the proposed NEN method was evaluated using a relatively small dataset. As a part of their ongoing research efforts, the authors are working towards developing a larger collection of bridge inspection reports for better evaluating the performance of the proposed NEN method. A similar performance level is expected in the evaluation.

In their future work, the authors also plan to further improve the performance of the proposed NEN method. Two main directions will be explored. First, for the candidate identifier concept generation, the authors plan to also include skip and reversed grams into the generated multi-grams. This would potentially address the errors introduced by only considering consecutive terms as grams. Second, for the candidate identifier concept ranking, the authors plan to test more advanced ranking methods and models, such as the Okapi Best Matching (BM25) model. A new ranking method will be developed, based on the testing results, to better balance the abstractness and the detailedness of the generated concepts for better supporting the subsequent bridge data analytics. These future research efforts would provide opportunities for further improvements.

At the policy level, one direction would be to work with bridge agencies, industry, and academia to streamline the data collection process in the bridge domain, where data could be pre-processed and normalized at the collection time. This would help establish more efficient and effective data management practices in the domain, which would result in high quality data for better data analytics performance for supporting enhanced decision making.

Acknowledgements. This material is based upon work supported by the Strategic Research Initiatives (SRI) Program by the College of Engineering at the University of Illinois at Urbana-Champaign.

References

1. McLinn, J.: Major bridge collapses in the US, and around the world. IEEE Trans. Reliab. **59**(3), 449–482 (2010)
2. Pearson-Kirk, D.: The benefits of bridge condition monitoring. In: Proceedings of the Institution of Civil Engineers – Bridge Engineers, vol. 161, no. 3, pp. 151–185 (2008)
3. Commonwealth Bureau of Roads: The condition of bridges on interstate highways. Commonwealth Bureau of Roads, Canberra (1986)
4. Organisation for Economic Cooperation and Development: The durability of concrete road bridges. Road Transport Research Program, Organisation for Economic Cooperation and Development, Paris (1988)
5. American Society of Civil Engineers: Report card for America's infrastructure. https://www.infrastructurereportcard.org/cat-item/bridges. Accessed 09 Jul 2017
6. National Transportation Safety Board: Highway accident report interstate 35W over the Mississippi River Minneapolis, Minnesota. National Transportation Safety Board, Washington, D.C. (2008)
7. Morcous, G., Lounis, Z., Cho, Y.: An integrated system for bridge management using probabilistic and mechanistic deterioration models: application to bridge decks. KSCE J. Civil Eng. **14**(4), 527–537 (2010)
8. Huang, Y.: Artificial neural network model of bridge deterioration. J. Perform. Constr. Facil. **24**(6), 597–602 (2010)
9. Liu, H., Madanat, S.: Adaptive optimisation methods in system-level bridge management. Struct. Infrastruct. Eng. **11**(7), 884–896 (2015)
10. Saeed, T.U., Moomen, M., Ahmed, A., Murillo-Hoyos, J., Volovski, M., Labi, S.: Performance evaluation and life prediction of highway concrete bridge superstructure across design types. J. Perform. Constr. Facil. **31**(5) (2017)
11. Liu, K., El-Gohary, N.: Semantic modeling of bridge deterioration knowledge for supporting big bridge data analytics. In: Proceedings of the 2016 ASCE Construction Research Congress, pp. 930–939. American Society of Civil Engineers, Reston (2016)
12. Liu, K., El-Gohary, N.: Similarity-based dependency parsing for extracting dependency relations from bridge inspection reports. In: Proceedings of the 2017 ASCE International Workshop on Computing in Civil Engineering, pp. 316–323. American Society of Civil Engineers, Reston (2017)
13. Liu, K., El-Gohary, N.: Feature discretization and selection methods for supporting bridge deterioration prediction. In: Proceedings of the 2018 ASCE Construction Research Congress. American Society of Civil Engineers, Reston (2018, in press)
14. Liu, K., El-Gohary, N.: Ontology-based semi-supervised conditional random fields for automated information extraction from bridge inspection reports. Autom. Constr. **81**, 313–323 (2017)
15. Liu, K., El-Gohary, N.: Semantic neural network ensemble for automated dependency relation extraction from bridge inspection reports. Automation in Construction (2017, Submitted)
16. Liu, K., El-Gohary, N.: Hierarchical spectral clustering for unsupervised linking of data extracted from bridge inspection reports. Advanced Engineering Informatics (2017, Submitted)
17. Federal Highway Administration: Developing advanced methods of assessing bridge performance. http://www.fhwa.dot.gov/publications/publicroads/09novdec/04.cfm. Accessed 13 Mar 2018

18. Popov, A.M., Adaskina Y.V., Andreyeva, D.A., Charabet, J.K., Moskvina, A.D., Protopopova, E.V., Yushina, T.A.: Named entity normalization for fact extraction task. In: Proceedings of the International Conference "Dialogue 2016". Computational Linguistics and Intellectual Technologies, Moscow, Russia (2016)
19. Liu, X., Zhou, M., Wei, F., Fu, Z., Zhou, X.: Joint inference of named entity recognition and normalization for tweets. In: Proceedings of the 50th Annual Meeting of the Association for Computational Linguistics: Long Papers, pp. 526–535. Association for Computational Linguistics, Stroudsburg (2002)
20. Cho, H., Choi, W., Lee, H.: A method for named entity normalization in biomedical articles: application to diseases and plants. BMC Bioinform. 18(1) (2017)
21. Li, H., Srihari, R.K., Niu, C., Li, W.: Location normalization for information extraction. In: Proceedings of the 19th International Conference on Computational Linguistics, pp. 1–7. Association for Computational Linguistics, Stroudsburg (2002)
22. Zhou, W., Yu, C., Smalheiser, N., Torvik, V., Hong, J.: Knowledge-intensive conceptual retrieval and passage extraction of biomedical literature. In: Proceedings of the 30th Annual International ACM SIGIR Conference on Research and Development in Information Retrieval, pp. 655–662. Association for Computing Machinery, New York (2007)
23. Cohen, A.M.: Unsupervised gene/protein named entity normalization using automatically extracted dictionaries. In: Proceedings of the ACL-ISMB Workshop on Linking Biological Literature, Ontologies and Databases: Mining Biological Semantics, pp. 17–24. Association for Computational Linguistics, Stroudsburg (2005)
24. Hanisch, D., Fundel, K., Mevissen, H.T., Zimmer, R., Fluck, J.: ProMiner: rule-based protein and gene entity recognition. BMC Bioinform. 6(1) (2005)
25. Wei, C.H., Kao, H.Y.: Cross-species gene normalization by species inference. BMC Bioinform. 12(8) (2011)
26. Campos, D., Matos, S., Oliveira, J.L.: A modular framework for biomedical concept recognition. BMC Bioinform. 14(1) (2013)
27. Jijkoun, V., Khalid, M.A., Marx, M., Rijke, M.D.: Named entity normalization in user generated content. In: Proceedings of the 2nd Workshop on Analytics for Noisy Unstructured Text Data, pp. 23–30. Association for Computing Machinery, New York (2008)
28. Khalid, M.A., Jijkoun, V., de Rijke, M.: The impact of named entity normalization on information retrieval for question answering. In: Macdonald, C., Ounis, I., Plachouras, V., Ruthven, I., White, R.W. (eds.) ECIR 2008. LNCS, vol. 4956, pp. 705–710. Springer, Heidelberg (2008). https://doi.org/10.1007/978-3-540-78646-7_83
29. Magdy, W., Darwish, K., Emam, O., Hassan, H.: Arabic cross-document person name normalization. In: Proceedings of the 2007 Workshop on Computational Approaches to Semitic Languages: Common Issues and Resources, pp. 25–32. Association for Computational Linguistics, Stroudsburg (2007)
30. Chrupala, G.: Normalizing tweets with edit scripts and recurrent neural embeddings. In: Proceedings of the 52nd Annual Meeting of the Association for Computational Linguistics, pp. 680–686. Association for Computational Linguistics, Stroudsburg (2014)
31. Liu, F., Weng, F., Jiang, X.: A broad-coverage normalization system for social media language. In: Proceedings of the 50th Annual Meeting of the Association for Computational Linguistics: Long Papers, pp. 1035–1044. Association for Computational Linguistics, Stroudsburg (2012)
32. Hassan, H., Menezes, A.: Social text normalization using contextual graph random walks. In: Proceedings of the 51st Annual Meeting of the Association for Computational Linguistics, pp. 1577–1586. Association for Computational Linguistics, Stroudsburg (2013)

33. Cook, P., Stevenson, S.: An unsupervised model for text message normalization. In: Proceedings of the Workshop on Computational Approaches to Linguistic Creativity, pp. 71–78. Association for Computational Linguistics, Stroudsburg (2009)
34. Leaman, R., Lu, Z.: TaggerOne: joint named entity recognition and normalization with semi-Markov models. Bioinformatics **32**(18), 2839–2846 (2016)
35. Bird, S., Loper, E., Klein, E.: Natural language toolkit. http://www.nltk.org/. Accessed 06 June 2017
36. Python Core Team: Python: A dynamic, open source programming language. http://www.python.org/. Accessed 06 June 2017

Semantic Description of Structural Health Monitoring Algorithms Using Building Information Modeling

Michael Theiler[✉], Kosmas Dragos, and Kay Smarsly

Bauhaus University Weimar, Coudraystr. 7, 99423 Weimar, Germany
michael.theiler@uni-weimar.de

Abstract. Information exchange among project stakeholders as part of structural life-cycle management has been gaining increasing interest in civil engineering. An integral part of structural life-cycle management is the operation and maintenance phase of structures, which is frequently associated with structural health monitoring (SHM). SHM has emerged as a novel methodology enabling the assessment of structural conditions by extracting information from structural response data and environmental data collected by sensors attached to structures. Representing a paradigm for exchanging information among stakeholders for structural life-cycle management, conventional building information, such as geometry, material and cost, is structured in so-called "building information models". These models are defined within building information modeling (BIM) standards, such as the Industry Foundation Classes (IFC). Furthermore, in recent research efforts, IFC-compliant descriptions of "monitoring-related information", i.e. information on SHM systems, have been reported. However, semantic descriptions of algorithms employed for SHM ("SHM-related algorithms") have not yet received adequate research attention. This paper introduces a semantic description approach for modeling and integrating SHM-related algorithms into IFC-based building information models. Specifically, this study focuses on algorithms embedded into wireless sensor nodes for automatically processing SHM data on board. The semantic description approach is validated by describing a wireless SHM system installed on a laboratory test structure designed and implemented with an embedded algorithm (fast Fourier transform). The expected outcome of this study is essentially an extension to the current IFC schema enabling the description of SHM-related algorithms in conjunction with SHM systems and structures to be monitored.

Keywords: Structural health monitoring · Building information modeling
Monitoring-related information · Semantic modeling · Metamodeling
Description of algorithms

1 Introduction

In recent years, building information modeling (BIM) has emerged as a promising paradigm in the architecture, engineering and construction industry for describing

© Springer International Publishing AG, part of Springer Nature 2018
I. F. C. Smith and B. Domer (Eds.): EG-ICE 2018, LNCS 10864, pp. 150–170, 2018.
https://doi.org/10.1007/978-3-319-91638-5_8

conventional information about structural life-cycle management [1]. Building information models are created for geometrically and semantically representing structures while offering full access and editability options to structure-related information throughout the structural life-cycle, which includes the planning phase, the construction phase, the operation and maintenance phase, and the demolition phase. BIM comprises tools, processes, and technologies for documentation purposes, and it typically builds on 3D geometrical models of structures supplemented by semantic information related to structural components [2]. BIM can advantageously be used to support all life-cycle phases. In the planning phase, structures can be optimized, e.g. with respect to design, cost, or durability, by combining BIM-based planning tools with analysis tools [3]. Furthermore, with BIM, discrepancies between plans and the structure being built can be semi-automatically documented in the construction phase [4], service intervals can be improved in the operation and maintenance phase [5], and in the demolition phase, the amount of waste produced during the demolition of structures can be estimated [6].

Due to ageing infrastructure, structural health monitoring (SHM) has been gaining an increasingly important role in the operation and maintenance phase of structural life-cycle management. SHM enables monitoring and assessing structural conditions, thus optimizing structural maintenance and enhancing structural safety [7]. In the past decades, SHM has been the topic of extensive research and has been successfully applied to large-scale engineering structures, such as bridges, wind turbines, and tunnels [8–11]. Furthermore, advances in informatics have introduced new techniques, such as artificial intelligence [12], autonomous software [13], biologically-inspired approaches [14], and agent-oriented concepts [15], which have substantially improved the performance and the applicability of SHM systems. Traditional SHM systems are composed of cable-connected components; however, in recent years, wireless SHM systems have been increasingly adopted in SHM offering several benefits compared to cable-based SHM systems, such as reduced installation time, lower costs, and higher flexibility. Since SHM is an integral part of the operation and maintenance phase in SHM-equipped structures, it is beneficial to enable semantic descriptions of SHM systems using BIM.

Drawing from the requirement for interoperability between building information models, SHM systems need to be semantically described in a holistic manner. Broadly speaking, the information related to SHM systems can be categorized into "sensor-related information" and into "monitoring-related information". For sensor-related information, several standards, modeling languages and ontologies have been developed, such as the Sensor Model Language (SensorML), the Semantic Sensor Network (SSN) Ontology, the Systems Modeling Language (SysML), and the Web Ontology Language (OWL) [16–19]. Furthermore, the IEEE 1451 standards family provides modeling capabilities for connecting sensors to microprocessors, instrumentation systems, and control/field networks [20]. Contrary to sensor-related information, the description of monitoring-related information is still an open research issue. Monitoring-related information encompasses information related to the SHM strategy, such as information about the semantic composition of SHM systems, about algorithms employed for data processing (SHM-related algorithms), or about the dynamics of SHM systems [21]. An accurate semantic description approach for monitoring-related information would facilitate tracking changes in SHM systems and substituting components of SHM systems. To this end, SHM system components to be described must be put into the context of the structures to be monitored, which has not yet received adequate attention and, thus, cannot be fully achieved with current BIM capabilities [22, 23].

In recent research efforts, monitoring-related information has been described using the Industry Foundation Classes (IFC), an open standard for the description of BIM-based models [24]. In particular, an extension of the IFC schema, referred to as "IFC Monitor" [25], has been proposed to describe SHM systems with structural systems to be monitored. As has been shown, the IFC Monitor extension facilitates the description of monitoring-related information, such as information about (i) semantic compositions of SHM systems, (ii) network topologies, and (iii) semantic relationships between components of SHM systems and components of structural systems to be monitored. In this study, the IFC Monitor extension is used as a basis, first, to generally describe SHM systems and, then, to represent SHM-related algorithms. Focusing on algorithms embedded into wireless sensor nodes for automatically executing SHM data analyses, this study advances BIM-based, IFC-compliant descriptions of SHM-related algorithms facilitating life-cycle documentations of SHM systems.

The paper is organized as follows. First, background information on semantically describing algorithms is provided, followed by a concise presentation of modeling capabilities of the current IFC schema. Next, based on the background information, a semantic description approach (semantic model) is developed serving as a technology-independent metamodel to describe SHM-related algorithms. Then, the IFC schema is extended to enable BIM-based descriptions of SHM-related algorithms in compliance with IFC modeling capabilities. Finally, to validate the semantic description approach, a wireless SHM system installed on a laboratory test structure with an embedded fast Fourier transform algorithm is described using the extended IFC schema.

2   Modeling of SHM-Related Algorithms

Strategies towards SHM usually involve collecting structural response data and environmental data, which are processed through algorithms to extract information on structural conditions. In this section, the existing capabilities for describing SHM-related algorithms are concisely presented. First, the semantic description of algorithms in general is explained, followed by a concise presentation of SHM-related algorithms commonly used for structural health monitoring. Then, the capabilities of the current IFC schema for describing SHM-related algorithms are illuminated.

2.1   Semantic Description of Algorithms

According to the ISO 9000 family of quality management systems standards [26], a "procedure" is referred to as a structured means to conduct activities or processes, including step-by-step descriptions of actions towards addressing problems. Algorithms consist of a sequence of components, which are executed for solving problems. As opposed to procedures, algorithms must terminate once a finite number of steps are executed, even if no solution to a problem can be found or if objectives of the problem have not been met [27]. Consequently, algorithms are often referred to as "effective procedures".

To ensure proper execution of algorithms, defining the chronological succession of components is essential. In Unified Modeling Language (UML) activity diagrams activity diagrams, the chronological succession of components is illustrated by arrows, referred to as control flow, which is strictly sequential and therefore linear. The simplest component of algorithms corresponds to a single command and is termed "statement". In addition to statements, Böhm and Jacopini [38] have stated essential to solve every problem with three elementary control structures: (i) "sequences", (ii) "selections", and (iii) "iterations". Each control structure has one input and one output, according to which the control flow executes the next algorithm component. A sequence is a block of algorithm components executed in a predefined order. A selection is often referred to as a conditional branch, the execution of which depends on meeting a predefined condition. An iteration contains an algorithm component that is executed repeatedly as long as a predefined condition is met. Exemplary illustrations of sequences, selections, and iterations are shown in Fig. 1.

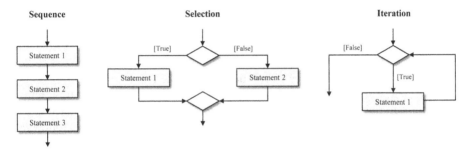

Fig. 1. Control flow of elementary control structures.

2.2   SHM-Related Algorithms

The main goal of SHM is to assess structural conditions using information derived from data collected by sensors that are attached to structures. To derive information from sensor data, different algorithms, depending on the specific objective of a SHM project, are applied. SHM-related algorithms can be categorized in groups based on common characteristics, such as the domain of applicability or the type analysis applied to the sensor data. For example, algorithms executed using sensor data in the form of time series are called time-domain algorithms, while algorithms using sensor data decomposed in terms of sinusoidal harmonic functions are termed frequency-domain algorithms. Furthermore, depending on whether physical principles of the structural behavior are considered or not, SHM-related algorithms are distinguished into physics-based algorithms and into data-driven algorithms, respectively. Given the diversity of SHM-related algorithms and the influence of the algorithm outcomes in decision making as part of the operation and maintenance phase of structural life-cycle management, the importance of efficient holistic semantic descriptions of SHM systems including monitoring-related information, and, by extension, SHM-related algorithms, comes to the forefront. In the next subsection, a concise description of current semantic description approaches for SHM systems is attempted, highlighting the shortcomings with respect to the description of SHM-related algorithms.

Table 1. Summary of commonly used SHM-related algorithms.

Algorithm	Domain	Analysis type
Fast Fourier transform	Frequency	Data-driven
Peak picking	Frequency	Data-driven
Frequency domain decomposition	Modal	Data-driven
Auto-regressive modeling	Time	Data-driven
Random decrement	Time	Data-driven
Stochastic subspace identification	Modal	Data-driven
Ibrahim time domain	Time	Data-driven
Artificial neural networks	Time/frequency	Data-driven
Direct integration	Time/frequency	Physics-based
Dynamic substructuring	Time	Physics-based

2.3 Existing Approaches for Semantic Description of SHM Systems

The following discussion focuses on approaches available for semantically describing SHM systems. Several modeling languages, models and ontologies have been introduced for describing sensor-related information. For describing SHM-related algorithms, emphasis in this study is placed on semantic description approaches following the BIM paradigm, as BIM-based standards are widely used in the architecture, engineering and construction industry and may provide a formal basis for documenting and exchanging SHM-related algorithms.

Non-BIM-Based Approaches. For semantically describing SHM systems, several sensor modeling languages and semantic models have been adopted, such as the Sensor Model Language (SensorML), the Semantic Sensor Network (SSN) Ontology, the Systems Modeling Language (SysML), and the Web Ontology Language (OWL). *SensorML*, which according to [28] is a useful standard for interpreting and pre-processing sensor data, offers possibilities for sensor representations via information models as well as XML encodings for describing sensors and processes related to sensor measurements [16]. The *SSN Ontology* integrates sensor technologies and semantic Web technologies towards describing sensors and sensor networks, and it supports the description of sensor-related information in terms of capabilities, measurement processes, observations, and deployments [17]. With respect to describing sensors, the SSN Ontology enables describing measuring options, measuring properties (e.g. accuracy, resolution), sensing processes, observations as well as deployment information of sensors. *SysML*, a standardized general-purpose modeling language proposed by the Object Management Group, provides tools to describe systems engineering applications, including sensor-based information [18]. The *Web Ontology Language* offers an explicit concept for the structure of processes enabling the description of control structures, such as sequences, selections, and iterations [29].

BIM-Based Approaches. With respect to BIM-based semantic descriptions of SHM systems, it has been demonstrated by Theiler and Smarsly [25] that a common semantic description of traditional building information and monitoring-related information helps categorize, document, update, and exchange monitoring-related information among all parties associated with the operation and maintenance phase of the structural life cycle. In the context of open BIM processes ensuring interoperability between different software, the IFC has been established to document and to exchange building information models. The IFC provide a formal basis for data storage and information exchange, thus enhancing the interoperability of building information models, which is a key requirement in BIM. The IFC semantic modeling approach is based on the "entity-relationship" (ER) concept, according to which physical objects and virtual components are referred to as "entities", whose characteristics are described as "attributes". Based on the relationships between the physical objects (or the virtual components), the entities are linked through "relationships", which are typically "objectified", i.e. modeled as separate entities pointing to other entities.

The basic entity, from which all entities with semantic significance are derived, is the *IfcRoot* entity. Objects, such as physical elements and activities, are defined using *IfcObjectDefinition* entities, from which *IfcObject* and *IfcProcess* entities are derived. Activities represented by entities derived from abstract *IfcProcess* entities are (i) events (*IfcEvent*), (ii) procedures (*IfcProcedure*), and (iii) tasks (*IfcTask*): Events trigger an action or response, procedures are used to describe sets of logical actions executed in response to events, and tasks represent identifiable work units.

Relationships between entities are described with *IfcRelationship* entities, from which entities representing objectified relationships are created. For example, for describing entities constituting parts of other entities, *IfcRelDecomposes* entities are adopted, and generic connections between two entities are defined by *IfcRelConnects* entities. Nesting relationships between entities are described with *IfcRelNest* entities, while the logical order of execution of different processes is modeled using *IfcRelSequence* entities [30].

Using the current version of the IFC schema (IFC4 – Addendum 2), which has been originally created for the building sector, a holistic BIM-based description of SHM systems is not possible, as entities to describe monitoring-related information are not fully supported in the IFC schema [22]. Nevertheless, partial description of monitoring-related information may be performed using existing entities. For example, sensor information in general can be described using the entity *IfcSensor*. Moreover, for integrating sensor information with respect to monitoring with emphasis on acceleration response data, Rio et al. have employed user-defined property sets of the IFC, proving that the representability of monitoring-related information through user-defined property sets is restricted [31]. Specifically for describing SHM-related algorithms, several IFC entities can be used, whose capabilities, however, need to be tested as these entities have been originally created to describe processes related to the construction industry. To tackle the aforementioned shortcomings of the current IFC schema with respect to describing SHM-related algorithms, an extension of the IFC schema is necessary. The semantic description approach (i.e. the semantic model), which will form the basis for the IFC schema extension, is described in the next section.

3   A Semantic Model for SHM-Related Algorithms

In this section, information relevant to describe algorithm components is integrated into a semantic model serving as a technology-independent metamodel for describing SHM-related algorithms. The semantic model is augmented with components describing SHM-related algorithms or, more precisely, describing statements and elementary control structures characterizing SHM-related algorithms in an object-oriented manner. The elementary control structures are semantically subdivided into components enabling consistent semantic descriptions of SHM-related algorithms.

As shown in Fig. 2, according to the semantic model, one process contains at least one algorithm, which is related to zero or more inputs and to one or more outputs. Furthermore, the domain and the analysis types of algorithms can be specified. Algorithms comprise one or more algorithm components, which are either statements (*Statement*) or elementary control structures (*ControlStructure*). In the semantic model, three subtypes of elementary control structures are distinguished: sequences, selections, and iterations. In the following paragraphs, the types of algorithm components, i.e. statements and subtypes of elementary control structures, contained in the semantic model are discussed in more detail.

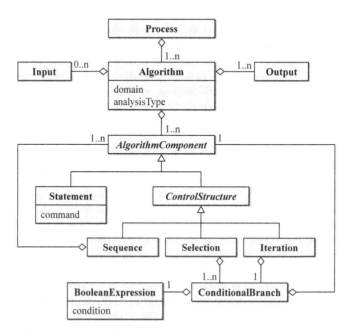

Fig. 2. Extract of the semantic model for describing SHM-related algorithms.

- **Statements.** Representing a basic, non-divisible component, statements refer to one command to be executed and are described by the subtype *Statement*. For the sake of simplicity, descriptions of statements are not further specified in the semantic model, because the description of statements depends on the target platform, i.e. on the underlying programming language. As an alternative, statements can be described textually, with pseudocode, or in mathematical notation for documentation purposes.
- **Sequences.** Sequences are described in the semantic model with the subtype *Sequence*. Since algorithm components contained in sequences must be executed sequentially, the *Sequence* subtype enables explicitly describing the control flow of algorithm components to be executed. The algorithm components can be simple, non-divisible commands (*Statement*) or elementary control structures, i.e. iterations, selections, or sequences.
- **Selections.** Selections are described using the subtype *Selection*. Conditions of selections and algorithm components bound to the conditions are described with conditional branches (*ConditionalBranch*). Conditional branches refer to Boolean expressions representing the conditions and to algorithm components representing the activity to be executed.
- **Iterations.** Iterations are described by the subtype *Iteration*. Similar to selections, conditions of iterations and algorithm components bound to the conditions are described with conditional branches (*ConditionalBranch*). By referring from a conditional branch to another algorithm component, algorithm components can be nested enabling, for example, nested iterations.

4   Extending the IFC Schema with Semantic Information on SHM-Related Algorithms

In this section, an IFC extension is presented proposing a mapping of the semantic model into the IFC schema. Capabilities from the current version of the IFC schema are reused to map the modeling requirements for a well-defined description of SHM-related algorithms. The IFC extension is based on the IFC Monitor extension previously introduced [25] to describe the semantic structure of SHM systems. With the IFC Monitor extension, the description of monitoring-related information is facilitated. Precisely, monitoring-related information includes information about (i) semantic compositions of SHM systems, (ii) network topologies, and (iii) semantic relationships between components of SHM systems and components of structural systems to be monitored. In this paper, the IFC Monitor extension is supplemented by entities to describe components of SHM-related algorithms and relationships among the algorithm components. Since the description of algorithm components is implemented hierarchically, the level of detail required to describe algorithms can case-specifically be adapted. The hierarchical description allows refining processes in subprocesses according to the level of detail required.

   As shown in Fig. 3, two entities *IfcRelSelection* and *IfcCondition* are added to the IFC schema enabling BIM-based descriptions of SHM-related algorithms related to SHM systems. *IfcRelSelection* entities extend *IfcRelSequence* entities relating two statements in a sequence. However, the sequence needs to be additionally linked to conditions that must be fulfilled for the sequence to be executed. As a result, conditions are described with *IfcCondition* entities containing Boolean expressions that must be evaluated at algorithm runtime. For simplicity, *IfcCondition* entities are described as strings. In addition to the two entities added for the description of algorithms, the entity *IfcSensorNode* has been added to the IFC schema in recent research efforts to describe sensor nodes contained in SHM systems.

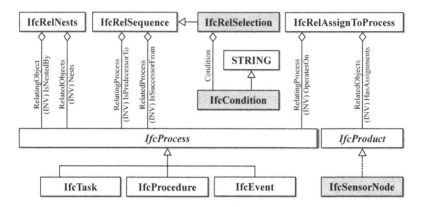

Fig. 3. Extract of the extended IFC schema with new entities and types gray-colored.

To avoid the specification of new entities, entities from the IFC schema are reused, provided that the entity specifications do not prohibit the use of the entities for describing SHM-related algorithms or, in general, algorithmic statements. In particular, entities of the type *IfcTask*, *IfcProcedure* and *IfcEvent* are reused. By definition, the aforementioned entities are intended to describe processes for the construction or for the installation of products. However, the entities are not explicitly restricted to these processes [30]. By reusing the IFC entities, SHM-related algorithms are described with *IfcTask* entities, while statements are described with *IfcProcedure* entities. Furthermore, *IfcEvent* entities are used to denote inputs and outputs of algorithms as well as to denote intermediate results of statements. Assigning components of SHM systems, such as sensor nodes, to processes is described with *IfcRelAssignToProcess* entities. With *IfcRelNests* entities, the relationship between algorithms (*IfcTask*) and algorithm components, such as statements (*IfcProcedure*), are described.

From a technical point of view, the IFC schema is defined in compliance with the EXPRESS data modeling language, formalized in ISO 10303-21:2016 [32]. Illustrating the definition of entities relevant for describing components of algorithms (*IfcCondition* and *IfcRelSelection*) and sensor nodes (*IfcSensorNode*), an extract of the extended IFC schema is shown in Listing 1. Listing 1 illuminates the definition of types, of entities (including the specification of supertypes of entities), and of entity-specific domain rules. Domain rules (also known as "where clauses") constrain the values of individual attributes. Combining different relationship entities, the description of elementary control structures in compliance with the IFC schema is shown in the following paragraphs.

```
...
TYPE IfcCondition = STRING(255);
END_TYPE;

ENTITY IfcRelSelection
  SUBTYPE OF (IfcRelSequence);
  Condition: IfcCondition;
END_ENTITY;

ENTITY IfcSensorNode
  SUBTYPE OF (IfcDistributionControlElement);
  WHERE
    ApplicableComponents: SIZEOF(QUERY(Rel <*
      SELF\IfcObjectDefinition.IsDecomposedBy | NOT(SIZEOF(QUERY(Comp <*
      Rel.RelatedObjects | NOT(SIZEOF(['IFC4.IFCSENSOR', 'IFC4.IFCACTUATOR',
      'IFC4.IFCCOMMUNICATIONSAPPLIANCE', 'IFC4.IFCELECTRICFLOWSTORAGEDEVICE']
      * TYPEOF(Comp)) = 1))) = 0))) = 0;
END_ENTITY;
...
```

Listing 1. Extract of the extended IFC schema demonstrating specifications of new entities.

Sequences. In IFC, sequences, as shown in Fig. 4, are described with *IfcRelSequence* entities. Using these entities, relationships describing the sequence of successive statements (*IfcProcedure*) are mapped with one *IfcRelSequence* entity for each relationship.

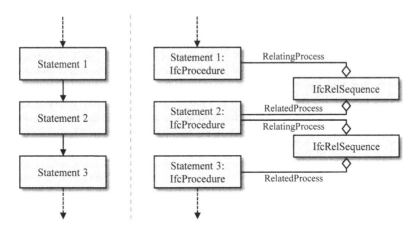

Fig. 4. Semantic description of sequences. (a) Example control flow; (b) corresponding IFC-compliant description.

Selections. Selections consist of statements and conditions on which the statements are bound. An example selection is shown Fig. 5a. After executing the first statement ("Statement 1"), a decision with respect to condition A and B is made, based on which Statement 2a or Statement 2b is executed. Statement 3 is executed regardless of the previous execution of statements. Figure 5b depicts the corresponding IFC-compliant description of selections, in which the four statements of the example selection are described with *IfcProcedure* entities. The connections between Statement 1 and Statements 2a and 2b are described by two *IfcRelSelection* entities, which refer to conditions A and B, respectively. Statement 3 is connected to Statements 2a and 2b using two *IfcRelSequence* entities closing the branches of the selection.

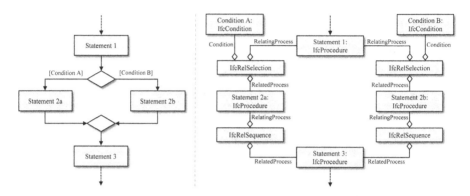

Fig. 5. Semantic description of selections. (a) Example control flow; (b) Corresponding IFC-compliant description.

Iterations. Iterations are described using the relationship entities *IfcRelSelection* and *IfcRelSequence*. In Fig. 6a, an example iteration is shown beginning with the first statement to be executed ("Statement 1"). Then, Statement 2 is repeatedly executed as long as condition A is met. If condition A is no longer met, condition B becomes true. The iteration is terminated and Statement 3 is executed. In Fig. 6b, the corresponding IFC-compliant description of iterations is shown. The three statements of the example iteration are described with *IfcProcedure* entities. An *IfcEvent* entity is added after the first statement that is connected with an *IfcRelSequence* entity to the statement representing an intermediate state ("State 1"). Subsequently, two possible paths are described through *IfcRelSelection* entities: Either condition A is fulfilled and Statement 2 is executed or condition B is fulfilled and Statement 3 is executed. In the first path, Statement 2 is related to *IfcEvent* "State 1" with an *IfcRelSequence* entity closing the loop of the iteration.

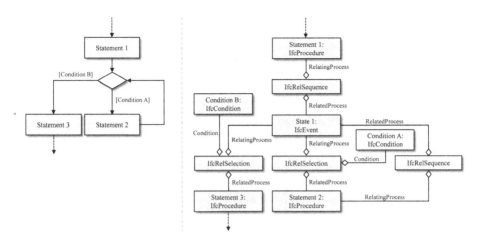

Fig. 6. Semantic description of iterations. (a) Example control flow; (b) Corresponding IFC-compliant description.

For verification purposes, test software of the official IFC certification program [33, 34] is used to check the syntactic and semantic correctness of the IFC extension proposed in this paper. For more details on the verification process, the interested reader is referred to [25]. In the following section, the BIM-based semantic description approach is validated focusing on documentation capabilities of the IFC schema extension.

5 Validation of the BIM-Based Description of SHM-Related Algorithms

To validate the BIM-based semantic description approach of SHM-related algorithms proposed in this study, the IFC schema extension is used to describe a wireless SHM system implemented with a fast Fourier transform (FFT) algorithm embedded into the wireless sensor nodes and installed on a laboratory structure. Since the validation test is performed on an existing SHM-equipped structure, the validation focuses on the documentation capabilities of the IFC schema extension, rather than on BIM-based design of SHM systems. First, the laboratory test structure and the wireless SHM system are presented, followed by a mathematical and semantic description of the embedded FFT algorithm. Next, the description of the laboratory test structure, of the wireless SHM system, and of the embedded FFT algorithm using the IFC schema extension is shown and validated, and the outcome of the IFC-compliant description is discussed.

5.1 Laboratory Test Structure and Wireless SHM System

For the validation test, a wireless SHM system is installed on a laboratory test structure comprising a four-story shear frame, shown in Fig. 7. Each story of the laboratory test structure consists of an aluminum slab of dimensions 300 mm × 200 mm × 15 mm (length × width × thickness) resting on four aluminum columns of cross section

Fig. 7. Wireless SHM system installed on a laboratory test structure for validation.

dimensions 20 mm × 2 mm (width × thickness). The columns are oriented so that the thickness of each cross section is aligned with the length of the plates. Each story has a height of 300 mm. The plate-to-column connections are considered fully fixed, while the columns are assumed to be clamped at the base.

The wireless SHM system installed on the laboratory test structure consists of four wireless sensor nodes, a base station, and a computer. As can be seen from Fig. 7, one sensor node is placed at the center of each plate. The sensor nodes selected for the validation test in this study are of type Percēv [35]. Each wireless sensor node possesses an 8-bit Atmel XMega 128A3U microprocessor operating at a speed of 32 MHz. In addition, a stream processing engine (SPE) with a 32-bit Atmel ATSAMG55J19 microprocessor is included that can be programmed to perform SHM-related tasks for data acquisition and for processing. In terms of memory, each SPE is equipped with 176 kB of RAM and with 512 kB of flash memory. Regarding wireless communication, wireless transceivers compliant with the IEEE 802.15.4 standard are integrated into the sensor node platform utilizing the ZigBee protocol. For structural health monitoring, the sensor nodes feature a 3-axial digital-output accelerometer and a thermistor. In addition, further sensor types can be connected to the sensor nodes, such as strain gauges or inclinometers.

5.2 Semantic Description of the FFT Algorithm Embedded into the Wireless Sensor Nodes

As shown in Table 1, for obtaining information on structural dynamic properties, several SHM-related algorithms are applicable in the frequency domain or in the modal domain. The first step for applying SHM-related algorithms in the frequency domain or in the modal domain involves decomposing the structural response data collected by sensors into sinusoidal harmonic functions, each at a different frequency, with a Fourier transform. The Fourier transform has been originally introduced as a tool in mathematics from representing a continuous function $f(t)$ of time t as a complex-valued function F of frequency ω, which is essentially an indefinite integral of function f, as shown in Eq. 1.

$$F(\omega) = \int_{-\infty}^{\infty} f(t)e^{-2\pi i\omega t} dt \tag{1}$$

Since structural response data is sampled at discrete time intervals, for applying the Fourier transform to discretized data the discrete Fourier transform (DFT) has been introduced, which is shown in Eq. 2. The integral is substituted by a sum of N complex values F, corresponding to N data points in the time series of the structural response data.

$$F_k = \sum_{n=0}^{N-1} f_k \cdot e^{-2\pi ik\frac{n}{N}} \quad k \in [0,N] \quad N \in \mathbb{Z} \tag{2}$$

From Eq. 2, it is evident that the computation of the DFT requires N^2 calculations, which renders the application of DFT computationally heavy for large time series. To overcome the heavy computational burden of the DFT, Cooley and Tukey [36] have introduced the fast Fourier transform, splitting the original DFT into smaller DFT computations of even-indexed terms and of odd-indexed terms and by combining the results to reconstruct the F complex series. The splitting into odd-indexed terms and even-indexed terms is performed in a recursive manner, thus reducing the computation load to $N \cdot \log N$ calculations. In Fig. 8, the FFT algorithm of Cooley and Tukey, for illustration purposes, is shown in its simplest form, the radix-2 decimation-in-time (DIT) FFT ("ditfft"). The ditfft2 is expressed in form of an activity diagram, which is used, in the following subsection, as a basis for describing the algorithm in conjunction with the wireless SHM system and the laboratory test structure to be monitored.

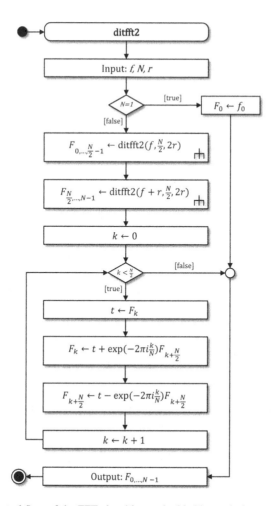

Fig. 8. Control flow of the FFT algorithm embedded into wireless sensor nodes.

5.3 IFC-Compliant Description and Validation

For validation, project-related information, the laboratory test structure, the wireless
SHM system, and the FFT algorithm embedded into the wireless sensor nodes is semantically described using the IFC extension materializing the semantic description
approach proposed in this study, resulting in an IFC model that contains the information
to be described (Fig. 9). The IFC model is created with the "apstex IFC Framework",
an open source software that allows reading, writing, creating, and modifying IFC
models [33].

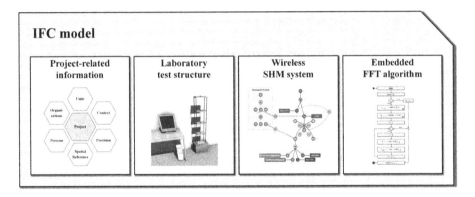

Fig. 9. Contents of the IFC model validated.

For data exchange between different software, IFC models are typically exchanged based on the standard for the exchange of product model data (STEP), formalized in ISO 10303-21:2016 [37]. In Listing 2, an extract of a STEP-based exchange file of the IFC model containing the information to be described is shown. First, general project-related information is described, followed by the description of the laboratory test structure. According to the physical system, the story height of the laboratory test structure is described by the "Elevation" attribute exchanged as the last parameter of each *IfcBuildingStorey* entity. In addition, structural components, such as slabs and columns, making up the laboratory test structure are described.

After describing the laboratory test structure, the wireless SHM system installed on the structure is described containing one sensor network characterized by a star topology. The sensor network contains one base station and four sensor nodes, which comprise acceleration sensors (accelerometers) and temperature sensors (thermistors).

Finally, the FFT algorithm embedded into the sensor nodes is described. Therefore, Listing 2 demonstrates an IFC-compliant description of the FFT algorithm ("ditfft2") depicted in Fig. 8. In Listing 2, the FFT algorithm is described with an *IfcTask* entity (#301). For describing the inputs and outputs of algorithms, *IfcEvent* entities are used, such as entity #302. In addition, the FFT algorithm contains several algorithm components, such as statements described with *IfcProcedure* entities (#303, #304, and #305). The nesting relationship between the algorithm and the algorithm components is described with an *IfcRelNests* entity (#307). Elementary control structures, i.e. sequences, selections, and iterations, are mapped combining different relationship entities. Here, selection relationships are described with *IfcRelSelection* entities (#308 and #309) containing predefined conditions to be met for executing the corresponding statements. Furthermore, sequence relationships are described with *IfcRelSequence* entities (#310).

```
/* Description of project-related information */
#1= IFCPROJECT($,#2,'Metaization concept for SHM',$,$,$,$,(#3),#4);
...
/* Description of the laboratory test structure */
#101= IFCBUILDING($,#2,'Laboratory test structure',$,$,#120,$,$,.ELEMENT.,
      $,$,#121);
#102= IFCBUILDINGSTOREY($,#2,'1st floor',$,$,#122,$,$,.ELEMENT.,0.);
#103= IFCBUILDINGSTOREY($,#2,'2nd floor',$,$,#123,$,$,.ELEMENT.,300.);
#104= IFCBUILDINGSTOREY($,#2,'3rd floor',$,$,#124,$,$,.ELEMENT.,600.);
#105= IFCBUILDINGSTOREY($,#2,'4th floor',$,$,#125,$,$,.ELEMENT.,900.);
#106= IFCSLAB($,#2,'Slab 1',$,$,#126,#127,$,.FLOOR.);
#107= IFCCOLUMN($,#2,'Column 1A',$,$,#128,#129,$,.COLUMN.);
...
/* Description of the wireless SHM system */
#201= IFCSHMSYSTEM($,#2,'Wireless SHM system',$,$);
#202= IFCSENSORNETWORK($,#2,'Sensor network',$,$,.STAR.);
#203= IFCSENSORNODE($,#2,'Base station',$,$,#220,#221,$);
#204= IFCSENSORNODE($,#2,'Sensor node 1',$,$,#222,#223,$);
#205= IFCSENSORNODE($,#2,'Sensor node 2',$,$,#224,#225,$);
#206= IFCSENSORNODE($,#2,'Sensor node 3',$,$,#226,#227,$);
#207= IFCSENSORNODE($,#2,'Sensor node 4',$,$,#228,#229,$);
#208= IFCSENSOR($,#2,'Acceleration sensor 1',$,$,#230,#231,$,
      .ACCELERATIONSENSOR.);
#209= IFCSENSOR($,#2,'Temperature sensor 1',$,$,#232,#233,$,
      .TEMPERATURESENSOR.);
...
/* Description of the embedded FFT algorithm */
#301= IFCTASK($,#2,'ditfft2','FFT algorithm (Cooley and Tukey)',$,$,$,$,$,
      .T.,$,$,$);
#302= IFCEVENT($,#2,'Input: f, N, r',$,$,$,$,.STARTEVENT.,$,$,$);
#303= IFCPROCEDURE($,#2,'F_0 = f_0','DFT base case',$,$,$,$);
#304= IFCPROCEDURE($,#2,'F_{0,...,N/2-1} = ditfft2(f,N/2,2r)',
      'DFT of f_0, f_{2r}, f_{4r}, ...',$,$,$,$);
#305= IFCPROCEDURE($,#2,'F_{N/2,...,N-1} = ditfft2(f+r,N/2,2r)',
      'DFT of f_r, f_{r+2r}, f_{r+4r}, ...',$,$,$,$);
#306= IFCRELASSIGNSTOPROCESS($,#2,'Relationship between sensor nodes and FFT
      algorithm',$,(#204,#205,#206,#207),.PRODUCT.,#301,$);
#307= IFCRELNESTS($,#2,'Relationship between FFT algorithm and algorithm
      components',$,#301,(#302,#303,#304,305,...));
#308= IFCRELSELECTION($,#2,'Selection 1A',$,#302,#303,$,$,$,'N=1');
#309= IFCRELSELECTION($,#2,'Selection 1B',$,#302,#304,$,$,$,'N>1');
#310= IFCRELSEQUENCE($,#2,'Sequence 1',$,#304,#305,$,$,$);
...
```

Listing 2. IFC-compliant description of project-related information, of the laboratory test structure, of the wireless SHM system, and of the embedded FFT algorithm (extract).

For validation purposes, the STEP-based exchange file of the IFC model is finally checked with the aforementioned test software used in the official IFC certification program. Adapted to the IFC extension, the test software validates, if the exchange file is free of syntactic errors and if the IFC model meets the semantic requirements of a well-defined IFC model. A detailed overview of criteria for the validation is provided in Table 2. The check of the IFC model with the test software showcases that the IFC model containing the laboratory test structure, the wireless SHM system, and the embedded FFT algorithm, is free of syntactic errors and meets all semantic requirements. Thus, it can be concluded that the IFC extension proposed in this study provides well-defined descriptions of SHM-related algorithms in compliance with the IFC standard. As a result, using the IFC extension, SHM-related algorithms can properly be described in conjunction with SHM systems and with structures to be monitored.

Table 2. Validation criteria and results.

Criteria	Result
Formal compliance according to the grammar defined in ISO 10303–21 (STEP)	✓
Conformance of header section with the header section schema	✓
Conformance of data section with the IFC Monitor schema	✓
Accordance of header section to IFC header definition	✓
Presence of non-optional attributes	✓
Accordance to geometry restrictions specified in the IFC documentation	✓
Conformance with implementers' agreements of the IFC standard	✓
Compliance with domain rules and uniqueness rules	✓

6   Summary and Conclusions

Building information modeling (BIM) has been widely applied in the architecture, engineering and construction industry as a paradigm for documenting and exchanging information among project stakeholders as part of structural life-cycle management. This information covers all phases of structural life-cycle management: planning, construction, operation and maintenance, and demolition. In recent years, as part of the operation and maintenance phase, structural health monitoring (SHM) has emerged as a novel method for assessing structural conditions. SHM involves collecting data from structures, such as structural response data and environmental data, via sensors and processing of the data for extracting information on the structural condition. Despite the widespread application of SHM, a formal description of SHM systems, enabling appropriate documentation and exchanging of monitoring-related information, is not possible yet with existing approaches. Current BIM-based approaches, in particular the Industry Foundation Classes (IFC) standard, focus only on the description of sensor-related information, while further aspects of monitoring-related information, such as data processing and analysis algorithms (SHM-related algorithms), are not covered.

This paper has presented a semantic description approach for SHM-related algorithms, which is realized with an extension of the current IFC schema. The semantic description approach proposed in this study enables describing various components of SHM-related algorithms as well as the relationships among the algorithm components. First, a semantic model for describing SHM-related algorithms has been created, followed by the development of a corresponding IFC-compliant mapping, by introducing entities for describing SHM-related algorithm components. The semantic description approach has been validated with respect to the documentation capabilities of the corresponding IFC schema extension through a wireless SHM system installed on a laboratory test structure with an algorithm for performing fast Fourier transform on acceleration response data embedded into the wireless sensor nodes. The validation test has proven the documentation capabilities of the semantic description approach, thus rendering the corresponding IFC schema extension a plausible tool for exchanging information on SHM-related algorithms using BIM.

Acknowledgments. This research is partially supported by the German Research Foundation (DFG) under grant SM 281/7-1. The financial support is gratefully appreciated. Any opinions, findings, conclusions, or recommendations expressed in this paper are those of the authors and do not necessarily reflect the views of the German Research Foundation.

References

1. EUBIM Taskgroup: Handbook for the introduction of building information modelling by the European public sector. Pan-European collaboration of public sector organizations across 21 countries (2017)
2. Eastman, C., Teicholz, P., Sacks, R., Liston, K.: BIM Handbook: A Guide to Building Information Modeling for Owners, Managers, Designers, Engineers, and Contractors. Wiley, Hoboken (2011)
3. Ninic, J., Koch, C., Stascheit, J.: An integrated platform for design and numerical analysis of shield tunnelling processes on different levels of detail. Adv. Eng. Softw. **112**, 165–179 (2017)
4. Kropp, C., Koch, C., König, M.: Interior construction state recognition with 4D BIM registered image sequences. Autom. Constr. **86**, 11–32 (2018)
5. Nical, A.K., Wodyński, W.: Enhancing facility management through BIM 6D. Procedia Eng. **164**, 299–306 (2016)
6. Cheng, J.C.P., Ma, L.Y.H.: A BIM-based system for demolition and renovation waste estimation and planning. Waste Manag. **33**(6), 1539–1551 (2013)
7. Doebling, S.W., Farrar, C.R., Prime, M.B.: A summary review of vibration-based damage identification methods. Shock Vib. Digest **30**(2), 91–105 (1998)
8. Jeong, S., Zhang, Y., O'Connor, S., Lynch, J.P., Sohn, H., Law, K.H.: A NoSQL data management infrastructure for bridge monitoring. Smart Struct. Syst. **17**(4), 669–690 (2016)
9. Smarsly, K., Hartmann, D., Law, K.H.: An integrated monitoring system for life-cycle management of wind turbines. Int. J. Smart Struct. Syst. **12**(2), 209–233 (2013)
10. Smarsly, K., Hartmann, D., Law, K.H.: A computational framework for life-cycle management of wind turbines incorporating structural health monitoring. Struct. Health Monit. Int. J. **12**(4), 359–376 (2013)
11. Feng, L., Yi, X., Zhu, D., Xie, X.Y., Wang, Y.: Damage detection of metro tunnel structure through transmissibility function and cross correlation analysis using local excitation and measurement. Mech. Syst. Sig. Process. **60**, 59–74 (2015)
12. Smarsly, K., Lehner, K., Hartmann, D.: Structural health monitoring based on artificial intelligence techniques. In: Proceedings of the International Workshop on Computing in Civil Engineering, Pittsburgh, PA, USA, 24 July 2007
13. Smarsly, K., Law, K.H., and König, M.: Resource-efficient wireless monitoring based on mobile agent migration. In: Proceedings of SPIE Health Monitoring of Structural and Biological Systems, San Diego, CA, USA, 06 March 2011
14. Peckens, C.A., Lynch, J.P.: Utilizing the cochlea as a bio-inspired compressive sensing technique. Smart Mater. Struct. **22**(10), 105027 (2013)
15. Bilek, J., Mittrup, I., Smarsly, K., Hartmann, D.: Agent-based concepts for the holistic modeling of concurrent processes in structural engineering. In: Proceedings of the 10th ISPE International Conference on Concurrent Engineering, Madeira, Portugal, 26 July 2003
16. Open Geospatial Consortium (OGC): OGC SensorML: Model and XML Encoding Standard. Wayland, MA, USA (2014)

17. W3C Incubator Group: Semantic Sensor Network XG Final Report. World Wide Web Consortium (W3C), Cambridge, MA, USA (2011)

18. Balmelli, L.: An overview of the systems modeling language for products and systems development. J. Object Technol. **6**(6), 149–177 (2018)

19. World Wide Web Consortium (W3C): OWL 2 Web Ontology Language Document Overview (Second Edition). https://www.w3.org/TR/owl2-overview/. Accessed 14 Jan 2018

20. Lee, K.B.: IEEE 1451: a standard in support of smart transducer networking. In: Proceedings of the 17th IEEE Instrumentation and Measurement Technology Conference, Baltimore, MD, USA, 01 April 2000

21. Smarsly, K., Theiler, M., Dragos, K.: IFC-based modeling of cyber-physical systems in civil engineering. In: Proceedings of the 24th International Workshop on Intelligent Computing in Engineering, Nottingham, UK, 10 July 2017

22. Theiler, M., Dragos, K., Smarsly, K.: BIM-based design of structural health monitoring systems. In: Proceedings of the 11th International Workshop on Structural Health Monitoring, Stanford, CA, USA, 12 September 2017

23. Legatiuk, D., Theiler, M., Dragos, K., Smarsly, K.: A categorical approach towards metamodeling cyber-physical systems. In: Proceedings of the 11th International Workshop on Structural Health Monitoring. Stanford, CA, USA, 12 September 2017

24. International Organization for Standardization (ISO): ISO 16739:2013 – Industry Foundation Classes (IFC) for data sharing in the construction and facility management industries. Geneva, Switzerland (2013)

25. Theiler, M., Smarsly, K.: IFC Monitor – An IFC extension for modeling structural health monitoring systems. Advanced Engineering Informatics (2018, Submitted)

26. International Organization for Standardization (ISO): ISO 9000:2015 – Quality management systems - Fundamentals and vocabulary. Geneva, Switzerland (2015)

27. Brett, A.C.: Procedures and algorithms. In: Linguistics 484 – Computational Linguistics – Grammars. Department of Linguistics, University of Victoria, British Columbia, Canada (2005)

28. Chen, C., Helal, S.: Sifting through the jungle of sensor standards. IEEE Pervasive Comput. **7**(4), 84–88 (2008)

29. Compton, M., Neuhaus, H., Taylor, K., Tran, K.-N.: Reasoning about sensors and compositions. In: Proceedings of the 2nd International Conference on Semantic Sensor Networks, Washington, DC, USA, 26 October 2009

30. BuildingSmart: IFC4 Documentation: Industry Foundation Classes – Version 4 Addendum 2. http://www.buildingsmart-tech.org/ifc/IFC4/Add2/html/. Accessed 24 Sept 2017

31. Rio, J., Ferreira, B., Pocas-Martins, J.: Expansion of IFC model with structural sensors [Expansión del modelo IFC con sensores estructurales]. Informes de la Construcción **65**(530), 219–228 (2013)

32. International Organization for Standardization (ISO): ISO 10303-11:2004 – Industrial automation systems and integration – Product data representation and exchange – Part 11: Description methods: The EXPRESS language reference manual. Geneva, Switzerland (2004)

33. Tauscher, E., Theiler, M.: apstex IFC Framework. http://www.apstex.com. Accessed 15 Jan 2018. Weimar, Germany

34. BuildingSMART International, iabi, AEC3 and APSTEX. B-Cert – The official platform for the buildingSMART IFC4 certification. http://www.b-cert.org. Accessed 15 Jan 2018. Berlin, Munich and Weimar, Germany

35. Civionics: Percēv System – Intelligent decisions driven by intelligent sensors (Product data sheet). Civionics, Ann Arbor, MI, USA (2018)

36. Cooley, J.W., Tukey, J.W.: An algorithm for the machine calculation of complex Fourier series. Math. Comput. **19**(90), 297–301 (1965)
37. International Organization for Standardization (ISO): ISO 10303-21:2016 – Industrial automation systems and integration – Product data representation and exchange – Part 21: Implementation methods: Clear text encoding of the exchange structure. Geneva, Switzerland (2016)
38. Böhm, C., Jacopini, G.: Flow diagrams, turing machines and languages with only two formation rules. Commun. ACM **9**(5), 366–371 (1966)

Development and Improvement of Deep Learning Based Automated Defect Detection for Sewer Pipe Inspection Using Faster R-CNN

Mingzhu Wang and Jack C. P. Cheng[✉]

Department of Civil and Environmental Engineering, The Hong Kong
University of Science and Technology, Hong Kong, China
mwangaz@connect.ust.hk, cejcheng@ust.hk

Abstract. Currently, visual inspection techniques, especially closed-circuit television (CCTV), are commonly utilized for sewer pipe inspection. Computer vision techniques are applied for automated interpretation of CCTV images to identify pipe defects. However, conventional computer vision techniques require complex handcrafted feature extraction and large amount of image pre-processing. In this study, a deep learning based approach is developed for sewer pipe defect detection using faster region-based convolutional neural network (faster R-CNN). 3000 images were collected from CCTV inspection videos of sewer pipes, among which 85% were used for training and validation and 15% are for testing. The detection model was trained and evaluated in terms of mean average precision (mAP), missing rate, detection speed and training time. The proposed approach is demonstrated to be applicable for detecting sewer pipe defects accurately with a high mAP and low missing rate. In addition, the initial model was improved by investigating the influence of dataset size, initialization network type and training mode, as well as network hyper-parameters on model performance. The improved model achieved a mAP of 83% and fast detection speed. This study has the potential for addressing similar object detection problems in the architecture, engineering and construction (AEC) industry and provides references when designing the deep learning models.

Keywords: Sewer pipe inspection · Defect detection
Computer vision · Deep learning
Faster region-based convolutional neural network (faster R-CNN)

1 Introduction

Sewer pipe systems form an important component of civil infrastructure which is designed to collect and transport waste water, storm water and ground water to treatment facilities. In the United States, there are over 800,000 miles of sewers and 500,000 miles of private lateral sewers that connect private property to public sewer pipes [1]. It was estimated that there are 19,500 sewer systems for handling an average daily flow of roughly 50 billion gallons of raw sewage but most of the sewer systems are between 30

© Springer International Publishing AG, part of Springer Nature 2018
I. F. C. Smith and B. Domer (Eds.): EG-ICE 2018, LNCS 10864, pp. 171–192, 2018.
https://doi.org/10.1007/978-3-319-91638-5_9

to 100 years old [2], making them susceptible to various pipe defects. Such defects can lead to serious social issues, construction incidents and heavy budget burden. For example, in the United States, there are at least 23,000 to 75,000 sewer sanitary overflows (SSOs) nationwide every year caused by pipe blockage, line breaks and water infiltration [3], leading to water quality problems, property losses and threats to public health. In addition, large amount of budget is needed for the maintenance of sewer pipe systems, e.g. US $297 billion is estimated to be required for waste water infrastructure over the next 25 years in the United States [1]. Therefore, it is important to detect pipe defects at an early stage such that further pipe deterioration can be prevented and existing defects can be repaired to maintain normal sewer operations.

Pipe inspection is essential for detecting defects of buried pipes. Visual inspection techniques such as closed-circuit television (CCTV) is most commonly utilized for underground pipe inspection. CCTV usually consists of a camera and an illumination device mounted on a tractor. During the inspection, the CCTV unit moves along the interior pipe wall and transmits the inspection video to an external monitor on the ground. When encountering a pipe defect or pipe lateral, the inspector would stop the unit and rotate and zoom the camera into the abnormal part. After the inspection, the inspector needs to watch the captured images or videos to identify the defect type and location. Such manual interpretation of the inspection images or videos is time-consuming, labor intensive and the results can be subjective and inaccurate. There is recently a trend of applying computer vision for interpreting the inspection images or videos automatically. However, conventional computer vision techniques require designing complex feature extractors and the training process is tedious. Due to the promising performance of deep learning in computer vision tasks such as image classification and object detection, deep learning based method is proposed in this study for identifying and locating the sewer pipe defects from CCTV images. The image features can be learned automatically in deep learning models and there is not much requirement of image pre-processing, which improves the detection accuracy and efficiency greatly.

2   Related Work

2.1   Conventional Computer Vision Techniques for Civil Infrastructure Inspection

With the wide development and application of visual inspection techniques for infrastructure, large number of inspection images or videos are generated during the inspection. Manual interpretation to obtain inspection results is required, which is inefficient and ineffective. Therefore, computer vision techniques have been investigated for automated interpretation of inspection images or videos. Most of the techniques applied in previous studies are image processing techniques, such as edge detection and morphological operations [4]. Although the noise reduction method [5] has been studied, prior knowledge of the images is still required for image processing. Generally, applications of conventional computer vision methods include image pre-processing, image segmentation, feature extraction and object recognition for different civil infrastructures [6]. Various vision-based tasks have been studied such as automated detection and dimension measurement of concrete cracks

[7], recognition of damage pattern changes and 3D visualization of cracks [8], and precise crack extraction [9]. Computer vision techniques have also been applied for underground sewer pipe inspection such as the segmentation and classification of sewer pipe images [10, 11] so as to obtain joints, laterals and defects for further condition assessment. Another application of image processing techniques is the automatic detection and segmentation of sewer pipe cracks [12, 13].

However, the image processing techniques mentioned above for defect detection of sewer pipes and other civil infrastructures require prior knowledge of the images for pre-processing. Complex feature extractors need to be designed manually, which is inefficient and not robust to image noise data. In addition, previous studies mainly focused on identification and property retrieval of single defect (mainly cracks). There has been limited research on the automated identification and localization of other common defects of underground sewer pipelines, such as tree root intrusion and water infiltration, which can lead to severe consequences.

2.2 Deep Learning Based Approaches for Image Classification and Object Detection

Deep learning has been widely developed and applied in various areas such as computer vision, speech recognition and natural language processing through various deep learning architectures, among which convolutional neural networks (CNNs) are commonly applied [14]. As shown in Fig. 1, a CNN model outputs the result for an input after processing through a stack of layers including convolution, activation, pooling, normalization and fully connection. Each layer is responsible for different functions and uses the result from the previous layer as the input. Compared with conventional approaches, CNNs require less image pre-processing and features are extracted through learning, so there is no requirement of expertise for manual design of complex feature extractors. Currently, there have been a few studies applying deep learning approaches for civil infrastructure such as for concrete crack detection [15, 16], tunnel inspection [17] and road crack detection [18]. However, the application of CNNs for infrastructure inspection is still in its infancy and there has been limited research using CNNs for sewer pipe defect detection.

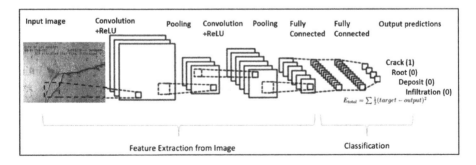

Fig. 1. Example architecture of CNN

CNNs are typically utilized for image classification and recognition but defect detection also requires the information of defect location. In previous studies, objects were detected using feature extractor based approach such as Haar detector [38], scale invariant feature transform (SIFT) [35] and histograms of oriented gradients (HOG) [12]. However, these methods require complex manual design of the feature extractor and tedious training process, which are inefficient and not very effective. The region-based convolutional neural network (R-CNN) is one type of a typical deep learning approach for object detection [19]. For an input image in R-CNN, region proposals are generated and each of them is forwarded into a CNN model extracting features, which is then fed into a classification layer. In the end, bounding box is predicted for the classified image. The main limitation of R-CNN is the tedious training and low detection speed. Hence, the fast R-CNN was developed [20], in which the region proposals are generated from the feature map and are then fed into two layers for classification and bounding box regression. The training time of fast R-CNN is reduced and the detection speed is improved. Nevertheless, the fast R-CNN still relies on selective search to generate region proposals, which can affect the model performance. Therefore, the faster R-CNN was developed based on the fast R-CNN [21] and the main difference is in the method to generate the region proposals. A faster R-CNN consists of a region proposal network (RPN) which is trained to generate region proposals and a fast R-CNN detector for feature detection and regression. The main characteristic of the faster R-CNN is that RPN and fast R-CNN detector can share convolution layers such that the computation cost can be greatly reduced. The number of region proposals generated by RPN is optimized and the quality is higher than those generated through selective search. Therefore, both the detection accuracy and detection speed are improved.

Faster R-CNN has been applied in some researches such as in pedestrian detection [22], face detection [23], real time vehicle detection and tracking [24–27] and traffic sign detection [28]. However, there have only been limited studies applying faster R-CNN in the architecture, engineering and construction (AEC) industry. A recent study [29] applying faster R-CNN for the detection of non-hardhat-use on construction sites indicated the potential of deep learning for object detection in construction management. So far, no study utilized the faster R-CNN for detecting defects for civil infrastructure, which is worthy of study.

3   Methodology for Automated Sewer Pipe Defect Detection Based on Faster R-CNN

Compared with state-of-the-art object detection approaches, faster R-CNN has high precision and recall value and achieved the highest mean average precision in the VOC 2012 dataset [30]. Therefore, the faster R-CNN is investigated and applied in this study for automated sewer pipe defect detection. As shown in Fig. 2, the overall workflow of the proposed automated defect detection approach using the faster R-CNN consists of image collection, augmentation and annotation, model training and model testing and evaluation.

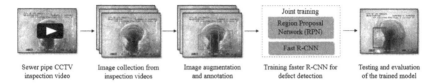

Fig. 2. Overall workflow of the proposed approach

3.1 The Developed Defect Detection Model Based on Faster R-CNN

A faster R-CNN model typically consists of a region proposal network (RPN) and fast R-CNN detector as illustrated in Fig. 3. There are three main steps applying faster R-CNN for object detection. Firstly, a convolutional neural network is utilized for feature extraction and a feature map is generated on the last layer. Based on the generated feature map, RPN generates region proposals with different aspect ratios and scales. In the third step, the generated regions proposals are fed into the fast R-CNN detector for classification and bounding box regression. Details of each step are explained in the following sections.

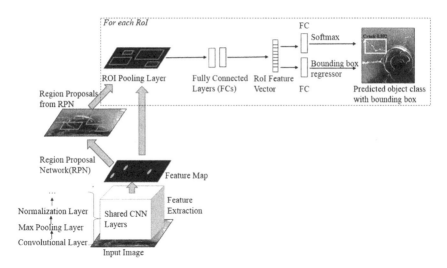

Fig. 3. Architecture of the developed faster R-CNN for sewer pipe defect detection

Feature Extraction Using CNN

Fast R-CNN utilizes convolution layers to extract features from images while RPN contains convolutional layers to produce region proposals. Therefore, several layers can be shared between RPN and fast R-CNN such that the computation cost can be reduced and region proposal quality can be improved. Zeiler-Fergus (ZF) network, proposed by Zeiler and Fergus [31], is a deep learning model developed with the function of visualizing different network layers. The model architecture was then adjusted and better performance was achieved than other popular models on the ImageNet classification dataset. Therefore, the CNN layers in the ZF network including 5 convolutional layers and 3 max pooling layers are applied for extracting image features in this study. The detailed architecture of the ZF network is shown in Fig. 8(a), there are 96 convolution kernels of size 7×7 in the first convolutional layer and 256 kernels of size 5×5 are used in the second convolutional layer. The kernel stride in both layers is 2 and in the following two layers, 384 convolution kernels of size 3×3 are applied at a stride of 1 and 256 kernels of size 3×3 are for the last convolutional layer.

As shown in Fig. 4, the convolutional layer utilizes a filter to slide over the pixel array of the input image, and the dot product between the filter and the subarray is calculated. The value from the dot product and the bias value are added to get the convolution result for the subarray. Such a convolution process is repeated for each subarray until the filter slides over the whole input volume. The initial weights of the filters are randomly assigned and the value of bias can be set according to the network configuration. The filter weights and the bias are adjusted continuously during the training process through the stochastic gradient descent (SGD) algorithm. The convolution output can be influenced by both the filter size and the convolution stride value. For example, the size of the output volume ($W_2 \times H_2 \times D_2$) is calculated as following:

$$W_2 = (W_1 - F + 2P)/S + 1 \tag{1}$$

$$H_2 = (H_1 - F + 2P)/S + 1 \tag{2}$$

$$D_2 = K \tag{3}$$

where W_1, H_1, and D_1 represents the width, height and depth of the input volume, K, F, S, P represents the number of filters, the width (which equals to the height) of the filter, the convolve stride and the number of zero padding respectively. Therefore, the parameters of the convolution operation can be adjusted such that better convolution results can be obtained.

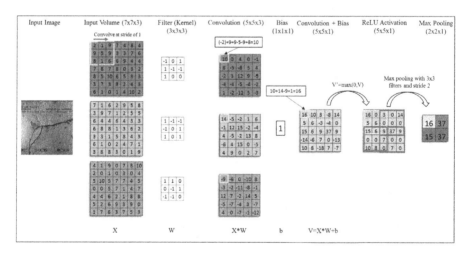

Fig. 4. Example of the process of convolution, ReLU activation and max pooling on a RGB image

The Rectified Linear Units (ReLU) function is typically used as the activation function in CNN models. ReLU applies the elementwise activation with the function f(x) = max(0, x), which has no bounded outputs in addition to those for negative inputs. The gradients of ReLU are always zero or one so the computation cost is reduced and the accuracy is increased. After the ReLU activation, max pooling is performed to reduce the spatial size of the input volume by taking the max values from the subarray of the input pixel array, as shown in Fig. 4. The dimension of the max pooling output $(W_2 \times H_2 \times D_2)$ is calculated as following:

$$W_2 = (W_1 - F)/S + 1 \tag{4}$$

$$H_2 = (H_1 - F)/S + 1 \tag{5}$$

$$D_2 = D_1 \tag{6}$$

where W_1, H_1 and D_1 represents the width, height and depth of the data after ReLU activation, F and S represents the pooling window size and pooling stride value. As different parameters of the pooling process result in different outputs, model performance can be different by adjusting the parameters. In the ZF network, the pooling layers are performed after the first, second and third ReLU activation layer respectively, using a sliding window of 3×3 at a stride of 2.

Normalization layers are applied to normalize the unbounded activation produced by the ReLU layer. High frequency features can be detected more easily as the pixel with larger value is more obvious after the local neighbourhood pixels are normalized. Local Response Normalization (LRN) is applied in the ZF network, which performs a sort of lateral inhibition and boost the more excited neurons [14]. Normalization can facilitate whitening, after which the data along the batch axis has a zero mean and unit variance. During whitening, the pixel value is calculated in Eq. (7):

$$\hat{x}^k = \frac{x^k - E(x^k)}{\sqrt{Var(x^k)}} \tag{7}$$

where $E(x^k)$ and $Var(x^k)$ is the mean and variance for pixels with the same x and y coordinates respectively. With the whitening process, the network can converge faster as correlation among the adjacent pixels is reduced.

In addition, to avoid the overfitting problem, a dropout layer is designed to disconnect part of the connections between the neurons on two adjacent layers with a certain dropout rate [32], which is set to be 0.5 in the ZF network.

Region Proposal Network (RPN) for Defect Detection
Instead of using selective search (SS), which is a typical method for generating region proposals in R-CNN and fast R-CNN, the region proposal network (RPN) is developed in faster R-CNN to generate object regions. RPN is developed based on the last convolutional layer and produces regions with a wide range of aspect ratios and scales using anchors. A small sliding window is proposed to slide over the feature map obtained from

the last sharable convolutional layer, and the sliding window is projected to a lower dimensional feature (256 dimension for ZF network). After convolution using two 1×1 filters and the activation with ReLU function, the extracted features are fed into a bounding box regression layer and a classification layer respectively. At each sliding window location, k region proposals are generated. The regression layer predicts 4k coordinates for the proposals while the classification layer outputs 2k scores which indicate the probabilities of the regions containing a defect or not.

Considering the large number of proposals generated by RPN that overlap with each other, non-maximum suppression (NMS) is utilized to reduce overlapping regions by merging proposals that have high intersection of union (IoU). After NMS, there are approximate 2000 proposals remaining, which are ranked according to the object scores, and only the top-N ranked proposals are kept. In this study, 2000 proposals are used for training and different number of proposals are evaluated during testing.

Fast R-CNN Detector
The region proposals generated through RPN are utilized as the input regions of interest (RoIs) for the fast R-CNN detector. For each RoI, the features from the convolutional layer are converted to a fixed-length vector through the RoI pooling layer. Each fixlength feature vector is fed into a sequence of fully connected layers and the final feature vector is fed into two layers: (1) the softmax layer producing probability scores for 5 classes as there are 4 types of defects as the data input of the model and another one class is the image background, and (2) the regression layer which outputs the relative coordinates of the bounding box.

3.2   The Model Training Process

RPN Training
Before conducting the RPN training, each region proposal is labelled to indicate the existence of an object (one type of pipe defect) in the region. RPN in faster R-CNN is trained using a multi-task loss function as shown in Eq. (8) [21].

$$L(\{p_i\}, \{t_i\}) = \frac{1}{N_{cls}} \sum_i L_{cls}(p_i, p_i^*) + \lambda \frac{1}{N_{reg}} \sum_i p_i^* L_{reg}(t_i, t_i^*) \qquad (8)$$

where i indicates the number of anchor, p_i represents the predicted probability of anchor i being one type of sewer pipe defect. p_i^* represents the ground-truth label of anchor i, where p_i^* equals to 1 if the anchor is a positive sample and 0 if it is negative. t_i is a vector indicating the coordinates of the predicted bounding box while t_i^* represents the ground-truth bounding box related to a positive anchor. N_{cls} and N_{reg} are two normalization factors for the two components and are weighted by a balancing parameter λ. With reference to related study, the value of N_{cls} is set to be 256 and N_{reg} equals to 2400 which is the approximate value of the number of anchor locations in the model. The balancing parameter λ is set to 10 such that both cls and reg terms are roughly weighted equally.

The aim of bounding box regression is to predict the accurate location of the proposed bounding boxes. The parameterization of the coordinates of the anchor is illustrated in the following equations [21]:

$$t_x = \frac{x - x_a}{w_a}, t_y = \frac{y - y_a}{h_a} \tag{9}$$

$$t_w = \log\frac{w}{w_a}, t_h = \log\frac{h}{h_a} \tag{10}$$

$$t_x^* = \frac{x^* - x_a}{w_a}, t_y^* = \frac{y^* - y_a}{h_a} \tag{11}$$

$$t_w^* = \log\frac{w^*}{w_a}, t_h^* = \log\frac{h^*}{h_a} \tag{12}$$

where $x, y, w,$ and h represents the centre coordinates and the width and height of the box. x, x_a and x^* indicate corresponding values for predicted box, anchor box and ground-truth box respectively. The same annotation method is used for the other three variables $y, w,$ and h.

The Log loss function is used to calculate the classification loss L_{cls} over two classes (object or not object). For the regression loss, $L_{reg}(t_i, t_i^*) = smooth_{L1}(t_i - t_i^*)$ where $smooth_{L1}$ is the robust regression loss function as shown in Eq. (13) [21].

$$smooth_{L1} = \begin{cases} 0.5x^2, & |x| < 1 \\ |x| - 0.5, & |x| \geq 1 \end{cases} \tag{13}$$

During the training, a set of k (k = 9 in this study) bounding box regressors without sharing weights are learned, each of which is responsible for one scale and one aspect ratio. Therefore, the model is able to predict boxes with various sizes.

Model Training
One typical training approach is four-step alternating training proposed by [21]. The first step is to train RPN in which the RPN network is initialized by a pre-trained ImageNet model and fined-tuned for generating region proposals. The generated proposals are used to train a separate fast R-CNN detector network in the second step. In the third step, the trained fast R-CNN detector is used to initialize the RPN training, during which the shared convolutional layers are fixed and only the unique layers of RPN are fine-tuned. Lastly, only the unique layers of fast R-CNN are trained and the shared convolutional layers are remained fixed. Consequently, a unified network is formed and the RPN and fast R-CNN share the same convolutional layers. Another training mode is approximate joint training. In this training mode, RPN and fast R-CNN are integrated into one network, which is trained using SGD. The region proposals are generated by feeding forward features and are then utilized for training fast R-CNN detector. During the backpropagation, the RPN loss and the fast R-CNN loss are

combined together for the shared layers [21]. This training process is easier to implement, but it ignores the derivatives in terms of the coordinates of the object proposals.

3.3 Model Evaluation

Precision and recall are typical indicators for most machine learning models e.g. single
object classification. However, using the conventional evaluation indicators is not
appropriate for the multiple object detection model as the prior distribution over objects
is not uniform [33]. Therefore, in this study, average precision and missing rate are used
to indicate the detection accuracy while detection speed and training time are used to
reflect computation cost.

Average Precision (AP)
The interpolated AP proposed by Salton and McGill [34] is applied for model evaluation
in this study, which is calculated using Eq. (14):

$$AP = \frac{1}{11} \sum_{r \in \{0,0.1,0.2,...,1\}} P_{interp}(r) \tag{14}$$

The precision at each recall level is interpolated by taking the maximum precision
measured for a model where the corresponding recall exceeds r:

$$P_{interp}(r) = \max_{\tilde{r}:\tilde{r} \geq r} p(\tilde{r}) \tag{15}$$

where $p(\tilde{r})$ is the measured precision at recall $\tilde{r}$. In the end, mean average precision
(mAP) for all the classes is calculated by Eq. (16) to compare the model performance.

$$mAP = \frac{1}{N_{cls}} \sum_{i} AP_i \tag{16}$$

Missing Rate
The missing rate is an evaluation index usually utilized in pedestrian detection models,
which is calculated with Eq. (17):

$$Missing\ rate = \frac{FN}{TP + FN} \tag{17}$$

The missing rate curve is used in this work by computing the missing rate over the
number of false positives per image, indicating the percentage of objects that are missed
during the detection.

Detection Speed
The detection speed of the faster R-CNN model in this study refers to the time required
by the whole defect detection process for each image. The speed is indicated by the
frames per second (FPS), which is the number of frames detected in one second.

Training Time

The time required for training the model reflect the computation cost the model, which is also one consideration when applying deep learning models in practice. Therefore, training time is one indicator evaluating the model performance and influential factors have also been investigated in the experiments.

4   Experiments and Results

The proposed model is aimed at automatically detecting four types of defects: tree root, crack, infiltration and deposit based on CCTV inspection images. Experiments are conducted to demonstrate the applicability of the proposed model as well as to improve model performance by investigating several influential factors.

4.1   Data Collection and Annotation

Available images used in this study are mainly captured from the sewer inspection videos in Pennsylvania, US. There are initially 1260 images containing four types of defects collected as shown in Fig. 5. Data augmentation is conducted to increase the dataset size through methods such as vertical and horizontal flips, rotation and scaling, color tuning i.e. adjustment of brightness, contrast and saturation, as shown in Fig. 6. After data augmentation, there are 3000 images used for training the model. All the training images are scaled down to the same size of 224×224 pixels.

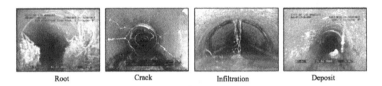

Root   Crack   Infiltration   Deposit

Fig. 5. Sample images of four types of sewer pipe defects

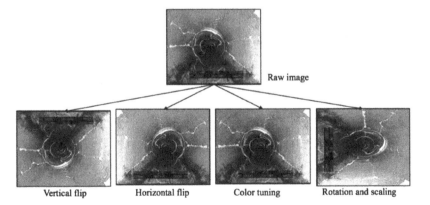

Raw image

Vertical flip   Horizontal flip   Color tuning   Rotation and scaling

Fig. 6. Examples of data augmentation

All the images collected and pre-processed are annotated with ground-truth bounding boxes and class labels using a graphical image annotation tool named LabelImage [35], providing ground-truth labels for training the detection model.

4.2 Experimental Setup

Three experiments are conducted respectively to investigate the influence of dataset size, network type and training mode, as well as network hyper-parameter on model performance. In each experiment, 75% of the dataset are used for training, 10% for validation and 15% for testing. All experiments are conducted using models developed based on Caffe [36], which provides libraries to build the architecture of deep learning models.

4.3 Experiment 1 and Results

The purpose of experiment 1 is to study the influence of the dataset size on the model performance. There are three dataset A, B and C with 1000, 2000, and 3000 images which are randomly selected from all the images. The ratio of defects over the number of images are kept the same in the three datasets to ensure the comparability of the model results. The proposed model, as introduced in Sect. 3.1 initialized by the ZF network is trained and tested with the three different datasets respectively. The results show that mAP of the model is increasing continuously with the increase of the dataset size. Specifically, the AP values of the four classes are also following a similar increasing trend except the AP for the deposit case, decreased with dataset B, after which it increased again. The precision-recall curve is computed to demonstrate the precision and recall value with different confidence thresholds as shown in Fig. 7. The detection for each defect using the model with dataset C has the highest curve, representing the best performance. The precision-recall curve also reflects that recall value increases while precision decreases in each detection. One possible reason is that there are fewer false negatives and more false positives predicted by the model with increase of the threshold. Since the purpose of defect detection is to identify and localize pipe defects to avoid further pipe deterioration, even though some detected objects are incorrectly identified, the situation is better than missing potential defects of sewer pipes (Table 1).

Table 1. mAP and AP of model using different datasets

Network	Dataset	mAP	AP			
			Root	Crack	Infiltration	Deposit
Original ZF	A	0.680	0.649	0.546	0.727	0.799
	B	0.763	0.735	0.794	0.759	0.765
	C	0.798	0.723	0.789	0.879	0.802

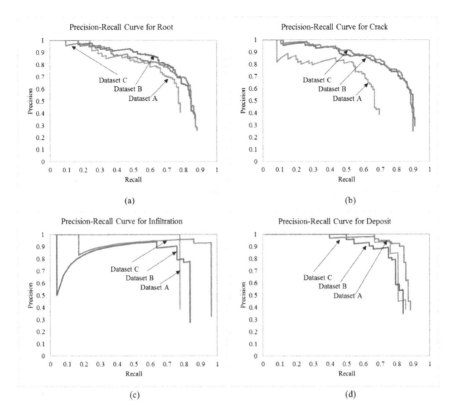

Fig. 7. Precision-recall curve for each class using the model with different dataset

4.4   Experiment 2 and Results

To study the influence of the initialization network types and the training modes on the detection performance, the proposed model is initialized with three different pre-trained networks. The first network is the ZF network, which is referred to as model S, for "small". The second one, VGG_CNN_M_1024 network [37], is referred as network M for "medium". The third one, the very deep VGG16 [38], is referred as network L, for "large", due to its deep architecture. The model initialized with network S, M, and L is trained with dataset C using alternating optimization training ("altopt") and approximate joint training ("end2end"), as introduced in Sect. 3.2.

As shown in Table 2, for the same dataset, models with network S and M achieved relatively high mAP as well as faster detection speed. Model S_A has the highest mAP of 79.8% and largest FPS of 20. Although model L_A also achieved the same highest mAP but the training time is much longer and the detection speed is much slower. Models with the training mode of "altopt" have slightly higher mAP values and faster detection speed but require a longer training time. The reason maybe that alternating optimization procedure between RPN and the fast R-CNN detector can improve the quality of the region proposals and facilitate feature extraction.

Table 2. Performance of models with different networks and training modes

Model	Architecture	Training mode	mAP	AP				FPS	Training time (h)
				Root	Crack	Infiltration	Deposit		
S_A	Network S+RPN	Altopt	0.798	0.737	0.727	0.871	0.857	20.408	6.053
S_E	Network S+RPN	End2end	0.792	0.726	0.769	0.878	0.794	18.868	5.760
M_A	Network M+RPN	Altopt	0.786	0.723	0.734	0.880	0.807	18.868	4.784
M_E	Network M+RPN	End2end	0.796	0.750	0.757	0.881	0.797	18.519	2.662
L_A	Network L+RPN	Altopt	0.798	0.729	0.737	0.890	0.837	8.197	14.762
L_E	Network L +RPN	End2end	0.761	0.706	0.757	0.786	0.795	6.849	10.969

In addition, the missing rate of each model in detecting each class is plotted. As shown in Fig. 8, the missing rate of all the models follows a decreasing trend with the increase of false positives detected. Generally, for each defect, rating curves of the models initialized with the same network and trained under the two training modes respectively are quite close to each other, indicating there is not much influence of the training modes on the missing rate. Although models with the approximate joint training yield relatively lower missing rate for detecting roots and cracks, alternating optimization training is slightly better for detecting infiltrations and deposits. Due to the high AP, fast detection rate, easier architecture as well as less training duration, model S_A was selected for further study in experiment 3.

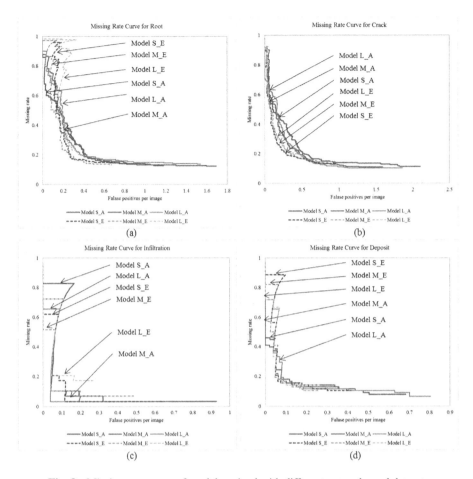

Fig. 8. Missing rate curve of models trained with different networks and datasets

4.5 Experiment 3 and Results

The objective of experiment 3 is to study the influence of the hyper-parameter and architecture of the network on the model performance. In this experiment, the architecture and hyper-parameters of the original ZF network are modified. As shown in Fig. 9 (adapted from [31]), two more convolutional layers followed by a max pooling layer are added at the end of the fifth convolutional layer. There are 384 kernels of size 3×3 at a convolution stride of 1 applied on both of the two added convolutional layers. The max pooling layer is configured with a 3×3 window at a stride of 2. As for the hyper-parameters, the size of the kernels used on the first convolutional layer of the shared network have been converted from 7×7 to 5×5. Similarly, the size of the kernels for the second convolutional layer are changed from 5×5 to 3×3. The stride of the second max pooling layer is set to 1. The modified model is trained with dataset A, B and C respectively, after which the performance is compared with the original model.

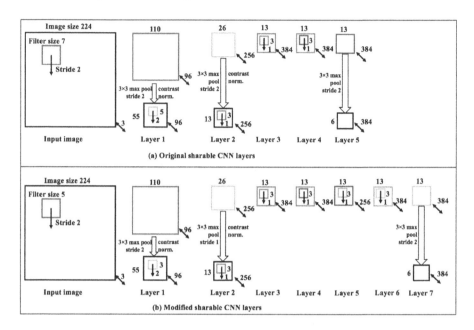

Fig. 9. Architecture of the sharable CNN layers in original and modified model

As shown in Table 3, the modified model achieved a great performance with a mAP of 83%. Specifically, the average precision (AP) of each detection has been improved. As illustrated in Fig. 10, the AUC of each modified model is higher than that of the original model after being trained with the same dataset. The overall performance of the modified models has been improved, although there are some fluctuations in certain groups (e.g. curve of model_C_M for infiltration is lower than model_C_O). As shown in Fig. 11, for each defect, the missing rate curve of the modified models trained with the same dataset is generally lower than that of the original models, indicating that fewer defects are missed than using modified models. In terms of the detection speed, although the FPS of the modified models has decreased, there is not much influence in practical detection as the detection accuracy has a higher priority compared with detection speed for sewer pipe inspection.

Table 3. Performance evaluation of the model with original ZF network and modified ZF network

Model	Network	Dataset	mAP	AP				FPS
				Root	Crack	Infiltration	Deposit	
Model_A_O	Original ZF	A	0.680	0.649	0.546	0.727	0.799	18.182
Model_B_O		B	0.763	0.735	0.794	0.759	0.765	19.608
Model_C_O		C	0.798	0.723	0.789	0.879	0.802	20.408
Model_A_M	Modified ZF	A	0.738	0.725	0.655	0.766	0.805	9.009
Model_B_M		B	0.781	0.759	0.767	0.799	0.801	9.174
Model_C_M		C	0.830	0.836	0.776	0.864	0.845	9.434

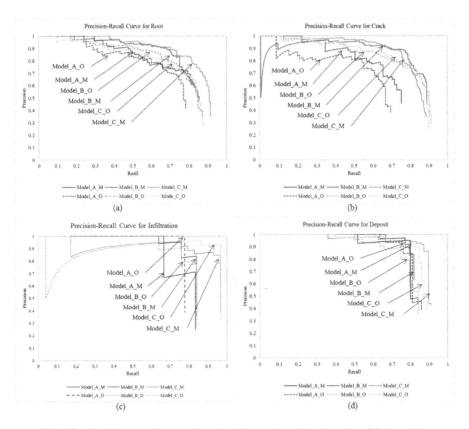

Fig. 10. Precision-recall curve for each defect using original and modified models

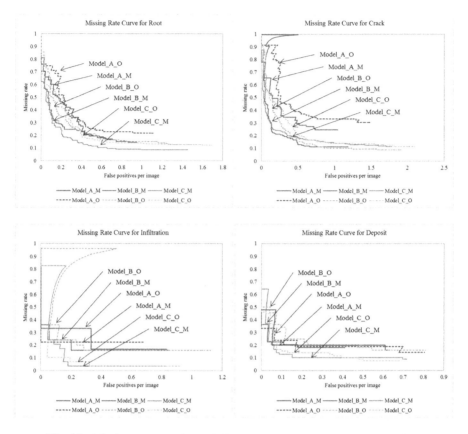

Fig. 11. Missing rate curve for each defect using original and modified models

5   Discussion

As indicated by the experiment results, dataset size, network type, and the hyper-parameters of a network can have influence on the performance of a defect detection model. Firstly, more training data may facilitate the model to learn the object features more accurately and comprehensively, leading to higher detection accuracy. Secondly, a deeper network can contribute to a higher average precision as more convolutional layers can extract more important features. However, the complex architecture and large number of parameters in deeper networks will increase the computation cost. In terms of the influence of hyper-parameters, experiment indicates that smaller sized kernels applied on convolutional layers are more likely to retain important features during convolution while smaller pooling stride of filters on the max pooling layer may prevent important information loss in the down sampling. But the computation cost also increased due to more architecture layers and smaller size of filter and stride. Therefore, there should be a trade-off between detection accuracy and the speed requirement when designing the architecture of object detection models.

Although the overall performance of the model with the modified network has been improved, there are some incorrect classifications. As shown in Fig. 12(a) and (c), the edge of the pipe joint and a piece of water infiltration near the joint are incorrectly classified as the pipe crack. Possible reasons for those incorrect detections is that the shape of pipe joint edge and infiltration are similar to that of cracks. Also, the joint edge on the image is brighter than its background, leading to a similar intensity change pattern to that of cracks. In addition, a long and dark deposit on the pipe interior wall is incorrectly detected as shown in Fig. 12(b), mainly because of its thin and long shape and the dark color. Therefore, the shape, color and intensity of an object influences the detection accuracy of the model.

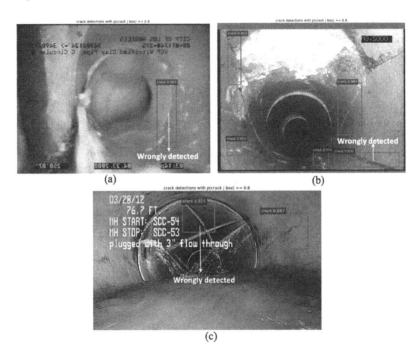

Fig. 12. Examples of incorrect detection

6   Conclusions

This study developed a deep learning based approach for identifying and locating sewer pipe defects automatically from CCTV images using the faster R-CNN model. Compared with conventional computer vision techniques, the proposed approach can reduce the time and labour for the interpretation of inspection images, increase defect detection accuracy and facilitate future condition assessment.

In addition, the accuracy of the model was improved, reaching a mAP of 83% by investigating several influential factors. Firstly, model trained with a larger dataset can learn the object features more comprehensively, leading to higher accuracy. Second, a deeper initialization network with more convolution layers can extract the image features more accurately and improve the accuracy. In addition, network hyper-parameters such as a smaller filter size and stride for convolution can increase convolution times while that on pooling layers can prevent too much information loss during down sampling, contributing to higher accuracy. However, a larger dataset, a deeper network or smaller filter size and stride may increase the computation cost of the detection model, resulting in longer training process and slower detection speed.

As the first trial of applying deep learning for sewer pipe defect detection, this study has the contribution in two aspects: (1) it paves the way for other users to apply the proposed approach on similar problems in the AEC industry; (2) the study on the influential factors provides insights for choosing an appropriate architecture and hyper-parameters when designing the model.

References

1. ASCE: Infrastructure Report Card (2017)
2. EPA: Why control sanitary sewer overflows, The United States (2004)
3. EPA: Report to Congress on Impacts and Control of Combined Sewer Overflows and Sanitary Sewer Overflows (2004)
4. Abdel-Qader, I., Abudayyeh, O., Kelly, M.E.: Analysis of edge-detection techniques for crack identification in bridges. J. Comput. Civil Eng. **17**(4), 255–263 (2003)
5. Yamaguchi, T., Nakamura, S., Saegusa, R., Hashimoto, S.: Image-based crack detection for real concrete surfaces. IEEJ Trans. Electr. Electron. Eng. **3**(1), 128–135 (2008)
6. Koch, C., Georgieva, K., Kasireddy, V., Akinci, B., Fieguth, P.: A review on computer vision based defect detection and condition assessment of concrete and asphalt civil infrastructure. Adv. Eng. Inform. **29**(2), 196–210 (2015)
7. Yu, S.-N., Jang, J.-H., Han, C.-S.: Auto inspection system using a mobile robot for detecting concrete cracks in a tunnel. Autom. Constr. **16**(3), 255–261 (2007)
8. Adhikari, R.S., Moselhi, O., Bagchi, A.: Image-based retrieval of concrete crack properties for bridge inspection. Autom. in Constr. **39**, 180–194 (2014)
9. Li, G., He, S., Ju, Y., Du, K.: Long-distance precision inspection method for bridge cracks with image processing. Autom. Constr. **41**, 83–95 (2014)
10. Sinha, S.K., Fieguth, P.W.: Morphological segmentation and classification of underground pipe images. Mach. Vis. Appl. **17**(1), 21–31 (2006)
11. Iyer, S., Sinha, S.K.: Segmentation of pipe images for crack detection in buried sewers. Comput.-Aided Civil Infrastruct. Eng. **21**(6), 395–410 (2006)
12. Sinha, S.K., Fieguth, P.W.: Automated detection of cracks in buried concrete pipe images. Autom. Constr. **15**(1), 58–72 (2006)
13. Halfawy, M.R., Hengmeechai, J.: Efficient algorithm for crack detection in sewer images from closed-circuit television inspections. J. Infrastruct. Syst. **20**(2), 04013014 (2014)
14. Krizhevsky, A., Sutskever, I., Hinton, G.E.: Imagenet classification with deep convolutional neural networks. In: Advances in Neural Information Processing Systems, pp. 1097–1105 (2012)
15. Cha, Y.-J., Choi, W., Büyüköztürk, O.: Deep learning-based crack damage detection using convolutional neural networks. Comput.-Aided Civil Infrastruct. Eng. **32**(5), 361–378 (2017)
16. Yokoyama, S., Matsumoto, T.: Development of an automatic detector of cracks in concrete using machine learning. Procedia Eng. **171**(Suppl. C), 1250–1255 (2017)

17. Makantasis, K., Protopapadakis, E., Doulamis, A., Doulamis, N., Loupos, C.: Deep convolutional neural networks for efficient vision based tunnel inspection. In: 2015 IEEE International Conference on Intelligent Computer Communication and Processing (ICCP), pp. 335–342. IEEE (2015)
18. Zhang, L., Yang, F., Zhang, Y.D., Zhu, Y.J.: Road crack detection using deep convolutional neural network. In: 2016 IEEE International Conference on Image Processing (ICIP), Phoenix, AZ, USA. IEEE (2016)
19. Girshick, R., Donahue, J., Darrell, T., Malik, J.: Rich feature hierarchies for accurate object detection and semantic segmentation. In: Proceedings of the IEEE Conference on Computer Vision and Pattern Recognition, pp. 580–587 (2014)
20. Girshick, R.: Fast R-CNN. In: Proceedings of the IEEE International Conference on Computer Vision, pp. 1440–1448 (2015)
21. Ren, S., He, K., Girshick, R., Sun, J.: Faster R-CNN: towards real-time object detection with region proposal networks. In: Advances in Neural Information Processing Systems, pp. 91–99 (2015)
22. Zhang, L., Lin, L., Liang, X., He, K.: Is faster R-CNN doing well for pedestrian detection? In: Leibe, B., Matas, J., Sebe, N., Welling, M. (eds.) ECCV 2016. LNCS, vol. 9906, pp. 443–457. Springer, Cham (2016). https://doi.org/10.1007/978-3-319-46475-6_28
23. Sun, X., Wu, P., Hoi, S.C.: Face detection using deep learning: an improved faster RCNN approach. arXiv preprint arXiv:1701.08289 (2017)
24. Yongjie, Z., Jian, W., Xin, Y.: Real-time vehicle detection and tracking in video based on faster R-CNN. J. Phys: Conf. Ser. **887**(1), 012068 (2017)
25. Ibadov, S., Ibadov, R., Kalmukov, B., Krutov, V.: Algorithm for detecting violations of traffic rules based on computer vision approaches. In: MATEC Web Conference, vol. 132, p. 05005 (2017)
26. Xu, Y., Yu, G., Wang, Y., Wu, X., Ma, Y.: Car detection from low-altitude UAV imagery with the faster R-CNN. J. Adv. Transp. **2017**, 10 (2017)
27. Jung, H., Choi, M.-K., Jung, J., Lee, J.-H., Kwon, S., Jung, W.Y.: ResNet-based vehicle classification and localization in traffic surveillance systems. In: 2017 IEEE Conference on Computer Vision and Pattern Recognition Workshops (CVPRW), pp. 934–940. IEEE (2017)
28. Zuo, Z., Yu, K., Zhou, Q., Wang, X., Li, T.: Traffic signs detection based on faster R-CNN. In: 2017 IEEE 37th International Conference on Distributed Computing Systems Workshops (ICDCSW), pp. 286–288. IEEE (2017)
29. Fang, Q., Li, H., Luo, X., Ding, L., Luo, H., Rose, T.M., An, W.: Detecting non-hardhat-use by a deep learning method from far-field surveillance videos. Autom. Constr. **85**(Suppl. C), 1–9 (2018)
30. VOC: PASCAL VOC Detection results, vol. 2017 (2012)
31. Zeiler, M.D., Fergus, R.: Visualizing and understanding convolutional networks. In: Fleet, D., Pajdla, T., Schiele, B., Tuytelaars, T. (eds.) ECCV 2014. LNCS, vol. 8689, pp. 818–833. Springer, Cham (2014). https://doi.org/10.1007/978-3-319-10590-1_53
32. Srivastava, N., Hinton, G., Krizhevsky, A., Sutskever, I., Salakhutdinov, R.: Dropout: a simple way to prevent neural networks from overfitting. J. Mach. Learn. Res. **15**(1), 1929–1958 (2014)
33. Everingham, M., Van Gool, L., Williams, C.K., Winn, J., Zisserman, A.: The Pascal visual object classes (VOC) challenge. Int. J. Comput. Vis. **88**(2), 303–338 (2010)
34. Salton, G., McGill, M.J.: Introduction to Modern Information Retrieval. McGraw-Hill, Inc., New York City (1986)
35. Tzutalin, LabelImg, vol. 2015, Git code

36. Jia, Y., Shelhamer, E., Donahue, J., Karayev, S., Long, J., Girshick, R., Guadarrama, S., Darrell, T.: Caffe: convolutional architecture for fast feature embedding. In: Proceedings of the 22nd ACM International Conference on Multimedia, pp. 675–678. ACM (2014)
37. Chatfield, K., Simonyan, K., Vedaldi, A., Zisserman, A.: Return of the devil in the details: delving deep into convolutional nets. arXiv preprint arXiv:1405.3531 (2014)
38. Simonyan, K., Zisserman, A.: Very deep convolutional networks for large-scale image recognition. arXiv preprint arXiv:1409.1556 (2014)

Smart HVAC Systems — Adjustable Airflow Direction

Milad Abedi[1], Farrokh Jazizadeh[1(✉)], Bert Huang[2], and Francine Battaglia[3]

[1] Department of Civil and Environmental Engineering, Virginia Tech, Blacksburg, VA 24061, USA
jazizade@vt.edu
[2] Department of Computer Science, Virginia Tech, Blacksburg, VA 24061, USA
[3] Department of Mechanical and Aerospace Engineering, University at Buffalo, Buffalo, NY 14260, USA

Abstract. Enhancing the thermal comfort level of the occupants has been the subject of several research efforts focused on controlling the Heating, Ventilation and Air-Conditioning (HVAC) systems with the objective of higher occupant-thermal-comfort. It has been demonstrated that improving occupants' thermal comfort often leads to savings in energy consumption. Also there are numerous studies that have directly aimed to optimize the energy consumption of the HVAC system while keeping the occupants' thermal comfort within an acceptable range. In majority of the cases the level of control over the actions of the HVAC system is restricted to controlling the temperature set-point for the thermal zone. This study aims to explore the benefits of creating a more flexible HVAC system, which can lead to improvements in occupant thermal comfort and energy consumption of the HVAC system. The envisioned HVAC system will be capable of adjusting the direction of the airflow at each diffusor thereby producing a wider range of actions. In this study, a Computational Fluid Dynamic (CFD) simulation of a room was used as a proxy for the real-world environment, and the results of the CFD model were generalized through a Gaussian Process Regression (GPR) model to provide higher resolution data. The benefits of enabling the HVAC system to control the direction of airflow at the point of diffusion have been evaluated in terms of occupant's thermal comfort and reduction in energy consumption.

Keywords: Airflow direction · HVAC · Thermal comfort
Computational Fluid Dynamics · Statistical learning

1 Introduction

Thermal comfort, defined as "that condition of mind which expresses satisfaction with the thermal environment and is assessed by subjective evaluation" [1], has been the subject of many research efforts during the last decades. While the comfort itself is a valid objective for research, it has also been established that increase in thermal comfort often leads to decrease in energy consumption. This is particularly encouraging due to the considerable contribution of HVAC systems to the total energy consumption. In the US, buildings are responsible for 40% of the total energy consumption [2], and 48% of

© Springer International Publishing AG, part of Springer Nature 2018
I. F. C. Smith and B. Domer (Eds.): EG-ICE 2018, LNCS 10864, pp. 193–209, 2018.
https://doi.org/10.1007/978-3-319-91638-5_10

the energy consumed in residential buildings is used by HVAC systems [3]. In commercial buildings, HVAC systems are responsible for 44% of the total energy consumption [4].

Current thermal comfort models such as the Predicted Mean Vote model [1] depend on a set of environmental and human parameters such as air temperature and metabolic rate. However, in real-world applications, lack of information about the specific occupant and the environment often leads to conservative assumptions. These assumptions in return lead to sub-optimal HVAC performance. Several research efforts [5–16] have focused on personalized HVAC control systems so as to adjust the HVAC system according to the occupant-specific thermal comfort tendencies to avoid making overly general assumptions. The other aspect of the problem, namely the estimation of relevant environmental parameters also presents a challenge especially considering the infeasibility of installing large number of sensors to better understand the environment. With the low number of sensing points, the condition of the environment is assumed to be one of relative uniformity thereby failing to take into account the effects of a non-uniform environment on the occupant's thermal comfort. Lack of sufficient awareness of the environment and the consequent simplistic assumptions also affect the actions taken by HVAC system to improve the occupant's thermal comfort. Aside from the lack of information about the environment, the inflexibility of HVAC system in terms of possible actions also limits the HVAC system's ability to produce an effective, environment-aware response. For instance, in a room with several diffusors, a change in one diffuser's airflow rate might be a sufficient action to ensure the thermal comfort of the occupant but the HVAC system's inability to control every single diffusor would limit the control to a change in airflow rate of all the diffusors which can be an ineffective action in terms of energy consumption.

In our previous studies [9–15] we have established methods of evaluating thermal comfort of occupants that could address the issue of lack of sufficient environment awareness in terms of its effect on evaluating the occupant's thermal comfort state. These methods also account for the natural differences in the occupant's thermal comfort parameters, thereby avoiding conservative assumptions regarding the parameters in question, which can in return lead to higher thermal satisfaction as well as lower energy consumption. In so doing, the occupant could be used as proxy for sensing points.

One of the potential merits of using the occupant as a proxy for sensing points is that the HVAC system might be able to take more specific actions to satisfy the occupant with lower energy consumption. Returning to the previous example of a room with multiple diffusors, having a real-time understanding of the occupant's thermal comfort state can help the HVAC control algorithm take more effective actions. To address the problem of lack of environmental information, we can use Artificial Intelligence (AI) learning algorithms that explore the environment and learn as they interact with it thereby alleviating the need for prior knowledge of the environment. One of such methods is Reinforcement Learning, where an agent learns how to behave in an unknown environment by interacting with it.

While the current state of the literature on flexible HVAC systems in terms of control within a thermal zone is very limited, a fair amount of research exists on a building level flexibility of HVAC systems. Tachwali et al. [17] designed a multi-zone HVAC controller equipped with a wireless sensor network that was capable of directing the airflow only to the occupied zones. In other studies, West et al. [18] and Ghahramani et al. [9] enabled a zone-level temperature set-point control for an HVAC system with the objective of further reducing running costs and CO2 emissions while maintaining occupant's thermal comfort. Through simulation of an entire floor with several rooms and offices and by using the occupancy data gathered from monitoring the real-world counterpart of the simulated model, Agarwal et al. [19] studied the benefits of a zone level temperature set-point control based on the occupancy state of each zone. In a subsequent paper, Agarwal et al. [20] explored the idea of using a network of occupancy detection sensors to enable a zone-level airflow control (on or off). Benefits of control over the components of the HVAC system has also been explored. Nassif et al. [21], in addition to the 70 zone-temperature set-points also controlled the inner components of the HVAC system such as supply duct static pressure, supply air temperature and chilled water supply temperature. In their study, Feldmeier and Paradiso [6] extended the level of control beyond the HVAC system, which was able to control zone-level temperature set-points, and enabled the control algorithm to open and close windows as well. While the smart control of the airflow direction by the HVAC system has not been properly studied, Fountain et al. [22] explored the benefits of allowing the users to control the direction of flow at the point of diffusion and also by using a desk fan. They concluded that enabling control over the air-movement can lead to higher thermal satisfaction.

As a first step in the way to designing and building more effective HVAC system, in this paper we have sought to answer the question of whether increasing the flexibility of the HVAC system in terms of control over the direction of airflow could lead to higher overall occupant thermal satisfaction with lower energy consumption. To do that a Computational Fluid Dynamic (CFD) model of a room was developed and used to study the effects of direction of airflow on the performance of the HVAC system. The performance of such a system was evaluated in term of energy consumption. The results of the analysis were used to gain insight into the promises of such a system and the challenges that the envisioned HVAC system would have to overcome.

2   Methodology

As noted, the objective of this paper is to investigate the effect of adjusting the direction of airflow on the energy consumption of the HVAC system while taking into consideration the thermal comfort state of the occupant. This objective has been pursued through a coupled simulation consisting of physics-based modeling and machine learning-based prediction algorithms. The simulation represents an occupant sitting in a room equipped with an HVAC system with adjustable airflow direction.

2.1   Environment

A CFD model in the commercial software ANSYS Fluent [23] was developed to serve as the simulation environment. The model represents a 6 m × 4 m × 2.5 m room with a single diffusor on one side and an exhaust on the other (Fig. 1(a)). Given the high computational cost of implementing the CFD model, the direction of the airflow was set to have a constant 30° angle with the ceiling so that the space of possible directions would become smaller and easier to explore. Equations for conservation of mass, momentum and energy were considered for an incompressible Newtonian fluid, and the Boussinesq model and the k – ε turbulence model were incorporated. The equations were solved by using the segregated Pressure-Based Navier-Stokes (PBNS) numerical solver and the Semi-Implicit Method for Pressure-Linked Equation (SIMPLE) algorithm was employed to solve the pressure-velocity coupling. Gradient and pressure spatial discretization was performed through the least squares cell based (LSCB) and the pressure staggering option (PRESTO!) approaches, respectively. For time derivative discretization, a first-order implicit method with a time step of 0.1 s was used. Discretization of energy, momentum, dissipation rate, turbulent kinetic energy and discrete ordinate was performed using a second-order upwind. Previous studies by Park and Battaglia [24] and Wang et al. [25] have validated the use of these equations and models for natural and forced convection in buildings. Through a grid resolution study the uniform grid spacing of 14.2 cm was chosen. A detailed validation of the grid cell size was performed in the studies by Park and Battaglia [24, 26] and guided the cell size used here.

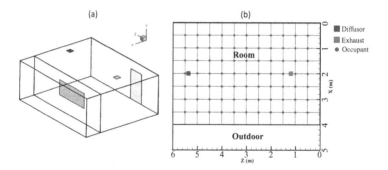

Fig. 1. (a) 3-D sketch of the simulated room. (b) The plan of the room in the CFD simulation. The considered occupant locations have been identified by red dots. (Color figure online)

The room is exposed to the warmer outside environment with a constant temperature of 30 °C (corresponding to a hot summer day) through a wall on one side of the room (Fig. 1). The solar intensity is constant at 1100 W/m^2, which represents a southern-facing window at a latitude of 37°N. The window shades are assumed to reflect solar radiation, but heat transfer is allowed through the windows. The stone façade of the exterior office walls is made of dolomite (thermal conductivity is 1.5 W/mK) and conduction is modeled through the exterior walls. The diffusor has been modeled using conventional 4-way louvre-bladed diffusors where the adjustable nature of the diffusor is defined as boundary conditions using velocity, flow area opening, and corresponding blade angles in each of the directions. The incoming airflow from the diffusor has a temperature of 13 °C and can be simulated at any direction and for any duration at the rate of 200 cfm (0.0944 m^3/s). In order for the CFD model to be representative of real-world scenarios the CFD model was started from an initial condition and it was allowed to run for 180 s without any diffusion. During this period, the room exchanged heat with the outside environment and thus a temperature gradient was created in the room. After the initial 180 s, the diffusor started to work and we continued to run the model with the diffusor turned on for an additional 420 s, while recording the results at 10 s time steps.

2.2 Occupant

For simplicity, we have assumed that the simulated room will only host one occupant. The occupant is assumed to be seated in a chair, the top of the head of the occupant being at a height of 1.2 m from the floor.

The occupant is assumed to be stationary. The computations have been carried out for 77 different locations for the occupant, corresponding to a mesh of 11 by 7, with 50 cm steps (Fig. 1(b)). This configuration corresponds to assuming a uniform probability distribution for the coordinates of the occupant in the room.

To evaluate the thermal comfort state of a simulated occupant at each step, a scaled version of the Proportion Comfortable model presented by Daum et al. [16] (Fig. 2(a)) was used. This model presents a relationship between the surrounding temperature and the thermal comfort index of the occupants. For this study, the aggregate thermal comfort graph was normalized so that its maximum equals 1 (Fig. 2(b)).

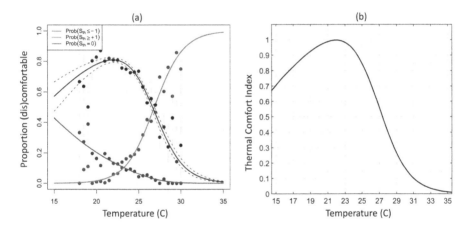

Fig. 2. Thermal comfort index versus temperature. (a) The original model taken from [16]. (b) The scaled model

By using this model, the thermal comfort index can be calculated based on the temperature in the vicinity of the occupant. At each time step of the CFD simulation, the temperature surrounding the occupant is calculated by averaging the temperature at three heights corresponding to the head, abdomen and ankles of the occupant. The average temperature is then fed into the aforementioned model, which in return outputs the thermal comfort index of the occupant.

2.3   Using Machine Learning Algorithms to Expand the Results of the CFD Simulation

Given the prohibitive computational cost of running the CFD model for every airflow direction of interest, simulations were carried out only for a total number of 6 airflow directions as illustrated in Fig. 3. A number of machine learning algorithms (Regression Models) were used to expand the results of the simulated 6 airflow directions to non-simulated directions of interest. Based on an empirical validation process, the Gaussian Regression Process (GPR) model was chosen. Using the CFD simulation results, a GPR model was trained that would allow us to evaluate the changes in the occupant's thermal comfort index in cases where the direction of airflow was not among the 6 simulated directions.

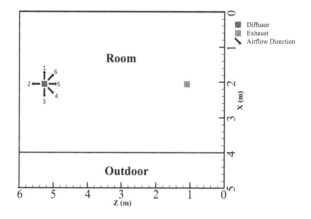

Fig. 3. The simulated airflow directions. All directions have a 30° angle with the ceiling.

Model Selection and Validation. Given that the intention behind using a regression model was to estimate the improvements in thermal comfort index in non-simulated directions, we have tailored our validation approach to correspond to this objective. To validate the performance of any regression model we completely eliminated the data belonging to a single chosen direction from the training set and used it as testing data instead. For instance, we trained the model based on the simulation results of directions 1, 2, 3, 5, 6 (leaving out direction 4). We then used the regression model to predict the results of the simulation for direction 4, and compared the regression model's predictions to the CFD simulation results.

This process was performed in each direction for all the 77 occupant locations as shown in Fig. 1(b). Table 1 represents the average and minimum values for the coefficient of determination (R^2) for the testing data in each of the tests in the case of the GPR model. For instance, the first row of Table 1 represents the validation results for the case where the CFD simulation data for direction 1 were eliminated from the GPR model's training set. The R^2 values were calculated based on the testing data (belonging to direction 1) and predictions of the GPR model that was trained on the data for remaining directions.

Table 1. Validation results for the GPR model

Eliminated direction	Average R^2	Minimum R^2
1	0.97	0.93
2	0.60	0.47
3	0.91	0.87
4	0.97	0.92
5	0.93	0.87
6	0.98	0.91

Selection of the regression model to generalize the results of the CFD analysis was done through an empirical validation process. The metric that was used for model selection is the average of all the R^2 values. For instance, the value of this metric for the GPR model is the average of all the values in the second column of Table 1. A number of well-known regression methods were tested, and based on the overall validation results (Table 2) the GPR model was selected. The Boosted Decision Tree Regression model, despite its higher R^2 score was not chosen for reasons that have been explained at the end of this section.

Table 2. Model selection based on average overall R^2

Regression method	Average overall R^2
Boosted Decision Tree Regression	0.98
Gaussian Process Regression	0.89
K Nearest Neighbors Regression (K = 5)	0.79
Multi-layer Perceptron Regression	0.58
Support Vector Regression	0.46
Linear Regression	0.45

In Table 1, note the lower value of the average and minimum R^2 in the case where the data belonging to direction 2 was eliminated from the training data. This is not surprising, because once we eliminated the data belonging to direction 2 there was no airflow direction in the training data that had a component in the same direction as direction 2 (all the other directions have an angle of $90°$ or more with direction 2). The results in Table 1 indicate that GPR is an accurate and reliable approach for our needs.

GPR Basics. [27] For a given data set of $D = \{(x_i, y_i)|i = 1, \ldots, n\}$ we define a model f that maps input X to output Y.

$$f(x) = X^T w, \qquad y = f(x) + \varepsilon \qquad (1)$$

Where w represents the model parameter vector and ε is the noise which is assumed to have a normal distribution as follows.

$$\varepsilon \sim \mathcal{N}(0, \sigma_n^2) \qquad (2)$$

Assuming that the training data are independent, the likelihood is defined as:

$$p(y|X, w) = \prod_{i=1}^{n} p(y_i|x_i, w) = \mathcal{N}(X^T w, \sigma_n^2 I) \tag{3}$$

Assuming a zero mean Gaussian prior probability with a covariance matrix of Σ_p we have:

$$w \sim \mathcal{N}(0, \Sigma_p) \tag{4}$$

$$p(w|y, X) = \frac{p(y|X, w)P(w)}{p(y|X)} \tag{5}$$

After some mathematical manipulation, we would arrive at the following conclusion.

$$p(w|X, y) \sim \mathcal{N}(\bar{w}, A^{-1}) \tag{6}$$

Where:

$$A = \frac{1}{\sigma_n^2} XX^T + \Sigma_p^{-1} \tag{7}$$

$$\bar{w} = \sigma_n^{-2} A^{-1} Xy \tag{8}$$

To make predictions for a test case we would average over all possible parameter values w, weighted by their posterior probabilities. Thus the predictive distribution for $f_* \triangleq f(X_*)$ at X_* is given by:

$$p(f_*|X_*, X, y) = \int p(f_*|X_*, w) p(w|X, y)dw = \mathcal{N}\left(\frac{1}{\sigma^2} X_*^T A^{-1} Xy, X_*^T A^{-1} X_*\right) \tag{9}$$

The strength of the GPR models stems partly from their capability in utilizing the notion of kernels (for further readings see Ref. [27]).

GPR Model Overview. Inputs to the GPR model are the airflow direction, the duration of airflow, and the initial thermal comfort index of the occupant (Fig. 4). The first two parameters, namely the direction and duration of airflow define the actions that the proposed HVAC system can take. The initial comfort index of the occupant encapsulates a number of human and environmental variables. The output of the GPR model is the amount of improvement in the thermal comfort index of the occupant as a result of the action that was taken by the HVAC system (Fig. 4).

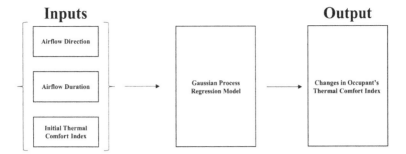

Fig. 4. Overview of the GPR model.

Evaluation of the Boosted Decision Tree Regression (BDTR) Model. While the hiher value of the average R^2 metric in the first glance suggests a superior performance for the BDTR model, upon closer inspection, we came to the conclusion that the BDTR model might not be representative of the CFD simulation results. Our analysis indicated that the BDTR model might have over-fitted the model to duration of flow (one of the inputs to the model) and as a result may have not been able to represent the effect of airflow direction on improvements in the occupant's thermal comfort index.

To show that the BDTR model does not capture the relationship between the direction of airflow and the model output, we trained the BDTR model by using the data belonging only to direction 2 and then used the trained model to predict the improvements in thermal comfort index for all the other directions. The average testing R^2 for this analysis was 0.98 which indicates that the results of the CFD simulation for airflow direction 2 was enough to predict the results for all the other direction, meaning that the airflow direction is inconsequential when it comes to improvements in the thermal comfort index of the occupant. If this were true, then the first hypothesis of this paper, namely that the direction of airflow has a significant effect on the thermal comfort index of the occupant would have been proven false. While R^2 is a well-known metric for validation or rejection of regression models, it is a single number and it does not provide enough insight into the underlying mechanism of the model. In order to gain further insight into the results of the BDTR model, we introduced the following error definition for any given data point in our data set.

$$Absolute\ Error_i = |PV_i - TV_i| \tag{10}$$

Where PV is the predicted value given by the regression model and TV is the true value obtained from the CFD simulation. To investigate the relationship between the BDTR model's performance and the Duration of Airflow parameter, a BDTR model and a GPR model were trained on the data belonging only to direction 2 and then they were used to predict the improvement in thermal comfort index for an occupant sitting at (X = 3.5, Z = 5.5) for all the other simulated airflow directions. Figure 5(a) represents the absolute error of the BDTR model's predictions and its relationship with the duration of airflow.

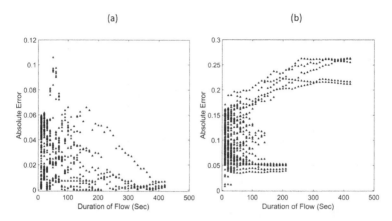

Fig. 5. Absolute prediction error of regression models trained only on the data belonging to airflow direction 2 (a) BDTR model (b) GPR model

As shown in Fig. 5(a), in the case of BDTR the data points that have a longer duration of flow have been predicted more accurately than those that have a lower duration of flow. This is not surprising, given our suspicion that the BDTR model gives more weight to the duration of flow than the other parameters. Long duration of flow creates a more uniform environment in the room and the effect of the direction of airflow is lessened compare to the situations where the duration of flow is limited. Therefore, in the situations with longer duration of flow, the duration of flow becomes the dominant parameter, which is why the BDTR model makes better predictions in those cases. For these reasons we suspect that the BDTR model has not been able to capture the relationships between the airflow direction parameters and the output, but instead has heavily relied on the duration of airflow to the detriment of the other parameters. The unrealistically high value of the coefficient of determination can be accounted for by the outlier effect, since the data points to which the model has shown the best fit are those that have a considerably longer duration of flow compared to the majority of the data points. In contrast to the BDTR model, the GPR model has not ignored the effects of airflow direction by relying heavily on the duration of flow parameter, which is why in Fig. 5(b) the values of absolute error of prediction for the GPR model have not followed the same trend as Fig. 5(a). Further analysis is required to determine if the BDTR model's overall performance is poor, but the represented evidence strongly indicates that the performance of the BDTR model is not as impressive as the R^2 values indicate. Given that such a comprehensive evaluation requires more data than available to us, in the interest of time and efficiency we have chosen to use the GPR model instead.

3   Results

3.1   Dynamics of the Environment

The presented results in this paper are intended to reflect the potentials that the proposed HVAC system has in terms of savings in energy consumption. Figure 6(a) presents the

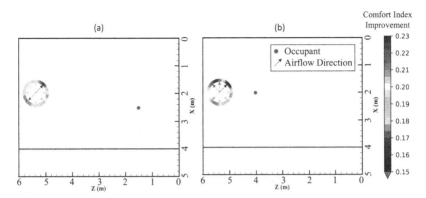

Fig. 6. Effect of direction of airflow on changes in the thermal comfort index (Duration = 60 s)

amount of improvement in the thermal comfort index of the occupant when the HVAC system has been working for a duration of 60 s in the CFD Model. By using the trained GPR Model the improvements in thermal comfort index for non-simulated directions have been computed.

According to Fig. 6(a) the suitable direction of the airflow for the given duration and environment is one that directs the airflow towards the occupant. Note that the shown energy-efficient airflow direction in Fig. 6(a) is not among the 6 simulated cases (Fig. 3), rather it is the prediction of the GPR Model.

Figure 6(b) shows the improvements in the thermal comfort index of an occupant sitting in a different location. Similar to Fig. 6(a) the results belong to the case, where the HVAC system has worked for a duration of 60 s. The contrasts between Fig. 6(a) and (b) shed light on challenges that the control system will have to face and overcome.

According to Fig. 6(b) in that situation the efficient direction of airflow is not in the direction of the occupant. As mentioned before, in our simulated CFD Model and the trained GPR Model the direction of the airflow has been constrained so that there exists a 30° angle between ceiling and the airflow direction. Thus if the occupant is sitting close to the diffusor, setting the airflow direction towards the occupant would result in a situation where the airflow passes above the head of the occupant by a distance. This limitation in the flexibility of the simulated HVAC system has made the problem of finding the efficient direction of airflow considerably more complex.

The energy-efficient direction of airflow in Fig. 6(b) is one that hits the walls first. Note that despite the geometrical symmetry of the room (with respect to the X = 2 line), the improvements in the thermal comfort index are not symmetric. This can be explained by taking into account that one of the walls is in contact with outside warm air which creates a temperature gradient within the room that causes the aforementioned non-symmetric behavior.

As demonstrated by the drawn contrasts between Fig. 6(a) and (b), the optimal behavior of the HVAC system is affected by many parameters such as the airflow dynamics of the room, the imposed temperature constraint and properties related to the occupant. In real-world applications other issues such as barriers (desks, monitors, etc.) can potentially cause further complexity. The control algorithm must be able to learn the optimal behavior despite all of these complexities, while requiring only a minimum number of sensors.

3.2 Energy Consumption

In this section, we have examined the potentials for reduction in energy consumption that the proposed flexibility in operation of HVAC system will be able to facilitate. A common practice in HVAC control studies is to define the thermal comfort as a constraint and then minimize the energy consumption of the system. For the purposes of this section, the minimum thermal comfort index will be set to 0.95.

The underlying hypothesis is that the energy consumption of a smart, comfort driven HVAC system is sensitive to the variations in the airflow direction at the point of diffusion. Using the CFD simulation and the trained GPR Model, we have computed the duration of airflow necessary for each airflow direction to bring the occupant to the desired thermal comfort index. Since the airflow rate is equal for all directions, for the purposes of this study we will assume that the energy consumption is proportional to the duration of airflow. However, we must be mindful that the relationship between airflow and energy consumption is not necessarily linear in all settings.

Figure 7 demonstrates the relationship between the horizontal angle of airflow and the duration of airflow (proportional to energy consumption). The horizontal axis shows the angle between the airflow direction and the direction of the occupant from the diffusor, while the vertical axis shows the duration of airflow required for the occupant to reach the desired thermal comfort index. Positive and negative values on the horizontal axis respectively indicate counter-clock-wise and clock-wise angles between the direction of the occupant and the direction of airflow. The solid line (red) shows the average results for the cases, in which the occupant is sitting at locations where $Z = 0.5$ or 1 or 1.5 (21 locations), with the shaded area representing a variation of one standard deviation from the average. The dash line (blue) belongs to the case where the occupant is sitting at $(X = 2.5, Z = 1.5)$. In Fig. 7 the efficient direction of airflow is the direction that blows the air in the direction of the occupant since this direction has a lower duration of airflow and therefore a lower level of energy consumption. Also note that the consistency of the results for different occupant location as demonstrated by a relatively narrow shaded area corresponding to a smaller standard deviation.

Figure 8 is similar to Fig. 7, except that the occupant is sitting closer to the diffusor at locations where $Z = 4.5$ or 5 or 5.5 for the solid line (red) and the corresponding location to the dash line (blue) is $(X = 2, Z = 4.5)$. Unlike the previous case, here the efficient angle of airflow is not at the same direction as the occupant's location. Note the more complex behavior and lack of consistency in Fig. 8 compared to Fig. 7 that is a result of the airflow dynamics of the room and the limitations of the HVAC system.

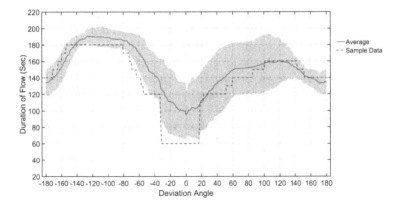

Fig. 7. Required duration of airflow in the CFD model that brings the occupant to the desired thermal comfort index versus the deviation angle from the location of the occupant. (Color figure online)

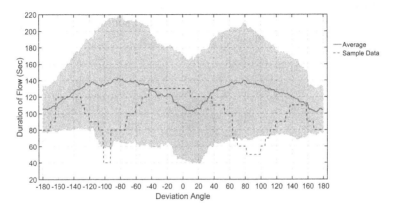

Fig. 8. Required duration of airflow in the CFD model that brings the occupant to the desired thermal comfort index versus the deviation angle from the location of the occupant. (Color figure online)

To examine the second hypothesis of this paper, namely that significant energy savings can be achieved by using flexible HVAC systems, we will assume a uniform probability distribution for the location of the occupant (occupant has an equal probability of sitting in any location in the room). To account for this assumption, we use the uniformly distributed occupant location presented in Fig. 1 and then we average over all user locations.

The percentage of energy savings for each direction is calculated in comparison to the uniform diffusion.

$$Energy\ Savings\ for\ direction\ i = 100 \times \left(1 - \frac{E_i}{E_{uniform}} \right) \tag{11}$$

E_i is defined as the amount of Energy needed to bring the occupant to the 0.95 thermal comfort index while diffusing the air in direction i. $E_{uniform}$ is defined as the amount of Energy needed to bring the occupant to the 0.95 thermal comfort index with a uniform diffusion. The average of the results for all the airflow directions (from 1 to 360° by a 1° step size) has been used as an estimate for uniform diffusion. As mentioned before, the airflow rate is constant in our simulations, so the energy consumption is proportional to the duration of airflow.

Assuming that a control algorithm can effectively identify the optimal airflow direction, we compute the Maximum Energy Savings for each occupant location.

$$Maximum\ Energy\ Savings = max_i \left(100 \times \left(1 - \frac{E_i}{E_{uniform}} \right) \right) \qquad (12)$$

For each one of the 77 occupant locations the Maximum Energy Savings has been calculated. According to the results, the average amount of energy saved by using the envisioned HVAC system with a competent control algorithm is 59% per cycle. The amount of the saved energy varies between 20% and 92% per cycle, depending on the location of the occupant. The histogram in Fig. 9 provides some insight into the potential savings that the proposed system can yield.

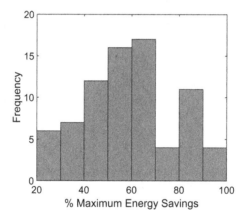

Fig. 9. Histogram of the Maximum Energy Savings per cycle achieved in the 77 considered occupant locations.

Figure 10 allows for a better understanding of the relationship between the occupant's location and the potential for savings in energy consumption by using the proposed platform. According to Fig. 10, in locations that are closer to the diffusor higher savings can be achieved. This should be taken into account when choosing the location of a diffusor or the number of diffusors in a real-world building. Note that the actual amount of energy savings brought on by the proposed HVAC system also depends on the number of heating/cooling cycles. It is likely that the envisioned HVAC system would have to go through a higher number of operation cycles compared to the case of uniform diffusion.

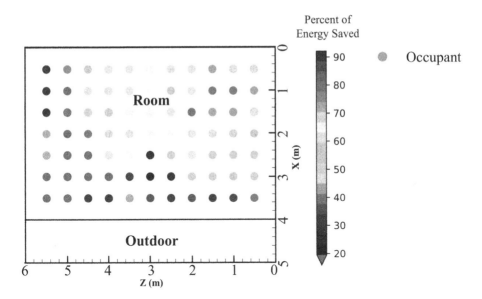

Fig. 10. Potential energy savings (per cycle) for each of the considered occupant locations.

4   Conclusion

In this paper, we introduced the idea of HVAC systems with more flexibility in terms of possible actions they can take within a thermal zone. A specific case of such HVAC systems, namely an HVAC system that is capable of adjusting the direction of airflow was investigated. A CFD model of the described setting was created and the results of the simulation were further generalized by using Gaussian Process Regression method to alleviate the need to perform a large number of computationally expensive CFD Simulations.

The results indicate that the idea of enabling the HVAC system to have control over the direction of airflow at the point of diffusion, offers a very promising prospect. The average energy savings of 59% per cycle (assumed to be proportional to the airflow duration) in comparison to a uniform-diffusion HVAC system calls for further research into this potentially effective and underexplored area of research.

Notwithstanding the demonstrated promise of the proposed ideas, the results show that a successful real-world design and implementation of such systems is predicated on effectively addressing the complexities and barrier that lie in the way. One of the challenges that such a system will face is the issue of designing an effective control algorithm. It was discussed in the previous sections that the optimal response at each state, as well as the potential for energy savings dramatically varies with parameters related to the occupant's location, the limitations of the HVAC system and the airflow dynamics of the thermal zone. Taking into account the infeasibility of installing a high number of sensors, the control algorithm must be capable of learning how to effectively control the HVAC system while using only a minimal amount of information. The envisioned HVAC system should also address the ventilation requirements. Our future line of research will focus on creating an interactive framework, in which an intelligent control algorithm would learn how to control the HVAC system. We are also in the process of designing and executing relevant empirical studies.

Acknowledgement. This material is based upon work supported by the Institute for Critical Technology and Applied Science (ICTAS) at Virginia Tech. Any opinions, findings, and conclusions or recommendations expressed in this material are those of the author(s) and do not necessarily reflect the views of the ICTAS.

References

1. American Society of Heating, Refrigerating and Air Conditioning Engineers: ANSI/ASHRAE Standard 55-2013: Thermal Environmental Conditions for Human Occupancy. ASHRAE (2013)
2. US Energy Information Administration. http://www.eia.gov/tools/faqs/faq.php?id=86&t=1. Accessed 10 Jan 2018
3. US Department of Energy. https://energy.gov/public-services/homes/heating-cooling. Accessed 10 Jan 2018
4. US Energy Information Administration. https://www.eia.gov/consumption/commercial/reports/2012/energyusage. Accessed 10 Jan 2018
5. Federspiel, C.C., Asada, H.: User-adaptable comfort control for HVAC systems. J. Dyn. Syst. Meas. Control **116**, 477–486 (1994)
6. Feldmeier, M., Paradiso, J.A.: Personalized HVAC control system. In: 2010 Internet of Things (IOT), pp. 1–8 (2010)
7. Erickson, V.L., Cerpa, A.E.: Thermovote. In: Proceedings of the Fourth ACM Workshop on Embedded Sensing Systems for Energy-Efficiency in Buildings - BuildSys 2012, pp. 9–16. ACM, Toronto (2012)
8. Gao, P.X., Keshav, S.: SPOT: a smart personalized office thermal control system. In: Proceedings of the Fourth International Conference on Future Energy Systems, pp. 237–246. ACM, Berkeley (2013)
9. Ghahramani, A., Jazizadeh, F., Becerik-Gerber, B.: A knowledge based approach for selecting energy-aware and comfort-driven HVAC temperature set points. Energy Build. **85**, 536–548 (2014)
10. Jazizadeh, F., Pradeep, S.: Can computers visually quantify human thermal comfort?: Short Paper. In: Proceedings of the 3rd ACM International Conference on Systems for Energy-Efficient Built Environments, pp. 95–98. ACM, Palo Alto (2016)
11. Jazizadeh, F., Ghahramani, A., Becerik-Gerber, B., Kichkaylo, T., Orosz, M.: User-led decentralized thermal comfort driven HVAC operations for improved efficiency in office buildings. Energy Build. **70**, 398–410 (2014)
12. Mansourifard, P., Jazizadeh, F., Krishnamachari, B., Becerik-Gerber, B.: Online learning for personalized room-level thermal control: a multi-armed bandit framework. In: Proceedings of the 5th ACM Workshop on Embedded Systems For Energy-Efficient Buildings, pp. 1–8. ACM, Roma (2013)
13. Jazizadeh, F., Marin, F.M., Becerik-Gerber, B.: A thermal preference scale for personalized comfort profile identification via participatory sensing. Build. Environ. **68**, 140–149 (2013)

14. Jazizadeh, F., Ghahramani, A., Becerik-Gerber, B., Kichkaylo, T., Orosz, M.: Personalized thermal comfort-driven control in HVAC-operated office buildings. In: 2013 Computing in Civil Engineering (2013)
15. Jazizadeh, F., Becerik-Gerber, B.: Toward adaptive comfort management in office buildings using participatory sensing for end user driven control. In: Proceedings of the Fourth ACM Workshop on Embedded Sensing Systems for Energy-Efficiency in Buildings, pp. 1–8. ACM (2012)
16. Daum, D., Haldi, F., Morel, N.: A personalized measure of thermal comfort for building controls. Build. Environ. **46**, 3–11 (2011)
17. Tachwali, Y., Refai, H., Fagan, J.E.: Minimizing HVAC energy consumption using a wireless sensor network. In: IECON 2007 - 33rd Annual Conference of the IEEE Industrial Electronics Society, pp. 439–444 (2007)
18. West, S.R., Ward, J.K., Wall, J.: Trial results from a model predictive control and optimisation system for commercial building HVAC. Energy Build. **72**, 271–279 (2014)
19. Agarwal, Y., Balaji, B., Gupta, R., Lyles, J., Wei, M., Weng, T.: Occupancy-driven energy management for smart building automation. In: Proceedings of the 2nd ACM Workshop on Embedded Sensing Systems for Energy-Efficiency in Building, pp. 1–6. ACM, Zurich (2010)
20. Agarwal, Y., Balaji, B., Dutta, S., Gupta, R.K., Weng, T.: Duty-cycling buildings aggressively: the next frontier in HVAC control. In: Proceedings of the 10th ACM/IEEE International Conference on Information Processing in Sensor Networks, pp. 246–257 (2011)
21. Nassif, N., Kajl, S., Sabourin, R.: Evolutionary algorithms for multi-objective optimization in HVAC system control strategy. In: 2004 Processing IEEE Annual Meeting of the Fuzzy Information, NAFIPS 2004, vol. 51, pp. 51–56 (2004)
22. Fountain, M., Arens, E., de Dear, R., Bauman, F., Miura, K.: Locally controlled air movement preferred in warm isothermal environments (1994)
23. ANSYS Inc.: ANSYS Fluent 16.0 Theory Guide. ANSYS Inc. (2015)
24. Park, D., Battaglia, F.: Effect of heat loads and ambient conditions on thermal comfort for single-sided ventilation. Build. Simul. **8**, 167–178 (2015)
25. Wang, J., Wang, S., Zhang, T., Battaglia, F.: Assessment of single-sided natural ventilation driven by buoyancy forces through variable window configurations. Energy Build. **139**, 762–779 (2017)
26. Park, D., Battaglia, F.: Application of a wall-solar chimney for passive ventilation of dwellings. J. Solar Energy Eng. **137**, 061006 (2015)
27. Rasmussen, C.E., William, C.K.I.: Gaussian Processes for Machine Learning. The MIT Press, Cambridge (2006)

Adaptive Approach for Sensor Placement Combining a Quantitative Strategy with Engineering Practice

Numa Joy Bertola[1,2(✉)] ⓘ and Ian F. C. Smith[1,2] ⓘ

[1] Future Cities Laboratory, Singapore-ETH Centre, ETH Zurich,
1 CREATE Way, CREATE Tower, Singapore 138602, Singapore
numa.bertola@epfl.ch
[2] Applied Computing and Mechanics Laboratory (IMAC), School of Architecture,
Civil and Environmental Engineering (ENAC), Swiss Federal Institute of Technology (EPFL),
1015 Lausanne, Switzerland

Abstract. Infrastructure-capacity challenges due to growing populations, increasing urbanization and ageing existing assets are widespread. The assessment of remaining life of existing infrastructure has the potential to improve decision-making on asset management. However, this task is challenging due to the difficulties in modelling of infrastructure behavior. Error-domain model falsification (EDMF) is an easy-to-use model-based structural-identification methodology where field measurements are used to improve knowledge of the real behavior of structures. This methodology accommodates aleatory and systematic uncertainties induced by sources such as modelling assumptions, boundary conditions and numerical computation. Field-measurements, collected during load tests, lead to the identification of bridge characteristics such as geometric and material properties as well as support conditions. Benefits of structural-identification practice depend upon the methodology chosen but also upon the choice of sensor type and its location. In spite of such obvious importance, sensor types and positions are usually chosen using only qualitative rules of thumb coming from engineering experience. A more rational strategy to design optimal sensor configuration is justified and this is the aim of the study described in this paper. First, two quantitative methodologies for sensor-configuration optimization are compared with the solution designed by engineers using experience only on a full-scale case study in Singapore. The first quantitative sensor-placement methodology selects sensor locations with the largest signal-to-noise ratio in model prediction. The second strategy maximizes the joint entropy of the sensor configuration, using the hierarchical algorithm for sensor-placement. The joint entropy evaluates redundant information between possible sensor locations to select locations delivering the largest information gain when coupled. The performance of sensor configurations is evaluated using two information-gain metrics: information gain and the expected number of candidate models using simulated measurements. The hierarchical algorithm outperforms the strategy based on the maximal signal-to-noise ratio and the sensor configuration chosen empirically without calculation. However, the sensor configuration proposed by the hierarchical algorithm may be non-intuitive for practitioners. Eventually, an adaptive approach, involving engineering judgement and the hierarchical algorithm is

© Springer International Publishing AG, part of Springer Nature 2018
I. F. C. Smith and B. Domer (Eds.): EG-ICE 2018, LNCS 10864, pp. 210–231, 2018.
https://doi.org/10.1007/978-3-319-91638-5_11

proposed to outperform engineering judgement and to avoid non-intuitive sensor configurations proposed by the hierarchical algorithm. Results highlight that information gain metrics combined with quantitative and qualitative strategies for sensor selection and placement lead to a useful tool for asset managers.

Keywords: Sensor placement · Structural identification · Hierarchical algorithm Model falsification

1   Introduction

Countries around the world are experiencing infrastructure-capacity challenges due to growing populations, increasing urbanization and ageing existing assets. Good infrastructure management strategies are necessary to fill the infrastructure gap which is estimated at 1 trillion USD/year (World Economic Forum 2014). Most large civil structures have a significant amount of reserve capacity due to the justifiably conservative nature of design and construction. Unfortunately, this reserve is rarely quantified, resulting in sub-optimal asset-management decisions. Knowledge of accurate load capacity of bridges can be exploited to extend lifetimes of existing structures, optimize retrofit designs and prioritize maintenance activities.

Field-measurements, collected during ambient vibration monitoring and through load testing, have been extensively used in the last decades to improve knowledge of the real behavior of structures (Catbas et al. 2013). Interpretation of the data provided by sensors is critical to accurately design structural models and subsequently extrapolate to the bridge reserve-capacity estimation. Such interpretation is a type of inverse engineering where causes (behavior models) are inferred from effects (measurements). Such inference is a fundamentally ambiguous task as many causes may explain the same effect, especially when modelling uncertainties are important at sensor locations. In the field of structural identification, inverse-problem difficulties have been recognized by many authors, for example Mottershead and Friswell (1993) and Beck and Au (2002).

Data-interpretation techniques, such as residual minimization (Mottershead et al. 2011) and Bayesian updating (Beck and Katafygiotis 1998; Katafygiotis and Beck 1998) are often employed. Smith (2016) observed that starting assumptions of such traditional model updating methodologies cannot be justified for large civil structures. They often result in biased identification due to important systematic uncertainties that modify correlation values between measurement points.

A multi-model approach was proposed (Raphael and Smith 1998; Robert-Nicoud et al. 2005a) to overcome challenges associated with inverse problems. In this method, structural-identification results consist of a set of candidate models that could explain the measurements taken from a structure. Goulet and Smith (2013) presented a probabilistic extension, called error-domain model falsification (EDMF). According to prior knowledge and engineering judgement, a population of model instances are generated. Then, model instances that differ significantly from measured values are falsified using threshold values that are derived probabilistically. Threshold bounds are obtained from uncertainty quantification and determined probabilistically using the Monte Carlo sampling and a target confidence level. In this methodology systematic uncertainties are transparently included and the use of uniform probability distributions increases robustness to unknown uncertainty correlations (Goulet and Smith 2013). This methodology has been successfully applied to fields such as wind simulation around buildings (Vernay et al. 2014), performance following earthquake damage (Reuland et al. 2017) and leak detection in water-supply networks (Moser et al. 2015).

Model updating outcomes depend on the measurement-system configuration. Sensor types and positions are typically chosen using only qualitative rules of thumb arising from engineering experience. Quantitative studies on optimal sensor locations for structural identification have been carried out using information theory to improve model-parameter estimation. Finding the optimal sensor configuration is usually formulated as a simple optimization task. Even though global-search optimization algorithms were proposed to determine optimal solutions (Kripakaran and Smith 2009), most authors have preferred to use greedy selection algorithms (Kammer 2005) to reduce the computational effort as the computational complexity of sensor-placement algorithm is exponential with respect to the number of sensors.

To evaluate sensor locations, approaches include maximizing the determinant of Fisher information matrix (Heredia-Zavoni and Esteva 1998; Udwadia 1994) and either minimizing the information entropy in posterior model-parameter distribution (Papadimitriou et al. 2000; Papadimitriou 2005) or maximizing information entropy in multiple-model predictions (Kripakaran and Smith 2009; Robert-Nicoud et al. 2005c). Another approach, presented by Goulet and Smith (2012) and extended by Pasquier et al. (2017), provides probabilistic estimations of the expected number of candidate models obtained with a sensor configuration using simulated measurements. The aim was to find the sensor configuration that minimizes the expected number of candidate models. The procedure was shown to be computationally costly because it requires the execution of the falsification procedure for a large number of simulated measurements and sensor locations (Moser et al. 2017).

Although entropy-based approaches have shown to be useful for finding near-optimal sensor configurations, most studies have involved inefficient search methods. Most authors assumed constant uncertainty levels at all sensor locations and have disregarded the mutual information between sensor locations. Papadimitriou and Lombaert (2012) included the effect of spatially-correlated prediction errors to correct the information entropy of model-parameter posterior distribution. Thus, the redundancy of information of neighboring sensors can be reduced by correcting entropy value. Yuen and Kuok (2015) showed that, for configurations involving multi-type of sensors, a strategy accounting for mutual information between sensors is required. Papadopoulou et al. (2014) introduced a methodology involving a hierarchical algorithm to examine sensor placement through maximizing the joint-entropy between sensor locations to account for mutual information. This sensor placement algorithm explicitly incorporates systematic uncertainties and was successfully applied to sensors for wind-around-building predictions (Papadopoulou et al. 2015).

As highlighted by Papadimitriou and Lombaert (2012), the optimal sensor placement for model-parameter estimation depends on the loading. In work on EDMF, the next sensor to add in the sensor configuration was associated with a pre-defined load test (Goulet and Smith 2012; Pasquier et al. 2017). In these studies of sensor-placement for structural identification, mutual information between multiple load tests is not considered within the sensor-placement methodology. Bertola et al. (2017) adapted the hierarchical sensor-placement algorithm for structural identification purposes and proposed a modification to consider mutual information between load tests. Results showed that the optimal sensor configuration differs significantly when redundant information between load tests is considered.

In the present study, two quantitative methodologies for sensor-configuration optimization are compared with the solution designed by engineers using only their experience on a full-scale case study. The first quantitative sensor-placement methodology selects sensor locations with the largest signal-to-noise ratio in model prediction. The second strategy maximizes the joint entropy of the sensor configuration, using the hierarchical algorithm for sensor-placement. The performance of sensor configurations is evaluated using two information-gain metrics: information gain and the expected number of candidate models using simulated measurements.

2   Structural Identification Through Model Falsification

Presented by Goulet and Smith (2013), error-domain model falsification (EDMF) is a model-based structural identification methodology using a multi-model approach. Model instances are instantiations of a model class, in which several combinations of possible parameter values $\theta_k = [\theta_1, \theta_2, \ldots, \theta_n]^T$ are assigned in order to generate an initial set of model instances Ω. Then, model-instance predictions are compared with field measurements of the structural behavior in order to identify candidate models among the initial set of model-instance population. Robert-Nicoud et al. (2005a) combined modelling and measurement uncertainties to determine boundaries of the falsification thresholds given a target reliability of identification ϕ. Model instances are falsified if the difference between predictions and field measurements exceeds the threshold boundaries at one or more sensor locations.

For each measurement location, $i \in \{1, \ldots, n_y\}$, model predictions and field measurements are linked to the true behavior using:

$$g_k(i, \Theta_k) + U_{i,g_k} = R_i = \hat{y}_i + U_{i,\hat{y}} \quad \forall i \in \{1, \ldots, n_y\} \tag{1}$$

where R_i corresponds to unknown real responses of a structure and $\hat{y}_i$ to the measured value at location i. Using a finite element analysis (FEA), predictions $g_k(i, \Theta_k)$ of the model class G_k are evaluated at location i. Θ_k is the set of instances of the parameter vector θ_k. U_{i,g_k} and $U_{i,\hat{y}}$ correspond to model-prediction uncertainties and measurement uncertainties, respectively. Equation (1) may be rearranged as:

$$g_k(i, \Theta_k) - \hat{y}_i = U_{i,c} = U_{i,\hat{y}} - U_{i,g_k} \tag{2}$$

where $U_{i,c}$ is the combined value of modelling and measurement uncertainties at location i. The left-hand side of Eq. (2) represents the difference between a model prediction and a field measurement.

The candidate-model selection, representing realistic sets of model-parameter values, involves the falsification of all model instances for which predictions cannot explain measurement data, given combined uncertainties and a target reliability of identification. The set of candidate models obtained after falsification is defined using Eq. (3).

$$\Omega_k'' = \left\{\theta_k \in \Omega_k \middle| \forall i \in \{1,\ldots,n_y\} u_{i,low} \le g_k(i,\Theta_k) - \hat{y}_i \le u_{i,high}\right\} \tag{3}$$

where Ω_k'' is the candidate model set (CMS) built of initial model instances, which have not been falsified. $u_{i,low}$ and $u_{i,high}$ are the lower and upper threshold bounds representing the shortest intervals through the probability density function (PDF) of combined uncertainties $f_{U_i}(u_i)$ at a measurement location i, including a probability of identification $1/n_y$. The Šidák correction $1/n_y$ (Šidák 1967) is used to maintain a constant level of confidence when multiple sensor measurements are compared to model-instance predictions (Eq. 4). The value for ϕ is usually set to 95%.

$$\forall i = 1,\ldots,n_y: \phi^{1/n_y} = \int_{u_{i,low}}^{u_{i,high}} f_{U_i}(u_i)du_i \tag{4}$$

All model instances that do belong to the CMS ($\theta_k \in \Omega_k''$) are labeled as candidate models. Since so little information is usually available to describe the shape of modelling-uncertainty distributions, every candidate model is set to be equally likely to be the correct model (Robert-Nicoud et al. 2005b). Thus, they are assigned an equal probability as expressed in Eq. (5).

$$\Pr\left(\Theta_k \in \Omega_k''\right) = \frac{1}{\int \theta_k \in \Omega_k'' d\theta_k} \tag{5}$$

Falsified model instances corresponding to model instances that do not belong to the CMS are assigned a null probability:

$$\Pr\left(\Theta_k \notin \Omega_k''\right) = 0 \tag{6}$$

Consequently Θ_k'', is the vector of random variables describing the realistic parameter values of the candidate model instances given measurement data. Its PDF is defined:

$$f_{\Theta_k''} = \begin{cases} \dfrac{1}{\int \theta_k \in \Omega_k'' d\theta_k}, & if \Theta_k \in \Omega_k'' \\ 0, & otherwise \end{cases} \tag{7}$$

If all initial model instances generated are falsified, the entire model class is falsified and thus $\Omega_k'' = \emptyset$. It means that no models are compatible with observations given model and measurement uncertainties. It is usually a sign of incorrect assumptions in the model-class definition, in the initial parameter values or in the uncertainty estimates (Pasquier and Smith 2016). This particular situation highlights one of the main advantages of

EDMF compared with traditional structural-identification approaches such as residual minimization. In this situation, the results of EDMF leads to a re-evaluation of assumptions and a new model class is generated.

3 Quantitative Sensor-Placement Strategies

In this section, the two model-based quantitative sensor-placement strategies, which are compared to the sensor configuration chosen by engineers without calculation are presented. This first strategy is based on the quantification of the average of predictions over the measurement uncertainties and is a conventional metric for engineers to evaluate sensor locations. The second measures the information content at possible sensor locations using the joint entropy.

A model-based sensor-placement strategy requires several preliminary steps. First, a finite-element model of a bridge is built to obtain reliable quantitative predictions of measurable variables such as deflection, strain or inclination at each possible sensor locations. A significant degree of non-parametric uncertainty is involved as numerical models always require geometrical and mathematical simplifications. Then, a sensitivity analysis is employed to evaluate the effects of variation in model-parameter values on model predictions. A small number of parameters, which have the highest impact on predictions, is then selected. After the design of several possible load tests, multiple model instances are generated using a sampling technique to obtain a discrete population of possible model-parameter values within plausible ranges. For each load test, model-instance predictions are computed. Each model instance is part of the initial model set, which is the dataset used in the quantitative sensor-placement strategies, that are described below.

3.1 Maximization of Signal-to-Noise Ratio

The first quantitative methodology uses the signal-to-noise ratio (SNR) to select sensor locations. It represents the quotient between the predicted quantity over the uncertainty at a certain location. A sensor location with a high signal-to-noise ratio means that the field measurements at this location will be large compared to sensor precision. As a multi-model approach is used, the signal-to-noise ratio is defined as the mean value of model-instance predictions divided by the measurement uncertainty at location i:

$$SNR = \frac{Signal}{Noise} = \frac{Mean\left(g_k\left(i,\Theta_k\right)\right)}{U_{i,y}} \tag{8}$$

The first quantitative methodology selects iteratively the sensor locations with the largest signal-to-noise ratio. Thus, a basic sequential algorithm is used in this sensor-placement strategy.

3.2 Hierarchical Algorithm

The second strategy uses a model-based sensor-placement algorithm. It requires definition of a sensor-placement objective function to evaluate possible sensor location and an optimization algorithm to reduce the number of combination of sensor configuration.

Sensor-Placement Objective Function

Information Entropy
The information obtained from prediction data is a major criterion for evaluating possible sensor locations. This can be evaluated using entropy from information theory (also known as Shannon's entropy or Information entropy). The information entropy $H(y_i)$ is a measure of disorder in information content (Eq. 9).

$$H(y_i) = -\sum_{j=1}^{N_{I,i}} P(y_{i,j}) \log_2 P(y_{i,j})$$

(9)

where y_i is an output variable, such as the deflection at a sensor location i, $P(y_{i,j})$ is the probability of the jth interval of a variable's distribution with $j \in \{1, \dots, N_{I,i}\}$, and $N_{I,i}$ is the maximum number of intervals at the ith location.

At a possible sensor location, the evaluation of the information entropy needs to create subsets of model-instance predictions. N intervals ($I_{w,i}$) are generated between the minimum and the maximum model-instance predictions at a possible sensor location. The constant width of the interval at this location is derived from the combination of measurement ($U_{i,y}$) and modelling ($U_{i,g}$) uncertainties with a level of confidence of 95%. Model instances in a subset cannot be distinguished from each other using an in-situ measurement falling in the middle of the interval during the falsification process. Thus, model instances in the same subset might not be discriminated using this sensor location. Another location is needed to further subdivide these subsets.

At each sensor location, the information entropy is computed (Eq. (9)) through counting the number of model instances $m_{i,j}$ in a subset, for which predictions fall within each interval and then calculating the probability of the interval as $P(y_{i,j}) = m_{i,j} / \sum_j m_{i,j}$. A location with a high information-entropy value of model predictions is considered as a good location (Robert-Nicoud et al. 2005c), meaning that this location is able to discriminate between model instances effectively.

Joint Entropy
Papadopoulou et al. (2014) introduced the joint entropy as a new sensor-placement objective function for system identification. The joint entropy is an information entropy measure associated with a set of locations, while assessing the mutual information of the locations. For a set of two sensors, it is defined in Eq. (10):

$$H(y_{i,i+1}) = -\sum_{k=1}^{N_{I,i+1}} \sum_{j=1}^{N_{I,i}} P(y_{i,j}, y_{i+1,k}) \log_2 P(y_{i,j}, y_{i+1,k})$$

(10)

where $k \in \{1, \dots, N_{I,i+1}\}$ and $N_{I,i+1}$ is the maximum number of intervals at the i + 1 location and $i + 1 \in \{1, \dots, n_s\}$ with n_s the number of potential sensor locations. The joint entropy is less than or equal to the sum of the individual entropies of the locations in the set (Eq. 11 - where I is the mutual information between sensor i and i + 1).

$$H(y_{i,i+1}) = H(y_i) + H(y_{i+1}) - I(y_{i,i+1}) \tag{11}$$

Optimization Algorithm - Hierarchical Algorithm

The hierarchical algorithm is a sequential algorithm (greedy search) in which model instances are organized in a tree structure and it was shown to perform better than traditional sequential algorithms with forward or backward strategies (Papadopoulou et al. 2014). The original version of the hierarchical algorithm (Fig. 2) accommodates only a single load test. To consider information from various load tests, a modification of the algorithm was proposed by Bertola et al. (2017).

At the root is the initial model set, and branches contain subsets of model-instance predictions. Branches from a node represent separations of the parent model set into smaller subsets that can potentially be divided using measurements from the new sensor added to the configuration. It allows the calculation of joint entropy of large sensor configurations, reducing the computational effort. At every iteration, the location with

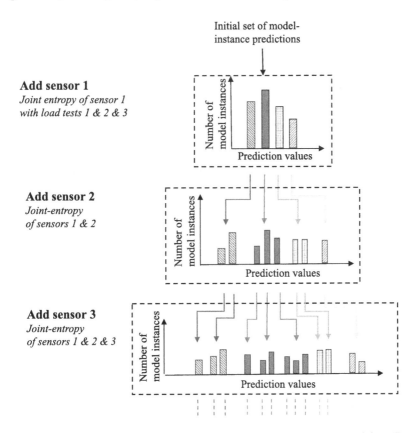

Fig. 1. Schematic of the hierarchical algorithm for sensor placement (adapted from Papadopoulou et al. (2014)).

the maximum joint entropy of the configuration is selected, allowing this sensor-placement algorithm to take into account mutual information between sensors according to the definition of the objective function.

A schematic overview of the tree structure of the hierarchical algorithm is presented in Fig. 1. The location with the largest joint-entropy value is added to the sensor configuration (sensor 1). At the top of the figure, intervals of model-instance predictions at this location are shown. Each subset of model instances is shown in a distinctive bar and clear spaces between bars are added for clarity only. To select the second sensor to add to the sensor configuration, information from the remaining unselected sensors is used to further divide each model-instances subset of Sensor 1. The configuration of Sensor 1 and Sensor 2 with the largest joint-entropy is selected and the second sensor is added to the sensor configuration.

This process is repeated at every iteration by adding a sensor to the sensor configuration, forming a hierarchy of model subsets. At each iteration, a location that has the highest potential to divide the existing subsets of model instances into smaller subsets is added to the sensor configuration. The process is repeated until all possible sensor locations are selected.

3.3   Evaluation of Sensor Configuration

Two information-gain metrics were chosen to evaluate the sensor configuration of the three sensor-placement strategies, following the metric comparison proposed by Papadopoulou et al. (2016). First, joint-entropy values are calculated for each sensor configuration to quantify the expected information gained. In order to be able to compare results from the three strategies, the code of the hierarchical algorithm is also used to assess the joint-entropy of the configurations chosen by the engineers without calculation and with the quantitative strategy based on the maximization of the signal-to-noise ratio. The joint entropy is the objective function of the hierarchical algorithm. However, as it is a greedy search, the solution proposed by this sensor-placement strategy may be suboptimal.

The second metric uses simulated measurements to provide probabilistic estimations of the expected candidate-model-set size for a sensor configuration, in a similar procedure as Papadopoulou et al. (2016). Simulated measurements were generated based on the model instances in the model class adding a random value taken from the combined uncertainties. Then, sensor locations are evaluated using the 50% quantile of the expected candidate-model-set size, as suggested by Pasquier et al. (2017).

4   Case Study Presentation

The full-scale case study was performed on a 32-year-old bridge in Singapore. The prestressed pre-cast concrete bridge is composed of 4 beams carrying three unidirectional traffic lanes over a simply-supported span of 32 m. The principal characteristics of the bridge are presented in Fig. 2.

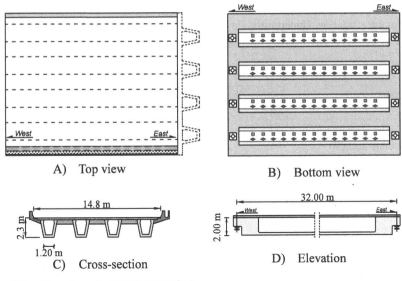

A) Top view   B) Bottom view

C) Cross-section   D) Elevation

- Possible inclinometer locations (Top view)
- Possible deflection-target locations (Bottom view)
- Possible strain-gauge locations (Bottom view)

Fig. 2. Bridge geometry showing the possible sensor locations: (A) Top view; (B) Bottom view; (C) Cross-section; (D) Elevation.

Sensors consisted of 2 inclinometers (I_i) to dispose on the parapet, 4 deflection targets (P_i) and 7 strain gauges (S_i) to dispose on the girders (Fig. 2: A; B). A laser tracker was positioned on the road below the bridge and used to measure deflections at target locations. Possible sensor locations were chosen to start 4 meters from the support (2 times the girder height) for strain gauges and deflection targets on the four main girders and 2 m from the support for the inclinometer on one parapet and are presented in Fig. 2 (A; B). To reduce the computational time, a discretization of possible sensor locations at every 2 m was chosen.

Five model parameters were identified as having the most influence on prediction values: the Young modulus of site-cast concrete of the deck E_{con}; the Young modulus of the precast concrete of the beams E_{pre}; the Young modulus of the concrete of the barrier E_{bar}; the rotational stiffness of the bearing devices K_{rot} and the vertical stiffness of the bearing devices K_{lon}. Their plausible ranges of values are estimated using engineering heuristics and are presented in Table 1. Non-structural elements, such as the asphalt pavement, are included in the numerical model, to reduce model-simplification uncertainties. Within this 5-parameter space, 1,000 initial model instances were generated using Latin Hypercube Sampling (LHS).

Table 1. Primary parameters considered and their initial intervals.

E_{com} [GPa]	E_{pre} [GPa]	E_{bar} [GPa]	K_{rot} log[Nmm/rad]	K_{lon} log([N/mm])
20–35	25–50	3–40	9–13	8–11

Table 2 presents the upper and lower bounds of model-class uncertainties and measurement uncertainties. Uncertainties are assumed to have uniform distributions and are estimated based on engineering judgment, sensor-supplier information and heuristics.

Table 2. Modelling and measurement uncertainties.

Uncertainty source	Displacements – (P)		Rotations – (I)		Strains – (S)	
	Min	Max	Min	Max	Min	Max
Model simplifications (%)	−5	13	−5	13	−5	13
Mesh refinement (%)	−1	1	−1	1	−1	1
Spatial variability (%)	–	–	–	–	−5	5
Additional uncertainty (%)	−1	1	−1	1	−1	1
Sensor precision	−0.05 mm	0.05 mm	−1 μrad	1 μrad	−2 με	2 με
Repeatability	−0.15 mm	0.15 mm	−4 μrad	4 μrad	−4 με	4 με
Sensor orientation (%)	–	–	–	–	0	6
Sensor installation (%)	–	–	−5	5	0	5

Three static load tests were successively performed on the bridge and the truck configurations are presented in Fig. 3. Load tests are composed of trucks of approximatively 32 tons. The repartition of the load on the three axles is 1/5; 2/5; 2/5 starting from the front. The first load test (LT1) is composed of six trucks (T_i) disposed on the bridge. The aim of LT1 is to maximize the deflection and strain in the precast beams. The second and third load tests (LT2 and LT3) dispose four trucks close to east and west support respectively. The aim of LT2 and LT3 is to maximize the inclination of the support. These load tests were chosen by the engineers based on their experience only.

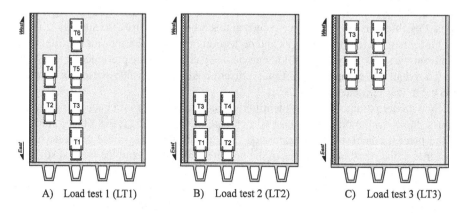

A) Load test 1 (LT1)   B) Load test 2 (LT2)   C) Load test 3 (LT3)

Fig. 3. Load-test presentation: (A) Load test 1; (B) Load test 2; (C) Load test 3.

4.1 Sensor Configuration Installed Based on Engineering Judgement

Two engineers designed the sensor configuration composed by the 13 available sensors (2 inclinometers, 4 deflection targets and 7 strain gauges) without use of any calculation. Both engineers have 5+ years of practical experience.

The choice of sensor configuration was discussed with the sensor suppliers in terms of feasibility of installation in the available time. The configuration presented in Fig. 4(A) was installed for load testing the bridge.

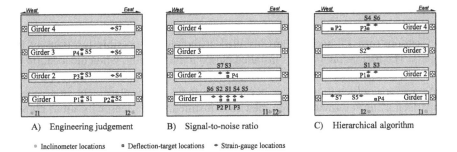

A) Engineering judgement   B) Signal-to-noise ratio   C) Hierarchical algorithm

⊙ Inclinometer locations   ▪ Deflection-target locations   ✦ Strain-gauge locations

Fig. 4. Sensor configurations: (A) Chosen by engineers without calculation; (B) Quantitative strategy based on the maximization of the signal-to-noise ratio; (C) Hierarchical algorithm – bottom view.

Several criteria were considered in this primarily qualitative design of the sensor configuration. First, locations with the largest signal strength were preferred. Therefore, girders at midspan are privileged locations for strain gauges and deflection targets. As the complete behaviour of the bridge needed to be monitored, at least one sensor on each girder was installed. Ultimately, to complete the sensor configuration, locations at quarter span were added.

5   Comparison of Sensor-Placement Strategies

In this section, sensor configurations using two quantitative strategies and using engineering judgement without calculation are compared. First, sensor configurations and sensor rankings from the sensor placement strategies are presented. Then, sensor configurations are compared using two information-gain metrics: the joint-entropy and the expected candidate-model-set size.

5.1   Sensor Configuration and Sensor-Type Ranking

Sensor configurations chosen based on engineering judgement and using two quantitative sensor-placement strategies are presented in Fig. 4. Each sensor configuration involves the same sensors: two inclinometers on the parapet; four deflections target and seven strain gauges on the four main girders. Even if the inclinometers are installed on the parapet, they are presented on a bottom view of the bridge for presentation purpose. As all sensor-placement strategies are based on a greedy selecting algorithm (Kammer 2005), sensors are named by the order of selection within their sensor type.

For strain gauges and deflections targets, engineers select sensor locations at quarter-span and mid-span on the four main girders of the bridge. Inclinometers are installed on the closest locations from the support on both side of the parapet (Fig. 4(A)).

The quantitative strategy based on the signal-to-noise ratio selects strain-gauge and deflection-target locations at mid-span on the first and second main girders. Inclinometers are installed in one side of the parapet on the closest possible locations from the support (Fig. 4(B)).

The hierarchical algorithm leads to selection of strain-gauge and deflection-target locations on the four main girders. Most sensors are placed closed to mid-span, even if some sensors (e.g. P2 and S7) are installed at the closest possible locations of the supports. The first inclinometer is installed closed to the support, while the location for the second inclinometer is selected closed to mid-span (Fig. 4(C)).

As sensor configurations differ between the three sensor-placement strategies, a comparison using information-gain metrics is justified. Some sensor locations chosen by the hierarchical algorithm, especially P2 and S7, could be non-intuitive for practitioners as locations selected have some small signal strengths compared with locations on the first girder at mid-span. The sensor configuration of the hierarchical algorithm requires further investigation to understand the selection of non-intuitive locations.

The sensor-type ranking is presented in Fig. 5 as a histogram with the sensor rank as vertical axis and the sensor identification as horizontal axis. Results of each sensor-placement strategy are presented with distinctive bars. It is important to mention that sensor locations are different for each strategy, only the order of sensor-type selection can thus be compared.

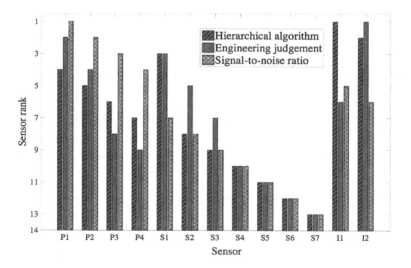

Fig. 5. Sensor-type ranking for three sensor-placement strategies.

Engineers chose iteratively sensors of each type starting with an inclinometer followed by a deflection target and then a strain gauge, starting with locations with large signal-to-noise ratio. The quantitative strategy based on the signal-to-noise ratio selected first all deflection targets, then all inclinometers and eventually all strain-gauges. The hierarchical algorithm selects the two inclinometers, then a strain gauge and then all deflection targets. Eventually, the remaining strain gauges are selected. The hierarchical algorithm assigns high rank to a sensor of each type showing that each type of sensors provides unique information.

It is observed that from the first or second sensor selected, the order of sensor-type selection differs for each sensor-placement strategy. A comparison of sensor configurations using information-gain metrics is thus justified and this is presented below.

5.2 Evaluation of Sensor Configuration

Two information-gain metrics are used to evaluate sensor configurations. The joint-entropy metric (Fig. 6) represents the ability of a sensor configuration to discriminate model-instance predictions, while the expected candidate-model-set-size metric (Fig. 7) provides estimation of the number of candidate models using simulated measurements for a sensor configuration.

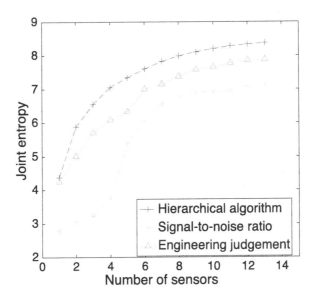

Fig. 6. Joint entropy of sensor configuration for three sensor-placement strategies as function of the number of sensors.

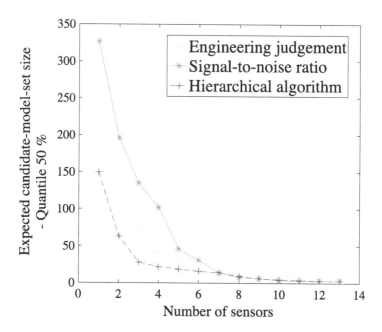

Fig. 7. Expected candidate-model-set size of sensor configuration for three sensor-placement strategies as function of the number of sensors.

The joint-entropy values of sensor configurations for the three sensor-placement strategies are presented in Fig. 6 as function of the number of sensors. For each sensor-placement strategy, the sensor selection follows their respective sensor rank (Fig. 5).

Sensor configurations selected by the hierarchical algorithm always performs better than other strategies in terms of joint entropy. The hierarchical algorithm is thus the most effective sensor-placement strategy in terms of joint entropy as information-gain metrics.

The quantitative strategy based on the maximal signal-to-noise ratio provides the smallest joint-entropy value for any number of sensors. As the signal-to-noise-ratio strategy under-performs other sensor-placement strategies in terms of the joint-entropy metric, it shows that this strategy selects sensor configurations providing larger redundant information between sensors. The quantitative strategy based on signal-to-noise ratio is thus not recommended for sensor placement.

For a small number of sensors ($N < 6$), the difference in terms of joint-entropy values is significant (13 to 15%) between sensor configurations chosen by engineers without calculation and proposed by the hierarchal algorithm. However, for a large number of sensors ($N \geq 6$), sensor configurations selected by engineers without calculation provides small difference of joint-entropy values (3 to 8%) with respect to hierarchical-algorithm sensor configurations. The final configuration chosen by engineers is shown to be very efficient as the difference with the hierarchical-algorithm sensor configuration is only 5% and to out-perform by 12% the sensor configuration selected using the signal-to-noise ratio. This result highlights the quality of engineering judgement.

An additional observation could explain the small difference of information gain between final sensor configurations. 39 sensor measurements were made on the bridge. As the static structure is a simple beam, the influence of the optimal sensor configuration over a suboptimal one is reduced for a large number of measurements. Results should be confirmed by another information-gain metric such as the expected candidate-model-set size presented below.

The expected candidate-model-set size of sensor configurations for the three sensor-placement strategies are presented in Fig. 7. From the 1000 model instances, 100,000 simulated measurements were generated adding a random value of combined uncertainties (Table 2). For each sensor configuration and for the three sensor-placement strategies, the falsification procedure was performed, and the cumulative distribution of the candidate-model-set (CMS) size was generated. The 50% quantiles of the cumulative distribution of the CMS size for the three sensor-placement strategies are compared as function of the number of sensors. The order of sensor selection follows the sensor ranks (Fig. 5).

The trends of the information-gain metric based on simulated measurements are mostly similar with trends of the joint-entropy information-gain metric. The main difference with the joint-entropy metric is that for a large number of sensors ($N \geq 7$), results from all sensor-placement strategies are very similar. For a small number of sensors ($N < 7$), sensor configurations selected by the hierarchical algorithm always perform better than other strategies in terms of expected candidate-model-set size. The hierarchical algorithm is thus the most effective sensor-placement strategy in terms of expected candidate-model-set size.

When there are less than 5 sensors, the difference in terms of expected candidate-model-set size is significant (8 to 35% difference) between sensor configurations chosen by engineers without calculation and proposed by the hierarchal algorithm. However, when the number of sensors is larger than 4, sensor configurations selected by engineers provide a similar expected candidate-model-set size (0 to 5% difference) with respect to hierarchical-algorithm sensor configurations. The configuration chosen by the engineers is shown to be efficient as no final difference with respect to solutions from quantitative strategies was observed.

For a small number of sensors ($N < 7$), sensor configurations selected by strategy based on the maximum signal-to-noise ratio provide largest expected candidate model-set size. This result confirms the previous observations of the joint-entropy information-gain metric (Fig. 6). As the signal-to-noise-ratio strategy under-performs other sensor-placement strategies in terms of information-gain metrics, it shows that this strategy selects sensor configurations providing larger redundant information between sensors. The quantitative strategy based on signal-to-noise ratio is thus not recommended for sensor placement for a small number of sensors ($N < 7$).

6   Adaptive Approach for Sensor Placement

In this section, the non-intuitive sensor-location selections of the hierarchical algorithm are discussed. First, the process of sensor selection of the hierarchical algorithm is detailed. Then, an adaptive approach for sensor placement, involving the hierarchical algorithm and engineering judgement without calculation is proposed. Eventually, this new approach is compared with previously introduced sensor-placement strategies in terms of sensor configurations, sensor ranking and information-gain metrics.

The difference between the maximum and minimum joint-entropy values of remaining possible locations divided by the mean value at each iteration of the sensor-placement process is presented in Fig. 8. An arbitrary threshold of 5% is proposed. Below that threshold, the selection of a suboptimal sensor location implies a decrease of joint-entropy bounded to 5% of the mean value.

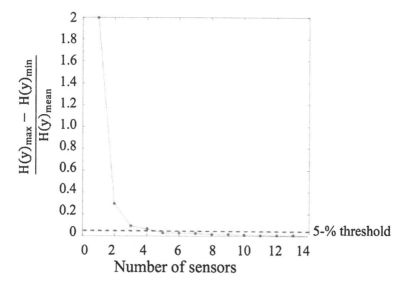

Fig. 8. Difference between the maximum and minimum joint-entropy value of possible sensor locations divided by the mean value at each iteration of sensor placement using the hierarchical algorithm.

It is observed that the difference of joint entropy between sensor locations decreases with increasing number of sensors, showing that it is less attractive to find the optimal location with increasing number of sensors. After 4 sensors in the sensor configuration, the difference between the maximum and minimum joint-entropy values divided by the mean value is below the 5% threshold. From the fifth sensor selection, all locations provide approximatively the same amount of new information. It means that the optimization of the sensor configuration only brings a minor improvement in terms of information gain when compared to the selection of a sensor location without calculation. Additionally, for more than four sensors ($N > 4$), the maximum joint-entropy is often achieved on non-intuitive locations on the bridge. For instance, the selection of P2 (Fig. 4(B)) requires to place the deflection target where the signal-to-noise was the smallest (i.e. close to the support on the least loaded girder). This selection increases only slightly the joint-entropy compared to a more intuitive location for engineers such as at mid-span on the most-loaded beam. If the intuitive location (mid-span on the most loaded beam was selected), the joint-entropy will decrease by 0.3%.

An adaptive approach for sensor-placement using both the hierarchical algorithm and engineering judgement is proposed below. First, sensor locations are selected using the hierarchical algorithm to guarantee to reach a sensor configuration with large information gain. Once the 5% threshold (Fig. 8) is reached, engineers select sensor locations for remaining sensors without calculation, allowing practical considerations in the design of the sensor configuration.

The sensor configuration of the adaptive approach is presented in Fig. 9, where sensor configurations chosen by engineers without calculation and proposed by the hierarchical algorithm are compared. Each sensor configuration involves the same sensors: two inclinometers on the parapet; four deflections target and seven strain gauges on the four main girders. Even if the inclinometers are installed on the parapet, they are presented on a bottom view of the bridge for presentation purposes.

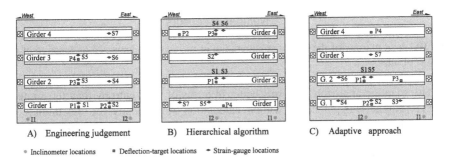

A) Engineering judgement   B) Hierarchical algorithm   C) Adaptive approach

* Inclinometer locations   ▪ Deflection-target locations   ◆ Strain-gauge locations

Fig. 9. Sensor configurations: (A) chosen by engineers without calculation; (B) hierarchical algorithm for sensor placement; (C) adaptive approach where (A) and (B) strategies are used – bottom view.

In the sensor configuration of the adaptive approach, most deflection-target and strain-gauge sensors are placed of the first and second girders at mid-span of quarter span similar to the sensor configuration selected by engineers without calculation, while inclinometer locations remain as selected by the hierarchical algorithm. The sensor configuration of the adaptive approach is thus a trade-off between sensor configurations of other sensor-placement strategies. Additionally, the adaptive approach avoids non-intuitive sensor locations on the fourth girder compared to the sensor configuration of the hierarchical algorithm. As the three sensor configurations differ, a comparison using the joint-entropy information-gain metric is presented below.

The joint-entropy value of the new sensor configuration based on an adaptive approach between the engineering judgement and hierarchical algorithm is presented in Fig. 10. Previous joint-entropy values from other sensor-placement strategies, except the signal-to-noise-ratio strategy, are also presented as benchmarks.

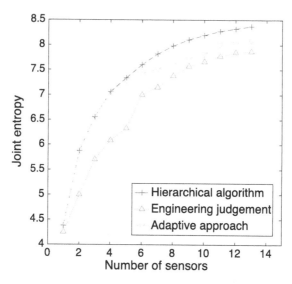

Fig. 10. Joint entropy of the sensor configuration of the adaptive approach as function of the number of sensors.

The adaptive approach performs better in terms of joint entropy than the strategy based on engineering judgement without calculation. Additionally, the maximum joint-entropy difference of the sensor configuration proposed by adaptive approach with respect to the sensor configuration proposed by the hierarchical algorithm is smaller than 5%. The adaptive approach for sensor-placement allows engineers to consider other criteria such as sensor cost, installation constraints and sensor reliability in the optimal sensor placement with only a small reduction of information gain compared to the hierarchical algorithm, thus avoiding globally inferior sensor locations.

7   Discussion

Sensor locations differ among strategies, thus indicating that the design of the sensor configuration is sensitive to the choice of sensor-placement strategy. The hierarchical algorithm outperforms other sensor-placement strategies in terms of both joint entropy and expected candidate-model-set size. The strategy based on the maximization of the signal-to-noise ratio results in a suboptimal sensor configuration with large redundancies in information provided by sensors. For a large number of sensors, engineers selected a good sensor configuration compared to sensor configurations of quantitative strategies without calculation. However, for a small number of sensors, the hierarchical algorithm significantly outperforms the configuration chosen by the engineers. An adaptive approach, using the hierarchical algorithm to select the first sensors and then, allowing engineers to select the remaining sensor locations was proposed in this study. Results show that the sensor configuration of the adaptive approach only slightly under-performs in terms of information gain the sensor configuration proposed by the algorithm and avoids inferior sensor locations according to additional criteria for sensor placement such as installation costs.

The following limitations of this study provide directions for future work. Three load tests were considered and designed by engineers without calculation. Load tests and sensor configurations should be optimized simultaneously to maximize the information gain from a sensor configuration. Additionally, to realize a successful monitoring campaign, optimizing a sensor configuration involves accommodating multiple contradictory and constraining criteria. However, in this study only information gain was considered when comparing sensor configurations from several sensor-placement strategies. Joint-entropy and expected-identifiability metrics to evaluate information gain were chosen following the information-gain-metric comparison proposed by Papadopoulou et al. (2016). A different information-gain metric, such as the prediction range, could have changed the evaluation of sensor configurations. While multiple criteria such as cost of monitoring, sensor-installation constraints and reliability to sensor failure are implicitly considered in the second stage, they could be considered in the first stage of an adaptive strategy. Finally, another limitation is that other engineers could have proposed different sensor-placement configurations.

The following limitations of the hierarchical algorithm are recognized. The greedy algorithm used in hierarchical algorithm does not necessarily lead to a global optimum. Additionally, the success of a model-based sensor-placement methodology depends on the numerical model that is used for predictions. Moreover, the sampling technique and the estimation of modelling uncertainties at sensor locations influence the optimal sensor configuration proposed by the quantitative strategies. An advantage of the hierarchical algorithm is the monotonic and bounded objective function. A stop criterion, for example an increase of joint entropy between two sensor configurations smaller than 0.1, could be introduced and considered in a multi-criteria-decision-making approach.

8   Conclusions

A rational sensor-placement methodology increases the performance of the structural-identification methodology by enhancing the model-instance discrimination. Specific conclusions are as follows:

- Using only the signal strength to configure sensors on a structure should be avoided.
- Sensor-placement algorithms such as hierarchical algorithm can increase the performance of a sensor configuration, especially if only a few sensors are placed.
- For large sensor configurations, an adaptive approach, which allows engineers to place sensors through taking into account practical considerations in a second step without compromising the information gain, has potential to become a useful tool for asset managers.

Future work will focus on the combination of optimization of sensor configuration and load tests simultaneously. Additionally, a multi-criteria-decision-making approach will be developed to include aspects such as cost and sensor-installation constraints, information gain criteria and sensor reliability explicitly in the determination of optimal sensor configurations. Eventually, the approach will be tested on several full-scale case studies.

Acknowledgments. This research was conducted at the Future Cities Laboratory at the Singapore-ETH Centre (SEC). The SEC was established as a collaboration between ETH Zurich and National Research Foundation (NRF) Singapore (FI 370074011) under the auspices of the NRF's Campus for Research Excellence and Technological Enterprise (CREATE) programme. The authors would like to acknowledge the support of the Land Transport Authority of Singapore (LTA) for the case study. Additionally, the authors are thankful to A. Costa, M. Papadopoulou, D. Vernay and M. Proverbio for their valuable input.

References

Beck, J.L., Au, S.-K.: Bayesian updating of structural models and reliability using Markov chain Monte Carlo simulation. J. Eng. Mech. **128**, 380–391 (2002)

Beck, J.L., Katafygiotis, L.S.: Updating models and their uncertainties. I: Bayesian statistical framework. J. Eng. Mech. **124**, 455–461 (1998)

Bertola, N.J., Papadopoulou, M., Vernay, D.G., Smith, I.F.C.: Optimal multi-type sensor placement for structural identification by static-load testing. Sensors **17**, 2904 (2017)

Catbas, F., Kijewski-Correa, T., Lynn, T., Aktan, A.: Structural Identification of Constructed Systems. American Society of Civil Engineers, Reston (2013)

Goulet, J.-A., Smith, I.F.C.: Structural identification with systematic errors and unknown uncertainty dependencies. Comput. Struct. **128**, 251–258 (2013)

Goulet, J.-A., Smith, I.F.C.: Performance-driven measurement system design for structural identification. J. Comput. Civ. Eng. **27**, 427–436 (2012)

Heredia-Zavoni, E., Esteva, L.: Optimal instrumentation of uncertain structural systems subject to earthquake ground motions. Earthq. Eng. Struct. Dyn. **27**, 343–362 (1998)

Kammer, D.C.: Sensor set expansion for modal vibration testing. Mech. Syst. Sig. Process. **19**, 700–713 (2005)

Katafygiotis, L.S., Beck, J.L.: Updating models and their uncertainties. II: model identifiability. J. Eng. Mech. **124**, 463–467 (1998)

Kripakaran, P., Smith, I.F.C.: Configuring and enhancing measurement systems for damage identification. Adv. Eng. Inform. **23**, 424–432 (2009)

Moser, G., Paal, S.G., Smith, I.F.C.: Measurement system design for leak detection in hydraulic pressurized networks. Struct. Infrastruct. Eng. **13**, 918–928 (2017)

Moser, G., Paal, S.G., Smith, I.F.C.: Performance comparison of reduced models for leak detection in water distribution networks. Adv. Eng. Inform. **29**, 714–726 (2015)

Mottershead, J.E., Friswell, M.I.: Model updating in structural dynamics: a survey. J. Sound Vib. **167**, 347–375 (1993)

Mottershead, J.E., Link, M., Friswell, M.I.: The sensitivity method in finite element model updating: a tutorial. Mech. Syst. Sig. Process. **25**, 2275–2296 (2011)

Papadimitriou, C.: Pareto optimal sensor locations for structural identification. Comput. Methods Appl. Mech. Eng. **194**, 1655–1673 (2005)

Papadimitriou, C., Beck, J.L., Au, S.-K.: Entropy-based optimal sensor location for structural model updating. J. Vib. Control **6**, 781–800 (2000)

Papadimitriou, C., Lombaert, G.: The effect of prediction error correlation on optimal sensor placement in structural dynamics. Mech. Syst. Sig. Process. **28**, 105–127 (2012)

Papadopoulou, M., Raphael, B., Smith, I.F.C., Sekhar, C.: Evaluating predictive performance of sensor configurations in wind studies around buildings. Adv. Eng. Inform. **30**, 127–142 (2016)

Papadopoulou, M., Raphael, B., Smith, I.F.C., Sekhar, C.: Optimal sensor placement for time-dependent systems: application to wind studies around buildings. J. Comput. Civ. Eng. **30**, 4015024 (2015)

Papadopoulou, M., Raphael, B., Smith, I.F.C., Sekhar, C.: Hierarchical sensor placement using joint entropy and the effect of modeling error. Entropy **16**, 5078–5101 (2014)

Pasquier, R., Goulet, J.-A., Smith, I.F.C.: Measurement system design for civil infrastructure using expected utility. Adv. Eng. Inform. **32**, 40–51 (2017)

Pasquier, R., Smith, I.F.C.: Iterative structural identification framework for evaluation of existing structures. Eng. Struct. **106**, 179–194 (2016)

Raphael, B., Smith, I.: Finding the right model for bridge diagnosis. In: Smith, I. (ed.) Artificial Intelligence in Structural Engineering. LNCS, vol. 1454, pp. 308–319. Springer, Heidelberg (1998). https://doi.org/10.1007/BFb0030459

Reuland, Y., Lestuzzi, P., Smith, I.F.C.: Data-interpretation methodologies for non-linear earthquake response predictions of damaged structures. Front. Built Environ. **3**, 43 (2017)

Robert-Nicoud, Y., Raphael, B., Burdet, O., Smith, I.F.C.: Model identification of bridges using measurement data. Comput. Civ. Infrastruct. Eng. **20**, 118–131 (2005a)

Robert-Nicoud, Y., Raphael, B., Smith, I.: System identification through model composition and stochastic search. J. Comput. Civ. Eng. **19**, 239–247 (2005b)

Robert-Nicoud, Y., Raphael, B., Smith, I.F.C.: Configuration of measurement systems using Shannon's entropy function. Comput. Struct. **83**, 599–612 (2005c)

Šidák, Z.: Rectangular confidence regions for the means of multivariate normal distributions. J. Am. Stat. Assoc. **62**, 626–633 (1967)

Smith, I.F.C.: Studies of sensor data interpretation for asset management of the built environment. Front. Built Environ. **2**, 2–8 (2016)

Udwadia, F.E.: Methodology for optimum sensor locations for parameter identification in dynamic systems. J. Eng. Mech. **120**, 368–390 (1994)

Vernay, D.G., Raphael, B., Smith, I.F.C.: Augmenting simulations of airflow around buildings using field measurements. Adv. Eng. Inform. **28**, 412–424 (2014)

World Economic Forum: Strategic infrastructure, steps to operate and maintain infrastructure efficiently and effectively (No. 180314). World Economic Forum, Davos (2014)

Yuen, K., Kuok, S.: Efficient Bayesian sensor placement algorithm for structural identification: a general approach for multi-type sensory systems. Earthq. Eng. Struct. Dyn. **44**, 757–774 (2015)

Multi-occupancy Indoor Thermal Condition Optimization in Consideration of Thermal Sensitivity

Wooyoung Jung[1] and Farrokh Jazizadeh[2(✉)]

[1] Virginia Polytechnic Institute and State University, 315B Patton Hall, 750 Drillfield Drive, Blacksburg, VA 24061, USA
jwyoungs@vt.edu
[2] Virginia Polytechnic Institute and State University, 200 Patton Hall, 750 Drillfield Drive, Blacksburg, VA 24061, USA
jazizadeh@vt.edu

Abstract. The primary criterion for assessing heating, ventilation, and air conditioning (HVAC) systems regarding thermal comfort is whether they are capable of satisfying more than 80% of occupants (i.e., acceptable condition). The predicted percentage of dissatisfied model proposes this value with the assumption that a neutral state is desired. However, recent studies cast light on personalized thermal comfort which demonstrates that occupants have diverse thermal preferences and respond differently to variations in temperature (i.e., thermal sensitivity). This study aims to shed light on the importance of taking thermal sensitivity into account in a multi-occupancy space, where the same thermal condition is shared, for thermal condition optimization, which was replicated in our multi-agent based (MAB) model. Each human agent (occupants' proxy) has its own properties (e.g., thermal preferences) and aims to create at least an acceptable condition for itself by providing feedback to a HVAC agent (HVAC systems' proxy). The HVAC agent optimizes the thermal condition based on feedback from human agents. Using this model, two operational scenarios have been explored: human agents have (1) the same (i.e., ignoring thermal sensitivity) and (2) personalized thermal sensitivities. The assessments demonstrate that integrating thermal sensitivity results in significantly different setpoint temperatures, increased thermal satisfactions of human agents and the number of satisfied human agents. In other words, thermal sensitivity is an important factor in improving the performance of HVAC systems.

Keywords: HVAC system · Multi-occupancy · Thermal sensitivity
Optimization · Multi agent-based model · Thermal comfort

1 Introduction

Current heating, ventilation, and air conditioning (HVAC) systems provide indoor conditions for a thermal zone (a group of spaces that are simultaneously controlled by HVAC systems) [1]. Accordingly, occupants frequently experience a multi-occupancy

© Springer International Publishing AG, part of Springer Nature 2018
I. F. C. Smith and B. Domer (Eds.): EG-ICE 2018, LNCS 10864, pp. 232–242, 2018.
https://doi.org/10.1007/978-3-319-91638-5_12

space, where individual thermal preferences, diversely presented throughout all thermal sensations [2], should be compromised for a collectively satisfactory environment. It is a well-known fact that a certain number of occupants remain dissatisfied due to such conflicts. As a proof, ASHRAE Standard 55 [3] indicates that an environment could be considered satisfactory when a majority (more than 80%) of occupants consider it acceptable, that is, some occupants will endure some level of discomfort in an acceptable environment. This criterion has been frequently employed to assess the performance of HVAC systems in providing a satisfactory thermal condition.

Recent works have revealed that individuals present different sensitivities with respect to variations in temperature [4–7]. This phenomenon has been referred to as thermal sensitivity in this paper. For example, one expresses discomfort quickly when the ambient temperature is decreasing but has higher tolerance to an increasing temperature. Another person might reveal the opposite. Daum et al. [5], who presented a probabilistic measure of personalized thermal comfort, used two separate discomfort probabilities (for being cold or hot) in their models. An overview of the experimental results in their study shows that these probability distributions manifest different parameters, reflecting varied thermal sensitivity to different thermal conditions. The same phenomenon was observed in our prior studies, during which individual thermal comfort profiles were presented [8–10]. In the wake of these findings, in assessment of HVAC performance, specifically when it comes to thermal comfort provision, the coupled effect of thermal preferences and sensitivities for multi-occupancy spaces should be taken into account.

However, in research and development studies, it is commonly assumed that thermal sensitivity are equally distributed [11–13] using the statement from ASHRAE [14] that a 3.0 °C (5.4 °F) of change in temperature is needed to influence thermal sensation. Thermal preferences played an exclusive role when indoor conditions are optimized in these studies. Consequently, the corresponding thermal comfort implications (e.g., the ratio of satisfied to dissatisfied occupants) might not reflect the actual potential.

This study aims to provide an insight on the importance of taking thermal sensitivity into account when an HVAC system seeks to provide a collective satisfactory condition. To this end, we have utilized a multi-agent based (MAB) modeling approach that replicates a multi-occupancy space where a single HVAC unit serves multiple occupants simultaneously. In a MAB model, autonomous individual elements (hereinafter agents) react to variations in the environment to achieve their own objectives [15]. In other words, an occupant can be described as a human agent and a HVAC system as an HVAC agent that controls the variations of ambient thermal conditions.

The rest of the paper is structured as follows. First, the second section discusses the limitations of conventional thermal comfort management in the context of personalized thermal sensitivity. In the third section, the MAB modeling characteristics are described in detail: (1) how each agent has been designed and how they interact with other agents to optimize indoor thermal conditions and (2) how this study investigates the influence of thermal sensitivity through the MAB model. The fourth section elaborates on the results of the analysis by explaining the influence of thermal sensitivity on the optimized setpoint temperature, thermal satisfaction of human agents, and number of satisfied agents. The paper is concluded in the fifth section with limitation and future work.

2   Previous Studies

ASHRAE Standard 55 [3] requires HVAC systems to be capable of maintaining a comfort zone defined by the predicted mean vote (PMV) model [16]. This model, adopted in HVAC standards at an international level [17], presumes that a neutral thermal sensation state is desired. As a consequence, current HVAC systems are designed to create the PMV-defined neutral state. This assumption has been challenged by Humphreys and Hancock [2], who reported the diversity of thermal preferences across all thermal sensations (from cold to hot). In detail, only 46.5% preferred the neutral state and 47.5% favored the slightly warm and warm states in their study. Considering this observation in contextual operations of the HVAC systems, individual thermal comfort should be taken into account to provide better conditions for occupants. Due to the advances of information technology (e.g., expansion of available datasets and advances in modeling), studies are focusing on investigating individuals [5], proposing methodologies for creating personally preferred conditions [18], and improving the performance of HVAC systems [10, 19, 20].

As personalized thermal preference information becomes available, a succeeding question emerges: Can an HVAC system provide a thermal condition that satisfies several personalized preferences. In his study, Lee [21] has mentioned the difficulties in meeting all separate thermal preferences requirements when occupants share a HVAC thermal zone. Since occupants often share a multi-occupancy space, it is pivotal to explore the influence of thermal sensitivity as one of the characteristics revealed in personalized measures of thermal comfort. Thermal sensitivity can be the key feature in a multi-occupancy room as it highly affects thermal discomfort. However, ASHRAE [14] considers a generalized thermal sensitivity by assuming that at least 3.0 °C (5.4 °F) is required to provoke a change in thermal sensations. Accordingly, studies assumed that individuals have a similar thermal sensitivity [11], or disregarded it in a multi-occupancy condition [22].

Therefore, in order to shed light on the importance of taking thermal sensitivity into account, this study compares two scenarios: (1) assuming generalized thermal sensitivity for all occupants like other previous studies and (2) taking personalized sensitivities into account. Each scenario was implemented in the MAB model that is elaborated in the following section.

3   Multi-agent Based Modeling

We have developed a MAB model that simulates a multi-occupancy space where individuals share a thermal zone. In a MAB model, an individual can be modeled with three characteristics of reactivity, pro-activity, and social ability [15]. The individual responds to variations in its environment, changes its behavior to achieve its own goals, and communicates with other agents. Hence, a well-developed MAB model could be a reliable replication of a thermal zone and its occupants. In the MAB model of this study, occupants are referred to as human agents and a HVAC unit as a HVAC agent.

3.1 Human Agents: Occupants' Proxy

A human agent has four properties as indicated in Table 1. This agent has been designed to represent how an occupant responds to the ambient environment. Temperature was considered as the only parameter of concern due to its major influence [23].

Table 1. Properties of human agents (i.e., occupants' proxies)

Properties	Description	In the MAB model
Thermal preference	Temperature that a human agent prefers	Randomly set within the range of 20 to 30 °C
Thermal satisfaction	Percentage of satisfaction with respect to current temperature	Maximized at the thermal preference (100%) and decreases otherwise with respect to thermal sensitivity
Acceptable condition	Temperature that a human agent thinks as acceptable	When the thermal satisfaction is above 39.35% (the value of $\mu \pm \sigma$ in a Gaussian distribution function)
Thermal sensitivity	Sensitivity to variations in temperature	Scenario 1: generalized thermal sensitivity using a linear function
		Scenario 2: personalized thermal sensitivities using a skewed probability distribution function

Each human agent prefers a specific temperature (thermal preference; e.g., 23.3 °C) which is randomly assigned within the range of 20 to 30 °C (typical indoor temperature [24]) by the model. Thermal satisfaction is maximized when human agent is at the desired temperature (100%) and decreases otherwise. Acceptable condition was designed based on a Gaussian distribution function which was utilized to present different thermal sensitivities. A Gaussian function has 39.35% when input values is within the range of one standard deviation from the mean value ($\mu \pm \sigma$) so that when thermal satisfaction becomes below 39.35%, it was recognized as unacceptable to human agents.

Thermal sensitivity was modeled using two scenarios. First, generalized thermal sensitivity is described as a linear relationship with thermal satisfaction ($f(x)$) so that an equally distributed thermal sensitivity was reflected in the model (Eq. (1)).

$$f(x) = 100 - s \times |x - \mu| \qquad (1)$$

where x indicates current temperature, μ thermal preference, and s thermal sensitivity. Specifically, we defined the acceptable temperature as 3.0 °C away from thermal preference on each side, as recommended in the generalized model of ASHRAE [14]. In other words, s is 20.22. In the second scenario, personalized thermal sensitivity was considered by a skewed distribution function (Eq. (2)).

$$f(x) = 100 \times 2 \times \exp\left(-\frac{(x - \mu)^2}{2\sigma^2}\right) \times \int_{-\infty}^{\alpha\left(\frac{x - \mu}{\sigma}\right)} \exp\left(-\frac{x^2}{2}\right) dx \qquad (2)$$

where x is current temperature, μ thermal preference, σ determines the breadth of thermal profile, and α decides which thermal sensitivity is steepened (either sensitive to high or low temperature). A positive skewness represents an occupant who is sensitive to lower temperature and vice versa. Two factors influencing thermal sensitivity (σ and α) were randomly assigned (σ: from 1 to 5 and α: from -4 to 4; these values were determined using the thermal profiles in [5, 6, 18]), thereby the diversity of thermal profiles was reflected in the second scenario.

Using theses aforesaid equations and values, thermal profiles were created and assigned to human agents in each scenario as shown in Fig. 1.

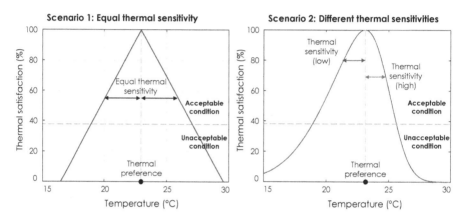

Fig. 1. A thermal profile of a human agent in two scenarios: (1) the generalized thermal sensitivity and (2) different thermal sensitivities.

Each human agent desires to maximize its own thermal satisfaction. Hence, it provides feedback to a HVAC agent (HVAC unit's proxy). This feedback shows whether the human agent wants an increase or decrease for the ambient temperature. The amount of thermal satisfaction with respect to a thermal change is also provided to the HVAC agent (Eq. (3)). In the case of having an unacceptable condition, the human agent provides a strong sign (Eq. (3) - the maximum feedback value of 100 in this MAB model) to further influence the decision made by the environmental agent (i.e., trying to put itself in priority).

$$\begin{cases} \textit{if acceptable condition} \rightarrow \begin{cases} \textit{if } x > \mu, \textit{feedback} = -df(x)/dx \\ \textit{if } x < \mu, \textit{feedback} = df(x)/dx \end{cases} \\ \textit{if unacceptable condition} \rightarrow \begin{cases} \textit{if } x > \mu, \textit{feedback} = -100 \\ \textit{if } x < \mu, \textit{feedback} = 100 \end{cases} \end{cases} \tag{3}$$

where x is the current (ambient) temperature, μ thermal preference, and $f(x)$ thermal satisfaction.

3.2   HVAC Agent: HVAC System's Proxy

The HVAC agent determines the setpoint temperature according to the feedback from human agents when the current temperature is not optimized. It sums all feedback from human agents and updates the setpoint temperature with the objective of maximizing the total thermal satisfaction (Eq. (4)).

$$
\begin{cases}
Objective\ function = \max_x \left(\sum_i f_i(x) \right) \\
if\ any\ feedback \rightarrow \begin{cases} if\ \sum feedback > 0 \rightarrow increase\ x \\ if\ \sum feedback < 0 \rightarrow decrease\ x \end{cases} \\
if\ no\ feedback \rightarrow stop\ (optimized)
\end{cases}
\tag{4}
$$

where x is the current (ambient) temperature, i is the number of human agent, and $f_i(x)$ is the ith human agent's thermal profile.

The initial temperature is randomly determined within the typical range of indoor temperature: 20 to 30 °C [24]. After that, human agents provide feedback until they become satisfied, and the HVAC agent optimizes the setpoint temperature as illustrated in Fig. 2, the flowchart of this MAB model.

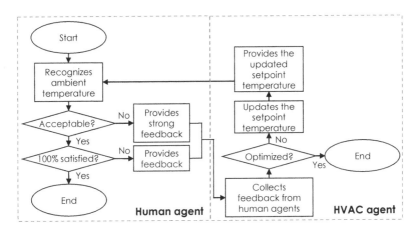

Fig. 2.   Flowchart of the interaction of human and HVAC agents

Using this optimization process through the MAB model, we analyzed the setpoint temperature, total thermal satisfaction, and number of human agents who are in an acceptable condition in both scenarios to check the influence of taking thermal sensitivity into consideration in a multi-occupancy space.

4   Results

In order to account for diverse occasions, a number of multi-occupancy scenarios were modeled: Two, three, and four human agents in a multi-occupancy space. In addition, three different sets of thermal preferences were selected in each case. Figure 3 illustrates one of the examples in our MAB simulations. To perform statistical analyses (paired-sample t-test), each case was run a thousand times, and then the results were analyzed. We used MATLAB for modelling and analyses.

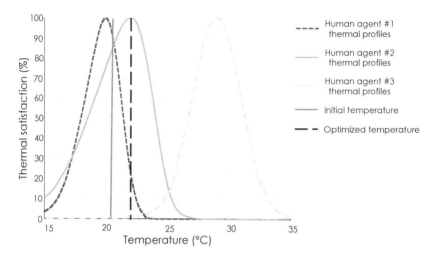

Fig. 3. Example of the MAB simulation.

As it relates to optimized setpoint temperature, the analyses demonstrated that thermal sensitivity played a role in every case (Table 2). There was a significant differ-ence between the mean and standard deviation values in two scenarios. Furthermore, the p-values from the paired-sample t-test had almost zero values, which further proves that the optimized setpoint temperatures were significantly affected when personalized thermal sensitivity of human agents were taken into account.

Table 2. Optimized setpoint temperature in both scenarios

# of human agents	The set of thermal preferences (°C)	Average optimized setpoint temperature (standard deviation; °C)		
		First scenario	Second scenario	P-value[*]
2	20, 24	23.19 (1.22)	22.25 (1.41)	0.00
	20, 28	24.71 (2.61)	24.30 (2.82)	0.00
	24, 29	25.72 (1.91)	26.03 (1.84)	0.00
3	19, 24, 28	25.59 (1.65)	24.40 (1.41)	0.00
	20, 22, 29	22.61 (0.83)	22.82 (1.58)	0.00
	21, 27, 29	26.69 (1.13)	26.38 (1.62)	0.00
4	20, 21, 28, 29	25.12 (2.81)	23.93 (2.38)	0.00
	20, 22, 24, 29	23.41 (0.83)	23.21 (0.91)	0.00
	20, 25, 27, 29	25.81 (0.91)	25.93 (1.01)	0.00

[*]From paired-sample t-test

Table 3 shows the average thermal satisfaction of human agents and as the results show, human agents in the second scenario manifested a significantly improved satisfaction in the optimized setpoint temperatures. Considering that the standard deviations in the second scenario were higher than the ones in the first scenario, it could be concluded that the optimized setpoint temperatures were better located by adapting personalized thermal sensitivity of human agents to maximize the total thermal satisfaction.

Table 3. Average thermal satisfaction of human agents in both scenarios

# of human agents	A set of thermal preferences (°C)	Average thermal satisfaction of human agents (standard deviation)		
		First scenario	Second scenario	P-value*
2	20, 24	60.00 (0.00)	70.96 (13.39)	0.00
	20, 28	34.86 (11.51)	44.02 (13.39)	0.00
	24, 29	50.00 (0.00)	62.04 (14.63)	0.00
3	19, 24, 28	40.00 (0.00)	48.32 (10.72)	0.00
	20, 22, 29	42.86 (5.58)	48.21 (10.39)	0.00
	21, 27, 29	44.23 (6.11)	52.24 (11.84)	0.00
4	20, 21, 28, 29	34.23 (9.85)	44.98 (12.52)	0.00
	20, 22, 24, 29	48.01 (4.15)	54.43 (8.70)	0.00
	20, 25, 27, 29	49.11 (4.53)	55.56 (8.77)	0.00

*From paired-sample t-test

Due to the increased thermal satisfactions of human agents, as indicated earlier, the number of satisfied human agents were also significantly increased (Table 4).

Table 4. Average number of satisfied human agents in both scenarios

# of human agents	A set of thermal preferences (°C)	Average number of satisfied human agents (standard deviation)		
		First scenario	Second scenario	P-value*
2	20, 24	1.91 (0.29)	1.73 (0.55)	0.00
	20, 28	0.00 (0.00)	0.85 (0.69)	0.00
	24, 29	2.00 (0.00)	1.46 (0.68)	0.00
3	19, 24, 28	1.00 (0.00)	1.48 (0.73)	0.00
	20, 22, 29	1.00 (0.00)	1.51 (0.62)	0.00
	21, 27, 29	1.00 (0.00)	1.64 (0.71)	0.00
4	20, 21, 28, 29	0.00 (0.00)	1.83 (0.95)	0.00
	20, 22, 24, 29	2.00 (0.00)	2.38 (0.61)	0.00
	20, 25, 27, 29	2.00 (0.00)	2.34 (0.65)	0.00

*From paired-sample t-test

These results demonstrate that thermal sensitivity plays a crucial role when we it comes to optimization of indoor thermal conditions, gauging thermal satisfaction, and quantifying the number of satisfied occupants in a multi-occupancy space.

5   Conclusion

This study aims to shed light on the importance of taking thermal sensitivity into consideration when indoor thermal conditions are controlled in a multi-occupancy space, which is commonly experienced by occupants. It was hypothesized that taking the diversity of personalized thermal sensitivity, one of the characteristics in personal thermal profiles, could impact thermal satisfaction of occupants as well as the optimized setpoint temperature. Using a MAB simulation environment, individual thermal comfort profiles were developed in two ways: Human agents had the same thermal preferences, but (1) with generalized thermal sensitivity in the first scenario and (2) with personalized thermal sensitivities in the second scenario. Each human agent aimed to create its own best thermal condition by interacting with the HVAC agent, which derived the optimized condition by maximizing the total thermal satisfaction of human agents. After several realizations, we compared the results in both scenarios. It was demonstrated that thermal sensitivity influenced (1) the optimized setpoint temperature, (2) thermal satisfactions of human agents, and (3) number of satisfied human agents. In the end, it was noticed that thermal sensitivity should be taken into account to better serve occupants. To leverage these results for improved air conditioning in multi-occupancy spaces, reliable personalized thermal comfort profiles should be developed and implemented in the control logic.

Although the interesting results were observed, there are a number of limitations that should be taken into account for real-world implementation of thermal sensitivity for control. Despite references to the previous studies that present actual thermal comfort profiles, we have used synthetically generated thermal profiles by random generation of distribution functions. Furthermore, we have assumed that the thermal conditioned air is uniformly distributed in a multi-occupancy space so that every human agent experienced the same average condition, which is not a realistic assumption. Therefore, we believe that the proposed MAB model has a potential for further expansion. The following improvements will be among the future directions of our research efforts:

- Taking occupant activities (i.e., impact of physical process on thermal sensations).
- Using actual thermal preference and sensitivity information in human subjects.
- Integration of multi-objective optimization for taking energy consumption into consideration.

Acknowledgement. This material is based upon work supported by the National Science Foundation under grant #1663513. Any opinions, findings, and conclusions or recommendations expressed in this material are those of the authors and do not necessarily reflect the views of the National Science Foundation.

References

1. Guo, W., Zhou, M.: Technologies toward thermal comfort-based and energy-efficient HVAC systems: a review. In: 2009 IEEE International Conference on Systems, Man and Cybernetics (2009)
2. Humphreys, M.A., Hancock, M.: Do people like to feel 'neutral'?: Exploring the variation of the desired thermal sensation on the ASHRAE scale. Energy Build. **39**(7), 867–874 (2007)
3. ASHRAE: Thermal Environmental Conditions for Human Occupancy. ASHRAE, Atlanta (2017)
4. Zhao, J., Lam, K.P., Loftness, V., Ydstie, B.E.: Occupant individual thermal comfort data analysis in an office. In: Sustainable Human-Building Ecosystems (2015)
5. Daum, D., Haldi, F., Morel, N.: A personalized measure of thermal comfort for building controls. Build. Environ. **46**(1), 3–11 (2011)
6. Ghahramani, A., Jazizadeh, F., Becerik-Gerber, B.: A knowledge based approach for selecting energy-aware and comfort-driven HVAC temperature set points. Energy Build. **85**, 536–548 (2014)
7. Jazizadeh, F., Jung, W.: Personalized thermal comfort through digital video images for energy-efficient HVAC control. Appl. Energy **109**, 82–100 (2018)
8. Jazizadeh, F., Becerik-Gerber, B.: Toward adaptive comfort management in office buildings using participatory sensing for end user driven control. In: Proceedings of the Fourth ACM Workshop on Embedded Sensing Systems for Energy-Efficiency in Buildings. ACM (2012)
9. Jazizadeh, F., Ghahramani, A., Becerik-Gerber, B., Kichkaylo, T., Orosz, M.: Human-building interaction framework for personalized thermal comfort-driven systems in office buildings. J. Comput. Civ. Eng. **28**, 2–16 (2013)
10. Jazizadeh, F., Ghahramani, A., Becerik-Gerber, B., Kichkaylo, T., Orosz, M.: User-led decentralized thermal comfort driven HVAC operations for improved efficiency in office buildings. Energy Build. **70**, 398–410 (2014)
11. Klein, L., Kwak, J.-Y., Kavulya, G., Jazizadeh, F., Becerik-Gerber, B., Varakantham, P., Tambe, M.: Coordinating occupant behavior for building energy and comfort management using multi-agent systems. Autom. Constr. **22**, 525–536 (2012)
12. Kwak, J.-Y., Varakantham, P., Maheswaran, R., Tambe, M., Jazizadeh, F., Kavulya, G., Klein, L., Becerik-Gerber, B., Hayes, T., Wood, W.: SAVES: a sustainable multiagent application to conserve building energy considering occupants. In: Proceedings of the 11th International Conference on Autonomous Agents and Multiagent Systems, vol. 1. 2012 International Foundation for Autonomous Agents and Multiagent Systems, Valencia, Spain. pp. 21–28 (2012)
13. Yang, R., Wang, L.: Development of multi-agent system for building energy and comfort management based on occupant behaviors. Energy Build. **56**(1), 1–7 (2013)
14. ASHRAE: ASHRAE Handbook Fundamentals. American Society of Heating, Refrigerating and Air-Conditioning Engineers, Atlanta (2013)
15. Wilensky, U., Rand, W.: Introduction to Agent-Based Modeling: Modeling Natural, Social, and Engineered Complex Systems with Netlogo. The MIT Press, Cambridge/London (2015)
16. Fanger, P.O.: Thermal Comfort: Analysis and Applications in Environmental Engineering. McGraw-Hill, New York (1972)
17. van Hoof, J.J.: Forty years of Fanger's model of thermal comfort: comfort for all? Indoor Air **18**(3), 182–201 (2008)
18. Jazizadeh, F., Ghahramani, A., Becerik-Gerber, B., Kichkaylo, T., Orosz, M.: Personalized thermal comfort driven control in HVAC operated office buildings. In: ASCE International Workshop on Computing in Civil Engineering (IWCCE) Conference (2013)

19. Erickson, V.L., Cerpa, A.E.: Thermovote: participatory sensing for efficient building HVAC conditioning. In: Proceedings of the Fourth ACM Workshop on Embedded Sensing Systems for Energy-Efficiency in Buildings, Toronto, Ontario, Canada, pp. 9–16. ACM (2012)
20. Jazizadeh, F., Ghahramani, A., Becerik-Gerber, B., Kichkaylo, T., Orosz, M.: Human-building interaction framework for personalized thermal comfort-driven systems in office buildings. J. Comput. Civ. Eng. **28**(1), 2–16 (2014)
21. Lee, J.: Conflict resolution in multi-agent based Intelligent Environments. Build. Environ. **45**(3), 574–585 (2010)
22. Li, D., Menassa, C.C., Kamat, V.R.: A personalized HVAC control smartphone application framework for improved human health and well-being. In: Computing in Civil Engineering 2017 (2017)
23. Jazizadeh, F., Marin, F.M., Becerik-Gerber, B.: A thermal preference scale for personalized comfort profile identification via participatory sensing. Build. Environ. **68**, 140–149 (2013)
24. Liu, W., Lian, Z., Liu, Y.: Heart rate variability at different thermal comfort levels. Eur. J. Appl. Physiol. **103**(3), 361–366 (2008)

BIM and Engineering Ontologies

Benefits and Limitations of Linked Data Approaches for Road Modeling and Data Exchange

Jakob Beetz[1] and André Borrmann[2(✉)]

[1] Chair of Computational Design, RWTH Aachen University of Technology,
Aachen, Germany
[2] Chair for Computational Modeling and Simulation,
Technical University Munich, Munich, Germany
`andre.borrmann@tum.de`

Abstract. The paper advocates the use of Linked Data approaches as a means of overcoming the limitations of conventional monolithic data modeling in the context of the de-facto heterogeneity of information systems and data models in the diverse fields of the digital built environment. It enriches the discussion by focusing on one specific sub-domain – the application of digital methods in road design, construction and operation which involves the exchange, management and querying of spatio-semantic data that typically stems from different data sources and involves diverse software systems and data models. It argues that semantic web techniques significantly simplify the integration of heterogeneous data models. In a case study, the German road data exchange standard OKSTRA is linked with the Dutch CB-NL and RWS object type libraries. Doing so, it is shown how nationally well-established and widespread standards can be integrated in order to perform cross-country querying of road data. As a basis for the cases study, OKSTRA was transferred into an OWL-based data format, resulting in the creation of okstraOWL. The paper discusses in detail strategies for realizing semi-automated mapping with the Dutch CB-NL and RWS object type library, including a detailed analysis of the advantages and limitations of the different options. Major emphasis is placed on finding spatially related entities. Finally, the paper discusses the capabilities of linking the data sets by presenting a number of exemplary SPARQL queries for answering real-world questions that require the integrated analysis of data sets in different data models.

Keywords: Linked Data · Infrastructure · Interoperability
Standardization · Road modeling

1 Introduction

1.1 Motivation

For many years, the effectiveness of the AEC industry has been drastically diminished by severe incompatibility problems between the software products

© Springer International Publishing AG, part of Springer Nature 2018
I. F. C. Smith and B. Domer (Eds.): EG-ICE 2018, LNCS 10864, pp. 245–261, 2018.
https://doi.org/10.1007/978-3-319-91638-5_13

employed in practice resulting in the loss of information whenever data is exchanged. Research into ways to overcome this issue started in the late 1980's. Back then, the development of an all-encompassing product model for every aspect of the building and construction sector seemed to be a viable solution. Based on this idea, the industry consortium buildingSMART International (bSI) has developed the Industry Foundation Classes (IFC) standard for the exchange of digital building models. Today, after 20 years of development, continuing improvement and extensions, the IFC model is the de-facto standard for data exchange in the building industry.

However, the complexity of the data model has already reached a critical limit: With more than 700 classes, thousands of attributes and a dense network of relationships between the classes [1], only a small number of experts is able to fully understand the functionality and behavior of the entire data model.

Nonetheless, even with this high level of complexity, many aspects of the construction domain are still not covered. This applies in particular to the infrastructure sector.

Although significant extension work for the infrastructure domain is currently being undertaken in the context of the bSI Infra Room, the resulting international standard will not be able to consider all aspects of national or local legacy road information standards, nor will it cover all related information domains, such as traffic or accident data. Taking a broader perspective, it becomes clear that a singular data model will never be able to integrate all relevant data from all domains in all cultural contexts for all application scenarios.

At the same time, it has become common sense in recent years, that the continued extension of the IFC data model without proper modularization, disentanglement and strategic, high-level architectural adjustments will further increase its complexity and reduce its manageability [2].

Given the de-facto existence of a large set of legacy data models in the construction and operation domain, the fundamental concepts of Linked Data seem to provide a promising solution to the challenges described above. Linked Data is based on the idea of making use of existing data formats from different domains mostly as-is, and to enable ways to relate them with each other through links between corresponding objects. The concept of Linked Data therefore contrasts with that of one all-embracing product model by respecting the existence of heterogeneous data sources.

Using the example of two national road data models and the international IFC standard, this paper presents how such integration can be performed from a technical point of view, and subsequently discusses the advantages and limitations of this approach. Figure 1 depicts the overall concept.

1.2 Linked Data

The notion of Linked Data is based on the idea of facilitating the connection, alignment and ultimately integration of heterogeneous data and information models by relying on a minimal set of common technologies and protocols: Known as the "Semantic Web Stack", a layered set of technologies is used as a

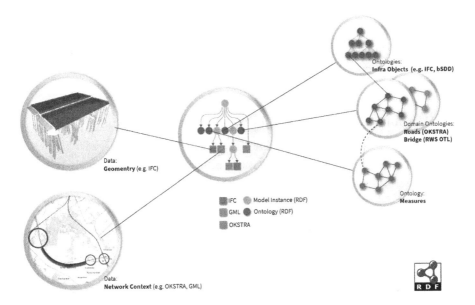

Fig. 1. Overview of the overall concept of multiple Linked Data vocabularies applied to legacy models

common platform to enable the creation of interoperable data models that can be connected across network boundaries.

Built on top of the common technological layers used for the World Wide Web such as HTTP, URIs and XML, at the core of the Linked Data and Semantic Web Technology stack is the Resource Description Framework (RDF): In RDF data, information and knowledge is expressed in the form of statements. Each statement is composed of a 3-tuple of resources, referred to as Subject, Predicate and Object (S, P, O). Each of the three resources can either be identified by a Universal Resource Identifier (URI, including URL, URNs etc.) or can be a literal value, usually with a simple data type from the XML Schema. By allowing arbitrary statements to be made about arbitrary resources residing at arbitrary locations, graph structures are composed of atomic statements that allow the expression of any data and information imaginable. While basic RDF offers simple constructs such as properties and lists, additional vocabularies from higher levels of the technological stack can be used that allow the uniform use of higher level concepts such as the notion of classes and subclasses, relationships and value range restrictions. The Ontology Web Language (OWL) vocabulary – which stems from the knowledge modeling domain – introduces formal logics, i.e. concepts that can be used to capture rules and knowledge that enable one to make explicit inferences from implicit information referred to as reasoning on the data or the schema itself.

A major challenge for making Linked Data work, however, is the identification and definition of appropriate resources in models and data sets that should be linked together. Ideally, these resources represent the identical physical or logical items or concepts. However, due to the diverging granularity and diverging semantics of the data models involved, identical objects often do not exist. The paper will discuss in detail the different categories of matching problems as well as potential solutions.

1.3 Vocabularies, Concept Libraries and Other Modular Data Models

One of advantages of the Linked Data approach is the ability to share meta-models, vocabularies and data sets across different knowledge domains, tools and platforms using homogeneous infrastructures and protocols [3]. In contrast to other data modeling and interoperability standards, Linked Data has the advantage of being self-documenting, queryable and extendable and of supporting the notion of sharing and reuse of meta-models from the ground up. Using the built-in notion of statements, mappings between different vocabularies both for concepts as well as their relations can easily be added and processed with the same tool chain that is used for the concrete data sets itself. By interconnecting different meta-models and instance data sets, a machine-readable, global web of data has been growing in a decentralized fashion over a number of years; similar to the network of information designed for the consumption by human readers known as the World Wide Web. This global data graph referred to as Linked Open Data Cloud currently consists of hundreds of vocabularies and classification systems that are interconnected. Even though it is not designed as a central hub, the Linked Data representation of the collaborative WikiPedia corpus, DBPedia [4] is currently the most interconnected data set and serves as a kind of nucleus for the Linked Open Data (LOD) Cloud. A prime example for useful vocabularies shared across engineering domains addresses the modeling of measures, units and quantities.

2 Existing Data Models for Road Infrastructure

While the road extensions of the IFC data model are still under development, there is a number of existing well-established data standards for representing and exchanging road data in use today.

2.1 InfraGML, CityGML

In the geospatial sector, two well-established domain models pertaining to infrastructural and urban artefacts including roads exist, that capture information valuable for infrastructure planning. The two standards are based on the Geographic Markup Language (GML, ISO 19136), an XML Schema-based information model for the spatial geometric description of geographic information that is developed and maintained by the Open Geospatial Consortium (OGC). Interestingly, the GML model has its technological roots in RDF and lends itself very well to Linked Data approaches. This opportunity is increasingly being used and numerous software implementations and products offer dedicated support for the efficient storage and spatial querying of large data sets. Specialized standards for both geometric descriptions (Well Known Text, WKT [5]) as well as queries (GeoSPARQL [6]) have been introduced to further enhance the support for Linked Data.

2.2 LandXML

LandXML is an open information exchange standard focused on modeling terrain, alignments and roads including a dedicated, independent geometry description format. With more than 200 classes and more than 1800 attributes, it is an extensive model that permits a complete and fine grained description of road infrastructure. The earlier versions 1.1 and 1.2 of the format are widely adapted in the road planning and construction domain. However, it must be noted that the organization maintaining the standard and the corresponding website LandXML.org is not a regular standardization body. An attempt to rescue and reuse the data model by the OGC led to a first version 2.0 in 2016, but this has not yet been picked up by software vendors.

2.3 OKSTRA

The German road data model OKSTRA (Objekt Katalog Strassen- und Verkehrswesen) makes it possible to describe road infrastructure on different granularity levels. It is a mandatory standard for data exchange processes in all public road construction projects in Germany. It relies on the GML standard and provides capabilities for describing the shape of a road in compliance with established engineering approaches, i.e. by combining horizontal and vertical alignment with a number of cross-sections. Apart from that it provides a rich set of semantics covering various aspects ranging from road design and condition rating to traffic and incident statistics.

With more than 1,800 classes and almost 14,000 attributes, the extent of the model is enormous. To reduce complexity and allow modular configuration for different use case scenarios, the data model is divided into 41 sub-schemas. Similar to the IFC, the original OKSTRA data model was modeled in the STEP EXPRESS language (ISO 10303-11 [7]). To better address contemporary industry practices and tool support however, the data modeling language was switched to UML from version 2.015 onwards and the defined data model is serialized as XMI [8].

2.4 IFC Alignment

The Ifc-Alignment project [9,10] is the first of the buildingSMART InfraRoom initiatives that has completed the full cycle of standardization and become part of the IFC revision 4.1. It is intended to serve as a common basis for future linear infrastructure extensions including IFC-Road, IFC-Railway and IFC-Bridge that can make common use e.g. of implicit parametric geometric descriptions of curves such as clothoids or Bloss curves. The alignment types have been adapted from existing data models such as LandXML and OKSTRA and integrated into the geometry descriptions of the IFC model.

2.5   RWS OTL, CB-NL

The Concept Library of the Netherlands (CB-NL) is an umbrella vocabulary intended as a bridge or pivot between different classification systems, vocabularies and data models used in the Netherlands. Currently it comprises 1557 concepts, among which 590 come from IMGeo (a Dutch CityGML extension), 491 from ETIM (electrotechnical equipment), 293 from NL/SfB (equivalent to Omniclass, Uniclass or DIN 276) and 57 from Rijkswaterstaat Object Type Library (RWS-OTL). The RWS-OTL is a modular ontology describing artefacts in the built environment as they are used by the Dutch Ministry for Infrastructure (RWS).

Overall, the RWS-OTL consists of 7,482 concepts that are connected via 10681 object relationships and 22,242 specializations (including restrictions, which also make use of subclassing mechanisms). Its current primary application is use in the context of requirement engineering for infrastructural projects, where concepts and their properties from the RWS-OTL are used to add additional semantics to geometrical models represented in the form of IFC or GML models. For this, an intermediary format stemming from the COINS [11] standard is used that is currently on track for international standardization as an "Information container for data drop" (ISO/CD 21597-1): It links concepts and properties from external vocabularies with files providing the 3D and 2D geometry of the facility under consideration.

3   Linked Data Migration and Integration Strategies

To employ Linked Data strategies and realize the advantages described in Sect. 1.2 the following strategies can be identified:

1. **Conversion and migration**
2. **Semantic payloads in legacy formats**
3. **Semantic containers.**

3.1   Basic Considerations: Formal Reasoning vs. Querying

Among the main advantages of formal ontologies expressed in OWL is the applicability of reasoning mechanisms for checking the consistency and correctness of schema and instance information. Generic inference engines (reasoners) can be applied to prove that the instance data provided in the ABox fulfills the requirements and constraints of the schema information provided in the TBox, see Fig. 2.

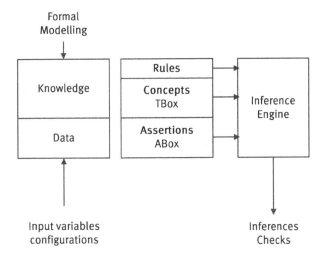

Fig. 2. Schematic depiction of inferences drawn from knowledge models (TBox), facts (ABox) and rules to derive new explicit knowledge from implicit facts

3.2   Linked Data

However, applying formal logic reasoning requires a very careful modeling of information and may involve significant computing resources: The effort of proving the consistency of ABox and TBox increases with the complexity of the data model and employed features of OWL for modeling constraints and boundary conditions. In addition, the extent of facts to be checked contributes to the required computing effort. Depending on the modeling approach taken, proofs may not be computed in a reasonable time frame or not be determined at all.

An easy workaround for the challenges involved with applying formal logic and reasoning is the employment of querying mechanisms such as the query language SPARQL. Applying a query language makes it possible to detect schema–instance inconsistencies through the formulation of corresponding queries. Such queries can be processed in a reasonable time span, also for very large data sets, but have the disadvantage of separating parts of the domain-specific logic and knowledge into external systems.

3.3   Challenges for Employing Linked Data Approaches

The greatest challenge for employing Linked Data approaches lies in the fact that data models with different origins and purposes typically implement different approaches in describing real-world objects and mental concepts. This results in differences in both coverage as well as granularity. While different types of traffic signs might be explicitly represented by individual classes in one data model, they might be subsumed by a more generic class in another one, or not modeled at all in a third one.

As 1-to-1 mappings of concepts can rarely be found in heterogeneous data models, the underlying semantics have to be carefully considered when defining links in order to avoid mis-matching and subsequent erroneous query results.

4   Case Study: Linking OKSTRA with Other Data Models

4.1   The OKSTRA Data Model

The OKSTRA standard is an object-oriented data model for representing road and traffic data. It was introduced by the German Ministry of Transport in the year 2000 as a means of harmonizing data exchange processes between software systems used for designing, constructing and operating roads. It has become a mandatory standard for exchanging road design data between roadway planners and the road authorities. Accordingly, OKSTRA is closely linked to the requirements of the German authorities. As road management in Germany is to a large extent under the control of the 16 federal states, OKSTRA provides mechanisms for state-specific extensions.

Originally, OKSTRA was defined using the data modeling language EXPRESS. From Version 2.015 onwards, the modeling language was changed to the more widespread Unified Modeling Language (UML). Accordingly, the schema is now represented in the XML metadata interchange format (XMI) and instance data is exchanged using XML documents.

OKSTRA consists of 41 sub-schemata addressing specific sub-domains of road design, construction and operation. This ranges from detailed design information including horizontal and vertical alignment as well as cross-sections to traffic signs and roadway condition data and traffic and accident statistics. OKSTRA is characterized by a very fine granularity and a high degree of detail. With more than 2,800 complex types and almost 14,000 attributes, the OKSTRA standard is among the most extensive road data models in the world.

A particularity of OKSTRA is its dynamic extension mechanisms. The "key tables" work similarly to the property sets of the IFC standard and make it possible to introduce extensions and modifications without the need to alter the schema. This provides flexibility, but at the same time reduces the possibilities for checking instance data for formal compliance with the data model. Another mechanism uses IDs to associate geometric objects with semantics provided by long lists of ID-to-concept mappings. These "domain semantics lists" (Fachbedeutungslisten) differ from state to state. They increase the complexity and represent a significant challenge for implementing linked data approaches.

For representing geometric (spatial) information, OKSTRA makes use of the Geographic Markup Language (GML) which itself implements the ISO 19107 Spatial Schema. Accordingly, a large part of the geometric information is provided by means of the GML types gml:Point, gml:Curve and gml:Surface or gml:MultiPoint, gml:MultiCurve, gml:MultiSurface, respectively. This is augmented by proprietary data types for describing more complex geometries required for representing aspects such as the alignment. To describe the shape of a road, OKSTRA basically provides a combination of 2D geometry for representing the horizontal and the vertical alignment as well as the cross-sections. This approach is similar to those implemented in LandXML, InfraGML and IFC-Alignment.

4.2 Making OKSTRA Available for Linked Data

In order to make OKSTRA and its instances available for Linked Data techniques and procedures, three steps are necessary:

1. Transforming the schema from EXPRESS, XMI or XSD into RDF, RDFS or OWL
2. Transforming instance data from XML or SPFF into RDF/XML, NTriples or Turtle
3. Making the instance data available through Linked Data infrastructure (e.g. SPARQL endpoints)

These three steps are discussed in the following sections.

4.3 Transformation of OKSTRA into okstraOWL

A number of research and development efforts can be found that have transformed data models from their underlying legacy schema modeling languages and formats such as NIAM, EXPRESS, or UML into Linked Data formats. The OntoSTEP initiative by NIST has proposed a generic transformation approach for EXPRESS-based models into OWL-DL [12]. Transformations of the IFC model from EXPRESS into OWL have been proposed in different variations in the past [13,14]. A first version of the ifcOWL transformation was standardized by the buildingSMART organization in 2016. The transformation approaches chosen for ifcOWL have been applied to OKSTRA and are discussed in the following sections.

As mentioned earlier, the transformation process is executed in three general stages. The following sections introduce the conversion of the schema.

URI Composition. One of the decisive factors for the usability of Linked Data vocabularies is the readability and ease of navigation of the resources used. A number of best practices have been suggested by other research and development initiatives and the W3C. Alongside the names of classes and properties themselves, offering a de-referenceable version of the schema contributes to adoption and uptake. For this, both a machine-readable and a human-readable version should be provided online that are automatically presented to the consumer via HTTP content negotiation either as HTML documentation (human) or as RDF/XML or as Turtle file (machine).

Data Types: Boxed/Unboxed. When modeling in RDFS or OWL, two main types of data can be identified: instances of objects and simple literal data types such as integer, float, string etc. In the original EXPRESS schemata as well as in the current XMI/XSD format both types are specified further using constraints to clarify the semantics and intended use. For example, for measuring length (`Achselement.Laenge:Meter` in S_Entwurf), the data type `Meter` is used that is defined as a type of `REAL` (EXPRESS: `TYPE Meter = REAL` in schema S_Allgemeine_Objekte) or `xsd:double` as an extension of the basictypes.xsd definitions in GML. To increase interoperability however, only simple XML Schema types are allowed in RDF and RDFS.

Different approaches to model the data type Meter can be chosen. In okstraOWL, we adopted the approach that was implemented in ifcOWL:

Listing 1.1. Boxed data types for the length measures in meters

```
okstra:Double
    rdf:type owl:Class ;
    rdfs:subClassOf
            [ rdf:type owl:Restriction ;
              owl:allValuesFrom xsd:double ;
              owl:onProperty :hasDouble
            ] .

okstra:Laenge_Achselement
    rdf:type owl:ObjectProperty ;
    rdfs:domain okstra:Achselement ;
    rdfs:range okstra:Meter .

okstra:Meter
    rdf:type owl:Class ;
    rdfs:subClassOf :Double .

okstra:hasDouble
    rdf:type owl:DatatypeProperty ;
    rdfs:domain okstra:Double ;
    rdfs:range xsd:double .
```

Classes and Names. The translation of the OKSTRA class structure including multiple inheritance can be realized by a simple transformation of `<element xmi` ↪ `:type="uml:Class">` of the XMI schema into `owl:Class` definitions. In OWL, all classes must be declared as being disjoint, i.e. instances can only be associated with exactly one class.

A critical question of representing large data models such as OKSTRA is the naming of classes. Although classes do have a unique name in OKSTRA, there is no unique name assumption (UNA) in Linked Data. For unambiguous identification, classes can be equipped with the UUID of the XMI model.

Listing 1.2. Boxed data types for the length measures in meters

```
okstra:Achse
        rdf:type owl:Class ;
        rdfs:label "Achse"^^xsd:string@de ;
        rdfs:label "Axis"^^xsd:string@en ;
          xmi:id "EAID_E4106DA8_B309_4197_A6A5_37570759D8B5"^^xsd:
              ↪ string
```

Attributes and Relations. In contrast to the 'locally' defined attributes of EXPRESS, XMI and XML Schema classes, definitions of properties and attributes in the form of `rdf:Property` and its subclasses `owl:DatatypeProperty` and `owl:ObjectProperty` are always 'global'. This is not without side effects: The attribute 'Laenge' (length) has different value ranges, types and measures in the context of different classes like meter or kilometer. A globally defined `rdf:Property` can only indirectly constrain the possible values using, for example, `owl:Restrictions`,

Key Tables. A notable feature of the OKSTRA model is the concept of the 488 core and even more regional 'key tables' (Schluesseltabellen) that require special attention due to the atypical data modeling style. Basically they represent lookup tables that can be used to add additional qualification to classes similar to indirectly modeled subclasses. For historic reasons they can either be modeled as references, embedded into the classes or captured in a compact form [15].

Aggregated Data/Collections. Ordered aggregation data types such as arrays or lists cannot be directly translated into OWL. The reason is that RDF and OWL are based on sets of elements. The mapping of ordered data types onto RDF is cumbersome and requires an additional layer to become processable by OWL-supporting inference engines [16,17]. Due to the low number of ordered collection data outside of geometrical elements which are covered in WKT, optional RDF lists have been adopted for okstraOWL. These can be kept in separate graphs that keep the main data files lightweight and allow DL-compatibility, but can be pulled into the graph on demand.

Integrating GML Geometry. With the transition from EXPRESS to UML/XMI in version 2.015, the previous geometry entities have been replaced by those of Geographic Markup Language (GML). As the GML format built on the Resource Description Framework (RDF) since its very beginning, a migration to Linked Data is a straightforward process.

In the approach implemented here, instantiated GML geometry is represented in RDF using "Well-Known text" (WKT). The basic idea of WKT is to represent points, lines, linestrings etc. by means of literal values (strings), as otherwise a significant syntactical overhead would be required when using `rdf:list` elements. The following listing shows an example.

Listing 1.3. Use of "well-known text" in RDF.

```
<sf:LineString rdf:about= "http://example.org/ApplicationSchema#
    ↪ EExactGeom">
    <geo:asWKT rdf:datatype= "http://www.opengis.net/ont/geosparql#
        ↪ wktLiteral">
        <![CDATA[
            <http://www.opengis.net/def/crs/OGC/1.3/CRS84>
            LineString((-83.4 34.0, -83.3 34.3))
        ]]>
    </geo:asWKT>
</sf:LineString>
```

4.4   okstraOWL Instance Data

In compliance with the conceptual foundations of Linked Data, okstraOWL instance data must fulfill the requirements of distributed networked environments. In contrast to conventional file-based approaches (as implemented by STEP Physical Files or XML instance files), the concept of a resource that can be identified and accessed by an URI plays a central role. Sending or downloading RDF files is only one of the many possible transportation forms.

Serialization. The serialization formats available for RDF such as RDF/XML, TURTLE, N-Triples, Notation3 (N3) etc. are content-wise equivalent, but vary in their suitability for different purposes.

– Where better readability is desired, TURTLE (.ttl) or N3 Notation should be used.
– Where fast import and export is required, N-Triples or N-Quads notations are recommended, as neither the XML Domain Object Model must be constructed nor prefixes resolved. The repetition of the URIs results in significantly increased file sizes, however the resulting files can be effectively compressed and easily archived.
– Through its standard XML structure, XML/RDF can be processed by standard XML (non-RDF) tools which are widely available.

For the reasons mentioned, the okstraXML schema has been published in both Turtle and RDF/XML notation.

Listing 1.4. Short example of the okstraOWL schema as RDF/XML

```
<owl:Class rdf:about="http://okstraowl.org/def/2017/okstraowl#Art_VES
    ↪ .03">
    <rdfs:label>Maximale Achslast</rdfs:label>
    <rdfs:subClassOf rdf:resource="http://okstraowl.org/def/2017/
        ↪ okstraowl#Schluesseltablle"/>
    <rdfs:subClassOf rdf:resource="http://okstraowl.org/def/2017/
        ↪ okstraowl#Art_VES"/>
</owl:Class>
```

4.5   Linking Instance Data

The creation of okstraOWL and the conversion of instance data provides the basis for linking OKSTRA data sets with other OWL-based data sets. As mentioned above, the focus of the case study lies on linking OKSTRA and CB-NL/RWS data sets.

As discussed above, the key for enabling the integrated analysis of data originating from different models is to find corresponding data items. Here we have to distinguish between two matching concepts:

1. Matching at schema level, i.e. matching of objects of the same category or type. For example, RWS objects describing roads must be matched with OKSTRA objects describing roads
2. Matching objects that represent the same identical object of the physical world, such as a road segment

Matching at schema level can be achieved through an semi-automated matching based on the similarities of the taxonomy of both data models. A challenge for matching lies in how to handle different granularities of the data models involved, both with respect to the inheritance hierarchy as well as the aggregation relationships. A typical example of the former is the OTL class *Kruisingsconstructie* (engl. crossing construction) with its subclasses *Overbrug* and *Brug* as opposed to the OKSTRA class *Bauwerk* (engl. engineering construction) which does not have any subclasses. A typical example for the latter is the containment structure Weginfrasysteemdeel → Brug → HoofdraagConstructie → Brugdrek as opposed to the rather simple containment structure of Bauwerk → Teilbauwerk in OKSTRA.

In the specific case of geometry-oriented data models, matching on instance level can be realized through spatial identification, i.e. objects that cover the same space are candidates for linking. To this end, spatial analysis functionalities can be applied, including identification of nearest neighbors or tests for spatial containment. In Fig. 3 the results of such linking processes between heterogeneous data sets are depicted showing school buildings near highways using queries on federated data sets that are introduced in the following section [18].

4.6   Integrated Analysis: Sample Queries

Two main use case scenarios have been identified to test the added value and viability of Linked Data approaches for road data captured in the OKSTRA format:

1. **Federated Queries** In this use case, a heavy goods transport is to be planned across borders of federal states. As a requirement, the road network structure should be queried across the individual data sets from the respective federal authorities and should span both network information pertaining to the topology as well as detailed information regarding, for example, the material qualities of the pavement, alignment curvatures etc.

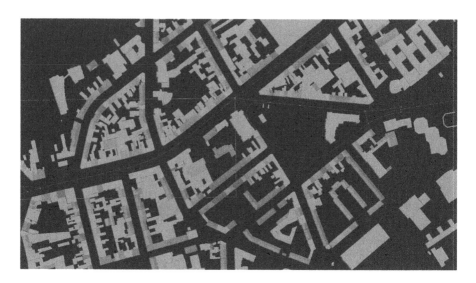

Fig. 3. Visualization of heterogeneous data sets in federated queries. Here schools (green) that are closer to highways sections (red) than 100 m. [18] (Color figure online)

2. **International Mappings** For use cases where other highway models need to be integrated, the capability of Linked Data approaches should be tested that make it possible to extend data processing scenarios within uniform models as described in use case 1 to heterogeneous models like Dutch road models using the RWS-OTL.

Approaches to mapping different data sets that are 'lifted' to RDF have been implemented in the context of this research in [18]. An example is provided in listing 1.5: Here, instance data sets of the proposed okstraOWL Linked Data format have been transformed for an inner city area of the town Aachen. For the investigated area, both a CityGML LOD 2 model as well as OKSTRA data from the road authority of the federal state of North-Rhine Westphalia are available and have been transformed into RDF. The GeoSPARQL language extension that has been implemented in a number of triple stores with SPARQL endpoint makes it possible to perform spatial analyses on the fly. In the example, all buildings with a building height greater than 20 m (provided as an explicit attribute in the CityGML model) are selected in the target area that are within a 50 m range of one of the highway-sections (German: Abschnitt) within the city limits.

Listing 1.5. A short example query using okstraOWL data in combination with CityGML data in an RDF format to query for tall buildings near highways

```
PREFIX geo: <http://www.opengis.net/ont/geosparql#>
PREFIX geof: <http://www.opengis.net/def/function/geosparql/>
PREFIX gml: <http://www.opengis.net/gml:>
PREFIX owl: <http://www.w3.org/2002/07/owl#>
PREFIX rdf: <http://www.w3.org/1999/02/22-rdf-syntax-ns#>
```

```
PREFIX rdfs: <http://www.w3.org/2000/01/rdf-schema#>
PREFIX xsd: <http://www.w3.org/2001/XMLSchema#>
PREFIX uom: <http://www.opengis.net/def/uom/OGC/1.0/>
PREFIX bldg: <http://www.opengis.net/citygml/building/1.0>
PREFIX okstra: <http://schema.okstra.de/2016/okstra:>
PREFIX co: <http://citygmlinteokstra.tue.nl/>


SELECT DISTINCT ?building ?height
WHERE { ?building rdf:type bldg:building .
        ?building geo:hasGeometry ?ageo .
        ?ageo geo:asWKT ?awkt .
        ?building bldg:measuredHeight ?height .
            ?b geo:hasGeometry ?bgeo .
        ?b rdf:type <http://schema.okstra.de/2016/Abschnitt> .
        ?bgeo geo:asWKT ?bwkt .
        FILTER (geof:distance(?awkt, ?bwkt,uom:metre) < 50)
        FILTER (xsd:double(?height) > 20)
        FILTER (?ageo != ?bgeo) .
}
```

5   Summary, Discussion and Outlook

This paper has presented an approach for integrating diverging road data models using Linked Data concepts and techniques. The necessity of applying linked data approaches has been motivated by the fact that a large set of national data models are in practical use, while new international data models are on the horizon, but not yet widely implemented. These data models are different in their purpose, structure, and extent. Experience over the last decades has shown that it is practically impossible to create a singular data model that covers all relevant data from all domains and all nations. By applying linked data approaches it becomes feasible to analyze the data represented across different data models in an integrated manner.

The approach has been demonstrated using a case study based on the German road data model OKSTRA. The goal of applying linked data approaches is to facilitate cross-national analysis of road and traffic data. A prerequisite for applying Linked Data approaches to OKSTRA is its conversion into an OWL-based data model. The challenges involved and the decisions taken have been discussed extensively in the paper. With the availability of the resulting okstraOWL schema and the corresponding instance data sets it becomes possible to link corresponding data objects and perform cross data-model queries.

The case study has shown promising results, but has also revealed challenges and limitations become apparent. In order to make Linked Data approaches work effectively and generate correct query results semantic alignment is required where semantically equal or similar elements of both data sets are associated with each other. For similar models the matching items can be identified using semi-automated matching methods. If the information coverage and granularity differs strongly between the models, matching must be performed manually.

Acknowledgments. The authors would like to thank J. Amann (TUM) and Y. Zheng (TUE) for their efforts in developing software prototypes implementing the concepts and case studies presented.

The research presented in this paper has been funded by the German Federal Highway Research Institute (BASt) under grant FE 01.0195/2015/AGB.

References

1. Amor, R., Jiang, Y., Chen, X.: BIM in 2007 - are we there yet. In: Proceedings of CIB W78 Conference on Bringing ITC Knowledge to Work, Maribor, Slovenia, pp. 26–29 (2007)
2. Laakso, M., Kiviniemi, A.: The IFC standard - a review of history, development and standardization. ITcon J. Inf. Technol. Constr. **17**, 134–161 (2012)
3. Bizer, C., Heath, T., Berners-Lee, T.: Linked data - the story so far. In: Semantic Services, Interoperability and Web Applications: Emerging Concepts, pp. 205–227 (2009)
4. Bizer, C., Lehmann, J., Kobilarov, G., Auer, S., Becker, C., Cyganiak, R., Hellmann, S.: DBpedia - a crystallization point for the web of data. Web Semant.: Sci. Serv. Agents World Wide Web **7**(3), 154–165 (2009)
5. Open Geospatial Consortium: Geographic information - well-known text representation of coordinate reference systems (2015)
6. Open Geospatial Consortium: GeoSPARQL - a geographic query language for RDF data (2012)
7. ISO10303-11:1994: Industrial automation systems and integration - Product data representation and exchange - Part 11: description methods: the EXPRESS language reference manual (1994)
8. Object Management Group: XML Metadata Interchange (XMI) Specification (2015)
9. Amann, J., Singer, D., Borrmann, A.: Extension of the upcoming IFC alignment standard with cross sections for road design. In: Proceedings of the ICCBEI 2015, Tokyo, Japan (2015)
10. Amann, J., Borrmann, A.: Embedding procedural knowledge into building information models: the IFC Procedural Language and its application for flexible transition curve representation. J. Comput. Civ. Eng. **30**(4), 1–14 (2016)
11. Willems, P., Schaap, H.: COINS 1.1 specs (Release 15/12/2014) - CoinsWiki
12. Krima, S., Barbau, R., Fiorentini, X., Sudarsan, R., Sriram, R.D.: Ontostep: OWL-DL ontology for STEP. National Institute of Standards and Technology, NISTIR 7561 (2009)
13. Beetz, J., van Leeuwen, J., de Vries, B.: IfcOWL: a case of transforming EXPRESS schemas into ontologies. AI EDAM **23**, 89–101 (2009)
14. Pauwels, P., Terkaj, W.: EXPRESS to OWL for construction industry: towards a recommendable and usable ifcOWL ontology. Autom. Constr. **63**, 100–133 (2016)
15. Hettwer, J., Portele, C.: T0006 Ableitung von OKSTRA®-XML aus der EXPRESS-Modellierung (2011)
16. Drummond, N., Rector, A.L., Stevens, R., Horridge, Moulton, G., Wang, H.G., Seidenberg, J.: Putting OWL in order: patterns for sequences in OWL. In: Proceedings of 2nd OWL Experiences and Directions Workshop, Athens (2006)

17. Pauwels, P., Terkaj, W., Krijnen, T., Beetz, J.: Coping with lists in the ifcOWL ontology. In: 22nd EG-ICE International Workshop, pp. 113–122 (2015)
18. Zheng, Y.: Improving the interoperability between city and infrastructure information. Integrating CityGML and OKSTRA data based on semantic web and linked data technology. Master's thesis, Eindhoven University of Technology (2017)

Engineering Informatics to Support Civil Systems Engineering Practice

Timo Hartmann[(✉)]

Civil Systems Engineering, TU Berlin, Berlin, Germany
`timo.hartmann@tu-berlin.de`

Abstract. Systems engineering is the interdisciplinary engineering field that focuses on the design of complex physical systems to optimize the system's performance over its life-cycle. To support such optimization efforts a number of computational modeling methods are required: ontological modeling, stochastic modeling, and process simulation modeling. Despite this need, the field of systems engineering has mainly focused on the development and discussion of managerial methods. This paper tries to provide a first starting point for a discussion about a framework to understand how the above mentioned computational methods can support system engineers. The paper introduces a first set of important methods and tries to integrate them in an overall framework for analysing engineered systems from different points of view. For each of the methods we also provide a simple illustrative example from our ongoing systems engineering teaching efforts at the TU Berlin.

1 Introduction

The basic idea behind systems engineering is that a high performing product can only be designed if each of the product's components and physical subsystems work in an integrated way together. An important aspect to allow engineers to understand the level of integration of a system is the modeling and simulation of a system to understand how well different design options of the system perform with respect to a set of previously defined requirements. These aspects of modeling and simulation have not yet been widely discussed in the scientific discourse. The discourse in the field of systems engineering is still mainly focused on the aspects of requirements engineering, as well as, the abstract modeling of system components and interfaces.

To start a discussion about the required computational methods to support systems engineering efforts, this position paper sets out to provide an overview of three important areas of advanced computing: Product modeling, process modeling and data analytics. We argue that a focus on these three areas will allow the field to move towards the simulation based integrated practice that is at the core of systems engineering philosophy. Among these areas, product modeling forms the basis for the other two as it allows to understand the different components of a complex engineered system together with its characteristics and interfaces.

© Springer International Publishing AG, part of Springer Nature 2018
I. F. C. Smith and B. Domer (Eds.): EG-ICE 2018, LNCS 10864, pp. 262–275, 2018.
https://doi.org/10.1007/978-3-319-91638-5_14

Based on well defined product models different physical and social processes that influence some or all of a system's components, such as structural dynamics, thermal behavior, or traffic loads can be simulated. The product models allow for the integration of different process models and simulations that allows for a holistic understanding of the behavior of the overall system upon the influence of the different physical and social processes. At the same time, advanced data analytics allows us to understand the current and historical behavior of different system components and their interrelation to each other. Data analytics allows an alternative to the process modeling and simulation area for predicting a system's behavior in instances where historical data is available about the behavior of a system or of some of its components.

The paper will briefly introduce these three areas and their computational underpinnings. To this end, the paper will show how system engineers can apply these computational methods to gain a better understanding about a system to support engineering work. The computational methods will be illustrated using simple class room examples that we use in our teaching modules at the civil systems engineering department at the TU Berlin. I close the paper by the introduction of a theoretical framework that combines the three areas and that can be used to organize system engineering efforts.

2   Systems Thinking in Engineering

Every product engineers design and commission, be it a bridge, road, or building, is comprised of sub-components that stand in relation to each other. Through this relation, the different elements form a whole reacting to certain environmental influences, supporting civil life, from crossing rivers, to driving safely, from providing shelter to the outside world. In this sense, we can conceptualize each civil product as a system of elements that stand in relation to each other and thus form a whole that is more than the individual elements in isolation.

In traditional systems thinking (Luhmann 1984; Ropohl 2012), there are at least three important concepts of systems that can foster understanding about the basic composition of civil engineered products. First, systems need to be understood as functional in relation to their environment. For the concept system to make sense a clear distinction between the system and its environment needs to be present. A system can then be defined as a collection of elements that receive information or physical stimulus from their environment, internally process these information and stimula and provide some type of output or reaction. This view on systems is often labeled as functional. The functional concept of systems allows us to understand questions such as "What is this thing" or "What does this thing do", while it specifically does not look at the inner composition of the system (Ropohl 2009).

While the functional concept treats the internal composition of the system as a black box, the structural concept looks into the system. A system also needs to be understood as a set of individual elements that stand in relation to each other. Each of the elements can be connected to each of the other elements in different ways. How elements are connected to each other defines the inner structure of the system. Therefore, this second concept is often called the structural concept of systems.

Finally, each of the elements of the system can itself be considered as a system that stands in relation to an environment. At the same time, the environment of each system can also be conceptualized as a system itself. Any reflection about a system can hence comprise different levels of super- and sub-systems, something that is often referred to as systems of systems thinking (Luzeaux et al. 2013).

While the traditional field of systems engineering as a framework to guide the engineering process of complex technical systems has evolved independent of systems thinking, the three above concepts of systems can be mapped well to the different main tasks prescribed by the systems engineering methodology. Systems engineering has recently evolved as the leading management practice across all the engineering disciplines and prescribes a set of iterative processes to be applied for designing, developing, operating, and maintaining complex engineered products throughout their life-cycle (Kapurch 2010). Systems engineering focuses on optimizing an engineered product as a whole, balancing each of the required components of the entire product to achieve some given product requirements.

Models, as abstract representations of reality, of the engineering product can be seen at the core of the systems engineering approach. As modern engineered products are highly complex, abstract models are required to understand the behavior of the products and allow for optimizing the product's design. Through models complex engineered products are simplified and conceptualized as systems, consisting of interacting elements, that together have to react to environmental conditions. The models are then used to define different alternatives for connecting components and then testing these alternatives towards the requirements during the design process. This allows engineers to theoretically understand the behavior of their product before developing and operating the product in the physical world.

The three concepts of systems thinking introduced above are at the core of understanding how to abstract good models to support the three main processes of systems engineering: Requirements management, interface management, and iterative and hierarchical component engineering. For one, each model needs to allow for understanding whether a engineered product can fulfill specific requirements for its functionality. To allow engineers to manage the requirements well, functional system models are required that can be used to evaluate the behavior of a system according to different changing environmental conditions.

At the same time, system engineering is concerned with defining the functional structure of the engineered products in terms of the products' components and their relations. Models need to support engineers to understand which components are required, how the different components need to be related, and how the related components together can react to different environmental conditions. Additionally, from a life-cycle perspective, engineers need to already understand in early design phases how components can be exchanged, maintained, and recycled at different life-cycle stages of an engineered product. To support these tasks structural system models of the engineering product are required.

Finally, the systems engineering approach prescribes a highly iterative process during which each of the components of a system are split up in their smaller components. The NASA systems engineering handbook (Kapurch 2010) for example suggests that every component of a system should be divided in sub-components until the sub-component can be acquired on the market or ordered at a third party supplier. These components at the lowest level of the product hierarchy then should be assembled to sub-components, the sub-components are then again assembled to higher level components till a final product that fulfills the requirements is engineered. To support this product engineering approach hierarchical system models are required.

Without a doubt, the computer has become an indispensable tool to support all of the above modeling tasks during systems engineering. Despite the ubiquitous presence of computers in everyday engineering, there is little discussion about computational support within the systems engineering community. The next section, therefore summarizes three important computational methods for supporting the above described systems engineering process focusing on the three areas of ontological modeling, stochastic data analytics, and process modeling and simulation.

3 Fundamental Informatics to Support Civil Systems Engineering

3.1 Ontologies and Product Modeling

The computational discipline of ontology engineering is concerned with the formal naming and the definition of entities, their properties, and the relation between entities within a specific domain of discourse (Noy et al. 2001). In that sense the engineering of an adequate ontology describing a civil engineered product is at the core of any systems engineering effort. Without formally defining and naming the different elements and environmental influences of a system together with the different possibilities to relate the elements with each other and with the environment no computational possibilities to support the engineering effort would be possible. Figure 1 shows an illustrative example of an ontology that models the different elements of a bridge.

While an ontology is a conceptual formalization of the logic behind the elements of a system and their relations (Krötzsch et al. 2012), engineering is also always concerned with the physical embodiment of the system in the real world. How an engineered product is geometrically configured is an important step towards the realization of the physical product. The product configuration is also important during the simulated evaluation of the different alternatives for the final product. Based on an ontology describing an engineered product conceptually, geometrical parameters help to link the conceptual description to the geometrical description of the product. Parameters allow engineers to capture design knowledge and intent within flexible models that are automatically

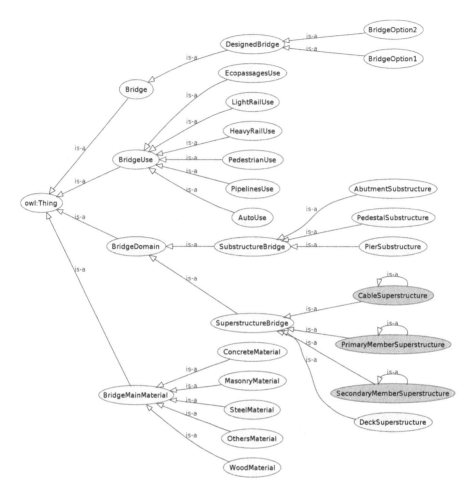

Fig. 1. Example of an ontology that conceptually models the different components of a bridge.

updated when the defined parameters change (Geyer 2008). Parameters also allow to define product family and parts that describe sub-elements of the engineered system (Pahl and Beitz 2013). Finally, parameters can be steered by computational algorithms to quickly generate a large number of possible physical configurations of a system for the purpose of evaluating the designs (Flager et al. 2009).

Figure 2 shows an example of a parametric model that can generate different geometrical configurations of a bridge based on two input parameters - bridge length and transversal span. This parametric model can be used to generate a large number of different bridge alternatives varying in length and transversal spans. This generation can be computationally steered.

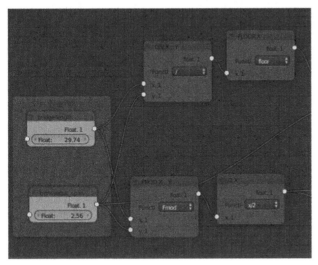

Fig. 2. Parametric model to generate the geometry of a bridge based on two input parameters. Upper part: The complete parametric model. Lower part: Detail of the model showing the two input parameters - bridge-length and transversal span

3.2   Data Analytics

Functional system models can only be established if the underlying relationship between the elements of a system are understood well. In cases such an understanding does not exist, the functional behavior of a system can still be represented with stochastic models (Matloff 2009).

Given a set of random observations about the stochastic behavior of a system or some environmental process that influences the system, statistical models can help to understand the random functional behavior of the system. Such an understanding, in turn, allows engineers to estimate the different possible conditions of the system behavior and how likely these conditions are. In particular, if an engineering effort is concerned with the safety of a system, a statistical model can help engineers to understand the magnitude of possible extreme conditions a system can be in to design systems that can withstand such conditions. Computationally engineers can for example use maximum likelihood methods to estimate the parameters for a given statistical model. To use maximum likelihood estimators, an engineer first assumes a possible joint density function for all observations. A more advanced method to estimate a probability density function for a given set of observations is the kernel density estimate. Kernel density estimation is a non-parametric method so that engineers do not need to make an a-priori assumption about an initial joint density function.

Next to the estimation of statistical models to estimate the stochastic behavior of a system or of an environmental process influencing the system, statistical testing methods can be applied to understand interaction effects between different elements of a system and different environmental influences of the system. A wide choice of statistical tests exists, but the two most commonly used tests are correlation tests and t-tests. Correlation tests allows to understand the connection of two elements based on a set of random observations of the behavior of the elements. The t-test on the other hand allows to compare two different groups of elements and can help engineers to understand whether two groups of systems or one system under two different environmental conditions behave significantly different.

To illustrate the above introduced basic statistical methods we use a data set collected for one of our earlier research studies (Ziari et al. 2016) with the aim to predict the deterioration behavior of roads according to different conditions based on a large data set of US highways collected by the Federal Highway Administration of the United States of America. The example is based on a very simple system model of the road, describing the road's physical composition as the thickness of the road's pavement layer and the thickness of its surface layer. As main performance measure for the quality of the road the roughness of the road's surface is used measured using the international roughness index. The road system is then influenced by a number of environmental processes related to the weather (annual average precipitation, annual average temperature, and annual average freeze index) and to traffic (annual average daily traffic, annual average daily truck traffic, single equivalent axle load). Observations for each of these system and environmental elements are collected from the freely available database of the Federal Highway Administration and the data set is described in detail in (Ziari et al. 2016).

As a start analyzing the data set, statistical models about the overall deterioration behavior of the road can be established using for example a maximum likelihood estimator. To understand the shape of the overall distribution the change in the roughness index of the roads after different years can be ploted as a histogram. Then suitable joint probability density functions can be choses. For example, in this case, a gamma distribution seems to be a good choice as it will allow us to estimate parameters that seem to provide good estimates for the deterioration of the road across the different time spans. Now a computational maximum likelihood estimator can be used to define the parameters for each time span and provide us with joint probability density functions that can be used to understand the deterioration behavior of the road better. Figure 3 provides a visual summary of the above described example.

Beyond standard mathematical tests, advanced machine learning methods allow for developing detailed prediction models of the behavior of a functional system based on a set of observations about the behavior of a system's elements

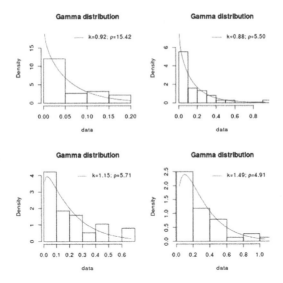

Fig. 3. Example of fitting a probability density function using the maximum likelihood estimator. Here we fit a gamma function to a data set that describes the deterioration of different road sections in the USA after one, two, three, and four years. The fitted function can then be used to sample values for stochastic simulations of road deteriorations

and its environment. Here the classical linear or non-linear regression methods require that an engineer defines a mathematical model of a system's structural behavior first. The classical regression methods will then estimate the parameters of the model based on a data set of previous observations. Advanced regression based methods, including support vector machines or artificial neural networks completely treat a functional system as a black box providing a mathematical model of the behavior of the system without any prior knowledge about the behavior of the system. A downside of these methods is, however, that they do not provide any new insights about the structural behavior of the system (Lantz 2013).

Bayesian and tree based machine learning methods are less accurate in their predictions of the functional behavior of a system. As an advantage, they provide insights into a system's structural behavior which often provides important insights for engineers (Lantz 2013). Finally, cluster based methods can provide categories for different behavioral states of a system grouped by environmental influences (Lantz 2013).

3.3   Process Modeling, Simulation, and Optimization

The above described statistical methods mainly help to understand the functional and, to a certain extent, the structural behavior of a system based on previously available observations of the system's behavior. In practice, often such observations are not available and therefore engineers have to rely on theoretical models that describe the structural behavior of a system. If implemented mathematically on a computer these models can be used to simulate the behavior of a system.

Traditionally, the core to many of these simulation methods are partial differential equations that model the change of some aspect of a system's behavior over time. Differential equations model the transition of a system's state assuming some underlying mathematical model involving the components of the system. Only simple linear partial differential equations can be solved analytical, so that computational solvers for partial differential equations have quickly become the norm within engineering practice (Farlow 1993).

Partial differential equations allow for modeling systems whose states are changing equally with each time step. Using functional programming techniques, however, also allow for modeling systems that change non-linearly. Such models are often referred to as discrete event methods and operate using an event queue that stores events that can be executed at arbitrary time steps. In particular, such discrete event simulation methods are valuable to model randomly occurring environmental events to provide a much deeper insight into a system's behavior than models that are based on partial differential equations only (Wainer and Mosterman 2016).

Simulation models based on partial differential equations can then be used to automate the analysis of the system models using the parametric modeling methods described earlier. Additionally, of course, variables describing environmental influences on the system can be varied in a similar manner. This allows for systematically changing the different initial input variables that either describe the behavior of the elements or the environment of the system. The range of all possible input variables is then often referred to as the parameter space. Combinatoric computational methods can be used to systematically analyse a large number of different alternatives within this parameter space. Such combinatoric analyses of the environmental factors modeled allow systems engineers to understand the behavior of a system under a large range of different outside factors. At the same time, different configurations of the parameters describing the system itself can be evaluated helping system engineers to develop optimal design configurations (Saltelli et al. 2000).

Each simulation result from the combination of different parameters can be considered as an observation in itself. Therefore, sets of simulation results can be analysed with the above described statistical methods. Such analysis allows for understanding relations between different parameters in the simulation models. This allows engineers to understand the importance of different parameters on the simulation outcome, a practice often referred to as sensitivity analysis (Saltelli et al. 2000). Parameters with little influence on the final outcome can be removed from the initial modeling equations and parameters with linear relations with each other can be represented as a single input factor (Forrester et al. 2008). Finally, machine learning methods can be used to train statistical prediction models. These prediction models can then be used instead of the partial differential based models which often allows to provide results in split seconds without running the often computationally expensive models (Forrester et al. 2008).

Often the parameter spaces are too large or the process models are too computationally expensive for simulating enough different parameter configurations so that system engineers can sufficiently understand how a system reacts to different environmental conditions and how a system can be ideally configured to cope with the different possible reactions. In these cases, computational sampling methods exist that can be applied to systematically search a vast design space using a well chosen amount of simulation runs (Saltelli et al. 2000). These sampling methods can be divided into purposeful samples that explore well chosen strata or in random samples that allow for an exploration according to the likelihood for the status of different environmental or system parameters. The stratified sampling methods help systems engineers to understand different well chosen groups of parameter configurations within different areas of the overall parameter space. This for example allows to include rare events that are of particular importance during safety engineering tasks. Random sampling methods, in turn, rather allow to understand system models with respect to their average and common behavior. To use statistical sampling methods a probabilistic distribution for environmental and system parameters needs to be assumed. This distribution can either be extracted from past observations using the above describe statistical methods or, alternatively, be assumed by specialists. Choosing sound distributions, in turn, allows to understand the general relation between elements of a system under general environmental conditions. Stratified sampling and statistical sampling can of course be combined in many different ways.

Finally, from a hierarchical system view, each of the sub-components of a system can itself be seen again as a functional system. In case enough observations about the behavior of such a functional system are available, each of the components can, in turn, be modeled using statistical computations techniques, in particular, using probability density modeling techniques, such as the maximum likelihood methods or kernel density estimates. Simulation models can than sample from the resulting probability density functions and the samples can serve as input for the theoretical structural system models. Environmental conditions can be modeled in the same manner. As samples from these probability density functions can provide arbitrary results, it is important to repeat the simulations multiple times sampling as many possibilities from the density functions as possible using so called Monte Carlo methods. The different simulation results, in turn, result in probabilistic distribution.

As an example, the above case of predicting road deterioration can be used again to illustrate the working of process model simulations in relation to sensitivity analysis and Monte Carlo methods. The example is based on a simple dynamic simulation model of two bridges that link two cities with each other. The model assumes that drivers tend to choose the bridge that is least deteriorated. At the same time, the more drivers travel over a bridge, the quicker the bridge deteriorates. We illustratively modeled these two processes for one of our

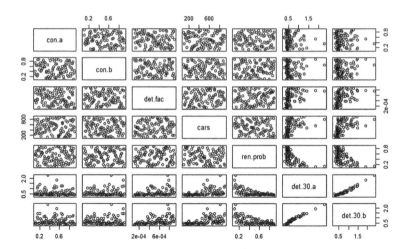

Fig. 4. Scatterplot resulting from a sensitivity analysis of a highly non-linear and stochastic model of road deterioration. The input variables of the initial road condition of two roads (con.a; con.b), the deterioration of the roads upon crossing of one car (det.fac), the number of crossing cars per year (cars), and the probability that a road is renovated in a year (ren.prob) are samples using the latin hypercube method. The output values road deterioration in 2030 of road a and road b (det.30.a, det.30.b) is simulated using a Monte Carlo approach. The scatterplot clearly shows that the initial road condition has little influence on the deterioration of the roads in 2013, while the deterioration factor and the number of cars have a positive influence, and the renovation probability a negative influence on the deterioration

teaching modules using two simple partial differential equations. Furthermore, the simple simulation model used stochastic distributed values the deterioration factor similar to the earlier introduced road example. To make the model highly non-linear we also assumed a certain probability that the bridge is renovated each year significantly reducing the existing road deterioration. We modeled this influence as a discrete event within the overall simulation model that can occur with a certain probability. A sensitivity analysis for this highly stochastic and non-linear model can for example sample the different parameter settings for each of the input values using a combined stratified and random sampling method (in this case the latin hypercube method) and based on the sampled parameter values can conduct a Monte Carlo simulation. A resulting scatter plot from this exercise is presented in Fig. 4. This scatterplot allows already to identify certain trends in the influence of the different input parameters on the bridge deterioration after a number of years.

4   Discussion

Figure 5 summarizes the presented computational methods within the concepts of the three different analytical views of systems. The behavior of functional

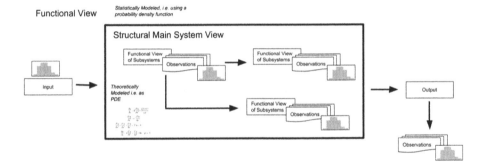

Fig. 5. Overall system based concepts of the paper

systems can be analyzed using statistical computational methods if there are a reasonable number of observations available about the input and behavior of a system. Systems can also be modeled using a functional view, by using partial differential equations and other computational simulation methods, such as discrete event simulations. These methods allow for the theoretical modeling of a system's behavior by describing the system's components and the relations between these components. The design of such functional simulation models requires an understanding of the system's components that can be gained through ontological modeling. Functional simulation models allow the evaluation of a large number of alternatives using parametric modeling methods that allow to systematically explore the combinatoric design space and the various environmental conditions a system might be subjected to. Finally, a hierarchical view of the system allows to combine statistical and theoretical modeling methods by the possibility to represent the behavior of selected components of a system through a stochastic functional model. In these cases, a system analysis based on simulation studies need to be subjected to Monte Carlo methods.

Table 1 summarizes the here presented computational methods that I consider as the basic methods within the overall toolkit of systems engineers. It is important to realize that these methods are just a suggestion of a set of basic methods and that I do not claim completeness. Other methods might be as relevant as the ones that are here presented. Candidates for further exploration would be for example optimization methods that allow to find optimal solutions within parametric search spaces. As quite some of the presented methods are computational very expensive methods to computationally parallelizise algorithms might also be important. Finally, the paper does not discuss any computational visualization methods. Nevertheless, I hope that this paper can provide a first starting point for future discussions about which of the methods are relevant and which are not.

The above summary of methods can provide academics with a good overview that can be used to design technically and computationally oriented systems engineering courses. The Bachelor and Master modules that we developed at the Technical University of Berlin can provide an example of how to integrate

Table 1. Overview of the introduced methods

Computational area	Computational method
Product system modeling	Ontology modeling
	Parametric modeling
Statistical system modeling	Maximum likelihood methods
	Kernel density estimates
	Correlation analysis
	t-Test
Theoretical system modeling	Partial differential equation solvers
	Discrete event simulation
	Sensitivity analysis
	Surrogate modeling
	Sampling methods
	Monte Carlo methods

the methods within a civil engineering curriculum. The summary can also help practitioners to understand how to support their practical system engineering efforts better using computational methods. In the end, if nothing more, we hope that the summary of computational methods together with my attempt to integrate the discussion into a system philosophical framework can help readers to better grasp the relevance of the introduced computational methods to support engineering tasks.

References

Farlow, S.J.: Partial differential equations for scientists and engineers. Courier Corporation, North Chelmsford (1993)

Flager, F., Welle, B., Bansal, P., Soremekun, G., Haymaker, J.: Multidisciplinary process integration and design optimization of a classroom building. J. Inf. Technol. Constr. (ITcon) **14**(38), 595–612 (2009)

Forrester, A., Keane, A., et al.: Engineering Design Via Surrogate Modelling: A Practical Guide. Wiley, Hoboken (2008)

Geyer, P.: Multidisciplinary grammars supporting design optimization of buildings. Res. Eng. Design **18**(4), 197–216 (2008)

Kapurch, S.J.: NASA Systems Engineering Handbook. Diane Publishing, Collingdale (2010)

Krötzsch, M., Simancik, F., Horrocks, I.: A description logic primer. arXiv preprint arXiv:1201.4089 (2012)

Lantz, B.: Machine Learning with R. Packt Publishing Ltd., Birmingham (2013)

Luhmann, N.: Soziale Systeme, vol. 478. Suhrkamp, Frankfurt am Main (1984)

Luzeaux, D., et al.: Systems of Systems. Wiley, Hoboken (2013)

Matloff, N.: From Algorithms to Z-scores: Probabilistic and Statistical Modeling in Computer Science. Creative Commons License (2009)

Noy, N.F., McGuinness, D.L., et al.: Ontology development 101: A guide to creating your first ontology (2001)

Pahl, G., Beitz, W.: Engineering Design: A Systematic Approach. Springer Science & Business Media, London (2013)

Ropohl, G.: Allgemeine Technologie: eine Systemtheorie der Technik. KIT Scientific Publishing, Karlsruhe (2009)

Ropohl, G.: Allgemeine Systemtheorie: Einführung in transdisziplinäres Denken. edition sigma, Berlin (2012)

Saltelli, A., Chan, K., Scott, E.M., et al.: Sensitivity Analysis, vol. 1. Wiley, New York (2000)

Wainer, G.A., Mosterman, P.J.: Discrete-Event Modeling and Simulation: Theory and Applications. CRC Press, Boca Raton (2016)

Ziari, H., Sobhani, J., Ayoubinejad, J., Hartmann, T.: Prediction of IRI in short and long terms for flexible pavements: ANN and GMDH methods. Int. J. Pavement Eng. **17**(9), 776–788 (2016)

Automated Approaches Towards BIM-Based Intelligent Decision Support in Design, Construction, and Facility Operations

Fernanda Leite[(✉)]

Department of Civil, Architectural and Environmental Engineering,
The University of Texas at Austin, 301 E Dean Keeton St. Stop C1752,
78712-1094, Austin, TX, USA
Fernanda.Leite@utexas.edu

Abstract. The architecture, engineering, construction and facility management (AECFM) industry has been experiencing many changes since inexpensive networked, mobile computing devices have become ubiquitous. With the rising amount of information and data generated in the life cycle of capital projects, information modeling and data interoperability have become a critical element in design, engineering, construction, and maintenance of capital facilities. Recent advances in Visualization, Information Modeling, and Simulation (VIMS) have the potential to address a number of these pressing challenges. The objective of this concept paper is to discuss challenges and ongoing research in three areas of study in VIMS: capturing experiential knowledge in building information modeling (BIM)-based design coordination; 4-dimensional modeling for site-specific safety planning; and automating the BIM upkeep process in the facility operations phase leveraging deep learning and computer vision.

Keywords: Building information modeling · BIM-based design coordination
4D safety modeling · Automated BIM upkeep

1   Introduction

The cost of computing has been in steady decline as the cost of virtually every other thing goes up. Natural resources are depleting and human populations are increasing apace. Sustainable development and construction has become an overarching theme in the Architecture, Engineering, Construction, and Facility Management (AECFM) industry. For many, it is not difficult to realize that computing is and will be a key enabler for achieving sustainability without sacrificing our living standard. Indeed, sensors and computers are playing increasingly important roles in today's capital project development. With the wide adoption of mobile computing in the AECFM industry, we have now entered into an era where information and data are ubiquitously generated and distributed, and, consequently, project organizations have been facing information and data that are generated at high velocity, large volume, and in a great variety of formats. With the rising amount of information and data generated in the life cycle of capital projects, information modeling has become a critical element in designing, engineering,

© Springer International Publishing AG, part of Springer Nature 2018
I. F. C. Smith and B. Domer (Eds.): EG-ICE 2018, LNCS 10864, pp. 276–286, 2018.
https://doi.org/10.1007/978-3-319-91638-5_15

constructing, and maintaining capital facilities (Leite et al. 2016). Recent advances in Visualization, Information Modeling and Simulation (VIMS) have the potential to address a number of these pressing challenges. The objective of this concept paper is to discuss challenges and ongoing research in three areas of study in VIMS: capturing experiential knowledge in building information modeling (BIM)-based design coordination; 4-dimensional modeling for site-specific safety planning; and automating the BIM upkeep process in the facility operations phase leveraging deep learning and computer vision.

2   Impacting Novice BIM-Based Design Coordination Performance Through Knowledge Embedded Systems

It is often said that experience is the best teacher, but what happens if the teacher is absent? How will the rising generation of construction professionals apply the insight of veteran practitioners, in an industry where recent economic turmoil has driven them to retire in droves? This is the motivation of my design coordination research at the University of Texas at Austin, in which we have been investigating how to capture tacit experiential knowledge in design coordination to train novice designers.

Decisions made and approaches taken in mechanical, electrical, and plumbing (MEP) design coordination largely depend on knowledge and expertise of professionals from multiple disciplines. The MEP design coordinator—who usually represents the general contractor or the main mechanical contractor—coordinates the effort of collecting and identifying clashes and collisions between systems. He or she asks clarifying questions during coordination meetings and often proposes solutions. During the process, the coordinator's tacit and experiential knowledge frequently is called upon and transferred to less experienced members of the team.

In recent years, the design coordinator usually was an experienced engineer who knew how to differentiate between critical and non-critical clashes, as well as how to prioritize clashes by importance and provide suggestions to the team—or even make decisions, based upon his or her expertise and experience. But increasingly, due to the recession's depletion of the ranks of veteran engineers from the United States industry, as well as the rising use of building information modeling (BIM), general contractors have started to rely more and more on novice engineers to run conflict resolution sessions. Although young engineers may be proficient in operating the coordination software systems, many have limited practical experience in MEP design and coordination.

While the use of BIM in MEP design coordination has greatly increased the amount and quality of available data, significant experiential knowledge still is needed for efficient, high-quality decision making; yet the process for bringing that knowledge to the table is faltering. We have conducted a study comparing the behaviors of experienced MEP coordinators with novices on model-based design coordination. Results show that experienced coordinators can locate relevant information and identify external information sources more efficiently, as compared to the novice coordinators. Experienced coordinators also are able to perform more in-depth analysis within the model, based on their experiences (Wang and Leite 2014a , Wang and Leite 2014b).

My team has been investigating whether novices' performance on coordination tasks will improve when experiential knowledge that has been extracted from past projects is made available to them through a software-enabled decision support system. Preliminary results show that such decision support significantly reduces the time spent on performing design coordination tasks and brings increased accuracy to clash resolutions.

With this vision of capturing experiential knowledge to train novice designers in mind, we have developed an approach to capture, represent and formalize experiential knowledge in design coordination to inform better design decisions, improve collaboration efficiency and train novice designers/engineers (Wang and Leite 2016). The approach systematically captures expert decisions during design coordination in an object-oriented, computer-interpretable manner and leverage database and machine learning techniques for knowledge reuse.

We now have a prototype system called TagPlus (illustrated in Fig. 1) that works as a plug-in for a widely used design coordination software system, Autodesk Navisworks. It captures design coordination decisions and stores each instance directly to related 3D objects. We then store this information in a database of MEP clashes and related expert solution descriptions, and use the information to train algorithms to learn from the knowledge (as illustrated in Fig. 2) and, ultimately, provide novice designers with a problem-based learning platform to enhance their performance in design coordination tasks. TagPlus is described in detail in Wang and Leite (2015).

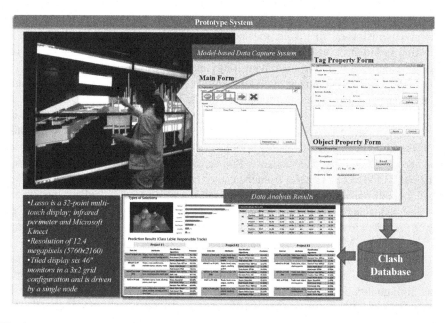

Fig. 1. TagPlus Prototype system to capture expert experiential knowledge in BIM-based MEP design coordination.

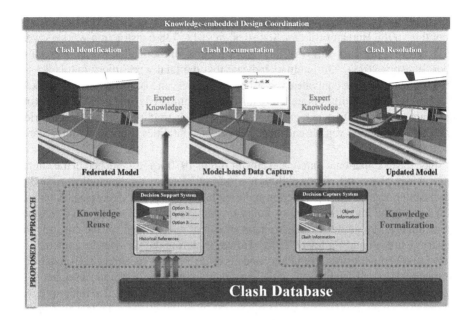

Fig. 2. Knowledge formalization and reuse in design coordination.

Tests with novices showed great potential for the knowledge-embedded approach. However, additional data is needed for more in-depth analysis. Based on the feedback from participants and direct observations in our experimental studies with novices, the information provided by the decision support system helped them understand the clashes more efficiently and effectively. Example responses: "It made it easier to understand the clashes", "I feel design intent and constraints are apt parameters in bringing in spatial and temporal context", "the suggestions were clear and usually correct and helped in making a decision" and "it saves time in providing all the information about the clash clearly". The decision support system also helped participants form a more organized structure to document clashes and solutions and facilitated wider consideration by including multiple factors (such as design intent and constraints) during the decision making process.

In summary, our current design coordination research results show the average time spent per clash was significantly reduced when decision support is available, however the accuracy of the predicted results still needs to be improved. These results illustrate how decision support would impact novices' performance and also shed light on the focus for future improvements on knowledge-embedded decision support systems.

3 4-Dimensional Modeling for Site-Specific Construction Safety Planning

Construction remains the second most hazardous industry especially due to the dangerous combination of pedestrian workers and heavy construction vehicles and machinery, such as dump trucks, dozers, and rollers (Bureau of Labor Statistics 2011). According to the Bureau of Labor Statistics, in 2011, 738 construction workers were killed, which represents 15.7% of fatal work injuries in the United States (Bureau of Labor Statistics 2011). 738 fatalities indicate that the fatal work injury rate is 9.1 for every 100,000 full-time equivalent construction workers, and U.S. construction workers are approximately 2.6 times more likely to be killed compared to the average fatal work injury rate for all industries, which is 3.5. Of the 738 construction industry fatal injuries, 39.3% are construction vehicle and machinery-related fatalities (Bureau of Labor Statistics 2011).

Since the Occupational Safety and Health Act of 1970 was established in the United States, which places the responsibility of construction safety on the employer, fatality and disabling rate in the construction industry has dramatically decreased. After this federal law came into effect, various injury prevention strategies have been developed and resulted in a significant improvement of safety management in the construction industry (Esmaeili and Hallowell 2012). However, during the last decade, construction safety improvement in terms of fatality and disabling rate has decelerated (Esmaeili and Hallowell 2012) and fatality rate in the construction industry is still much higher than other industries (Bureau of Labor Statistics 2011). Therefore, innovative injury prevention practices such as integration of project schedules and information technology can be leveraged to significantly improve current construction safety management practices.

To address the safety issues related to the dynamic nature of the construction industry, Yi and Langford (2006) emphasize the importance of integration between safety management and scheduling. Hazardous situations vary according to different project activities and a construction project schedule should be considered for safety planning, especially for hazard identification (Yi and Langford 2006). However, current safety planning approaches do not consider a project schedule to address when and where hazards are expected and safety controls are required. In addition, current safety plans do not address possible hazards which might be caused by multiple activities and specific temporal and spatial information. In order to create more effective site-specific safety plans, it is important to integrate safety planning and project schedules.

Another challenge of site-specific safety planning is lack of safety sources utilized. While information technology-based approaches, such as Building Information Modeling (BIM), have been widely used for project planning and progress monitoring, construction safety planning is still highly dependent on traditional sources such as 2D drawings, paper-based regulations, and tacit information. As a result, current safety planning approaches limit the capability to identify and analyze hazards prior to construction and can potentially be improved with the integration of information technology.

I envision that the construction safety planning process can be systematically formalized through a 4-dimensional (4D) environment, which integrates 3D and time, to address site-specific temporal and spatial safety information. Figure 3 illustrates an overview of the research developed by my team (Choe and Leite 2017a; Choe and Leite 2017b).

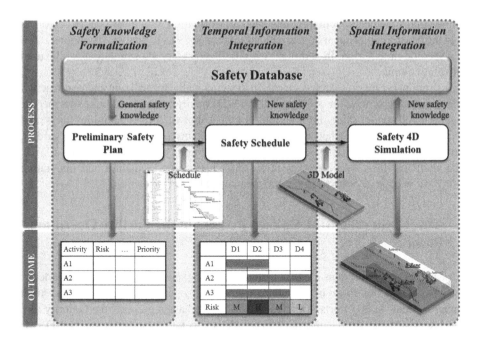

Fig. 3. Overview of 4D-modeling for site-specific safety planning research.

The safety planning approach includes: (1) safety database development, and (2) site-specific temporal and spatial information integration. The safety database is described in detail in Choe and Leite (2017a), where we compare safety risk of different construction trades in terms of common hazard types and sources of injuries, and propose a safety reference for reliable safety risk assessment. The safety risk analysis presented in Choe and Leite (2017a) can be used as a general safety reference by safety managers to understand the dynamic nature of safety risk. It can also aid in preparing safety actions, such as inspections or training, more effectively by focusing on high-risk occupations, hazard types, or sources of injury.

The site-specific temporal and spatial information integration is described in detail in Choe and Leite (2017b), where we present a formalized 4-dimensional (4D) construction safety planning process that addresses site-specific temporal and spatial safety information integration. We integrated safety data, which includes general safety knowledge, site-specific temporal and spatial information, from a project schedule and a 3-dimensional (3D) model.

I envision that safety personnel will be able to devise a preliminary safety plan including prioritizing risky activities and preparing proper responses in early stages of the project without site-specific information. This preliminary safety plan will be integrated with a project schedule to incorporate safety knowledge and site-specific temporal information. The temporal information integration process will allow identifying and prioritizing work period risk with baseline safety data in the preliminary safety plan. The safety schedule will be integrated with a project 3D model (i.e. BIM) in order to extract site-specific spatial information. Safety 4D simulation, which integrates general safety data, site-specific temporal and spatial information, will allow safety personnel to identify safety impacts of concurrent activities as well as to analyze dangerous zones in a specific time period. In addition, this visualized safety 4D simulation can be used for safety training.

In summary, this research focused on systematically formalizing the construction safety planning process in a 4-dimensional (4D) environment to address site-specific temporal and spatial safety information. Findings show that risky activities, days, and zones can be prioritized when a project schedule contains activity information regarding number of workers including occupation types and zoning plan (Choe and Leite 2017b). The challenge lies on automating safety information representation and integrating safety knowledge in order to streamline site-specific safety planning.

4   Automating the BIM Upkeep Process in the Facility Operations Phase

Infrastructure and buildings are designed to have long, useful life spans in the order of decades. Many buildings in the world are still in operation after centuries, amid numerous renovation efforts. This long operational phase represents the majority of a building's lifecycle, yet the information regarded to operations and maintenance (O&M) as well as for renovations is rarely kept up-to-date, even if the facilities themselves are dynamic in nature and as-built conditions frequently change.

Lack of up-to-date as-built information impacts decisions made during operation and maintenance, increasing costs for searching, validating, and/or recreating facility information that was supposed to be already available (Fallon and Palmer 2007). Gallaher et al. (2004) estimated that O&M personnel spend an annual cost of $4.8 billion in the United States capital facilities industry verifying that documentation accurately represents as is conditions, and another $613 million converting that information into a usable format (Gallaher et al. 2004). A database and a data model would be the best practice for preserving such information over a structure's lifecycle, and the rapidly adopted use of Building Information Models (BIMs) potentially could have been the ideal solution. Unfortunately, BIMs are currently mostly used for project management purposes during the construction phase.

The reason behind the lack of widespread adoption of BIMs for O&M is the enormous undertaking of updating project BIMs for every single change that occurs. Manually updating BIMs over a structure's long lifecycle is cumbersome and extremely error prone. Hence, human operators and contractors are often unwilling and negligent in keeping the BIMs up-to-date. Even if the participants were willing, it is difficult to determine whether the updates are correct and/or any information is missing. Hence, computerized automation of the process seems to be essential in order for such information to be useful, timely, and accurate.

My team at the University of Texas at Austin, along with colleagues at Drexel University (James Lo and Ko Nishino), are working on a National Science Foundation project called LivingBIM. This research aims to demonstrate how automatic and continuous updates of BIM in a given structure are possible and how such updates can be of benefit to the long lifecycle of facilities and structures.

To help automate this process, computer vision is leveraged to sense the environment and to provide decision-making inputs for updating the BIM database. Computer vision in an open world encounters an extremely challenging problem: identifying a detected object. It can be argued that in the situation of a built environment, the expected objects are less dynamic in variety, and better yet, the BIM database itself can be used as a resource to provide contextual identification for a detected object. With the complexity of object identification reduced, the iterative process of BIM updating via machine vision over a long period of time can train the machine vision process itself continuously, which can then improve the quality of detection and reduce the possibility of false positives and other errors.

Within the first year, our team has (1) conducted interviews with facility management professionals, (2) designed and presented a new building point cloud segmentation method, and have (3) begun creating and curating a training dataset in order to eventually apply deep learning methods to the problem of semantic segmentation of building system scans (Figs. 4 and 5). Our team conducted a series of hour-long face-to-face interviews with people involved in facility operations and maintenance to identify current information practices. This was done in an effort to define a scope for the project, identify what information a BIM should contain in order to be useful to personnel in the facility management (FM) space, and evaluate the receptivity of FM to new technology. Once the relevant BIM content was identified, we began to explore what content could be provided by computer vision. We decided on deep learning as the avenue for data processing as these emerging semantic segmentation methods have demonstrated a level of unprecedented versatility. Rather than hand engineering an algorithm to identify a single type of object in a few types of scenarios, deep learning holds the promise of identifying many different types of objects in a similarly diverse range of scenarios. Unfortunately, there is no existing dataset whereby deep learning networks can be trained to classify or semantically segment building systems. Our team has been exploring different possibilities for how such a dataset can be created. Synthetic RGB-D (color + depth) images could be generated using 3D computer modeling and photo-realistic rendering. Scans could be collected and then manually annotated. In the process of manually annotating scans, we developed a new 6D DBSCAN based approach to segmenting point clouds as a preprocessing step to manually grouping clusters into semantically meaningful groups (Czerniawski et al. 2018).

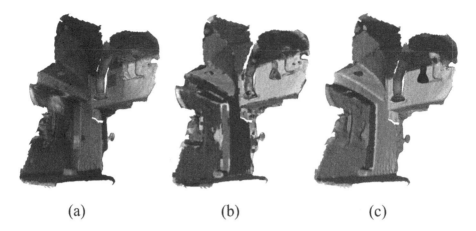

(a)   (b)   (c)

Fig. 4. 3D reconstruction created using a commodity range camera depicting part of a building facility; (a) the original scan with captured color texture; (b) scan pre-segmented using the 6D DBSCAN based segmentation method; and (c) scan semantically segmented (Color figure online)

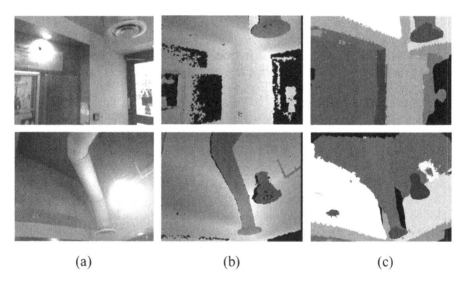

(a)   (b)   (c)

Fig. 5. 2D images collected using a commodity range camera depicting part of a building facility; (a) RGB color channels; (b) depth channel; (c) semantic segmentation of the 2D images (Color figure online)

Once a sufficiently large dataset has been created, we will move on to training neural networks to semantically segment scans, and then ultimately use those segmented scans to perform automated 3D modeling. Our initial annotated dataset for 3D reconstructions of building facilities, which we call 3DFacilities, is presented in detail in Czerniawski and Leite (2018). The dataset currently contains over 11,000 individual RGB-D frames comprising 50 annotated scene reconstructions. It is our hope that this database, leveraging the success of deep learning, will contribute to the Scan-to-BIM research community.

5   Conclusions

The objective of this concept paper was to discuss challenges and ongoing research in three areas of study in VIMS: capturing experiential knowledge in building information modeling (BIM)-based design coordination; 4-dimensional modeling for site-specific safety planning; and automating the BIM upkeep process in the facility operations phase leveraging deep learning and computer vision. Our design coordination research results show the average time spent per clash was significantly reduced when decision support is available, however the accuracy of the predicted results still need to be improved. These results illustrate how decision support would impact novices' performance and also shed light on the focus for future improvements on knowledge-embedded decision support systems. Our research on 4D modeling for site-specific safety planning focuses on systematically formalizing the construction safety planning process in a 4D environment to address site-specific temporal and spatial safety information. The challenge in this research area lies on automating safety information representation and integrating safety knowledge in order to streamline site-specific safety planning. In our work thus far on automating BIM upkeep for facility management (FM), we conducted interviews with FM personnel which helped us identify key information classes that any FM BIM should contain, and we have begun to create the deep learning data processing pipeline required to convert computer vision inputs into a semantically rich BIMs. It is our hope that our 3DFacilities database will contribute to the Scan-to-BIM research community.

With the rising amount of information and data generated in the life cycle of capital projects, information modeling has become a critical element when addressing challenges in the project lifecycle. The sample research projects presented in this paper illustrate how proper information modeling, integration, and visualization can potentially benefit various phases of the project lifecycle, helping the industry as a whole deliver capital projects more effectively and sustain resilient facilities and infrastructure.

Acknowledgments. This research was supported, in part, by the National Science Foundation (NSF) under award number 1562438. Their support is gratefully acknowledged. Any opinions, findings and conclusions, or recommendations expressed in this material are those of the authors and do not necessarily reflect the views of the National Science Foundation. Mention of trade names in this article does not imply endorsement by the University of Texas at Austin or NSF.

References

Bureau of Labor Statistics: Revisions to the 2011 Census of Fatal Occupational Injuries (CFOI) Counts. United States Department of Labor, Washington, DC (2011)

Choe, S., Leite, F.: Assessing safety risk among different construction trades: a quantitative approach. ASCE J. Constr. Eng. Manag. **143**(5), 04016133 (2017a). https://doi.org/10.1061/(asce)co.1943-7862.0001237

Choe, S.; Leite, F.: Construction safety planning: site-specific temporal and spatial information integration. Autom. Constr. **84**, 335–344 (2017b). https://doi.org/10.1016/j.autcon.2017.09.007

Czerniawski, T., Leite, F.: 3DFacilities: annotated 3D reconstructions of building facilities. In: Proceedings of the 25th Annual Workshop of the European Group for Intelligent Computing in Engineering (EG-ICE), École Polytechnique Fédérale de Lausanne (EPFL), Lausanne, Switzerland, 15 p. (2018)

Czerniawski, T., Sankaran, B., Nahangi, M., Haas, C., Leite, F.: 6D DBSCAN-based segmentation of building point clouds for planar object classification. Autom. Constr. **88**, 44–58 (2018). https://doi.org/10.1016/j.autcon.2017.12.029

Esmaeili, B., Hallowell, M.: Attribute-based risk model for measuring safety risk of struck-by accidents. In: Proceedings of Construction Research Congress 2012, West Lafayette, ID, pp. 289–298 (2012)

Fallon, K.K., Palmer, M.E.: General Buildings Information Handover Guide: Principles, Methodology and Case Studies. National Institute of Standards and Technology (2007)

Gallaher, M.P., O'Connor, A.C., Gilday, L.T.: Cost Analysis of Inadequate Interoperability in the U.S. Capital Facilities Industry. National Institute of Standards and Technology (2004)

Leite, F., Cho, Y., Behzadan, A., Lee, S., Choe, S., Fang, Y., Akhavian, R., Hwang, S.: Visualization, information modeling and simulation grand challenges in the construction industry. ASCE J. Comput. Civil Eng. (2016). https://doi.org/10.1061/(asce)cp.1943-5487.0000604

Wang, L., Leite, F.: Formalized knowledge representation for spatial conflict coordination of mechanical, electrical and plumbing (MEP) systems in new building projects. Autom. Constr. **64**, 20–26 (2016). https://doi.org/10.1016/j.autcon.2015.12.020

Wang, L., Leite, F.: Process knowledge capture in BIM-based mechanical, electrical, plumbing design coordination meetings. ASCE J. Comput. Civil Eng. (2015). https://doi.org/10.1061/(asce)cp.1943-5487.0000484

Wang, L., Leite, F.: Impacting novice design coordination performance through problem-based learning. In: Proceedings of the 21th Annual Workshop of the European Group for Intelligent Computing in Engineering (EG-ICE), Cardiff University, Cardiff, United Kingdom (2014a)

Wang, L., Leite, F.: Comparison of experienced and novice BIM coordinators in performing mechanical, electrical and plumbing (MEP) coordination tasks. In: Proceedings of the 2014 Construction Research Congress, Atlanta, GA (2014b)

Yi, K.-J., Langford, D.: Schedule-based risk estimation and safety planning for construction projects. J. Constr. Eng. Manag. **132**(6), 626–635 (2006)

Digital Construction Permit: A Round Trip Between GIS and IFC

Sébastien Chognard[(✉)], Alain Dubois, Yacine Benmansour,
Elie Torri, and Bernd Domer[(✉)]

Hepia, Geneva, Switzerland
{sebastien.chognard,alain.dubois,yacine.benmansour,
elie.intorri,bernd.domer}@hesge.ch

Abstract. Building design and surrounding environment are influencing each other. Environment is usually described by a Geographic Information System (GIS), while buildings are often designed with Building Information Modeling (BIM) software. Despite some differences on technology and standards, GIS and BIM deal with geometrical data and attributes. Possible links between GIS and BIM using the City Geographic Markup Language (CityGML) and the Industry Foundation Classes (IFC) as standard exchange formats have been studied [1–4].

The present work establishes an exchange between IFC and GIS features. As an open format, IFC files can be handled by AEC-related software. It is therefore of interest, if IFC can be used for a roundtrip between GIS and BIM.

A three-step translation protocol has been developed and tested: (1) Data from GIS had to be transformed into an IFC reference environment model. (2) A test building has been designed. Imported environmental elements have been edited as well. (3) The exported IFC file was then imported into GIS data sets in order to update existing data.

The process employed the FME software to convert GIS to IFC and back. Data management tasks have been delegated to a database complying with the IFC format (BIMserver). The accurate import and export of data has been monitored over the entire data exchange process.

This study uses the development of a digital construction permit submission procedure for the canton of Geneva in Switzerland.

Keywords: GIS · BIM · IFC · Convergence of GIS and BIM
Digital building permit · GIS-BIM round trip

1 Introduction

Requesting a construction permit is an important milestone of a project. Administrative procedures vary from country to country and are furthermore often state and city specific. Sometimes, designers are obliged to re-introduce data already present in numerical building models into specific forms. This is a waste of time and might cause data inconsistencies.

After submission to authorities, the length of the procedure cannot be influenced by the requester. It depends on the organization of the administrative workflow, communication and collaboration among the participating departments and if code

© Springer International Publishing AG, part of Springer Nature 2018
I. F. C. Smith and B. Domer (Eds.): EG-ICE 2018, LNCS 10864, pp. 287–306, 2018.
https://doi.org/10.1007/978-3-319-91638-5_16

compliance checking is supported by numerical models instead of being done manually on printed plans. The uncertainty concerning the length of the control procedure makes it difficult to determine a precise date for the start of construction.

Geneva's authorities are aware of this issue and commissioned a web-based approval system for projects of minor importance (marked "APA" in Fig. 1). The system optimizes the workflow and is mainly based on an exchange of electronic documents with encapsulated information [5].

Singapore is one of the pioneers in streamlining the construction permit procedure. The Corenet web-based platform accepts BIM-Files for requesting a building permit [6]. Templates are provided for major BIM software (Revit and Archicad) and building inspectors are controlling native files. A web tool informs the qualified person (e.g. the designer) in detail about the progress of the procedure.

Controlling a project might be quite complex and includes aesthetics, conformity with dimensions and distances defined in local building zones, energy consumption, fire and earthquake security, accessibility for handicapped persons, structural safety and others. Automated building code checking is proposed since a while, see for example [7–9]. A preliminary report from Fiatech [10], investigating into code compliance checking using a rule checking engine based on IFC (Solibri), suggests that an automatic process might be too complicated to establish. This is mainly due to the fact, that building standards and zonal regulations have been formulated to be processed by humans and not by computers. Dimyadi and Amor [11] give an overview of systems for code compliance checking and propose a framework where rules of building codes are introduced in a legal data exchange format and tested against an IFC based building model.

The work presented by this paper does not cover the part of automated code checking procedures or provides proposals to change internal procedures of building control authorities. It concentrates on the way data is exchanged between designers and

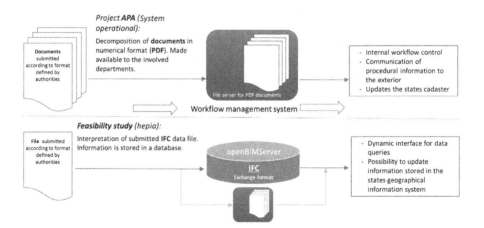

Fig. 1. New numerical approval system for construction projects of minor importance (above) and proposed system for the full construction project procedure.

building inspectors as well as internal data communication during the administrative procedure. The procedure for a full building permit (DD) in the canton of Geneva, Switzerland is used as an example. Approximately 80% of the information asked by authorities for a full building permit (DD) is either directly accessible via a digital model (BIM) or can be derived (calculated) from it.

Replacing ten identical paper copies by the submission of numerical documents in the case of the numerical "APA" procedure can be considered as a major improvement. Nevertheless, data present in PDF documents is not processed directly or managed by a database. Information is not bundled but scattered in multiple files. A data management platform, based on the IFC-format, might be able to increase the performance of the system by using one single IFC file for data exchange (see Fig. 1).

2   Complementarity of GIS and BIM and How This Might Improve Planning and Administrative Procedures

GIS and BIM are describing built environment in different ways. Standards for inter-operable data structures are mainly provided by the OGC[1] in the case of GIS and buildingSMART in the case of BIM. Complementarity of GIS and BIM is acknowledged by researchers [1–4, 12]. Discussions with designers show their big interest to combine both information sources in a reference model. Unfortunately, communication between the two systems has not yet been formalized.

BIM systems concentrate on the building itself. The upcoming standard "IFC5" will extend data structures to describe linear infrastructural constructions, such as tunnels and bridges as well. So far, managing the built environment like with GIS – systems is not possible (and might never be). The actual version of IFC does not provide object classes to integrate trees or landscape elements, for example.

GIS systems are mostly used to manage data on a territorial scale, whereas BIM is used on a building scale. The different scales can be combined and used to integrate in order to manage multiple buildings (BIM) on a large territory (GIS) [13, 14].

Figure 2 shows a comparison. Main standards for GIS are InfraGML and CityGML, the BIM standard is called IFC. OGC and buildingSMART plan to harmonize InfraGML and IFC5. The OpenInfraPlatform [15] proposes a conversion between the two and supports also the local German standard for road data (OKSTRA).

Construction impacts the environment: whether by its presence, its energy consumption, or by generating the need to extend or construct infrastructure. The maximum constructible volume is defined through zonal regulations which are limiting the buildings height, describe approved roof forms and define other geometrical details. Minimum distances towards existing buildings have to be respected. GIS can benefit from an update with BIM data from executed projects.

This leads to the idea to investigate, if GIS data could be transformed into a BIM compatible format (IFC), used as a basis for project development in a BIM environment and if "as built" data can be re-introduced into the GIS system for an update. In

---

[1] OGC: Open Geospatial Consortium.

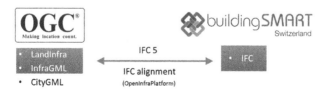

Fig. 2. Comparison of GIS and BIM

the case of Geneva, the cantonal geographic information system (SITG) is very rich and well managed and therefore a good candidate to test the procedure. Figure 3 shows the possible round trip and the following objectives have been fixed to test its feasibility:

- Evaluate the IFC data structure for collaborative work and its applicability for the building permit procedure: can all necessary information be included in one single file and does the import and export of IFC - data work?
- Use available GIS data as a valid starting point for the creation of a reference model for project development.

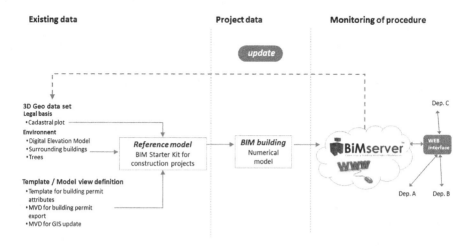

Fig. 3. Roundtrip from GIS to BIM to GIS, starting at the left with the reference model, using a collaborative platform (BIMserver) for the building permit procedure and updating the GIS system at the end

- Check that the procedure can be applied by professionals using standard BIM programs.
- Investigate how information can be centrally stored, managed and retrieved in order to be integrated into the validation procedure of a building permit for the case of Geneva
- Update the territorial database with actual project data at the end of construction.

3   Towards a Digital Construction Permit

3.1   Usability of IFC for Building Permit Evaluation

The amount of paper documents to be provided when requesting a building permit in Geneva and the number of fields to be filled in gives a discouraging high number: an average full construction permit is accompanied by 45 documents, with more than 20 fields per form.

This feasibility study does not provide an exhaustive testing of all present forms and fields. The strategy chosen was to define information categories and then test if they can be communicated and stored into an IFC file for data exchange. Three main categories (1–3) and three sub-categories (A–C) have been identified (Table 1). Categories depend on data origin (GIS, BIM or calculated) and subcategories define if IFC can provide the required data structure (object and attribute, object only, nothing). A data object of each category has been implemented and observed during the round trip.

Table 1. Data categories used for testing procedures

Category		Correspondence between building permit forms, territorial information and IFC object
1		Information is stored in the GIS system and can be exported to a BIM software
	A	Direct import : A corresponding IFC object and properties exist
	B	Indirect import, no property : A corresponding IFC object exists, but a property has to be created
	C	Indirect import, no IFC object : A corresponding IFC object with the property have to be created.
2		Information is not stored in the GIS system and has to be created during project phases
	A	Direct: A corresponding IFC object and properties exist
	B	Indirect, no property : A corresponding IFC object exists, but a property has to be created
	C	Indirect, no IFC object : A corresponding IFC object with the property have to be created.
3		Calculable: Information can be calculated by using data introduced during project phase

3.2 From GIS to BIM (IFC): Creating a Reference Model for Project Development

3.2.1 Data Source and Selection for the Reference Model

The reference model provides the numerical basis for the development of a construction project. It shall contain all available and public accessible territorial information. This study considers only aboveground data.

In Geneva, administration and public companies formed an interest group to manage the cantonal geographical data [16] already in 1991. At the present, the "Territorial Information System" (SITG), consolidates 882 different layers. 68.6% of these are open data [17]. Information is managed and published using GIS server (ESRI geodatabases and geoservices), which is accessible under http://ge.ch/sitg.

Usually, the following basic data types (vectors) are used in spatial data models: points (zero-dimensional object, 0D), lines (one-dimensional, 1D) and polygons (two-dimensional, 2D) [18]. Today, the majority of GIS systems manage three-dimensional objects (3D) as for example the multipatch layer in the case of ESRI. A layer of each data type is selected (except polyline) to test if it can be transformed into the IFC format. Polyline objects have not been evaluated because they are very similar to polygon objects. All used features are public domain and can be downloaded from the SITG site [17]. Data from the following SITG layers has been used:

Point Feature: *SIPV_ICA_ARBRE_ISOLE* contains data about isolated trees. Isolated trees are trees which are not part of a forest. This open data feature is managed by the "Conservatoire et Jardin botaniques" of Geneva.

Polygon Feature: *CAD_PARCELLE_MENSU* draws the official plot according to the cadaster. This open data feature is managed by the «Département de l'aménagement, du logement et de l'énergie Direction de la mensuration officielle».

3D Multipatch Layers: Five layers are used to represent buildings:

- *CAD_BATI3D_BASE*: building footprint
- *CAD_BATI3D_BASIC_FACADE*: exterior walls
- *CAD_BATI3D_BASIC_TOIT*: roof
- *CAD_BATI3D_SP_FACADE*: wall details
- *CAD_BATI3D_SP_TOIT*: roof details (dormers, roof openings, etc.)

A combination of these five layers forms the 3D building model of Geneva. The layer *CAD_BATI3D_PROJECT* represents the global volume of a projected building. All layer are open data and managed by the «Département de l'aménagement, du logement et de l'énergie Direction de la mensuration officielle».

Raster Feature: *MNA_TERRAIN* is the Digital Elevation Model (DEM) of Geneva. The model uses data obtained by a LIDAR flight. Its resolution is 50 cm per pixel. DEM is open data and managed by the «Département de l'aménagement, du logement et de l'énergie Direction de la mensuration officielle».

The reference model will be composed out of this data and includes information about the ground, the neighboring buildings, the building plot and the trees. A lot more details can be potentially obtained through the SITG.

Proposals for an automatic conversion from GIS (CityGML) to IFC have been made [1, 4, 19]. This study uses a tool specialized on data conversion (FME). This commercial software, created by the Safe Software Company, could be described as the "Swiss army knife" for data conversion. The FME platform is able to connect and transform hundreds of formats, including IFC [20]. In the present case, multiple different formats had to be converted into IFC. Although FME provides a pre-configured GIS-IFC converter, some particularities how georeferenced and geometrical data is managed are worth mentioning.

3.2.2 Georeferenced Data

Data from GIS systems are georeferenced. The SITG uses the Swiss CH1903 + _LV95 (EPSG 2056) coordinate system. IFC files and BIM software support georeferenced data as well, but they employ the WGS 84 system (longitude/latitude) and for practical reasons two reference points for a project:

- The project base point, defining the projects origin (0, 0, 0)
- The survey point, representing a known point for correct building orientation within the chosen coordinate system.

Both points have been placed at the same location, which is called the centroid of the initial parcel. A centroid is defined as the center of gravity of a polygon and most GIS software as well as the employed conversion software provide functions for its calculation.

It has been observed, that the FME standard mapping from CH1903+_LV95 (GIS) to WGS84 (BIM) did not export the resulting WGS84 coordinates to IFC. An alternative solution had to be developed: GIS and BIM systems use the metric system for length measurement. Dimensions are varying: CH1903+_LV95 communicates in meters, BIM in millimeters. Furthermore, the 2017 version of FME does not transfer the units used to IFC. Therefore, all coordinates were converted from meters to millimeters, then translated to transform the centroid of the plot into the new origin (0, 0, 0). Additionally, original coordinates of the centroid are stored in CH1903+_LV95 format in order to be able to do the reverse operation (see Sect. 3.4).

3.2.3 Geometrical and Alpha-Numerical Data

IFC objects require full 3D data. They are modeled as volumes. GIS however, uses still a lot 2D representation or 3D planar objects. As a result, GIS objects have to be converted into volumes. This can be done by extrusion. Data from the five layers representing the 3D building is modeled as surface objects (multipatch). Walls and roofs had to be extruded for their conversion into IFC. The extrusion could not consider the precise thickness of the building elements, since this information is not present in the system. A few centimeters have been used as a default value. Figure 4 shows on the left an exploded view of 3D planar objects in GIS. The objects obtained by extrusion in FME and conversion into an IFC data structure are visualized on the right. Extrusion is clearly visible at the buildings' roof.

Importing an IFC file with object geometries produced by extrusion can cause difficulties. Extruding walls to the interior of the building provokes intersections. This

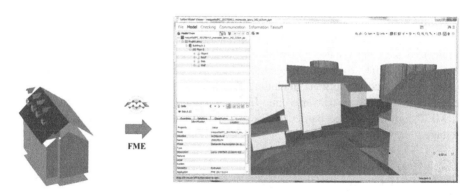

Fig. 4. Extrusion of 3D planar GIS data into 3D volume IFC objects

is considered as an error by Revit and the software stops importing the IFC file. Converting the geometry from "Solid" to "Brep" solves this problem.

Classes like IFCBuildingElementProxy are easier to handle, since they have less geometrical restrictions. It is tempting to export all GIS objects into this class, but the main advantage of BIM and its class hierarchy, the semantics, will be lost. Therefore, the IfcBuildingElementProxy class has only been used for GIS objects without a corresponding IFC class. In this study, trees are exported by default into the IFCBbuildingElementProxy.

When converting trees into IFC, 2D point data has to be transformed into 3D objects with a volume. Important parameters for a tree are the volume occupied by its crown and its maximum height. The SITG layer SIPV_ICA_ARBRE_ISOLE provides these attributes (see Table 2).

Table 2. SIPV_ICA_ARBRE_ISOLE layers fields used to construct the tree geometry

Layer field	Attribute
Hauteur totale	Maximum tree height
Diametre de la couronne	Crown diameter
Diametre du tronc	Trunk diameter
Hauteur de tronc	Height where the crown begins

Trees are represented as two superposed cylinders to show the volume occupied. The cylinder at the bottom represents the trunk and the cylinder at the top represents the crown. If the attribute field is not documented, a default value is assigned. Figure 5 shows the result for a tree in the IFC model.

Not all attributes needed are necessarily provided by the reference project. Missing fields are requested from the user by a pop up when the FME script is started. These are for example the project name, the name of the client, the name of the designer etc. These attributes are exported directly into corresponding IFC classes and do not require any transformation.

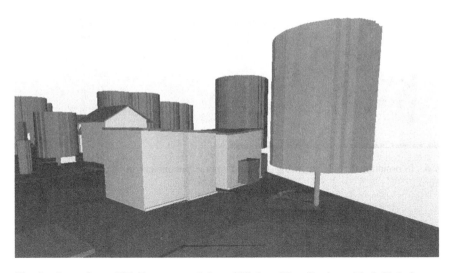

Fig. 5. A tree in an IFC file composed from GIS data. Visualization with Solibri viewer.

3.3   Project Development Phase

During the project development phase, two aspects had to be checked:

- The correct import of the reference model created by the conversion software into the BIM software package
- The correct transfer of data structures added to the IFC building objects in order to fulfil information requirements of the building permit procedure and their export using a model view definition

3.3.1   Reference Model Import

The reference IFC-File has been tested with two major BIM software packages (Archicad and Revit). The IFC file is imported into the BIM software. When an error occurred during import, the FME converter had to be modified, as mentioned in Sect. 3.2.3. When the file has been imported without errors, it has been exported directly without any modification. The exported model has then been checked using the Solibri viewer to check if all initial GIS information is present?

Importing the reference model into Archicad with default parameters resulted in information losses (see Fig. 6).

A new translator with custom import settings had to be created. Geometrical conversion settings had to be chosen as shown in Fig. 7. Using the custom translator (File > Interoperability > IFC), GIS-data imports correctly via IFC into the BIM software.

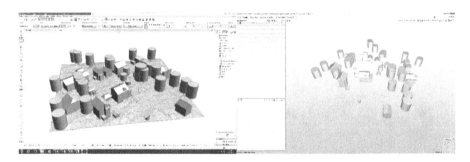

Fig. 6. Information loss when using standard import parameters in Archicad (visualized by Solibri)

Fig. 7. IFC translator setup for the IFC import into Archicad

3.3.2 3D Digitalization and Attributes Parameters

Not all information needed for the building permit procedure can be provided by the GIS. Whenever possible, attributes are stored in existing IFC classes and their properties but some attributes do not exist in IFC.

Adding an attribute to an IFC class is done by creating a property set (IfcPropertySet) adding the necessary attributes (IfcPropertySingleValue) and establishing a link (IfcRelDefinesByProperties) between this property set and an existing object (case 2.B Table 1) or a newly created object (case 2.C Table 1).

The two BIM software packages evaluated can handle these manipulation via their user interface. Revit uses the notion of "Families". Creating a new parameter in Archicad modifies directly the IFC scheme. If object and parameter category are connected, they will correctly be exported.

For example, an IfcPropertySet "planting" is created and linked to the IFCBuildingElementProxy (which contains the tree object). All tree related attributes (properties) are added to the element: as soon as a tree is created.

All these modifications are saved as a re-usable template.

3.3.3   Exportation of the "Building Permit" Model

The final model contains all IFC classes and properties needed for the building permit deposit, together with all other project-related data. The "Model view definition" (MVD) defines, which IFC classes have to be exported.

Solibri model viewer has been used to check the exported IFC file, containing the reference model, added properties and the building to be constructed. The export settings are defined thanks to the checking of the IFC in Solibri and the two IFC files exported from Revit and Archicad are identical and contain all necessary information.

3.4   From IFC to GIS: Updating Territorial Data with "as Built" Data

To convert IFC data to GIS, the same software that created the reference model (see Sect. 3.2) has been used: FME. First, all georeferencing is recovered, then geometry and attributes are written to GIS layers.

Coordinates of elements inserted using the BIM software are related to the project base point. For example, a vertex from a building wall, with the coordinates (10 000, 20 000), is at 10 000 mm on the x-axis and at 20 000 mm on the y-axis with respect to the project base point. As the CH1903+_LV95 is expressed in meters, and the coordinates of the project base point are assumed to be for example (N 1 178 379.666, E 2 449 443.114), then the coordinates of the vertex into the CH1903+_LV95 system would be equal to (N 1 178 399.666, E 2 449 453.114). Projecting the model leads to a conversion into meters, followed by a translation caused by the coordinates of the project base point given in Swiss coordinates. These coordinates are integrated into the model by a PropertySet connected to the IfcSite. The process is the exact reverse of which is being done for the reference model (see Sect. 3.2.2).

The SITG accepts only the global volume of the construction without details concerning roof and façade. Therefore, the representation can be reduced to a LOD 200 (BIM standard) or LOD 2 (CityGML standard). FME selects IfcRoof-, IfcWall- and IfcSlab-objects, simplifies the geometry and exports in multipatch format.

Trees are localized by a point in the layer SIPV_ICA_ARBRE_ISOLE. Transforming a 3D volume object (IFC) into a point feature (GIS) is possible using the centroid point. In FME, first the "centerPointExtractor" tool extracts the coordinates of the gravity center of the object (x, y, z). Then the "VertexCreator" tool with the option "replaceWithPoint" replaces the geometry of the object with a point geometry (the coordinates of the point are set with the output of the "centerPointExtractor" tool). The "VertexCreator" tool switch only the geometry property, so attributes property are not affected.

When geometry and attributes are modified, the conversion from this data into GIS layers is a straightforward. Figure 8 shows the process for trees.

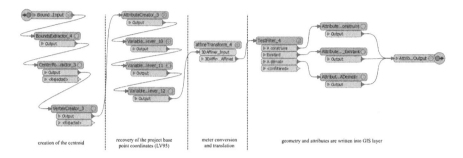

Fig. 8. FME procedure for converting an IFC file into GIS layers (process for tree objects)

3.5   BIM Data Storage, Management and Retrieval: Collaborative Platforms

3.5.1   Defining the Requirements for the Collaborative Platform

Following Swiss planning procedures, a project submitted to obtain a building permit is already very detailed. Not all information is needed during the procedure and control tasks at the building authority are distributed between multiple departments.

Therefore, a predefined export (Model View Definition) is implemented and tested for two major BIM Software packages. The same method is applied by Singapore's BCA (Building control authority).

Collaborative platforms are very popular to share information. Many cloud-based services are proposed, but they sometimes accept only data from the product line of a software supplier or cannot be tailored to the very specific needs of the building permit procedure. As a public administration, the Geneva state authorities cannot and do not want to use a proprietary product. "BIMserver" has been chosen as an open collaborative platform and IFC as the exchange file format. The part of the digital construction permit application is imagined to be organized as a BIM level three system.

BIMserver is an open source (GNU Affero GPL) java platform developed by the Open source BIMcollective. Its objective is to support the collaborative process in architecture and building engineering. It can be installed as a local application (using JAR file and a Java Virtual Machine), or as a server (using WAR file and Tomcat). BIMserver allows to store IFC files into an open source DB Berkeley [21] and to manage the versioning of this file. It offers different API in an open framework [22–24]. In the scope of this project, BIMserver has been installed as a server.

Account management for users is provided. IFC Data can accessed through a web interface (BIMViews), through a command line tool or through a HTTP/SOAP protocol. SOAP is a protocol specification for exchange of structured information [25]. Thus a language that writes XML encoded messages and sends HTTP requests can access to IFC data placed on BIMserver. Requests can made by a local or a web application.

3.5.2   Web Interface to Access the IFC Model Stored in BIMserver

The IFC file exported from the BIM software has been filtered by the Model View Definition during the export from BIM software. It contains the complete information for all departments participating in the building permit procedure.

A web interface can help to provide targeted data. Additionally, as BIMserver manages the versioning of IFC for a project, the web interface may allow a department to access to different versions of a project and ensure an effective follow-up of modifications.

A local python filter

Python is an interpreted high level programming language. The python packages "requests" and "requests_toolbelt" allow python to send HTTP requests. Many languages can send HTTP requests but python is the main scripting language for GIS procedures. Figure 9 shows an example of a python request which informs about the number of projects stored on the BIMserver. The request has two main parts, the token (Fig. 9 num. 1) and the request (Fig. 9 num. 2).

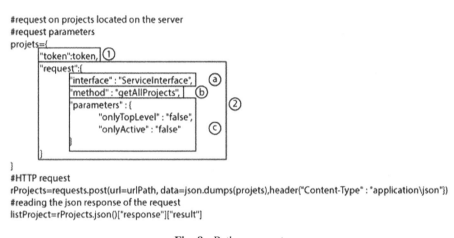

```
#request on projects located on the server
#request parameters
projets={
        "token":token, ①
        "request":{
                'interface' : "ServiceInterface',   ⓐ
                'method" : "getAllProjects",   ⓑ
                'parameters" : {                              ②
                        "onlyTopLevel" : "false",
                        "onlyActive" : "false"   ⓒ
                }
        }
}
#HTTP request
rProjects=requests.post(url=urlPath, data=json.dumps(projets),header("Content-Type" : "application\json"})
#reading the json response of the request
listProject=rProjects.json()["response"]["result"]
```

Fig. 9. Python request

The token attribute is a unique code, guaranteeing protected data access. A log request with access parameters (id and password) has to be send to obtain a user-token for subsequent use.

The request attribute is a list of three elements: the method called (2.b), its parameter (2.c) and the family of the method (2.a). This request is an equivalent to a common method call that could be write as:

```
ServiceInterface.getAllProjects(onlyTopLevel = False,
onlyActive = False)
```

The response sent by the server is JSON formatted and can be interpreted by python. The method getDataObjectByOid allows to read attributes from an object thanks to its identifier (OID). The IFC hierarchy tree can be travelled thanks to this method and attributes value can be accessed.

A lot of requests are necessary to access to the value searched, since one request is necessary for each node change in the IFC hierarchy tree. Figure 10 shows the result of a python script which gives the surface area of rooms according to their floor. The script is executed on a shell without a specific user interface. An interface can be created using JavaScript.

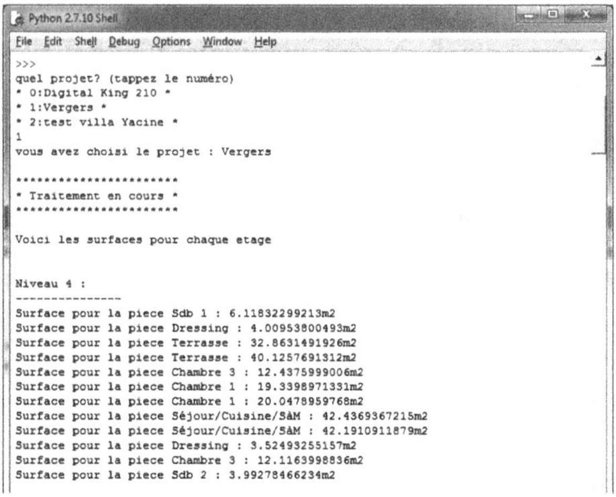

Fig. 10. Script python on IDL shell

A web interface filter

JavaScript is a programming language for the creation of interactive webpages and supported by all modern web browsers [26]. It allows HTTP requests, employing the same semantic as python (Fig. 11).

Figure 12 shows a prototype of a web interface using JavaScript. When the web page is loaded, the request shown in Fig. 11 retrieves all projects stored on BIMserver

```
var projets={
    "token": token,
    "request": {
        "interface": "ServiceInterface",
        "method": "getAllProjects",
        "parameters": {
            "onlyTopLevel": "false",
            "onlyActive":"false"
        }
    }
};
var requestProjets=$.ajax({
    url:urlPath,
    type:'post',
    data:JSON.stringify(projets),
    contentType:'application/json',
    dataType:'text',
    async:false
});
```

Fig. 11. Javascript request

Fig. 12. Web interface for reading IFC data from BIMserver

and create a drop-down list. The building inspector can select a project of interest and detailed information is shown on the screen.

4   Results and Discussion

4.1   Evaluation of IFC Data Structure

The IFC data structure has been tested according to test cases defined in Table 1: direct import/export when IFC provided an equivalent property, creation of properties when an equivalent IfcObject could be identified and using IfcProxy when there was no such object.

This procedure was evaluated with two main BIM software packages and proven to be operational. The IfC format 2 × 3 has been used for converting, importing and exporting data, since some incompatibilities occurred with the IFC 4 interfaces of the used software. The use of IfcProxy objects destroys unfortunately the inherent semantics of the IfC data model.

It can be concluded, that construction permit data can be communicated using IFC as a data exchange format.

4.2   Reference Model (GIS to IFC)

The reference model should contain all available GIS data within a perimeter around a construction site. Data has been transformed into IFC and can be used as a valuable starting point for designing the new project. It helps to integrate a project into its environment. Transformation of data has been tested for different forms of GIS representation, as there are point feature, polygon feature, 3D multipatch and raster feature. The model created by the transformation script includes a ground model extract from the Digital Elevation Model, the emplacement and the volume occupied surrounding buildings and isolated trees.

Figure 13 below shows initial GIS data represented as a 2D view on ArcGIS desktop (top left), as well as a 3D view on ArcScene (top right). The model exported from GIS, transformed and imported into the BIM software is shown below. The reference model is an exact transcription of the exported GIS data. So far, the reference model provides only a low level of details (LOD 2, according CityGML). The currently created reference model does not separate the buildings into floors and rooms, as proposed by the IFC hierarchy.

It may allow creating rules as a no overlap rule with an IFCWall.

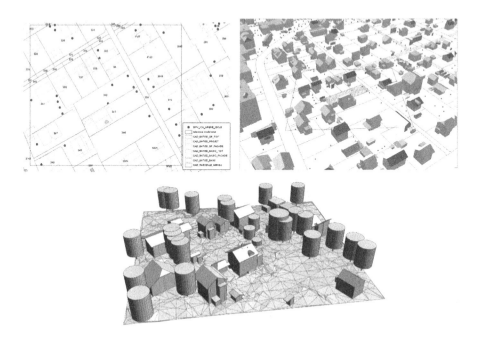

Fig. 13. IFC reference model (bottom) created using GIS data (top)

At the present time, IFC does not support vegetation objects. Trees are introduced into the IFC structure by creating a new IFCBuildingElementProxy object. Unfortunately, storing objects in an IFCBuildingElementProxy class does not provide the same semantical richness as if there would be a corresponding object.

4.3   Project Development, Using a Reference Model and Exporting Valid Building Permit Information

The introduction of the reference model as well as additional data structures needed to communicate relevant building permit information has been checked with two major BIM software packages. No major difficulties have been encountered, but differences how the tools are managing import and export of geometry and data had to be addressed.

When working on a project, designers have to apply special procedures in order not to destroy data-integrity. As an example, trees cannot simply be deleted with the standard command, otherwise data will be lost. The designer has to change attributes of the object directly to keep the traceability and for correct data export.

4.4   Data Storage and Management

A collaborative platform allows to manage IFC file data. BIMserver offers file versioning. Building models are updated by loading a new file onto the server. Inspectors have always access to the newest data as well as to previous project versions.

BIMserver offers different API which can handle HTTP requests. Data can be accessed by different methods. Local or web-based applications can be implemented to filer and calculate specific data. Each inspector can access to specific data and calculate their indicators.

BIMserver is a modular framework with the possibility to create API's directly connected to IFC data. The difference between the custom API solution and the web interface is the location of the process. The web interface using JavaScript located on the client side (front-end.). The custom API is on the server side (back-end). The front end solution involves many requests from the client to the server, where requests used by the back-end solution are local and will therefore be more time-efficient. Custom API seems to be the solution of choice.

4.5   Introducing Updated Project Data into the GIS

Figure 14 shows a comparison between the GIS data made available for the reference model and the GIS data obtained by exporting an IFC file of a construction project from the BIM software: both layers, the one coming from the reference model and the second from a construction project are perfectly overlapping. This demonstrates that accuracy of coordinate data does not decrease when data is transformed during the diverse import and export operations.

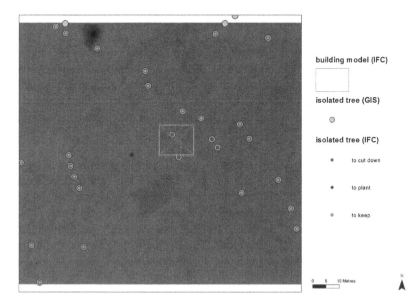

Fig. 14. Comparative mapping of original GIS data and data exported from the final IFC model

Additionally, comparison of the reference model and the updated IFC project file allows to keep track of modifications. The colored dots inside the tree location points indicate their status: existing, to be planted, to be cut. With a reference model extracted from GIS and is meant to be re-introduced again into GIS, the BIM user needs to manage the data correctly. In fact, a tree may be located on the future building site. The user should not simply delete the tree but modify its attribute. When BIM data will be transferred back into a GIS layer, the destruction of the tree is not reported in the GIS feature if the object is deleted. So far, the deletion of an object has not been coupled with an attribute modification.

5 Conclusions and Future Work

The feasibility study showed that data exchange between GIS and BIM is beneficial for both sides. The digital construction permit has been used as an example. Designers can import a reference model which contains available information concerning the build environment compiled from official data sources (the Geneva Territory Information System, SITG). This data is converted by a specialized software (FME) into an IFC file. Different GIS data types, like point feature, multipatch feature or raster feature have been tested. Interoperability has been evaluated with two BIM software packages (Archicad and Revit). The level of detail of the reference model can easily be increased, considering the potential of available GIS data.

Although Geneva's SITG is considered as the most complete, well-structured and reliable GIS system in Switzerland, its initial conception in 1991 did not foresee a possible interaction with numerical building models (BIM). So far, information is organized into layers, using data in diverse formats and from different sources. A migration towards a GIS data structure providing a bigger semantical richness, like CityGML or InfraGML, would be beneficial for GIS-BIM interaction.

The templates developed for the two tested BIM software packages provided, combined with the reference model, the necessary basis to extract an IFC file which potentially carries all information needed for the building permit procedure. At the end of the project, it was possible to introduce "as-built" information in the GIS database. The fact that imported GIS objects, like trees, cannot be erased with commands normally used when designing, is distracting. When such a system will be commissioned for practice, other techniques to compare the initial with the "as-built" situation have to be developed.

BIMserver has proven its usability as a cooperative platform for the building permit control procedure. It allows to share information with all involved departments. Information can easily be filtered and distributed via web browsers and Javascript. Query options can rapidly be adapted when procedures or laws are changing. Uploading an IFC model onto the BIMserver offers a possibility for first simple controls, like completeness of transmitted data. This avoids that designers lose their time because of missing documents and that administration starts to work on an incomplete project.

So far, the study concentrated on data exchange, transformation and management. A representation form of building codes and construction rules which supports building inspectors during the checking procedure are still to be done. Building codes are not formulated in a way that they can be understood by computers.

Acknowledgements. Financing and support by Geneva state authorities is gratefully acknowledged.

References

1. El-Mekawy, M., Östman, A., Shahzad, K.: Towards interoperating CityGML and IFC building models: a unified model based approach. In: Kolbe, T.H., König, G., Nagel, C. (eds.) Advances in 3D Geo-Information Sciences, pp. 73–93. Springer, Heidelberg (2011). https://doi.org/10.1007/978-3-642-12670-3_5
2. Cheng, J., Deng, Y., Du, Q.: Mapping between BIM models and 3D GIS city models of different levels of detail. In: 13th International Conference on Construction Applications of Virtual Reality, London, pp. 30–31 (2013)
3. Devys, E., Gesquière, G.: Interopérabilité et intégration des données et modèles urbains: standards, normes et tendances pour les SIG. Modélisation Ville Modè Au Proj. Urbain Réf. DRI Paris, pp. 92–103 (2012)
4. de Laat, R., van Berlo, L.: Integration of BIM and GIS: the development of the CityGML GeoBIM extension. In: Kolbe, T., König, G., Nagel, C. (eds.) Advances in 3D Geo-Information Sciences. Lecture Notes in Geoinformation and Cartography. Springer, Heidelberg (2011). https://doi.org/10.1007/978-3-642-12670-3_13
5. Demander en ligne une autorisation de construire en procédure accélérée (APA). https://www.ge.ch/demander-ligne-autorisation-construire-procedure-acceleree-apa
6. E-Info. https://www.corenet.gov.sg/general/e-info.aspx
7. Eastman, C., Lee, J., Jeong, Y., Lee, J.: Automatic rule-based checking of building designs. Autom. Constr. **18**, 1011–1033 (2009)
8. Preidel, C., Borrmann, A.: Automated code compliance checking based on a visual language and building information modeling. In: Proceedings of the International Symposium on Automation and Robotics in Construction, ISARC, p. 1. Vilnius Gediminas Technical University, Department of Construction Economics & Property (2015)
9. Zhang, S., Teizer, J., Lee, J.-K., Eastman, C.M., Venugopal, M.: Building Information Modeling (BIM) and safety: automatic safety checking of construction models and schedules. Autom. Constr. **29**, 183–195 (2013)
10. AutoCodes project Phase 1 proof of concept final report.pdf
11. Dimyadi, J., Amor, R.: Automated building code compliance checking - where is it at? Presented at the Proceedings of CIB WBC, 6 May 2013
12. Deng, Y., Cheng, J.C.P., Anumba, C.: Mapping between BIM and 3D GIS in different levels of detail using schema mediation and instance comparison. Autom. Constr. **67**, 1–21 (2016)
13. Zhang, X., Arayici, Y., Wu, S., Abbott, C., Aouad, G.F.: Integrating BIM and GIS for large-scale facilities asset management: a critical review. Presented at the Twelfth International Conference on Civil, Structural and Environmental Engineering Computing, Funchal, Madeira, Portugal, 2 September 2009
14. Kang, T.W., Hong, C.H.: A study on software architecture for effective BIM/GIS-based facility management data integration. Autom. Constr. **54**, 25–38 (2015)

15. TUM Open Infra Platform - Lehrstuhl für Computergestützte Modellierung und Simulation der TU München. https://www.cms.bgu.tum.de/de/forschung/projekte/31-forschung/projekte/397-tum-open-infra-platform

16. SITG: Définition. /sitg/le-sitg

17. Catalogue—SITG. http://ge.ch/sitg/sitg_catalog/sitg_donnees

18. Rigaux, P., Scholl, M., Voisard, A.: Spatial Databases: With Application to GIS. Elsevier, Amsterdam (2001)

19. Donkers, S., Ledoux, H., Zhao, J., Stoter, J.: Automatic conversion of IFC datasets to geometrically and semantically correct CityGML LOD3 buildings: automatic conversion of IFC datasets to CityGML LOD3 buildings. Trans. GIS **20**, 547–569 (2016)

20. Safe Software—FME—Integrate Data, Applications, Web Services. https://www.safe.com

21. Oracle Berkeley DB. http://www.oracle.com/technetwork/database/berkeleydb/overview/index-085366.html

22. Beetz, J., van Berlo, L., de Laat, R., van den Helm, P.: Bimserver. org – an open source IFC model server. In: Proceedings of the CIP W78 Conference (2010)

23. Beetz, J., de Laat, R., van Berlo, L., van den Helm, P.: Towards an open building information model server. In: Proceedings of the 10th International Conference on Design & Decision Support Systems in Architecture and Urban Planning, The Netherlands (2010)

24. Open source BIMserver. http://bimserver.org/

25. SOAP (2018). https://en.wikipedia.org/w/index.php?title=SOAP&oldid=819451188

26. JavaScript (2017). https://en.wikipedia.org/w/index.php?title=JavaScript&oldid=817437479

Standardized Names for Object Types and Attributes as Basis for Cooperation Between Planning and Building

Laura Böger[1([✉])], Wolfgang Huhnt[1], and Siegfried Wernik[2]

[1] Technische Universität Berlin, Straße des 17. Juni 135, 10623 Berlin, Germany
`laura.c.boeger@tu-berlin.de`
[2] DhochN Digital Engineering GmbH, Lützowstr. 102, 10785 Berlin, Germany

Abstract. When using Building Information Modeling (BIM), it is expected to increase interorganizational collaboration in the construction industry. To reach this goal, it is necessary to use open standards for model exchange such as the Industry Foundation Classes (IFC). The non-profit organization buildingSMART defines this standard. IFC provides object types and attributes, which describe properties of objects. The IFC standard do not address possible values for attributes; but beside coordinated names for object types and attributes, coordinated values for attributes are required. This is necessary for the evaluation of digital models for different purposes. Several approaches in the fields of ontology and classification systems address this issue. However, at present time there is no clear distinction between prerequisites that modeled objects have to fulfill and products, which satisfy these requirements. Suppliers or construction companies at the interface between planning and construction propose products for the modelled requirements of the planning process. This paper describes an approach that bases on a dictionary, which provides standardized object types, attributes and values. A project database and a database with products, called supplier database, use this dictionary as a basis. Resulting from the modeling phase, the project database is ultimately mapped with the supplier database to propose products that fulfill the requirements. The approach presented in this paper can be regarded as a next step in using a standard that already exists: the buildingSMART Data Dictionary.

Keywords: Building Information Modeling (BIM)
Industry Foundation Classes (IFC) · buildingSMART Data Dictionary (bSDD)

1 Introduction

For some time, the use of Building Information Modeling (BIM) in the Architectural, Engineering and Construction (AEC) industry is commonly accepted in practice, e.g. (Borrmann et al. 2015). The Industry Foundation Classes (IFC) is an open data standard for BIM, which supports an interorganizational collaboration during the planning process and is present in leading BIM software (Laakso and Kiviniemi 2012). The exchange of data relies not only on the use of identical data structures for the exchange.

© Springer International Publishing AG, part of Springer Nature 2018
I. F. C. Smith and B. Domer (Eds.): EG-ICE 2018, LNCS 10864, pp. 307–324, 2018.
https://doi.org/10.1007/978-3-319-91638-5_17

Furthermore, every project participant must use coordinated terms. Due to the fragmentation of the AEC industry it is difficult to communicate efficient and effectively. Information inconsistencies and problems with regulatory compliance are a result (Rezgui et al. 2010). The aim of IFC is an open interoperability that would enable the seamless flow of production and maintenance information as well as reduce redundancies (Laakso and Kiviniemi 2011). Thus, coordinated terms are required.

This paper describes a concept that supports the exchange of data between planning and construction in a beneficial way using coordinated terms. Moreover, we focus on using coordinated terms during the planning phase. We integrate suppliers of building materials and built-in components to support the selection of building materials and building components.

The paper has the following structure: First, Sect. 2 gives an overview of the basic problems that lead to this approach. The following Sect. 3 summarizes the current status of data exchange in the AEC industry. It presents the buildingSMART Data Dictionary (bSDD), which addresses the use of standardized terms. Section 3 also describes a similar attempt to this paper that uses a standardized basis together with the bSDD as a starting point for modeling in projects. Section 4 explains the solution concept, starting with the needed databases. Section 5 presents a prototype for Autodesk Revit to demonstrate the functioning of the approach in planning processes. A demonstration of the solution concept and the workflow with the presented prototype shows Sect. 6. The results are conclusively discussed in Sects. 7, and 8 summarizes the paper and gives an outlook to the following steps.

2   Problem Description

The standard IFC was created to serve the BIM interoperability needs of the AEC industry. However, instead of achieving an improved collaboration in the planning process due to its open access, the exchange of BIM data is dominated by proprietary solutions (Laakso and Kiviniemi 2012). This leads to the presumption that the standard is not sufficient for the demands of the industry.

IFC provides object types and attributes to describe properties of objects. It does not address possible values for attributes; but beside coordinated names for object types and attributes, coordinated values for attributes are required. This is necessary for the evaluation of digital models for different purposes.

When an object is specified in the modeling phase, it is essential for the tendering phase to store all anticipated values in the attributes of that object. A BIM project is mostly a collaboration of many planners, so it is highly probable that some values are stored more than once in the same project under different names. In the worst case, planners use *different* values to describe the same attribute. This leads to the necessity of standard names for object types, their attributes, and the values that are used to describe prerequisites.

Currently, there is no clear distinction between prerequisite that modeled objects have to fulfill and products, which satisfy these requirements. The aim is to create a coordinated conceptualization so that every object, whether in a project or as a product, uses identical attributes and coordinated terms.

However, we cannot prescribe such a structure for all projects in AEC. Projects differ in their focus, in number and specialization of project participants, etc. Therefore, we always require a project specific preparation phase to select required object types, attributes and possible values for these attributes. This leads to a need of a common basis that stores an amount of standardized object types, which can be selected to fulfill the requirements for every different project.

Such a concept is already addressed by bSDD. We expand the focus of the use of bSDD in such a way that we show how suppliers can be integrated. Our goal is to automate and therefore simplify the process of proposing building materials and built-in components and to distinguish clearly between requirements and selected products.

To create a common basis for both, projects and suppliers, it is necessary to reconcile all needed terms. This is challenging in more than one way. The chosen conceptualities must be explicit to facilitate working with this basis. Otherwise, it is likely that people refuse to work with it because of the additional expense to understand it. Further on, this basis must be topical, which leads to the need of a supervisory authority that removes redundancies as well as incomprehensible terms (and replaces them). This is the task for further development of bSDD.

We show in this paper the potential that bSDD can have at the interface between planning and construction.

3   Related Work

The following chapter gives an overview of standards in the AEC industry, focusing on data exchange and classifications. In its last section, it presents a project to show the benefits of using bSDD during a modeling phase of a project.

3.1   Standardized Models for Data Exchange

A first approach for the development of a lossless data exchange between CAD systems started already in the 1970s, as described for instance in (Borrmann et al. 2015). However, this exchange was limited to a description of geometry. Efforts for further standards led via Standard for the Exchange of Product Model Data (STEP) eventually to the in 1995 founded International Alliance for Interoperability (IAI). In 1997, IAI published a first version of IFC. IAI renamed itself to buildingSMART in 2005. Since 2013, EN ISO 16739 standardizes IFC. (Borrmann et al. 2015; buildingSMART Homepage 2018; DIN 2017).

The data modeling language for IFC is EXPRESS (ISO 2004; DIN 2017). In EXPRESS, the term entity describes a unit of data. Entities have attributes. Attributes can base on an elementary data type, or they can be relations to other entities. They are divided in mandatory (e.g. the identifier) and optional. The schema is extensive but also complex and has redundancies (Eastman et al. 2010; Belsky et al. 2016). Furthermore, IFC can be difficult to utilize, due to a lack of specific task-oriented exchange content.

This leads to incomplete and incompatible data exchange, when the coordination of specific information that has to be included in the IFC view is incorrect (Eastman et al. 2010). In other words, the classification can be unreliable because the export tool may not match the intended classification, which can be context specific (Belsky et al. 2016). van Berlo et al. (2012) describes another problem with IFC: users prefer to receive data that only contains information they need at a given time; but simultaneously, the exact need of information from engineers is unclear. This is a result of the lack of information agreement, and it is seen as a crucial threshold that must be overtaken.

3.2 Coordinated Terms: Ontologies and Classification Systems

Coordinated terms can be the basis for a common understanding in architectural and civil engineering projects. Examples are the classification systems OmniClass (Omni-Class Homepage 2018), ETIM (ETIM international Homepage 2018) or eCl@ss (eCl@ss Homepage 2018). OmniClass, for instance, describes its standard as a strategy to classify the built environment and that it provides a standardized basis for classifying information (About OmniClass 2018).

When talking about standard terms or classification for object types and attributes, it is necessary to explain the term ontology, which defines conceptualizations. The World Wide Web Consortium (W3C), ontologies provide services such as semantic search and retrieval of web resources (W3C Homepage 2018; De Nicola et al. 2009). According to (Gruber 1993, page 1), "an *ontology* is an explicit specification of a conceptualization." The classification systems that are mentioned before are all based specific self-defined ontologies. When every participant uses the same terms of the defined vocabulary, ambiguity can be excluded. Because of the problems with IFC described in Sect. 3.1, users are interested in semantic web technologies. This led for instance to the development of a Web Ontology Language (OWL) version of the IFC schema, called ifcOWL (Terkaj and Šojić 2015).

buildingSMART developed a platform for using different ontologies, the buildingS-MART Data Dictionary (bSDD). It bases on a generic standardized data model (buildingSMART Data Dictionary Homepage 2018). Conceptualities need to be specified, so as a conclusion bSDD provides a library of object types and attributes. It supports the identification of objects in the built environment and their properties, while terms are standardized per language (buildingSMART Data Dictionary Homepage 2018). The difference between the notions in bSDD and IFC is that the Data Dictionary is for general terms, whereas the class hierarchy in IFC is at a very detailed level.

The aim of bSDD is to create data transparency with its openness and internationality, which shall lead to shared reusable object libraries.

3.3 An Approach with bSDD

In 2012 started a research project called "freeBIM Tirol"[1] that focused on the definition of component properties to ensure an ideal collaboration between different BIM teams. A database, called a server for properties, was created to store, complement and edit attributes of building components and materials; the project serves as the basis for ÖNORM A6241-2 (b.i.m.m. 2018). The aim was to match these properties subsequently with bSDD and to complement the dictionary with missing data.

Every parameter has its own identifier, which provides explicitness of the used term. When using a BIM software, the parameters are mapped onto the properties of the software. This creates a link between the identifiers and the data of a BIM model.

The project database contains the following elements: components, parameters and values. Components and parameters have identifiers, names and descriptions; in addition, parameters are assigned to a component. The stored values are standard values for the parameters, defined by standards like Eurocode (freeBIM Merkmalsserver 2018).

In June 2016, the project started its second phase and is now addressing two main goals: Firstly, to create a higher acceptance for BIM in the planning process trough facilitating the starting phase with their property server; secondly, to support the tendering and to create bill of quantities automatically (freeBIM project description 2018).

4   Solution Concept

This paper presents an approach that uses bSDD as a basis for the modeling phase. In addition to the presented project freeBIM, the aim is to enable the possibility of automatic product proposals at the end of the modeling phase and thus to integrate suppliers into the flow of data. The following chapter describes the sequences that are necessary to reach this goal.

4.1 Setting Up the Databases

For the procedure from standardized terms from bSDD to an automatic proposal of products that fit the requirements from the modeling phase, three types of databases must be available. The first one is the already described bSDD, the second one needs to store product descriptions and their specified values. The supplier or provider of products must specify the second type of database. The third database stores all determinations of the BIM project.

The later presented prototype uses a database, which fulfills all requirements of bSDD. Furthermore, databases from different suppliers with different product descriptions for an automatic proposal of products is needed. To demonstrate the procedure, all

---

[1] "freeBIM Tirol" is a collaboration between Universität Innsbruck, Austria, and the companies CAD Anwendungen MUIGG KG, Austria, b.i.m.m., Germany and inndata Datentechnik GmbH, Austria.

databases were independently created as embedded relational database management systems (RDBMS), namely Java-based H2 (H2 Database Homepage 2018).

Data Dictionary. The created database for the data dictionary adopts the concept of buildingSMART. It is later addressed as simply data dictionary to prevent confusion with the bSDD.

The database contains standardized object types, e.g. wall, window or door. Beside a Universally Unique Identifier (UUID), there is one name for the object type for each language. Additionally, the database stores the creator as well as the date of creation and the topicality of the object type.

Every object type has a number of standardized attributes. Their basic structure is similar to the object type: UUID, names per language, creator, date of creation and topicality. Furthermore, a type of the attribute is stored, which defines a distinction between the memory structures such as floating point number, integer number or character strings. Later in the modeling phase this shall give the user an information about the expected value for the attribute. If the attribute has floating point numbers, a unit is stored as well. Figure 1 shows a detail from the database.

UUID	ENGLISH	UNIT	TYPEOFATTRIBUTE
25d45068-ab47-4a5a-a7da-ef60c5e238b8	thermal transmittance	6cb01def-c44f-46ef-9447-99d0cd49e673	attribute with double value
471d17f8-617e-487a-8754-d4364e190921	fire protection class	-	attribute with string values

Fig. 1. A detail from the SQL database of the data dictionary using dBeaver (dBeaver Homepage 2018)

Every attribute is only stored once in the database. If different object types have the same attribute, for instance, a door and a window both have the attribute "height", they are referring to the same attribute, identifiable trough a UUID. Values for attributes that are standardized, for instance by Eurocode, are already stored in the data dictionary. Every possible value is stored together with its underlying standard. Values that depend on the object type and that are defined by the same standard, for example the fire protection class in Eurocode, are stored together. Later in the progress, the modeler has to choose a reasonable value.

Supplier Database. The database that stores products has a similar structure as the data dictionary. Subsequently, a schema for the supplier databases is described. Unlike the data dictionary, which is unique and only needed once, every provider or supplier can create an amount of databases for their products. Only the structure must remain the same.

First, there need to be a selection of an object type from the data dictionary that fit the product. For instance, a window manufacturer would assign the object type "window" to his products. Subsequently, it is necessary to select an amount of attributes from the previously chosen object type. The available values for the product define the needed attributes; in a next step, the values must be stored as well. Figure 2 illustrates the procedure.

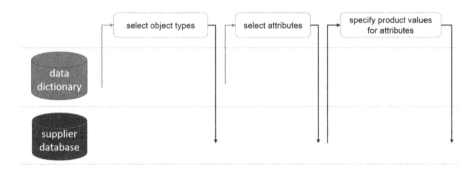

Fig. 2. Setting up a supplier database

4.2 Executing a Project

For every project, all relevant information is stored in one or more databases of the same schema.

At the beginning, all participants must agree about the project language. In a next step, a selection of object types and attributes from the data dictionary is stored in the database. Both, object types and attributes bring their identifiers as well as their names in the previously chosen language. Attributes keep their type for values such as integer number, floating point number or character string. Units for attributes with floating point numbers as values and standardized values from the data dictionary are stored as well. This process is called project preparation phase. Figure 3 demonstrates the process.

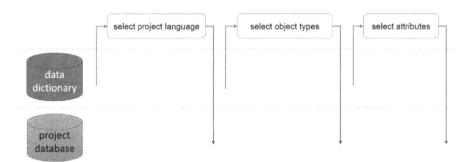

Fig. 3. Project preparation phase

The preparation phase is separated from the chosen BIM modeling software. At the beginning, these steps are platform-independent for every project, while later in the process, the modeling obviously differs depending on the specific BIM modeling software.

The definition of requirements follows the selection of attributes. This includes a specification of values for every selected attribute in every object in the BIM model. The values are stored in the project database. Figure 4 illustrates the modeling phase.

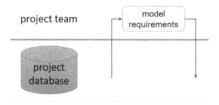

Fig. 4. Modeling phase

The specification of values is divided into two different attribute categories: either standardized values for the attribute exist or not. If there are standardized values, only a selection is possible, whereas without these standards every value is feasible, as long as it fits to the data type (floating point number, integer number, character strings).

Automatic Generation of Product Proposals. Based on the decisions in the modeling phase, an automatic proposal of products from different suppliers is possible. Every database bases on the data dictionary. Terms are explicit; this prevents redundancies and simplifies the product selection.

Two different kinds of teams are involved in this procedure: Firstly, the project team making the specifications that are stored in the project database. Secondly, the supplier team creates and updates the supplier database. Several supplier teams are possible.

Supplier teams propose products, based on the information in the project database. Afterwards, the project team can select products and store them in the project database. Figure 5 gives an overview of the process.

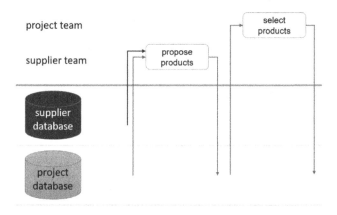

Fig. 5. Product selection

5   Prototype Implementation for Project Preparation and Modeling

This chapter presents a prototype implementation for the project preparation and the modeling phase using Autodesk Revit 2018.

The prototype uses as a basis the data dictionary, as described in Sect. 4.2. Revit is addressed through an add-in that uses the Revit API. A web service provides the connection between the data dictionary and the Revit add-in. In fact, the web service is a remote procedure call (RPC) that provides sequences, which are defined in Java and can be executed in the programming language of the add-in, C#. Thereby, it is possible to access the data dictionary (H2 database) via add-in. The only possible operation is to read data from the data dictionary; it is not possible to change the content of the dictionary through the add-in.

Every operation for the modeling phase is stored in the project database. The add-in accesses the project database the same way it does with the data dictionary. Differences to the data dictionary are functionalities to write, read and change data in this database. Java provides the needed operations for this, so the dictionary can be accessed through a RPC. Figure 6 illustrates the described schema.

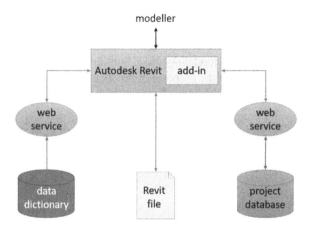

Fig. 6. Interaction between web services and add-in

The following processes all start with the launch of a new Revit file. The project preparation phase, which is theoretical platform-independent, is integrated in Revit to control every decision just with one tool. When starting a new Revit project, the add-in asks the user to select a language and object types. Both are stored in the database, as shown before in Fig. 3. The next step, called preparation phase for modeling with Revit, is to assign the object types to existing Revit categories. It is not possible to create additional categories via Revit API. However, it is possible to assign an object type to multiple categories. The mapping between object type and Revit category is stored in the project database.

The selection of the attributes follows the selection of the object type. The attributes are stored in the database and the add-in creates for every attribute a shared parameter in Revit. Afterwards, it creates a binding between the shared parameters and the categories, which is equivalent to the relation between attributes and object types. Figure 7 illustrates the procedure.

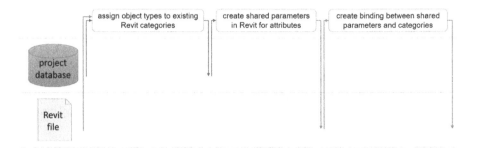

Fig. 7. Preparation phase for modeling with Autodesk Revit

After the preparation, the modeling phase in Revit begins. Every new placed object in the project leads to a new dialog from the add-in to store values for attributes. This dialog depends on if the category is assigned to an object type and stored in the database or not. The values, or precisely the requirements for the modelled object, are stored in the database as well as in the Revit file. Figure 8 shows the interaction between the database and the Revit file in the modeling phase. Subsequently, all needed data is stored in the project database, to make the proposal of products available in the next step.

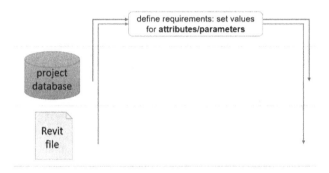

Fig. 8. Modeling phase with Autodesk Revit

6 Example

The following chapter demonstrates the in Sect. 5 described concept. The example shows the procedure by means of the object type "window".

First, there will be an overview of stored attributes in the data dictionary. The stored attributes are later used in the supplier database as well as in the project.

6.1 Attributes and Possible Values for Windows in the Data Dictionary

As described in Sect. 4.1, the database for the data dictionary stores object types, their attributes and, if existing, standardized values. Figure 9 shows a detail from the table for object types in the database. This example demonstrates the procedure from the data dictionary to a product proposal with three attributes: the thermal transmittance, the water tightness and the index for sound reduction. Figure 10 shows these attributes in the data dictionary.

⊞ UUID	⊞ ENGLISH
4db63cd4-ff35-4c64-a21b-3a5174ac0296	window
44073e26-22fd-47ed-9172-9a0309f20af1	door
80e06e32-f655-475e-b627-3eb3154b4f02	wall

Fig. 9. Detail from the table for object types in the data dictionary

⊞ UUID	⊞ ENGLISH	⊞ TYPEOFATTRIBUTE
3f19b2b7-c091-4bbb-b05b-46297b8146c5	thermal transmittance	attribute with double value
c7a8e475-985d-46b2-a2c4-67741e3f8e3a	sound reduction index	attribute with double value
390170e2-8283-4313-bee8-849c6f27d586	water tightness	attribute with string values

Fig. 10. Detail from the table for attributes in the data dictionary

The attribute "water tightness" has standardized values from standard DIN EN 12208 (DIN 2000). Figure 11 shows a detail from the stored standardized values.

⊞ UUIDATTRIBUTE	⊞ STANDARD	⊞ VALUE
390170e2-8283-4313-bee8-849c6f27d586	DIN EN	0
390170e2-8283-4313-bee8-849c6f27d586	DIN EN	1A
390170e2-8283-4313-bee8-849c6f27d586	DIN EN	1B
390170e2-8283-4313-bee8-849c6f27d586	DIN EN	2A
390170e2-8283-4313-bee8-849c6f27d586	DIN EN	2B
390170e2-8283-4313-bee8-849c6f27d586	DIN EN	3A
390170e2-8283-4313-bee8-849c6f27d586	DIN EN	3B
cc533600-2862-4c3a-bd07-323e9f3daf3e	EN	E 30
cc533600-2862-4c3a-bd07-323e9f3daf3e	EN	E 15

Fig. 11. Detail from the table for relations between attributes and standardized values

6.2   Products for Windows in a Supplier Database

To create a database with supplier product descriptions, it is necessary to use the data dictionary as a basis, as described in Sect. 4.1. After the selection of object types for a product description, follows a selection of attributes, which apply to the values of the product. The database stores the product description together with its assigned object type, as seen in Fig. 12.

Every product has attributes from the data dictionary and the database stores the values from the product, either chosen from the standardized values or selected by the supplier. Figure 13(a) shows the selected string values for this example, Fig. 13(b) shows floating point numbers.

⊞ UUID	⊞ ENGLISH	⊞ UUIDOBJECTTYPE	⊞ CREATOR
a0904c8a-72e2-440d-aa4a-9d2984b98503	Product A	4db63cd4-ff35-4c64-a21b-3a5174ac0296	supplier A
bfc85302-e3dc-436c-af64-0cac5ed1426b	Product B	4db63cd4-ff35-4c64-a21b-3a5174ac0296	supplier A
43698e36-61c8-4a63-b260-4e8eec1fea2d	Product C	4db63cd4-ff35-4c64-a21b-3a5174ac0296	supplier A

Fig. 12. Detail from the supplier database with products and their object types

(a)
⊞ UUIDPRODUCT	⊞ UUIDATTRIBUTE	⊞ VALUE
a0904c8a-72e2-440d-aa4a-9d2984b98503	390170e2-8283-4313-bee8-849c6f27d586	9A
bfc85302-e3dc-436c-af64-0cac5ed1426b	390170e2-8283-4313-bee8-849c6f27d586	9A
43698e36-61c8-4a63-b260-4e8eec1fea2d	390170e2-8283-4313-bee8-849c6f27d586	9A

(b)
⊞ UUIDPRODUCT	⊞ UUIDATTRIBUTE	⊞ VALUE
a0904c8a-72e2-440d-aa4a-9d2984b98503	3f19b2b7-c091-4bbb-b05b-46297b8146c5	1,2
a0904c8a-72e2-440d-aa4a-9d2984b98503	c7a8e475-985d-46b2-a2c4-67741e3f8e3a	41
bfc85302-e3dc-436c-af64-0cac5ed1426b	3f19b2b7-c091-4bbb-b05b-46297b8146c5	0,9
bfc85302-e3dc-436c-af64-0cac5ed1426b	c7a8e475-985d-46b2-a2c4-67741e3f8e3a	48
43698e36-61c8-4a63-b260-4e8eec1fea2d	3f19b2b7-c091-4bbb-b05b-46297b8146c5	0,92
43698e36-61c8-4a63-b260-4e8eec1fea2d	c7a8e475-985d-46b2-a2c4-67741e3f8e3a	45

Fig. 13. Selected values for the products

6.3 Modeling Phase

For preparing a modeling phase, it is necessary to start the web service. The next step is to open a new Revit file in the program.

After starting the preparation phase, the process follows the steps described in Sect. 4.2. It starts with the selection of the project language, which is English in this example. This is followed by the selection of the object types, in this example "window". The next dialog asks the user to choose attributes from the object type for the project.

Figure 14 shows the dialog windows for the described sequence. If the attribute has standardized values, an abbreviation of the used standard is part of the description, as shown in Fig. 14(c). It can happen that different standards standardize identical attributes. In this case, the data dictionary supports uses with these different standards. The users have to select a specific standard for their project. After the selection of the attributes, the user must assign the chosen object types to one or more Revit categories. Figure 15 shows the dialog window in Revit. In the background, the in Sect. 5 described procedure (creating shared parameters and bindings) is performed. This completes the project preparation phase with Revit.

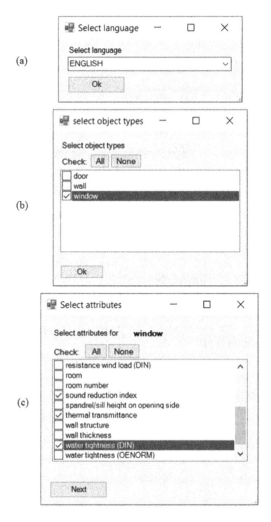

Fig. 14. Selection of language, object types and attributes in the project preparation

320 L. Böger et al.

Fig. 15. Assignment between object type and Revit category

In the modeling phase, the user chooses values as requirements for the objects. For every placed object in the Revit file that belongs to a category with an object type, a new dialog window appears. It contains all chosen attributes. The text field for the value gives the user an information about the kind of value that is demanded (integer number, floating point number, character string). If the attribute has standardized values, only a selection is possible. Figure 16 shows the dialog before the specification of a standardized value, Fig. 17 shows it afterwards.

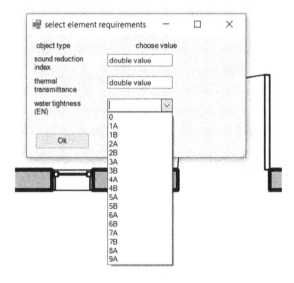

Fig. 16. Specification of requirements for the placed window in Revit

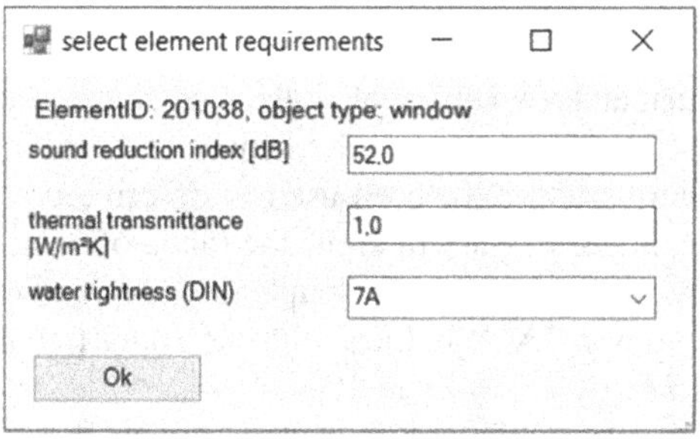

Fig. 17.   Chosen requirements for the placed window

The identifier (ID) of the Revit element is stored in the database, together with the values and their relation to the object. Figure 18(a) shows the six-digit ID in Revit for the placed window, Fig. 18(b) the relation between the object type and Fig. 18(c) the selected values.

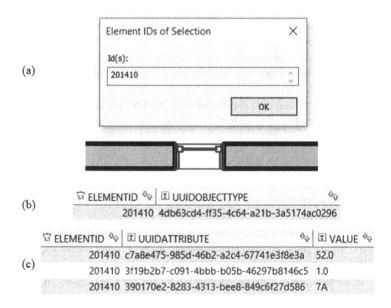

(a)

(b)

(c)

Fig. 18.   Interaction of identifiers in the project database

This must be done for every object in the Revit project. Of course, every object can have different values for the chosen attributes. If all objects including their attribute values are stored in the project database, the modeling phase concludes.

6.4   Product Proposals and Their Selections

The product proposal demands two different kinds of databases: a project and a supplier database. The terms used to specify the requirements and stored in the project database synchronize with the terms that have been used to describe products in the supplier database. At this point, it is necessary to know the range of values for every attribute. This can be illustrated with the presented example: the specified requirement for water tightness in the example was 7A. Windows with the water tightness 8A and 9A also fulfill the requirement 7A.

The example includes three different products. Products B and C fulfill the requirements from the project database, which leads to their proposal[2]. Subsequently the project team chooses one of these products.

7   Discussion

The presented approach relies on a correct and functional data dictionary. The development of buildingSMART for bSDD is far driven. However, there is still a lot of work to do; and it is a challenge to set up such a data dictionary for AEC sector. It makes no sense that individual countries develop such a dictionary. buildingSMART is international; and it can be the right organization to organize such a necessary development. Associations and standardization organizations from all over the world must contribute to such a data dictionary.

We tried to show the benefit of using data dictionary in the interaction of project work and suppliers for building materials and built-in components. The example is simplified. We know that real projects require much more attributes to describe requirements.

Using such an approach in real projects requires a rethinking of the use of standards in this field. It is necessary to use standardized data structures for data exchange; but without coordinated terms, evaluation of digital models by different persons for different applications is not possible.

Another challenge will be the organization of such a data dictionary. Terms defined in the data dictionary must be understandable by users. Project preparation phases do have a significant influence on the entire project. At present time, we discuss the necessity of BIM execution plans; and the selection of terms must be an integral part of these plans.

We showed the functioning using Autodesk Revit as a BIM modeling software. Other modeling software can be integrated. The concept itself is not restricted to a specific modeling software as long as objects have identifiers and attributes can be assigned to objects.

---

[2] **Requirements**: sound reduction index: 52.0 dB, thermal transmittance: 1.0 W/m²K, water tightness: 7A; **Product A**: sound reduction index: 41.0 dB, thermal transmittance: 1.2 W/m²K, water tightness: 9A; **Product B**: sound reduction index: 48.0 dB, thermal transmittance: 0.9 W/m²K, water tightness: 9A; **Product C**: sound reduction index: 45.0 dB, thermal transmittance: 0.92 W/m²K, water tightness: 9A.

We are convinced that such an approach cannot solve all problems. The presented prototype addresses only semantical data. The need to exchange geometry still exists. Therefore, data dictionaries will not replace data exchange; but they can improve the efficiency in the AEC sector. Coordinated terms facilitate the communication between project participants. They can simplify processes that rely on explicit terms, such as choosing attributes for objects and they can be used in algorithms replacing error-prone human work by the work of computers.

8 Summary and Outlook

The described concept bases on a data dictionary that is reliable and up-to-date. Object types and attributes are reduced to only one name per language, which simplifies the structure. To improve the selection of values, the data dictionary stores standardized values as well.

Supplier use this dictionary and create their own database based upon them. Suppliers adopt standardized values, while they can also chose other values independently. The project starts with a preparation phase to select object types and attributes from the data dictionary. In the modeling phase, the project team specifies requirements, which eventually lead to product proposals based on the databases of suppliers after completion of the modeling. The next step is to create an automation for product proposals to facilitate this process.

The definition of explicit terms for an interorganizational collaboration is essential to create a seamless flow between the phases of a project. The described procedure shall improve the process between preparation, modeling and product selection. Thereby, it is possible to reduce mistakes and redundancies in the process, which leads to a more effective way to finish projects in the AEC industry.

The example presented in this paper is simple. In our next steps, we want to expand the use of a data dictionary to more types of objects, more attributes, and more standards and accepted technical regulations. Further developments are necessary to support the selection of product proposals in a more sophisticated way. This is especially true to the selection of products. The future will show whether approaches such as the presented prototype will influence the AEC sector so that we can benefit from the use of coordinated terms in our field.

Acknowledgements. The authors thank Eric Robaszewski. He implemented the add-in for Revit as part of his student research project "Standardisierte Bezeichnungen für Objekttypen und Attribute als Grundlage zur Zusammenarbeit zwischen Planung und Ausführung" at Technische Universität Berlin.

References

About OmniClass. http://www.omniclass.org/about/. Accessed 11 Jan 2018
b.i.m.m. about freeBIM Tirol. https://bimm.eu/portfolio-posts/freebim-tirol/. Accessed 10 Jan 2018

Belsky, M., Sacks, R., Brilakis, I.: Semantic enrichment for building information modeling. Comput.-Aided Civ. Infrastruct. Eng. **31**, 261–274 (2016)

Borrmann, A., König, M., Koch, C., Beetz, J.: Building Information Modeling – Technologi- sche Grundlagen und industrielle Praxis. Springer Vieweg, Wiesbaden (2015)

buildingSMART Data Dictionary Homepage. https://www.buildingsmart.org/standards/standa rds-tools-services/data-dictionary/. Accessed 10 Jan 2018

buildingSMART Homepage. https://www.buildingsmart.org/. Accessed 10 Jan 2018

dBeaver Homepage. https://dbeaver.jkiss.org/. Accessed 11 Jan 2018

De Nicola, A., Missikoff, M., Navigli, R.: A software engineering approach to ontology building. Inf. Syst. **35**, 258–275 (2009)

DIN: Deutsches Institut für Normung e.V. DIN EN 12208. https://www.beuth.de/de/norm/din-en-12208/23757934. Accessed 13 Jan 2018 (2000)

DIN: Deutsches Institut für Normung e.V. DIN EN ISO 16739. https://www.beuth.de/de/norm/din-en-iso-16739/263869392. Accessed 10 Jan 2018 (2017)

Eastman, C.E., Jeong, Y.-S., Sacks, R., Kaner, I.: Exchange model and exchange object concepts for implementation of national bim standards. J. Comput. Civ. Eng. **24**(1), 25–34 (2010)

eCl@ss Homepage. https://www.eclass.eu/. Accessed 11 Jan 2018

ETIM international Homepage. https://www.etim-international.com/. Accessed 11 Jan 2018

freeBIM Merkmalsserver. http://www.freebim.at/Info_2016. Accessed 10 Jan 2018

freeBIM project description. http://www.freebim.at/Beschreibung_2016/. Accessed 10 Jan 2018

Gruber, T.R.: A translation approach to portable ontology specifications. Knowl. Acquisit. **5**(2), 199–220 (1993)

H2 Database Homepage. http://www.h2database.com/html/main.html. Accessed 11 Jan 2018

ISO: International Organization for Standardization ISO 10303-11 (2004). https://www.iso.org/standard/38047.html. Accessed 10 Jan 2018

Laakso, M., Kiviniemi, A.: A review of IFC Standardization – interoperability through complementary development approaches. In: CIB W078 2011 Conference, Sophia Antipolis, France (2011)

Laakso, M., Kiviniemi, A.: The IFC standard – a review of history, development and standardization. J. Inf. Technol. Constr. **17**, 134–161 (2012)

OmniClass Homepage. http://www.omniclass.org/. Accessed 11 Jan 2018

Rezgui, Y., Hopfe, C.J., Vorakulpipat, C.: Generations of knowledge management in the architecture, engineering and construction industry: an evolutionary perspective. Adv. Eng. Inform. **24**, 219–228 (2010)

Terkaj, W., Šojić, A.: Ontology-based representation of IFC EXPRESS rules: an enhancement of the ifcOWL ontology. Autom. Constr. **57**, 188–201 (2015)

van Berlo, L.A.H.M., Beetz, J., Bos, P., Hendriks, H., van Tongeren, R.C.J.: Collaborative engineering with IFC: new insights and technology. In: Gudnason, G., Scherer, R. (eds.) 9th European Conference on Product and Process Modelling, pp. 811–818. Routledge, United Kingdom (2012)

W3C Homepage. https://www.w3.org/. Accessed 15 Jan 2018

The Emulation and Simulation of Internet of Things Devices for Building Information Modelling (BIM)

Steven Arthur[✉], Haijiang Li, and Robert Lark

School of Engineering, Cardiff University, 14-17 The Parade, Cardiff CF24 3AA, UK
{arthurs,lih,lark}@cardiff.ac.uk

Abstract. The most significant recent development in the AEC industry has been the adoption of Building Information Modelling (BIM), but its full potential is far from being fully exploited. The Internet of Things (IoT) provides a rich source of new data for BIM. BIM can provide a framework for the organization and analysis of IoT data. Each IoT solution can require thousands of sensors creating a continuous stream of varied data.

A connection between BIM and the IoT throughout the lifecycle would result in many new possibilities. This paper examines emulating or simulating large numbers of IoT devices to explore the potential of effectively linking BIM with the IoT.

With emulation, the complete outwardly observable behavior of real historical IoT devices is mimicked and matched. The alternative to emulation is simulation where an abstract model of the IoT network is created programmatically using rules.

Emulating and simulating devices reduces the barriers to carrying out the development required to enable BIM to utilize the full potential of the IoT.

Keywords: BIM · IoT · Simulation · Emulation
Building Information Modelling · Internet of Things

1   Introduction

Many industries have been changed, created or have even disappeared because of disruptive technology. Travel, journalism, television, music, advertising and many more have been fundamentally changed. The history and status quo of the AEC domain is very different.

The AEC industry has been slow to adapt to technological change, resulting in stagnation or even decline over the last 40 years [1]. Many factors have slowed the adoption of new technology. There is a great amount of fragmentation in the AEC industry [2] and a large project could involve dozens of subcontractors, architectural and engineering firms, managers, etc. Furthermore, the parties involved vary from project to project which makes it difficult to develop systems which persist. Competition in the industry creates a disincentive to invest in expensive new technology when working on any one project despite long-term advantages. Other factors include concerns about the benefits

© Springer International Publishing AG, part of Springer Nature 2018
I. F. C. Smith and B. Domer (Eds.): EG-ICE 2018, LNCS 10864, pp. 325–338, 2018.
https://doi.org/10.1007/978-3-319-91638-5_18

being too small to justify the initial costs and a conservative approach from senior leadership [3]. The purpose of this research is to lower the barriers to implementing IoT technology by using emulation and simulation.

The situation in relation to technological inertia is slowly beginning to change. The most significant recent development has been the adoption of BIM, a digital representation of the physical and functional characteristics of buildings or infrastructure. The first steps came in the 1970s with Computer-Aided Design (CAD). In 2002, Autodesk released a paper entitled "Building Information Modelling" [4] and BIM has been central to technological change in the industry since. The full potential of BIM is far from being fully exploited. Data is either not collected from potential sources or the expertise is not available to make use of it. More projects would benefit from making use of new software, mobile devices, the Internet and sensors.

Undertaking BIM research using the required number of IoT devices is limited by the vast practical challenges and cost involved. This paper examines application-focused methodologies for emulating or simulating large numbers of IoT devices. This can enable greater exploration of the potential of effectively linking BIM with the IoT.

1.1 Building Information Modelling (BIM)

At its core, BIM is a standardized digital representation of a built asset (such as a building or bridge). This contains data and information linking to spatial relationships, geographic information and properties of building components (e.g. the materials used). More importantly, BIM is a process of standardization, sharing structured data and managing all the data associated with a building from conception to demolition. With the model at the center, the aim is for all parties to collaborate on the same rich pool of data, but this has not yet been fully achieved. The current situation results in untapped insights from potentially rich data sources.

BIM has opened the AEC domain to the possibilities of technological change but the scale of the data, required integration of autonomously orchestrated processes, need for seamless collaborative networking and required data intelligence demand new solutions. Fulfilling the potential of BIM will require the leveraging of new technology. Those that embrace technological change can reap the benefits and become more competitive, as has happened in many other industries.

The adoption of BIM can result in a significant reduction in costs over the lifecycle of a project by detecting issues (such as clashes) early on. Combined with reduced completion times, improved buildings and better safety, the case for adopting BIM is overwhelming and BIM is gaining traction across the world. BIM has been mandatory for all public-sector projects in the UK since April 2016 [5].

Currently, the preconstruction stages widely adopt BIM but it is used progressively less in the later stages of the lifecycle [6]. The BIM Maturity Model has three levels [7]. Up to Maturity Level 2 is very well defined but Level 3 is under development. To implement BIM up to Level 3 requires integrated BIM (iBIM) and Lifecycle Management in order to take advantage of the rich information provided by BIMs [8, 9]. The BIM guidelines do not specify a methodology for adapting or incorporating BIMs in an operational built environment. Integrating the IoT with BIM would help to achieve BIM Level 3.

1.2   The Internet of Things

The Internet of Things (IoT) consists of sensors and other devices which send and receive live data via the Internet or other networks. Radio frequency identification (RFID) tags can be embedded in real world devices and monitored remotely. The term the Internet of Things was first used by Kevin Ashton in 1999 [10] but is now widespread. The IoT market is predicted to reach $267 billion by 2020 [11] with a total of 20 billion devices by the same year [12].

1.3   Connecting BIM and the IoT

This paper looks at emulating and simulating IoT devices to make it more practical and efficient to research the integration of BIM and the IoT. Several approaches have already been proposed to make the actual connection between BIM and real-time data [13–15]. Although making this connection isn't the focus of this paper, it would be useful to briefly explore how this connection can be made.

Current approaches to combining sensor data with BIMs reported in the literature are theoretical or apply only to very specific domains. Some advances, such as the proposed Building Information Modelling Sensor Language (BIMSL) [16] have contributed to the effort. There are many alternative sensor data markup languages such as SensorML and future research could explore the most efficient way to integrate the dynamic data.

Research into making the connection between BIM and the IoT often builds on what is already available. Currently, facility managers use Building Management Systems (BMS). A BMS is a computer-based control system installed in buildings that controls and monitors the building's mechanical and electrical equipment. It is logical to combine BIMs with the existing BMS to improve their functionality (which includes planning maintenance, assessing the safety of the environment and improving operability). The data from the BMS can be hosted in the cloud by connecting the BMS to the Internet. This would make the BMS a part of the IoT. One advantage of using the cloud is that it allows for multi-tenancy, enabling resources to be shared across multiple users. Khalid et al. [17] introduces the idea of information-rich BIMs providing real-time information through BMS instead of the static information normally associated with them. This enables facility managers to better interact with the built environment in real-time.

Pasini et al. [18] presented a framework for managing information in the operational stage of buildings. Different sources of data collected in real-time were integrated into the BIM process by extending the interoperable and neutral schema of IFC. The IFC (Industry Foundation Classes) specification is an open data format used widely throughout BIM applications. BIMs are populated using data gathered through remote sensors. This data determines parameters in BIMs, changes parameters and possibly even modifies models. A converter was developed to constantly access the data through web services and output it into the IFC format.

The techniques described in this subsection are intended for physical devices. This paper will look at emulating/simulating these devices with virtual devices which other systems (such as a BMS) will be unable to differentiate from the real thing.

2   Methods

The tools for emulation and simulation are hosted using a combination of on-site hardware and Microsoft Azure in the cloud. Microsoft Azure is a set of cloud services that developers use to build, deploy and manage applications. The advantages of using on-site hardware include privacy, control and no usage charges. The on-site hardware used includes three Intel i7 computers each with 4 cores, 64 GB RAM and 4 TB of storage. All computers were running Windows Server 2016.

For emulation a combination of SQL Server, Enzo Unified and Azure IoT Hub were used. For simulation a combination of Contiki, Cooja and VMware were used.

2.1   Tools Used for Emulation

Enzo Unified and SQL Server. Enzo Unified is a Data as a Service Platform that can be used with SQL Server for the emulation of live IoT networks [19]. Enzo Unified facilitates communication between SQL Server and Azure IoT Hub. Enzo Unified allows the virtual connection of IoT devices to emulate scenarios quickly, securely and with resiliency. Its features include messaging for specific IoT detection events, cross IoT device communication and logging asynchronously.

Enzo Unified abstracts the underlying cloud APIs, allowing T-SQL (Microsoft's proprietary extension to SQL) commands to be executed against a scalable IoT cloud platform such as Azure IoT Hub as shown in Fig. 1.

Fig. 1. Enzo Unified facilitates communication between T-SQL and Azure IoT Hub [19].

The emulated devices are indistinguishable from real devices and thousands or even millions of them can be connected, monitored and managed.

Enzo Unified can be run on a server or IoT simulations can be created using REST commands from an Internet browser using Enzo Online. Enzo Online is an HTTP Protocol Bridge with all functionality in the cloud as a service. Enzo Online has the advantage that services can be configured once and reused from any language/platform through HTTPS calls.

Enzo Unified serves as the bridge between SQL Server and the Azure IoT Hub environment by allowing SQL Server to send test messages to Azure IoT Hub.

Azure IoT Hub. Azure IoT Hub is a service provided by Microsoft to implement IoT solutions. The advantages of Azure IoT Hub include its scalability, multiple communication options, extensive device libraries and seamless integration with Azure Stream Analytics (to carry out powerful real-time analytics of the data stream). This research was awarded a Microsoft Azure Research Award which was used to pay for the Azure services but there are also free alternatives to Azure IoT Hub such as Apache Nifi. The data collected in the Azure IoT Hub can be analyzed using other Azure tools such as Stream Analytics or Azure Machine Learning Studio.

Azure IoT Hub receives data from IoT devices (or virtual IoT devices in this case) to facilitate further actions or analysis. It therefore acts as a proxy for a BMS in this research.

2.2   Tools Used for Simulation

Contiki and VMware. Contiki is a popular open-source operating system used for the IoT. It connects IoT microcontrollers to the Internet and is a powerful toolbox for building complex wireless systems. Contiki fully supports standard IPv6 and IPv4 for Internet-enabled devices to communicate. It also supports recent low-power wireless standards such as RPL, 6lowpan and CoAP [20]. It has a high degree of performance and security, making it an ideal operating system for the IoT.

Instant Contiki has been used for this research. Instant Contiki is an Ubuntu Linux virtual machine that runs in VMWare player and has Contiki and all the development tools, compilers and Cooja installed for convenience.

Cooja. The programming on Contiki is performed using Cooja. Cooja is a network simulator that can be used to simulate large or small networks of Contiki motes. Motes are the RFID microcontrollers, sensors and any other wireless devices that are connected and must communicate over the IoT. The base libraries of IoT microcontrollers and sensors are available in the C programming language and can be imported. Virtual IoT devices can be programmed, controlled and monitored with back-end C programs to get the desired results.

In this research Cooja is used for simulation purposes but it can be used for physical sensors as well. A great advantage of using Cooja for simulation is that the motes use the same firmware as actual physical devices [21]. Virtual motes can be imported in the simulation area so that they can be viewed and analyzed.

Sink motes (which receive incoming events from another object) and sender motes (which send events) can be simulated. When the simulation is complete, the overall activities carried out during the simulations can be analyzed. Cooja produces log data, charts, visual representations and tables to facilitate analysis. Data can also be copied or exported for further analysis using data mining and machine learning tools.

3   Implementation

The emulation/simulation implementations are described separately in the next subsections and discussed further in Sect. 4.

3.1 Emulation Implementation

For the emulation of IoT devices, an example building with eight temperature sensors and four humidity sensors was used. The devices were first created using T-SQL. A full list of the twelve sensors created is shown in Fig. 2.

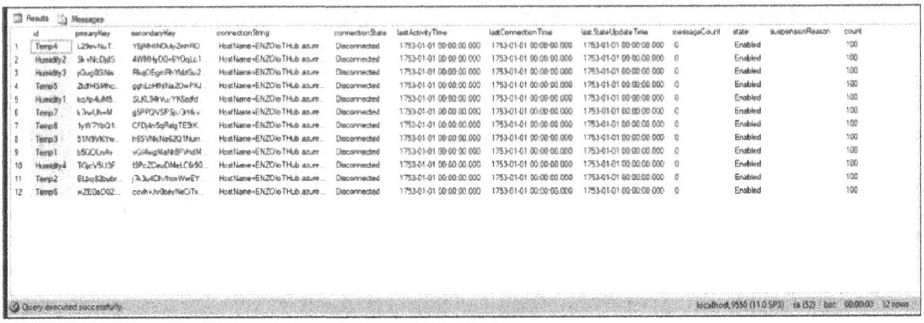

	id	primaryKey	secondaryKey	connectionString	connectionState	lastActivityTime	lastConnectionTime	lastStateUpdateTime	messageCount	state	suspensionReason	count
1	Temp4	L29evNuT...	YEjMHtNOuyZmhRO...	HostName=ENZOIoTHub.azure...	Disconnected	1753-01-01 00:00:00.000	1753-01-01 00:00:00.000	1753-01-01 00:00:00.000	0	Enabled		100
2	Humidity2	Sk+NcDjdS...	4WMHyD0+6YOqLc1...	HostName=ENZOIoTHub.azure...	Disconnected	1753-01-01 00:00:00.000	1753-01-01 00:00:00.000	1753-01-01 00:00:00.000	0	Enabled		100
3	Humidity3	yGug0GNs...	RkqOEgnRhYldzGu2...	HostName=ENZOIoTHub.azure...	Disconnected	1753-01-01 00:00:00.000	1753-01-01 00:00:00.000	1753-01-01 00:00:00.000	0	Enabled		100
4	Temp5	ZbdHSMhc...	gghLcHfhINa2OwPXJ...	HostName=ENZOIoTHub.azure...	Disconnected	1753-01-01 00:00:00.000	1753-01-01 00:00:00.000	1753-01-01 00:00:00.000	0	Enabled		100
5	Humidity1	koXp4uM5...	SUKL94tVu/YKSzdfd...	HostName=ENZOIoTHub.azure...	Disconnected	1753-01-01 00:00:00.000	1753-01-01 00:00:00.000	1753-01-01 00:00:00.000	0	Enabled		100
6	Temp7	k7rwUh+M...	g5PPQVSPSp/3Hkv...	HostName=ENZOIoTHub.azure...	Disconnected	1753-01-01 00:00:00.000	1753-01-01 00:00:00.000	1753-01-01 00:00:00.000	0	Enabled		100
7	Temp8	1yW7YbQ1...	CFDj4n5qRelgTE3tK...	HostName=ENZOIoTHub.azure...	Disconnected	1753-01-01 00:00:00.000	1753-01-01 00:00:00.000	1753-01-01 00:00:00.000	0	Enabled		100
8	Temp3	51N9VKYw...	h6SVNkNa62Q1Num...	HostName=ENZOIoTHub.azure...	Disconnected	1753-01-01 00:00:00.000	1753-01-01 00:00:00.000	1753-01-01 00:00:00.000	0	Enabled		100
9	Temp1	b5GOLnAv...	vGi4wgMaNbBFVndM...	HostName=ENZOIoTHub.azure...	Disconnected	1753-01-01 00:00:00.000	1753-01-01 00:00:00.000	1753-01-01 00:00:00.000	0	Enabled		100
10	Humidity4	TGjcV5U3F...	t9PcZCeuDMeLC6r90...	HostName=ENZOIoTHub.azure...	Disconnected	1753-01-01 00:00:00.000	1753-01-01 00:00:00.000	1753-01-01 00:00:00.000	0	Enabled		100
11	Temp2	ELbo82bubr...	j7k3u4Dh/hoxWwEY...	HostName=ENZOIoTHub.azure...	Disconnected	1753-01-01 00:00:00.000	1753-01-01 00:00:00.000	1753-01-01 00:00:00.000	0	Enabled		100
12	Temp6	wZE0aDQ2...	covh+Jv9beyNeCiTx...	HostName=ENZOIoTHub.azure...	Disconnected	1753-01-01 00:00:00.000	1753-01-01 00:00:00.000	1753-01-01 00:00:00.000	0	Enabled		100

Fig. 2. The twelve devices available in Azure IoT Hub.

For emulation, the data can come from whatever source is suitable e.g. historical data from similar sensors/scenarios. Whatever data source is used, the data can be used to populate the relevant T-SQL commands. The statement shown below sends dummy data to Azure IoT Hub from the eight virtual temperature sensors.

```
EXEC bsc.AzureIoTHub.SendTestData
    2400,
    60000,
    'Temp1,Temp2,Temp3,Temp4,Temp5,Temp6,Temp7,Temp8',
    '{"deviceId":"#deviceid()",
    "location":"BIMBuilding1",
    "measurementValue":#rnddouble(0,35),
    "measurementType":"temperature",
    "localTimestamp":"#utcnow()"}'
```

Each temperature sensor sends 300 messages (i.e. 2400 in total) at 60,000 ms (i.e. 1 min) intervals. Each message contains the ID of the device, a random temperature in the range of 0–35 °C, the measurement type (i.e. temperature) and the timestamp. Time stamping is important for event detection & sequencing and can also be used for post event analysis. A sample of the temperature messages is shown in Fig. 3.

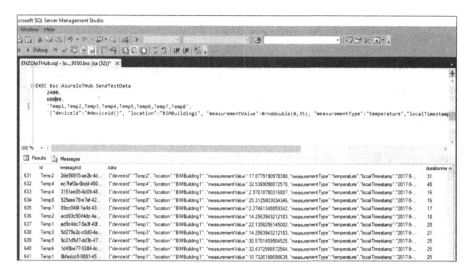

Fig. 3. Sample of messages sent from virtual temperature sensors.

A similar statement sent 300 messages data from each of the four humidity sensors (1200 in total) but this time with a measurement type of humidity in the range of 0–100%. The statement is shown below.

```
EXEC bsc.AzureIoTHub.SendTestData
    1200,
    60000,
    'Humidity1,Humidity2,Humidity3,Humidity4',
    '{"deviceId":"#deviceid()",
    "location":"BIMBuilding1",
    "measurementValue":#rnddouble(0,100),
    "measurementType":"humidity",
    "localTimestamp":"#utcnow()"}'
```

A sample of the 1200 humidity messages is shown in Fig. 4.

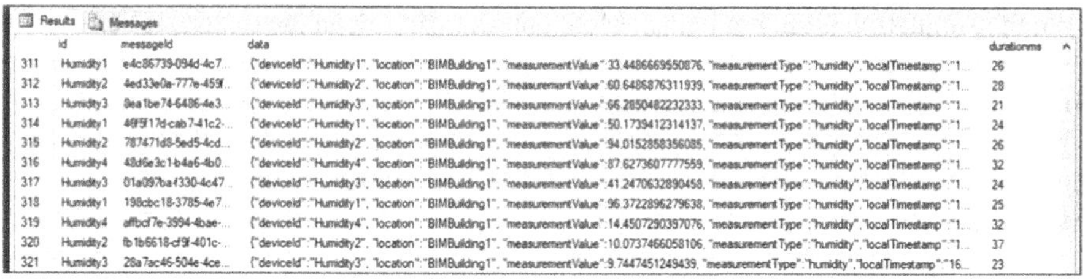

Fig. 4. Sample of messages sent from virtual humidity sensors.

The 3600 messages sent from the 12 devices are now available in the Azure IoT Hub for further analytics as shown in Fig. 5.

Fig. 5. Messages and devices displayed in Azure IoT Hub.

3.2 Simulation Implementation

Cooja is used to simulate a small network of Contiki motes (i.e. devices). A new simulation was created with the relevant building area and radio medium (UDGM) being specified. The simulation was carried out in a virtual building with dimensions of 100 m × 100 m. A sink mote (to receive events) and the sender motes (i.e. the devices) were then set up. As with the emulation implementation, twelve devices were created in total (eight temperature sensors and four humidity sensors). The simulation interface is shown in Fig. 6.

The simulation can be run in real-time or speeded up for convenience. The output from the simulation is shown in the "Mote output" window in the top right. Scripts can be used to control the simulation and change parameters such as the duration of the simulation – a sample script is shown in the "Simulation script area" in the middle. A whole range of statistics and data about the simulation are available in the "Sensor Data Collect with Contiki" window on the right. These statistics for each mote include Average Power Consumption, Temperature, Humidity, Network Hops, Latency etc. A timeline of all the activity during the simulation is shown in the "Timeline" window at the bottom. The "Network" window on the left is shown in more detail in Fig. 7.

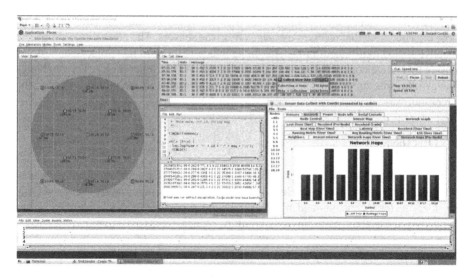

Fig. 6. Simulation interface in Cooja.

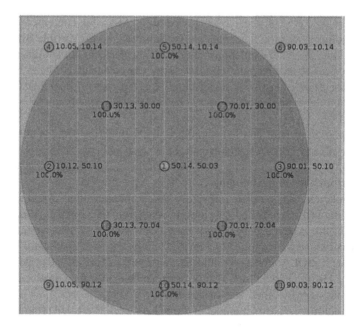

Fig. 7. Animated network visualization in Cooja.

For the duration of the simulation the "Network" window shows an animation of the simulation in real-time (or speeded up if preferred). The building is 100 m × 100 m with the right-hand wall shown as a dark grey line in the "Network" window. Each small square represents an area of 10 m x 10 m. The position of each mote is shown next to it. The temperature sensors are shown in yellow (motes 4, 5, 6, 2, 3, 9, 10 and 11) and the humidity sensors are shown in purple (motes 13, 17, 16 and 18). The central blue mote is a sink mote that receives messages from the sensors. The green circle shows the effective radio environment of the sink mote which helps with mote placement. Motes outside this range communicate with the sink mote via the other motes. The blue lines between the sink mote and sensors shows the radio traffic at the moment in time the screenshot was taken.

4 Discussion

New Technologies are increasingly affecting the AEC industry and modifying the way buildings are conceived and developed [18]. Buildings are increasingly seen as service providers to the occupants and not just financial products. Indeed, stakeholders are demanding these changes to improve comfort, reduce energy consumption and maximize performance. Information collected using the IoT can inform stakeholders about the buildings themselves and the behavior of the occupants. The behavior predicted by emulation and simulation can be correlated with real measurement leading to ongoing improvements.

Developing BIM practices and technologies can improve the connection of virtual BIMs with the delivered physical assets in operation. Modeling combined with emulation/simulation provides the fundamentals for designing highly flexible BIMs that can evolve over time. With the emulations/simulations in place, additional services such as cognitive services & face recognition for security can be added. BIM can be used as a framework for establishing how devices are expected to work together. Monitoring variations from the expected behavior can help identify device issues or maintenance requirements.

The integration of BIM and IoT simplifies the engineering process underlying the combination of sensor data with the physical elements and constructive characteristics of the building. It enables a comparison between the measured performance with the expected performance of the building.

With emulation, the complete outwardly observable behavior of real existing IoT devices is mimicked and matched. The message data from the virtual devices is received by Azure IoT Hub, which behaves as if the devices were virtual. This would also be the case if this technique were applied to a BMS. Dummy data was used in this implementation, but the T-SQL statements could be generated in various ways depending on requirements. Historical data from real sensors can be read from a database to recreate different scenarios or modified versions of them.

With simulation, an abstract model of the IoT network is created programmatically using rules, random generation or a mixture of the two. Using this method, various real IoT devices can be simulated as well as their interaction with each other. The simulation is a good approximation because the same firmware is used on the virtual devices as the real ones. Simulations can help establish where sensors should be placed, which are the best sensors to use, how to maximize the cost-effectiveness of achieving a certain result and what problems may occur.

Various scenarios can be emulated/simulated to narrow down to a few options which could be validated in the field to determine the best one. The accuracy and completeness of the data can then be rigorously validated and checked by an expert.

4.1 The Benefits of Bringing BIM and the IoT Together

The IoT provides a rich source of new data for BIM. Data that comes from BIMs (such as spatial and component data) can provide a framework for the organization and analysis of IoT data in a way that is useful for the operation of a building [22].

The IoT, BIM (buildings and infrastructure) and Data Analytics complement each other with the IoT providing a continuous stream of varied data. Big Data from the IoT (traffic congestion, energy consumption, pressure readings from a bridge etc.) can be collected and analyzed to optimize decision-making and boost operational efficiency. Rather than being archived or just used for its immediate purpose, data coming from apparently unrelated systems can provide valuable, unique and actionable insights using machine learning or Big Data Analytics. Stream Analytics can be used to provide useful insights from live IoT data in real-time (e.g. checking for the deterioration of a bridge), allowing predictive maintenance [1] and the detection of problems in advance. This not only offers obvious safety benefits but can also help to reduce costs. Parts can be replaced when required instead of at set intervals based on a worst-case scenario.

The huge amount of IoT data that will increasingly be generated by buildings and infrastructure means that they can provide services [18]. Integrating BIM and the IoT will enhance functionality and asset tracking in the operations stage, and help to move toward cognitive buildings. Collaboration between projects increases the data available and the potential for even deeper insights. IoT data from whole districts or even entire Smart Cities can be analyzed together for insights into urban planning, weather, traffic, fire, etc.

Connecting any asset, machine, system or site to the Internet has an almost limitless range of BIM uses throughout the lifecycle. These include measuring and enhancing facility performance, automation and control, improving safety, energy management, optimizing inventories and security [1].

Live data (from environmental controls, wireless assets, building control/monitoring systems, etc.) can be collected throughout the lifecycle of a building and used to measure and improve comfort and facility performance. Identifying problems early can result in huge savings. The IoT could save $1 trillion dollars a year in maintenance, services and consumables by 2022 [23]. Types of sensors include environmental controls, building equipment, cameras, water and waste, environmental protection, smart electricity grid access, wireless assets, power, building control/monitoring system, access control, mobile tools and lighting.

A relationship between the BIMs and associated IoT devices throughout the lifecycle would result in many new possibilities. For example, design and construction alliances could be partially paid on the basis of the performance of a building over the lifecycle using data supplied by IoT sensors and adjudicated by smart contracts [24].

Tender systems could also be based on "Value" rather than lowest price. This value proposition can extend into the life cycle of the building with a new funding model for design and construction. A contract could carry over into post occupancy, delivering reward based on data supplied by IoT sensors and adjudicated by smart contracts. For example, remaining payments could be based on energy performance.

4.2   Why Emulate/Simulate?

Emulation/simulation of IoT networks can be used for modeling or proof of concept. Emulation (using Enzo Unified) or simulation (using Cooja) can be used to test different scenarios when the resources required to test combinations of real devices would be prohibitive. Emulation/simulation can be used to inform decisions before implementing the chosen option in the field.

The Architecture for BIM-IoT Emulation/Simulation/Implementation is shown in Fig. 8.

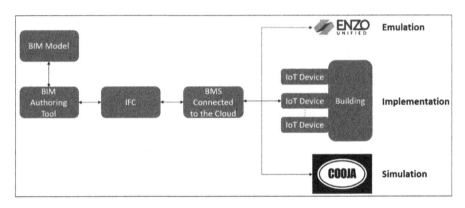

Fig. 8. BIM-IoT simulation architecture.

The BMS receives data from either a field implementation, emulation or simulation and behaves in the same way regardless of the source of the data. Emulating and simulating devices reduces the barriers to carrying out the development required to enable BIM to utilize the full potential of the IoT.

Although various research into linking BIM and the IoT have been discussed in this paper, they have often not been validated practically because of the associated challenges or are specific to certain domains. Emulation/simulation can help to address both issues. Although practical validation on a small scale is desirable, emulation and simulation enable validation of concepts on a scale that may not be possible using real devices because of resource limitations. Emulation and simulation paradigms can also be modified to suit different scenarios and devices relatively easily.

5   Conclusion and Future Work

The IoT will undoubtedly play an important role in the future of the AEC industry. Architects, Engineers, operators and owners of built assets will all want to harness all available information to generate insight that they can use to become more efficient, save money and make peoples' lives better. This article has explored emulating or simulating IoT devices for BIM to bring this about.

It has been demonstrated that devices can be emulated using T-SQL statements combined with a Data as a Service Platform such as Enzo Unified. Devices can also be simulated using tools such as the IoT operating system Contiki combined with a network simulator such as Cooja. As IoT devices proliferate and BIM is embraced, tools such as these will be required to ensure the connection of these important technologies isn't impeded.

There is a great deal of scope for future work. Further development will enable historical data from real devices to be read from a database for emulation. Simulations must be made more elaborate and reproduce real-life scenarios. The results of emulation and simulation must be validated against real devices in the field and improved as necessary. Multiple building and infrastructure projects could be considered simultaneously. IoT data from whole districts or even entire Smart Cities can be analyzed together for insights into urban planning, weather, traffic, fire, etc. Big Data Analytics and powerful hardware would be required for the consideration of an entire city [25].

There will be ongoing hurdles to overcome. There will be compatibility issues between the disparate technologies and in the AEC domain there is still a lingering resistance to change. However, these issues have been common in other fields and have been overcome as change was embraced. With determination, this can be overcome as the long-term advantages become irresistible. Emulation and simulation can help to lower the barriers and enable the required development of BIM-IoT integration.

References

1. Castagnino, S.: What's the future of the construction industry?—World Economic Forum. https://www.weforum.org/agenda/2016/04/building-in-the-fourth-industrial-revolution/
2. Weippert, A., Kajewski, S.L.: AEC industry culture: a need for change. In: CIB World Building Congress 2004, Building for the Future, pp. 1–10 (2004)
3. Migilinskas, D., Popov, V., Juocevicius, V., Ustinovichius, L.: The benefits, obstacles and problems of practical bim implementation. Procedia Eng. 57, 767–774 (2013)
4. Autodesk: AUTODESK ® REVIT ® WHITE PAPER Building Information Modeling for Sustainable Design. Autodesk Revit White Pap. (2005)
5. Designing Buildings Wiki: Federated building information model - Designing Buildings Wiki. https://www.designingbuildings.co.uk/wiki/Federated_building_information_model
6. Bilal, M., Oyedele, L.O., Qadir, J., Munir, K., Ajayi, S.O., Akinade, O.O., Owolabi, H.A., Alaka, H.A., Pasha, M.: Big data in the construction industry: a review of present status, opportunities, and future trends. Adv. Eng. Inform. 30, 500–521 (2016)
7. BIM Level 2. http://bim-level2.org/en/
8. Motawa, I., Almarshad, A.: Case-based reasoning and BIM systems for asset management. Built Environ. Proj. Asset Manag. 5, 233–247 (2015)
9. Harty, J., Kouider, T., Paterson, G.: Getting to grips with BIM: a guide for small and medium-sized architecture, engineering and construction firms
10. Gaurav, K.: Programming Internet of Things using Contiki and Cooja - Open Source for You. http://opensourceforu.com/2017/06/programming-internet-things-using-contiki-cooja/

11. Columbus, L.: Internet of Things Market to Reach $267B by 2020. https://www.forbes.com/sites/louiscolumbus/2017/01/29/internet-of-things-market-to-reach-267b-by-2020/#1a20c7cb609b
12. Tung, L.: IoT devices will outnumber the world's population this year for the first time—ZDNet. http://www.zdnet.com/article/iot-devices-will-outnumber-the-worlds-population-this-year-for-the-first-time/
13. Riaz, Z., Arslan, M., Kiani, A.K., Azhar, S.: CoSMoS: a BIM and wireless sensor based integrated solution for worker safety in confined spaces. Autom. Constr. **45**, 96–106 (2014)
14. Guven, G., Ergen, E., Erberik, M.A., Kurc, O., Birgönül, M.T.: Providing guidance for evacuation during an emergency based on a real-time damage and vulnerability assessment of facilities. In: Computing in Civil Engineering, pp. 586–593. American Society of Civil Engineers, Reston (2012)
15. Dong, B., O'Neill, Z., Li, Z.: A BIM-enabled information infrastructure for building energy fault detection and diagnostics. Autom. Constr. **44**, 197–211 (2014)
16. Alves, M., Carreira, P., Aguiar Costa, A.: BIMSL: a generic approach to the integration of building information models with real-time sensor data. Autom. Constr. **84**, 304–314 (2017)
17. Khalid, M.U., Bashir, M.K., Newport, D.: Development of a building information modelling (BIM)-based real-time data integration system using a building management system (BMS). In: Dastbaz, M., Gorse, C., Moncaster, A. (eds.) Building Information Modelling, Building Performance, Design and Smart Construction, pp. 93–104. Springer, Cham (2017). https://doi.org/10.1007/978-3-319-50346-2_7
18. Pasini, D., Ventura, S.M., Rinaldi, S., Bellagente, P., Flammini, A., Ciribini, A.L.C.: Exploiting Internet of Things and building information modeling framework for management of cognitive buildings. In: 2016 IEEE International Smart Cities Conference, vol. 40545387, pp. 1–6 (2016)
19. Roggero, H.: Enzo—Data as a Service Platform. http://www.enzounified.com/
20. Contiki: The Open Source Operating System for the Internet of Things. http://www.contiki-os.org/
21. Thomson, C.: Cooja Simulator Manual (2016)
22. Haines, B.: Does BIM have a role in the Internet of Things?—FM Systems. https://fmsystems.com/blog/does-bim-have-a-role-in-the-internet-of-things/
23. OCT. TOP READER PICK Top 10 Predictions for IT in 2017 and Beyond—Information Management. https://www.information-management.com/slideshow/oct-top-reader-pick-top-10-predictions-for-it-in-2017-and-beyond#slide-10
24. Matthews, M.: BIM & Blockchain Examples 1 - BIM + Blockchain Malachy Mathews. https://sites.google.com/site/bimblockchainmalachymathews/bim-blockchain-examples
25. Correa, F.R.: Is BIM big enough to take advantage of big data analytics? (2015)

Using IFC to Support Enclosure Fire Dynamics Simulation

Johannes Dimyadi[1]([⊠])(iD), Wawan Solihin[2](iD), and Robert Amor[1](iD)

[1] University of Auckland, Auckland, New Zealand
{jdim006,trebor}@cs.auckland.ac.nz
[2] NovaCITYNETS Pte. Ltd., Singapore, Singapore
wsolihin@outlook.com

Abstract. One objective of the performance-based design (PBD) of fire safety in buildings is to ensure occupants have an adequate time to escape the effects of the fire unharmed. A commonly accepted threshold of the safe evacuation time is the time it takes for the fire to compromise the escape routes rendering them untenable. This is a complex computational problem that often requires simulations to solve given the geometry of the building, plausible fire scenarios, thermo-physical properties of building materials and furnishing, as well as the environmental conditions.

Conventionally, the input data preparation for such simulations is time consuming and error-prone as it involves tedious manual measurement and data transcription from paper-based drawings and specification documents. The recent uptake of ISO-based building information modelling (BIM) among building designers means that such information should become more readily available. However, sharing information from such a highly complex data model as BIM with downstream applications such as fire dynamics simulations can be challenging due to the lack of a practical method for querying spatial data. This paper explores two methods of sharing BIM information with an industry standard enclosure fire dynamics simulation tool. The paper further describes potential future work in using the simulation output to help auditing a given scenario against a set of compliance criteria. A four-storey sample building model is presented in the paper to illustrate both approaches.

Keywords: BIM · IFC · FDS · Geometric representation

1 Introduction

1.1 Sharing Building Information Modelling (BIM) Data

The BIM (Building Information Modelling) technology has enabled a collaborative approach to design and construct buildings in recent years as it is progressively being adopted by building design practitioners. BIM has the potential of making available one set of common building information to share among processes and applications in a building project. One way of achieving this, in theory, is by using the ISO16739 IFC (Industry Foundation Classes) data model [1]. IFC is a highly-structured, rich and

© Springer International Publishing AG, part of Springer Nature 2018
I. F. C. Smith and B. Domer (Eds.): EG-ICE 2018, LNCS 10864, pp. 339–360, 2018.
https://doi.org/10.1007/978-3-319-91638-5_19

necessarily complex data model to represent every physical and functional aspect of such a complex object as a building. Extracting the geometry and spatial data from an IFC file is a significant undertaking due to the complexity of the data structure. Although commercial tools offering such data extract functionality are available, they are proprietary in nature and offer limited query capabilities and integration options with other software interfaces. Non-proprietary tools such as the open source BIM-server [2] are also available and may be used as a common platform to share building information, but additional development work is needed to augment its basic querying capabilities. There are also software add-ons, such as SimLab IFC Importer for SketchUp [3] and IfcBlender [4] for Blender [5], but they are designed to extend the capabilities of specific 3D model authoring software applications with the IFC import and export functionality.

Recent research to address the gap has seen the development of BIMRL (BIM Rule Language) that offers an efficient IFC data querying capability that supports multiple geometric representations [6]. BIMRL can act as an independent IFC query engine to service any software interface that requires BIM data for any application.

This paper describes the use of BIMRL as a query engine to provide the required BIM data from an IFC file for mapping to the input data specification of a fire dynamics simulator. The paper also presents a comparative approach of getting BIM data using Blender 3D modelling application [5] with third-party software add-ons to achieve the same objective.

1.2 Fire Safety Compliant Design Objectives

The fire safety of occupants is one of the most important considerations when designing a building. Every legal framework in the world would stipulate some forms of requirement for a building to be designed with an adequate means of escape for occupants in the event of an emergency. An adequate means of escape from a fire in a building is commonly measured in terms of the time it takes for occupants to reach a safe point outside the building before the escape routes become compromised by the effects of the fire. Another common objective is to ensure that the structural integrity is maintained sufficiently for fire- fighting operations. This can represent a complex engineering design problem involving several fire safety science principles that deal with how fire develops, its impact on the structure, and how toxic products of combustion would spread within a building enclosure.

Building codes and regulations traditionally prescribe solutions that are based on a typical building with a limited set of parameters. These "one-size-fits-all" prescriptive requirements specify exactly how a building must be constructed so that it can be deemed to satisfy the safety objectives. Modern legal frameworks incorporate the performance-based design (PBD) approach that allows designers to offer a unique and innovative solution that would satisfy the performance objectives, which are usually qualitative in nature. The PBD approach often requires that the design solution be validated using established scientific principles to demonstrate that it is valid for the building and its intended usage throughout its entire life-cycle. Fire engineers often resort to numerical simulations for this purpose, which requires an accurate geometry of the space and essential information such as the furnishing, fenestration, thermo-physical properties of the building materials, and environmental conditions.

1.3   Enclosure Fire Dynamics Simulations

Enclosure Fire Dynamics pertains to the study of the fire behavior and the environmental response to the fire within an enclosure where there is a limited supply of fuel and oxygen. There are three common physics based approaches to simulating enclosure fire dynamics, namely lumped parameter or "zone models", computational fluid dynamics (CFD) models based on classical turbulence modelling techniques, and large eddy simulations (LES) techniques [7]. The latter provides the most realistic description of fire phenomena developed to date.

Two commonly used software tools in the industry today for simulating enclosure fire dynamics are B-RISK, a combined probabilistic/deterministic "zone model" developed by BRANZ (Building Research Association of New Zealand) [8] and FDS (Fire Dynamics Simulator), a CFD model developed by NIST in the US [9]. These tools represent two different types of computational fire model with distinct underlying philosophies in representing fire scenarios within an enclosure. Consequently, they also have different approaches in representing the building geometry for simulation purposes. Zone models such as B-RIK treat a building as a series of rectangular rooms interconnected to each other or to the outdoor by common openings of specified dimensions. CFD models such as FDS rely on the exact placement of solid objects, openings, and an accurate geometry of the building to determine the interaction between the fire and the environment in each enclosure.

This paper will mainly focus on the transfer of information from IFC-based BIM to FDS.

1.4   FDS (Fire Dynamics Simulator)

FDS (version 6.6 at the time of writing) defines each fire scenario within a three-dimensional computational domain consisting of rectilinear meshes with each mesh divided into three-dimensional cuboid cells [9]. FDS treats solid objects within the computational domain as flow obstructions, whereas openings such as doors and windows as flow passages. FDS employs LES numerical techniques to solve large scale hydrodynamics turbulence appropriate for low speed, thermally-driven fluid flow with an emphasis on smoke and heat transport from fires. Calculations occur in each cell and the result of the calculations become a new set of input parameters to the calculations in the adjoining cells. Depending on the input specification, FDS can determine various aspects of a simulated enclosure fire incident such as the level of thermal radiation and convection, the amount of fire products generate, and the level of concentrations of certain gas species. Some of the simulation output parameters can be used in an audit to determine if the assumed fire scenarios would be acceptable against prescribed legal thresholds.

The outcome of FDS simulation can be visualised in a number of ways using the companion tool SmokeView [10], depending on the output parameters specified in the input file.

1.5 Similar Research

Similar research was conducted in 2007 to investigate the use of a purpose-built IFCSTEP Parser tool, developed at the University of Christchurch in New Zealand, to extract a subset of the IFC data model for specific applications in the fire engineering domain [11]. A software interface, IFCSTEP-FDS, was developed in a subsequent research project to map the building geometry information extracted by the IFCSTEP Parser tool to an input dataset for FDS [12]. Several single-storey building models were used in the research to illustrate the approach. As IFCSTEP was intended to be a generic IFC parser for a specific domain, some calculations were necessary in the mapping process to suit the FDS specification.

IFCSTEP Parser was a research tool that only supported the axis-aligned bounding box (AABB) geometry representation. Consequently, it is limited to parsing objects that conform to the AABB geometry. Another limitation of IfcSTEP parser is the dependency on a specific software library that no longer supports later versions of the IFC specification.

2 FDS Input and Output Data Modelling

2.1 Geometry Specification in FDS

FDS treats solid obstructions such as walls within a building as a series of orthogonal cuboids with respect to each other. Each cuboid is represented by a bounding box and specified using the coordinates of the Lower Left Bottom (LLB) and Upper Right Top (URT) corners. The object is defined using the OBST namelist group in a line of data specification between & and/delimiters, as follows:

&OBST XB = *LLBx,URTx,LLBy,URTy,LLBz,URTz*, SURF_ID = "Wall"/

In the above solid obstruction data specification, *LLBx* denotes the x-coordinate of the LLB corner of the bounding box, and *URTy* denotes the y-coordinate of the URT corner of the bounding box, etc. The SURF_ID is an optional parameter that identifies which specification of boundary condition parameters is applicable to this solid obstruction. For example, a SURF namelist group with ID = "Wall" may specify the material composition and properties of the object. Boundary conditions of solid obstructions may also be specified with surface temperature, heat-flux, and other quantities or as a fire source. Another relevant parameter on the SURF namelist group is GEOMETRY = "CYLINDRICAL" or"SPHERICAL", which is useful to represent non-planar objects such as conduits or services ducts.

The computational efficiency in FDS is partly achieved using a rectilinear numerical grid system, which is geometrically satisfactory for most building elements. However, this may represent a limitation when certain objects have geometric features that do not conform to the rectilinear grid. In such a case, the non-conforming objects must be voxelised into multiple orthogonal cuboids that conform to the grid (Fig. 1). For example, a wall that is non-orthogonal with respect to the axes must be transformed into a set of voxels that best approximate its original shape while conforming to the grid. In terms of calculations, the impact of this "sawtooth" profile on the boundary conditions is currently handled by removing one of the vorticity terms in the equations of the flow solver, which is triggered by a Boolean parameter input specification on the affected object. The future release of FDS is planned to employ a high-order immersed-boundary method (IBM) of calculations for better handling this phenomenon.

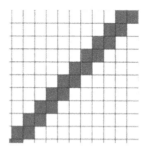

Fig. 1. Voxelised representation of a non-orthogonal object

2.2   Data Requirements for FDS

The following IFC elements are required for the purposes of FDS simulation:

- Walls (internal and external)
- Openings in walls (for doors and windows)
- Slabs
- Major structural columns or beams
- Stairs
- Major furnishing items such as desks, cabinets, or major equipment.

For solid obstructions such as walls, slabs, and major columns or beams, the following properties and attributes are also required:

- The Globally Unique Identifier (GUID) of the object
- The short and long name as well as description of the object
- Coordinates of LLB and URT corners of each object represented as a bounding box (in the World Coordinates System)
- For openings, an additional data is required, i.e. the sill height. This is particularly relevant for windows or any opening that is at certain height above the floor level.
- The materials composition of walls, their layer index, name, and thickness.

3   Querying and Extracting IFC Data

There are several considerations that influence the preferred approaches in getting the appropriate data from IFC. One important consideration is the ease of getting the right information. IFC is a standard specification designed for data exchange, which makes it very verbose and explicit. While it is an open standard that allows everyone to "see" the specification and the data, one will still need quite an in-depth understanding of the concept and the structure. This is made worse when one tries to connect two domains that deal with the same basic information but in a different view point and in different details, such as IFC and FDS. Many have tried to build the "bridge" between the two systems. In general, such system becomes difficult to manage because of the burden to deal with both systems in rather detailed knowledge.

The rise of an approach to treat IFC as a database, as evidenced in the gaining of popularity of the open source BIMserver [2], provides a little relief to this woe, but it is still inadequate. One of the difficulties is getting the right geometry data. The geometry by nature is complex, and there is no exception with IFC. As alluded to in Sect. 1 of this paper, for example, BIMServer can serve the IFC geometry data, but it still requires the consuming application to re-construct the data into the appropriate form needed for the application.

3.1   The BIMRL Approach

The following are two main considerations behind the use of the BIMRL query language approach to share BIM data with FDS:

1. BIMRL is a simplified database representation of the IFC model. As a database, it allows flexible queries to be performed against the data. This includes a pre-check process to ensure the model has everything required to generate a good quality data needed for FDS. Being built on top of a standard RDBMS (Relational Database Management System), BIMRL queries can be performed using standard SQL statements given certain level of knowledge on its simplified schema and an understanding of the IFC data structure [13]. Using a generic tool like BIMRL releases the burden for the application to deal with a lot of details in parsing the IFC data.

2. BIMRL has a built-in concept to support multiple geometry representations [14]. This concept allows integrated queries for both building elements and their geometries. This includes not only the specification to re-construct the geometry, but the shapes of the final geometry. BIMRL generates five geometric representations for each object, i.e. AABB, OBB, Octree approximation, triangulated Polyhedron, and BREP (Boundary Representation) by a set of enriched boundary faces (Fig. 2). This may represent a redundancy, but also a flexibility of having different level of details available for various applications. For example, AABB data is adequate to represent orthogonal wall objects for FDS data, but the Octree cells representation is necessary

to represent voxelized objects in the case of non-orthogonal walls or objects with a complex profile. All five geometry representations are pre-computed and persisted in the database for querying efficiency.

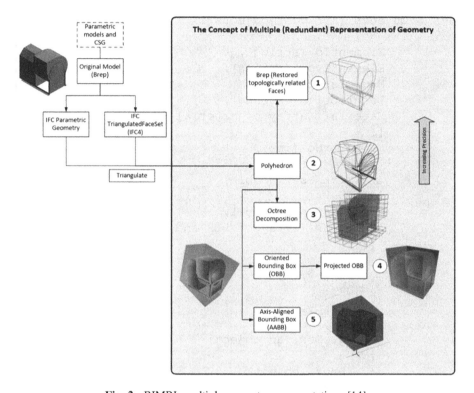

Fig. 2. BIMRL multiple geometry representations [14]

Given its support for multiple geometry representations, BIMRL can extract the required data for output in a form that would minimise downstream calculations needed for the mapping to FDS. BIMRL can express the query output in JSON (Javascript Object Notation) [15], which is most suitable for data exchange using web service applications. Below is the data requirements schema (in JSON) that can be used to design the corresponding BIMRL query:

```
{
    StoreyId (string),
    StoreyName (string),
    StoreyLongName (string),
    Objects (Array of objects):
    {
        ElementId (string),
        ElementType (string),
        Name (string),
        Description (string),
        Material (array of material objects):
        [{
            LayerNo (int),
            Name (string),
            Thickness (double)
        }]
        IsOrthogonal (bool),
        CellBbox (array of LLB and URT coordinates)
        [{
            LLB:
            {x, y, z}
            URT:
            {x, y, z}
        }]
        SingleBox (an object)
        {
            Bbox (object),
            Openings (an array of objects)
            [{
                SillHeight (double),
                Bbox (CellBbox object)
            }]
        }
    }
}
```

BIMRL supports two types of data query, namely a standard triplet form and the un-interpreted SQL pass-through. Below is an excerpt of the BIMRL triplet query based on the data requirements schema:

```
CHECK
//Collect relevant objects, i.e. IfcWall (and
IfcWallStandardCase), IfcSlab, IfcColumn, and IfcStair
from the model into Set1
{(IfcWall, IfcSlab, IfcColumn, IfcStair) E
      Collect E.ElementId Eguid, E.ElementType Etype,
      E.Name Ename, E.Description Edesc, E.container cont
} as Set1;

//Collect all external walls (with IsExternal property
equals to TRUE) and add them into Set2
{IfcWall W Where Property(W,IsExternal)='true'
   Collect W.ElementId Eguid, Property(W,IsExternal)
   ExternalWall
} as Set2;

//Evaluate data after a Left Outer Join between Set1 and
Set2 based on the element guid (marking all objects plus
the external walls)
EVALUATE FireDataOutput(Eguid, Etype, Ename, Edesc,
   cont,"e:\\ifc2fds\\FDSOut.json") From Set1
   Left Outer Join Set2 using (Eguid);

//Print the result to the UI and to the JSON output file
ACTION print result;
```

In the above query, if the element returned an IfcWall object, then the query further checks to see if the object has a property "IsExternal" with a value of "true" indicating that it is an external wall. This is useful to identify as external walls can then be set with a transparency value in FDS to improve the visualisation of the simulation output. The extent of the computational domain can also be aligned with the outer face of the walls.

Based on the actual object geometry, BIMRL can automatically determine which geometric representation (AABB or Octree Cells) is suitable to represent the object for FDS. As explained earlier, Octree Cells would produce voxels to conform to the FDS geometry specification.

3.2   The Blender Approach

Blender is a community supported open-source generic 3D modelling tool that supports Python scripting natively for extending its basic functionality [5]. Consequently, there are many open-source add-ons available. IfcBlender is one of these add-ons, which is part of the IfcOpenShell software toolkit developed by Thomas Krijnen at the University of Eindhoven in the Netherlands [4]. IfcBlender adds the IFC geometry import functionality to Blender. Another add-on relevant for the work described in this paper is BlenderFDS [16], which allows one to compile the required data from within the Blender's modelling environment to create the input dataset for FDS.

The IFC model import for Blender is a straightforward and relatively efficient process. Once the building model is imported, the object geometry and main properties (GUID, name, and description) would then be readily available for access.

4   Generating FDS Input Data

FDS is a command line software application without any graphical user interface. Each fire scenario is defined in a single text file containing namelist groups describing different aspects of the scenario to be simulated such as the duration of the simulation, the size of the computational domain, the specification of solid obstructions, openings, and material properties, boundary conditions, and output quantities, and so on.

Several third-party pre-processors are available to assist with the creation of the FDS input. Exemplar commercial tools include Pyrosim [17], and more recently CYPECAD MEP. Exemplar open-source software add-ons and scripts include BlenderFDS [17] for Blender, 3dsolid2fds [18] for AutoCAD, and step2fds [19]. Neither FDS nor these third-party user-interface tools currently support extracting data directly from the IFC.

4.1   The BIMRL Approach

BIMRL uses a specified data requirements schema (in JSON) as the basis for a query on a given IFC model. The query extracts the required information and outputs the result in the specified form (in JSON), which is then parsed by a JSON parser and mapped to the FDS input dataset in a single process (Fig. 3). For this exercise, the BIMRL query result is made available as a physical file for processing by a purpose-built FDS input data mapping interface, which incorporates a JSON parser. An alternative data exchange method could be via a web service application, which enables a remote application to make use of the query service provided by BIMRL.

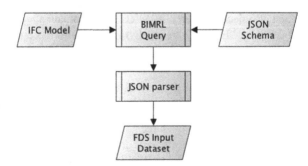

Fig. 3. IFC to FDS data mapping using BIMRL

The BIMRL approach enables the FDS data mapping process to be integrated, for example, with an automated compliance audit framework that can interface with FDS to support the PBD approach.

4.2   The Blender Approach

The Blender approach uses two software add-ons to achieve the same objective. Firstly, IfcBlender add-on tool is used to import the geometry of the IFC model of the sample building. Once imported, the next step is to use the BlenderFDS add-on interface to manually classify individual objects into the desired type of representation, i.e. either as AABB or as Voxels. This is a time-consuming process that is dependent on the placement and geometry of the object in relation to the intended computational grid in FDS. As each object is classified, BlenderFDS would create the resulting OBST namelist group formatted line of data for that object and save it into a collection. Eventually, all objects are classified and the lines of data in the collection can then be compiled and exported as the required FDS input dataset (Fig. 4).

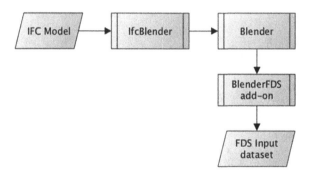

Fig. 4. IFC to FDS data mapping using Blender

BlenderFDS is an interface within the Blender modelling environment to guide the user in creating the FDS input data, which includes non-geometrical information such as material properties definition, computational domain setup and other parameters. However, these information needs to be entered manually by the user as part of the FDS input data modelling.

The Blender approach effectively provides a graphical user-interface to FDS with the advantage of being able to share the BIM geometry data.

5   Worked Example

A sample four-storey building model has been selected to illustrate the approach of sharing BIM data described in this paper. This building model was originally developed by the regulatory authority in New Zealand as a test case for the performance-based compliant fire safety design verification method [20]. The actual model used for the work described in this paper was developed using ARCHICAD 20 and exported to IFC2x3.

Figure 5 shows the exported model being viewed in the IFC viewer tool, a part of the IFC Tools Project by APSTEX. New features such as fenestrations and a non-orthogonal internal wall have been added to the model to demonstrate the challenges associated with mapping the geometry data to suit the input specification of FDS.

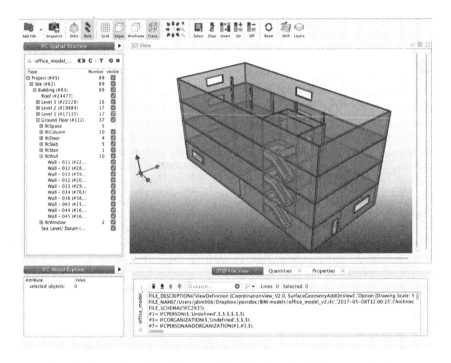

Fig. 5. The IFC model of the sample building in the IfcViewer application

Each level of the building accommodates open plan offices. Figure 6 is the ground level layout plan showing two offices separated by an internal wall with an inclined middle section (i.e. "Wall – 044").

The upper levels (levels 2 to 4) of the building has a typical floor layout, which is shown in Fig. 7. An internal stairwell provides access to all levels through a corridor on each level. The stairwell also serves as a single means of escape for occupants during an emergency.

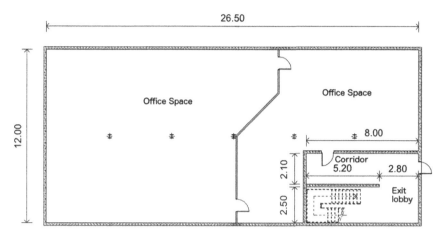

Fig. 6. Ground level layout plan

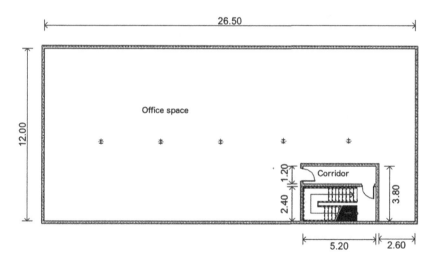

Fig. 7. Typical upper levels layout plan

5.1 The BIMRL Approach

The IFC model of the sample building is imported into BIMRL and processed by extracting every elements and properties from the model and storing them into the database. Additionally, five geometric representations of each object are generated and stored in the database. Figure 8 shows a geometric representation of the entire building model in BIMRL.

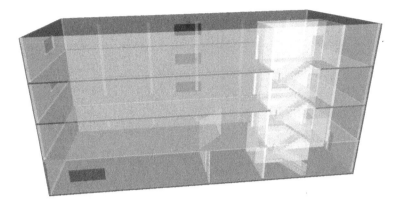

Fig. 8. A geometric representation of the building model in BIMRL

The execution of the query produced a large JSON output, which is due to the large number of voxels generated for the slabs that have a cut-out profile around the stairwell and also due to the representation of the stairs (Fig. 9).

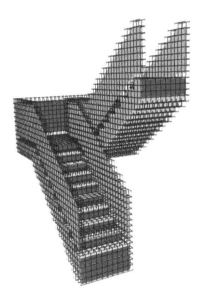

Fig. 9. The Octree Cells (level 8) representation of the Stairs

Below is an excerpt of the query output for the 'Wall – 011' object that is orthogonal with respect to the axes and has an opening, so the AABB geometry representation is appropriate for the object.

```json
{
    "ElementId":"19ALpexd7GHBgVjZM16DWk",
    "ElementType":"IFCWALLSTANDARDCASE",
    "Name":"Wall - 011",
    "Description":"",
    "Materials":[
        {
            "LayerNo":1,
            "Name":"Concrete - Structural",
            "Thickness":0.2
        }
    ],
    "IsOrthogonal":true,
    "IsExternal":false,
    "CellBbox":null,
    "SingleBbox":{
        "Bbox":{
            "LLB":{
                "x":19.2672109375,
                "y":12.5232998046875,
                "z":0
            },
            "URT":{
                "x":27.467150390625,
                "y":12.7232998046875,
                "z":3.2
            }
        },
        "Openings":[
            {
                "SillHeight":0,
                "Bbox":{
                    "LLB":{
                        "x":20.54610072752,
                        "y":12.1232997142,
                        "z":0
                    },
                    "URT":{
                        "x":21.44610072752,
                        "y":12.7232997142,
                        "z":2.1
                    }
                }
            }
        ]
    }
}
]
```

Another example is 'Wall – 044', which is the inclined middle section of the internal timber-framed wall on the ground level, which is subject to voxelization (Fig. 10). Below is an excerpt of the query result showing 2 out of 29 voxels generated.

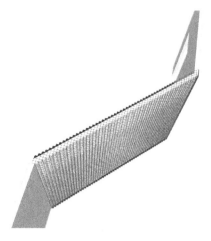

Fig. 10. AABB and Octree Cells representations of different sections of a wall

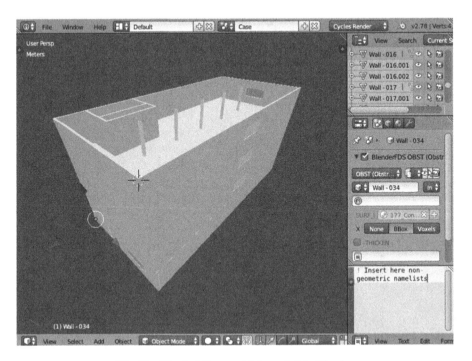

Fig. 11. The building model imported to Blender

```
{
    "ElementId":"2dZqvRyzIpHuQM7C0wKNZH",
    "ElementType":"IFCWALL",
    "Name":"Wall - 044",
    "Description":"",
    "Materials":[
        {
            "LayerNo":1,
            "Name":"Timber - Wall",
            "Thickness":0.09
        }
    ],
    "IsOrthogonal":false,
    "CellBbox":[
        {
            "LLB":{
                "x":14.464227971062398,
                "y":13.697208381771718,
                "z":-0.0141062499999989
            },
            "URT":{
                "x":14.573928952424797,
                "y":13.757635718506444,
                "z":3.1010312500000000167
            }
        },
        {
            "LLB":{
                "x":14.9073928952424797,
                "y":14.133208381771718,
                "z":-0.0140624999999989
            },
            "URT":{
                "x":15.008629933787197,
                "y":14.234635718506444,
                "z":3.101703125000000167
            }
        }
```

5.2   The Blender Approach

Figure 11 shows the IFC model of the sample building imported into Blender using the IfcBlender add-on tool.

The next step is to create the FDS input data by selecting each object in the model individually (Fig. 12) using the BlenderFDS user-interface and specify if the object is to be represented as AABB or voxels. Additionally, the material composition (SURF ID namelist group) can be selected for the object, if it has been defined.

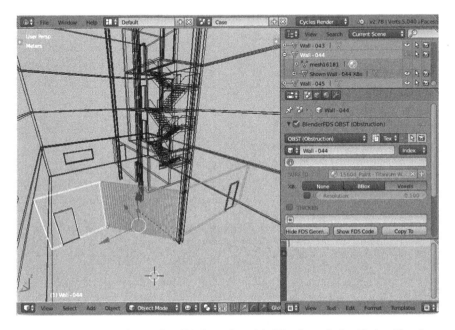

Fig. 12. The non-orthogonal wall being selected in Blender and classified as Voxels

Objects can be selected graphically or from the list of objects. Once an object has been classified, its classification and other properties can be copied to other objects.

5.3   Generated FDS Input Data

The non-geometrical information such as the simulation parameters are specific to FDS that must either entered by the user, either via a set of default values (using the BIMRL approach) or manually through a user interface (in the case of Blender).

The material composition of walls and its thickness are generally specified in BIM, so the information can be extracted and used in the material property specification in the FDS input file, as shown below. FDS can represent a composite material by specifying the mass fraction of each component, i.e. MATL_MASS_FRACTION.

```
&MATL ID='Concrete - Structural',
      FYI='',
      SPECIFIC_HEAT=1.04,
      CONDUCTIVITY=1.8,
      DENSITY=2280.0/

&SURF ID='Wall - 020',
      COLOR='INVISIBLE',
      BACKING='INSULATED',
      MATL_ID(1,1)='Concrete',
      MATL_MASS_FRACTION(1,1)=1.0,
      THICKNESS(1)=0.20/
```

The thermo-physical properties of the material such as its specific heat, conductivity and density are all assumed initial default values. As a good practice, it is expected that any simulation input data would be checked for validity and appropriateness by the user before the simulation is executed. As part of the validity check, the properties of objects may be changed to more appropriate values depending on the application or scenario.

Below is an excerpt of the generated obstruction specification for 2 different walls in FDS. The first wall, 'Wall – 044', is represented by 29 voxels. The second wall, 'Wall – 020' is represented as a simple AABB.

```
// Wall - 044 represented by 29 voxels
&OBST ID='Wall - 044_0'
      XB=14.464,14.573,13.697,13.757,-0.001,3.101 /
&OBST ID='Wall - 044_1'
      XB=14.907,15.009,14.133,14.235,-0.001,3.101 /


// Wall - 020 external wall
&OBST ID='Wall - 020'
      XB=0.767,27.667,7.523,7.723,3.200,6.400,
SURF_ID='Wall - 020' /
```

Both approaches generated almost identical FDS input files. In general, the BIMRL approach produces a lot more voxels than those by BlenderFDS. This is partly due to the high level of Octree Cells selected for those objects in BIMRL. The generated FDS input file is then executed with a zero simulation duration to produce a set of geometry data that can be visualised using SmokeView (Figs. 13 and 14).

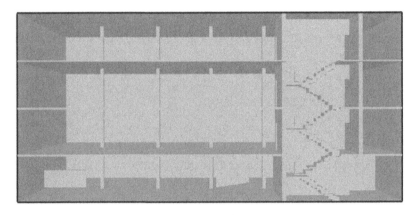

Fig. 13. The sample building model as represented in FDS, viewed in SmokeView

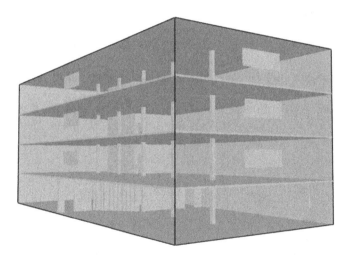

Fig. 14. Another view of the sample building as represented in FDS, viewed in SmokeView

6   Discussions and Conclusion

Two comparative approaches to share IFC geometrical data with the FDS simulation tool has been described in this paper. The BIMRL approach offers a customised query given a data requirements schema, which may include non-geometrical IFC data such as single value properties of certain objects. This is superior to the Blender approach where only geometrical data can be imported. Furthermore, the Blender approach relies on the IfcBlender software add-on with a predefined mapping definition hard-coded into the tool that cannot be modified easily.

Although the BIMRL approach allows extracting some of the semantical data pertinent to fire dynamics simulation such as thermo-physical properties of materials from an IFC model, the actual data may not be present in the architectural model unless it has been enriched with such information by a fire design engineer. Another set of information essential to enclosure fire dynamics simulations is the characteristics of the fire such as its location, type of ignition source, and the potential energy release based on the configuration of combustible materials in the enclosure. Fire design specific parameters are unlikely, if not inappropriate, to be incorporated into the IFC model during the design phase, but would be provided directly into the simulation input dataset as part of a good fire engineering design practice.

The BIMRL approach has an added potential to be integrated with, for example, an automated compliance audit framework that can interface with FDS by generating an input data for it and then using the simulation output (in a comma-delimited format) in a compliance audit process in conjunction with specified normative criteria.

There are two other approaches similar to the Blender's workflow that have not been described in this paper. They involve using commercial tools such as Pyrosim and CYPECAD MED and intermediate data exchanges in proprietary formats, which lacks transparency. These alternative approaches provide a good user-interface for FDS input data modelling with the advantage of being able to share BIM geometry data.

Future work may include an investigation for an optimised method of representing voxels in BIMRL. Another potential future work is a case study of auditing certain quantities in the FDS simulation output for compliance with specified criteria.

References

1. ISO 16739: ISO 16739: 2013 Industry Foundation Classes (IFC) for data sharing in the construction and facility management industries. International Organization for Standardization, Geneva (2013)
2. Beetz, J., van Berlo, L.: Bimserver.org - an open source IFC model server. In: Proceedings of CIB W78 International Conference, Cairo, Egypt, pp. 1–8 (2010)
3. Schreyer, A.C.: Architectural Design with SketchUp: 3D Modeling, Extensions, BIM, Rendering, Making, and Scripting. Wiley, Hoboken (2016)
4. Krijnen, T.: IfcOpenShell. http://ifcopenshell.org/. Accessed 19 Mar 2018
5. Brito, A.: Blender 3D: Architecture, Buildings, and Scenery. Packt Publishing Limited, Birmingham (2008)
6. Dimyadi, J., Eastman, C., Amor, R., Solihin, W., Eastman, C., Amor, R.: Integrating the BIM rule language into compliant design audit processes. In: Proceedings of the 33th CIB W78 International Conference 2016, pp. 1–10. Queensland Institute of Technology, Brisbane, Australia (2016)
7. Baum, H.R.: Simulating enclosure fire dynamics. In: US National Research Council Workshop to Foster Improved Fire Safety, pp. 107–116 (2003)
8. Baker, G., Wade, C., Spearpoint, M., Fleischmann, C.: Developing probabilistic design fires for performance-based fire safety engineering. Procedia Eng. **62**, 639–647 (2013). https://doi.org/10.1016/j.proeng.2013.08.109
9. McGrattan, K., McDermott, R., Weinschenk, C., Overholt, K., Hostikka, S., Floyd, J.: Fire Dynamics Simulator User's Guide. National Institute of Standards and Technology (2015)
10. Forney, G.P.: Smokeview (Version 6) A Tool for Visualizing Fire Dynamics Simulation Data Volume II: Technical Reference Guide (2013)

11. Spearpoint, M.J., Dimyadi, J.: Sharing fire engineering simulation data using the ifc building information model. In: International Congress on Modelling and Simulation - MODSIM07, Christchurch, New Zealand (2007)
12. Dimyadi, J., Spearpoint, M., Amor, R.: Sharing building information using the IFC data model for FDS fire simulation. In: Karlsson, B. (ed.) Proceedings of 9th International Symposium on Fire Safety Science, Karlsruhe, pp. 1329–1340. IAFSS (2008)
13. Solihin, W., Eastman, C., Lee, Y.C., Yang, D.H.: A simplified relational database schema for transformation of BIM data into a query-efficient and spatially enabled database. Autom. Constr. **84** (2017). https://doi.org/10.1016/j.autcon.2017.10.002
14. Solihin, W., Eastman, C., Lee, Y.C.: Multiple representation approach to achieve high-performance spatial queries of 3D BIM data using a relational database. Autom. Constr. **81**, 369–388 (2017). https://doi.org/10.1016/j.autcon.2017.03.014
15. Peng, D., Cao, L., Xu, W.: Using JSON for data exchanging in web service applications. J. Comput. Inf. Syst. **7**, 5883–5890 (2011)
16. Gissi, E., Bartola, R., De Santis, N., Valpreda, F., Faletti, G., Overholt, K., Dimyadi, J., Orvieto, R.: Blueprint for Blender + FDS (2009)
17. Thunderhead Engineering: PyroSim: A Model Construction Tool for Fire Dynamics Simulator (FDS) (2010)
18. Dimyadi, J.: 3dsolid2fds. https://sites.google.com/site/jdimyadi/3dsolid2fds. Accessed 19 Mar 2018
19. Wolfris: STEP2FDS. https://github.com/wolfris/step2fds. Accessed 19 Mar 2018
20. MBIE: C/VM2 Verification Method: Framework for Fire Safety Design For New Zealand Building Code Clauses C1-C6 Protection from Fire. The Ministry of Business, Innovation and Employment, Wellington, New Zealand (2014)

A Semantic Web-Based Approach for Generating Parametric Models Using RDF

Farhad Sadeghineko[1]([✉]) [iD], Bimal Kumar[1] [iD], and Warren Chan[2]

[1] Construction and Surveying Department, Glasgow Caledonian University,
Glasgow, G4 0BA, UK
{farhad.sadeghineko,b.kumar}@gcu.ac.uk
[2] Computer, Communications and Interactive Systems, Glasgow Caledonian University,
Glasgow, G4 0BA, UK
warren.chan@gcu.ac.uk

Abstract. Semantic-rich 3D parametric models, like Building Information Models (BIMs) are becoming the main information source during the entire life-span of an asset. The use of BIM in existing buildings has been hampered by the challenges surrounding the limitations of existing technologies for developing retrofit models. Some progress has been recently made in generating non-parametric models from the Point Cloud Data (PCD). However, a proper fully developed parametric model is still some way away. In this paper, challenges are addressed by reviewing the state-of-the-art before presenting our approach. The aim of our approach is to apply the Semantic Web Technologies for generating parametric models using PCD as primary data. The Semantic Web as a set of standards and technologies is used for providing an appropriate framework for storing, sharing, and reusing the semantics of information on the web. Building elements are recognized in PCD, and the concept of Resource Description Framework (RDF) as a Semantic Web technology and a standard model for interchanging the data on the web is then used to markup detected elements. The RDF data is then standardized to Industry Foundation Classes (IFC) as an open standard building data model to generate the parametric model of the asset utilizing BIM software that supports IFC. Some parts of this ongoing research are performed manually, and the future work is to implement the process automatically. Primary results are quite promising and should be of interest to the modeling of all kinds of assets, in particular, Historical Building Information Modelling (HBIM).

Keywords: Building Information Modelling (BIM) · Semantic Web
Resource Description Framework (RDF)

1 Introduction

Building Information Modelling (BIM) is utilized in Architecture, Engineering, and Construction (AEC), Facility Management (FM), and other domains to provide information concerning the building [1]. Semantic-rich three-dimensional parametric models, like Building Information Models (BIMs) are fast becoming the main source of information during the entire life-cycle of an asset [2–4]. The use of BIM impacts

© Springer International Publishing AG, part of Springer Nature 2018
I. F. C. Smith and B. Domer (Eds.): EG-ICE 2018, LNCS 10864, pp. 361–377, 2018.
https://doi.org/10.1007/978-3-319-91638-5_20

different aspects of an asset consisting in the precision of the planning phase, the decision-making process, the improvement of data management, the enhancement of the productivity, flexibility, energy efficiency, sustainability, and safety in construction [2, 5–8]. Accurate BIMs improve the performance and facility management of an asset [9]. As a matter of fact, after the completion of construction, BIMs that are mapped from the as-designed condition of an asset do not necessarily match to the originally constructed building (as-is condition) due to the changes applied to the building during the construction process in different stages [10]. On the other hand, in some unique circumstances like existing assets and historical environments, the asset may not have a proper 3D model – the only available data are 2D drawings and corresponding documents. Hence several approaches have been proposed during the past years to make the process of capturing BIMs as effective and efficient as possible by developing automated or semi-automated approaches to map parametric models. The general workflow of capturing BIMs using 3D point measurements gathered from the asset can be classified into two directions including 'Scan and BIMs' and 'Scan to BIMs' (Fig. 1) [11, 12]. In the case of the availability of the CAD model, the process of capturing BIMs is performed through 'Scan and BIMs' procedure [11]. On the other hand, in unique circumstances, such as in existing buildings and historical environments, in which 2D documents are the only available data, BIMs are mapped adopting 'Scan to BIMs' approach [12].

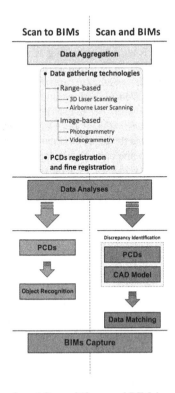

Fig. 1. The general workflow of 'Scan and BIMs' and 'Scan to BIMs'.

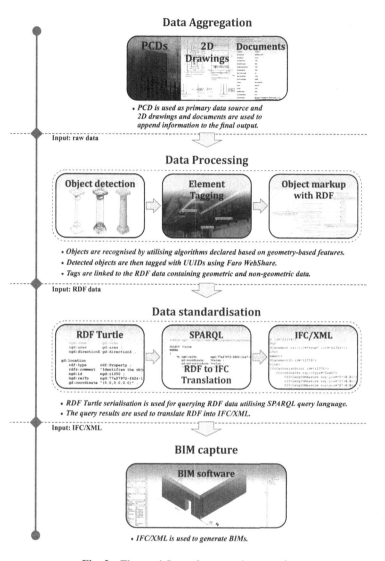

Fig. 2. The workflow of proposed approach.

Historic Building Information Modelling (HBIM) has lately achieved significant attention in developing a suitable BIM framework concerning the modelling of historical monuments. The quality of the represented model, its geometric reliability [1] and, more significantly, the required asset information embedded in the generated models play a key role in elaborating a suitable HBIM framework. A detailed and semantic representation of HBIM can be useful to address an appropriate LoD in advancing the HBIM framework. While the use of BIM in new construction projects has lately gained significant momentum, its use in existing assets, specifically historic buildings, has been hampered by challenges surrounding the limitations of existing technologies for capturing retrofit models [2, 13]. A variety of different technologies are available for gathering the data from an existing asset in the form of images or point measurements, including image-based and range-based methods. Photogrammetry and Videogrammetry are the most commonly adopted methods in the image-based domain [4, 14–16]. 3D laser scanning technology as a range-based method is an accurate, popular, and commonly used method for extracting the data from an existing asset in the form of Point Cloud Data (PCD) [2, 4, 14]. The challenging part of generating parametric models is to record and analyse the information included in PCDs. Although some progress has been recently made in generating non-parametric models from PCDs, a proper full-blown parametric model is still some way away.

This paper reviews the state-of-the-art to address the challenges involved in generating parametric models and managing the large-scale information (metadata) embedded in models before proposing our approach. A Semantic Web-based approach is proposed in this paper to generate parametric models and to manage the required asset information. The workflow of this ongoing project can be classified into four general steps consisting of (1) Data Aggregation, (2) Data Processing, (3) Data Standardization, and (4) BIM Capture (Fig. 2). PCD extracted from 3D laser scanner is used as the primary input data along with corresponding 2D drawings and related documents to improve the final results. In the data processing step, building elements are recognized in PCD, and the concept of RDF is then used to mark up detected objects. The challenging part of this approach is the data standardization process where the RDF data as a Semantic Web key technology needs to be translated to Industry Foundation Classes (IFC). The final step is to import IFC as an open source data model into any BIM software that supports IFC schema.

2 Methodology

The research gap and the challenges involved in capturing semantic-rich three-dimensional parametric models are identified by reviewing academic journals, conference proceedings, books, and applied application (e.g. reports, buildingSMART, openBIM, RDF core and APIs, etc.) that contribute to the implementation of BIM and HBIM for new buildings and retrofit assets. The focus of this review is on three key subjects, including (1) BIM process and its use in the construction industry along with associated applications used in new and existing buildings, (2) construction-related technologies, such as remote sensing (e.g. 3D laser scanning), (3) The use of Semantic Web standards, technologies, and applications in construction and other domains (e.g. RDF, SPARQL, etc.). A keyword search approach is applied to limit the scope of resources. The main keywords that are used are 'Building Information Modelling (BIM)', 'Historic Building Information Modelling (HBIM)', 'Parametric Modelling', 'Semantic Web', 'Resource Description Framework or Format (RDF)', SPARQL Protocol And RDF Query Language (SPARQL), and 'Industry Foundation Classes (IFC)'. The Semantic Web-related technologies are investigated to identify an appropriate architecture for marking up the detected elements and managing the large-scale information embedded in parametric models. The 'Apache Jena API' (for generating RDF graphs), 'W3C SPARQL' query language, 'IFC Open Tool' (for generating IFC), and Autodesk Revit 2016 (BIM modeller) are utilized to implement the data standardization and BIM capture processes.

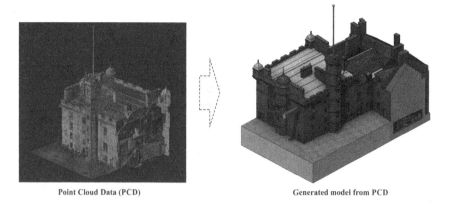

Point Cloud Data (PCD)   Generated model from PCD

Fig. 3. Edinburgh Castle model generated from PCDs (source: Historic Environment Scotland, 2016).

3 Related Work

In the past years or so, varying studies have been carried out to develop automated or semi-automated approaches for capturing parametric models, utilizing PCDs as the main data source. The proposed approaches can be classified into two general classes consisting of 'Scan and BIMs' and 'Scan to BIMs' (Fig. 1). A variety of different data collection technologies and methods are available in the construction industry for capturing the data from a new built projects or existing assets. However, 3D laser scanning (range-based) is the most popular and adopted technology among other methods owing to the data accuracy and geometric information sufficiency [2, 10, 14, 15]. The process of generating BIMs, in either case, comprises several common steps and the difference between developed approaches relies on the availability of the CAD model. In new building projects, if the CAD model is accessible, the scanned data (PCD) is matched and compared to the CAD model to identify the discrepancies between existing data sets for generating BIMs (Scan and BIMs). On the other hand, if the asset does not have an existing model, BIMs are captured by identifying elements inside the PCD (Scan to BIMs). Several approaches have been proposed in the literature to generate parametric models using the geometric features embedded in PCD, such as lines, boundaries, 2D & 3D primitives, and so forth. Moreover, approaches proposed in the literature are supported by various declared algorithms to assist the process and to move from manually generating BIMs, which is time-consuming, tedious and error-prone due to the human intervention [5, 17, 18], towards an automated or semi-automated practice. Most of the approaches are declared based on the geometric features that are embedded in PCDs. In Gao et al. [11] a variety of different algorithms have been declared to detect the geometric relationship between elements in PCD and the corresponding CAD model in a real-world mechanical project. In this approach, geometry-related features are used to identify geometric primitives and to project the as-is (as-built) condition. The datasets, PCD and the available CAD model, are then matched together to identify the discrepancies, such as shape, location, dimension, and composition, between the as-designed model and as-is condition for capturing accurate as-built models. Other geometric specifications, such as region-based, primitive-based, and distribution-based characteristics, are employed in similar proposed methods for generating accurate BIMs [6, 11, 19].

On the other hand, in some unique circumstances, particularly historical environments, the existing asset may not have a 3D CAD model, and the only available information includes 2D drawings and related documents. In this case, the retrofit models need to be generated from the data collected from the building (typically PCD captured by 3D laser scanner). Most approaches that are developed based on this method (Scan to BIMs) use PCD as the main data source. The approach proposed in Zhang et al. [12] focuses on detecting and extracting the planar patches of an existing asset. In this method different aspects of geometric features, like the relationship between points and linear characteristics, are used to recognize the boundaries and surfaces (geometric primitives) of 3D shapes. A similar approach is proposed in Xiong et al. [17] to capture interior building elements, such as walls, floors, ceilings, windows, and openings. The spatial-related characteristics like the connectivity, relative distance, and the contextual relationship between point elements and corresponding building components, is used to identify and extract planar patches. The detected surfaces are then interconnected to form 3D geometric primitives that are clustered in different categories (wall, floor, door, etc.) afterwards. Other similar approaches, such as Budroni and Boehm [20, 21], Adan and Huber [22, 23], and Okorn et al. [24] have also been developed based on the geometric features for detecting geometric primitives of a 3D shape and constructing building elements based on the identified shapes.

The use of BIM in historic environments has been recently increased among heritage communities concerning the generation and representation of comprehensive and intelligent 3D models. 3D parametric models in HBIM are used for different purposes, such as restoration, conservation, retrofitting, building analyses, and more importantly the facility management [3, 25–27]. While different methods have been developed for capturing BIMs in new environment and retrofit assets (non-historical buildings), the development of approaches for generating semantic-rich parametric models in heritage domain has recently gained a lot of momentum. One of the challenges involved in using BIM in historical environments is that historic buildings, compared to new build projects, include more complex components and shapes [27, 28] that are not supported by commercial BIM software. Moreover, commercial BIM software are generally designed to model new buildings and are limited to irregular and complex geometries that occur in HBIM [3, 29]. The approach proposed in Oreni et al. [26] focuses on the restoration requirements of a historical building. In this approach different features of NURBS (Non-Uniform Rational Base-Spline) have been utilized to reconstruct geometric objects focusing on the mutual relationship between them using PCD as the main data source. The detected geometric elements are then converted into building components. A similar method is proposed in Barrazetti et al. [27] to capture parametric objects of an existing building as well as a historic bridge using NURBS characteristics.

The workflow of the proposed approach starts with extracting the discontinuity lines and corresponding surfaces from PCDs using the NURBS attributes, and the geometric shapes are generated by interconnecting the extracted planar patches.

Fig. 4. RDF statement (triple).

```
<rdf:RDF
    xmlns:RDFTriple="http://www.example.com/simpleRdfTriples/"
    xmlns:rdf="http://www.w3.org/1999/02/22-rdf-syntax-ns#">
  <rdf:Description rdf:about="http://www.example.com/simpleRdfTriples/Subject">
    <RDFTriple:Predicate rdf:resource="http://www.example.com/simpleRdfTriples/Object"/>
    <RDFTriple:Predicate>Literal Object</RDFTriple:Predicate>
  </rdf:Description>
</rdf:RDF>
```

Fig. 5. RDF/XML format for the RDF graph in Fig. 4.

```
# filename: rdfTriple.ttl

@prefix rdf: <http://www.w3.org/1999/02/22-rdf-syntax-ns#> .
@prefix RDFTriple: <http://www.example.com/simpleRdfTriples#> .

RDFTriple:Subject
      RDFTriple:predicate RDFTriple:Object ;
      RDFTriple:Predicate "Literal Object" .
```

Fig. 6. RDF Turtle format for the RDF graph in Fig. 4.

Despite mathematic-based methods, there are other approaches proposed in the literature that focus on developing libraries of building elements for capturing BIMs in HBIM domain [30]. In Dore and Murphy [3] a semi-automated approach is developed that is based on a library of different building elements supported by a rule-based algorithm. In this method, building elements, extracted from the range-based (PCD) and image-based (images) technologies, are matched to the components that are created and stored in a pre-defined library for capturing retrofit BIMs. More information regarding the creation of building elements library can be found in Murphy et al. [30]. In addition, there are other proposed approaches, which are developed based on element libraries and architectural ontologies, for manually or semi-automatically BIMs generation using PCD as the main data source [1, 31, 32].

Fig. 7. Tagging building elements in Faro WebShare [44].

4   Challenges and Limitations

Although some progress has been recently made in the generation of building geometries or parametric models using PCD as the main data source, a proper full-blown parametric model is still some way away. The fact is that the process of extracting appropriate details of an existing asset, including the accuracy of geometries as well as the level of auto-mation, varies from one method to another. Hence, one single declared method cannot be used for different objects and environments sufficiently [33]. Moreover, the structure of developed approaches is based on the project requirements, such as the accuracy of models, the real representation of the model, information attached to the extracted geometries, the Level of Detail (LoD), etc. Different types of challenges are involved in extracting the information from PCDs and generating corresponding building compo-nents. The integration of BIM software and data collection technologies is the most common limitation [34], particularly in historical environments owing to the complexity and unique form of each building component. New build projects contain regular shapes and components while historical buildings contain building elements with irregular shapes that remain as simple geometry primitives during the process of capturing BIMs due to the limitation of commercial BIM software. The level of required information embedded in extracted models, which is an important part of Building Information Modelling process, is another challenge involved in BIM capture. Furthermore, the process of attaching required asset information to the captured elements is the chal-lenging part of generating semantic-rich parametric models in HBIM, and this part is currently carried out manually. The Edinburgh Castle BIM project (Fig. 3), as a case study in this ongoing research, carried out by Historic Environment Scotland (HES) could be a good example for mapping BIMs from PCD manually. The management and manipulation of large-scale information embedded in extracted elements and BIM models during the asset lifespan is another challenge that needs to be addressed for developing a suitable BIM framework for retrofit assets and historical buildings.

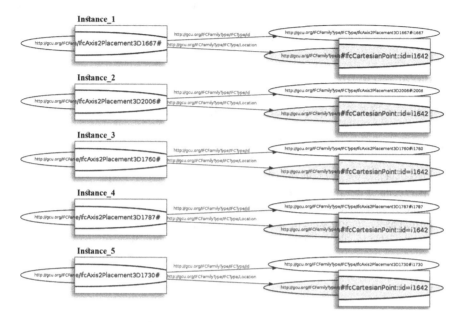

Fig. 8. RDF sub-graphs for five different instances (subjects) that contain same value for the location property.

5 Semantic Web Technologies

Semantic Web (SW) as a set of technologies and standards provides a suitable frame-work for the store, share, and reuse of the information [35] on the web. In the past years or so, the use of SW technologies has gained growing levels of popularity and interest in different domains, including the AEC. In McGibbney and Kumar [36] the SW technology is used for creating a framework (model) for the legislation in AEC domain. Another example of the SW use could be the case study carried out by Hernandez et al. [37, 38] in cultural heritage domain. Resource Description Frame-work or Format (RDF), as a structure on the web, is a commonly used SW technology (also known as SW standard format) for describing and interchanging the information in the form of metadata [39]. RDF is structured based on a simple architecture, and the basic logic of RDF makes it capable to manage and process large-scale data, and it also supports a variety of different contexts [40]. The representation of RDF is based on simple statements also known as triples. An RDF statement consists of a subject (instance), predicate (property), and an object (value). RDF graph is constructed by matching the subject to the object through the predicate (Fig. 4). The subject and predicate are declared as URIs, and the object can be declared either as a URI or literal value (string value) [41, 42]. The concept of RDF supports varying formats, such as RDF XML, RDF Turtle, etc. The

RDF XML format for the same RDF graph illustrated in Fig. 4 is shown in Fig. 5, and the Turtle version for the same graph is shown in Fig. 6. The RDF graph data compared to other graph databases (DBs), such as Relational DBs and Hierarchical DBs, does not have a concept of root or hierarchy which enables RDF to relate resources to another without any hierarchical relationships between them [40].

6   Parametric Modelling

The general workflow of the proposed approach, as described in Fig. 2, consists of four steps starting with the data acquisition. PCD is the main source of data in this project, and other related data, like 2D drawings and corresponding documents, are used in addition to the PCD to facilitate the final result. The second step is to process the collected data and use the concept of RDF to mark up elements identified in PCD. The principal focus of this project is the data standardization process as the challenging part of this ongoing research where RDF data as a serialization needs to be translated into IFC format as a data model. The final step of the proposed method is to use the IFC to generate the BIM model by importing the IFC data model into BIM software that support IFC.

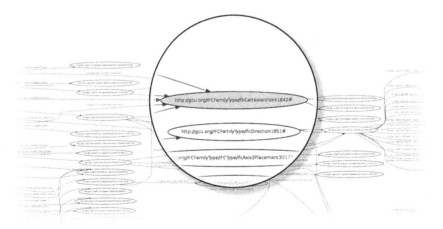

Fig. 9. Shared value for five instances in RDF graph generated by merging sub-graphs.

6.1   RDF Markup and Data Standardization

The first step in data processing section is the object recognition process. Building elements are recognized using the geometric feature in PCD. As mentioned in Sect. 3, several approaches have been developed for detecting building object in PCD, but with a varying of success. The elements that are detected in PCD are geometric primitives that do not contain required asset information needed to facilitate the BIM process and the future management of an asset. In this project, we use the concept of RDF to mark up identified elements and to append required asset information to building objects. The recognized building elements are first tagged by a GUID (Globally Unique IDentifier) or UUID (Universally Unique IDentifier) which is then linked with the corresponding RDF graph or any other RDF serializations, like .ttl, .xml, .json, etc. There are different commercial software available that can be used for tagging elements (assigning the GUID to elements) directly in PCD, such as FARO WebShare (Fig. 7). The use of RDF provides the fundamentals for the analysis, management, and interoperability of large-scale information [43]. The interoperability feature of RDF is used for sharing the information throughout the process efficiently. In a building, including new, retrofit, and historical assets, different detected elements might share similar information, and in current practice, the data is attached to the element individually. However, RDF provides the opportunity to merge similar information and exchange semantic information [40] that can be used among different building components. The sharing characteristic of RDF accordingly reduces the size of the information. The associated information for an element is firstly declared in separate RDF sub-graphs (Fig. 8), and the main RDF graph is generated by merging sub-graphs. In Fig. 9, an RDF graph (merged graph model) for a wall demonstrates an IfcCartesianPoint with a unique id (i1642) that is a shared value for five different instances (sub-graphs that are declared separately) and an instance for the next corresponding values. Instead of declaring the value for each instance separately, RDF automatically identifies and merges similar values and represents an individual value for different subjects (in this case, five instances) which reduce the scale of the information accordingly.

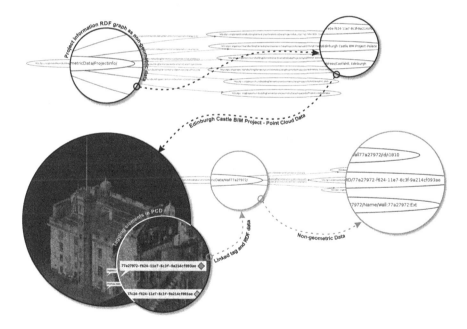

Fig. 10. Marking up building elements using the concept of RDF.

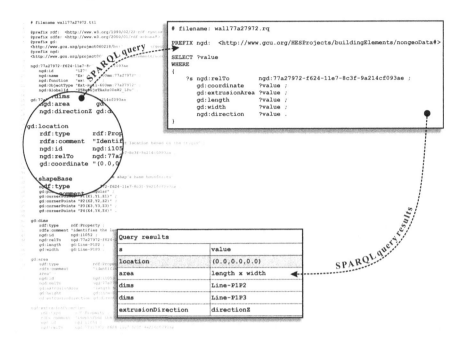

Fig. 11. Extracting the information from RDF data (RDF Turtle format) using SPARQL query language.

A parametric model contains two types of information, consisting of geometric information (e.g. location, dimension, area, element relationship, etc.) and non-geometric information that cannot be extracted from PCD (e.g. name, GUID, material, and other required asset information). The concept of RDF offers the opportunity to manage different information with varying vocabularies. The information in the form of RDF serializations linked with the tags in PCD (Fig. 10) is stored, shared on the web along with the corresponding model as the linked data. In other words, if the information for a building element changes in the model or in RDF data during the life-cycle of an asset, the alterations will be applied to the project accordingly. The other advantage of using RDF for managing the information is that stored data can be reused for other building components in different projects. In general terms, the use of SW technologies enhances and facilitates the access to the data archives, the data navigation process, metadata representation with multiple formats, the integration between multiple data sources with different vocabularies and structures, etc.

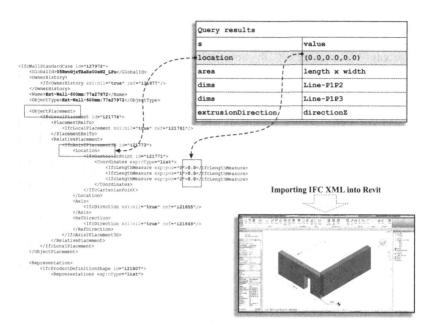

Fig. 12. Using SPARQL query results to translate RDF data to IFC XML format, and creating the IFC XML to generate the parametric model in Autodesk Revit BIM software.

The challenging part of this ongoing research is the data standardization process. In this step, primary RDF data as a serialization, which is a set of byte streams stored in a file or memory and can be reconstructed and reused later if required, needs to be translated to IFC as a data model and the common and globally used standard data format within the construction industry for the information integration and exchange [2, 5]. The first step of this process is to extract the information from RDF data that is used to mark up elements in PCD by linking RDF to the tags. We use SPARQL (Sparql Protocol And RDF Query Language) – as the standard query language designed for Semantic Web – to query and pull data from RDF. SPARQL is not limited to the RDF data and it can be also applied to other data serialisation [45, 46]. One of the advantages of SPARQL is that it can be applied to either a single RDF statement or to an RDF graph that is structured by merged sub-graphs. In this project, the Turtle format of RDF is used to extract required information for the translation process. The SPARQL query results – information extracted from RDF data – are then used to generate corresponding entities for IFC XML. For example, The RDF statement for a wall consists of an UUID (the tag of the wall in PCD linked to the corresponding RDF data as the subject represented by an URI), location as the property of the wall (predicate represented by an URI), and the value of the property (object represented as a literal or URI). The SPARQL query language is then used to extract the data associated with the wall by querying for the location value (object) which is a point coordinate(x, y, z) (Fig. 11). The query results (data extracted form RDF Turtle) are then used to implement the RDF to IFC translation process. The IFC XML ObjectPlacement entity as a sub-entity of IfcWall or

IfcWallStandardCase is then used to locate the wall in project according to the project origin point (Fig. 12). Depending on the structure of the wall, IfcWall or IfcWallStandardCase entity is used in IFC to represent a wall, including geometric and non-geometric data. The non-geometric data, such as Name, ObjectType, identifier (id), and GlobalId as sub-entities for the wall entity, are accordingly appended to the corresponding element. The same process can be applied to other entities, such as the wall layouts and materials, and other elements like doors and windows and corresponding openings. The final step is to import the generated IFC XML into any BIM software that supports IFC format to map parametric models.

7   Conclusion

The aim of the proposed approach in this paper is to address challenges and limitations involved in generating parametric models for retrofit assets, particularly historical buildings, and to provide a suitable BIM framework for mapping BIMs. Several approaches have been recently developed to detect and model building components using PCD as the main data source. However, a proper parametric model is still some way away. The approach presented in this paper uses the concept of Semantic Web technologies to provide an effective and efficient solution to address identified challenges. The use of RDF as a Semantic Web technology makes the proposed method capable of managing the large-scale information involved in the parametric modelling process. RDF also gives the opportunity to produce large-scale databases of identified objects, that are labelled throughout the process, using simple RDF statements, and to share the stored information with the same components identified in one project and similar objects in other projects. Several approaches have been structured based on object libraries, and this advantage of Semantic Web technologies can be a proper solution for dealing with metadata.

With regard to retrofit assets, building models change during the life-cycle of an asset owing to the alterations produced during the remodeling process, and consequently the corresponding information change. In our approach, we use the concept of RDF to provide a suitable solution for simplifying and manipulating the information during applied changes. The third step of the proposed approach, data standardization, is the core and challenging part of this ongoing research where RDF as a Semantic Web technology and a serialization needs to be translated to IFC as an open source data model. Currently, some steps of this research are carried out manually, and the next step of this work is to change the workflow of the proposed method to an automated process. The primary results of this research are quite promising and should be of interest to the modelling of all kinds of building components, particularly historical buildings.

Acknowledgement. Authors would like to express their gratitude to Dr. Vajira Premadasa of Historic Environment Scotland for providing assistance and support in the research presented in this paper.

References

1. Quattrini, R., Malinverni, E., Clini, P., Nespeca, R., Orlietti, E.: From TLS to HBIM. High quality semantically-aware 3D modeling of complex architecture. Int. Arch. Photogramm., Remote Sens. Spat. Inf. Sci. **40**(5), 367–374 (2015)
2. Volk, R., Stengel, J., Schultmann, F.: Building information modeling (BIM) for existing buildings - literature review and future needs. Autom. Constr. **38**, 109–127 (2014)
3. Dore, C., Murphy, M.: Historic building information modelling (HBIM). In: Handbook of Research on Emerging Digital Tools for Architectural Surveying, Modeling, and Representation, vol. 1, pp. 239–280 (2015)
4. Brumana, R., Oreni, D., Cuca, B., Binda, L., Condoleo, P., Triggiani, M.: Strategy for integrated surveying techniques finalized to interpretive models in a byzantine church, Mesopotam Albania. Int. J. Archit. Herit. **8**(6), 886–924 (2014)
5. Zhang, S., Teizer, J., Lee, J.-K., Eastman, C.M., Venugopal, M.: Building information modeling (BIM) and safety: automatic safety checking of construction models and schedules. Autom. Constr. **29**, 183–195 (2013)
6. Gao, T., Akinci, B., Ergan, S., Garrett, J.: An approach to combine progressively captured point clouds for BIM update. Adv. Eng. Inform. **29**(4), 1001–1012 (2015)
7. Brilakis, I., Lourakis, M., Sacks, R., Savarese, S., Christodoulou, S., Teizer, J., Makhmalbaf, A.: Toward automated generation of parametric BIMs based on hybrid video and laser scanning data. Adv. Eng. Inform. **24**(4), 456–465 (2010)
8. Hayne, G., Kumar, B., Hare, B.: The development of a framework for a design for safety BIM tool. In: Computing in Civil and Building Engineering 2014, Orlando, pp. 49–56 (2014)
9. Turkan, Y., Bosche, F., Haas, C.T., Haas, R.: Automated progress tracking using 4D schedule and 3D sensing technologies. Autom. Constr. **22**, 414–421 (2012)
10. Tang, P., Huber, D., Akinci, B., Lipman, R., Lytle, A.: Automatic reconstruction of as-built building information models from laser-scanned point clouds: a review of related techniques. Autom. Constr. **19**(7), 829–843 (2010)
11. Gao, T., Ergan, S., Akinci, B., Garrett, J.: Evaluation of different features for matching point clouds to building information models. J. Comput. Civil Eng. **30**(1), 1–13 (2014)
12. Zhang, G., Vela, P.A., Karasev, P., Brilakis, I.: A sparsity-inducing optimization-based algorithm for planar patches extraction from noisy point-cloud data. Comput.-Aided Civil Infrastruct. Eng. **30**(2), 85–102 (2015)
13. Chevrier, C., Charbonneau, N., Grussenmeyer, P., Perrin, J.P.: Parametric documenting of built heritage: 3D virtual reconstruction of architectural details. Int. J. Archit. Comput. **8**(2), 135–150 (2010)
14. Bosche, F., Forster, A., Valero, E.: 3D Surveying Technologies and Applications: Point Clouds and Beyond. Heriot-Watt University, Edinburgh (2015)
15. Bosche, F.: Automated recognition of 3D CAD model objects in laser scans and calculation of as-built dimensions for dimensional compliance control in construction. Adv. Eng. Inform. **24**(1), 107–118 (2010)
16. Golparvar-Fard, M., Bohn, J., Teizer, J., Savarese, S., Pena-Mora, F.: Evaluation of image-based modeling and laser scanning accuracy for emerging automated performance monitoring techniques. Autom. Constr. **20**(8), 1143–1155 (2011)
17. Xiong, X., Adan, A., Akinci, B., Huber, D.: Automatic creation of semantically rich 3D building models from laser scanner data. Autom. Constr. **31**, 325–337 (2013)
18. Son, H., Kim, C.: Automatic segmentation and 3D modeling of pipelines into constituent parts from laser-scan data of the built environment. Autom. Constr. **68**, 203–211 (2016)

19. Huber, D., Akinci, B., Oliver, A.A., Anil, E., Okorn, B.E., Xiong, X.: Methods for automatically modeling and representing as-built building information models. In: Proceedings of the NSF CMMI Research Innovation Conference, Atlanta (2011)
20. Budroni, A., Bohm, J.: Automated 3D reconstruction of interiors from point clouds. Int. J. Archit. Comput. **8**(1), 55–73 (2010a)
21. Budroni, A., Bohm, J.: Automatic 3D modelling of indoor Manhattan-world scenes from laser data. In: Proceedings of the International Archives of Photogrammetry, Remote Sensing and Spatial Information Sciences, pp. 115–120 (2010b)
22. Adan, A., Huber, D.: Reconstruction of wall surfaces under occlusion and clutter in 3D indoor environments. Robotics Institute, Carnegie Mellon University, Pittsburgh, PA CMU-RI-TR-10-12 (2010)
23. Adan, A., Huber, D.: 3D reconstruction of interior wall surfaces under occlusion and clutter. In: 3D Imaging, Modeling, Processing, Visualization and Transmission (3DIMPVT), pp. 275–281. IEEE (2011)
24. Okorn, B., Xiong, X., Akinci, B., Huber, D.: Toward automated modeling of floor plans. In: Proceedings of the Symposium on 3D Data Processing, Visualization and Transmission, vol. 2 (2010)
25. Oreni, D., Brumana, R., Georgopoulos, A., Cuca, B.: HBIM for conservation and management of built heritage: towards a library of vaults and wooden bean floors. ISPRS Ann. Photogramm., Remote Sens. Spat. Inf. Sci. **5**, W1 (2013)
26. Oreni, D., Brumana, R., Della Torre, S., Banfi, F., Previtali, M.: Survey turned into HBIM: the restoration and the work involved concerning the Basilica di Collemaggio after the earthquake (L'Aquila). ISPRS Ann. Photogramm., Remote Sens. Spat. Inf. Sci. **2**(5), 267–273 (2014)
27. Barazzetti, L., Banfi, F., Brumana, R., Previtali, M., Roncoroni, F.: BIM from laser scans… not just for buildings: NURBS-based parametric modeling of a medieval bridge. ISPRS Ann. Photogramm., Remote Sens. Spat. Inf. Sci. **3**(5), 51–56 (2016)
28. Barazzetti, L., Banfi, F., Brumana, R., Gusmeroli, G., Oreni, D., Previtali, M., Roncoroni, F., Schiantarelli, G.: BIM from laser clouds and finite element analysis: combining structural analysis and geometric complexity. Int. Arch. Photogramm., Remote Sens. Spat. Inf. Sci. **40**(5), 345–350 (2015)
29. Murphy, M., McGovern, E., Pavia, S.: Historic building information modelling (HBIM). Struct. Surv. **27**(4), 311–327 (2009)
30. Murphy, M., McGovern, E., Pavia, S.: Historic building information modelling–adding intelligence to laser and image based surveys of European classical architecture. ISPRS J. Photogramm. Remote Sens. **76**, 89–102 (2013)
31. Attar, R., Prabhu, V., Glueck, M., Khan, A.: 210 King Street: a dataset for integrated performance assessment. In: Proceedings of the 2010 Spring Simulation Multiconference, Society for Computer Simulation International, pp. 177–180 (2009)
32. Chevrier, C., Perrin, J.P.: Generation of architectural parametric components: cultural heritage 3D modelling. In: Joining Languages, Cultures and Visions – CAADFutures 2009, Les Presses de l'Universit de Montral, pp. 105–118 (2009)
33. Fassi, F., Achille, C., Fregonese, L.: Surveying and modelling the main spire of Milan Cathedral using multiple data sources. Photogramm. Rec. **26**(136), 462–487 (2011)
34. Apollonio, F.I., Gaiani, M., Sun, Z.: BIM-based modeling and data enrichment of classical architectural buildings. SCIRES-IT-Sci. Res. Inf. Technol. **2**(2), 41–62 (2012)
35. Yu, L.: A Developer's Guide to the Semantic Web. Springer Science & Business Media, Berlin (2011). https://doi.org/10.1007/978-3-662-43796-4

36. McGibbney, L.J., Kumar, B.: A framework for regulatory ontology construction within AEC domain. In: Ontology in the AEC Industry, pp. 193–215 (2015)
37. Hernandez, F., Rodrigo, L., Contreras, J., Carbone, F.: Building a cultural heritage ontology for Cantabria. In: Annual Conference of CIDOC, pp. 1–14 (2008)
38. Hernandez, F., Rodrigo, L., Contreras, J., Carbone, F.: Cantabria cultural heritage semantic portal. In: Proceedings of the 2007 International Conference on Semantic Web Challenge, vol. 259, pp. 9–16 (2007)
39. Domingue, J., Fensel, D., Hendler, J.A.: Handbook of Semantic Web Technologies. Springer Science & Business Media, Berlin (2011). https://doi.org/10.1007/978-3-540-92913-0
40. Powers, S.: Practical RDF: Solving Problems with the Resource Description Framework. O'Reilly Media Inc., Sebastopol (2003)
41. Cyganiak, R., Wood, D., Lanthaler, M.: W3C recommendation homepage. https://www.w3.org/TR/rdf11-concepts/. Accessed 10 Sept 2017
42. Klyne, G., Carroll, J.J.: W3C recommendation homepage. https://www.w3.org/TR/2004/REC-rdf-concepts-20040210/#section-Concepts. Accessed 10 Sept 2017
43. Antoniou, G., Van Harmelen, F.: A Semantic Web Primer, 2nd edn. MIT Press, Cambridge (2008)
44. Dolphin, J.: The application of building information modelling to the UK nuclear decommissioning industry. M.Sc. Dissertation, Glasgow Caledonian University, Glasgow (2016)
45. DuCharme, B.: Learning SPARQL: Querying and Updating with SPARQL 1.1. O'Reilly Media, Inc., Sebastopol (2013)
46. Cure, B., Blin, G.: RDF Database Systems: Triples Storage and SPARQL Query Processing. Morgan Kaufmann, Burlington (2014)

A Proposal for the Integration of Information Requirements Within Infrastructure Digital Construction

Jaliya Goonetillake$^{(\boxtimes)}$, Robert Lark, and Haijiang Li

School of Engineering, Cardiff University, Queens Building, The Parade,
Cardiff CF24 3AA, UK
GoonetillakeJF@cardiff.ac.uk

Abstract. There has been rapid development and adoption of the digital construction process globally, and this has led to the production of vast volumes of asset information. Following the implementation of the process on an highways project in the United Kingdom, it was observed that the current BIM process could potentially lead to an overload of information which could diminish the value of implementing the process. It was also observed that some of the asset information could be of great value, but had not been specified in the information requirements. To address these issues, a programme of research is proposed which will be broken down into three main stages. These will include a review of the implementation of the process on an existing infrastructure project, the establishment of a formalized approach to establish these requirements through discussions with industry experts, and the development of a framework which will facilitate the extraction of information that brings the most value to the user. This paper presents the first of these stages, and then introduces the approaches that will be taken to address the next two stages to create the framework for the generation of valued information requirements.

Keywords: Building Information Management (BIM)
Business Process Management (BPM) · BIM adoption · Digital construction

1 Introduction

The construction industry has benefitted greatly since its adoption of Building Information Management (BIM) processes and tools, especially during the design and construction phases. The adoption of digital construction has been driven forward by government mandates such as those set by the UK government [1]. A major part of the BIM process is the management of information over the lifecycle of a project. To standardize the construction information exchange format, Industry Foundation Classes (IFC) developed and maintained by buildingSMART International [2], are widely accepted as the leading information exchange format in the industry. Great advances have been made in its adoption in the buildings industry, however, the drive has been slower in large infrastructure projects.

© Springer International Publishing AG, part of Springer Nature 2018
I. F. C. Smith and B. Domer (Eds.): EG-ICE 2018, LNCS 10864, pp. 378–390, 2018.
https://doi.org/10.1007/978-3-319-91638-5_21

The challenge with the adoption of BIM open standards in infrastructure are the large footprints of these projects. For example when considering highways infrastructure, as of 2015 it was estimated that there were 245,900 miles of road in Great Britain [3]. This road network will continue to expand, but also will need to be constantly maintained. It will be challenging as well as unfeasible to integrate existing information of such expansive networks into proposed BIM exchange formats such as Industry Foundation Classes (IFC) or its Model View Definitions.

Along with this, it will be challenging to manipulate and securely store the volume of data being generated throughout the lifecycle of such assets is therefore necessary to understand the requirements of the various users over the lifecycle of an asset and filter out the information that is of greatest value to that particular user.

This paper will describe a programme of research that is now underway that will discuss and review previous work that has attempted to address this issue, then propose a framework that might be used to identify what data is required at each stage of an infrastructure project with a view to creating a mechanism in which captured information can be queried in accordance with the defined requirements. A recent highways infrastructure project was used to identify the potential research gaps that have to be addressed to achieve the above and to provide a case study of the implementation of current BIM processes in accordance with UK BIM standards and protocols and this is discussed in Sect. 4.

2   Hypothesis, Aims and Objectives

The aim of this research is to identify a variety of asset information requirements for linear infrastructure projects, to categorise them by various 'uses' and to establish a mechanism for identifying the value of this information. The specific objectives are detailed below:

1. Implement the Building Information Management process on a highway project using current industry standards.
2. Record lessons learnt and attempt to find solutions or give recommendations on how issues that are identified could be tackled.
3. Understand the influence BIM has throughout the lifecycle of an asset, in particular linear infrastructure such as highways.
4. Classify the various uses that the BIM data that has been collected can have, and quantify the value of implementing the BIM process as recommended.

3   Methodology

The research will be divided into three stages, with separate projects that will back up each stage:

- **Stage 1** - General overview and current practice – The Eastern Bay Link project (EBL)

- **Stage 2** - Focus on value and information exchange – Workshop series with industry experts to understand the information exchange requirements over the lifecycle of a linear asset
- **Stage 3** - Implementation and validation – A trial on an infrastructure project.

As of the second year of this programme, Stage 1 is close to completion with writing up underway and all the data having been collected. Stage 2 has involved a series of workshops with a panel of experts involved in various stages of the lifecycles of linear assets, the outputs of which are now being analysed.

Following the first two phases of the research, a common issue that has been identified in linear infrastructure projects attempting to implement BIM is that even though large volumes of data are generated both during and after construction, it is not clear what the value of this data is and so there is real uncertainty as to what information should be collected and then used.

One of the hoped for outcomes of the workshops was to identify the various roles over the lifecycle of a project so as to be able to create various view definitions depending on these roles. The challenge faced on most projects is that the most asset managers do not see potential value in the information that is being captured by the BIM process.

The current research is therefore attempting to further analyze the various 'uses' and roles that have been defined, and quantify or qualify them. The next stage of the research will then be to create a mechanism which will help stakeholders decide what information will be of the most value to them.

3.1   The Eastern Bay Link (EBL)

The EBL was a project that the Welsh Government initiated to improve traffic flow and make the Cardiff Bay more accessible from the east of the UK. It is a 1.2 km long elevated dual carriageway which comprises a composite viaduct structure which is just over 700 m long.

It was decided that the BIM process, as defined by the British Standards 1192 series, should be followed and trialled to better understand the challenges associated with implementing such a process. The project coincided with the half way point of the research programme, and was used as a case study to identify the gaps that exist in implementing BIM on a real-life project.

3.2   Workshop Series

A series of workshops were carried out by the research team's industry partners, which involved getting experts involved with various stages of infrastructure projects together to discuss and share their knowledge. The intention of this series of workshops was to attempt to align current practice with the BIM process and technology. This was done by collating global BIM standards and then having discussions with regard to information exchanges and processes at the various gateways of a project.

One major gap that was identified on the EBL project was the uncertainty as to what project information should be shared, and how it could be done. Also the general feasibility of implementing the process project wide can prove to be challenging at the start. One question that constantly arose was what was the value of the process, and whether it was feasible to complete certain tasks related to it. For example the Level of Information (LOI) for most of the EBL was found to be too high, as the asset manager only required a set amount of information to manage the asset. As a result, there was a waste of time and resources to collect and structure this additional information, and the asset manager now has to store and sift through all of this information. A counter argument is that this additional information, if archived separately, could be extremely valuable in the future, for example when major maintenance works have to take place.

The workshop series attempted to tackle these issues by attempting to understand the various requirements of all the stakeholders of a typical infrastructure project. One of the targets was to then be able to create a Model View Definition (MVD) for highways and airports with the aim of being able to filter information for separate roles depending on their requirements. Another goal was to identify various scenarios and define various decisions and processes that could be triggered by this to enable them to be represented using Business Process Model and Notation (BPMN) and Decision Model and Notation techniques as will be discussed further in Sect. 3.2.

From a research perspective this series of workshops aided in understanding the various stakeholder requirements over the course of an infrastructure project. Prior to the workshop a literature review was undertaken, and it was decided that it would be useful to categorize various parts of the process into what are known as 'BIM uses' similar to those defined by Succar et al. [4] and Kreider and Messner [5]. By being able to categorize them into various sections and then using the outputs of the workshops as a guideline, it was possible to better understand the value or the hidden costs that the various uses bring into the BIM process.

3.3 Framework Validation

The final stage of the research that has yet to be undertaken will involve implementing the framework and the mechanisms that are being developed on a different infrastructure project to validate the technique. It is expected that this project will also be useful in further refining the relevant BIM uses and would play a role in validating the hypothesis.

4 Review of Related Work

The intent of this research is to focus on the potential untapped value of the information collected on site and the manner in which it could be shared and manipulated. The highways project that is being used as a case study for the research shows that a large volume of data are generated, however as the value of this data is not recognized it generally goes to waste or can overload systems with an excessive volume of information. A similar observation was made by Kenny [6] in a discussion with a panel of experts, where they stated that there is a potential overload of construction data, however there is also untapped potential in this vast volume of data.

The key is to be able to identify a manner in which it can be defined who finds what information the most useful, and when. The next step could then be to create a mechanism in which the information models could be interrogated based on this perceived value. This requires decision processes and criteria to be modeled and uploaded into an engine which can be used as a mechanism to interrogate this model.

4.1   BIM Adoption

In the UK, the National BIM Report for 2017 [7] states that following the Level 2 BIM mandate in 2016, 60% of practices use BIM, and 95% expect to adopt it within the next three years. The next target by the NBS in the UK is to extend this use into the operation of assets over their lifetimes, which is where a large portion of the cost of an asset arises. When the BIM process is implemented in the UK, it is widely acknowledged that it is used mainly during the construction phases of a project. Given the state of the art, the benefits of implementing the process include clash detection, cost estimation, scheduling, quality management, and health and safety. These topics have also been observed to be the most researched in academia, as was observed by Bradley et al. [8] who analyzed 84 publications that address the infrastructure sector and found that more than half only addressed design and construction.

The UK BIM adoption is being driven by the 1192 series of standards, the CIC BIM Protocol, which is a supplementary legal agreement incorporated into construction contracts, as well as various best practice guides and templates of documents that are expected to be produced if implementing the standards in the UK. The 1192 series [9] currently consists of 6 standards which cover the codes of practice, implementation during capital/delivery phases, the operational phases, collaborative production of information, and security requirements.

When observing the adoption of the process in the United States, the National BIM Standards – United States Version 3 (NBIMS – US V3), [10] which is the third version of an ongoing project of buildingSMART, is used as the industry standard. This series of standards has been tailored to incorporate various existing standards such as the National CAD Standards (NCS). The U.S. Department of Transportation also have a series of guidelines and studies covering surveying, 3D data, Construction, Post-Construction and education for 3D Engineered Models and e-Construction. Similarly countries such as Singapore, Australia, Finland, Sweden, Norway and Germany have their respective BIM adoption strategies based on their current construction strategies.

4.2   Business Process Management (BPM)

As the research aims to identify the value that different sets of information bring to various users, a particular mechanism will have to be created to ensure that the information can be filtered based on this. It was decided that a similar technology/modelling method to that adopted by BuildingSMART in their Information Delivery Manuals (IDM) [11] will be used.

Information Delivery Manuals (IDM) are used to specify the business requirements of the users to identify the information that is required to carry out a particular process during the lifecycle of an asset. The aim of IDM's are to define processes, specify the IFC capabilities required to support these defined process, identify the actors involved in these processes, and are provided in a format that is useful for the target group for this information.

However, there can also be great value in other factors that are not necessarily defined by a particular requirement of a target group. Therefore, as observed in the project, and in industry, a large volume of potentially valuable information will not be integrated into the Asset Information Model (AIM). The Asset Information Model (AIM) as defined by the PAS 1192:3 [12], is the asset information and data as specified by the clients/asset managers requirements. The idea of the research that is currently being undertaken is to use similar components of the IDM as specified in the standards which include the information requirements, process maps, and their various functional parts.

The processes will then be modeled using the web service-based XML execution language for Business Process Management (BPM) systems. To specify these processes Business Process Model and Notation (BPMN), which is maintained by the Object Management Group (OMG) [13] will need to be used. BPMN's follow a flowchart method to model the sequence of steps that are required for a particular process. The BPMN's will have various 'swim lanes' which are defined by the particular roles of the participants, and within this series of swim lanes there will be certain tasks that will be defined and triggered by certain events.

To model and describe repeatable decisions, Decision Model and Notation (DMN), which is a standard also published by the Object Management Group [14], will also be used for the research. These standards were developed to complement BPMN's by moving process logic into decisions. It will provide a mechanism to input certain information and have an output (a decision) based on what has been defined within the DMN.

Using these standards will ensure that both the decision models and the process models can be exchanged via an Extensible Markup Language (XML) [15] representation.

To create this BPM system, it was decided that an open-source platform such as Camunda [16] or Activiti [17] will be used. The intension is to create the BPMN and DMN Engine, and also to use the open source Camunda modeler to model the BPMN and DMN diagrams.

Such an Engine should be able to execute most of the symbols specified in the latest BPMN standards [18]; which cover the requirements of this research. This should then also integrate with a Decision Engine which should be able to execute decision tables from within the BPMN process.

The intention is that the information modeling will be carried out using the ifcXML [19] format which is the XML representation of the Industry Foundation Classes (IFC) schema. The reason for the development of ifcXML by BuildingSMART, was to allow a broader range of applications especially for Web services to access data related to the built environment.

5   Case Study – The Eastern Bay Link (EBL)

5.1   Introduction

The Cardiff Bay area has been developed and several infrastructure projects have been carried out in this area, both as a tourist attraction as well as an area with several employment sites and apartment complexes. Another factor was to provide a more direct route between the A232 and the bay area.

The dual carriageway was designed to cross access roads and a live railway which carries hot steel billets between two factories within that area. The construction site was within the premises of the Cardiff dock authority and as a result a certain level of coordination was needed to ensure operations ran smoothly.

The viaduct itself consists of two concrete structures as well as a steel and concrete structure which spans the railway line. The transition structure to the existing roundabout consists of an embankment which was built using a by-product of the material used from an adjacent factory in the dock area.

5.2   Project Requirements

The design was to comply with the standards and advice notes contained in the Design Manual for Roads and Bridges (DMRB) and also included the Local Council's design standards as applicable. Alongside these requirements the application of Building Information Management was required as all stakeholders believed that it would be an ideal project to implement the process, and it would also coincide with the government mandate set for the implementation of Level 2 BIM.

The BS1192/PAS1192 series of standards were expected to be followed which included the manner in which documentation was to be shared and structured, and to improve coordination between various parties involved within the project. Another aspect of BIM included the creation of data rich models and information structured in a standardized format, which could then be integrated with the asset management system at handover.

5.3   Information Exchange and Structure

One of the greatest challenges when attempting to implement the BIM process was that most of the technology, systems and standards were created with the intention of implementing the process on buildings. However, there has been little work done in implementing the process in highways infrastructure and attempting to standardize the way in which data is structured and handed over to the client for use in the operational stages of a project.

Given the uncertainty as to how the information should be structured, and what documentation and format was needed, it was decided that it would be best to start creating the project information model and then understand what asset information could be collected, and handed over in a useful format.

The asset databases were initially produced by the designers, and then had to be updated as the project progressed and linked to the Project Information Model (PIM) as seen in Fig. 1. This embedded data was then extracted into Comma Separated Value (CSV) format from the Asset Information Model (AIM).

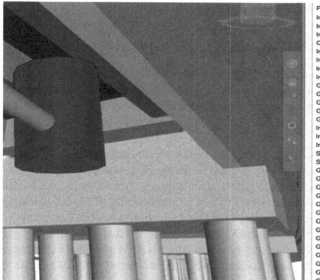

Property
Information:Name
Information:Description
Information:Modified By
General:Layer name
Information:Color
Information:Linetype
Information:Lineweight
Information:General Object Type
General:Style Name
General:Structure XSize
Geometry:Structure Rotation Angle
Geometry:Structure Northing
Geometry:Structure Easting
Insertion Rim Behavior:Insertion Rim ...
Insertion Rim Behavior:Surface Adjust.
Insertion Rim Behavior:Automatic Surf...
Sump Behavior:Sump Elevation
Sump Behavior:Sump Depth
Geometry:Connected Pipes
General:Connected Pipe Outer Botto...
General:Connected Pipe Invert Elevat.
General:Connected Pipe Center Elev...
General:Connected Pipe Crown Elev...
General:Connected Pipe Outer Top E...
General:Connected Pipe Inner Diame.
General:Connected Pipe Inner Height
General:Connected Pipe Outer Diam...
General:Connected Pipe Outer Height
General:Connected Pipe Flow Directi...
General:Connected Pipe Direction
General:Connected Pipe Shape
General:Connected Pipe Wall Thickn...

Fig. 1. Example of information that could be extracted from model elements

5.4   Research Methodology

Over the course of the Eastern Bay Link project, the lessons learned have been recorded to aid the suppliers as well as assist with identifying the issues and benefits of adopting BIM by the industry. The Eastern Bay Link project can be considered to be a pilot project, as one of the main objectives was to determine the benefits of BIM and optimize the process in similar projects in the future. The benefits of using the process can vary across stakeholders and the approach to implementing it can be different from project to project. This is due to the standards not being specific enough, and the technology that is used having shortcomings.

5.5   Guidelines Used

According to Bakis et al. [21] the most appropriate method of investigating the benefits of information technologies is through case studies as this method allows the analysis of the more holistic and meaningful characteristics of real-life events. As a result of this several case studies were reviewed to analyze how the process can be improved on the current project, and also help with documenting where the short-comings are with the current process.

As a part of creating a roadmap of where the shortcomings lie, the intention is to document how the process was followed at each of the 8 RIBA (Royal Institute of British Architects) stages, while attempting to follow the recommendations in accordance with the guidance provided by Fairhead [22]. The intention is to communicate with all the stakeholders by the end of the process to observe how they used BIM and what short-comings they observed in implementing the process.

5.6 Assessment of Available Standards, Methods and Procedures

There is a lack of case studies of this type that are related to highways infrastructure, especially from a contractor's perspective. As a result of this, most of the previous work related to highways has been observed through discussions with managers on similar projects in the UK, and through reports similar to that which has been produced by the BIM Task Group.

During the initial period of the research, a significant amount of time was invested in analyzing the various types of software and technology that is already available and frequently used in industry. The strengths and weaknesses of these various tools, and their uses were analyzed as it plays a major role in implementing BIM, and assessing the value it brings to the process, for example clash detection of various elements.

The initial intention was to attempt to observe whether it would be feasible to use IFC as a file format. However, the current version which is IFC4 is lacking in highways design, and as a result has led to difficulties with issues associated with linking data to models.

The Common Data Environment (CDE) which is currently being used on the project can also lead to the issue of the ownership of the files and the linking of the information to the federated model. It is still uncertain how links to the model will be maintained once it has been placed in the client's database.

5.7 Identified Gap

One of the biggest issues with the project was that both the industry standards and employers requirements were ambiguous. It was not feasible to collect all the asset information and as a result there was a lack of standard processes in place to ensure accurate as-built information was being collected. The result was that there was a vast volume of information that will probably be discarded by the asset managers.

The issue is that this information could be of great value in the future when major maintenance works take place, for example. It was observed that most projects are similar, where historical data of an asset does not exist or even if the information does exist it will be very difficult to manipulate.

6 Discussion and Proposed System Design

In an ideal scenario there will be a central location/locations in which information can be stored which can then be extracted when needed, depending on the requirement for the information. To do this it will be necessary to create several view definitions depending on the use to the stakeholders, as shown in Fig. 2.

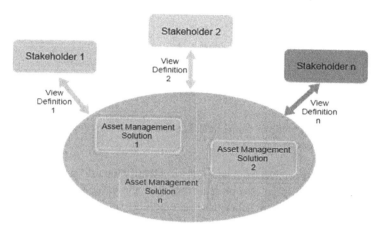

Fig. 2. The concept of mining the Asset Information Model (AIM)

The challenge on the EBL project was that the information that needed to be collected was not well defined at the start, and as a result it was decided that all the information generated would be stored and named in accordance to the naming convention defined by the guide to the BS 1192 [23]. As a result the information produced was vast and difficult to manipulate and use effectively. If the required usage of this data had been defined clearly at the start more value could have been added to the information that was collected and shared amongst the stakeholders of the project.

There is value in having this data in a format that can be queried easily. The current British standards state that the next stage of the implementing the BIM process, would include the adoption of the open and neutral format for buildings and infrastructure; Industry Foundation Classes (IFC).

If the information is produced in this format or a corresponding Model View Definition (MVD), this would allow the information to be integrated with a compatible asset management system.

However, after observing the data management processes currently being used in industry, as well as getting the opinion of industry experts through the structured workshops, it has been concluded that most existing asset management systems would not be able to easily integrate data structures such as IFCs. Also, it is not feasible in many cases as IFCs for infrastructure have not been sufficiently developed currently.

This research is therefore attempting to propose a middle ground in which the necessary information could be collected on site, and then integrated into an asset management system bringing value to all the parties involved in a project.

The intent is to be able to facilitate the manner in which information is shared between stakeholders by identifying the components that have most value in terms of their ability to be integrated into each other's systems as illustrated in Fig. 3.

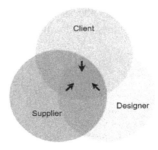

Fig. 3. The eventual outcome of the research is to identify which information can potentially bring the most value to each stakeholder

To be able to do this it has been necessary to identify the information that can bring the most value at each stage of a project from strategic definition to operation of the asset. The novelty of the research then lies in attempting to model these various processes and decisions in a machine readable format, using Business Process Model and Notation (BPMN) and Decision Model and Notation (DMN). The aim is then to be able to then be able to upload these BPMN and DMN into an execution engine.

The information models created for the Eastern Bay Link (EBL) project are currently being expressed in XML format. A custom application will then be created to allow an execution engine to be linked to the BIM server through its service APIs [24]. The ultimate aim is to be able to query the Information Models as specified by the execution engine (see Fig. 4). This will allow users to acquire the asset data that is of most value to them.

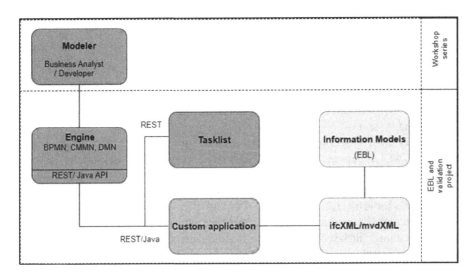

Fig. 4. The proposed framework

7   Conclusion and Future Work

The strategy discussed in this paper addresses two key aspects of the information management process. One is how to take account of the value of the information with respect to the specific project or asset requirements. The other is the technological developments that are required to ensure better information governance. Initially the BIM process was implemented on an infrastructure project (the Eastern Bay Link in f) to identify the potential gaps in the application of BIM to an infrastructure project by industry. A literature review was also conducted in parallel with this in order to try and validate the case study observations and reinforce the premise of the proposed research. Following the identification of the potential research topics, the data collected from the Eastern Bay Link together with that from a series of structured workshops with a panel of experts has identified the need to quantify the value of the data that is collected and to explore how the processes and decisions that are needed to quantify the perceived value can be modeled. This phase of the research is now underway. To map out the decisions and processes it has been decided that Decision Model and Notation (DMN) and Business Process Model and Notation (BPMN) will be used respectively. The final step of the research will then be to develop an Engine and API in which these decision and process models can be used. With the overflow of untapped construction data, the proposed mechanism should be of real value, especially when managing large assets such as highway networks.

Acknowledgements. The Dawnus Ferrovial Agroman Joint Venture (DFAJV), and Ferrovial Agroman.

References

1. HM Government: Building Information Modelling (2012)
2. BuildingSMART International: Industry Foundation Classes - Version 4 - Addendum 2. http://www.buildingsmart-tech.org/ifc/IFC4/Add2/html/
3. Department for Transport: Road Lengths in Great Britain (2016)
4. Succar, B., Saleeb, N., Sher, W.: Model uses: foundations for a modular requirements clarification language. In: Australasian Universities Building Education (AUBEA2016), pp. 1–12 (2016)
5. Kreider, R.G., Messner, J.I.: The uses of BIM classifying and selecting BIM uses, pp. 0–22 (2013)
6. Kenny, J.: Round table: have we reached information overload? (2017)
7. National Building Specification (NBS): National BIM report (2017)
8. Bradley, A., Li, H., Lark, R., Dunn, S.: BIM for infrastructure: an overall review and constructor perspective. Autom. Constr. **71**, 139–152 (2016)
9. British Standards Institution: BIM level 2. http://bim-level2.org/en/
10. BuildingSMART International: National BIM Standard - United States: Version 3 - Scope (2015)
11. BuildingSMART International: Information delivery manual guide to components and development methods (2010)

12. British Standards Institution: PAS 1192-3:2014 - specification for information management for the operational phase of assets using building information modelling (2014)
13. Object Management Group (OMG): Business process model and notation (BPMN) version 2.0. Business **50**, 170 (2011)
14. Object Management Group: Decision model and notation version 1.1, p. 172 (2016)
15. World Wide Web Consortium (W3C): Extensible Markup Language (XML) (2016)
16. Camunda BPM: Camunda BPM documentation - version 7.8. https://docs.camunda.org/manual/7.8/
17. Activiti: Activiti BPM. https://www.activiti.org/
18. Camunda BPM: BPMN 2.0 implementation - coverage. https://docs.camunda.org/manual/7.8/reference/bpmn20/
19. Thomas, L., Matthias, W.: ifcXML4 specification methodology (2012)
20. Barlish, K., Sullivan, K.: How to measure the benefits of BIM - a case study approach. Autom. Constr. **24**, 149–159 (2012)
21. Bakis, N., Kagioglou, M., Aouad, G.: Evaluating the business benefits of information systems. In: 3rd International SCRI Symposium on Salford Centre for Research and Innovation. University of Salford, pp. 280–294 (2006)
22. Fairhead, R.: RIBA Plan of Work 2013 Guide: Information Exchanges. RIBA Publishing, London (2015)
23. Richards, M.: Building Information Management: A Standard Framework and Guide to BS 1192. British Standards Institution, London (2010)
24. BIMServer.org: BIM Server - Service Interfaces. https://github.com/opensourceBIM/BIMserver/wiki/Service-Interfaces

Use Cases for Improved Analysis of Energy and Comfort Related Parameters Based on BIM and BEMS Data

Filip Petrushevski[1(✉)], Maryam Montazer[2], Stefan Seifried[3],
Christian Schiefer[4], Gerhard Zucker[1], Thomas Preindl[3], Georg Suter[2],
and Wolfgang Kastner[3]

[1] AIT Austrian Institute of Technology, Vienna, Austria
filip.petrushevski@ait.ac.at
[2] Design Computing Group, TU Wien, Vienna, Austria
[3] Automation Systems Group, TU Wien, Vienna, Austria
[4] Caverion Austria, Vienna, Austria

Abstract. A facility passes through several life cycle phases: conceptual design, design development, construction, use, reuse, remodeling, and demolition. In each phase, documents are created by architects, engineers, technical planners, and contractors that reflect the facility's state at certain points in time. Information exchange is achieved with commercial or open data exchange standards. Using building information modeling (BIM), complex three-dimensional and semantically rich building models are feasible that facilitate planning and data exchange in project teams and through the whole lifecycle. Such models have significant potential not only for design and construction, but also to improve building operation. This paper investigates how BIM may be applied to improve operational efficiency in facilities. More specifically, the aim is to achieve improved reporting and visualization of energy and comfort related parameters, as well as their engineering and commissioning, by application of BIM in combination with building energy management systems (BEMS). We present use cases that will guide the development of a novel dynamic BIM concept in which facility data are combined with building management system data. As a conclusion, an analysis of the feasibility of the use cases in terms of information availability is provided.

Keywords: BIM · BEMS · Energy · Comfort

1 Introduction

The energy used by buildings makes a significant part of the whole energy consumption [1]. This has a huge impact on the costs for the operation of the building but also indirectly influences the climate change especially if the consumed energy does not come from renewable sources and its production generates big amounts of greenhouse gas emissions. According to the International Energy Agency "assertive action is needed now across all countries to improve global average energy use per capita by at least 10% by 2025 using energy-efficient and low-carbon building

© Springer International Publishing AG, part of Springer Nature 2018
I. F. C. Smith and B. Domer (Eds.): EG-ICE 2018, LNCS 10864, pp. 391–413, 2018.
https://doi.org/10.1007/978-3-319-91638-5_22

technologies" [2]. By using effective energy management, measures can be applied to reduce the energy consumption and with that reduce the operational costs and the negative environmental impact. However, these measures usually influence the comfort of the occupants inside the buildings, which includes but it is not limited to the thermal comfort, the indoor air quality (IAQ) and the visual comfort. The motivation to invest into systems that support the building operators to effectively manage the building energy consumption usually called building energy management systems (BEMS) is to help them find the optimal balance between the otherwise conflicting goals for the occupants' comfort and the energy consumption. These systems can be independent systems or can be an integral part of a more general building management system (BMS) responsible also for other functions and domains such as fire alarm or access control systems.

The life-cycle of each facility consists of most of these phases: conceptual design, design development, construction, use, reuse, remodeling, and demolition. The work by stakeholders involved in each of the phases such as architects, engineers, technical planners, and contractors is documented. However, completely different formats are used in different stages and by different stakeholders. The documentation from each phase represents the facility's state at a certain point in time. For example, in the conceptual phase, only simplified site and building models are used as a starting point to develop more detailed planning in different disciplines such as architecture, structural engineering, mechanical engineering or electrical engineering. The designs and plans are used all through construction with every change documented back into the plans. The utilization of different proprietary and open formats makes the data exchange very difficult. The Building Information Modeling (BIM) is designed to overcome the issues above, by providing complex geometrical and semantically rich building models with the potential to provide interdisciplinary data exchange and integration between several stakeholders and life-cycle phases. Although such models are mostly used for the design, construction, and refurbishment, they have a significant potential to improve building operation and usage since they might contain valuable information providing the building operators with detailed insight and understanding of the building and its systems structure and operation.

This paper investigates how BIM may be applied during building operation to improve operational efficiency in facilities through the improved analytics of energy and comfort related parameters. More specifically, the aim is to achieve improved reporting and visualization of those parameters by combining BIM with BEMS as an independent system or part of a BMS. Furthermore, the same concept could be used for engineering and commissioning of the subsystems. Use cases are presented that will guide the development of a novel dynamic BIM concept in which more static facility data are combined with more dynamic BMS data. The paper is organized as follows: the related work and the state-of-the-art in areas related to the topic are presented in the following Sect. 2; in Sect. 3, the use cases for the improved analysis of energy and comfort related parameters are presented and described in a structured way; Sect. 4 gives an overview of the information requirements to be provided within the use cases; finally, Sect. 5 concludes the paper and presents a plan for the future work.

2   Related Work

This work is influenced by the state-of-the-art in the related fields of BEMS, BIM, computer-aided facility management (CAFM), as well as ontologies and reasoning. In the following, a general overview of each field, recent related work and its relation to this work is presented.

2.1   Building Energy Management Systems

A BEMS is a system that manages the energy flows within, into and out of the building. An important part of every facility is its energy systems including the management of the energy consumption, distribution, production, and storage. Thus, BEMS are responsible for managing the energy supply, storage, distribution, and consumption. The energy supply can be external from an energy grid such as power grid, gas, or district heating (and recently cooling), or internal (also called building integrated) in the form of a photovoltaic system, solar-thermal system, or combined heat and power (CHP) system. In case the facility produces more energy than its needs, the excess energy can be fed back to the grids (in the form of smart grid integration) or stored locally for self-consumption (for example, for charging electric vehicles). The storage is usually in the form of thermal storage or electric batteries. For storing thermal energy, mainly water is used as a storage medium but also phase changing materials (PCM) in special storage containers or the ground in the vicinity of the building. Electric energy was stored in lead-acid batteries in the past (mainly for uninterrupted power supply (UPS) of critical systems such as server rooms), but recently lithium-ion based batteries are increasingly used. The distribution of energy within the building takes place indirectly through internal subsystems such as heating, ventilation, and air conditioning (HVAC) or lighting systems. The end consumption depends on the specific components and units within those subsystems in the form of air handling units (AHUs), fan coils, radiators, concrete core activation, capillary tube mats, ventilation outlets or luminaires.

As previously mentioned, BEMS are either stand-alone or part of a BMS, along with a building automation system (BAS) or a building control system (BCS) depending on the level of control and the size of the system. Largely integrated systems also cover other domains and functionalities such as security and access control, fire protection, elevators, indoor navigation, or infotainment systems.

When it comes to the management of the energy consumed by the HVAC system as the biggest consumer in most facilities, different automation, and control strategies can be applied. Most old systems use thermostats, static operational schedules or control strategies that specify a fixed dependency between two variables (for example, outdoor temperature and heating/cooling). However, more advanced systems could use model predictive control (MPC) where the building, its systems or some of their parts are modeled as a so-called digital twin. Such a model may then be used to predict, e.g., the energy loads. In systems that are integrated with smart grids demand side management and demand response, e.g., based on multi-agent systems [3], could be used. For maximizing self-consumption of locally produced energy, load shifting strategies are beneficial. Instead of setting the control strategies only once during commissioning of the facility (or maybe during re-commissioning), modern systems favor the concept of continuous commissioning where the strategies are continuously adapted to external conditions and usage.

Different forms of BEMS are in use already for decades [4]. However, in the past, they were implemented mostly as stand-alone systems with hard-coded variables and hard-wired sensors and actuators. Nowadays, the modern BEMS solutions are offering more flexibility and scalability which on the one hand influences the rapidly increasing acceptance but on the other hand introduces issues such as complexity and stability of facility operation.

Due to large amounts of diverse data in BEMS, it is becoming unfeasible to extract relevant information that could be beneficial for building operation optimization. Thus, using computational intelligence methods, such as artificial neural networks, fuzzy logic or evolutionary algorithms, has a potential to improve energy management in buildings through situational awareness and more efficient, dynamic and adaptive control [5]. Furthermore, this could be achieved by implementing and deploying advanced data analytics to improve the energy efficiency of the building by long-term proactive and adaptive energy management [6]. Machine learning algorithms can be applied to the rest also to forecast the energy consumption in facilities [7]. Molina-Solana et al. give a comprehensive overview of additional data science techniques and tools such as classification, regression, clustering, association rules, sequence discovery, anomaly detection, and time series analysis that could be applied to building energy management [8]. They discuss use cases in different domains of building energy management such as prediction of building energy load, building operation, analysis of infrastructures and retrofitting, fault detection and prevention, economic analysis of electric consumption, and energy fraud detection. According to them, but also others [9], technological trends such as smart metering, big data, Internet of Things (IoT), edge computing and cloud computing are expected to have a significant impact on energy management. However, additional important issues like privacy concerns and uncertainties arise.

Many previous studiesaddress the integration of BIM (Sect. 2.2) with BEMS. For example, Ock et al. developed a conceptual framework that integrates BIM information with simulations for real-time weather-responsive control [10]. They focus on the control of the artificial lighting and optimization of the heating and cooling energy use based on simulations that use BIM as a source. Dong et al. developed an information infrastructure for fault detection and diagnostics that is enabled by BIM [11]. For better support of holistic building energy management, different data sources can be integrated using a combination of BIM principles and semantic web technologies [12]. This approach uses a semantic model in the form of ontology (Sect. 2.4) that is used to generate rules for the adaptive management of the building. The solution has an integrated web-based interface that is used to visualize both the monitoring data and the suggestions for improvement.

The future development of advanced BEMS solutions can benefit significantly from the recent trend of IoT (see for example [13]). Especially interesting are wireless sensor networks for easy deployment and extensions of BEMS for building retrofitting in outdated buildings [14]. However, this introduces additional problems such as vulnerability to unauthorized network access or complexity of setting up wireless links

[15]. Several production scale commercial platforms for IoT and data analytics are available that have a potential to deal with these issues [16–18].

Big players in the BEMS industry are continuously improving their solutions into the direction of analysis of energy and comfort related parameters (see for example [19–23]). Also, recent notable newcomers (for example [24, 25]) are promising more advanced analysis, and some of them already use semantic modeling to support the optimization algorithms [26]. However, the development of full integration of BIM within BEMS for improved visualization and reporting of energy and comfort related data is still in the early stage. This is most probably due to the lack of standardized formats suitable for information modeling of operational data and the effort related to the manual recreation of the missing information.

2.2   Building Information Models

During the different phases of a building project, a large number of documents is generated which are shared among project members. Information exchange is achieved via commercial or open data exchange standards. Nowadays, with powerful BIM software, it is possible to exchange richly structured information during the whole project lifecycle.

Building information modeling (BIM) refers to an approach for providing a semantically rich data model to represent the building information during the whole project lifecycle. A BIM model allows project participants (e.g., architects, engineers, technical planners, contractors and facility managers) to collaborate [27, 28]. A key feature of a BIM system isis parametrized building objects that enable rapid authoring of building models [27].

There are two popular open data exchange standards for BIM: Industry Foundation Classes (IFC) [29] and Green Building XML (gbXML) [30]. Industry Foundation Classes (IFC) is a neutral, open data standard for BIM which is defined in the STEP-EXPRESS data modeling language [31]. In this data schema, information about entities in the Architecture, Engineering, and Construction (AEC), relationships between them, processes and other behavioral data are defined. Recent releases are IFC 2x3 and IFC 2x4 (IFC 4).

From the energy management point of view, entities for HVAC, lighting and electrical system components are modeled in IFC 2x3. Recently, in IFC 4, new HVAC-related entities are modeled, including IfcSensor (to model sensor measurements) and IfcSpatialZone (to model HVAC zones) [32]. Although IFC pursues a comprehensive and expressive approach, utilization of BIM models is more prevalent in the design phase of building projects. Relevant data in the building operation phase in general and in BEMS specifically are still insufficiently represented. For instance, a sensor (data-point) of a BMS can only be rudimentarily modeled in IFC.

The gbXML standard adopts a down-top approach and is developed based on extensible markup language (XML) format. XML is a general-purpose data modeling language and has less expressive power and greater simplicity in comparison with EXPRESS. Due to gbXML's capability to reuse information from energy simulation and its extensibility, it is suitable for information exchange between BIM software (e.g., Autodesk's Revit and Graphisoft's ArchiCAD) and energy analysis software (e.g., DOE-2, e-QUEST, and HAP) [33]. Similar to IFC, support for modeling BMS data is limited in gbXML.

Information exchange between BIM applications is done via files or model servers. IFC-based model servers have been developed to support collaborative design workflows [34]. They can be accessed by queries with rudimentary functionality. To develop a data interface between BIM systems, model view definitions (MVD) can be helpful. MVD refers to a subset of IFC schema which is required to satisfy certain Exchange Requirements in the AEC industry [35]. MVDs based on IFC 2x3 are views for coordination, structural analysis, and basic FM handover. Recently, two additional MVDs for IFC 4 have been developed for reference and design transfer [36].

A requirement in the operation phase concerns the compilation of equipment lists, product data sheets, warranties, spare parts lists, or maintenance plans. The Construction Operations Building Information Exchange (COBie) is a subset of the IFC data model that defines how information may be captured during design and construction and handed over to facility managers in the operation phase. Information provided by designers includes floor, space, and equipment layout, while contractors provide model and serial numbers of installed equipment [37]. There are four alternative COBie representations: IFC STP, IFC XML, SpreadsheetML and COBieLite. The most common COBie representation is the spreadsheet format which can be exported from a BIM and imported to computerized maintenance management systems (CMMS) and CAFM systems [38].

2.3   Computer-Aided Facility Management

Buildings and facilities are complex systems of systems, which require a multi-disciplinary and holistic approach to ensure their efficient operation. According to the International Facility Management Association (IFMA), facility management (FM) "encompasses multiple disciplines to ensure functionality of the built environment by integrating people, place, process and technology" [39]. CAFM systems leverage information and communication technologies (ICT) to handle the complexity of large buildings and the large amounts of data accumulated during their operation. These systems contain information about the property, such as floor plans and descriptions of physical spaces. One of the goals of CAFM systems is to enable reporting on the energy consumption of the building. CAFM also provides location information about the equipment of a plant. FM strives for a cost and energy efficient coordination of buildings with their users and organizations. Typical FM applications include space management, equipment, and IT infrastructure management. CAFM systems are used in large public or commercial buildings. Space representation in CAFM systems is schematic in the form of two-dimensional models. CAFM systems have simplified interfaces with BIM software and are database-oriented (see for example [40, 41]). Relational or spatially enabled databases are used. Since the access is predominantly via Structured Query Language (SQL), these systems can be integrated with enterprise resource planning (ERP) software. Due to gaps in software interoperability between BIM and CAFM, much of the valuable semantic information is lost [42].

2.4   Ontologies and Reasoning

The notion of an ontology is defined as a "formal, explicit specification of a shared conceptualization" [43]. The term "conceptualization" refers to an abstract model of an artifact, part of a system, by having identified the relevant concepts, their properties, and relations. The terms formal and explicit mean that the model can be processed by machines as well as by humans. Furthermore, types of concepts and their usage constraints are explicitly defined. Hence, ontologies provide the means to formally model the structure of a system including its relevant classes, instances, relations, and restrictions. Reasoning in ontologies is the derivation of facts that are not expressed explicitly by the ontology. On the one hand, reasoning helps to design and maintain high-quality ontologies - keeping them meaningful, correct, minimally redundant, and richly axiomatized [44]. On the other hand, ontology reasoning enables the answer of queries about ontology classes and instances as well as alignment and integration of multiple ontologies.

Over time, several ontologies emerged covering the domain of buildings, automation, and smart energy usage simultaneously. A prime representative for this class of ontologies is Colibri, which aims at enabling intelligent control of energy supply and demand. It was first described in [45] and enables the semantic modeling of structural parts of buildings as well as building services. Following the ontology engineering methodology described in [46], Colibri incorporates existing ontologies like DogOnt [47] or ThinkHome [48] to achieve its goals. The ontology comprises of four major parts: building structure, devices and appliances, data services, and control services. The building structure is abstractly described using the concept of zones and includes building parts, floors or rooms. As required, zones may be put into a spatial context using relative arrangement (e.g., *Zone A* is below *Zone B*). Devices and appliances, part of building services, are modeled by subclasses of the *BuildingResource* class. However, there is no available class to model the flow between different devices, part of the same building service (e.g., dampers, fans, or compressors part of a variable air volume unit). The *DataService* concept then represents data generated by before-mentioned devices and appliances, but also external data sources. The semantic description of the data (e.g., temperature, humidity) itself is done utilizing the *ParameterConfiguration* class. Relations to control variables are modeled using the *ParameterVariation* class, which combines the nature of the data value change with boundary conditions. Further, the *ControlService* class denotes components able to influence specific datapoints actively. Finally, it is noteworthy, that Colibri also provides a well-defined interface to various systems based on the Resource Description Framework (RDF) and the WebSocket protocol. Another approach is Brick, an ontology explicitly designed for the modeling of metadata about BMS. The Brick ontology is the result of an extensive study of different BMS installed on different buildings across Europe and the United States. In contrast to the ontologies mentioned before, the Brick schema aims to enable the description of many parts of a BMS as possible [49]. The Brick schema builds upon the groundwork of different schemata emphasizing the usage of building metadata. From Project Haystack [50], Brick borrows the concept of tags and combines it with an underlying ontology to describe hierarchies, relationships, and properties for the description of building metadata. The concept of tags refers to name-value pairs describing a fact or an attribute of an entity. Hence, tags may be combined into so-called tagsets, which allow the grouping of several tags into a single entity without losing the semantic relations of individual tags. Further, this avoids the use of complicated tag names. Beside the most fundamental class, the Point, the three classes *Location, Equipment,* and *Measurement* comprise the top layer of the hierarchy. Several relationship concepts such as *isPartOf, isInputOf, isOutputOf* or *Feeds* enable the descriptive interlinking of different classes. Finally, the concept of *FunctionBlocks* enables the modeling of logical groups of *Points* and *Equipment.*

3   Use Cases

Facility managers use BEMS to control indoor environmental conditions in buildings. BEMS and CAFM systems are operated separately. In this section, we present use cases that will guide the development of a dynamic BIM for BEMS concept in which facility data are combined with BEMS data.

Capabilities of BIM systems to visualize dynamic processes that occur in a building are currently limited. Hence, to support decision making during the operational phase of a building, a dynamic BIM that provides data on current energy consumption and comfort related parameters is desirable. The potential stakeholders of such a dynamic BIM include developers of smart building solutions, facility or building managers, and developers of building codes and standards [51]. Informed by equipment and indoor environment sensor data collected by BEMS and visualized by a dynamic BIM system, facility managers could identify energy savings potential in buildings. Linking live or recorded data from sensors, meters, and loggers in buildings with BIMs could improve fault detection and decision-making of building managers.

However, a main challenge in the realization of a dynamic BIM concerns the integration of heterogeneous information from different data sources and formats [32]. In this work it is anticipated, that a dynamic BIM may be derived semi-automatically from available design, operational and maintenance data with semantic and geometric reasoning. Further, the requirements of existing facilities where existing data may be incomplete and have low information content are considered. This means that current approaches for new construction that are based on reuse of richly structured BIM from the design phase are not immediately applicable to existing facilities. However, it is precisely existing facilities that often have a high potential for improving energy effectiveness and comfort. The requirement of incomplete and poorly structured base data affects the definition of the data model and workflows for partially automated generation of the dynamic BIM.

The following use cases are based on literature research, the experience of the authors and qualitative interviews conducted with representatives of relevant stakeholders in building operations, like facility managers and energy efficiency consultants. The interview guidelines were implemented using a semi-structured approach. Such approaches combine specific questions (to bring forth the foreseen information), and open-ended questions (to elicit unexpected types of information) [52]. Hence it allowed the guided collection of qualitative data from real-world stakeholders without interference by the interviewers. An analysis of the interview transcripts led to individual use cases per interview partner, which were further studied to find similarities and joint issues. Next, the found use-cases were merged and harmonized were applicable and refined with the necessary information flows. A notable recurring theme among the found use cases was the use of visual inspection and reporting for analyzing energy and comfort parameters.

3.1   Visualization and Reporting Use Cases

The visualization and reporting use cases are shown in the UML use case diagram [53] in Fig. 1. The use cases vary from visualization of data-point values to visualization of building alarms, preprocessed data, logging data and radiant cooling/heating elements in a spatial context, as well as reporting of energy consumption. Actors in these use cases are the facility manager or the more specialized role of an energy manager.

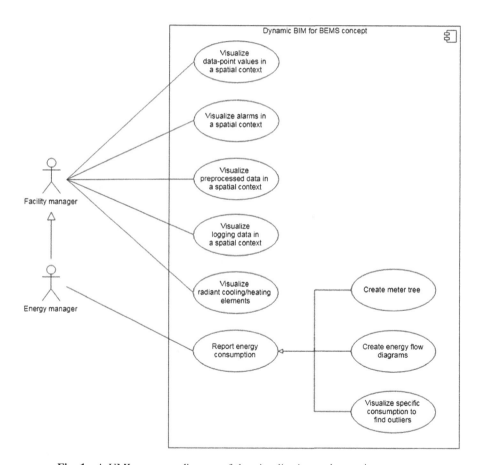

Fig. 1. A UML use case diagram of the visualization and reporting use cases

Use case UC1 'Visualization of data-point values in a spatial context' is described in Table 1. The use case addresses limited capabilities in BEMS to visualize data-point values in the context of rooms and zones in which they are located. A BIM model would be a simplified bare bone model containing essential information which are derived from defined and validated requirements. Data maps that combine space layout data retrieved from a BIM with BEMS data enable facility managers to scan large amounts of data for salient patterns effectively. For instance, temperature differences of sensors located in adjacent zones that exceed a predefined threshold may be highlighted with 2D, 2.5D or 3D visualizations of room layouts and color-coded temperature data. Color coding methods, such as heat maps, facilitate the detection of potential anomalies (e.g., temperature difference greater than a given threshold) and spatial granularity of data-points, respectively. Visualizations of time-series data may be animated. Visualization of room functions from BIM may provide facility managers with useful additional information. For example, server rooms and offices may have different temperature set points, and therefore the threshold for temperatures differences in server rooms may be higher than the threshold for temperature differences between offices.

Table 1. Use case UC1 'Visualize data-point values in a spatial context'

Use case ID	UC1
Use case name	Visualize data-point values in a spatial context
Use case description	Readings for one or more data-point values are retrieved from B(E)MS. They are visualized in the context of their zones or zone regions, which are obtained from BIM
Actor(s)	Facility manager
Trigger	On-demand or automatic check
Basic flow	1. A set of data-points (e.g., all temperature, CO_2 or humidity sensors on a given floor), as specified by the facility manager, is retrieved from BIM together with their zone contexts and HVAC terminals (supply air diffusers, return air grilles, fan coil units) in zones 2. Readings for data-points are retrieved from B(E)MS 3. Zones, zone regions, or data-points locations are colored based on their proximity. For example, temperature differences of sensors in adjacent zones that exceed a predefined threshold may be highlighted
Necessary information	1. Access to data-points in B(E)MS (e.g., trending data for temperature, CO_2 or humidity sensor, thermostat setpoints) 2. Rooms geometry, functions 3. HVAC zones geometry 4. HVAC terminals locations

Use case UC2 'Visualize alarms in a spatial context' is described in Table 2. Alarms are events that are triggered automatically by a BEMS. An example of an alarm is a zone temperature value exceeding a preconfigured upper threshold. Different types of alarms are located in their spatial context. This makes it is easier for facility managers to group related alarms and interpret their messages. The flow and required data for this use case are similar to the visualization of data points (UC1).

Table 2. Use case UC2 'Visualize alarms in a spatial context'

Use case ID	UC2
Use case name	Visualize alarms in a spatial context
Use case description	A list of alarms is retrieved from B(E)MS. They are visualized in the context of their zones or zone regions, which are obtained from BIM
Actor(s)	Facility manager
Trigger	Manual
Basic flow	1. Retrieve a list of actual alarms (location of alarms, alarm messages) from BEMS 2. Retrieve zones that contain alarm locations 3. Visualize the position of the alarms in zones
Necessary information	1. Location of alarm values (i.e., containing zones, objects) 2. Current alarm values 3. Building geometric information (shapes of zones, rooms, etc.) 4. Geometric information of HVAC/electrical installation

Use case UC3 'Visualize and compare preprocessed data in a spatial context' is described in Table 3. Such a use case could lead to a deeper insight into the operation of a building. Further, this enables the identification of gaps between the design and operation phase of a building and even non-intended tenant behavior. This is especially true when a spatial context is added to both the preprocessed and live data, and spatial proximity allows for correlation of diverse data. For example, simulation of solar radiation intensity combined with a weather forecasting service can identify zones that are prone to overheating. Hence, the facility manager could be aware of the affected zones and can readjust the heating system. Sometimes unusual sensor readings, despite the absence of equipment failure, can be accounted to non-obvious sources (weather, holidays, and one-time events in the affected space). In this case, the abnormal reading can be explained by correlating the values with other sensors and data sources (weather forecast, calendars or weather station readings) in the contextual neighborhood. The source and type of the preprocessed data can be manifold and may range from building energy simulation results and weather forecasting services to construction phase calculations about the building and technical equipment. However, the preprocessed data is usually not readily available in the BIM.

Use case UC4 'Visualize logging data in a spatial context' is described in Table 4. In the buildings with limited or no B(E)MS system, loggers may be deployed for data collection to monitor indoor air quality conditions or plug loads. Therefore, visualization of the spatial distribution of loggers together with their readings enables facility managers to detect and localize anomalous reading patterns faster and easier. For instance, if loggers are near each other, coloring may be done to highlight differences in data values (like in UC1), and if loggers are spread out, coloring may be done based on an absolute range. Locations of loggers may change over time and need to be tracked in

Table 3. Use case UC3 'Visualize and compare preprocessed data in a spatial context'

Use case ID	UC3
Use case name	Visualize and compare preprocessed data in a spatial context
Use case description	Preprocessed data and live data are visualized and compared by adding spatial context to both of them. Spatial proximity is used to derive correlations of diverse data
Actor(s)	Facility manager
Trigger	On-demand or automatic
Basic flow	1. A data-point from the BEMS is requested 2. Its spatial context is retrieved from BIM 3. External data sources that correspond with the BEMS data-point are prompted 4. Readings from the external data-points and the BEMS data-point are visualized (i.e., superimposed)
Necessary information	1. BEMS data-points 2. BIM geometry information 3. External data sources (examples): a. Weather service b. Energy simulation results c. Calendar with public holidays

Table 4. Use case UC4 'Visualize logging data in a spatial context'

Use case ID	UC4
Use case name	Visualize logging data in a spatial context
Use case description	A set of loggers and their readings are retrieved from logging database. They are visualized in the context of their zones or zone regions, which are obtained from BIM
Actor(s)	Facility manager
Trigger	On-demand
Basic flow	1. A set of loggers (e.g., all temperature/CO_2/humidity sensors) is retrieved from BIM for a given time window together with their zone contexts and HVAC terminals (supply air diffusers, return air grilles, fan coil units) in zones 2. Readings for loggers and the time window are retrieved from the logging database 3. Zones, zone regions, or logger locations are colored according to data values
Necessary information	1. Access to logger data 2. Loggers locations 3. Rooms geometry, functions, adjacency 4. HVAC zones geometry, adjacency 5. HVAC terminals locations

BIM. Loggers may be deployed in multiple buildings at the same time and may need to be visualized. In case of long time intervals, loggers and their data may need to be visualized for multiple locations. This could be useful if different areas of a building are to be covered with a small number of loggers (e.g. for plug load loggers but challenging for indoor air quality (IAQ) loggers due to different weather conditions).

Use case UC5 'Visualize logging data in radiant cooling/heating elements' is presented in Table 5. The concrete core activated ceilings compared to radiators are not easily recognizable and tangible. Therefore, visualization of supplied areas by showing supplied zone borders by one valve, showing thermally activated zones and marking the areas with dew point problems can help facility managers to identify comfort problems more easily. In this use case, regarding each zone, zone borders, as well as the actual valve position and dew point sensor values, are retrieved from BIM and BEMS, respectively. Through investigation of retrieved values, the zone layout with valve position range as well as the zones with dew point problems is identified and visualized through 2D, 2.5D or 3D visualization and color-coded information.

Use case UC6 'Report energy consumption' as described in Table 6 provides energy managers with useful information to prepare energy management reports and energy consumption to the property management. Some parts of these mentioned processes such as visualization of specific consumption to find outliers, the creation of meter tree and energy flow diagrams can be automated. In this use case, a list of all

Table 5. Use case UC5 'Visualize radiant cooling/heating elements'

Use case ID	UC5
Use case name	Visualize radiant cooling/heating elements
Use case description	Actual valve position and dew point sensor values are retrieved from BEMS. They are visualized in the context of their zones or zone borders which are obtained from BIM
Actor(s)	Facility manager
Trigger	On-demand
Basic flow	1. Choose a floor (or part of it) 2. Find a list of all zones N in the chosen part 3. Show the borders of the zones 4. For each zone n from the list N a. Ask the actual valve position b. If the value is larger than zero, put the (z, n, b) triple into list S, where b is a Boolean value, indicating that zone z has an open valve by the value of n c. Ask the actual dew point sensor value d. If value is one, but the double (z, b) into the list M where b is a Boolean value, indicating that zone z has a dew point problem 5. Visualize the zone layout using colored valve position range (blue-red) 6. Mark all zones in a list M
Necessary information	1. Actual valve position (and dew point sensor value) in BEMS available 2. Assignment of geometrical areas to concrete core activated zones 3. Assignment of valves (and dew point sensors) to zones

Table 6. Use case UC6 'Report energy consumption'

Use case ID	UC6
Use case name	Report energy consumption
Use case description	Energy managers often have to provide energy management reports and energy consumption to the property management. Following parts can be automated: 1. Create meter tree (relation of meters to zones and plants) 2. Create energy flow diagrams 3. A visualization of specific consumption to find outliers
Actor(s)	Energy manager
Trigger	On-demand
Basic flow	1. Collect a list of all meters M from the BEMS 2. For each meter m in the list M a. Ask the actual power value b. Ask the actual consumption value c. Ask the pre-defined previous time period (month, year,..) value d. Calculate the difference => consumption of pre-defined time period e. Divide the consumption of m by the related zone area f. Find a list of all sub-meters S g. Find a list of all previous (hierarchy up) meters P h. Sum up consumption of all sub-meters in list S and compare to m i. If the sum is significantly higher or lower than the value of m, then put the information to list W 3. Create a visualization based on lists P and S 4. Create energy flow diagram based on consumption and P and S 5. Compare all specific values calculated in e) and put information of outliers to list W 6. Visualize the zone measured by meter m, layout using colored consumption range (blue-red) 7. Create a list with all deviations stored in list W
Necessary information	1. Meter values available in BEMS (incl. historical data) 2. Semantic information of zone (area) 3. Assignment of meters to zones 4. Assignment of meters to plants 5. Assignment of plants to zones

existing meters (M) together with their actual power value, actual consumption value and pre-defined previous time period are retrieved from the BEMS, and the related zone geometries and zone area of each meter are retrieved from the BIM. Also, assignment of meters to zones, meters to plants and plants to zones can be done by ontologies. As the output, the differences between actual consumption value and pre-defined time period consumption value of each meter per its related zone area is calculated and visualized via colored consumption range (e.g. red and blue). Also, regarding of each meter in M, a list of sub-meters (S) and previous meters (P) is retrieved and visualized, and then, through comparison of sum up consumption of all meters, the information of outliers and deviations are calculated, stored in a list (W) and reported. Finally, energy flow diagrams based on the consumption and the metering hierarchy (i.e., M, P, and S) are visualized via Sankey diagrams.

3.2   Engineering and Commissioning Use Cases

Apart from operational analytics of energy and comfort related parameters, the approach of using a combination of dynamic BIM and BEMS could also be useful for more advanced analysis of the building systems' parameters during their (re)engineering or (re)commissioning. Involved actors are engineers from different domains who are occasionally appointed to analyze and improve the configuration of the building systems. Here, a couple of examples of such engineering and commissioning use cases is presented. Figure 2 shows them in a UML use case diagram.

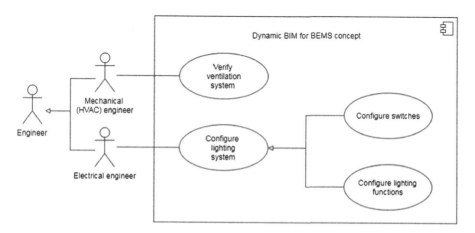

Fig. 2. A UML use case diagram of the engineering and commissioning use cases

A key benefit of a digital building model as it is provided in BIM is the ability to employ it for increasing the quality of engineering the technical systems that are required for building services like HVAC, lighting and other energy-intensive services. The task of commissioning includes the configuration and testing of technical systems according to the intended installation and planning of the equipment. The digital model can be employed as a blueprint by using semantic and spatial reasoning for energy systems.

Use case UC7 (Table 7) covers the verification of a ventilation system using the provided layout of energy provisioning, duct systems and distribution components like variable air volume (VAV) controllers, flaps and sensory equipment for temperature and air quality (e.g. CO_2 sensors). Given that the system is operational the use case envisions to spatially analyze the path from energy provisioning to the end point of the airflow, which may be offices or halls. The result is a graph that shows the paths from source to the different destinations. An annotated model like BIM supports this process by allowing the identification of the functionality of different components. I.e., an airflow starts ventilation, may pass through different flaps, is conditioned by heating

Table 7. Use case UC7 'Verify ventilation system'

Use case ID	UC7
Use case name	Verify ventilation system
Use case description	Validation of the engineering and installation of ventilation by combining structural BIM information with control and operation data from BEMS
Actor(s)	Mechanical (HVAC) engineer
Trigger	On-demand
Basic flow	1. Relevant components are extracted from the BIM: fans, ducts, flaps, heating coils, cooling coils, humidifiers, etc 2. Spatial reasoning to extract duct topology 3. Assignment of control signals to components 4. Deriving a test pattern of switch states to validate actual installation against topology in BIM 5. Execution of test patterns and recording of monitoring data to determine measured impact and compare to the expected impact 6. Reporting deviation detected during validation
Necessary information	1. Semantically annotated energy components and their relations in BIM 2. Access to control signals and monitoring data of BEMS for switch states, flap positions, airflows and temperatures

coils, cooling coils or humidifiers, may be split down to different distribution paths and reaches its endpoint, which may be equipped with a motor flap or a VAV. These components should be semantically annotated to building service classes, allowing to derive the airflow paths.

In a next step, the operation data from the BEMS is separated into control data and sensory data. Using the control data, the operation states of equipment is determined to allow to decide when, e.g., a fan is operating and which temperature the incoming airflow has. Using the switch state of flaps and other equipment an expectation on the impact in the endpoint can be created and compared with the measured data, e.g., the indoor air data. While the data will be noisy and there will be crosstalk in parts of the system that are not intended to be addressed, the expectation is that for a given control state a specific part of the building shall be reached. The control and operation information gathered from BEMS allow to validate the engineering state of the ventilation system and compare it with the intended operation. It highlights problems like an undersupplied room or incorrectly supplied rooms. Based on these symptoms the problem can be narrowed down to incorrect engineering, but possibly also to equipment failure or incorrect usage by inhabitants.

Commissioning is today a manual and error-prone task where the building services are brought to operation state by providing configuration information. Buildings that are equipped with a building automation system are commonly undergoing permanent reconfiguration due to reconstruction, changes in ownership structure or changing tenants. This means that commissioning is a recurring task that has to be repeated when the framework conditions change.

Use case UC8 employs the digital model for a lighting application (Table 8). Again, a semantically annotated BIM allows identifying relevant building equipment

Table 8. Use case UC8 'Configure lighting system'

Use case ID	UC8
Use case name	Configure lighting system
Use case description	Lighting system configuration upon first commissioning and refurbishment, addressing both light switch assignment and lighting function
Actor(s)	Electrical engineer
Trigger	On-demand
Basic flow	1. Room plan is extracted from the BIM containing updates during refurbishment; also has to contain assigned room function like office, meeting room, canteen 2. Spatial reasoning makes an assignment of light actuators to light sources 3. Engineer uses suggested assignments and implements or adapts them 4. Reasoner suggests actuator functionalities based on room function like constant light, daylight controlled, auto-on or timed 5. Engineer uses suggested functions and implements or adapts them
Necessary information	1. Semantically annotated light components and their relations in BIM

like light, switches, dimmers and presence detectors. Furthermore, the building's zones should be annotated with a usage scenario like office, hall, meeting room, canteen, etc. Given the location of equipment and the room functions, the system can support the commissioning process in two steps: first, it can make suggestions how to link light switches with lights. While this is a consideration for the building's planning phase, a building can easily be modified by indoor refurbishment that changes the floorplan and adds or removes zones. When refitting the BIM, it, therefore, makes sense to suggest new configurations for coupling switching and lights. The second, straight-forward advantage is that the system suggests lighting functions that depend on the room functions: offices require either constant light or daylight controlled lighting, halls that are equipped with motion detectors need lights with auto-on and a timeout after the last motion, while other areas may be equipped with dimmable light equipment. Since the variations of different room functions are limited within a building, but still, each zone requires commissioning, supporting this repetitive task will increase commissioning speed and quality as well as energy efficiency.

4   Requirements

For each of these and other use cases specific information is required. Thus, information requirements are identified together with their possible origin. For example, access to data-points in BEMS (e.g., trending data for temperature, CO_2 or humidity sensors, as well as thermostat set-points), logger locations, room and zone geometry, functions and adjacency, and HVAC terminals location are all required to visualize the data-point values in a spatial context. In addition to the BEMS data-points and geometry information from BIM, additional external data sources such as a weather service, energy simulation results or calendar with public holidays are necessary for the visualization of preprocessed data in a spatial context.

4.1 Functional Requirements

An implementation of the proposed use cases is foremost in need of an approach to make use of the provided heterogeneous data sources. Thereby, in this work, functional requirements revolve around the ability to interconnect and analyze data from the stated sources in a single unified context provided by an overarching model.

As for interconnection with external systems, the first functional requirement is the possibility to read arbitrary data from varying sources. Those data sources do not only differ in their respective data models, but also in their mode of operation. A distinction can be made between dynamic or operational data sources (e.g., live sensor readings) and static data sources (e.g., the spatial position of objects). In the case of the former, historical access to data values are needed for several use cases. Hence, additional functionality canto sample and store values locally from external data sources is needed.

In Table 9 functional requirements for an overarching system model as well as for the semantic reasoning have been summarized and mapped to the use cases. The main challenge is to build a semantic model for an overarching system model which is abstract enough to hide minor details, yet provide enough expressive power to model all information present in the BIM as well in the BEMS. Another requirement is the interconnection of different bits of information using through the semantic model. This enables the cross-reference of data values from formerly disjoint sources, like linking the spatial position of a sensor stored in BIM with the corresponding live readings provided by the BEMS.

Table 9. Functional requirements

ID	Base use case	Description
SR1	All UCs	The BIM4BEMS Model shall be able to represent all objects in BIM
SR2	All UCs	The BIM4BEMS Model shall be able to represent all objects on which information is provided by the BEMS
SR3	All UCs	It shall be possible to connect the information of sensors from BIM semantically with the data-points provided by the BEMS
SR4	All UCs	Objects in the building known to BIM as well as BEMS shall be connectable in the model
SR5	UC4	It shall be possible to import new models into the BIM4BEMS Model to augment it

4.2   Non-Functional Requirements

Ease of setting up, using, and maintaining a BIM4BEMS model is a key non-functional requirement for its applicability to real buildings. This and other non-functional requirements are summarized in Table 10. They are relevant for all use cases.

Table 10. Non-functional requirements

ID	Base use case	Description
NSR1	All UCs	The BIM4BEMS Model shall be easy to setup, use and maintain for buildings with basic as well as advanced BEMS
NSR2	All UCs	The BIM4BEMS Model shall be easy to setup, use and maintain for rudimentary as well as detailed documentation of as-built conditions
NSR3	All UCs	Visualization and interaction with the BIM4BEMS model shall be according to the domain expertise and IT skills of facility and energy managers
NSR4	All UCs	The BIM4BEMS Model shall utilize existing open standards for data interoperability and BMS protocols
NSR5	All UCs	The BIM4BEMS model shall be protected against security threats

To realize these benefits, efforts to configure the model should be minimized. Furthermore, ensuring its effective and regular use by facility and energy managers and engineers demands that data visualization and interaction of users with the model are designed according to their domain knowledge, expertise, and IT skills. Since buildings are modified over time, modifications should be updated in the BIM4BEMS model without significant user effort. Ideally, the BIM4BEMS model is maintained by facility managers or technicians rather than IT specialists. Workflows, which address these issues, are being developed to setup and maintain the BIM4BEMS model.

To address the technical complexity of integrating BIM and BEMS data and achieve reliable and robust operation, the use of existing, ideally open standards for data interoperability (such as IFC or gbXML) and BMS protocols (such as BACnet, LonWorks, or EIB/KNX) is important.

Finally, as it accesses, integrates and visualizes data from different sources and may be available to users in multiple locations, the BIM4BEMS model should operate in an environment that is protected against security threats that may cause loss of data, data inconsistency, or harm to buildings or its occupants.

5   Conclusion and Outlook

The feasibility of each use case always depends on the availability of the necessary information. Other factors also influence the feasibility of implementation and deployment, such as stakeholder interests and their conflicts, or the economic profitability and return on investment, which is out of the scope of this paper. The information that is required can be divided into two main categories: static and dynamic.

Static information is information related to the building itself as well as its components. This includes but is not limited to: building geometric information (wings, floors, rooms and zones geometry, their functions and adjacency); geometry and location of HVAC equipment (terminals, valves, installations) and electrical installations including lighting; loggers' properties and location; positioning of alarms and their containment into zones or association with equipment components. Currently, this information is stored in different formats and documents such as site plans, floor layouts, system layouts (e.g., ventilation layouts or fire protection layouts), or room tables. However, part of the necessary information for some use cases is not easily available mostly because it is insufficiently documented or not documented at all. Furthermore, the documentation is usually not prepared in a format that is easy to integrate into a more dynamic model, so some manual or semi-automatic processing is required.

Dynamic information is information which originates from the B(E)MS and represents some parameter (data-point) related to the building operation or is external information that could be used for the improvement of the operation. Thus, to support the use cases the following B(E)MS information access is necessary: trending data for temperature, CO_2, or humidity sensors, thermostat set-points; alarm values; logger data; meter values (including historical data). Additionally, external information, for example, weather forecast, energy simulation results, or calendar with public holidays, is required.

To conclude, based on the analysis the use cases UC1, UC3, and UC4 of the visualization and reporting use cases are more feasible since they require information from sources that are already available in either BIM or B(E)MS. On the other side, use cases such as UC2 and UC5 require more detailed information such as detailed assignment of alarms to a particular location or detailed location of valves which is normally not available neither in BIM nor B(E)MS, and thus these use cases are less feasible. UC6 is partially feasible because it requires access to historical data of many meters and sub-meters that are usually not present. The engineering and commissioning use cases UC7 and UC8 could be feasible if a semantic annotation of components is available in BIM. However, existing BIM components usually lack the required details of semantic information. In future, component manufacturers might provide instead of only geometry and general description a more detailed semantic information which will increase the feasibility of these use cases.

As future work, further development and implementation of the use cases into a proof-of-concept framework is foreseen. For this purpose, a dynamic BIM for BEMS concept model is defined. Furthermore, the model creation and update workflows will be defined as formal process models using the Business Process Modeling Notation (BPMN) [54]. The presented use cases and the proof-of-concept framework will be validated with a real building and the involved stakeholders. The findings are going to be made available to the BIM, FM and HVAC industry to expand the BIM specifications toward building operation.

Acknowledgment. This work was funded under the project "Building Information Modeling for Building Energy Management Systems" (BIM4BEMS) by the FFG (Austrian Research Promotion Agency) program City of Tomorrow (project number 854677).

References

1. International Energy Agency: Energy Technology Perspectives 2016 - Towards Sustainable Urban Energy Systems. OECD/IEA (2016)
2. International Energy Agency: Tracking Clean Energy Progress 2017. OECD/IEA (2017)
3. Hurtado, L., Nguyen, P., Kling, W., Zeiler, W.: Building energy management systems—Optimization of comfort and energy use. In: 2013 48th International Universities' Power Engineering Conference (UPEC) (2013)
4. Virk, G.S., Alkadhimi, K.I.H., Cheung, J.M., Loveday, D.L.: Advanced control techniques for BEMS. In: Rao, R.B.K.N., Hope, A.D. (eds.) COMADEM 89 International: Proceedings of the First International Congress on Condition Monitoring and Diagnostic Engineering Management (COMADEM), pp. 463–468. Springer, Boston (1989). https://doi.org/10.1007/978-1-4684-8905-7_74
5. Manic, M., Wijayasekara, D., Amarasinghe, K., Rodriguez-Andina, J.J.: Building energy management systems: the age of intelligent and adaptive buildings. IEEE Ind. Electron. Mag. **10**(1), 25–39 (2016)
6. Schachinger, D., Gaida, S., Kastner, W., Petrushevski, F., Reinthaler, C., Sipetic, M., Zucker, G.: An advanced data analytics framework for energy efficiency in buildings. In: 2016 IEEE 21st International Conference on Emerging Technologies and Factory Automation (ETFA) (2016)
7. Sipetic, M., Petrushevski, F., Judex, F.: Comparison of machine learning algorithms for forecasting of residential complex energy consumption. In: 24th Workshop of the European Group for Intelligent Computing in Engineering, Nottingham, UK (2017)
8. Molina-Solana, M., Ros, M., Ruiz, M.D., Gómez-Romero, J., Martin-Bautista, M.: Data science for building energy management: a review. Renew. Sustain. Energy Rev. **70**, 598–609 (2017)
9. Navigant Research: Research report: Market Data: Building Energy Management Systems, September 2017. https://www.navigantresearch.com/research/market-data-building-energy-management-systems. Accessed Jan 2018
10. Ock, J., Issa, R.R., Flood, I.: Smart building energy management systems (BEMS) simulation conceptual framework. In: Winter Simulation Conference (WSC) 2016 (2016)
11. Dong, B., O'Neill, Z., Li, Z.: A BIM-enabled information infrastructure for building energy fault detection and diagnostics. Autom. Constr. **44**, 197–211 (2014)
12. McGlinn, K., Yuce, B., Wicaksono, H., Howell, S., Rezgui, Y.: Usability evaluation of a web-based tool for supporting holistic building energy management. Autom. Constr. **84**, 154–165 (2017)
13. Minoli, D., Sohraby, K., Occhiogrosso, B.: IoT considerations, requirements, and architectures for smart buildings—energy optimization and next-generation building management systems. IEEE Internet Things J. **4**(1), 269–283 (2017)
14. Kazmi, A.H., O'grady, M.J., Delaney, D.T., Ruzzelli, A.G., O'hare, G.M.: A review of wireless-sensor-network-enabled building energy management systems. ACM Trans. Sens. Netw. (TOSN) **10**(4), 66 (2014)

15. Coates, A., Hammoudeh, M., Holmes, K.G.: Internet of things for buildings monitoring: experiences and challenges. In: Proceedings of the International Conference on Future Networks and Distributed Systems (2017)
16. IBM: Watson Internet of Things (2018). https://www.ibm.com/internet-of-things. Accessed Jan 2018
17. Microsoft: Microsoft Azure (2018). https://azure.microsoft.com. Accessed Jan 2018
18. Siemens: MindSphere (2018). https://siemens.mindsphere.io/. Accessed Jan 2018
19. Honeywell: Honeywell Building Solutions (2018). https://buildingsolutions.honeywell.com. Accessed Jan 2018
20. Johnson Controls: Johnson Controls Building Management (2018). http://www.johnsoncontrols.com/buildings/building-management. Accessed Jan 2018
21. Pacific Controls: Pacific Controls Integrated Building Automation (2018). http://www.pacificcontrols.net/solutions/integrated-building-automation.html. Accessed Jan 2018
22. Schneider Electric: Schneider Electric Smart Building Solutions (2018). https://www.schneider-electric.com/en/work/solutions/system/s1/buildings-systems.jsp. Accessed Jan 2018
23. Siemens: Siemens Building Technologies (2018). http://www.buildingtechnologies.siemens.com/bt/global/en/buildingautomation-hvac/building-automation/pages/building-automation-system.aspx. Accessed Jan 2018
24. Building IQ (2018). https://buildingiq.com/. Accessed Jan 2018
25. Nantum: Prescriptive Data (2018). http://www.prescriptivedata.io/. Accessed Jan 2018
26. SkyFoundry: SkySpark (2018). https://skyfoundry.com/skyspark/. Accessed Jan 2018
27. Eastman, C., Teicholz, P., Sacks, R., Liston, K.: BIM Handbook, A Guide to Building Information Modeling for Owners, Managers, Designers, Engineers, and Contractors. Wiley, Hoboken (2008)
28. Howard, R., Björk, B.: Building information modelling–Experts' views on standardisation and industry deployment. Adv. Eng. Inform. **22**, 271–280 (2008)
29. ISO 16739: Industry Foundation Classes (IFC) for data sharing in the construction and facility management industries, "International Organization for Standardization" (2013). https://www.iso.org/standard/51622.html. Accessed Jan 2018
30. Green Building XML (gbXML) Schema, Inc.: Open Green Building XML Schema: a Building Information Modeling solution for our green world (2018). http://www.gbxml.org. Accessed Jan 2018
31. Model support group of BuildingSMART Alliance: Industry foundation classes, IFC4 official release (2013). http://www.buildingsmart-tech.org/ifc/IFC4/final/html/index.htm. Accessed Jan 2018
32. Wang, H., Gluhak, A., Meissner, S., Tafazoli, H.: Integration of BIM and live sensing information to monitor building energy performance. In: The CIB 30th Intternational Conference on Application of IT in AEC Industry, Beijing, China (2013)
33. Dong, B., Lam, K.P., Huang, Y., Dobbs, G.M.: A comparative study of the IFC and gbXML informational infrastructures for data exchange in computational design support environments Geometry information. In: Building Simulation 2007 (2007)
34. Adachi, Y.: Overview of IFC model server framework. In: eWork and eBusiness in Architecture, Engineering and Construction. CRC Press, Boca Raton (2002)
35. Chipman, T., Liebich, T., Weise, M.: mvdXMl specification 1.1. Model Support Group (MSG) of buildingSMART International Ltd. (2016)
36. Model Support Group of BuildingSMART: Model View Definition (MVD) speciification, buildingSMART International Ltd. (2018). http://www.buildingsmart-tech.org/specifications/ifc-view-definition

37. East, E.: Construction Operations Building information exchange (COBie): Requirements Definition. U.S. Army, Engineer Research and Development Center, Washington, D.C. (2007)
38. National BIM Standard: Information Exchange Standards, Construction Operation Building information exchange (COBie) – Version 2.4, National Institute of Building Sciences buildingSMART alliance, US (2015)
39. IFMA: International Facility Management Association (2018) https://www.ifma.org/about/what-is-facility-management. Accessed Jan 2018
40. ARCHIBUS, Inc.: ARCHIBUS. www.archibus.com. Accessed Jan 2018
41. ProFMSoftware: "ArchiFM," vintoCON Ltd. http://www.archifm.net/. Accessed Jan 2018
42. Pärn, E., Edwards, D., Sing, M.: The building information modelling trajectory in facilities management: a review. Autom. Constr. **75**, 45–55 (2017)
43. Studer, R., Benjamins, R., Fensel, D.: Knowledge engineering: principles and methods. Data Knowl. Eng. **25**, 161–198 (1998)
44. Baader, F., Horrocks, I., Sattler, U.: Description logics. In: Staab, S., Studer, R. (eds.) Handbook on Ontologies. INFOSYS, pp. 3–28. Springer, Heidelberg (2004). https://doi.org/10.1007/978-3-540-24750-0_1
45. Schachinger, D., Kastner, W.: Semantics for smart control of building automation. In: Proceedings of the IEEE 25th International Symposium on Industrial Electronics (ISIE) (2016)
46. Sure, Y., Staab, S., Studer, R.: Ontology engineering methodology. In: Staab, S., Studer, R. (eds.) Handbook on Ontologies. IHIS, pp. 135–152. Springer, Heidelberg (2009). https://doi.org/10.1007/978-3-540-92673-3_6
47. Bonino, D., Corno, F.: DogOnt - ontology modeling for intelligent domotic environments. In: Sheth, A., Staab, S., Dean, M., Paolucci, M., Maynard, D., Finin, T., Thirunarayan, K. (eds.) ISWC 2008. LNCS, vol. 5318, pp. 790–803. Springer, Heidelberg (2008). https://doi.org/10.1007/978-3-540-88564-1_51
48. Kofler, M., Reinisch, C., Kastner, W.: A semantic representation of energy-related information in future smart homes. Energy Build. **47**, 169–179 (2012)
49. Balaji, B., Bhattacharya, A., Fierro, G., Gao, J., Gluck, J., Hong, D., Johansen, A., Koh, J., Ploennigs, J., Agarwal, Y., Berges, M., Culler, D., Gupta, R., Kjaergaard, M.B., Srivastava, M., Whitehouse, K.: Brick: towards a unified metadata schema for buildings. In: Proceedings of the 3rd ACM International Conference on Systems for Energy-Efficient Built Environments, Palo Alto, CA, USA (2016)
50. Haystack, P.: Project Haystack. https://project-haystack.org. Accessed 11 Jan 2018
51. Volkov, A., Chelyshkov, P., Lysenko, D.: Information management in the application of BIM in construction. The roles and functions of the participants of the construction process. Procedia Eng. **153**, 828–832 (2016)
52. Hove, S.E., Anda, B.: Experiences from conducting semi-structured interviews in empirical software engineering research. In: 11th IEEE International Software Metrics Symposium (METRICS 2005) (2005)
53. Object Management Group: OMG Unified Modeling Language (OMG UML) Version 2.5 Specification (2015). http://www.omg.org/spec/UML/2.5
54. Object Management Group: Business Process Model And Notation BPMN Version 2.0 (2011). http://www.omg.org/spec/BPMN/2.0/

Building Information Modeling (BIM) Applications in an Education Context

Alcínia Zita Sampaio[✉]

Department of Civil Engineering and Architecture, University of Lisbon,
Av. Rovisco Pais, 1049-001 Lisbon, Portugal
zita@civil.ist.utl.pt

Abstract. Teaching Architecture and Civil Engineering requires a permanent updating of knowledge concerning procedures and technologies used in Construction industry. In this sense, the school should seek to adapt its curriculum to include innovative issues to support a better construction. The Building Information Modeling (BIM) methodology involves the concept of information centralized in a unique geometric model and promotes collaboration between all participants. An important role of teaching is to organize actions to stimulate the insertion of new issues in school. The present report presents several uses of the 3D/BIM model, the main limitations found in the development a nD/BIM models and the most remarkable benefits of the BIM methodology when supporting multitasks, within an education context. Several examples of BIM applications developed by students as MSc researchers are described in detail: 2D/BIM technical drawing representations; conflict analysis based in a 3D/BIM model; coordination of construction project supported on a 3D/BIM model; structural analyses using 3D/BIM models; 4D/BIM model for construction planning; materials take-off supporting 5D/BIM models; energetic analyses based on 6D/BIM model; development of 7D/BIM model in maintenance activity. The concept of multiuse of the 3D/BIM model becomes very clear for students, from the development of different nD/BIM models. The objective is to add competitive skills in the training of future civil engineers.

Keywords: BIM methodology · nD/BIM models · Engineering training
Competitive skills

1 Introduction

The methodology Building Information Modeling (BIM) is an approach that is essentially based on the integration of processes, supported by a data-rich 3D model which allows to seamlessly tracking the whole life-cycle of a construction [1]. The methodology BIM, involving the concept of information centralized in a unique virtual geometric model, is changing deeply the way how information is managed within the construction sector, and is strongly supported in advanced modeling technology. BIM combines the parametric three-dimension (3D) modeling and a height level of information, on the generation of a virtual digital model, the 3D/BIM model. As such, it is expected that the whole process becomes more accessible to the multiple entities that

© Springer International Publishing AG, part of Springer Nature 2018
I. F. C. Smith and B. Domer (Eds.): EG-ICE 2018, LNCS 10864, pp. 414–428, 2018.
https://doi.org/10.1007/978-3-319-91638-5_23

collaborate in the enterprise either while developing the design and later in the management of the building [2]. Future engineers should be trained in the large spectrum allowed by BIM methodology.

One important competence of teaching is to promote the introduction of new knowledge that can enrich the student. In this sense the teacher must analyze the best method of providing knowledge to the student. One of the methods is to drive the direction of masters' theses for the topic, BIM, in order to be able to explore the different applications that the engineer can perform with the available BIM tools [3]. The BIM theme was introduced in the Civil Engineering Department only 3 years ago and it is offered to students of the first curricular year. As so, at this level only the handling of basic BIM tool is taught. Senior students have a better understanding of what is the activity of the engineer and some idea that the BIM methodology has been applied in all sectors all over the world. So it is important that the finalists' student earn that competence before leaving school.

Several aspects were study within MSc researches in order to generate nD/BIM models focuses on a wide perspective of the BIM used in the construction industry. The main objective of the presented education strategy is to add competitive skills in the training of future architects and civil engineers [4]. The text describes several research works developed by MSc students, remarking the positive achievements and contributes to the construction field. As the works developed by MSc students, are normally the first contact with BIM, the study cases projects are of low complexity, and the range of studied situations, are of course limited in order to achieve academic reports with the depth and extension appropriate.

2   Training and Education

The implementation of BIM covers various sectors of the construction industry [5]. The text presents several uses of the BIM model to support the analysis of inconsistency between disciplines, the planning and construction management, the take-off of quantities of material and the structural design process. All were developed in an educational context. Based on the presentation of studies applied to real situations there were identified the main benefits and limitations in the generation of nD/BIM models. The nD directions of the BIM use are based on a proper relationship and collaboration among team members in order to optimize the process of development of the project [6]. The required collaboration is based on features provided by a sustained methodology and an effective interoperability of BIM tools.

The capabilities that have been demonstrated in recent reports, together with the dissemination of technological advances achievements, should be known by the users. The school, within its educational mission, has the role of encouraging the students, future engineers and architects, to acquire new knowledge on BIM issue. So, the future engineers and architects should obtain new knowledge concerning BIM concept and multiuse. In the context of the education activity in a Civil Engineering and Architectural school some topics of BIM application were developed by students within MSc research works [7]. The present text describes several of these research works. The students have been conducting research works concerning nD/BIM applications addressing various activities related to the areas of architecture, structures and construction (Fig. 1):

- Generation and analysis of **structural** 3D/BIM model [8];
- **Conflict analysis** based on 3D/BIM model [9];
- Establishment of **parametric objects** applied in the architectural 3D/BIM model [10];
- Planning [11] and management [12] of the **construction** supported on 4D/BIM model;
- Take-off of **quantities** of materials from project supported on 5D/BIM model [13];
- **Maintenance** of buildings supported on 6D/BIM model [14].

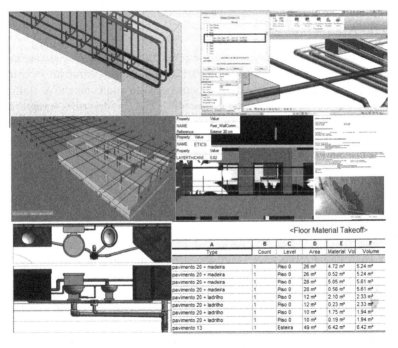

Fig. 1. nD/BIM didactic models – structural design, management and construction planning, maintenance, conflict analyses and materials take-off.

The objective with the introduction of BIM methodology, at the last level of the student's school training, is to enable the future engineer with basic knowledge: in handling BIM tools and in learning how to use them for running usual work, normally developed based in traditional software. In this context, the study cases are real-projects but the focus to be analyzed is selected in order give to each student a unique perspective to follow (structures, planning construction or takeoff material).

3   BIM Concept and Multiuse

The reference to BIM methodology includes the combination of a set of technologies related to the generation of the model and with the handling of their data, and the ability to promote a high level of interdisciplinary collaboration, desirable in the development and analysis of the project, contributing to achieve better productivity and quality in the design, construction and maintenance of buildings [1]. Basic BIM technology supports a clear and precise communication between architects, engineers, builders, facility managers and owners, with their activities based on the BIM model that allows the centralization of all the information, which is being raised along the development of a project. The practical concept of BIM points, currently, two essential aspects:

- The **generation** of a three-dimensional (3D) geometric model containing all the information associated with the idealization and development of a project;
- The **use** of data, able to be provided by the model, in the various activities that are usually carried over a project.

After the 3D/BIM model is created containing the information considered relevant, it can be used to establish distinct tasks: technical drawings generation, conflict detection analyses; construction planning definition; take-off of quantities of material; energy study; maintenance strategy.

Due to the consistency of design data with quality data and construction process with quality control process, BIM can generate and maintain information produced during the whole life-cycle of a building project—from design to maintenance—and can be applied to various fields [2]. BIM can be considered as a digital representation of a building, an object-oriented 3D model, and a repository of project information to facilitate interoperability and exchange of information between software. Therefore, BIM data-rich model allows the extraction of data, appropriate to various users' needs, and the generation of information that can be used to make decisions, to improve the process of delivering the facility and to create better products [6].

A BIM model constitutes a complete and full database, not only concerning the geometric data, the most visible part of the process, but also the materials applied in the building and its mechanical and physical characteristics [15]. The methodology BIM interferes with all aspects involved in a building project:

- The **initial** stage when the form of the building is generated (architecture);
- The different phases of the **structural** study (structural solution design, analysis and production of technical drawings);
- The **quantification** of materials and budgets and the **construction** planning process (definition of geometric model for each construction phase and cost estimation);
- And later in the post-occupation period of the building (**management** and **maintenance**).

3.1   Generation of Drawings and Sections Views (3D/BIM)

The graphical documentation associated with the project is made up of plants, vertical sections, elevations and construction details. As the digital 3D/BIM model is formed of parametric objects, it contains all the information associated with the composition of each component. The BIM tools admit the ability to manipulate the BIM data is in order to obtain different type of drawings and perspectives of the model. For example, a plant is automatically obtained by the application of a horizontal section made by a secant plane located in a higher level than the top level of the windows (Fig. 2).

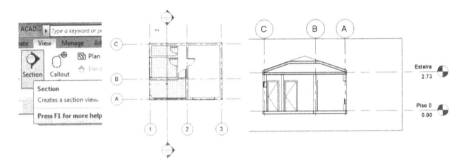

Fig. 2.   Plan representation and section view [16].

On the representation a vertical cut, the location of the intersection plane is shown over a plan view (intersection plan line, name and guidance). The plant drawing that is automatically obtained contains a reduced amount of information. The BIM tool allows adding the missing information such as dimensions and designation of each room and correspondent area [10]. In addition, vertical cuts can be applied over the 3D/BIM model. It allows to shown in a perspective view the interior of the building and the graphical representation of each material (Fig. 3).

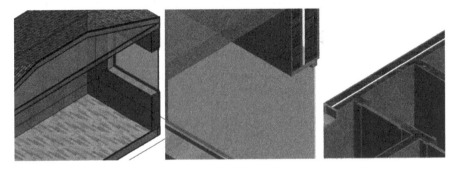

Fig. 3.   Representation in vertical cut applied over the model [16].

The graphic documentation set that can be obtained from the model is one of the advantages of BIM, when compared with the traditional process, emphasizing the ability of automation, updating, adding details, and material composition of elements. To this end, the drawings can be organized by selecting drawings, tables, supplementary schemes details and other information. The software automatically creates a sheet with all these elements, each representing a certain range, which is automatically actualized when the 3D/BIM model is changed. This BIM capacity avoids the representation of incoherent, incorrect or outdated information, as is frequent in CAD drawings when a project is submitted to adjustments.

3.2 Interoperability Analyses in Structural Design (3D/BIM)

The main objective of the researches consists of a comparative analysis between the traditional process and the BIM methodology, focusing on the structural component of the project. Two didactic works were carried out. The studies allow the identification of limitations and problems resulting from the analysis of two specific cases, and the proposed recommendations and best practices to promote achieving a higher degree of efficiency.

In a research work, conducted by Azevedo [17], a structural *Revit* model was created over a *Revit* architecture model. The preliminary design of the structural elements geometry was carried out based on the architectural constraints of the building, the imposed actions, and the used materials, and next the *Revit* structural model was transposed to the structural software, *SAP2000*. In the process the degree of interoperability between software were analyzed. It was analyzed the type of information that is maintained or amended, and which adaptations were necessary to make in order to obtain a correct analytical model. Although the transposition cannot be described as the ideal methodology, taking into account constraints that condition the efficiency of BIM model, it has significant advantages compared with the traditional process (Fig. 4):

- The **transposition** of data between the *Revit* and *SAP2000* is conducted only in one direction (not allowing subsequent updates in the original *Revit* model).
- The main **advantages** are: decrease of the amount of errors and inconsistencies in the structural design; decrease of the total project duration; increase of the overall efficiency;
- However some **limitations** are found in this process: unidirectional information workflow (updates not supported); limitations on the type of elements transferred; difficulty in transposing slabs openings; inability to transfer alignments (grids); failure to recognize the constraints of foundations.

Fig. 4. *Revit* models (architecture and structural) and SAP2000 models.

In a second research work performed by Oliveira [8], after doing the safety check for structural elements and the detailing of rebar in *Robot*, it was necessary to transfer all the information back for the BIM model, but this process is still very limited (Fig. 5):

• Regarding the **slab**, *Revit* does not recognize the rebar information exported by *Robot*. It is however possible, to create a *dwg* file in *Robot*, specifying the detail drawings of reinforcement;
• The transposition process of information related to **beam** details between the calculation and modeling software admits some degree of integration; however, the results are still not satisfactory. It becomes necessary to set directly in *Revit*, the rebar on each beam. There are still many limitations to full integration between *Revit* and *Robot*;
• Contrary to what occurs for beams, the exportation of detailed rebar information for **columns** between *Robot* and *Revit* is carried out without any difficulties. This takes importance if a higher level of detail is desirable and for the account of material;
• For the **foundation beams** some problems occur when exporting detail information about the reinforcement and it should be considered the correct splices of rebar in the connection between columns and foundations to improve the quality of drawings.

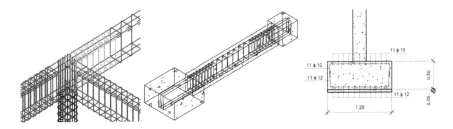

Fig. 5. Adjustments performed in *Revit* of rebar detailing transferred from *Robot*.

BIM methodology has become particularly popular in the construction industry however it has been difficult to spread the use of this within structural engineering workplaces. There is, therefore, the need to demonstrate that this is a valid methodology, which using the BIM tools is advantageous even when directed at the structural design. It should be noted that the detail of reinforcement developed for the structural elements, is possible by two alternatives; by recourse to the structural calculation software *Robot* or trough *Revit*. Both possibilities show different levels of automation and rectifications for the results are commonly necessary due to the inconsistency of data.

3.3   Conflict Analysis Between Disciplines (3D/BIM)

The BIM methodology and tools associated with it present themselves as an excellent asset to support the process of conflict analysis, as they make it possible to merge all disciplines in an integrated virtual environment, the 3D/BIM model. The aim of the study conducted by [9] was to evaluate the practical capabilities of the BIM concept in the conflict analysis between building services, namely, the water supply and drainage systems design, and the architectural and structural design. As such, it was developed a 3D/BIM model containing the components: architecture, structures and building services. The model was analyzed oriented to the clash detection between elements from all disciplines and for that the *Clash Detective* function in *Revit* was used. This work contributes to demonstrate the advantages of BIM in the conciliation and coordination between different specialties, as well as the benefits of its application in conflict analysis in an engineering design.

The BIM tools admit to overlap three design disciplines and support the analyses of conflicts verified between elements belonging to distinct disciplines. There are applications such as *Tekla BIMsight*, *Solibri Model Checker* or *Navisworks* with additional capabilities aimed at conflict analysis. The algorithm of conflict detection can evaluate two modes of inconsistency:

- Conflict detection based on **geometry** consists in checking for intersections between 3D elements of different specialties;
- Analyze based on **rules** that allow to detect cases that do not check for compliance with regulations or rules previously defined by the user (minimum distance between elements or the space for people circulation may not be obstructed by systems elements).

Tekla BIMsight can be used on the analysis between the specialties Mechanical, Electrical, and Plumbing (MEP) and structures. First, the two components, both created in a BIM modeler software, must be are exported to *Tekla*, in IFC compatible format. The two models are then overlapped and the conflict detection is activated by selecting the rule named *MEP vs Structure*. A list of points of conflicts is returned from the analysis. The perspective of Fig. 6 allows the visualization of several collision points marked with a symbol.

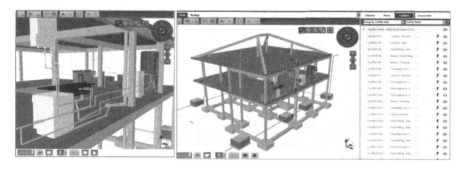

Fig. 6. Geometric conflict detection between MEP and Structures disciplines.

Then, it must be carried out a detailed analysis of each occurrence because duplicate events can be considered and some conflicts are inevitability. The conflicting situations adjustments cannot be carried out directly in *Tekla BIMsight*, which constitutes a limitation of most of the BIM viewers, and corrections must be performed in a BIM modeler tool (Fig. 7).

Fig. 7. Correction solutions carried out in conflict spots.

3.4 Visual Simulation of Construction Planning (4D/BIM)

Planning and scheduling in construction, involves the sequence of activities both in space and in time, taking into account the allocation and resource acquisition, quantities and space constraints amongst others. Using the *Revit* software the architectural and infrastructure models of a project were generated [11]. To create a 4D model the *Navisworks* software was used to allow the interconnections amongst sets of 3D elements of the BIM model, with the planned tasks stablished. For that the link between construction tasks and groups of elements of the 3D/BIM model is needed. The *Navisworks* BIM viewer admits the integration of 3D/BIM model with the construction planning established in the *Gant* schedule using the *Microsoft Project* software. This process corresponds to the generation of a 4D/BIM model of the building construction (Fig. 8).

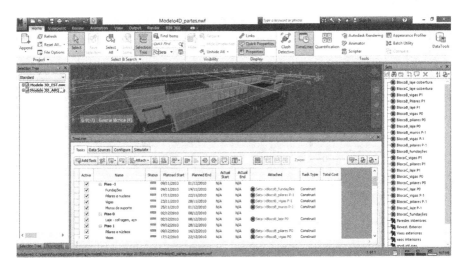

Fig. 8. Generation of a model 4D/BIM using *Navisworks* BIM viewer.

The 4D/model allows the visual simulation of the building construction. It allows the detection of eventual conflict in work and supports the definition of logistics planning in the shipyard and the coordination of the equipment and material supply. The application is easily manipulated using mobile devices at the construction site. The real construction and the planed process can be compared. In accordance with the specific situation found the 4D/BIM model admits to update the timeline (delays and advances), the inclusion of new elements and the redefinition of groups associated with each task [18].

3.5   Take-Off of Material Quantities (5D/BIM)

The 3D/BIM model allows obtaining the amount of materials from the project and in distinct design phases. The information associated with each parametric object can be added when needed [10]. For example, to obtain the cost estimation of a project, it is necessary to add the unit cost to each type of parametric object. Depending on the number and type of parameters that were associated with the parametric object, it is possible to automatically obtain several types of tables containing lists of elements and quantities related with the parameters of the objects [13]. So those tables can cover several fields: surface area of the elements, the safety coefficient, the sound reduction level, individual and global cost, thermal transmission coefficient or the function, trademark and manufacturer of components.

For example, it is possible to obtain from a structural BIM model, a table with the number of reinforced concrete columns of the project. The procedure to obtaining the table starts with: the creation of a new folder, *New Schedules/Quantities*; the selecting of the elements type, *Structural Columns*; the selection of required fields or parameters. Table 1 illustrates the list of columns of a project, considering the name, the type of material and the volume per element. Table 2 presents another list concerning the floor elements.

Table 1.   Take-off table of columns from a 3D/BIM model

Scheduled fields (in order)	Structural Column Schedule				
Type					
Count	A	B	C	D	E
Family	Type	Count	Family	Volume	Structural Material
Structural Material					
Volume	P1 200 x 200m	1	M_Concrete-Rectangular-Column	0.11 m³	Concrete, Cast-in-Place gray
	P1 200 x 200m	1	M_Concrete-Rectangular-Column	0.11 m³	Concrete, Cast-in-Place gray
	P1 200 x 200m	1	M_Concrete-Rectangular-Column	0.11 m³	Concrete, Cast-in-Place gray
	P1 200 x 200m	1	M_Concrete-Rectangular-Column	0.11 m³	Concrete, Cast-in-Place gray
	P2 200 x 300m	1	M_Concrete-Rectangular-Column	0.16 m³	Concrete, Cast-in-Place gray
	P2 200 x 300m	1	M_Concrete-Rectangular-Column	0.16 m³	Concrete, Cast-in-Place gray
	P2 200 x 300m	1	M_Concrete-Rectangular-Column	0.16 m³	Concrete, Cast-in-Place gray
	P2 200 x 300m	1	M_Concrete-Rectangular-Column	0.16 m³	Concrete, Cast-in-Place gray

Table 2. Table of quantities of floor materials

Scheduled fields (in order):	<Floor Material Takeoff>						
Type Count Level Area Material: Volume Volume Family and Type Structural Material	**A**	**B**	**C**	**D**	**E**	**F**	**G**
	Type	Count	Level	Area	Material: Vol	Volume	Family and Type
	pavimento 20 + madeira	1	Piso 0	26 m²	4.72 m³	5.24 m³	Floor: paviment
	pavimento 20 + madeira	1	Piso 0	26 m²	0.52 m³	5.24 m³	Floor: paviment
	pavimento 20 + madeira	1	Piso 0	28 m²	5.05 m³	5.61 m³	Floor: paviment
	pavimento 20 + madeira	1	Piso 0	28 m²	0.56 m³	5.61 m³	Floor: paviment
	pavimento 20 + ladrilho	1	Piso 0	12 m²	2.10 m³	2.33 m³	Floor: paviment
	pavimento 20 + ladrilho	1	Piso 0	12 m²	0.23 m³	2.33 m³	Floor: paviment
	pavimento 20 + ladrilho	1	Piso 0	10 m²	1.75 m³	1.94 m³	Floor: paviment
	pavimento 20 + ladrilho	1	Piso 0	10 m²	0.19 m³	1.94 m³	Floor: paviment
	pavimento 13	1	Esteira	49 m²	6.42 m³	6.42 m³	Floor: paviment

3.6   Energy Analysis Support (6D/BIM)

The analysis of energy sustainability performed over a BIM model is named a 6D/BIM application. One of the factors to consider in selecting particular constructive system is the ability to reduce energy consumption in a building, providing, at the same time, the conditions of comfort required.

Regarding the environmental behavior simulation, *Revit* allows the user to transfer the 3D/BIM model, using the IFC format, to other software such as *Ecotec*, *Equest* or *Energyplus* [10]. Revit includes *Green Building Studio* functionality that allows the energy simulation, on the BIM model. So, in an initial design the decision-making can be substantiated in a comparative analysis of results relating to environmental perform-ance, reducing carbon dioxide emissions and economic energy consumption [19]. The parameter concerning the thermal transmission coefficient is a characteristic of the objects of the BIM model. This fiscal characteristic of the objects is used on the energetic simulation performed by the software. Thus, the results may be obtained from the energy simulation, and at different stages of the project (Fig. 9).

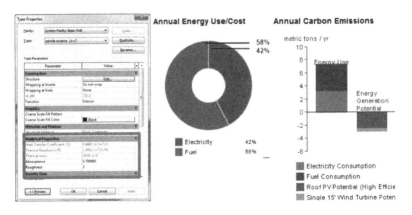

Fig. 9. Thermal properties and energy analysis result.

3.7   Building Maintenance Activity (7D/BIM)

Maintenance is one of the activities that can be explored with BIM, as all the information of the building, from various disciplines, is centered on a unique BIM model. A 7D/BIM application can support the inspection of buildings, when integrated with the *Navisworks* BIM viewer. An inspection program was developed in by Simões [14]. It contains a database organized by construction component (exterior and interior walls and roof) related to the most frequently anomalies verified in each type of component and associated to recommended repair methods (Fig. 10).

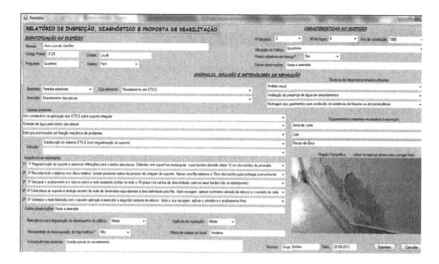

Fig. 10.   Inspection program interface.

In a building during an inspection visit, the engineer can manipulate the BIM model using a mobile device. The *Navisworks* allows incorporating both the BIM model and the inspection application. Then when the user is faced with an anomaly, detected over a component of the real building, can select the corresponding model element, and can:

- Consult the **composition** of the element (thickness and material of each layer), and the relevant parameters for maintenance that have been associated to the respective parametric object;
- Run the **inspection program** and fill out an inspection sheet, including photographs taken in the real building;
- **Archive** the inspection sheet in *pdf* format and link the report to the correspondent BIM model element.

Once completed the inspection visit to the building and linked each anomaly report to the model (Fig. 11), the engineering, supported in the information allowed by the BIM model, can draw up a sustainable rehabilitation work or a preventive maintenance plane.

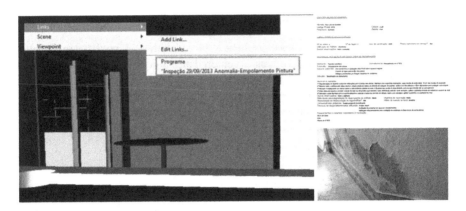

Fig. 11. Consulting an inspection report on a BIM model.

4 Conclusions

The report exposes several aspects of BIM methodology, from the generation of 3D/BIM models to the definition of 7D/BIM models. The use of BIM methodology for the development of construction management emerged several situations that expose the benefits of using BIM. So, the potential of BIM to support a transformation of the processes of design and construction has been evident and reported in the multi-sectors described.

Concerning the 3D/BIM model the automatic definition of drawings and sections, the analyses of conflict between disciplines and the structural analyses support in the methodology were described and the main benefits and limitations were worked out. During the creation and usage of 4D/5D/6D/7D BIM models, some very positive points where found, from which the following ones are highlighted: The ability to visualize the schedule and the 4D simulation show that *Navisworks* can be a useful tool to support the project planning, in a collaborative environment, as intended in the BIM methodology; the BIM model allows obtaining tables covering several fields concerning surface area of the elements, volume of materials, individual and global cost (5D/BIM model); *Revit* includes the *Green Building Studio* plugin a functionality that allows the energy simulation (6D/BIM model), in an initial design, allowing a comparative analysis of results relating to environmental performance, reducing carbon dioxide emissions and economic energy consumption; the developed 7D/BIM application demonstrates clearly how BIM can support building inspections when integrated with a BIM viewer.

The text enabled the knowledge of the subject BIM within an education context but oriented to the real activity. Research on the subject has exposed several objects of study covering BIM, from its origin to its application in the Construction sector, seeking to know the reasons for his development and how this methodology has been developed. The multiuse methodology applied over the 3D/BIM model becomes very clear to the new professionals as the students developed different nD/BIM models within their research works. The main objective of this strategy was to add skills in the training of future architects and civil engineers, in an innovative area of growing demand in the national and international construction. After the student perform successfully the study set out to achieve, the young engineer has the ability, in a project, to carry out an adequate analysis of the application of the methodology BIM and of what resources he can use in its development. Of course, as each student studied only one perspective of the BIM application, he will meet better the scope he studied. But the BIM concept and use are cross at any direction of BIM and the student has the necessary knowledge to develop BIM also in other areas of work.

References

1. Azhar, S., Hein, M., Sketo, B.: Building information modeling (BIM): benefits, risks and challenges (2008). http://ascpro.ascweb.org/chair/paper/CPGT182002008.pdf. Accessed 09 Jan 2018
2. Eadie, R., Browne, M., Odeyinka, H., McKeown, C., McNiff, S.: BIM implementation throughout the UK construction project life-cycle: an analysis. Autom. Constr. **36**, 145–151 (2013). http://dx.doi.org/10.1016/j.autcon.2013.09.001. Accessed 09 Jan 2018
3. Sampaio, A.Z., Berdeja, E.P.: Collaborative BIM environment as a support to conflict analysis in building design. In: 4th Experiment@ International Conference 2017 - exp.at'17, Faro, Portugal (2017). Accessed 09 Jan 2018. ISBN 978-989-99894-0-5
4. Sampaio, A.Z., Simões, D.: Maintenance of buildings supported on BIM methodology. In: XIV DBMC - Durability of Building Materials and Components (paper DBMC-p083.pdf, abst.), p. 83. RILEM Publications S.A.R.L., Ghent (2017). e-ISBN 978-2-35158-159-9
5. Succar, B., Sher, W., Williams, A.: An integrated approach to BIM competency assessment, acquisition and application. Autom. Constr. **35**, 174–189 (2013). https://doi.org/10.1016/j.autcon.2013.05.016. Accessed 09 Jan 2018
6. Chen, L.J., Luo, H.: A BIM-based construction quality management model and its applications. Autom. Constr. **46**, 64–73 (2014). http://dx.doi.org/10.1016/j.autcon.2014.05.009. Accessed 09 Jan 2018
7. Sampaio, A.Z., Simões, D.G., Berdeja, E.P.: BIM tools used in maintenance of buildings and on conflict detection. In: Delgado, J.M.P.Q. (ed.) Sustainable Construction. BPR, vol. 8, pp. 163–183. Springer, Singapore (2016). https://doi.org/10.1007/978-981-10-0651-7_8. ISBN 978-981-10-0651-7, Print ISBN 978-981-10-0650-0
8. Oliveira, J.D.: Analysis of the implementation of BIM in structural project. M.Sc. thesis in Civil Engineering, University of Lisbon, Lisbon (2016). (in Portuguese)
9. Berdeja, E.P.: Conflict analysis in a BIM base project. M.Sc. thesis in Civil Engineering, University of Lisbon, Lisbon (2014). (in Portuguese)
10. Araújo, L.: Development of a walls' library to BIM methodology. M.Sc. thesis in Civil Engineering, University of Lisbon, Lisbon (2016). (in Portuguese)
11. Mota, C.: 4D Model in construction planning based on BIM technology. M.Sc. thesis in Civil Engineering, University of Lisbon, Lisbon (2015). (in Portuguese)
12. Silva, D.: Construction management supported on a BIM model. M.Sc. thesis in Civil Engineering, University of Lisbon, Lisbon (2015). (in Portuguese)
13. Silva, B.: BIM methodology as a support to the quantity take-off from projects. M.Sc. thesis in Civil Engineering, University of Lisbon, Lisbon (2016). (in Portuguese)
14. Simões, D.G.: Maintenance of buildings supported on BIM model. M.Sc. thesis in Civil Engineering, University of Lisbon, Lisbon (2013). (in Portuguese)

15. Gu, N., London, K.: Understanding and facilitating BIM adoption in the AEC industry. Autom. Constr. **19**, 988–999 (2010). http://dx.doi.org/10.1016/j.autcon.2010.09.002. Accessed 09 Jan 2018
16. Sampaio, A.Z.: BIM model - generation of architectural model. Didactic text of syllabus Computer Aided Design, University of Lisbon, Lisbon (2017). (in Portuguese)
17. Azevedo, V.: BIM model analysis in the structural design perspective. M.Sc. thesis in Civil Engineering, University of Lisbon, Portugal (2014). (in Portuguese)
18. Sampaio, A.Z., Mota, C.: BIM model of structures used in construction planning. In: National Meeting of Structural Concrete, Coimbra, Portugal, vol. 4, 10 p. (2016). (in Portuguese). http://be2016.dec.uc.pt/. Accessed 09 Jan 2018
19. Coelho, E.: Establishment of parametric objects in BIM floors applied in buildings. M.Sc. thesis in Civil Engineering, University of Lisbon, Lisbon (2017). (in Portuguese)

Data Exchange Requirement Analysis for Value for Money Assessment in Public-Private Partnerships

Guoqian Ren[1(⊠)], Haijiang Li[1], Yi Jiao[2], and Weishuai Zhang[3]

[1] Cardiff School of Engineering, Cardiff University, Cardiff, UK
{RenG,lih}@cardiff.ac.uk
[2] Luban Soft Ltd., Shanghai, People's Republic of China
[3] BoGuang Digital Ltd., Jinan, People's Republic of China

Abstract. Value for money (VfM) as the lifecycle assessment approach in publicprivate partnerships (PPP) essentially covers the overall project performance in both qualitative and quantitative ways. However, the performance measurement in VfM is still lacking supporting data in the project lifecycle. Based on the performance structure of the VfM quantitative assessment, this article developed a data extraction scheme integrated with building information modelling (BIM). The domain of modules mainly covers buildings, civil engineering and highways according to a related measurement standard. By extracting the data types from the original BIM model, the filtered information can facilitate a quantitative assessment by obtaining the required data automatically.

Keywords: Public-private partnership · Value for money
Building information modelling · Data exchange

1 Introduction

The assessment method defined as the value for money (VfM) analysis is widely used around the world by public infrastructure agencies examining the public-private partnership (PPP) approach as a potential project delivery method [1]. The VfM analysis within it is not simply a typical financial-orientated supervision scheme that could also be applied to all procurement phases as a project development tool [2]. Due to the public sector goals in the PPP contract, the quantitative processes of private parties with their project management schemes are challenging currently. A recent report published by the World Bank Group indicated that even in countries with well established PPP programmes, the approach of the VfM assessment is often the subject of controversy and debate [3]. The World Bank Group's clients are trying to develop means that are more systematic for PPP project identification, yet they still lack functional data support. In this way, engineering procurement data may support the VfM assessment highly in most of the public works like civil infrastructures [4]. To stress this possibility, this paper introduces building information modelling (BIM) as one of the essential information supports for VfM.

© Springer International Publishing AG, part of Springer Nature 2018
I. F. C. Smith and B. Domer (Eds.): EG-ICE 2018, LNCS 10864, pp. 429–446, 2018.
https://doi.org/10.1007/978-3-319-91638-5_24

BIM technology has been increasingly accepted in the architecture, engineering and construction (AEC) industries in the last decades. It represents the standardised process of project development, and it uses a digital model to simulate the project lifecycle of a building facility [5]. BIM nowadays is not only an object-oriented modelling process, but it is also becoming part of an intelligent information management platform concerning both internal and external project information. The real-time costs throughout the design, construction and operation stages can be obtained from BIM so that the value chain for clients can be guaranteed [6]. As the primary information carrier within BIM, the Industrial Foundation Class (IFC) standards are the bottom data support of the BIM data dictionary for information exchange requirements [7]. Beyond this, the Information Delivery Manual (IDM) is defined to capture the business processes and provide user information exchange requirements and specifications. Its functional part refers to objects or attributes that have been recognised as critical features in IFC data structures. The domain-specific Model View Definition (MVD) is programming as a technical solution for formalising special-purpose knowledge.

Because no robust standard defines the requirements for a data exchange in a VfM assessment, this currently results in a manual acquisition [8]. This paper proposes modules for the model view and data exchange method from a BIM model followed by the VfM definition. To achieve this goal, the paper will decompose the structure of the VfM quantitative assessment first and then propose a formalised data exchange requirement for a quantitative assessment collected from different AEC regulations, so the information delivery for VfM can be defined progressively. It then presents the data exchange framework for VfM (DFV) by using IFC as the data foundation to deliver standardised information for a VfM quantitative assessment.

2   The Current Status of VfM in PPP

A PPP, as the conclusive procurement concept of the build-operate-transfer (BOT), private finance initiative (PFI) and franchise model, gradually covers multiple mega-construction projects [9]. Unlike conventional procurement, the public sector has to pay a significant proportion of the capital costs of the project up front, followed by an ongoing expense for operation and maintenance over the project lifecycle [10]. A PPP/PFI procurement strategy led by the public sector could stress fair cooperation with a private partner by setting up a special purpose vehicle (SPV) for the targeted project. All the capital needs and financing appraisals are operated by both parties, stressing the effectiveness of financial control and lifecycle management.

In the UK, to simulate private participants, a new PF2 approach is proposed to replace the original PFI procurement strategy. It starts to improve the access of social capital and institutional investors to join the venture of long-term public procurement by providing low-risk capital structures and a better supervision system for asset securitisation [11]. In 2012, HM Treasury withdrew its quantitative tool, and the updated PF2 guidance is now under development. Practice in China, which involves a massive infrastructure of construction and a PPP project library of more than 14,000 projects, was proposed to use the PPP procurement model, and it is basing its PPP structure on the PFI procedure.

As a vital process of project argumentation, VfM supports project sponsors in building up the original logic of whether to perform the PPP procurement model or use the traditional methods, such build and transfer (BT). It is regarded as a lifecycle assessment process, and it can progress not only starting from the early stage of project demonstration, but it can also update dynamically throughout the entire project flow, through the bid or post-bid evaluation [12]. The various VfM approaches commonly used in different regions demonstrate that because VfM methodologies are developed in most countries, more detailed explanations and measurement approaches are required to enhance the level of performance (Table 1).

Table 1. VfM application status

Country	VfM application status	Legal framework	VfM related toolkit	Info query platform
Turkey	No specific methodoloy developed	No	No	No
China	Methodology developed (only qualitative assessment provided)	Guidelines for the operation of Public-Private Partnership (trial)	Government and social capital cooperation project value for money assessment guidelines	No
Indonesia	No specific methodoloy developed	The Presidential Regulation No. 38 of 2015; The Ministry of National Development Planning/National Development Planning Agency (BAPPENAS) Regulation No. 4 of 2015; The Government Goods and Services Procurement Policy (LKPP) Regulation No. 19 of 2015	No	No
Brazil	No specific methodology developed	The General Law for PublicPrivate Partnerships	Public-Private Partnership in Roads and Highways (P3 Toolkit, 2013	No
India	Specific methodology developed	General Financial Rules; Model RFQ & RFP; Model concession agreements	PPP Structuring Toolkit	No
UK	Specific methodology developed	Public procurement law; PFI/PF2	Value for money assessment guidance; Assessing value for money; CIPFA Toolkit	No

(*continued*)

Table 1. (*continued*)

Country	VfM application status	Legal framework	VfM related toolkit	Info query platform
France	Specific methodology developed	PPP and concession law (two regimes)	MAPPP guidance template for the Preliminary Assessment; Reference guide for a financial model for the Preliminary Assessment	No
USA	Specific methodology developed	Different PPP laws in different states	Value for money analysis for P3 s; P3-VALUE Analytical Tool	No
Chile	No specific methodology developed	Concessions Law and regulations	No	No
South Africa	Specific methodology developed	National Treasury PPP Practice Note	Public-Private Partnership Manual, South Africa	No
Canada	Specific methodology developed	P3 s guidance for public sponsors	PPP public sector value for money guidance	No
Australia	Specific methodology developed	National PPP Policy Framework	Value for money guidance	No

The quantitative VfM method is frequently abrogated due to feasibility issues. The project data currently used for financial accounting are historical and not specific. This is most likely due to the inadequate performance of the VfM assessment from the beginning of the project lifecycle [13]. The information acquired manually from multiple sources and resources brings about issues with the information exchange. The weakness of the current PPP/PFI practice indicates the aspects of cost overrun and information transparency that are unable to guarantee the project goals [14].

BIM, introduced in the early 1990 s, is considered the foundation of project information development in construction engineering projects [15]. 'Building information management' is the accepted way to describe the application of BIM as it stresses more on the information interaction and transmission. It is a digital process designed to guide project construction and operations. In project-based industries, the collaborative relationships between different contract sectors and organisations are required to be more integrated to reshape traditional procurement activities. Today, BIM is designed to build low-cost, integrated working systems in infrastructure projects [16]. The development of BIM to date suggests it has the potential to work with PPP models by challenging electronic procurement [17].

It seems the lack of supporting data and unstable toolkits concerning VfM processes could be improved by integrating with BIM, which presupposes the need for all-inclusive information that contains lifecycle functionalities to deal with change [18]. Thus, it is necessary to build a VfM strategy that can provide more valuable deliverables by considering lifecycle performance. The information in BIM concerned with the VfM is hardly distinguished by software, and in most cases, the BIM model in the large-scale project contains typically vast data lines that make it difficult to obtain the information needed for evaluations. Referenced by the concepts of IDM and MVD, which indicate that different users of BIM data have different needs in different domains [19], this article proposes a possible method of clarifying the information exchange for VfM that is mainly focused on the quantitative assessment and then develop a tool that can extract the related data type within the BIM model automatically.

3   Analysis of VfM Quantitative Assessment

As a vital assessment used to reflect on the economic benefits of a project directly, a quantitative measurement requires a more direct measurement of a procurement strategy. The public sector comparator (PSC), originally used in the UK, is now widely regarded as an effective means in quantitative assessment around the world [20].

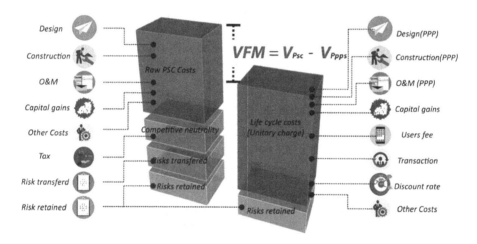

Fig. 1. Structure of the quantitative assessment using PSC method

The above paragraph (Fig. 1) suggests that a PSC-based VfM quantitative strategy could be decomposed effectively by using different knowledge domains from engineering finance schemes. The costs of PSC are calculated by setting up a fictional model using a traditional public procurement strategy, which is carried out from the programming level until financial close [4]. The calculated cost of using PPP (PPPs) as the procurement model must always be less than the cost likely to be incurred if using a traditional public procurement model. The calculation of the PSC-related formula is shown below:

$$V_{psc} = V_{raw} + V_{cn} + V_r \tag{1}$$

$$V_{ppps} = V_{lcc} + V_r' \tag{2}$$

Where V_{psc} (value of PSC) is structured based on the traditional procurement strategy composed of mainly three parts. Within it, V_{raw} represents the resource costs through the entire lifecycle, while V_{cn} represents the value of competitive neutrality, which is based on beneficial factor adjustments, such as differences in state taxation rates and interest rates and differences in regulatory costs. It is used to guarantee that the government provision of a good or service has no advantage over the private sector. V_r represents the quantitative value of risk-related costs that contain external and internal project aspects. In the PPP procurement strategy proposed are shadow prices (V_{ppps}), where V_{lcc} is given by the subsidy based on the lifecycle costs of using social capitals, while V_r' is the risk costs remaining in the public sector.

$$V_{lcc} = C_{ca} + V_{raw}'(1 + r) + C_o \tag{3}$$

V_{lcc} could be decomposed based on Formula 3, where C_{ca} stands for the public investment allowance during the project design to the construction stage, V_{raw}' represents the resource costs of authorising private sectors, r is the respected profit margin and C_o is the other costs of the public sector.

$$V_{raw} = C_{CapEX} + C_{OpEX} + Co \tag{4}$$

$$C_{CapEX} \approx \sum_k^n C^k U^k \tag{5}$$

C_{CapEX} the capitalised cost of project design and construction, excluding capital gains
C_{OpEX} the cost of project operation and maintenance, excluding thirdparty income
k the particular item of the project work breakdown structure C the corresponding quantities of engineering work item
U the overall unit price that contains the costs of labor, materials and equipment.

Based on both calculation schemes, it can be seen that the lifecycle resource costs are an essential constituent, and they influence the extent unitary charge during the franchise period. Due to project type differences, the scheme used to forecast the Operation and maintenance (O&M) expenditure may vary along the project lifecycle [21]. Based on this fact, the cost institution still lacks evidence of enough inventory to cover most public facilities, such as railways and highways. The information in the project's early stage plays a vital role in estimating the capitalised cost, and it could provide fundamental support for estimating the O&M expenditure [22].

As shown in Fig. 2, which represents the structure of PSC, the expenditure incurred in procuring the asset and the costs incurred by the authority in operating the asset or running the project services could relate to BIM within their information scope. This paper suggests that a quantitative assessment using the PSC method could be expressed more efficiently and thoroughly by the application of BIM and propose related data extraction method corresponding to the information required.

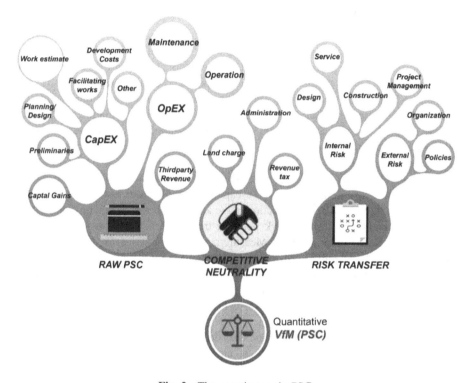

Fig. 2. The constituents in PSC

4   Data Exchange Analysis for VfM Quantitative Assessment

MVD, as the application format (normally written in XML language) proposed by buildingSMART, defines a legal information subset covers all IFC concepts (entities, attributes, relationships, quantity definitions, etc.). It represents the software requirement specification for the implementation of an IFC interface to satisfy the exchange requirements from IDM. These standardised data models support information extraction and sharing across different domains. Based on the published information exchange standard, the current practice of BIM also indicates that the exportation of IFC data from the project model has the potential to support lifecycle performance measurement [23] and the VfM assessment process [18].

To conduct the automatic data exchange process in a VfM assessment, this section presents related IFC entities and data attributes sourced manually from different project standards. It references the MVD procedure of defining the information exchange requirement of VfM and proposes a model view software tool for the consistency of the required information so that the related IFC entities could be automatically collected from a digital model. A case model is presented in this section, and it shows that the data screening could simplify the process of obtaining useful data from BIM.

4.1 Define Related IFC Datatype for Quantitative Assessment

The IFC data model is an object-based file format developed by buildingSMART, which is an international organisation aiming to facilitate information exchange in the AEC industry. IFC is registered in the official International Standard ISO 16739:2013. The version IFC 2×3 is widely used as the cooperation format in most BIM software companies. The defined data within IFC entities cover most of the project's internal domain models, such as architecture, facility management, cost estimating and HVAC. IFC 4, released by ISO 16739-21 in 2013 was designed to cover overall project procurement aspects and to use a more efficient way to present the semantic relations between entities [24].

The following table lists an example that shows the related IFC 4 entities corresponding to the work items covering the capital expenditures (CapEx) and the operating expenses (OpEX). The classification in the left column represents the quantities of works for different engineering work items in the early cost estimates. The classification references the New Rules of Measurement (NRM) series for buildings, Civil Engineering Standard Method of Measurement (CESMM) for civil engineering works and Method of Measurement for Highway Works (MMHW) for highways. The related unit linking to cost value could be obtained from pricing book for construction and building maintenance. The right column lists the corresponding data types and required attributes of an IFC-based presentation.

The data type used in the preliminaries has defined the data type related to labor and other construction resources, and the related attributes are defined in the quantity sets of IFC. The quantities extracted from BIM could support the measurement of work estimates greatly. The cost constituent in this section references the NRM standard mainly for buildings in most cases; the related data could be found in the IFC quantity set section or sometimes in the IFC property set section. Based on the detailed measurement conditions, the information provided by the above data type could not provide the exact information needed to add more constraints. For example, to extract the total gross area of office space, the keyword 'office' should be screened out first.

The quantities extracted from BIM do not yet support project maintenance, and there is no specific cost maintenance/repair classification for civil works. The information provided in the early design stage still lacks project practice to be included in the budget calculation. Based on the building maintenance price book (BICS) classification, the associated data type in the IFC structure could be defined initially, and it could potentially start to build details of 'maintenance and repair' linking with BIM. The cost constituent in this section references the Royal Institution of Chartered Surveyors (RICS) standard mainly for building maintenance process to stress the possibility of using existing data from BIM to support the budget forecast in the O&M stage.

Table 2. IFC datatype response to VfM quantitative assessment

Cost constituent	Group element	Unit related	Related IFC entity type	Related Ifc attribute type
Preliminaries	Labour site huts/formworks	weeks weeks/nr	IfcLaborResource IfcConstructionProductResource	IfcQuantityCount
	General equipment	weeks/nr	IfcConstructionEquipmentResource	IfcQuantityTime
Planning/ Design		m²/km²	IfcSite; IfcBuilding; IfcBuildingStorey; IfcSlab	IfcQuantityArea
Work estimates	Facilitating works	item/m²/ m³	IfcSite; IfcSlab; IfcBuildingStorey; IfcWall; IfcColumn; IfcConstructionProductResource; IfcSpace	IfcQuantityArea; IfcQuantityCount
	Substructure	nr/m/m²/ m³	IfcSlab; IfcWall; IfcColumn; IfcPile; IfcBeam	IfcQuantityArea; IfcQuantityCount; IfcQuantityLength; IfcQuantityVolume
	Superstructure	m²/nr	IfcSlab; IfcCloumn; IfcBeam; IfcRoof; IfcStair; IfcRamp; IfcWall; IfcDoor; IfcWindow	IfcQuantityArea; IfcQuantityLength; IfcQuantityCount
	Internal finishes	m²	IfcWall; IfcSlab; IfcCovering	IfcQuantityArea
	Fittings/ furnishings/ equipment	Nr	IfcFurnishing	IfcQuantityCount
	Services	m²/nr	IfcBuilding; IfcBuildingStorey; IfcSpace; IfcTransportElement	IfcQuantityArea
	External works	m²	IfcSlab; IfcWall; IfcSite; IfcBuildingStorey; IfcBeam	IfcQuantityArea
Building maintenance	Scaffolding		IfcWall	IfcQuantityArea
	Demolitions/ alterations	m²/m/nr	IfcWall; IfcChimney; IfcBoiler; IfcWindow; IfcDoor	IfcQuantityArea; IfcQuantityCount
	Excavations	m³/m²	IfcSpace	IfcQuantityArea; IfcQuantityVolume
	Concrete work	m³/m²/ nr	IfcBeam; IfcColumn; IfcSlab	IfcQuantityArea; IfcQuantityVolume; IfcQuantityCount
	Underpinning/ stone-work	m²/nr	IfcWall; IfcBeam; IfcSpace; IfcSlab	IfcQuantityArea; IfcQuantityVolume
	Reroofing	m²/nr/m	IfcRoof; IfcChimney	IfcQuantityArea; IfcQuantityCount; IfcQuantityLength
	Woodwork	m²/nr/m	IfcWall; IfcCovering; IfcSlab; IfcFloor; IfcWindow; IfcStairs; IfcFurniture; IfcPipeSegment	IfcQuantityArea; IfcQuantityCount; IfcQuantityLength
	Plumbing	m/nr	IfcPipeSegment; IfcSanitaryTerminal; IfcFurniture; IfcTank; IfcFlowStorageDevice; IfcSpaceHeater; IfcBoiler	IfcQuantityCount; IfcQuantityLength
	Internal/external finishes	m²/nr	IfcSlab; IfcCovering; IfcWall	IfcQuantityCount; IfcQuantityArea
	Glazing Repairs	m/nr/m²	IfcWindows	IfcQuantityArea; IfcQuantityLength
	Painting/Decorating	m²/m	IfcWall; IfcSlab; IfcWindows; IfcPipe Segment; IfcDoor; IfcRailing	IfcQuantityArea; IfcQuantityLength

4.2   Information Delivery for VfM Quantitative Assessment

Table 2 lists the data type related to the VfM quantitative assessment, while Table 3 shows a proposed sample of related cost items. This table illustrates the relationships between model entities and attributes and to what extent that information is needed for assessment. For example, if the assessment needs the visualisation support, such as the geometry, extrusion or colour of the product material, the related datasets should be specified for the data extraction. It is worth mentioning that in most cases, the related entities and attributes could also match the other cost items, and one cost item could relate to different objects/entities.

Table 3. IDM table for VfM quantitative assessment (partly)

Cost item	Information items/object	Attribute set	Attributes	VfM agreements
Design budget (floor area method)	Building; building floor	Spatial composition	Context	Not related
		Spatial decomposition	Spatial element	Not related
		Spatial container	Related element/product	Not related
			Annotation	Not related
		Quantity sets	Gross floor area	Related
		Product placement	Local placement	Not related
			Grid placement	Not related
		Geometry	Shape/solid forms	Related
Up floor (elemental method)	Building slab systems	Geometry	Shape/solid forms	Related
		Material	Material type	Related
		Quantity sets	Gross area	Related
			Width	Related
		Properties for objects	Function	Related
			Nominal thickness	Related
			Reference	Related
			Structural material	Related
			Metadata	Not related
		Assignment	Structural objects	Not related
			Part of building element	Not related

(continued)

Table 3. (*continued*)

Cost item	Information items/object	Attribute set	Attributes	VfM agreements
Scaffolding (functional unit method)	Internal/external wall systems	Geometry	Shape/solid forms	Related
		Material	Material type	Related
		Quantity sets	Gross area	Related
			Height	Related
		Properties for objects	Function	Related
		Assignment	Reference	Related
			Structural material	Related
			Metadata	Not related
			Structural objects	Not related
			Part of building element	Not related

The definition of information needed for VfM in this paper references the concept of MVD and IDM which was created to cover the knowledge map of a VfM quantitative assessment and it represents the related hierarchy of the embedded data type in IFC 4. It is a similar MVD-based approach by using XML editors writing up in raw format to apply the data exchange requirement functioning on the BIM model. The rules written in this scheme use the existing IFC 4 Knowledge. The concept templates related to attribute sets could correspond by using the datasets in IFC 4. For example, the requirement of the extract 'Geometry' of floor slab could reference the IFC 4 geometry sets, such as 'body geometry,' 'box geometry' or 'surface geometry' and go a step further to check whether the 'IfcShapeRepresentation' dataset is in 'IfcSlab.' The filtered document could be outputted by setting up a list of constraints to check the related attributes in IFCXML.

To identify the scope of the DFV tool, the authors used the information indices in NRM, CESMM4, MMHW and BICS, which contain 65 classes of cost items that relate to buildings, civil engineering works and highways. Those items cover the most aspects across the construction cost domain. In the NRM, the cost measurement method is defined in different ways. For example, the quantities for construction, maintenance and renewal works can be determined using the value of the total gross floor area of the built assets or by projecting the value of functional units. And also in certain circumstances, for either newly built or existing assets, the elemental method is a new approach for measuring the estimated capital building and maintenance costs. The elemental method takes the significant elements of the building works and provides breakdown structure estimates. According to the present status, this article references the three measurement methods among different measurement standards, and it plans to make the MVD-based data exchange tool functional at the beginning of PPP project identification. Using the MVD concepts, the categorised rule sets were coded and implemented for checking the required IFC data type. The checking rule includes the existence of the data type, attributes and reference. Once the data type exists in the IFC file, the type check will retrieve the inheritance of it and locate the related attributes, references and data aggregates.

4.3   Rules for Data Exchange

Based on the circumstances, the rules for checking related IFC data types state that the target IFC data type will be checked first and then the acquired attributes will be located (Fig. 3). The attributes in IFC most related to the cost estimates are the physical quantities linking with the related projects or objects.

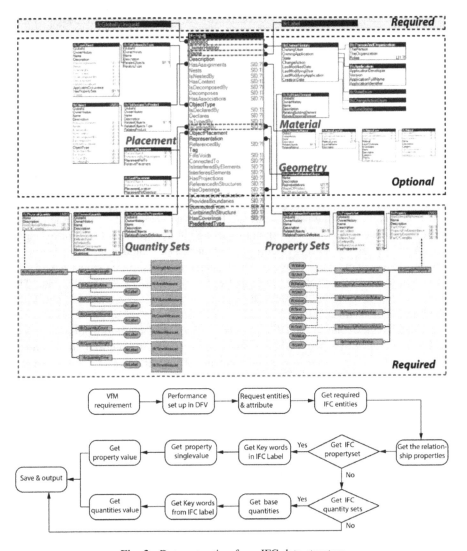

Fig. 3. Data extraction from IFC data structure

According to the NRM, the cost estimates during the project's early stage should be performed based on the available information. The information in BIM could support the cost estimates by providing the correlated value from simplicity to complexity and from the initial concept model to the federated model. For example, to measure the cost of wall finishes, the gross side area as the defined physical quantity in the 'IfcWall' could be used to capture the value directly. In the IFC scheme, the objectified relationship represented in 'IfcRelDefinesByProperties' has been set to source the property set definitions and objects. Moreover, 'name' and 'IfcMaterial' also be located by programming.

This functional data type can be defined as 'optional' for the user in the proposed DFV; from the operation interface, users can select from the following options to activate the rule functions: (1) options that decompose the quantitative assessment, (2) options that decompose the measurement methods and (3) options that decompose the quantity types linking to the unit rates. Because there is no current 'standard modeling way' to store the attributes due to object complexity, as in Revit, sometimes IFC property sets are used to store useful data annotations, which are hardly written into IFC quantity sets. The rules also cover the aspects of IFC property sets when necessary.

This paper proposes a school BIM model created in Autodesk Revit as shown in Fig. 4 that satisfies most aspects of cost items. Through the process of quantifying the relevance of different entities to the particular type of measurement, this DFV tool enables a more convenient and efficient quantitative analysis for PPP projects in the early project justification stage.

The present DFV is defined to be operated during the strategic assessment until detailed design approval, because the current rules of data extraction do not deal with

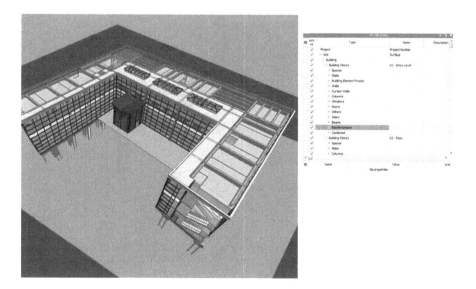

Fig. 4. Cases studies model for data exchange

the construction stage, which requires higher precision computations of the digital model quantities. For many PPP projects published using a new build project proposed by local authorities, the information might be rich enough to be stored using the IFC data format within the BIM model.

In the project-planning phase, the information could be sourced using the data type 'IfcSite' so that the planning-related attributes or documentation could be stored and located in the model. The attributes relating to the performance of 'temporary road,' 'cleaning area' or the 'building pad' can also be traced to different IFC data types. Likewise, the information in the early building design stage can be extracted from data type 'IfcBuilding,' 'IfcBuildingStorey' or 'IfcSlab.' The detailed design afterward is supposed to contribute to the formal cost plan, which includes the estimates of the basic site, building, indoor space and structure design. The maintenance works could also be

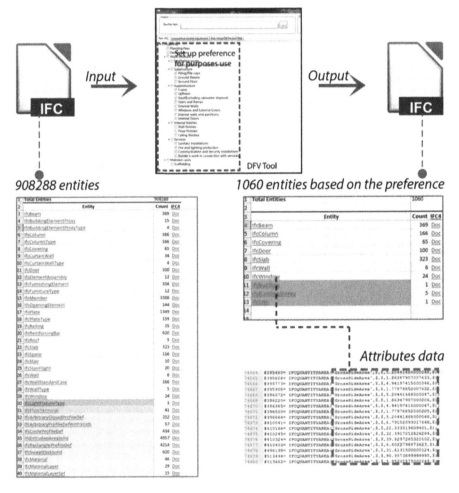

Fig. 5. Cases studies for data extraction on BIM model

measured using the physical model attributes that are similar to those used in build cost estimates. IFC entities, such as 'IfcSlab' and 'IfcWall,' can respond to various cost items in a 'superstructure' and 'internal finishes' class. 'IfcSpace' as a particular entity to represent an area or volume within a building can be decomposed in areas wherein the functionalities of building spaces, such as 'office' or 'meeting room,' can be located. By setting up constraints and rules, these spaces with their related objects and attributes could be extracted to measure the construction and maintenance cost items.

As showed in Fig. 5, the input IFC file could be obtained from Revit or any other BIM software which cover most of the physical and documentation features. Extracting related data is hardly processed by using initial BIM model. In the case model, 908288 entities are contained in the initial input. Based on the preference of cost estimates in PSC estimates, the corresponding cost items are selected and screened with only 1060 entities. Within it, the attributes data could be obtained from either IfcElementQuantity or IfcPropertySet. The lightweight data are proposed to remain IFC format and could be used for further development to support budget department and Value for money quantitative analysis.

For the existing PPP projects or the projects that have already established a planning and design scheme, these data could be captured more systematically, and the value calculated in the quantitative assessment can support the project's approval largely. The outputs of the DFV are still IFCXML data sheets that contain the useful information sets defined in this article. The DFV can be used for different circumstances by BIMbased context projects, in which the arrogating agents, such as the clients and project managers, can use such a BIM-based tool to stream the data for VfM.

5 Discussions

BIM-based procurement management can play an essential role in PPP. Project-domain professionals can identify the intents of the requirements of mapped IFC entities and related attributes. Moreover, the formalized data requirement extracted from the engineering digital model is designed to support the VfM assessment lifecycle rather than only functioning during the project justification stage, especially in the existing project, which is required to be operated in a PPP model and which must access the justification process and re-evaluate project values. BIM, with extensive implementation in building and civil works, could support directly the evaluation of time and could help project managers continuously to establish a well-organized information management platform. The data delivery in BIM follows international standards, which indicate that different models translated from different sectors could 'talk in the same language'. The idea of DFV is established to guide the BIM to support the procurement strategies and provide functional tools in the first step. The current development is still limited in the following aspects:

For data-level aspects, even the ISO defines the AEC-related data types in IFC; there is still a lack of consensus in AEC sectors when it comes to storing the internal project data in the appropriate place. The case study model also failed to extract the value from the corresponding data type because the value there is empty. The understanding between software companies and users could complicate data management, which could be improved in the future.

For information-level aspects, the IFC is still in development alone with practice. IFC 2×3 is the most widely used version among most software companies, while some IFC data types are hardly used by AEC sectors. AEC companies often ignore entities without physical substance, likely due to the diversity of construction products. As IFC 4 has a more efficient way of managing entity relations, for example, construction resource elements can relate to the IFC data type, which is defined as 'IfcConstructionResource'. It has its sub-entities that relate to equipment, product, crew and labour resources, but they are not yet stored properly in BIM.

For the knowledge-level aspects, the external element hardly links with IFC, which also requires other methods that could cooperate with the BIM system to manage the performance of the entire lifecycle.

This article references the concept of IDM and MVD that function on VfM assessment but did not show the entire workflow defined by National Building Information Model Standard (NBIMS). This is due to the implementation area in PPP covers different types of engineering costs catalogues, and also the project internal stages such as preliminaries build-up and maintenance also require more complicated extension of data standardization. The logic idea and DFV tool with its interface proposed in this article is trying to stress the possibility of defining standardized information delivery process for PPP project justification. With the development, all the coded rules in XML language can be put into IFC validation like IfcDoc for MVD validation. Different type of engineering projects could also be classified by based on domain performances.

6 Conclusion and Future Works

As a lifecycle project management concept, PPP focuses on procurement benefits that require a lifecycle information exchange and management platform, and it is here that BIM can play an important role. The information processes applied in VfM still use traditional measures, which are limited in terms of both automation and the accuracy of decision-making. Thus, it is necessary to build a VfM strategy that can provide more valuable deliverables.

Even currently, a few public projects have started to use BIM as their information management platform in construction stages. To stress further the lifecycle assessment aspects, BIM is still limited in covering the overall performance of the project. Based on the potentiality of BIM, this paper proposes a BIM-based approach that functions during the project's early stage and that stresses the possibility that information attached to the digital model could ensure the measurement is being achieved in real time along with the project flow.

The PSC-based approach is now using static, historical data that is usually inappropriate. By decomposing the VfM structure, the supporting information contained within the quantitative assessment could be memorised and transmitted using the open neutral data format. This paper proposes an IFC 4-based data extraction scheme. The outputs of the framework could not only support the VfM assessment lifecycle, but also function as a means of verification for PPP business cases and even take a step further toward performance appraisal after contract signature. Future works should stress project quality aspects and create a semantic structure combined with PPP domain knowledge so that a comprehensive VfM assessment can be performed.

References

1. Cheng, Z., Ke, Y., Lin, J., Yang, Z., Cai, J.: Spatio-temporal dynamics of public private partnership projects in China. Int. J. Proj. Manag. **34**(7), 1242–1251 (2016)
2. Kweun, J.Y., Wheeler, P.K., Gifford, J.L.: Evaluating highway public-private partnerships: evidence from U.S. value for money studies. Transp. Policy **62**, 12–20 (2017)
3. World Bank Institute and Public-Private Infrastructure Advisory Facility: Value-forMoney Analysis-Practices and Challenges: How Governments Choose When to Use PPP to Deliver Public Infrastructure and Services (2013)
4. Grimsey, D., Lewis, M.K.: Are public private partnerships value for money? Evaluating alternative approaches and comparing academic and practitioner views. Account. Forum **29**(4), 345–378 (2005)
5. Cheng, J.C.P., Ma, L.Y.H.: A BIM-based system for demolition and renovation waste estimation and planning. Waste Manag. **33**(6), 1539–1551 (2013)
6. Smith, P.: BIM & the 5D Project Cost Manager. Procedia - Soc. Behav. Sci. **119**, 475–484 (2014)
7. Grilo, A., Zutshi, A., Jardim-Goncalves, R., Steiger-Garcao, A.: Construction collaborative networks: the case study of a building information modelling-based office building project. Int. J. Comput. Integr. Manuf. **26**, 1–14 (2012)
8. Ibem, E.O., Laryea, S.: Survey of digital technologies in procurement of construction projects. Autom. Constr. **46**, 11–21 (2014)
9. Regan, M., Smith, J., Love, P.E.D.: Financing of public private partnerships: transactional evidence from Australian toll roads. Case Stud. Transp. Policy **5**(2), 267–278 (2017)
10. HM Treasury: Private Finance Initiative and Private Finance 2 Projects. HM Treasury, March 2015
11. HM Treasury: A new approach to public private partnerships, December 2012
12. Henjewele, C., Sun, M., Fewings, P.: Critical parameters influencing value for money variations in PFI projects in the healthcare and transport sectors. Constr. Manag. Econ. **29**(8), 825–839 (2011)
13. National Audit Office: Review of the VFM assessment process for PFI. October 2013
14. Hall, D.: Why Public-Private Partnerships Don't Work the many advantages of the public alternative. Public Service International (2014)
15. van Nederveen, G.A., Tolman, F.P.: Modelling multiple views on buildings. Autom. Constr. **1**(3), 215–224 (1992)
16. Bradley, A., Li, H., Lark, R., Dunn, S.: BIM for infrastructure: an overall review and constructor perspective. Autom. Constr. **71**, 139–152 (2016)
17. Grilo, A., Jardim-Goncalves, R.: Challenging electronic procurement in the AEC sector: a BIM-based integrated perspective. Autom. Constr. **20**(2), 107–114 (2011)
18. Ren, G., Li, H.: BIM based value for money assessment in public-private partnership. In: Camarinha-Matos, Luis M., Afsarmanesh, H., Fornasiero, R. (eds.) PRO-VE 2017. IAICT, vol. 506, pp. 51–62. Springer, Cham (2017). https://doi.org/10.1007/978-3-319-65151-4_5
19. International Standards Organization: Building information modelling - Information delivery manual - Part 1: Methodology and format, p. 34 (2010)

20. Ismail, K., Takim, R., Nawawi, A.H.: A public sector comparator (PSC) for value for money (VFM) assessment tools. Asian Soc. Sci. **8**(7), 192–201 (2012)
21. World Bank: Public-Private Partnerships Reference Guide (2014)
22. Kehily, D., Woods, T.: Linking effective whole life cycle cost data to parametric building information models using BIM technologies requirements to parametric building information models using BIM technologies. CITA BIM Gather. **2013**, 1–9 (2013)
23. Love, P.E.D., Liu, J., Matthews, J., Sing, C.P., Smith, J.: Future proofing PPPs: lifecycle performance measurement and building information modelling. Autom. Constr. **56**, 26–35 (2015)
24. Liebich, T.: IFC4 – The new buildingSMART Standard. BuildingSMART, no. IFC4. Overview, p. 25 (2013)

Towards an Ontology-based Approach for Information Interoperability Between BIM and Facility Management

Weiwei Chen, Keyu Chen, and Jack C. P. Cheng[✉]

The Department of Civil and Environmental Engineering,
The Hong Kong University of Science and Technology, Kowloon, Hong Kong
{wchenau, kchenal}@connect.ust.hk, cejcheng@ust.hk

Abstract. Building information modeling (BIM) brings interoperability to the architecture, engineering, construction and facility management (AEC/FM) industry by providing an information backbone throughout a building's lifecycle. Information interoperability or data mapping is critical for seamless information sharing between BIM and FM, because the approaches to information representation in BIM and in FM systems are different. The geometric and semantic information in BIM can be represented by IFC schema, while the FM data is commonly represented in a corresponding relational database. Even though COBie is a neutral data format to deliver information from BIM to FM, the data structure of COBie does not incomplete to represent all information from BIM to FM. Therefore, there is a lack of an appropriate solution to smoothly integrate BIM with FM. This paper aims to address the information interoperability issue and propose an ontology-based methodology framework for data mapping between BIM and FM. Based on the proposed framework, an ontology approach is developed as a tool to facilitate the facility knowledge management and to improve the data mapping process. Finally, a case application about facility maintenance activity is implemented to demonstrate the feasibility of the ontology approach.

Keywords: Building information modeling · Facility management
Information interoperability · Ontology · IFC · COBie

1 Introduction

Inadequate interoperability among model-based applications costs 15.8 billion dollars by losing its efficiency in the U.S. facilities, of which a 10.6 billion dollar loss occurs during operation and maintenance (O&M) [1]. Data interoperability is crucial to construction projects that have multiple stakeholders, including owners, general contractors, equipment suppliers, material suppliers, and others. Information is essential for supporting efficient and effective building maintenance and daily operations. However, in facility management (FM), due to a lack of data integration, more than 80% of the time is spent looking for relevant information [2]. Building Information Modelling (BIM) aims to provide a means to support the seamless exchange of information throughout the lifecycle of buildings through the integration of different technologies,

© Springer International Publishing AG, part of Springer Nature 2018
I. F. C. Smith and B. Domer (Eds.): EG-ICE 2018, LNCS 10864, pp. 447–469, 2018.
https://doi.org/10.1007/978-3-319-91638-5_25

while supporting industry stakeholders' processes. BIM can contribute to FM both as a source and a repository of information to support the planning and management of building maintenance activities in both new and existing buildings [3]. Ding et al. [4] further reinforced these findings and revealed that BIM enables a 98% reduction in the amount of time used for updating FM databases.

With the emergence of data specification such as COBie (Construction Operation Building information exchange) and the IFC (Industry Foundation Classes) open standard, there has been an increasing interest in developing approaches that can integrate BIM data into FM system. The Sydney Opera House case study demonstrated some existing FM systems (such as Mainpac, HARDCAT and TRIM) for facility information management, and illustrated how IFC and BIM can support data consistency and information interoperability in FM [5]. Information interoperability issues related to integration of BIM data with existing FM systems may be partly resolved through the use of ISO 16739 certification [6]. The IFC specification within ISO 16739 is an open and neutral data file format for data sharing and exchange within construction and FM, support greater integration between BIM software vendors. IFC is the only object oriented 3D vendor-neutral BIM data format for the semantic information of building objects [7]. IFC models have been used as the file format for transferring BIM data into computerized aided facility management (CAFM) tools due to the lack of interoperability between existing CAFM tools and the growing number of commercially available BIM packages. Emerging literature on data integration between BIM and FM show that software interoperability remains a significant and persistent obstacle [8, 9]. Additionally, Patacas et al. [10] suggested that their study case highlighted shortcomings in the IFC/COBie standards and available tools. In order to facilitate the information delivery from BIM to FM, data integration and exchange from different domains, which may vary in data structure and data type, is needed. For example, Chen et al. [11] extended the IFC schema to represent the facility maintenance management information in BIM models, and applied COBie data to transfer BIM data into FM system for automatic maintenance work order scheduling.

Currently, some researchers leveraged ontology approaches to solve the information interoperability problem in the AEC/FM industry. Das et al. [12] studied an ontology-based web service framework for construction supply chain collaboration and management, and suggested security was enhanced with access control and a data model for the distributed databases was also presented for data storage and retrieval. Deng et al. [13] developed a referent ontology called Semantic City Model to map BIM models into GIS models, and finally illustrated that the developed methodology can achieve automatic data mapping between IFC and CityGML. Costin and Eastman [14] suggested that with the increased demand of ontologies in the AEC/FM industry, it is necessary to be standardization and consensus in the development of the ontologies to ensure seamless transfer of information as well as realizing the full benefits of ontologies. However, there is a lack of studies on the data integration of BIM and FM using ontology schema or ontology methodology.

Therefore, the purpose of this paper is to present a methodology framework based on the ontology approach for integrating BIM and FM and to solve the information interoperability and data sharing problems in the AEC/FM industry. This study proposes an ontology approach built with the web ontology language (OWL) based on

COBie data to help retrieve information from an IFC model, transfer data into COBie data standard, and finally deliver BIM data into FM systems. In this paper, the following sections are as follows. Section 2 illustrates the research background and related work, and the proposed methodology is elaborated in Sect. 3. In Sect. 4, an example and result are illustrated to verify the feasibility of the proposed methodology, followed by conclusions in Sect. 5.

2 Research Background and Related Work

2.1 Introduction to IFC and COBie

IFC is an object-based file format with a data model developed by buildingSMART (formerly the International Alliance for Interoperability, IAI) to facilitate interoperability in the AEC industry, and is a commonly used collaboration format in BIM based projects [15]. IFC supports a wide range of geometric representations as well as rich semantic information. Currently, the IFC data format [16] is considered a major data exchange schema standard for BIM. IFC files contain data about building objects and connections between those objects. Each IFC file is made of object classes, relation classes, and resource classes. Object classes identify an IFC object, its ownership, and functional units. Relation classes define the multiple relations between object classes and their functional units, whereas resource classes describe functional units through a set of attributes. Previous research has focused on extracting and managing building component information using IFC files during design and construction, and proposed solutions for design evaluation, construction cost estimating, and construction management [17]. Furthermore, managing information using IFC files during the FM phase has started to gain more attention in recent years, and research efforts have led to development of methods, such as IFC-based indoor path planning [18]. The IFC data of representing a wall in BIM models is illustrated in Fig. 1. As shown in Fig. 1, IFC can represent geometric information, such as length and height. In addition, IFC can store

```
#184= IFCRECTANGLEPROFILEDEF(.AREA.,$,#183,3507.50000000003,124.999999999989);
#185= IFCAXIS2PLACEMENT3D(#6,$,$);
#186= IFCEXTRUDEDAREASOLID(#184,#185,#19,2579.99999999876);
#187= IFCCOLOURRGB($,0.501960784313725,0.501960784313725,0.501960784313725);
#188= IFCSURFACESTYLERENDERING(#187,0.,$,$,$,$,IFCNORMALISEDRATIOMEASURE(0.5),IFCSPECULAREXPONENT(64.),.NOTDEFINED.);
#189= IFCSURFACESTYLE('Default Wall',.BOTH.,(#188));
#191= IFCPRESENTATIONSTYLEASSIGNMENT((#189));
#193= IFCSTYLEDITEM(#186,(#191),$);
#196= IFCSHAPEREPRESENTATION(#88,'Body','SweptSolid',(#186));
#199= IFCPRODUCTDEFINITIONSHAPE($,$,(#178,#196));
#203= IFCWALLSTANDARDCASE('21cZUVhov28P$mjU5m7Uua',#41,'Basic Wall:Generic - 125mm:305762',$,'Basic Wall:Generic - 125mm:305775',#172,#199,'305762');
#212= IFCMATERIAL('Default Wall');
#215= IFCPRESENTATIONSTYLEASSIGNMENT(($,#215),$);
#217= IFCSTYLEDITEM($,(#215),$);
#219= IFCSTYLEDREPRESENTATION(#83,'Style','Material',(#217));
#222= IFCMATERIALDEFINITIONREPRESENTATION($,$,(#219),#212);
#225= IFCMATERIALLAYER(#212,125.,$);
#227= IFCMATERIALLAYERSET((#225),'Basic Wall:Generic - 125mm');
#230= IFCMATERIALLAYERSETUSAGE(#227,.AXIS2.,.NEGATIVE.,62.5);
#231= IFCWALLTYPE('21cZUVhov28P$mjU5m7Uuf',#41,'Basic Wall:Generic - 125mm',$,$,(#305,#307,#309,#311,#313),$,'305775',$,.STANDARD.);
#233= IFCPROPERTYSINGLEVALUE('Base Constraint',$,IFCLABEL('Level: Level 1'),$);
#234= IFCPROPERTYSINGLEVALUE('Base Extension Distance',$,IFCLENGTHMEASURE(0.),$);
#235= IFCPROPERTYSINGLEVALUE('Base is Attached',$,IFCBOOLEAN(.F.),$);
#236= IFCPROPERTYSINGLEVALUE('Base Offset',$,IFCLENGTHMEASURE(0.),$);
#237= IFCPROPERTYSINGLEVALUE('Location Line',$,IFCIDENTIFIER('Finish Face: Exterior'),$);
#238= IFCPROPERTYSINGLEVALUE('Related to Mass',$,IFCBOOLEAN(.F.),$);
```

Fig. 1. Part of IFC data of a wall in a BIM model

various kinds of semantic information, such as owner information, modification history of model, and cost and schedule of building components. BIM models based on IFC can be used for various tasks during the construction, such as in feasibility studies, tendering [19], code checking, and operation management [20].

COBie was created in 2007 as a new way for designers and contractors to directly provide electronic operations, maintenance, and asset management information [21]. COBie is a vendor neutral, IFC-based data exchange specification that describes the information exchange between the construction and operations phases of a project. It is a performance-based specification for facility asset information delivery. COBie is a standard data model for information delivery from the construction stage to O&M stage The COBie-compliant Excel file consists of 16 separate spreadsheets that capture project data from different lifecycle phases. Table 1 identifies each COBie worksheet, the purpose of the worksheet, and the facility lifecycle when the data is captured. We can see that not whole COBie information can be exported from BIM models, and other part information is generated from the O & M period.

In BIM models, IFC can provide geometric information and semantic information, while the neutral data format, COBie data, should provide much more information, such as spatial data, asset details, documentations and graphical information. Additionally, neutral data format, such as COBie, can support processes during the operation of

Table 1. Standard COBie worksheets

COBie Worksheet	Purpose	Lifecycle when data is capture
Contact	Capture data providers and manufacturers contact information	All
Facility	Facility description and measurement standards	Design
Floor	Identifies floors or levels	Design
Space	Identifies rooms or spaces	Design
Zones	Identifies zones	Design
Type	Identifies equipment, parts, or materials and warranty information	Design/Construction
Component	Identifies each equipment, part, or material instance and installation information	Design/Construction
Systems	Associates building components with building system	Design/Construction
Job	Identifies operations and maintenance procedures	Construction/Commissioning
Resource	Special materials, tools or training required to complete a Job Task	Construction/Commissioning
Spare	Identifies spare parts lists	Construction/Commissioning
Documents	Indexes submittal documents	All
Issues	Identifies other issues including operational safety issues	All
Coordinates	Applies coordinates to a facility, floor, space or component	All

buildings like space management, asset management, maintenance planning, energy management and reconstruction projects during the lifecycle.

In fact, in order to support information exchanges according to the industry's business processes, IFC and COBie are continuously being developed by build-ingSMART with input from the AEC/FM industry. Some standards, including PAS 1192-2: 2013 [22], PAS 1192-3:2014 [23], and ISO 16739 [6], allow data models to be structured in a universal way, allowing owners and their project teams to define attributes unambiguously, enabling product data to be exchanged between designers, suppliers, constructors and operators [2]. The definition of COBie data drops has also been introduced in the UK in order to capture and check the client's requirements throughout the lifecycle of a building. Data drops specify the data requirements at key stages of building lifecycle development and are aligned with RIBA Plan of Work stages [24]. The need for the provision of structured data for asset information models has been recognized in PAS1192-3:2014 [23], which specifies an information man-agement methodology for the operational phase of building assets.

2.2   Ontology and Ontology Research in BIM-Based FM

In fact, ontologies are widely used in information retrieval [25], schema development, and development of search engines [26]. When dealing with knowledge from multiple domains, a reference ontology could serve as a medium for carrying knowledge and thus facilitate interoperability between domains [27]. More specifically Burton-Jones et al. [28] presented ontology quality metrics: "syntactic (richness and correctness), semantic (meaningfulness, consistency and clarity), pragmatic (number of classes and properties, accuracy and relevance), and social (extent of usage by other ontologies and number of times used)". Ontologies can be seen as means to describe important aspects of a domain on the basis of a formal semantic language. An ontology provides a shared vocabulary, which can be used to model a domain, that is, the type of objects and/or concepts that exist, and their properties and relations. A properly developed ontology consists of five components. The components of an ontology, as shown in Table 2, include 1) terms, 2) definitions, 3) properties types, 4) classes, and 5) a class hierarchy. These components are the basis for all ontologies [25].

Table 2. Components of an ontology

Ontology Component	Description	Synonyms
Terms	A word or expression that has a precise meaning in some uses or is peculiar to a science, art, profession, or subject	Names, Words
Definitions	An exact statement or description of the nature, scope, or meaning of something	Description, Explanation
Properties types	A quality or feature regarded as a characteristic or inherent part of someone or something	Property, Characteristic
Classes	A group, set, or kind sharing common attributes	Types, Concepts
Class hierarchy	An arrangement or classification of things according to relative importance or inclusiveness	Structure, Organization

One possibility for an ontology representation is the Semantic Web technology or OWL Web Ontology Language [29]. OWL is the richest representation language of the Semantic Web initiative of the World Wide Web Consortium (W3C), with its capabilities based on the Resource Description Framework (RDF) and resource description framework schema (RDFS) [30]. Recommended by the W3C and as an open standard, OWL was originally designed to facilitate machine-readable linking of documents on the World Wide Web. Main constructs in OWL are concepts, individuals and properties. A concept denotes a construct that can have members belonging to that concept and sub-concepts in order to form hierarchies. The concrete members of such concepts are individuals that represent entities in the modeled domain of discourse. Attributes of these entities and connections between individuals are further described by a set of properties. These can be differentiated into two types: an object property establishes connections between different individuals, thus allowing interconnections to be modeled; and a data type property connects a specific individual to a value of a specified data type (e.g., extensible markup language (XML) data type). With the help of these properties, logical axioms can be phrased that aid in describing concepts and members. They can also be used in equivalence relations in order to enable logical reasoning on stored facts [29].

Therefore, ontology matching and mapping has become an interesting topic as it plays an important role in joining heterogeneous ontologies to work together [31, 32]. Some researchers leveraged the ontology approach to solve the information interoperability problem in the AEC industry. Wang et al. [33] used ontology to represent and reason on context-sensitive construction information as an alternative way of construction information management. As a relatively new field, BIM ontology research needs more exploration. Jung and Joo [34] noted that ontology research for BIM, especially on the hierarchy structure of BIM objects, is still rare. IfcOWL [35] is by far the most complete effort to lift the IFC specification onto the ontology level. However, because most of the ontology elements generated are strictly rooted in the IFC specification, its flexibility in different application scenarios is somewhat restricted. Lee et al. [36] studied the information interoperability about the validation testing on data format of BIM and FM. Until now, there is a lack of studies on information interoperability of BIM and FM based on ontology.

2.3 Challenges of Data Interoperability Between BIM and FM

Inadequate data integration is a constant issue amongst building information models because of differences in syntax, schema or semantics. Multiple levels of data interoperability exist. Semantic interoperability is the one most applied to BIM data integration with other systems. Semantic heterogeneity of data results from different meanings or interpretations of data that may arise from various contexts. Hence, data integration and interoperability are inextricably linked when discussing BIM and other systems, including FM system, that need to integrate with it. Data interoperability issues related to the integration of BIM data with existing FM systems may be partly resolved through the use of ISO 16739 certification.

The IFC specification within ISO 16739 is an open and neutral data file format for data sharing and exchange within construction and FM, affording greater integration between BIM software vendors. The applications of mapping between BIM and IFC have been discussed by several scholars. Hassanain et al. [16] proposed an IFC-based data model for integrated maintenance management for roofing systems. Hassanain et al. [17] presented a general object-oriented schema for asset maintenance management that supports information exchange from the construction period to the O&M period. Pastacas, et al. [10, 37] assessed IFC and COBie can support how much facility managers' information requirements. They indicated that part of COBie data can be exported from IFC 4, however other part cannot be exported from IFC and generated in the O&M stage.

Based on the aforementioned literature review, the challenges of data interoperability between IFC and COBie are shown as follows:

(1) The first challenge is that the facility information requirement for FM is different from geometric and semantic information on BIM models. In other words, BIM models can only provide parts of the information for FM.

(2) The second challenge is that the data schema of FM systems is different from the data schema in BIM models. Because BIM data can be represented in the IFC schema, while FM data can be represented in COBie data or other relational data base schema.

(3) The third challenge is about the methods of data storage. BIM data can be stored in BIM models, which can be represented in several different ways, such as IFC or XML. While FM data is usually stored in relational database, such as Excel or Access database.

3   Methodology

In this study, a methodology framework is proposed for data mapping between IFC and COBie. The methodology framework aims to achieve the goal of bidirectional mapping between BIM and FM system. The proposed methodology framework consists of three components: (1) a developed ontology-based framework for mapping data between IFC and COBie, (2) identification of the facility information requirement for data mapping between IFC and COBie, (3) ontology-based FM data representation.

3.1   Proposed Ontology-Based Methodology Framework for Data Integration

Figure 2 is the general methodology framework of the bidirectional information integration between BIM and FM based on ontology. In this proposed framework, the IFC schema is explored firstly to find these entities which represent building components and spaces. The relationship between entities and attributes of entities is regarded as semantic information for data mapping. While the geometric information is directly mapped into the geometric information of COBie data. There are some necessary documents generated in the O&M period, such as maintenance work orders and specifications, which are not stored in BIM models and thus cannot be delivered from

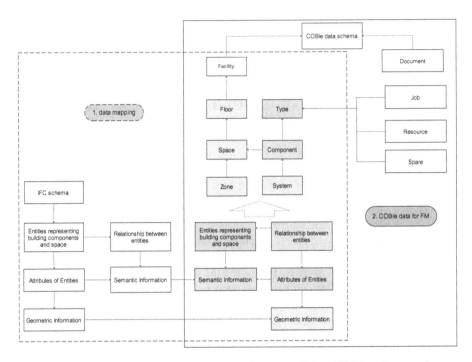

Fig. 2. General framework of data integration between BIM and FM based on ontology

BIM models. Information on documents, spares, resources and jobs is represented in COBie data schema, but not represented in IFC schema.

This methodology framework consists of two parts: (1) data mapping between IFC schema and part of COBie data schema, and (2) the whole COBie data schema. Specifically, IFC schema and COBie schema are decomposed into many pieces, and the corresponding information types are illustrated in details. In data mapping part, IFC schema is divided into five parts, namely, (1) entities representing building components and space, (2) relationship between entities, (3) attributes of entities, (4) semantic information, and (5) geometric information. Correspondingly, the data types in COBie schema can be represented in these five data types. "Floor", "Space", and "Zone" mainly include geometric information. "Components" represents the entities of IFC schema, while "System" makes use of the relationship between entities. In addition, "Type" is generated from the attributes of entities. After data mapping, the COBie data can be extracted from BIM models.

Furthermore, based on the methodology framework, this study is explored in the following steps: (1) identify the facility information requirement, (2) transfer geometric and semantic information from IFC to COBie, (3) use ontology approach to represent COBie data to match the corresponding data in IFC, and (4) import COBie data into FM system based on ontology approach.

3.2 Identification of Facility Information Requirement

In order to map IFC data into COBie and FM system, the first step is to identify what kind of information is required in FM activities. The information requirements of various facility activities are different. The main facility information requirements in some facility activities are listed as follows: (1) information on warranties, spare/replacement parts, preventive maintenance tasks and resources, etc. (2) the operation about equipment and machines in buildings, start-up/ shut-down procedures, and troubleshooting procedures, and (3) space measurement, fixed or movable properties, and space-function capabilities.

In addition, according to the definition of Level of Detail (LOD) about BIM models, the LOD of BIM models for FM is required to achieve LOD 400 and LOD 500 (as-built model). As-built model contains information relating to the architectural, structural, civil and MEP elements with links to operation, maintenance, and asset data. Additional information and data for equipment and space planning may be included, such as product data, maintenance manuals, photos, warranty data, manufacturer information and contacts.

In fact, BIM models cannot provide complete information for FM based on Fig. 2. Pastacas, et al. [10, 37] also assessed IFC and COBie can support how much facility managers' information requirements. Based on specification of asset information requirement PAS 1192-2:2013 [22], standards of PAS 1192-3:2014 [23] and buildingSMART 2014b [16], an initial analysis was carried to evaluate the support of asset register information requirements by IFC/COBie data entities. The following Table 3

Table 3. Evaluation of IFC and COBie support for asset register requirements

Asset register information requirements (BSI, 2012)	IFC 4	COBie 2.4 (Spreadsheet xml)
(a) Identification number or unique reference for the asset;	SerialNumber (Pset_ManufacturerOccurrence)	Component sheet - SerialNumber
		Component sheet – BarCode
	BarCode (Pset_ManufacturerOccurrence)	Component sheet– TagNumber
		Component sheet - AssetIdentifier
(b) Make and/or model;	ModelReference (Pset_ManufacturerTypeInformation)	Type sheet - ModelReference
(c) Manufacturer;	Manufacturer (Pset_ManufacturerTypeInformation)	Type sheet – Manufacturer
(d) Vendor, if different to manufacturer;	Manufacturer (Pset_ManufacturerTypeInformation)	Type sheet - Manufacturer
(e) Date of manufacture;	ProductionYear (Pset_ManufacturerTypeInformation)	

(continued)

Table 3. (*continued*)

Asset register information requirements (BSI, 2012)	IFC 4	COBie 2.4 (Spreadsheet xml)
(f) Date of acquisition, installation or completion of construction;	AcquisitionDate (Pset_ManufacturerOccurrence)	Component sheet - InstallationDate
		Component sheet - WarrantyStartDate
(g) Location of asset;	WarrantyStartDate (Pset_Warranty) IfcSpace	Component sheet - Space
(h) Whether or not access equipment is required;	IfcTask	Job sheet
(i) Whether or not the asset is subject to a permit-to-work requirement	IfcTask	Job sheet
(j) Initial cost;	IfcCostValue	
(k) Predicted lifetime;	ExpectedLife (Pset_ServiceLife)	Type sheet - Expected Life
(l) Specification;		Type sheet - all
(m) Replacement cycle;	IfcTask	Job sheet
(n) Cost breakdown;		
(o) Servicing requirements, including type and frequency of service;	IfcTask	Job sheet
(p) Other maintenance required;	IfcTask	Job sheet
(q) Maintenance costs;	ReplacementCost	Type sheet - ReplacementCost
(r) Accumulated depreciation;		
(s) Written-down value;		
(t) Source of components and spare parts, where applicable		Type sheet - Manufacturer
(u) Energy consumption and, where applicable, energy-efficiency rating;	SustainabilityPerformance Description/Environmental (IfcTypeObjectProperty)	Type sheet - Sustainability Performance
(v) Identification of hazardous or other risks to people or property.	Pset_Risk	
Total number of unsupported attributes	3/22	6/22

illustrates the evaluation result of IFC and COBie support for asset register requirement. Table 3 indicates that 3 of 22 attributes are not supported by IFC, and 6 of 22 attributes are not supported by COBie. It illustrates that part of COBie data can be exported from IFC 4, while the other part cannot be obtained from BIM models. Therefore, not only the facility information requirement, but also the information resources need to be identified in FM.

Based on the specification of asset information requirement (PAS 1192:2013) [22], the information checklist of BIM-FM model is proposed in Table 4. As seen in Table 4, information supported for FM is from three aspects, namely, BIM models,

Table 4. The information checklist of FM model

Profile	Information Type	System Class	To be- checked from BIM(IFC)/COBie/FM System)
Basic parameters	Basic information	Equipment name	BIM (IFC)
		Developing BIM model of equipment	BIM (IFC)
		Appearance description (word)	FM System
		Appearance example (picture)	FM System
Model parameters	Geometric information	Size(length – width -height)	BIM (IFC)
		Material	BIM (IFC)
		Elevation	BIM (IFC)
		Special detail of model (word/picture)	FM System
	Equipment detail information	Equipment number	BIM (IFC)
		OmniClass number	BIM (IFC)
		Brand/Manufacturer	COBie
		Location (area/floor/room)	BIM (IFC)
		Price/cost data	COBie
		Purchase date	COBie
		Responsible person	COBie
		Equipment specification	COBie
		Equipment type	BIM (IFC)
		Equipment function	BIM (IFC)
		Equipment units	BIM`(IFC)
		Equipment professional information	COBie
		Other require by owner	FM System
External links information	Supplementary information	Warranty	COBie
		Assembly process	FM System
		Operation manual	FM System
		2D drawing	FM System
		Equipment performance table	FM System
		Manufacture information	COBie
		Upgrades	FM System
		Damages/deterioration	FM System
	Maintenance records	Equipment resume	FM System
		History maintenance records	FM System
		Checklist	FM System
		Record book of maintenance staff	FM System
		Maintenance schedule	FM System
		Replacement	FM System

COBie data and FM system. In order to deliver BIM data/ IFC data from BIM models to support FM activities, an ontology-based approach for FM data representation is developed in Sect. 3.3.

3.3 Ontology-Based FM Data Representation

According to the PAS-1192-2:2013 standard [22], an asset information model should include a graphical model, non-graphical data, and documentation. Graphical models and part of the non-graphical data can be obtained from BIM models, while the other part of non-graphical data and documentation, such as information on maintenance activities, cannot be obtained from BIM models and are usually stored in FM systems. In BIM models, there are geometric information and semantic information. Therefore, the first step is to transfer the graphical model (geometric information) and non-graphical data (semantic information) from BIM models to FM data, and the second step is to represent the other part of non-graphical data and documentation in COBie data format.

Transfer Geometric and Semantic Information from BIM Model to FM data
In order to map data from BIM models to FM system, the key point is to know what information in BIM models has been represented in IFC data format. The following information is contained in the IFC schema based on IFC standard: (1) coordinate mapping, (2) geographical elements (features, contours, regions, etc.), (3) shape, space, space structure, (4) building elements (wall, door, window, roof, stairs, etc.), (5) relations between elements (holes, chases, voids, zones), (6) connectivity (services, structure, building), (7) zones (fire, workstation, rising ducts, shafts), (8) systems (piping, ducting, cable, structural, etc.), (9) HVAC equipment (chillers, fans, bumps, boilers, etc.), (10) controls, instruments (sensor, actuator, controller, gauge, meter), (11) electrical elements (transformers, motors, generators, etc.), (12) sanitary element, (13) fire protection elements, structural elements, furniture, etc.

Because there are geometric information and semantic information in BIM models. Transferring BIM data to FM data is considered in two parts. In geometric information aspect, the X coordinate and Y coordinate of Point 1 and Point 2, length, and width in Fig. 3a can be directly exported from BIM models. The geometric information can represent walls, space, etc.

In semantic information aspect, lines and points have no value unless the information provides a common understanding by all team members. Normally, the geometric representation in BIM models cannot be directly used in FM activities. For example, in Fig. 3a geometric representation and relationship of rectangles, the point P1 and point P2 have less value for FM, and the connections between points and lines create meanings. Therefore, the exchanging information about connections makes sense. In Fig. 3, the value of the connection information transcends the value of the geometric information. Extracting the connection information and relationship is necessary and valuable.

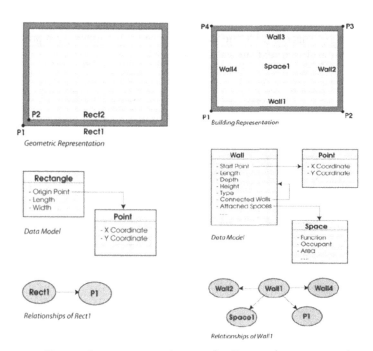

a. Geometric representation and relationship of rectangles   b. Geometric representation and relationship of walls

Fig. 3. Geometric representation and relationship among points, walls and spaces

In addition, in semantic information aspect, the attributes of each component are valuable for FM. Based on the literature review, ontologies can be seen as means to describe important aspects of a domain on the basis of a formal semantic language. The ontology and OWL can represent the objects, properties, individuals, data properties, etc., which will be used to represent the BIM data for information integration. Except the geometric information, such as start point, length, depth, and height, the semantic information, including type, connected walls, function and occupant, is also represented in Fig. 3b.

Basic Ontology Development of COBie for Data Integration
The aforementioned second step is to represent the other part of non-graphical data and documentation in COBie data format. In COBie neutral data format, information is divided into new categories, namely, facility, floor, building systems, spaces, product type, and named components, as shown in the COBie data structure (Fig. 4). In addition, manufacture products, documents, job plans, and resource are collected in construction phase, and not from BIM models. The basic information requirement for

FM and the relationship between different types are also illustrated in Fig. 4. In order to make sure the IFC data and COBie data consistently, the ontology representative of COBie data is developed and shown as follows.

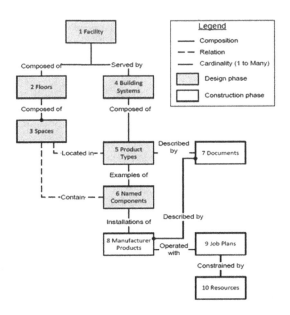

Fig. 4. COBie data structure

In this study, the ontology management tool, Protégé [38], is used for developing and managing ontologies. As shown in Fig. 5, class hierarchy of entities and entity relations can be created easily in Protégé through the add buttons on the "class hierarchy" and "object hierarchy" interfaces. The ontology can be viewed through the Ontograph interface provided by Protégé. The ontology can be saved as an OWL file and published by placing it on a server through file transfer methods like File transfer Protocol. After being published, the OWL file can be viewed in XML format on a browser and queried through SPARQL, a RDF query language using the Internationalized Resource Identifiers (IRI) to identify the location of the ontology.

Figure 5 shows the corresponding class hierarchy of the resulting. In Fig. 5, A represents the data location of ontology, and the ontology data can be stored in .owl file format, .XML file format, or .RDF file format. B represents the class hierarchy of entities, which correspondingly means the data structure. C represents the relationship of product type with other entities. The developed ontology also illustrates the class hierarchy of entities in ontology graph, as shown in the D part of Fig. 5. Moreover, E shows the object properties of entities.

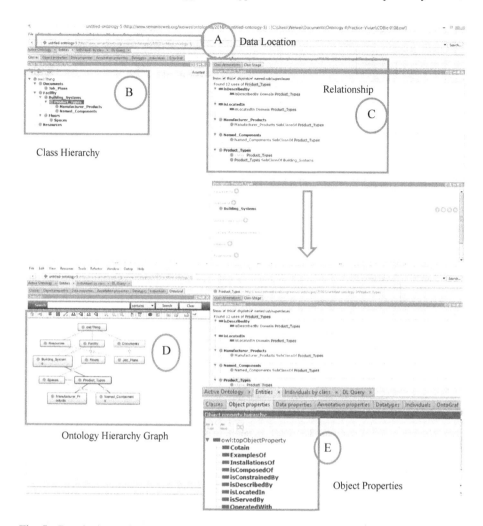

Fig. 5. Developing and publishing COBie ontologies using Protégé ontology management tool

Unified Modeling Language Representation

Since the Protégé interface cannot clearly show all the entities and their relationships in one view, Fig. 6 shows the schematic diagrams for the complete Unified Modeling Language (UML) models of COBie domain ontology. The ontology specifies the concepts and relationships required to describe the semantics of data being exchanged. The COBie UML data schema is developed based on the standard PAS 1192-4:2014 [23]. Figure 6 illustrates the detailed entities, relationship, and properties to represent data types of FM data.

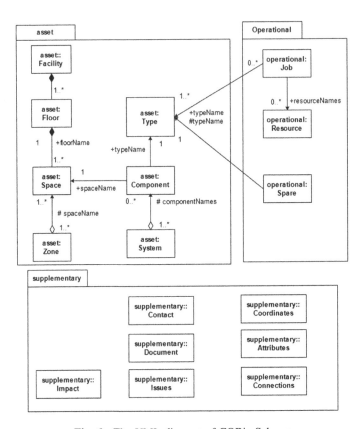

Fig. 6. The UML diagram of COBie Schema

4 Result and Discussion

In order to validate the proposed ontology-based methodology framework of information interoperability for BIM and FM, we explored the facility maintenance process and came up with the facility information requirement of maintenance activities. The UML diagram of facility information requirement of maintenance activities is shown in Fig. 7. The facility information requirement consists of ten classes, namely, inspection request, required maintenance trade, maintenance request, required tool type, resource, maintenance team, work order, required tools, required equipment, and required materials. Specifically, the corresponding attributes of each class is illustrated in detail in Fig. 7. For example, work order includes 11 properties, such as activityID, buildingID, emergency level, etc.

In addition, the ontology representation of facility information requirement of maintenance activities is developed using Protégé ontology management tool. The class hierarchy, ontology hierarchy graph, and corresponding object properties are shown in Fig. 8. In the class hierarchy, inspection request, maintenance request, maintenance team, and work order are the first classes. Required tool type and resource

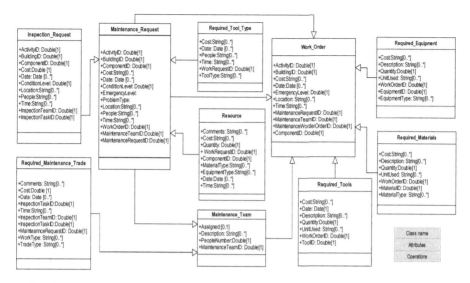

Fig. 7. The UML diagram of facility information requirement of maintenance activities

are sub classes of maintenance request. Required maintenance trade is the sub class of maintenance team. Required equipment, required materials, and required tools are sub classes of work order. The relationships between work order and other classes, such as required equipment, required materials and required tools are clearly represented in Fig. 8. Similarly, the relationship between other classes are also elaborated in the ontology schema. In addition, the corresponding object properties of all classes are listed, and the ontology hierarchy graph is shown in Fig. 8.

In this case, Autodesk Revit is selected as the BIM software, while ARCHIBUS is selected as the FM system. In the facility information requirement of maintenance activities, part of information is exported from BIM models based on IFC, while other part of information is generated during the O&M process. Firstly, the required information is extracted from BIM models, and COBie extension plug-in for Revit is applied to export data from BIM models to COBie spreadsheets. COBie extension plug-in for Revit can be set to export the expected information from BIM models, as shown in Fig. 9.

After obtaining the COBie data from BIM models, the attributes of COBie data and attributes of data stored in FM database should be mapped one by one. Figure 10 shows the attribute mapping between COBie data and FM data in ARCHBUS. In Fig. 10, the "a" column represents the attribute names in COBie spreadsheets. The "b" column represents the field names of attributes in FM system, while the "c" column represents the corresponding table names of attributes in FM system. The "attribute name" is selected as an example to be imported from COBie spreadsheet into FM system. The "name" in the field of FM system is the corresponding one of the "attribute name" in COBie, and the "name" in the field of FM system is stored in the "attribute"

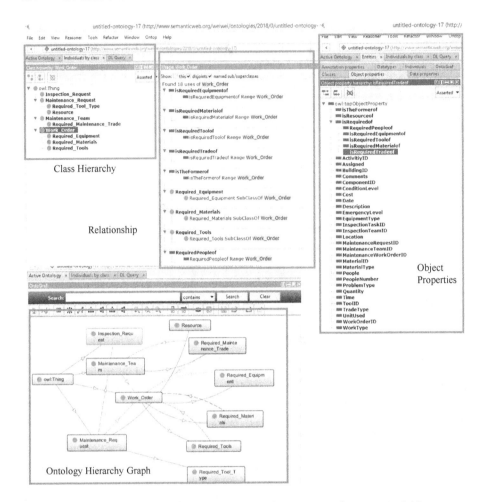

Fig. 8. Ontology of facility information requirement on maintenance activities

table of FM system. After finding the corresponding attributes and tables, a COBie connector is developed to import COBie data into FM system, as shown in Fig. 10 and Fig. 11.

Figure 11 illustrates the process of importing COBie data into corresponding fields in FM system using connector. The process of setting connector is illustrated as follows. Firstly, the connector properties are set. "COBie_attributes" is selected as the connector code, and Excel file connect type is chosen as the connector type. Secondly,

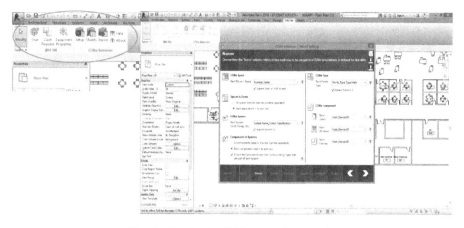

Fig. 9. The Revit COBie extension Plug-in

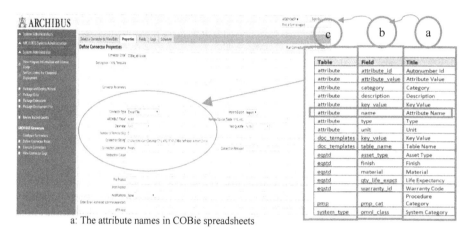

a: The attribute names in COBie spreadsheets

b: The field names of attributes in FM system

c: The table names of attributes in FM system

Fig. 10. Attribute mapping between COBie data and FM system

the connector field of "name" is edited to match the corresponding "attribute name" in COBie. Thirdly, define the COBie connector filed to import COBie "attribute name" into "name" field in FM system. Therefore, the data mapping is achieved based on the developed ontology approach.

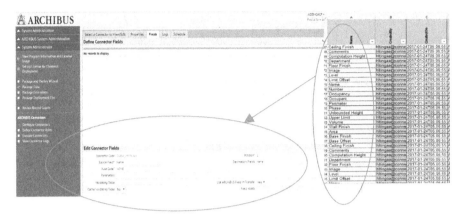

a. Edit connector field in FM system

b. Import COBie "attribute name" into "name" field in FM system

Fig. 11. Import COBie data into corresponding fields in FM system using connector

5   Conclusions

This paper presents a methodology framework to map IFC and COBie data based on an ontology approach, which is developed to solve the information interoperability problem between BIM and FM. The representation schema in the IFC domain and the COBie domain are illustrated in detail. Ontology technology is applied to successfully transfer data from BIM to COBie, and finally import COBie data into FM system.

In this paper, the geometric and semantic information mapping has been explained respectively, and it elaborates that BIM cannot provide complete information for FM. Therefore, facility information requirement is explored and required information is represented to use ontology approach and Protégé ontology management tool for FM. In addition, the proposed methodology framework is applied into facility maintenance activities to verify the feasibility. The result shows that facility maintenance information can be successfully mapped from BIM models into COBie data, and finally be imported into FM system. However, sometimes there is data loss between BIM and FM system. In addition, there is a limitation that the data in columns have to be imported from COBie sheets into FM system by configuration manually, and the information is imported column by column, which is not efficiency. In the future, a data mapping engine would be developed to dynamically deliver information from BIM models to FM system.

References

1. Lavy, S., Jawadekar, S.: A case study of using BIM and COBie for facility management. Int. J. Facil. Manag. **5**(2) (2014)
2. Atkin, B., Brooks, A.: Total facilities management. John Wiley & Sons, Hoboken (2009). ISBN 978-1-118-65538-2
3. Volk, R., Stengel, J., Schultmann, F.: Building information modeling (BIM) for existing buildings—literature review and future needs. Autom. Constr. **38**, 109–127 (2014). https://doi.org/10.1016/j.autcon.2013.10.023
4. Ding, L., Drogemuller, R., Akhurst, P., Hough, R., Bull, S., Linning, C.: Towards sustainable facilities management, In: Technology, Design and Process Innovation in the Built Environment, pp. 373–392. Taylor & Francis (2009)
5. Sabol, L.: Building information modeling & facility management. IFMA World Workplace, 2–13 (2008)
6. ISO16739:2013, Industry Foundation Classes (IFC) for data sharing in the construction and facility management industries. https://www.iso.org/standard/51622.html. Accessed 14 Sept 2017
7. Thein, V.: Industry foundation classes (IFC) BIM interoperability through a vendor-independent file format. Bentley Sustaining Infrastructure, USA (2011)
8. Ghosh, A., Chasey, A.: Structuring data needs for effective integration of building information modeling (BIM) with healthcare facilities management. In: 7th International Structural Engineering and Construction Conference: New Developments in Structural Engineering and Construction, ISEC 2013, Research Publishing Services (2013). https://doi.org/10.3850/978-981-07-5354-2_fam-5-324
9. Kiviniemi, A., Codinhoto, R.: Challenges in the implementation of BIM for FM—Case Manchester Town Hall complex. In: Computing in Civil and Building Engineering, pp. 665–672 (2014). https://doi.org/10.1061/9780784413616.083
10. Patacas, J., Dawood, N., Kassem, M.: Evaluation of IFC and COBie as data sources for asset register creation and service life planning. In: Proceedings of the 14th International Conference on Construction Applications of Virtual Reality & Islamic Architecture, Sharjah (2014). http://tees.openrepository.com/tees/bitstream/10149/559488/2/559488.pdf
11. Chen, W., Chen, K., Cheng, J.C., Wang, Q., Gan, V.J.: BIM-based framework for automatic scheduling of facility maintenance work orders. Autom. Constr. **91**, 15–30 (2018). https://doi.org/10.1016/j.autcon.2018.03.007
12. Das, M., Cheng, J.C., Law, K.H.: An ontology-based web service framework for construction supply chain collaboration and management. Eng. Constr. Archit. Manag. **22**(5), 551–572 (2015). https://doi.org/10.1108/ECAM-07-2014-0089
13. Deng, Y., Cheng, J.C., Anumba, C.: Mapping between BIM and 3D GIS in different levels of detail using schema mediation and instance comparison. Autom. Constr. **67**, 1–21 (2016). https://doi.org/10.1016/j.autcon.2016.03.006
14. Costin, A., Eastman, C.: Requirements for ontology development in the AECO Industry. In: LC3 2017: Volume I – Proceedings of the Joint Conference on Computing in Construction (JC3), Heraklion, Greece, pp. 533–540 (2017). https://doi.org/10.24928/JC3-2017/0149
15. East, W.E.: buildingSMART alliance information exchanges: Means and Methods (2013). http://www.nibs.org/?page=bsa_cobiemm. Accessed 17 July 2017
16. buildingSMART, 2014a, IFC Overview. http://www.buildingsmart-tech.org/specifications/ifc-overview. Accessed 17 July 2017

17. Zhang, X.-Y., Hu, Z.-Z., Wang, H.-W., Kassem, M.: An industry foundation classes (IFC) web-based approach and platform for bi-directional conversion of structural analysis models. In: Computing in Civil and Building Engineering, pp. 390–397 (2014). https://doi.org/10.1061/9780784413616.049

18. Lin, Y.-C., Su, Y.-C.: Developing mobile-and BIM-based integrated visual facility maintenance management system. Sci. World J. **2013**, 1–10 (2013). https://doi.org/10.1155/2013/124249

19. Ma, Z.L., Wu, Z.H., Wu, S., Zhe, L.: Application and extension of the IFC standard in construction cost estimating for tendering in China. Autom. Constr. **20**(2), 196–204 (2011). https://doi.org/10.1016/j.autcon.2010.09.017

20. Hassanain, M.A., Froese, T.M., Vanier, D.J.: Development of a maintenance management model based on IAI standards. Artif. Intell. Eng. **15**(2), 177–193 (2001). https://doi.org/10.1016/S0954-1810(01)00015-2

21. COBie. What is COBie? (2017). https://www.thenbs.com/knowledge/what-is-cobie. Accessed 12 Jan 2017

22. BSI, PAS 1192-2:2013 Specification for information management for the capital/delivery phase of construction projects using building information modelling, BSI Standards Limited. http://www.bimhealth.co.uk/uploads/pdfs/PAS_1192_2_2013.pdf. Accessed 10 Sept 2016

23. BSI, PAS 1192-4:2014: Collaborative production of information. Fulfilling employer's information exchange requirements using COBie. Code of practice. https://shop.bsigroup.com/forms/PASs/BS-1192-4-2014/. Accessed 20 Oct 2017

24. Leon, M., Laing, R., Malins, J., Salman, H.: Development and testing of a design protocol for computer mediated multidisciplinary collaboration during the concept stages with application to the built environment. Proc. Environ. Sci. **22**, 108–119 (2014). https://doi.org/10.1016/j.proenv.2014.11.011

25. Gruber, T.R.: Toward principles for the design of ontologies used for knowledge sharing? Int. J. Hum Comput Stud. **43**(5–6), 907–928 (1995). https://doi.org/10.1006/ijhc.1995.1081

26. Gomez-Perez, A., Fernández-López, M., Corcho, O.: Ontological engineering: with examples from the areas of knowledge management, e-commerce and the semantic web. Springer Science & Business Media, Heidelberg (2006). https://doi.org/10.1007/b97353. ISBN 1-85233-551-3

27. Kitamura, Y., Takafuji, S., Mizoguchi, R.: Towards a reference ontology for functional knowledge interoperability. In: ASME Conference Proceedings, vol. 48078, pp. 111–120 (2007). https://doi.org/10.1115/detc2007-35373

28. Burton-Jones, A., Storey, V.C., Sugumaran, V.P., Ahluwalia, P.: A semiotic metrics suite for assessing the quality of ontologies. Data Knowl. Eng. **55**(1), 84–102 (2005). https://doi.org/10.1016/j.datak.2004.11.010

29. OWL2: Web Ontology Language (2009). http://www.w3.org/TR/owl2-overview/. Accessed 19 Dec 2017

30. Allemang, D., Hendler, J.: Semantic web for the working ontologist: effective modeling in RDFS and OWL. Elsevier, Amsterdam (2011). ISBN 978-0-12-385965-5

31. Paolucci, M., Kawamura, T., Payne, T.R., Sycara, K.: Semantic matching of web services capabilities. In: Horrocks, I., Hendler, J. (eds.) ISWC 2002. LNCS, vol. 2342, pp. 333–347. Springer, Heidelberg (2002). https://doi.org/10.1007/3-540-48005-6_26

32. Cheng, C.P., Lau, G.T., Pan, J., Law, K.H., Jones, A.: Domain-specific ontology mapping by corpus-based semantic similarity. In: Proceedings of 2008 NSF CMMI Engineering Research and Innovation Conference. Knoxville, Tennessee (2008). http://eig.stanford.edu/publications/jack_cheng/NSF08.pdf

33. Wang, H.-H., Boukamp, F., Elghamrawy, T.: Ontology-based approach to context representation and reasoning for managing context-sensitive construction information. J. Comput. Civ. Eng. **25**(5), 331–346 (2010). https://doi.org/10.1061/(ASCE)CP.1943-5487. 0000094

34. Jung, Y., Joo, M.: Building information modelling (BIM) framework for practical implementation. Autom. Const. **20**(2), 126–133 (2011). https://doi.org/10.1016/j.autcon. 2010.09.010

35. Beetz, J., Van Leeuwen, J., De Vries, B.: IfcOWL: a case of transforming EXPRESS schemas into ontologies. Ai Edam **23**(1), 89–101 (2009). https://doi.org/10.1017/ S0890060409000122

36. Lee Y., Yang F., Eastman C.M., Roper K.O.: Modularized validation of a building information model according to the specifications of the facility management handover and COBie. In: LC3 2017: Volume I – Proceedings of the Joint Conference on Computing in Construction (JC3), Heraklion, Greece, pp. 279–288 (2017). https://doi.org/10.24928/JC3-2017/0080

37. Patacas, J., Dawood, N., Vukovic, V., Kassem, M.: BIM for facilities management, evaluating BIM standards in asset register creation and service life planning. J. Inf. Technol. Constr. **20**(20), 313–331 (2015). http://www.itcon.org/2015/20

38. Stanford Center for Biomedical Informatics Research. Research, Protege (2014). http://protege.stanford.edu/. Accessed 20 Sept 2017

Utilising the Potential of Standardised BIM Models by a Fundamental Transformation of Collaboration Processes

Katharina Klemt-Albert[1]([✉]), Philipp Hagedorn[1], and Torben Pullmann[2]

[1] Institute of Construction Management and Digital Engineering,
Leibniz Universität Hannover, Hannover, Germany
{klemt-albert,hagedorn}@icom.uni-hannover.de
[2] albert.ing GmbH, Frankfurt, Germany
t.pullmann@albert-ing.com

Abstract. The digital method Building Information Modelling (BIM) offers a large potential for the construction industry. In addition to the three-dimensional geometry representation including derived visualizations, the key advantage of BIM is semantic object-based information management. A European case study verifies that failing communication and collaboration processes are the main impediment to BIM adoption. Furthermore, these processes remained nearly constant during the last years. One reason for this stagnation is a lack of usable and efficient information management and communication. To face these issues, the presented approach will sketch a natural model-based information management and collaboration workflow. The approach focuses on the standardisation of collaboration processes, data and issue management and their implementation into a Common Data Environment (CDE).

Keywords: Project planning · Collaboration · Workflows · Standardisation
Information management · Common Data Environment
Building Information Modelling

1 Introduction

The key advantage of Building Information Modelling (BIM) is the semantic object-based information management and the integration of multi-dimensional information levels. Whereas the general usage of 3D models significantly increases, semantic object-orientated building models are used in less than 30 of the engineering offices in Germany. Furthermore, less than 15% of the evaluated companies are integrating multi-dimensional process information into their BIM workflow [1]. A European case study verifies that failing communication and collaboration processes are the main impediment to BIM adoption [2]. Furthermore, these processes remained nearly constant during the last years.

© Springer International Publishing AG, part of Springer Nature 2018
I. F. C. Smith and B. Domer (Eds.): EG-ICE 2018, LNCS 10864, pp. 470–486, 2018.
https://doi.org/10.1007/978-3-319-91638-5_26

Hence, an important reason for this stagnation is a lack of usable and efficient information management and communication. As described by Shafiq et al. [3], the long-running established collaboration processes in the construction industry are "document-centric and challenged by the introduction of Building Information Modelling". While most engineers working with BIM are highly engaged to apply model-based planning processes, while avoiding further changes and keeping the proven structure-based information management at the same time. Over the last 20 years, the structured document management was transferred from paper-based artificial repositories to digital document management systems [4]. However, these artificial structures are limited to documents and do not follow natural planning workflows.

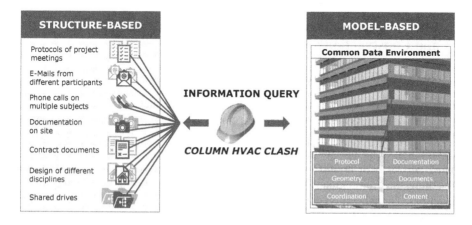

Fig. 1. Structure-based vs model-based information management

To find the relevant information, for instance on an HVAC clash with a column, the coordinator has to review several folders to find the structural and HVAC plans (see Fig. 1). There is no consistent documentation of information and coordination within today's information management. The current workflow proceeds in artificially established structures which follow the organisation of bookshelves and ring files and do not correspond to the real building topology. Actually, human's natural chain of thought is object-related. The use of semantic BIM models can support the engineers with more intuitive hence logical queries delivering high-quality information. In consequence, a transformation of information management is required, to enable that involved engineers can follow the logical paths and processes to communicate and gain the information they need.

Besides the structure-based information management, further problems concerning collaboration within the planning processes were identified by Alazmeh et al. [5] as follows: First, the currentness of information and the insufficient information exchange are addressed as long-lasting problems in collaboration. Second, the disregard of BIM-based information delivery and visual communication methods brought through 3D-models emerged as an impediment for optimized collaboration. In addition, Alreshidi et al. [6] found out that consistency and compatibility are the most common data issues within construction projects. As a result of a qualitative scientific survey of project managers in different fields of construction, communication was seen as the key factor causing complexity in construction projects by nearly 50% of the project managers [7]. Consequently, there is a strong need for a fundamental transformation of collaboration in construction. Another case review from the UK stated that the overall construction industry has to improve cultural understandings of sharing and transferring information within a project dramatically [8]. The concluding research question is how a usable and efficient information management can be developed for construction projects using information and communication technologies and advanced Building Information Modelling.

2   Information Management in AEC (Architecture, Engineering and Construction)

2.1   State-of-the-Art of BIM-Based Information Management

In the last decades, several information management instruments and other approaches have been developed. Document Management Systems (DMS) and Information Management Systems (IMS) were employed for management of corporate knowledge. According to Craig and Sommerville [8], about 12% of project knowledge existed in a shared environment in 2002. With the further development of Building Information Modelling, the information management gained effectiveness with the exchange of 3D model-based collaboration data, which was stated by Singh et al. [9]. The implementation of analysing and checking tools increases the interest in participating in the BIM method. Collaboration management is not any longer a corporate and internal topic but needs to integrate various project participants leading to central model concepts like Model Server or BIM Server. By 2015, the 20% of interrogated design companies worked on a shared model using a model server. However, shared models do not embody the whole project knowledge and information. Another 69% of the companies acknowledged that they keep comparing different revisions of the models with 2D documents and drawings [1].

Server-based collaboration in the construction industry was established with the implementation of the BIM Collaboration Format (BCF) [10]. First server-based collaboration was introduced by Beetz et al. [11] with BIMserver and its IFC-model-based collaboration. With model-server, not only issues can be exchanged and conflicts transformed from drawing-based markups to model-based issue management, but collaborative BIM processes are implemented for instance with the approach of van Berlo and Krijnen [10]. To achieve an optimal use of processual collaboration, the aggregation of all relevant data is included within the building model. Major advantage can be gained by utilising the digital model as a Single Source of Truth (SSoT) as stated by Poirer et al. and Sanchez et al. [12, 13]. Accordingly, the SSoT is the only reliable source of all relevant data for every project participant during the planning and construction process [12, 14]. The planning process completely relies on the information stored in the model so that other concurrent information is incidental and has no legal relevance. To accomplish this, working results must be stored entirely in the digital model and reliable information can only be retrieved from the SSoT. This attaches a huge importance of legal aspects and contractual design to the model.

However, a large bulk of data in a single centralised model leads to a very unmanageable model so that in the end planners deny using it. Dossick et al. [15] denoted the SSoT as an "ideological pitfall" in the case that data is not delivered according the specific addressees. To avoid this "pitfall", the model server can be extended into a Common Data Environment (CDE) bringing models, information and documents together in a queryable environment and allowing cloud-based collaboration.

Concluding from the state-of-the-art review, the following stages of Information Management evolve delivering a certain degree of collaboration (see Fig. 2). Whereas DMS and IMS provide a medium collaboration level on documents and information, the change in collaboration is achieved by using shared building models, model server and cloud-based collaboration. Defining the CDE as a single source of truth leads to a holistic (and obligatory) model-based collaboration.

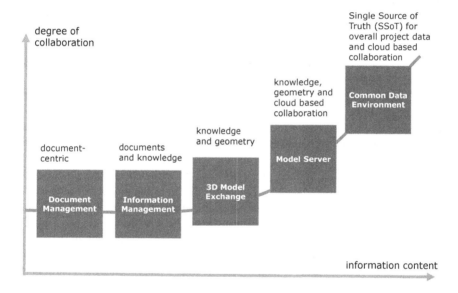

Fig. 2. Information content and degree of collaboration

2.2 Common Data Environment Concept

A server-based Common Data Environment as specified in PAS 1192 [16] can remedy to avoid information overflow. The CDE provides part models and coordination views. The need for part models for different disciplines were outlined by Eastman et al. [17]. To retrieve the linkage between the part models a coordination view or coordination model is commonly implemented. Relevant project data can be stored as semantic linked data. Furthermore, collaboration processes, information on costs, appointments and quality as well as documentation and as-built updating in terms of the SSoT-approach are included in the CDE. With this, the CDE functions as a source of information and an archive for documentation concurrently [19]. The new model-based location of data and information lead to the development of new processes. Especially, the possibility to access information via advanced semantical and model-based queries creates plenty of new use cases. The linked knowledge and recent development in ICT facilitate further research projects.

Information management using BIM and CDE in the construction industry is standardised in some countries. One of the pioneers is the British Standardization Institution with PAS 1192-2:2013 [16]. Moreover, various BIM protocols like the CIC BIM Protocol (UK) [18] or the Singapore BIM Guide propose the use of a Common Data Environment or equivalent information management techniques. In Singapore, an approach to Common Data Environment workflows is defined in four steps [20]. In the first step, individual disciplines create models according to predefined deliverables. The second step is to check and review each part model and forwarding it to a cross-disciplinary model coordination sharing the information with other disciplines. After the authorisation of the coordination model by a BIM Manager, the third step is the validated design output and the last step the archiving of the project. Parts of this workflow were described in the previous version of the PAS 1192-2:2007. Furthermore, the UK government premises organizations to implement a Common Data Environment to achieve the Level 2 BIM Maturity. In 2017, the International Organization for Standardization (ISO) drafted an adoption of the British Standard PAS 1192 as the ISO 19650 [21].

With respect to information management, a distinction between explicit and implicit knowledge has to be taken into account. Explicit knowledge is the part of knowledge that can directly be conceived and is non-encoded ("what"). On the opposite, implicit knowledge is the part that is bound to personal experience and intuition ("how"). Explicit knowledge like the unambiguous information of a construction project (e.g. technical models, specification and defined processes) can be included in a document-centric repository. Implementing a data-based platform linked to the model not only explicit knowledge becomes dramatically more accessible. Indeed, the more exciting point is the implicit knowledge linking the engineering expertise with the model: The aspiration of a CDE should be a platform for scrutinising details, recognising complex relations, and developing solutions for the team of engineers. Having this in mind, another significant component of CDEs is the embedded communication between project participants.

2.3   Content and Requirements of a CDE

As described above, CDEs contain the overall project data including documents, models, knowledge and collaboration. But certain users and projects demand different contents and operations. Figure 3 contains a general overview of contents and related operations as minimal requirements derived from the previous paragraph.

Models are essential within a CDE. Regarding different levels of authorisation within a role concept, it is opportune to use part models for each discipline instead of a centralised shared model. The platform must be able to upload revisions of part models into a repository while history and ownership of each need to be recorded. Merging various part models into a common coordination view is also necessary. As a consequence, functionalities like versioning and comparisons must be provided by the CDE in order to be able to review changes between revisions. With respect to different authorisation levels, the status of each part model must be managed individually to ensure security and consistency during the data exchange workflow.

Comprehensive Information focuses on locking, sharing and accessing data with participants according to individual authorisation. The data exchange and authorisation workflows are described in Sect. 3. Querying different kinds of data using search, filter and selection options leads to the creation of a large amount of different exportable reports. The possibility to import and link *Documents* and *Drawings* with model elements is a functional requirement. Furthermore, it is necessary that both can be exported according to the level of authorisation. Another important function is the bidirectional interface between 2D drawings and 3D models: drawings need to be derived from the model for the on-site purpose. But, existent drawings also need to be compared to the corresponding section of the 3D model to detect differences and determine the right model revision.

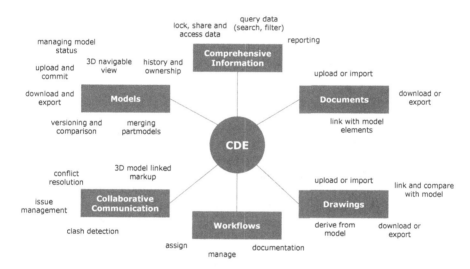

Fig. 3. Content and required processes within a Common Data Environment

To facilitate and enhance collaboration and documentation, it is necessary to integrate a *Workflow* management into a CDE. The workflow management substitutes the analogue decentralized communication and technically represents the transfer of responsibility between participants. Therefore, workflows need to be assignable, manageable and completely documented. For *Collaborative Communication*, clash detection is one standard application. Especially when merging part models into a collaborative view, clash detection and conflict resolutions should be conducted to align the part models. To guarantee the usability, the complete workflow of markup, issues and conflicts should be performed model-related on the platform. This process offers major advantages to the project participants: Issues are always linked to the model in a defined revision and to a specific object. Furthermore, the complete workflow is documented.

3   Definition of Collaboration Processes Within a CDE

In this approach, we extrapolate from minimum requirements of CDEs to a definition of collaboration processes. Therefore, project roles can be described as seen in Fig. 4. Subsequently, workflows for model processing and issue resolving are defined.

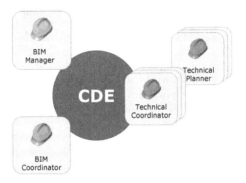

Fig. 4. Project roles

3.1   Model Processing

The model processing workflow starts with the *Information Author* who is a technical planner of a certain discipline. He creates a corresponding part model (see Fig. 5). Since the model is drawn up in a native authoring software and not in the CDE, the *Work in Progress* state is attributed to part models and revisions when uploaded firstly. As long as part models remain in this state, they are not shared with other disciplines and visible only for the authoring technical planners and their technical coordinator (see Table 1).

The *Technical Coordinator* of each discipline can check and review the corresponding part model. He has either to approve or to decline the content. If he declines, it will be archived on the server. Due to the consistency of the documentation, the declined revisions cannot be deleted. The information author can now upload an edited revision of the part model.

If the part model is set into the *approved* state by the technical coordinator, it is visible for the *BIM Coordinator* (see Table 1). The BIM coordinator has the right to set the status of the approved part models to *shared*. After that, the part model is irrevocably *shared* and visible for all technical planners and coordinators. For further collaboration, the BIM Coordinator creates a coordination view with a set of *approved* or *shared* part models. The state of the coordination view depends on the lowest state of the included part models. Consequential, a whole coordination view is only *shared*, when all included part models are *shared*. The coordination view is then visible for all technical planners, that participate in the view. Necessarily, a coordination view has to be *shared* to proceed in the workflow.

The relationship between coordination view and part models is left-total. This means, a coordination view contains at least one or more part models. On the other hand, part models can be contained by one or more coordination views or by zero (if they were declined and archived by the technical coordinator). The set of part models of a coordination view is locked, hence a partial change is not possible. Additionally, it is not possible to add more than one revision of a part model to the view. Due to consistency in the planning process, changes in part models always lead to adding a new view. With this characterisation, a coordination view can be compared to the analogue indexed 2D plan comparison.

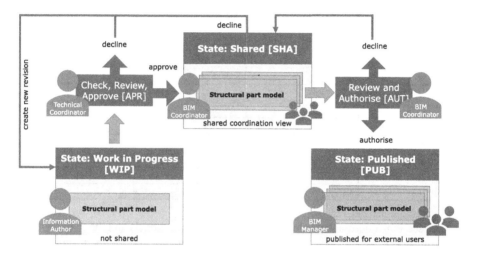

Fig. 5. Workflow of model processing

During the *shared* state in the coordination view, clash detections and logic checks are performed by the BIM coordinator. The detailed workflow of issue resolving is described in the following section. When all issues are solved, the coordination view can be reviewed and *authorised* by the BIM Coordinator. *Authorised* elements are visible for the role *BIM Manager*. It is noteworthy, that the authorisation can be withdrawn until the status is changed to *published*. A coordination view can be published by the BIM manager. Actually, if the status is set to *published*, the view and included part models are visible to all process participants and also to all external users of the CDE (e.g. clients).

The roles and rights according to the workflow sketched before are summarised in Table 1. The table shows the privileges per user for the current model states, e.g. the approved state can be set by the technical coordinator and extends view rights to the BIM Coordinator

The table distinguishes between the read and set rights for each status. The read right allows users to access part models with the corresponding status. The set right allows users to transfer part models of coordination views into the corresponding status. The information author is always able to see his own work whereas it is not visible for technical planners of other disciplines until the revision is *shared* by a BIM coordinator. Furthermore, the technical coordinator of a discipline can always see revisions of his own discipline. Once the technical coordinator *approves* a revision, it is visible for the

BIM coordinator immediately. Once the status is changed to *shared*, technical planners of other disciplines can view the revision.

Table 1. Authorisation concept

Current State	Right	Technical Planner in Information Author role	Technical Planner	Technical Coordinator	BIM Coordinator	BIM Manager	External User
Part model rights							
Work in Progress [WIP]	Set to state	WIP (initial)		APR			
	View	x		x			
In Approval [APR]	Set to state				SHA		
	View	x		x	x		
Shared [SHA]	Set to state				AUT		
	View	x	x	x	x	x	
Coordination view rights							
In Authorisation [AUT]	Set to state					PUB	
	View	x	x	x	x	x	
Published [PUB]	Set to state						
	View	x	x	x	x	x	x

The section "coordination view" refers to a set of part models and their shared revisions in a coordination view. Generally, a coordination view has the read status of the included part models. If the BIM Coordinator *authorises* the view, the BIM Manager has read rights and can *publish* it. This is the only state which permits reading rights to external users.

3.2   Resolving Issues

The workflow of issue resolving starts with the delivery of part model revisions by technical planners into a *shared* coordination view managed by a BIM Coordinator (see Fig. 6). Nevertheless, every upload of part models proceeds according to the defined workflow of model processing. If the BIM coordinator performs a clash detection in which results in a conflict between two disciplines, this conflict is distributed as an issue on the CDE platform. The involved technical planners are notified about the detected clash. Usually, one of the technical planners is responsible for the conflict and the needed change respectively correction. The other one then is the depending technical planner.

According to the expertise of the BIM Coordinator, it is either him or the depending technical planner who assigns the issue to the responsible planner. This includes markups and further information. For a BCF conform issue, at least a title, a type, a status and a responsible person need to be defined. Information can be committed as a description of the conflict or as attached documents and screenshots. With this information, the responsible planner can create a new revision and deliver it to the BIM coordinator. The coordinator now runs out another conflict check and reviews the revision. Then, he either decides that the problem is resolved or not. If the problem is resolved, the revision is integrated into a new coordination view to proceed within the model processing workflow. As long as the problem is not resolved, the responsible technical planners are responsible to deliver corrected revisions.

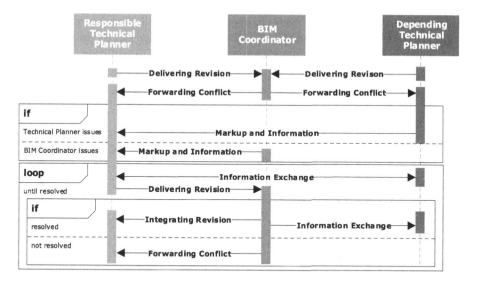

Fig. 6. Workflow of issue resolving

The use of BIM Collaboration Format (BCF) for resolving issues leads to a read-only list of conflicts in most cases [10]. Therefore, a necessary step is to implement the comment function of BCF into the workflow of resolving issues to provide a collaborative discussion setup. Because of the comment function, depending and responsible technical planners and BIM coordinator can communicate easily during the issue resolving process in order to achieve a quick conflict resolution. With this, the CDE not only features explicit knowledge but also enables an exchange of implicit knowledge among project participants.

Using BCF export functionality, the issues and their comments are useable within external software to support the natural user environment with known software applications and tools. Usually, an external system allows to add new issues, modify parts of existing issues like status and responsibility, and allows to extend existing issues by further comments. When importing back the extended BCF files, the CDE has to ensure that imported information is treated in a way that all modifications are documented, no information is hidden, and imported information about the original author is only handled in an informative way. Since BCF files are not protected against manipulation, the use is a potential risk for the consistency of a CDE. To avoid tampering of data, the uploading person is always the technical author and fully responsible for the imported information.

4   Software Implementation and Use Case Scenario

The defined workflows were proven in several railway and road infrastructure projects. Therefore, the processes were implemented into the CDE platform Squirrel. To concretise the approach, a use case scenario has been extracted from a realised project. The project has been the construction of an electrified railway bridge planned using the platform Squirrel. The use case is supported by screenshots from the software.

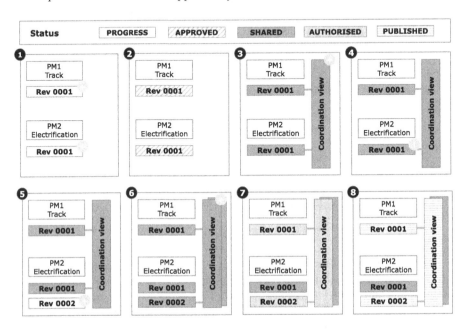

Fig. 7. Use case setup

Figure 7 shows the setup of the use case in eight steps. Each step contains the status of the observed part models and coordination views. Whenever a new part model revision or coordination view is created, it is marked with a "+" sign. To achieve a better comprehensibility, the figure shows only the track planning and the electrification planning in detail.

1. **Uploading part models**

First, the planners for the track and electrification design upload their part model file to the platform. In both cases, the first upload leads to a part model revision 0001, because it is the first uploaded file in either part model. According to the authorisation level, the electrification planner and track planner can see their own revisions, but also all other revisions that are shared. The uploaded revisions are in the status PROGRESS (see Fig. 7).

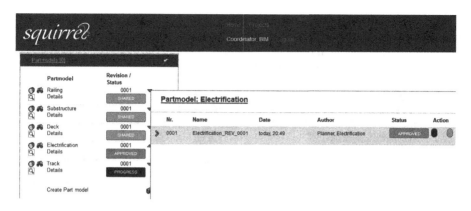

Fig. 8. Uploading, approving and sharing part models in the CDE platform

2. Approving part model revisions

The respective technical coordinators approve the part model revisions of their discipline to forward it to the BIM coordinator (see Fig. 8). In some projects, there might be only one physical person for technical planner and technical coordinator in each discipline. To approve a part model revision on the platform, the technical coordinator selects the part model and opens the detail box. This box offers the history of all revision of a part model with detailed information on author, status and date. Moreover, it offers possibilities to compare two revisions with a graphical 3D comparison. In this box, the technical coordinator changes the status from PROGRESS to APPROVED.

3. Sharing part model revisions and creating a coordination view

In Fig. 8, the BIM coordinator is logged in to the CDE. The 3D view offers a synopsis of all shared and approved part models in their most recent revision. Furthermore, the part model container gives an overview about all part models of the project. The BIM Manager selects an approved revision and sets the status to SHARED with the button in the action column.

For the creation of a coordination view, at least all selected revisions need to be SHARED. Opening the container Coordination view, the BIM Coordinator can create a new coordination view. This container displays the summary of created coordination views. By clicking on a coordination view, the linked part model revisions are activated and concurrently locked in the part model container. Additionally, the 3D view is updated with the coordination view. This view can now be accessed by all participating disciplines.

4. Identifying conflicts, assigning issues, delivering information

Using the coordination view, the BIM coordinator can review the part models e.g. with a geometric clash detection or a logic check. In this case, a geometric clash detection delivered a clash between the track and the electrification. As marked in Fig. 9, the suspension of the overhead wiring intersects the clearance gauge of the track line. This clash leads to the creation of an issue, which can be done within the issue container.

Besides the creation of issues out of identified conflicts, BCF issues can be imported or exported. Issues are always attached to a coordination view to keep the consistent set of revisions. With the creation of an issue, the screenshot of the clash is provided on the platform as well as in an export of the BCF issue.

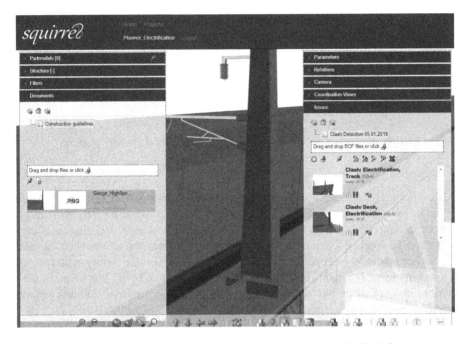

Fig. 9. Identifying clashes and providing information in the CDE platform

In addition to the visual and textual description of the issue, the BIM coordinator of technical planners can attach documents to a clash or to a set of objects. In this case, the guideline with geometric dimensions is attached to the clearance gauge to supply further information. The type of issues can be information, warning, error or unknown, according to the BCF-Standard.

5. Forwarding the issue to the electrification planner

The BIM coordinator assigns the issue to the responsible electrification planner (see Fig. 10), who then is informed about new and updated issues.

The issue container features a read/unread and type filter, to distinguish between issues (e.g. displaying only open unread error issues). The planners and coordinators communicate issue-related directly in the issue dialogue so that the responsible planner designates a revision in which the issue is solved or other questions can be answered and discussed directly in the environment with the track planner or BIM coordinator. The major advantage of the BCF conform issue management and the exportable BCF files is the return of the BCF file into the native authoring tool. With this, the electrification planner can easily import the issue into his native environment and change the height of the overhead wiring.

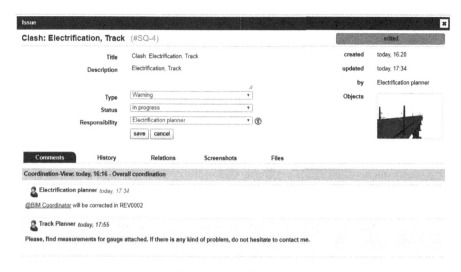

Fig. 10. Issue dialogue

6. Uploading resolved revision

After the correction of the conflict, a new revision of the part model is uploaded by the electrification planner with the status progress. Of course, this revision has to be approved and shared again. With the shared revision, the BIM Coordinator creates a new coordination view, which is now without clashes.

7. Reviewing and authorising the coordination view

Besides the clash detection, the BIM coordinator has the function to review and authorise the coordination view for the BIM manager. This involves obvious planning inconsistencies as well as violations of the project-specific BIM execution plan. The BIM Coordinator may also apply automated rules or use external tools for automated tests.

8. Publishing the coordination view

The BIM manager is the last actor in this workflow. He decides whether the delivered coordination view has the quality to be published for external users of the CDE. So finally, the coordination view and all inherent revisions have the status published (Fig. 11).

Published versions are visible for external participants which have no other view rights during the planning process. While in published state, the information may be locally archived, or used as confident basis for further planning steps. A later removal of the published state does not guarantee privacy of the information. For this reason, all versions which once have been published may not be set to any other state.

The use case scenario before has been proofed with 19 participants during a BIM collaboration workshop at the X Lab at Leibniz Universität Hannover. The participants took the roles of technical planner, coordinator, BIM Coordinator, BIM Manager, client

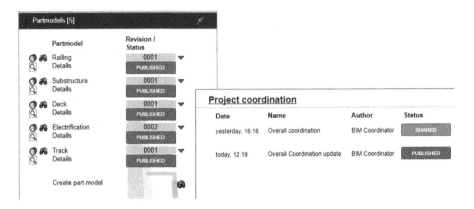

Fig. 11. Published coordination view and inherent revisions

and quality manager according their individual domain as engineering professionals. The evaluation was measured after a basic training with three different scenarios from road and railway infrastructure projects. In general, the presented collaboration processes were described as positive and enhanced. Especially the issue management was experienced as direct communication and as a short distance between participants. Figure 12 shows the evaluation of collaboration processes in usability and added value. Around 5% rated the process usability as poor, 21% as good and 74% as very good. The question of added value evaluated that 5% voted for poor, 16% for good and 79% for very good.

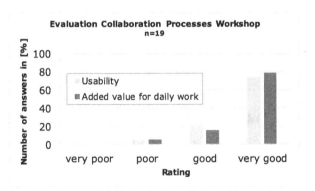

Fig. 12. Evaluation of collaboration processes

5   Conclusion and Outlook

The presented approach of developing a CDE concept with integrated workflows and embedded communication complies with the requirements for a collaborative information management of construction projects and bridges asymmetries in information and the information gap between different project participants.

The evaluation of information management led to specific requirements of collaboration platforms. Based on these specifications, workflows were defined, implemented into the CDE and demonstrated in a use case scenario. The developed workflows are applicable for most projects in civil, structural, railway and infrastructure engineering. Beyond the adoption of a more collaborative culture, it is important that all participants have access to the complete stock of information and get easily the information they need. Thus, a CDE with the developed features becomes an usable and efficient tool for information management.

For the presented development, the British Standard is a reasonable basis for CDE collaboration and precise information sharing dependent on object status and user role. Using a CDE with highly interconnected information structures, integrated with semantical and geometrical model data, participants benefit from an advanced level of intuitive information retrieval which goes far beyond the capabilities of conventional document management processes.

In following steps, aspects of data security according to consistency and documentation should be evaluated and possibly standardised. Especially, CDEs have to assure consistency of the complete content whenever anything is added, modified or deleted. All actions have to be traceable and transparent. The CDE as SSOT circumvents all possible kinds of undesired manipulations caused by direct or indirect user actions (e.g. file imports). This provides a trustworthy and transparent collaboration environment and ensures the right information at the right time.

As a conclusion, specified CDEs can significantly enhance the communication in construction projects. Universal implementation of a CDE as a single source of truth (SSOT) will have relevant impact on sociological perspectives and the mode of operation of each participant. Ideally, a CDE alleviates communication overhead, prevents false accusations and enables establishment of a productivity encouraging error management culture. With further investigation, many more aspects of the use of CDE as SSOT will be observed and integrated into the concepts.

References

1. Braun, S., Köhler-Hammer, C., Rieck, A.: Ergebnisse der BIM-Studie für Planer und Ausführende. Digitale Planungs-und Fertigungsmethoden. FRAUNHOFER - Institut für Arbeitswirtschaft und Organisation IAO, Stuttgart (2015)
2. Bernstein, H.M., Gudgel, J.E., Jones, S.A.: The Business Value of BIM in Europe: Getting Building Information Modeling to the Bottom Line in the United Kingdom, France and Germany. SmartMarket report (2010)
3. Shafiq, M.T., Matthews, J., Lockley, S.R.: A study of BIM collaboration requirements and available features in existing model collaboration systems. J. Inf. Technol. Constr. (ITcon) **18**, 148–161 (2013)
4. Björk, B.-C.: The impact of electronic document management on construction information management. In: International Council for Research and Innovation in Building and Construction, Aarhus (2002)
5. Alazmeh, N., Underwood, J., Coates, S.P.: Implementing a BIM collaborative workflow in the UK construction market. Int. J. Sustain. Dev. Plan. **13**(1), 24–35 (2018)

6. Alreshidi, E., Mourshed, M., Rezgui, Y.: Requirements for cloud-based BIM governance solutions to facilitate team collaboration in construction projects. Requir. Eng. **23**(1), 1–31 (2018). https://doi.org/10.1007/s00766-016-0254-6

7. Klemt-Albert, K.: BIM – Was ist Realität? Was noch Vision? 39. Massivbauseminar: Digitalisierung im Bauwesen, Technische Universität Darmstadt (2017)

8. Craig, N., Sommerville, J.: Information management systems on construction projects: case reviews. Rec. Manag. J. **16**(3), 131–148 (2006). https://doi.org/10.1108/09565690610713192

9. Singh, V., Gu, N., Wang, X.: A theoretical framework of a BIM-based multi-disciplinary collaboration platform. Autom. Constr. **20**(2), 134–144 (2011). https://doi.org/10.1016/j.autcon.2010.09.011

10. van Berlo, L., Krijnen, T.: Using the BIM collaboration format in a server based workflow. Procedia Environ. Sci. **22**, 325–332 (2014). https://doi.org/10.1016/j.proenv.2014.11.031

11. Beetz, J., van Berlo, L., de Laat, R., et al.: BIMserver. org – an open source IFC model server. In: Proceedings of the CIB W78 2010: 27th International Conference (2010)

12. Sanchez, A.X., Hampson, K.D., Vaux, S. (eds.): Delivering Value with BIM: A Whole-of-Life Approach. Routledge an imprint of Taylor & Francis Group, London, New York (2016)

13. Poirier, E.A., Forgues, D., Staub-French, S.: Understanding the impact of BIM on collaboration: a Canadian case study. Build. Res. Inf. **45**(6), 681–695 (2017). https://doi.org/10.1080/09613218.2017.1324724

14. Klemt-Albert, K., Bahlau, S.: BIM-Modell als Single Source of Truth. Bauwirtschaft, Wolters Kluwer Deutschland (Nr. 2017/2), p. 74 (2017)

15. Anderson, A., Marsters, A., Dossick, C.S., et al.: Construction to operations exchange: challenges of implementing COBie and BIM in a large owner organization. In: ASCE Construction Research Congress, pp. 688–697 (2012)

16. The British Standards Institution: Specification for information management for the capital/delivery phase of construction projects using building information modelling 91.010.01 (PAS 1192-2) (2013)

17. Solihin, W., Eastman, C., Lee, Y.C.: A framework for fully integrated building information models in a federated environment. Adv. Eng. Inform. **30**(2), 168–189 (2016). https://doi.org/10.1016/j.aei.2016.02.007

18. Beale & Company Solicitors LLP, BIM Task Group: CIC Building Information Modeling (BIM) Protocol: Standard Protocol for use in projects using Building Information Models. Construction Industry Council (CIC), London (2013)

19. Preidel, C., Borrmann, A., Oberender, C.-H., et al.: Seamless integration of common data environment access into BIM authoring applications: the BIM integration framework. In: European Conference on Product and Process Modelling, vol. 11 (2016)

20. Building and Construction Authority: Singapore BIM Guide: Version 1.0 (2012)

21. DIN EN ISO 19650-1: Organization of information about construction works - Information management using building information modelling. Part 1: Concepts and principles (2017)

Author Index

Printed in the United States
By Bookmasters